ANGEL

THE CASEFILES VOLUME I

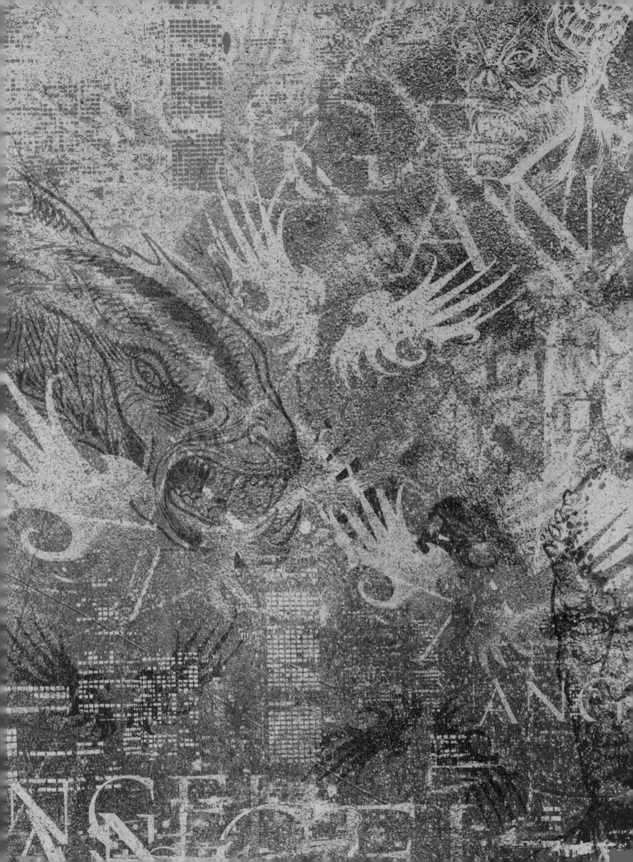

ANGEL

THE CASEFILES VOLUME 1

**NANCY HOLDER, JEFF MARIOTTE,
AND MARYELIZABETH HART**

DEDICATIONS

To my wonderful nieces and nephews: Richard, Teresa, Skylah, and Ian Wilkinson; Sandra and Bill Morehouse; and David Wilkinson. For Linda Lankford, who keeps me sane, and for Maryelizabeth and Jeff, who don't. And for Michael Reaves. —*NH*

To my two co-authors, who can make such an enormous undertaking seem like . . . well, an enormous undertaking with good company. —*JM*

To my parents, who probably never envisioned my reading *Carrie* and checking dozens of books out of the library leading to works like this. And to Nan, for the invitation to join in the fun. —*MeH*

ACKNOWLEDGMENTS

Our deepest gratitude: first, to David Boreanaz, who took time out of his insanely busy schedule to talk with us; to Caroline Kallas and Debbie Olshan, who rock our world; and to David Greenwalt and his writing team for rocking Angel's world. Our deepest gratitude to the entire cast and crew of *Angel*, who work so hard to bring us this most excellent show, and yet made sure they were available for interviews and follow-up questions. To all the Bronzers, and to Anne Cox, Allie Costa, Angela Rienstra, and Pat-mom. Here's to Las Vegas and many other fine PBP venues, long may they wave. To the Wednesday night MG B/A group. And with total West Coast love to the Pocket Team Extraordinaire: Lisa Clancy, Micol Ostow, and Liz Shiflett. We so owe you. Oh, yeah, and thanks to some guy named Joss Whedon, whoever he is.

Special thanks to the following people: Kristina Peterson, Brenda Bowen, Alan Smagler, Ellen Krieger, Lauren Ackerman, Russell Gordon, Sammy Yuen, Nancy Pines, Lisa Feuer, Donna O'Neill, Linda Dingler, Twisne Fan, Rebecca Springer, Scott Shannon and Patricia MacDonald

First Pocket Books edition May 2002
™ and © by Twentieth Century Fox Film Corporation.
Video grabs courtesy of Omni Graphic Solutions
All rights reserved.

Pocket Books
An imprint of Simon & Schuster Uk Ltd.
Africa House, 64-78 Kingsway London WC2B 6AH
www.simonsays.co.uk
All rights reserved, including the right of reproduction in whole or in part in any form.

Designed by: Lili Schwartz
Editor: Lisa A. Clancy
Editorial Team: Elizabeth Shiflett and Micol Ostow

Printed in the United States of America
2 4 6 8 10 9 7 5 3 1
A CIP catalogue record for this book is available from the British Library
ISBN 0-7434-4959-2

DEDICATIONS

To my wonderful nieces and nephews: Richard, Teresa, Skylah,
and Ian Wilkinson; Sandra and Bill Morehouse; and David Wilkinson.
For Linda Lankford, who keeps me sane, and for Maryelizabeth
and Jeff, who don't. And for Michael Reaves. —*NH*

To my two co-authors, who can make such an enormous undertaking
seem like . . . well, an enormous undertaking with good company. —*JM*

To my parents, who probably never envisioned my reading *Carrie*
and checking dozens of books out of the library leading to works like this.
And to Nan, for the invitation to join in the fun. —*MeH*

ACKNOWLEDGMENTS

Our deepest gratitude: first, to David Boreanaz, who took time out of his insanely busy schedule to talk with us; to Caroline Kallas and Debbie Olshan, who rock our world; and to David Greenwalt and his writing team for rocking Angel's world. Our deepest gratitude to the entire cast and crew of *Angel*, who work so hard to bring us this most excellent show, and yet made sure they were available for interviews and follow-up questions. To all the Bronzers, and to Anne Cox, Allie Costa, Angela Rienstra, and Pat-mom. Here's to Las Vegas and many other fine PBP venues, long may they wave. To the Wednesday night MG B/A group. And with total West Coast love to the S&S Team Extraordinaire: Lisa Clancy, Micol Ostow, and Liz Shiflett. We so owe you. Oh, yeah, and thanks to some guy named Joss Whedon, whoever he is.

CONTENTS

FOREWORD

In case there were any doubters (no, we didn't think so), with *Angel*, Joss Whedon has proven that he's no one-hit wonder. It wasn't good enough for him to turn a show with the unlikely title of *Buffy the Vampire Slayer* into one of the best, most critically acclaimed, most beloved programs on television. He had to do it all over again, with *Angel*. Simpler name, equally unlikely premise. An evil vampire gets his soul back, gains a conscience, and tries to atone for his sins by moving to Los Angeles and working as a private investigator.

The beauty of both *Buffy* and *Angel* is this: when you convince a friend who hasn't watched to tune one in—after the expected concerns because of the title and/or premise—and he or she turns to you afterward, that stunned expression on his or her face, and says, "But it's so good."

And it is—*they* are—both so good. We watched a lot of *Angel*—a *lot* of *Angel*—in order to be able to write this book. Watching so closely, one can see how carefully crafted every aspect of the show is. With many shows, that kind of close attention could be painful. With *Angel*, it's a joy. The show rewards close viewing. "It's so good."

We hope our enthusiasm for the world that Joss Whedon and David Greenwalt and some of the best writers, directors, and actors in television have created is evident in these pages. We had a great time putting this together for you. Enjoy.

—NANCY HOLDER, JEFF MARIOTTE, AND MARYELIZABETH HART

CHARACTER GUIDE

ANGEL (Liam, Angelus)

"You don't know what evil is."

Angel is a one-of-a-kind hero: the only vampire on earth with a soul. His road to L.A. has been a rocky journey . . . and the difficulties are not over yet.

In 1753 he was still a twenty-something human named Liam, a layabout who got drunk in the taverns of Galway every night and slept around with courtesans and loose girls. His merchant father disapproved of him, despairing of the man he might become, and it was hard to tell which came first, Liam's bad behavior or his father's low opinion of his son.

Then, one fateful night, Darla, a beautiful vampire, watched Liam brawling in a pub. Smitten with him, she lured him down an alley with promises to show him the world and a better life. Then she turned him into a vampire. She waited by his grave for him to rise and helped him through his transformation into vampiric eternal life. Among his first kills were the members of his family.

He took his vampire name, Angelus, from his little sister's assumption that Liam had returned to the family as an angel. Thus the girl invited him in, and he ruthlessly slaughtered everyone, showing his father exactly what kind of man he had become.

Darla understood that Liam wanted to be free of his father's influence and, in a show of her power over him, encouraged Liam to kill the man. The headstrong Liam/Angel did so, not realizing that he would now never win the man over. But the desire for his father's approval faded with the human part of him, as he learned to bring down prey, savor human blood, and make love with the tempestuous Darla.

Angel and Darla lived and loved for over a hundred years. In 1760 they arrived in the court of the Master, Darla's sire and the head of the Order of Aurelius, but Angelus and the Master instantly locked horns, and Angelus and Darla left to terrorize Europe on their own. Angelus became the scourge of Europe, the most vicious vampire in existence. For him it wasn't about the kill, it was about the torture leading up to the kill.

In the late 1700s Darla and Angel met up with another pair of vampire lovers—Elizabeth and James—both of whom survived only to fatefully encounter the reformed Angel in present-day L.A.

Darla brought a girl named Drusilla to Angel's attention in 1860. The young woman was cursed with visions, and fled to a convent after Angel slaughtered her family. First Angelus drove her crazy. Then he turned her, becoming her sire.

In 1880 Drusilla went on to turn a love-struck young poet named William, who learned the value of torture at his grandsire's knee. Because of his preference for utilizing railroad spikes as implements of torture, he became known as William the Bloody, or Spike.

Thus Angel, Darla, Drusilla, and Spike were Angel's first vampiric family.

They roamed Europe, together, in pairs, and singly, cutting a wide swath of terror and destruction. It was during this time that Angelus took on another protégé, Penn, who adopted the habit of scratching a cross in the cheek of his victims.

Angel and Darla were hotly pursued by a vampire hunter named Daniel Holtz, a man determined to drive the soulless creatures from the world. He cornered them many times, once in a burning barn where Darla showed her true colors and abandoned Angel to take his own chances (he escaped and forgave her), and again when he had Angel in an inquisitor's chamber, but Darla showed up to rescue her "dear boy." They let Holtz survive that encounter because they had better plans for him. Having learned the location of Holtz's family, they used it against him—killing his wife and newborn son and turning his beloved daughter into a vampire. Holtz, a step behind them, was forced to kill his own daughter. Angelus showed Holtz the true value of his family: they were a liability. Holtz vowed revenge. . . .

One night in Borsa, Romania, in 1898, Darla presented Angel with a birthday present: a lovely Gypsy girl. He killed the young woman, not knowing she was a favorite of her clan. Her family cursed him with a spell to restore his soul while he still walked as a vampire. Horrified, he was now tormented by every single evil act he had committed, every person he had gleefully tortured and mercilessly killed. Unknown to Angel, the spell would remain in effect until he experienced a moment of true happiness. Ostensibly, this happiness would allow him a respite from his suffering, so the Gypsies did not want this to happen. (It is unclear if they knew this "moment" would bring the demonic nature of Angelus to the fore, but the clan could monitor his situation from a distance, and as the years progressed and Angel became more humanlike because of his contact with Buffy the Vampire Slayer, the clan sent a representative to observe him in Sunnydale and be sure that happiness would never be his. Her name was Janna of the Kalderash clan, though for the purposes of blending into contemporary society she went by the name Jenny Calendar.)

Back in the late 1890s, Darla was equally horrified that her paramour had been polluted with a soul and drove him from her presence. But Angel couldn't stay away from her. He tried to feed off innocent humans to prove his worth to her, but his newly returned conscience prevented him from following through. He was content to feed off the periphery of society—the criminals, the malcontents. When Darla discovered this, she ordered him to drink of an innocent, a baby, to prove his love and his worth. Unable to do so, he fled from her anger during the Boxer Rebellion in China in 1900, just as his "grandson" Spike was coming into his own, having finally killed a Slayer.

Eventually Angel went a bit mad, living in alleyways and feeding off rats until 1997, when a demon named Whistler offered him the chance to "become" someone, to actually do something with his unlife. Whistler took Angel to L.A. where he saw Buffy Summers from afar. He witnessed her calling to become the Slayer and decided to help her.

Angel waited for her to arrive at the Hellmouth in Sunnydale and warned her of the impending Armageddon called "the Harvest," during which his grandsire, the Master, would escape the underground church in which he was currently imprisoned. Angel occasionally showed up to let the Slayer know about subsequent impending evils. He and Buffy began to fall into deep like, and Angel revealed to her his vampiric nature.

At this point, Darla——back in the service of the Master—reentered Angel's life. Darla attempted to come between Buffy and Angel by making Buffy think he had attacked Buffy's mother. Predictably, Buffy hunted him; just as predictably, Darla tried to kill her. Forced to choose between Darla and Buffy, Angel staked Darla.

Shortly afterward, Buffy confronted the Master in his underground prison. He killed her, though her friend Xander Harris was able to revive her when Angel was not (no breath, hence no CPR). The Master was now free and preparing to open the Hellmouth. Buffy killed him.

Angel and Buffy continued to fight side-by-side, falling in love along the way, and on her seventeenth birthday they made love. This single moment of true happiness changed Angel back into the soulless Angelus, who then stalked and tormented Buffy by trying to kill all her friends, succeeding only in killing Jenny Calendar as she was about to restore his soul, in defiance of her clan curse. To stop his plan to end the world, Buffy had no choice but to send him to Hell, even though his soul had been magically restored at the last moment by Buffy's friend, Willow.

After centuries of demon time spent in torment, Angel emerged from Hell, not certain why he had been freed. Wild from pain and torture, Angel hunted like an animal again until Buffy rescued him. When he in turn saved her from a dangerous human, he began to reclaim his humanity. But guilt over the death of Jenny, the pain he had visited upon Buffy and her friends, and memories of his past crimes haunted him, and he tried to kill himself in atonement. Knowing he was too weak-willed to actually kill himself, he tried the most passive way possible: waiting for the sun to rise. Even a desperate Buffy couldn't persuade him back inside, but the hand of The Powers That Be interceded, and the sunrise was delayed by a miraculous snowfall in Southern California on Christmas morning. Accepting that he was sent back from a hell dimension for a reason, Angel agreed to try to live in this world again.

ngel Cordelia Doyle Wesley Gunn The Host Fred Darla Lindsey Lilah Kate Buff
ate The Oracles Faith Holland Drusilla Anne Angel Cordelia Doyle Wesley Gun
he Ho Drusill
nne Kat
uffy Ann
ngel e Hos
red D Drusill
Cordeli Dar
inds Drusill
nne Gun
he Lila
Kate Ang
Cord e Hos
red Buf
he Anr
ngel Wesle
uffy Ann
ngel e Ho
red D Drusill
Cordeli Dar
indsey Drusil
nne Gun
he Ho Lila
Kate B Ang
Cordeli e Ho
red D Buf
The Or Anr
uffy Drusil
ngel Wesl
Doyle Ang

He also tried to resume his relationship with Buffy . . . minus the lovemaking. Their bond was tested many times, most pointedly by the evil, long-lived mayor of Sunnydale who quite succinctly and forcefully pointed out that their relationship couldn't work: Angel would live forever, and while her lifespan was shortened by her work as the Slayer, Buffy would still live long enough to know all that she had given up to be with a man who could never truly be with her and give her a family. Buffy and Angel agreed that the mayor was evil and therefore could not possibly understand their love, but both knew differently. Angel was already contemplating their nonfuture when Buffy's mother kindly but firmly reminded him that Buffy was sometimes just a girl in love, and all she could see of tomorrow was Angel. Shortly thereafter, Angel told Buffy he was leaving Sunnydale, even though he knew it would break her heart.

When he was fatally poisoned by the rogue Slayer Faith, Buffy forced Angel to drink of her because he needed the blood of a Slayer to live. The act nearly killed her, and he was then assured that leaving was the right thing to do. Especially now that he had the blood of a Slayer, an innocent human, in his mouth. After they successfully defeated the mayor of Sunnydale in an apocalyptic graduation ceremony, Angel walked out of Buffy's life, thinking that he would never see his one true love again.

At first he lived alone in Los Angeles, battling evil in a haphazard way. Since tasting the blood of his soul mate, his craving was reactivated, and he found it difficult not to drink from human beings. The half-demon Doyle arrived to prevent him from backsliding on his vow not to take human lives or drink their blood, and helped set him on a more focused course of finding redemption as a warrior for the side of good. Through Doyle's painful visions, The Powers That Be began to use Angel as their champion, whether it was to give Cordelia Chase a purpose in life or to rescue innocent children from assassination.

"I'm game."

Once, Angel returned to Sunnydale in secret to help Buffy in battle. When she learned that he had "stalked" her, she came to Los Angeles to confront him. While she was there, they battled a Mohra demon, whose blood enabled Angel to become human again. With Angel freed of the Gypsy curse, the two resumed their passionate relationship. But it quickly became clear to Angel that without his vampiric strength or agility, he was a liability to the Slayer. He also learned that his being taken out of the struggle between good and evil would cause harm to the mission of helping others and hasten Buffy's death. He asked the Oracles to turn him back into a vampire, sacrificing his own human life to save Buffy's.

While attempting to save Brachen demons (Doyle's relatives) from the purist demons known as the Scourge, Angel was again put in a situation that required the ultimate sacrifice: his life. But this time Doyle saved Angel's life by sacrificing his own in a perceived atonement for a previous wrong. Angel's new family was wrenched apart.

Shortly thereafter, as Angel and Cordelia grieved for their coworker and friend, ex-Watcher Wesley Wyndam-Pryce arrived on the doorstep of Angel Investigations. Happy to see a familiar face from their Sunnydale days, and willing to put their past disagreements (mostly over the fate of Faith the previous year) behind them, Angel offered Wesley a job, now giving Wesley purpose and thus saving another life in exchange for Doyle's. And Cordy became indispensable to him as she carried Doyle's link to The Powers That Be. Angel's family had changed.

During a mission to save three seer children from certain death, he felt compelled to steal an artifact from the Wolfram & Hart vaults. The Scroll of Aberjian, translated by Wesley, contained a prophecy about a vampire with a soul. At first it appeared to signify Angel's death, and Cordy and Wes became concerned that Angel had nothing to live for. But in the end, Wesley found an alternate meaning in the words and realized that Angel might be given another chance at being human if he worked toward redemption. Once more, Angel had hope of life as a mortal being . . . if he continued the good fight.

"Don't believe everything you're foretold."

Angel continued to seek redemption not by grace but through good works, though an accidental killing of a good demon who was trying to protect someone opened Angel's eyes to the need for him to stop trying to accrue a body count. He was not going to attain redemption after a certain number of good works. The work itself is the reward.

After a demon named Vocah blew up his office/subterranean apartment, Angel selected an old hotel for the new offices of Angel Investigations: the Hyperion Hotel, the scene of one of his past crimes. The loner Angel of the 1950s essentially handed over the lives of the hotel's residents to the Thesulac demon who resided there, feeding off their paranoia. Today's Angel, with the help of his friends Cordelia, Wesley, and a streetwise guy named Charles Gunn, was finally able to banish this demon and put to rest his own demons about that time in his life. The gang moved in.

Angel began to have dreams of Darla, his sire, in which she catered to him and pleasured him. He woke up very tired (and cranky) and his obsession with Darla took its toll on his effectiveness on the mission. What he was not aware of is that she was actually *alive* again, raised by W&H. She was administering a magic powder to him to make him have vivid dreams . . . which she augmented with her bodily presence in his bedroom.

Once he actually met up with her, he saw that Darla had been brought back as a human being. Far from being delighted with her reincarnation, however, she hated the pounding in her chest. She begged Angel to change her into a vampire, but he refused. He found her trying to lure other vampires into turning her, and interfered.

After a time, as Darla's soul "strengthened" its presence, Angel learned that she was dying of the syphilis that was about to kill her in human life, back when she was a courtesan. Angel promised to stay with her—she would not die alone—and she accepted her fate with grace, wanting to die with real humanity.

Alas, such was not to be. W&H, fearing that Darla has not distracted Angel from their activities but only strengthened his resolve to do good, located Drusilla and brought her in to change her own grandsire. A captive Angel was forced to watch as his old "family" came full circle.

Angel had always walked close to the edge of good and evil, and now he landed squarely in the territory of the damned as he locked thirty of W&H's top attorneys in Holland Manners's wine cellar with Dru and the newly thirsty Darla.

He divested himself of the protesting Cordelia, Wesley, and Gunn, leaving them in the lurch both emotionally and financially, and walked away.

"You're all fired."

Then he hunkered down into training mode, preparing himself for battle against the combined forces of the soulless Darla and Dru. The two vampire women had been amassing a gang of the best and the brightest to burn L.A. to the ground. He vowed to stop them, and there was a sense of urgency to his preparations—Darla had finally chosen good over evil and now, forcibly changed, she was doing horrible things. With Angelus always just below the surface of his persona, did the same fate await him?

Angel managed to set them both on fire, but they escaped. He continued his downward spiral. After she recovered, Darla approached him, and Angel, desperate to feel something, *anything*, after being shown the ways of the world by Holland, made love to her, knowing it would change him into Angelus. But rather than providing him with any happiness at all, much less true happiness, the act filled him with despair. Darla knew that she had finally lost him—and Angel knew that he had reached rock bottom.

Kate Lockley, the cop Angel worked with and flirted with ever so slightly over the past two years, had been fired from the LAPD for poor judgment and an obsession with the supernatural after vampires killed her father, the father whose approval she always sought and never received before he died. She tried to commit suicide, and Angel saved her. They finally connected, as one person to another—the true healing of them both.

When Wesley was shot by a zombie cop, Angel tried to reconnect with his family, but he was firmly rebuffed. He tried again, offering to work for them, not the other way around, and they warily took him back on as an employee. But tensions were high among the group, and it seemed that nothing would be forgiven . . . until he bought Cordelia a stunning wardrobe and melted her icy heart. The rest of the team gradually fell into line behind her, though the dynamic changed. Wesley was the nominal leader, a position he thought would impress *his* father, even though the team still depended on Angel. But Angel depended on them as well, emotionally, especially Cordelia. Cordy was also still his link to The Powers That Be.

On a mission to another dimension to rescue Cordelia, the demon inside Angel burst through the vampire and human masks. It was a hideous, mindless creature, drawn to blood. The only person who was unafraid of the Angelbeast was a woman nicknamed Fred, also captive in this strange world. She looked on the darkest parts of Angel's persona and still accepted him, actually falling for the "handsome man" who rescued her.

By the time Angel and the others returned from the alternate dimension of Pylea, Angel was a changed man in many ways. Over the course of his time in Los Angeles, he has had an epiphany, realizing that there is absolutely no way he can ever atone for what he has done. Though he had started running after the carrot of "Shanshu," seeking to deserve the restoration of his humanity, Angel discovered humanity has its evil side as well, as the dead Holland Manners pointed out to him. To strive for goodness is not the same as striving to be a human being.

Seeing this with great clarity, Angel made the brave decision to leave off seeking his "Shanshu." He wanted to do good things because that's what good people (and vampires!) do. He hoped to alleviate suffering simply because people shouldn't suffer, and not because he might get to become a person someday if he helped enough people.

"If nothing we do matters, then all that matters is what we do."

With the addition of the vulnerable, intelligent, slightly wacky Fred, Angel thinks his new life is complete. But the line between friends and family was blurred when Darla returned to Angel's life, bearing him incredible news . . . and a vengeful Holtz followed her straight into the heart of Angel's family.

Angel is played by David Boreanaz. He appears in every episode.

CORDELIA CHASE (Cordy, Cor)

"I'm not a sniveling, whiny little crybuffy. I'm the nastiest girl in Sunnydale history. I take crap from no one."

Cordelia was the richest, the most popular, and the snobbiest girl at Sunnydale High School. She and her cadre, "the Cordettes," decided what, where, and who were in and out. Buffy and her friends, Willow Rosenberg and Xander Harris, were most definitely out.

Cordelia crushed on Angel the first time she saw him, and she was totally baffled that he preferred Buffy. Learning that he was a vampire was also a setback, but then on prom night of sophomore year she joined—albeit reluctantly—in the battle against the various and sundry demons that emerged. And she did it all without breaking a nail.

After that fateful night, she became a de facto member of the Scooby Gang. Her two biggest talents were blurting out the one thing everyone else was too polite to mention and providing transportation to and from supernatural crises. She also needed mucho rescuing from jilted boyfriends and jealous girls.

She was perhaps the only person more surprised than Xander when they hooked up during junior year. Despite how embarrassed she was to be seen with him at first, she eventually stuck up for their relationship. She was extremely hurt when she discovered Xander and Willow locked in a desperate kiss when they believed themselves about to die at Spike's hand. Humiliated to be cheated on by a loser, Cordy accidentally conjured up a vengeance demon. Luckily, the spell was reversed (and now the reformed vengeance demon is engaged to Xander, but that's another story). Despite her best intentions, Cordy was continually drawn back into the Slayer's circle, at first reluctantly, then eagerly when Faith's new Watcher, a dashing young British man named Wesley Wyndam-Pryce arrived during her senior year. They flirted and even danced together at the prom, but their first and second kisses were so disastrous, they agreed to part as friends.

Though she was accepted at many colleges, shortly before graduation, Cordelia learned her parents had been busted for tax evasion, and Cordy went from riches to rags overnight. With nothing to lose but her pride, she left Sunnydale to take Hollywood by storm.

She ran into Angel at a Hollywood party. To impress him, she fabricated a successful acting career and carefree starlet lifestyle, but the truth was she was living in a dump, on the verge of starvation. After Angel rescued her from the vampire Russell Winters, she employed herself as his office manager. And thus Angel Investigations was born. Cordelia got herself better digs, complete with a helpful poltergeist named Dennis.

Much to her horror, Cordelia found herself attracted to Angel's half-demon sidekick Doyle. This was bad déjà vu: Xander Harris had been such a "fixer-upper" that she lost her social cachet by publicly dating him. Done with charity work, she had hopes of bagging someone rich and handsome, but Doyle was none of those things. In fact the first rich and handsome man Cordy slept with turned out to just be using her as a surrogate mother to gestate demon spawn. As Cordy learned, not only is sex bad (which Angel heartily agreed with), she now had people she could trust to help her.

But just when she let down her guard and allowed Doyle to warm her heart, he died heroically—and transferred his vision gift to her via a kiss.

Now it was Cordy who had the brain-splitting visions, providing crucial information to the team, which expanded again with the arrival of Wesley. Even though she tried to unload the visions on first Angel and then Wesley via a kiss, they remained with her. She was now Angel's link to The Powers That Be.

The visions extracted a heavy physical and mental toll, and she finally lost it completely when the demon Vocah—to distract Angel from the ritual to raise Darla—broke down her defenses, causing her to have hundreds of simultaneous visions, all focusing on the pain and misery of others. Freed from her nightmare—again, by her compatriots—Cordy vowed anew to help with the good fight, and declared finally that she, Wesley, and Angel were a family.

"I can't give up my visions . . . they're part of who I am now."

It might have been best for Cordelia if she could give up her visions: each one was getting progressively worse, taking its toll on her. The others in Angel Investigations grew increasingly worried about her.

In one year Cordelia moved from being a clerical disaster interested in landing a rich husband to a young woman whose world falls down around her ears when Angel, who had become her best friend, abandoned her to pursue the mystery of Darla's return to life.

Cordelia experienced many trials by heartbreak: her intuition about the danger a revived Darla posed was absolutely on target, and after Angel delivered a critical wound to their professional and personal relationships, it was she who rallied and persuaded Gunn and Wesley to reopen Angel Investigations, albeit under a different, yet to be determined, name. Committed to the cause of helping, now that her (two) eyes had been opened to the pain and suffering in the world, she devoted herself to the family that nourished her—Gunn, Wesley, and Angel. She stopped dating altogether and had few friends (except Harmony, an evil vampire who just broke up with her honey bunny, the returned Spike, but again, that's another story).

In addition to guiding the group with her visions, she battled the bad alongside her men. Not only was she always prepared to kill Angel should Angelus be resurrected, but she rescued Gunn on her own, cracking the skull of one of his homeboys when she thought he was attacking her newly acquired big brother. She showed Wesley how to loosen up and lose his stiff upper lip, but took command when he was shot.

Needless to say, her acting career, friendships, and indeed all relationships outside of the Angel team suffered. As Wesley told the a post-epiphany Angel, "Our Cordelia is not the carefree person she once was." She was the one person Angel had the hardest time reconciling with, but she was also the most important one, simply because, as she said, he hurt her feelings. The two were on their way to regaining the solid friendship that they had when Vocah put her out of commission a year earlier. Angel was determined to prove himself worthy of her friendship, even going so far as to celebrate—regardless of expense—when she landed a national commercial, and to then defend her honor when the director treated her like a piece of meat.

But Cordelia's biggest test—which she passed with flying colors—was when she was inadvertently whisked to the Host's dimension, Pylea. When Angel led Wes, Gunn, and the Host into that dimension to rescue her, risking their lives, they needed no other reason than "It's Cordelia."

In Pylea, first declared a "cow," then elevated to a cow princess because of her visions, Cordy held the lives of her friends, and many others, in her hands. She had wanted to be a princess all her life—or rather, to return to being a princess—and once her wish was granted, she rose to the occasion. At first she saw only the perks—not having to shovel through demon horse poop, as for example, and the yum-miness that her Groosalugg consort turned out to be. Then she tried to save the body (and therefore, the life) of Lorne, the Host, and was reminded of her calling.

The Groosalugg was ready to "take the burden" from her—that is, take her visioning power for his own, and it was then that Cordelia had her own epiphany: the visions were part of who she was. They were not only her responsibility, but something she would not willingly give up.

Groo also invited her to stay and rule Pylea, and it was a bit of a temptation—to be rich again, pampered, and treated well—but such things were no longer for her.

Freely choosing her life back in the Earth dimension, Cordelia returned from Pylea. But the question remained: Since she is "only" human, will the visions that were skull-splitting for even the half-demon Doyle, finally prove to be too much for her?

Cordelia Chase is played by Charisma Carpenter, who, as a cast regular, has appeared in every episode.

ALLEN FRANCIS DOYLE (Doyle)

"We all got something to atone for."

Doyle was Angel's hard-drinking messenger, sent to him by The Powers That Be, to help Angel be an effective warrior on the side of good. He did this via extremely painful visions that contained information about some-one who needed saving. Sometimes he received a lot of information and sometimes it was very sketchy. But getting it was always painful.

He was human on his mother's side and Brachen demon on his father's side. He was stronger and had more acute senses when he wore his demon form—looking like a blue, spiny hedgehog with human fea-tures—but he was ashamed of his demonic heritage. Hoping to spare him from knowing about his demon blood, his mother decided to see if he "presented" before she told him. When he turned twenty-one, his demon side emerged, and by then he was already married to Harry (Harriet). They both freaked out, although once the initial shock wore off, Harry assured him that she thought it actually wonderful that he was part demon. He didn't believe her and became bitter and impossible to live with.

Once a happily married third-grade schoolteacher who volunteered at a food co-op, Doyle became a drunk living in a flophouse. When he was approached by another Brachen demon, who begged him to help the clan escape the relentless approach of the Scourge, Doyle refused. That was when he had his first vision, mentally observing the slaughter of his own demonic people. Then he was sent to help Angel.

Angel was concerned about Doyle's insistence on walking the path of self-destruction: drinking too much, gambling, and owing large sums to bookies and loan sharks, many of whom were not human. More than once, Angel had to save him from scummy bad guys. Doyle continually insisted that he was not a hero like Angel, but he could definitely be counted on in a battle or when Angel or Cordelia's life was in danger.

9

Especially Cordelia's. From the moment he met the former beauty queen, Doyle was smitten. But her apparent, growing dislike for demons—based solely on the evil ones they battled every day—caused him to hide his true nature from her, all the while defending her from evil boyfriends of the human variety. When Harry resurfaced requesting a formal divorce, Cordelia actually experienced a twinge of jealousy. But before Doyle could reveal his true nature to her, the Scourge appeared. This violent band of purebred demons threatened to annihilate all traces of human life that their Beacon could reach. Doyle, finally at peace with his demonic heritage, knowingly sacrificed himself to save Angel and the day. But before he died, he revealed his Brachen appearance—and his love—to Cordelia, and passed on his vision gift to her with a glowing kiss.

Doyle was played by Glenn Quinn and appeared in episodes #1 through 9 of Season One.

WESLEY WYNDAM-PRYCE (Wes)

"And that's why I became a rogue demon hunter."

Wesley was originally sent to Sunnydale by the Watchers Council of Britain to replace Rupert Giles, who was acting as Watcher for both Buffy and Faith. Stuffy and priggish, Wesley alienated both Slayers and they virtually ignored him from day one. This annoyed him, but that altered no one's opinion of him as an interloper . . . except for Cordelia Chase. From the first sight, she was quite taken with him, and he with her. Their lustful attraction went unfulfilled until a kiss revealed to them that sparkage between them was not in the offing.

After Faith went over to the dark side, Angel kidnapped her and tried to reach her, finding a connection between her situation and his own. He was on the verge of making headway when Wesley intruded and took her into custody. His plan was to remand her to the Council for punishment. She escaped and went from very bad to even worse, and Angel was furious with Wesley.

Without a charge, Wesley planned to return to England, but he stayed in Sunnydale when it became clear to all that there was going to be a showdown between the Scooby Gang and the Mayor on graduation day. He even approached the Council about curing Angel after Faith poisoned him. Though the Council refused, on principle, to "save" a vampire, Wesley stayed on in Sunnydale to help in the final battle, where he was assigned to back up . . . Angel. Wesley was knocked out very early on in the confrontation, though he was heard whimpering in his usual way when he was carted off by the paramedics once the smoke cleared.

"What's a rogue demon?"

Then the Council fired him, and he became a self-proclaimed rogue demon hunter. He arrived in Los Angeles tracking a demon who was killing and mutilating both humans and demons and found himself face-to-face with Angel. At first he suspected the old boy of committing the crimes, but as they began to work together he grew to understand why Angel was in Los Angeles and what he was about.

With Doyle dead, Wesley coincidentally arrived in Los Angeles to replace him as the third member of Angel Investigations. His arrival was greeted with another of Cordelia's kisses, this one with a little more sparkage—but it turned out she was only trying desperately to pass on Doyle's gift. And The Powers weren't for Wesley.

After his first adventure with Angel and Cordelia, Wesley was invited to breakfast (scrambled eggs and toast), and then invited to join the payroll. Over time he became part of the family. He grew more confident and less nerdy as time passed. He risked his life time and again for his friends and served as primary researcher of the supernatural, a skill honed from his days as a Watcher.

When a possessed boy pointed out that Wesley lacked the support and love of his own father, the ex-Watcher was shamed before his friends. But when the same boy told Angel that Wesley planned to kill the vampire, Angel threw his support behind Wesley, saying he would only be disappointed in Wes if he *didn't* kill Angel, should he turn evil. Wesley was reassured by this profession and regained his footing. He had faith that anyone with a soul can be redeemed.

However, that faith in people was sorely tested by Faith, after she arrived in town and agreed to work for Wolfram & Hart and take Angel out. When Angel seemed uninterested in being drawn into that game, she kidnapped Wesley and brutally tortured him. He stood up to her courageously, not pulling any punches as he stated his belief that she was too evil and insane to be redeemed. Once he freed himself and went after her, he was shocked to find her in Angel's arms, weeping. She wanted to change, wanted to reform. Grudgingly, Wesley eventually accepted the possibility of Faith's redemption.

Then three Council operatives arrived in L.A. and Wes was offered his old life back if he would turn the rogue Slayer in to the Council. They enlisted his aid in capturing her—or so they thought. His price was the assurance of safety for Angel, which made the operatives privately laugh. Finally they agreed, and he left for Angel's apartment . . . where he immediately clued Angel and the others into what was going on, making his affiliation plain. Clearly, Wesley was still part of the team.

After the demon Vocah stole the Scroll of Aberjian from Angel's office, Wesley was severely injured in a bomb blast that was meant to kill the whole gang. He wound up in the hospital, but still managed to translate the scroll and protectively look in on Cordelia. Once the crisis was past, he, Angel, and Cordy reconvened at Cordelia's apartment, and Cordelia pronounced them a family. Wesley happily assumed his place as part of that family.

"Why do people keep putting me in charge of things?"

When Wesley arrived in Los Angeles, he still smacked of British self-importance. But being fired from the Council seasoned him a bit. Now fully part of the Angel Investigations family, he had adventures of his own, in which he was the primary actor . . . and he got the girl: namely Virginia Bryce, whose father was planning to sacrifice her to the Goddess Yeska in return for more riches and power. Wesley pretended to be Angel to get the gig, but it was pure Wesley Wyndam-Pryce who saved her. And who she chose to be with.

Angel's abandonment hit Wesley hard, too, but like Cordelia, he agreed to take on the job Angel should have been doing—protecting people from evil. He found in Gunn a good friend, to both their surprise, perhaps because as he accepted more and more responsibility his strengths were more openly displayed. They often worked as a team, and it was while trying to save Gunn from going up against the bad zombie cops all by himself that Wesley was shot, almost fatally.

11

When Angel asked to rejoin the agency, he deferred to Wesley, who called the shots and did so very well. Wesley, too, found healing through redefinition—far from being the screw-up his father assumed he was, he had been tested and found to be a levelheaded leader of his own "family." The once shy, stammering demon hunter who hinted around about staying for breakfast was now the commander of an entire operation, who Angel is not able to fire because Wesley had claimed his own place in the fight against the bad.

Heartbreak occurred for Wesley when Virginia left him. Though she spent her entire life among the boogedy-boogedy, she couldn't handle the violence surrounding Wesley's vocation. It was he, not she, who realized that she had to go, and he parted from her with grace and maturity—a far cry from the geeky Watcher who lusted after Cordelia.

But it was during the group's adventures in Pylea that Wesley truly came into his own. He was elected by the rebels to be their new leader, and Wesley made the hard decisions, ordering strategic sacrifices of some lives to save other men and women. Even the street-hardened Gunn was impressed by the iron will and excellent soldiering of his friend.

Wesley no longer needs to prove himself. He has the quiet confidence of someone who knows who and what he is: a fighter and a leader. He is no longer simply a walking reference book, nor a schlub who never gets the chicks. As he returns from Pylea, the question remains, how does the new Wesley figure into the equation that is Angel Investigations?

Wesley is played by Alexis Denisof, who joined the cast in episode #10 of Season One and appears in every subsequent episode of Season One and Two.

CHARLES GUNN

"I was never going to let anything happen to you. I was supposed to protect you. You were my sister."

Charles Gunn was the leader of a band of vampire fighters. They lived like guerilla soldiers in their perpetual street war against the bloodsuckers. When he met Angel, he couldn't believe that there was such a thing as a good vampire and nearly killed him. It was only when Angel saved Alonna (before she was changed) that Gunn spared Angel and agreed to parley with this unusual vampire.

Gunn's beloved sister was Alonna, and she was changed by the vampires to provoke Gunn into doing something stupid and fatal. His heart broke as he staked her.

Later he also agreed to help Angel by distracting the vampire detectors employed by Wolfram & Hart, leaving Angel free to conduct his rescue mission of the three seer children . . . and steal the Scroll of Aberjian.

He remained a contact for Angel whenever the vamp needed backup muscle. When Cordelia and Wesley were both hospitalized after run-ins with Vocah, Angel turned to Gunn to protect his "family" while Angel went after Wolfram & Hart.

> **"I've got a plan. . . . We die horribly and painfully, you go to Hell, and I spend eternity in the arms of Baby Jesus."**

In Season Two, Gunn moved from being a loner who depended on no one to a team player who understood that there is strength in numbers—as in battle, so in life. He was moved by Cordelia's insistence on caring about him and her willingness to defend him to the death, if need be. The death of his sister made him become more aloof, more on guard, more disciplined than he was before Alonna had been changed.

Then George, one of his old homeys, died on his watch, and Gunn realized that he couldn't do it all alone. Even if he had set himself up as someone who could save everyone, he was not. Though he governed his street fighters with an authoritarian hand, it didn't work. People still die; they fall through the cracks, they make their own bad choices, they lose in battle. Worse, he couldn't be everywhere at once, working with the Angel folks while at the same time trying to take care of all the concerns of his other family.

What Gunn realized was that all the individuals in both camps were his family—he was the bridge that united them all—and that he had to work with others to keep the family strong. His impressions of nearly every person (Angel included) in his life were expanded: Far from being "Stick-figure Barbie," Cordelia is a capable young woman (okay, still liking the clothes). Angel, his fallen hero, returned strengthened by his humility and his desire to find the proper role for himself. Wesley, once an effete Englishman with a weird and seemingly unnecessary job title (Watcher? Who watches? Just do it!), became a stirring commander whom Gunn was happy to follow.

Gunn doesn't step down, or step back . . . he steps in—into the community of those who fight for good, for the people. Now that he no longer has to isolate and protect himself from life . . . what will life hold in store for him?

> **"We still kill some vampires, yes?!"**

Charles Gunn is played by J. August Richards, and he appeared in episode #20 and 22 of Season One and every episode of Season Two.

THE HOST (Lorne/Krevlornswath of the Deathwok Clan)

"Excuse me, I'm the Host, have you met me? I never shut up."
Big, bold, and very green, the Host is an anagogic demon, a being who can read people's auras and foretell their futures—but only if they sing. Accordingly, he opened Caritas, a dual-purpose karaoke bar and demon sanctuary, where the rules—no concealed weapons and no devouring the clientele—keep all demons safe from one another. (There's a few big loopholes there, but they get worked out. Eventually.) He loves music and he belts the tunes out with a hot set of pipes—which is actually very strange, as the gang learns he comes from Pylea, a dimensional plane where music simply does not exist.

In Pylea he was a lonely misfit who brought shame to his family, the Deathwok Clan, because he figured there was more to life than the

13

ancient traditions of hunting, gathering, and the sacred joust. Lorne stumbled upon a dimensional portal that took him to L.A. He loves the flash and glamour—he'd probably be equally happy in Vegas—and he built Caritas right on the ground where the portal dumped him.

He met Angel and Company because Wesley brought Cordelia and Angel to Caritas to meet a stoolie named Merl. The cheeky Host was "smitten" with Angel at once—or maybe it was his long coat—and when things went badly awry with a) Cordelia's recent vision and b) Merl's evasive and damaging "information," the Host read Angel's aura (after a halting rendition of "Mandy") and steered him gently toward the right course to take—in this case, down the middle of a Los Angeles street on a jousting charger.

Their relationship became one of a flippant, flashy teacher and his brooding, distracted mentee. The Host listened to the team's problems, offered them drinks and an open mike. He's not above being fooled, like when his favorite bartender Ramon betrayed him and Angel, but he'd rather make love, not war.

As Angel sank deeper and deeper into depression and very murky moral ground during the Wolfram & Hart games with Darla, the Host sought him out in the hotel and valiantly tried to get him back in the game. He succeeded, in the crisis afforded by a young grad student who wanted to freeze time so his girlfriend would love him forever. Angel acted and, in fact, went on to have an epiphany: He's gonna do good simply for the sake of doing good. The Host was delighted.

But then Landok, one of the Host's cousins from his homeworld, fell through a dimensional portal and spilled the beans about "Lorne's" past. Forces on all sides—including the real psychic Lorne sometimes consults—pressured Lorne to return to Pylea, one of the catalysts being that Cordelia had accidentally been transported there, and he reluctantly went home again.

"Did I mention the part where I don't go?"

In Pylea, he was the most grata-less persona ever, rejected by everyone, including his bearded mother. His brother, Numfar, danced the Dance of Shame while Lorne sighed for the comforts and colors and music of Los Angeles.

The final indignity came when he was beheaded, but he was overjoyed when he realized that his body, which was secretly returned to his family seat by the Groosalugg, was not thrown into the maggot pile by his mom. Therefore she must have some feeling for him, beyond wishing him dead and scattered to the four winds.

Lorne returned to Los Angeles more certain than ever that he wouldn't go back to Pylea. But he definitely needed to go, one last time.

"I always said I would never go back. But I needed to go . . ."

The Host is played by Andy Hallett, and he appeared in episodes #1, 3, 5, 6, 9, 11, 13, and through the end of Season Two.

FRED (Winifred Burkle)

"Bad things always happen here."

Fred is a young woman in a vision of Cordy's, last seen in the library where she worked. A physics student, she apparently vanished into thin air.

As Angel and Co. worked their way through the details about her disappearance, Cordelia was accidentally sucked through a portal to the otherplace of Pylea . . . the Host's homeworld. Eventually, all of Team Angel ended up there—and it was Cordelia who first met Fred where they were imprisoned among other humans and forced to work. Fred was pretty wacko and extremely skittish—the result of having been first a slave, and then a fugitive, for over five years.

When Fred was recaptured, Angel received the honor of beheading her. Instead, he rescued her, and she led him to safety in her "tree." There she had been working on mathematical equations, although she couldn't remember why. Angel gently reminded her of her life back in the Earth dimension, but Fred wasn't sure what was real anymore.

When the hideous demon that resides inside Angel manifested itself, Fred was not afraid of it. Like the maiden with the unicorn, her innocence had a calming influence on him. When he was not Angelbeast, she fed him her weirdo concoction of Crug-grain, thistles, and Kalla-berries. A resourceful girl, she killed the Captain of the Guard when he attempted to take them prisoner.

When Angel, the Host, Gunn, Wesley, and Cordelia got ready to escape, they brought Fred with them in Angel's Chevy as it barreled through the portal. She's back in L.A. now, staying with Angel in the hotel, and it looks like there'll be a bit of a readjustment for the strange girl. . . .

"Fish tacos on every corner."

Fred is played by Amy Acker, and she appeared in episodes #19 through 22 of Season Two. She is a cast regular for Season Three.

DARLA

"I can show you the world."

The story of Darla slowly unfolds, starting with a flashback to Galway, 1753, the night when she transformed Angel into a vampire. Deeply smitten with him, she exulted as he was reborn, and guided him into his first kills—among them, his entire human family. When, after the killing of the Gypsy girl in 1898, Angel's soul was restored, Darla was repulsed by him—although her love for him was still very much alive. In a frenzy of grief and rage, she banished him from her presence.

When they met again, almost a hundred years later, she was back in the service of her sire, the Master, and a reformed Angel was serving at the side of the Slayer. Though she tried to lure Angel back to the fold, he killed her. Shocked, she dissolved into ash. . . .

In Los Angeles a few years later, Wolfram & Hart summoned the demon Vocah to conduct a raising, to bring back one who could defeat or distract Angel. That "one" turned out to be Darla, who was completely freaked out that she was back among the conscious undead . . . or was she?

"It was so long ago, I don't even remember my real name."

While Buffy may be Angel's soul mate, Darla was his obsession.

Realizing this, Wolfram & Hart raised her, bringing her back to this plane of existence. However, she returned not as a vampire, but as a human being. At first, confused about why she was brought back human, she conformed to their plans, nearly succeeding in driving Angel crazy in dreams and drugged visitations. She began to let him "see" her as a woman with her "husband" in a restaurant, walking in Santa Monica, providing Angel with blurry glimpses of her here and there. He was tormented, and she was glad. His sire Darla was the closest thing to a wife Angel ever had, and she would not tolerate being a woman scorned.

But nor did she particularly relish being a human woman. She hated the heartbeat in her chest, she declared to Angel, in defiance of all of Wolfram & Hart's plans, and wanted with all that heart to become a vampire again. Angel refused to be the one to change her, telling her that the vampire life she led him into was no gift, but a pronouncement of doom and misery. Aware that this meant he was rejecting her as well, she tried to understand him, tried to figure out what it was he found so attractive about being human.

But time was running out for Darla. In her first life, in colonial America, she was dying of syphilis, in her case an occupational hazard. It was then the Master came to her bedside and changed her into a vampire. Now, the syphilis had returned and was too far along to be cured by modern means. She was terrified of dying. Angel underwent a magical trial to save her, but the result was what neither of them expected . . . Angel and Darla learned that Darla would not be healed of her syphilis: she had already used up her chance to be "reborn" in the human mold. Surprisingly Darla accepted her imminent death. Influenced by Angel's encouragement, she decided she was meant to die the way she should have in Colonial days. Darla wanted only to be a good person, deserving of Angel's love in the end.

"Life's too short. Believe me, I know. Four hundred years, and it's still too short."

But Wolfram & Hart, specifically the love-struck lawyer Lindsey McDonald, wasn't ready to let her go. Lindsey tracked down Drusilla and offered the madwoman a chance to change her own grandsire. The idea appealed to Dru, and she arrived in L.A. in time to "save" grandma by changing her back into a vampire while a bound, helpless Angel looked on.

After her second change, Darla maintained a relationship with W&H, but on her own terms. She sent the firm a "fifteen-body memo" to let them know that she was not their puppet any longer. Sparing both Lindsey and Lilah, she waited to see which of them would survive at the firm, not returning the love Lindsey showered on her.

She also ran with Drusilla, who was now both Darla's sire and her "granddaughter," as Dru was sired by Angel. Drusilla called Darla "Grandmother," something Darla didn't love, but Dru was from the old days when Angelus (and Spike) were part of her vampire family. Though Darla had her moments when Dru's insanity grated on her, it was better to have a crazed companion than no one.

> **"Why is everyone trying to make this about Angel? For God's sake, can't a woman
> wreak a little havoc without there being a man involved?"**

Darla also still carried a torch for Angel . . . until he badly burned her in a terrible gasoline fire. She is surprised by the brutality and darkness within him, and allowed Lindsey McDonald to provide her safe harbor until she healed. Then she tried once more to get her "dear boy" back by coming to him at his lowest point.

But his moment of true happiness did not occur . . . because he didn't love her.

Awash in misery, Darla left Angel, left Lindsey, left L.A.

But actions have consequences, and Darla was gifted with a new soul in an unexpected way, and soon finds herself in a role she never expected: loving mother.

Darla is played by Julie Benz and appears in episodes #15, 18, and 22 of Season One, as well as #1, 3, 4, 5, 7, 9, 10, 11, 15, and 16 of Season Two.

LINDSEY MCDONALD

> **"Me, I'm unreliable, I've got evil hand issues and I'm bored
> with this crap. Besides, I'm leaving, you want to chase me?
> Be my guest."**

Sexy, driven Lindsey McDonald was one of the rising young stars at Wolfram & Hart. He started out life in dire poverty, watching the system grind down his father, and vowed that he would never be anybody's victim. After a sterling career in law school, he showed incredible initiative at W&H, helping evil and/or demonic clients escape the long arm of the law time and again.

Lindsey was alerted to the presence of "a new player in town" when Angel dispatched Lindsey's vampire client, Russell Winters. Lindsey kept his eye on Angel and tried to put him out of the game, from setting the law on him to hiring Faith to kill him. None of his plans succeeded.

> **"I want out."**

When W&H hired a powerful woman named Virginia Brewer to kill three children who were gifted with marvelous seeing powers, the brutality of the planned murders sickened Lindsey. He appealed to Angel, telling him he wanted to leave Wolfram & Hart for good. Angel enlisted him in defending the three children, which included helping Angel infiltrate W&H.

Holland Manners, Lindsey's mentor at the firm, realized that Lindsey was wavering and had a long talk with him. After the caper was concluded, he lured Lindsey back into the fold with a better job title, a huge raise . . . and Holland's office. The older man was "going upstairs" to a better position as well.

The stakes upped for his soul, Lindsey found he could be bought after all. His crisis of conscience was over, and he went back to W&H.

He resumed his campaign against Angel, assisting with a mysterious ritual to raise a new enemy to fight the vampire. A demon named Vocah was called in to perform the rite, but was astounded to discover that during Lindsey's brief trip to the side of good, Angel lifted the scroll containing the Prophecy

17

of Aberjian from the W&H vaults. The words of Anatole, contained within the scroll, were required for the raising.

Vocah insisted that W&H leave the retrieving of the scroll to him, and Lindsey and the others obeyed. Vocah came through, putting Wesley and Cordelia out of action and into the hospital.

The raising began, and Angel arrived to stop it. As Angel battled Vocah, an angered Lindsey snatched up the scroll and successfully performed the raising, losing his hand to Angel afterward.

For Lindsey McDonald, there were new scores to settle.

"It's a good plan and I'll tell you why, because of the his-finding-you-instead part."

His attempts to remove Angel resulted in a deadlock. Holland Manners had informed Lindsey that the point was not to kill Angel, merely to turn him evil (into Angelus) or sideline him. They realized that Angel was pivotal to the endgame Wolfram & Hart were playing; it's which side he would be on that remained unclear. So Lindsey had to be content to keep him alive while Wolfram & Hart tried to turn him dark.

Lindsey had tottered back and forth between good and evil ever since Angel came to L.A. He was so brilliant and cagey that, truthfully, even his law firm's machinations were beginning to feel pointless. Added to that his heartache over Darla's obvious preference for Angel, and he saw no reason in prolonging the pain.

Lindsey more clearly became the Cain to Angel's Abel as Season Two unfolded. In a triangle with Darla, they were wound tightly together, and that bond became stronger for all the interaction between them: At first conspiring against Angel, eager to kill him and be done with all the hassle he represents, Lindsey was forced to work with him to solve the mystery of the new hand his ever-supportive employers provided. The humans whose bits were being sliced off, slowly but surely, by the lab that gave him his hand, disgusted even Lindsey.

Lindsey missed the music he could make with his guitar; in Caritas, he sang his heart out for the psychic Host . . . and with his new hand he was *good*. He moved everyone in the club—even Angel, who tried to mask his jealousy with really stupid wisecracks. Lindsey loved Darla with a real, shining love. And he displayed kindness in saving Lilah's life, by pointing out her loyalty, how hard she'd worked . . . and the dirt she had on the people who were about to execute her.

". . . L.A.? You can have it."

There was much good in Lindsey, including his parting words to Angel, in the form of advice about how to deal with W&H. In his laid-back gear of jeans, shirt, and kicker boots, piled into his truck, he took what was left of his soul and headed for somewhere else, somewhere to start over.

Assuming he evaded the cops . . .

Lindsey is played by Christian Kane. He appeared in episodes #1, 18, 19, 21, and 22 of Season One, and #1, 5, 7, 9, 10, 11, 15, 16, and 18 of Season Two.

LILAH MORGAN

"Green is my favorite color, I look good in diamonds, and I love riding in limousines."

Lilah Morgan is a beautiful, ambitious, and ruthless attorney at Wolfram & Hart. The competition between her and Lindsey grew as each tried to be the one to put Angel out of commission. She actually offered the vampire a job at W&H after she plucked him from the demon gladiatorial games run by the MacNamara brothers. She was also present at the raising of Darla, though she backed off when things got out of hand.

> **"I heard Henderson actually pulled her firstborn out of company daycare to offer it up . . . brownnoser. My mother was right . . . I should have had children."**

Lilah Morgan

Current Assignment:
Co-Vice-President
for Special Projects

Junior Associate, 1994
Senior Associate, 1997
Junior Partner, 2000

Graduate of Mortonson University
School of Law, 1994, with high honors
Law Review, 1992-94
Recruited by Los Angeles office,
supervised by Holland Manners

OPEN   CLOSE

After Holland Manners's death in the wine cellar incident, his successor Nathan Reed decided to pair Lilah and Lindsey together to run the Special Projects Division. The firm would watch their effectiveness, judge their performances, and eventually cull the herd—one would stay and have a new job title, and one would go and have a new headstone.

Lilah was exceedingly nervous about this state of affairs, terrified that she would end up with the headstone. The far more sanguine Lindsey made her crazy with his *laissez*-die attitude, and she figured he must be up to things that he was not sharing with her. She looked through his stuff, she tried to make nice to Darla, she wore a wire to entrap him, and she even tried to seduce him.

When Angel surprised her by waiting for her in her car, she nearly came unhinged. As her failures continued to mount up—the loss of Bethany, the psychokinetic girl whose father was abusing her; the loss of the Big Hold-up cash; the wine-cellar slaughter; and her seeming lack of day-to-day preparation, in contrast to the more composed Lindsey—she feared for her life. Never mind that in most of her fiascoes she worked with Lindsey. Though he was clearly in trouble for his mistakes, he had a better Teflon coating than she did. So when the firm rewarded Lindsey with a new hand, she figured her days were numbered.

She was right. As their review period came to an end, Lindsey was in and she was out. But just as she was about to be executed and Lindsey celebrated, Lindsey handed the job to her and split. Lilah missed dying by seconds . . . on second thought, she didn't miss it at all.

A more confident Lilah stepped up to the plate in Lindsey's absence. Now if she could only figure out how to thwart Angel. . . .

Lilah Morgan is played by Stephanie Romanov. She appeared in episodes #1, 18, 19, 21, and 22 of Season One, and in #1, 4, 10, 11, 12, 15, and 18 of Season Two.

KATE LOCKLEY

> **"You've got some pretty weird stuff for a veterinarian."**

Kate Lockley was a detective on the LAPD force. She and Angel both lied to each other the first time they met, and they never quite managed to establish a bond of trust. She was working undercover, trying to find a killer, and he was doing the same. She initially didn't tell him she was a cop and he didn't reveal his vampire nature to her. Though she believed him to be the killer, he saved her from the real killer and they began an acquaintance of sorts, even sharing information to get to Dr. Ronald Meltzer, although she was highly suspicious of his lack of P.I. credentials.

Meanwhile, she was trying to deal with her relationship with her father, Trevor. After her mother died, he shut down emotionally. Kate was starved for love and attention, but he never provided it. She tried for a long time to be good enough for him, including following him into police work, but she eventually gave up. When she was cursed by Allen Lloyd's Talking Stick, she opened up and stated her case. Unfortunately

she did so in a room full of her father's friends and coworkers, and while most of them were similarly affected, her father, now retired from the force, never held the stick and so he remained desensitized. While under the influence of the Talking Stick she also demonstrated her affection for Angel. The morning after, her father remained his cold self, and Kate put distance between herself and Angel.

When Angel's old protégé, Penn, hit town, Angel and Kate found themselves on a collision course to discover his identity and whereabouts. Again Kate was worried that the mysterious Angel was the killer. When she finally discovered that the killer was a vampire and saw Angel go to "vamp face" to battle the creature, she emotionally turned against Angel—although in her bid to drive a two-by-four through Penn's chest, she purposely avoided doing the same to Angel. But she made it clear that they were no longer friends, and never would be.

That notion was cemented when her father was murdered by vampires. True, he was running demonic drugs for their boss, but Kate couldn't get past the notion that evil things—things just like Angel—brutally killed the man whose love she never managed to win. From then on, it was war between her and Angel . . . a war that escalated when she discovered—from Lindsey McDonald, of all people— that Angel was harboring a wanted criminal: Faith. When he wouldn't surrender the Slayer, Kate turned hard cop and threatened Angel with a sunlit jail cell until he would divulge Faith's location. She meant it, too, and Angel was about to be fatally locked up when Faith arrived and turned herself in.

From then on, Kate tried to be in on every investigation that had a supernatural bent to it. The rest of the force ridiculed her for it, but Kate didn't care. She was a woman on a mission: to rid the city of Angel's kind.

Poor Kate. During the past year, she had to come to grips with the death of her father, the knowledge that L.A. is crawling with evil of the supernatural kind, and ridicule from her fellow officers for trying to defeat that evil. Worst of all, Angel let her down terribly. He instigated the slaughter of thirty people she was sworn to protect—the lawyers at Wolfram & Hart. Kate had no personal love for W&H, but they had sworn out a complaint against Angel, predicting their demise at his hands—accurately, it would appear, except that Angel chose to let Dru and Darla to do his dirty work.

Angel and Kate still crossed paths, and they still knocked heads, as when she helped with the zombie cop investigation. But as a result of that particular case, Internal Affairs investigated her, and the police department fired her. Left with no identity, no friends, no family, Kate sought to end her own life.

But she reached out one more time . . . to Angel, the one person on the planet to whom she still felt any kind of connection. She made a suicide attempt that was clearly a plea for help as she phoned Angel, so needing him to care enough to save her life . . . on many levels. When he arrived, finding her unconscious, he entered her apartment—her world—without any difficulty. The fact that Angel showed, and the fact that he was able to enter and save her despite never having been invited in, gave Kate the hope that she needed to go on. What will happen to her is anybody's guess . . . but she will now be able to face it with more courage and self-respect than before she reached out, and Angel reached back.

"I think maybe we're not alone in this. . . . Because I never invited you in."

Kate Lockley is played by Elisabeth Rohm. She appeared in episodes #2, 4, 5, 6, 11, 14, 15, 18, 19, and 22 of Season One, and episodes #5, 8, 10, 14, 15, and 16 of Season Two.

BUFFY ANNE SUMMERS

"I felt your heart beat."

Buffy the Vampire Slayer was, is, and always will be Angel's soul mate. She knows it, and he knows it, and though she has tried to move on, all other men walk in the sunlight. Angel is her shadow side, the true other half of her, and though they cannot be together as lovers, no man or God or Powers That Be can sever the deep bond between them.

The Slayer was called in Los Angeles in 1997, and Angel was there. He secretly watched her terror as she began to train and made her first kills, and he fell in love with her. He vowed to help her, even though he had cut himself off from all humanity and vampiredom (which he did again, when he exiled himself to Los Angeles).

Buffy's relationship with Angel stalled early on when she discovered that he was a vampire. A Slayer to the core, she went after him, sparing him after he killed Darla, one of his own kind. Buffy learned that he had been "cursed" with the return of his soul so that he might spend his immortal life regretting the suffering he caused as Angelus, once the most vicious vampire to walk the earth.

They continued to fight the good fight side-by-side. Soon Buffy loved Angel with all her soul, literally, and gave herself to him on the night of her seventeenth birthday. Their perfect love ripped his soul away from him.

Things looked very dire. Then Buffy and her best friend, Willow, discovered a spell that would return Angel's soul to his body. Buffy tracked down Angel, who had set a rite in motion to suck every living thing on the planet into Hell. By the time she found him, the rite could only be reversed by the sacrifice of Angel himself. Though Willow had clearly succeeded and Angel's soul had returned, Buffy still sacrificed him to save the world.

Ultimately Angel was returned from a hell dimension by The Powers That Be. Still in residual physical and emotional pain, he and Buffy tried to stay away from each other. Driven by his need for her and scared for her safety, Angel even tried to kill himself on Christmas Day. He knew he wasn't strong enough to do it himself, so he merely waited for the sun to come up. Buffy and The Powers That Be saved him and convinced him that life was worth living. Angel and Buffy resumed a loving, but platonic, relationship.

When Buffy returned from the big city, she met Faith, who proved to be a rogue Slayer, insanely jealous of the affection and attention Buffy received from everyone, including Angel. She poisoned Angel to distract Buffy from the evil mayor's plans for demonhood. Buffy saved Angel, but in the process lost him forever when he decided he could no longer be around her. Angel left Sunnydale, ending up in L.A.

Buffy later learned that Angel had covertly returned to Sunnydale to help her fight the revenge-seeking spirits of some Native American warriors and went to Los Angeles to confront him. While she was there he was magically transformed into a human man. Once again they made love. Buffy was aware that life with Angel as a regular human would be difficult, but she still wanted him. However, Angel quickly realized he wasn't as valuable in a fight, and when he learned this vulnerability would cost Buffy—and countless others—her life, he went to The Powers That Be and asked them to change him back. They agreed.

When Angel told Buffy that he asked The Powers That Be to make him a vampire again in order to protect her, she was devastated. But The Powers made sure that she, like everyone else—except Angel—forgot that the transformation ever occurred.

The next time she came to L.A. was when she learned that Faith had gone there. She was determined to protect Angel from the evil Slayer . . . and then discovered that Angel had taken Faith under his wing, determined to rehabilitate her. Buffy was stunned and hurt, and her parting from Angel was not good. . . .

"What, you came back here because you thought of something more hurtful to say, and you would've phoned, but the look on my face was just so funny?"

Angel went back to Sunnydale to apologize; he didn't want to leave things that way. He met Buffy's new boyfriend, Riley, and it became clear to him that Buffy had moved on, even though Riley wouldn't last a few more months. Not because Riley didn't love her—he did—but because he felt she didn't love him in return.

When Buffy's mother died, Angel traveled to Sunnydale (again) to be with Buffy . . . until the sun came up. He offered to stay as long as she wanted him to, but both agreed she'd need to be strong on her own.

Upon their triumphant return from Pylea, with the rescued, adoring Fred in tow, the Angel Investigations team found Willow Rosenberg waiting for them. And Angel knew instantly that she was there with news of Buffy, and that it wasn't good.

> **ANGEL:** "You still my girl?"
> **BUFFY:** "Always."

Buffy Summers is played by Sarah Michelle Gellar. She appeared in episodes #8 and 19 of Season One.

BROTHER AND SISTER ORACLES

"Now, the Oracles are finicky and unpredictable." —*Doyle*

The Oracles are higher beings who can commune with The Powers That Be (aka TPTB) and provide worthy supplicants with cryptic hints about what is to come—provided they get some swag in return.

On Angel's first encounter with the Oracles, he sacrificed his watch, and the second time he offered an antique Chinese vase. On that occasion, the two agreed to refold time and "swallow" the twenty-four hours when Angel became human.

Doyle was the one who told Angel about the Oracles. He led Angel to "The Gateway for Lost Souls,"

a portal beneath the post office. From there, Angel is magickally brought into the never-ending chamber where the Oracles grant audiences. Doyle himself is barred from their presence—he's a mere messenger, while Angel is a full warrior for the side of good. Like both Angel and Doyle, the Oracles owe fealty to The Powers That Be.

Angel first approached them after he had been rendered human by the Mohra demon's blood. While this allowed him to enjoy a relationship with Buffy (and also to enjoy ice cream), it also hampered his ability to fight the good fight, and—he learned—would ultimately hasten Buffy's demise. He asked to be restored to his warrior status, and the Oracles granted this, along with a little memory wipe to all involved in the preceding hot-and-heavy twenty-four hours. Except Angel. Once again, his memories would weigh on him.

Later, when a grief-stricken Angel approached the Oracles to restore Doyle, they dismissed his request as beneath them, assuring him that he would still have contact to TPTB, as in the saying "When a door closes, a window opens." He left their chambers to discover that Doyle had "gifted" Cordelia with the power of his visions before he sacrificed himself to the save the Brachen clan.

Unfortunately, the demon Vocah was also able to enter the Oracles' chamber. To cut Angel off from TPTB, he killed both Oracles. The Sister's ghost had one last conversation with Angel to tell him, in her cryptic Delphi way of course, how to stop the raising, of which Vocah was a part. Though Angel failed to stop the raising, TPTB still communicate with him through Cordelia, aka Vision Girl.

The Oracles were played by Randall Slavin (the Brother) and Carey Cannon (the Sister), and appeared in Episodes #8, 10, and 22 of Season One.

FAITH

"I gotta be the first Slayer in history to be sponsored by a vampire."

In every generation, there is one girl called to become the Slayer. It is she, and she alone, who will fight the demons, the vampires, and the forces of darkness. . . .

Except in practice it doesn't always work that way. On prom night in 1997, Buffy Summers, the Vampire Slayer, died at the hands of the Master. Xander Harris revived her with CPR. But as she was momentarily technically dead, another Slayer was called to carry on the line. This was Kendra. Thus, for the first time, there were two Slayers at the same time. Then Drusilla killed Kendra, and Faith was called.

Faith's first Watcher was tortured to death before her eyes by the vampire Kakistos, and Faith high-tailed it to Sunnydale to hook up with Buffy. For a time, Buffy's Watcher, Giles, took care of both Slayers. When Giles was fired by the Council of Watchers, Wesley Wyndam-Pryce, who had been assigned to Faith, took over training duties for both girls, though they rarely paid him any attention.

Angel Cordelia Doyle Wesley Gunn The Host Fred Darla Lindsey Lilah Kate Bu
Kate The Oracles Faith Holland Drusilla Anne Angel Cordelia Doyle Wesley Gu
The Ho Drus
Anne A Ka
Buffy An
Angel e Ho
Fred D Drus
Cordeli Da
Lindsey Drus
Anne A Gu
The Ho Lil
Kate B Ang
Cordeli e Ho
Fred D Bu
The Or An
Angel Wes
Buffy An
Angel e Ho
Fred D Drus
Cordeli Da
Lindsey Drus
Anne A Gu
The Ho Lil
Kate B
Cordeli Ho
Fred D Bu
The Or An
Buffy Isi
Angel
Doyle Ang

Reeling from the constantly changing authorities, as well as the betrayal by a fake interim Watcher, Gwendolyn Post, who lied to Faith at the same time Buffy kept secrets from her, Faith accidentally took a human life. The burden of that act, plus her already unstable mental condition, took their toll: She snapped. She allied herself with the evil mayor of Sunnydale and tried to distract Buffy from his Ascension by shooting Angel with a poisoned crossbow bolt. Only the blood of a Slayer could save him, and Buffy came after Faith to make her provide it. Badly beaten, Faith escaped Buffy, but she lapsed into a coma for eight months.

When she woke up, angry to discover the mayor had been killed, that Buffy and Angel had split up, that she was wanted for murder, and that she really had nothing left in the world, Faith traded bodies with Buffy, using magic left to her by the vanquished mayor. She tried to kill Buffy's mother and slept with Buffy's boyfriend, Riley. Buffy defeated her again, switching their bodies back, and Faith fled Sunnydale, eventually ending up in Los Angeles.

Lindsey McDonald, Lilah Morgan, and Lee Mercer hired Faith for fifteen thousand dollars to assassinate Angel. She clocked Cordelia and tortured Wesley, but she couldn't get Angel to do what she really wanted, which was to put her out of her misery . . . permanently. Angel believed that she could be redeemed and even defied an angry, vengeful Buffy in favor of defending Faith. So far, his trust has borne fruit: Faith turned herself into the police, and she is incarcerated in a Los Angeles jail.

> **FAITH:** "The road to redemption is a rocky path."
> **ANGEL:** "That it is."
> **FAITH:** "Think we might make it?"
> **ANGEL:** "We might."

Faith and Angel have clearly developed a strong bond, predicated on the fact that each has done terrible things for which they are now willing to pay. At the beginning of Season Two, Angel visited Faith in jail, where the Slayer is willingly serving her time. It's a tough road, though, for she has to restrain herself from using her powers of slayage, even when she's being beaten or threatened with a homemade shiv. But contact with Angel . . . and his faith in her . . . keeps her going.

Faith is played by Eliza Dushku. She appeared in episodes #18 and 19 of Season One, as well as episode #1 of Season Two.

HOLLAND MANNERS

"I did a lot of crazy things when I was your age, searching and all. It took me a while to realize how the world is put together and where I belonged in it. And actually, the world isn't that complicated for those who know how to use it."

Holland Manners was Lindsey McDonald's superior at Wolfram & Hart. He handpicked Lindsey when Lindsey was a sophomore at law school, seeing the potential in the young man. He was aware of Lindsey's betrayal in the matter of the seer children, yet when Lindsey came back to take his punishment, Holland rewarded him with a promotion. He was moving up, too.

Holland was present for the raising of Darla, and it was clear that he envisioned great things arising from her arrival.

Ever-cool, professional Holland still never got his hands dirty, though he orchestrated various murders, executions, tampering with witnesses, and creating tortured childhoods for the brutal assassins in the employ of Wolfram & Hart. A terrifying father figure, he had a special affection for Lindsey, and he groomed the young man to rise like a star, even reminding Lindsey to make time for a personal connection now and then. After all, Holland had a lovely trophy wife who played hostess to her husband's proud wine tastings in his former-bomb-shelter wine cellar. Though he died in the wine cellar, and at the hands (or teeth) of the vampires he employed, he continues to work for W&H—his contract extends beyond death. It is he who acted as Angel's guide to the "Home Office," a sort of Faustian journey which resulted in Angel's realization that Earth's the best place for evil, or what is redemption for?

> **"Our firm has always been here in one form or another. The Inquisition, the Khmer Rouge . . . we were here the first time a caveman clubbed his neighbor and watched in fascination as his brains oozed out in the dirt. We're in the hearts and minds of every living being and that, friend, is what's making things so difficult for you. The senior partners are evil and powerful beyond imagination, and you can try to fight them, but that's the source of their power. The world doesn't work in spite of evil, Angel. It works with us. It works because of us."**

Holland also appeared posthumously in the promo video for Anne's East Hills Teen Center at the Big Hold-up, his warm, fuzzy image a chilling counterpoint to the man he was in life . . . and still is, in death.

Holland Manners was played by Sam Anderson, and appeared in episodes #21 and 22 of Season One and #4, 7, 8, 10, 12, and 15 of Season Two.

DRUSILLA (Dru)

> **"I didn't like that barkeeper.**
> **I can't get his eyes off my fingers."**

Except for nearly dying in the fire her sire set specifically to kill her, Angel's vampire "daughter" Drusilla is happy to be back in the loop after having been run out of Sunnydale a few years earlier. Wolfram & Hart located her and brought her to Los Angeles to change back Darla, her "grandmother," and Dru was more than happy to do so. She treated Darla's rebirth into vampiric life with the tenderness and anticipation of a new mother. Doting on Darla, happy to be hanging out, she loved the shopping, the partying, and the killing. But after Angel set the two of them on fire, she and Darla parted ways.

Drusilla is played by Juliet Landau and appears in episodes #5, 7, 10, and 11 of Season Two.

ANNE STEELE (Lily, Chantarelle)

"It'll wash."

"Anne Steele" is actually Lily, who was also Chantarelle, Sister Sunshine, and a number of other personas as the lost waif staggered through life. She was one of Sunnydale's Goths, following the promise of Ford,

worshipping the Lost Ones, eager to become a vampire through the good graces of Spike, until she saw what a vampire really was: a ravening, bloodsucking beast. Buffy and her gang saved Lily and most of the others, and Lily fled Sunnydale, eventually ending up in the big city. . . .

. . . Where she and a new boyfriend lived on the streets, scrounging for hand-outs and making money donating blood (ironic, huh?). But the blood drive was a front for a demon overlord looking for fresh servants for his own hell region.

Lily was rescued from the hell dimension by Buffy, who had fled to the city after killing Angel, and now saved the girl from the path she was going down. Buffy gave Lily her waitressing job, and her middle name—Anne—but more importantly, Buffy gave her some self-respect and some hope.

Now Anne runs the East Hills Teen Center for runaways in L.A., and she runs it well. But it was a financial struggle to make it from month to month—there are so many kids on the street—and she was getting pretty low on donations when a guardian angel stepped forward: Lindsey McDonald, of the law firm Wolfram & Hart. The firm organized the Big Hold-up for her, a charity bash during which famous actors and actresses pretended to hold up the attendees for big, fat donations.

Angel, who "accidentally" ran into her on the street, and then stopped by the shelter with a "dona-tion" of Cordelia's clothes, told her the whole thing was a scam. W&H was planning to steal almost all the money. He had been keeping her under surveillance because of her connection to them—an admis-sion that frightened her, half-convincing her that Angel was a psycho-stalker.

Eventually, his powers of persuasion prevailed over Lindsey's charm. Angel told her he had proof on tape, and she agreed to expose W&H during the Big Hold-up. She managed to get to the tape player that was run-ning W&H's self-serving promo about her shelter, only to discover, like everyone else, that Angel did not, in fact, have the goods on the firm. His tape was of Cordy and Wesley fooling around with a video camera.

But his purpose was served. In trying to stop the (imaginary) tape exposé, Lilah, Lindsey, and the firm were humiliated and distracted. In the fracas, a nemesis of Angel's, Boone, jacked the donations . . . which Angel later gave to Anne. Though she was mad at being used by Angel merely to one-up the law firm, and there was blood all over the money, she accepted the tainted wealth, muttering, "It'll wash."

Later Anne provided haven at her shelter when zombie cops went on a rampage. She had known Gunn from her time on the streets and was happy to help him and Wesley out. She acquitted herself well as the protector of street kids as she once was. After all, that's just what she herself was before some-one took an interest and lent her more than a handout.

Anne Steele is played by Julia Lee, and she appeared in episodes #12 and 14 of Season Two.

EPISODE GUIDE

THE KEY

It's not just an episode guide. It's not just a dessert topping. It's The Key to the glory that is Angel. Presented for your perusal . . . all the nifty bits about the world of Broody Guy:

FROM THE FILES OF ANGEL INVESTIGATIONS

Title of the ep, who wrote it, who directed it, and who stopped by to act in it.
Case #: episode number

ACTION TAKEN: beautiful and moving recap of the events of the ep, including the Resolution, and whether the file got put in the "Case Closed" cabinet, lost by Cordelia, or has yet to be concluded.

DOSSIERS: a description of the Client; any Victims; the Suspects, i.e., whodunit and who might have dun it; and Civilian Support—people and things other than Team Angel that helped with the case.

CONTINUITY: elements of the case that resonated through the rest of the season, such as, if Cordelia finally manages to buy enough shoes to assure her own perfect moment of happiness (no peeking ahead!).

QUOTE OF THE WEEK: Like there's only *one*.

THE DEVIL IS IN THE DETAILS

EXPENSES: proof positive that crimefighting is not cheap.

WEAPONRY: the stabby, firey, mangly bits.

THE PLAN: rarely followed, often yearned for.

DEMONS, DEMONS, DEMONS: is a Kailiff demon lime green or mauve? Do Mohra demons crave salt, and what about that Goddess Yeska, anyway?
With a subsection of The Vampire Rules (can Angel have his picture taken? If so, will he *smile* for it?) so you can play along at home.

AS SCENE IN L.A.: locations of the locations.

THE PEN IS MIGHTIER

FINAL CUT: it's in the script but not in the episode.

POP CULTURE: we keep current so you don't have to!

OUR HEROES: from hours of interviews on set and by phone, sound *bites* from the cast and crew.

SIX DEGREES OF . . . : linking the actors and crew through their work, i.e., Christian Kane and Julie Benz were both on *Fame L.A.*

TRACKS: karaoke, compositions, and music cues.

Angel Episode Guide

SEASON ONE

EPISODE NUMBER	EPISODE NAME	ORIGINAL U.S. AIR DATE
1ADH01	"City Of"	October 5, 1999
1ADH02	"Lonely Heart"	October 12, 1999
1ADH03	"In the Dark"	October 19, 1999
1ADH04	"I Fall to Pieces"	October 26, 1999
1ADH05	"Rm w/a Vu"	November 2, 1999
1ADH06	"Sense and Sensitivity"	November 9, 1999
1ADH07	"The Bachelor Party"	November 16, 1999
1ADH08	"I Will Remember You"	November 23, 1999
1ADH09	"Hero"	November 30, 1999
1ADH10	"Parting Gifts"	December 14, 1999
1ADH11	"Somnambulist"	January 18, 2000
1ADH12	"Expecting"	January 25, 2000
1ADH13	"She"	February 8, 2000
1ADH14	"I've Got You Under My Skin"	February 15, 2000
1ADH15	"The Prodigal"	February 22, 2000
1ADH16	"The Ring"	February 29, 2000
1ADH17	"Eternity"	April 4, 2000
1ADH18	"Five by Five"	April 25, 2000
1ADH19	"Sanctuary"	May 2, 2000
1ADH20	"War Zone"	May 9, 2000
1ADH21	"Blind Date"	May 16, 2000
1ADH22	"To Shanshu in L.A."	May 23, 2000

STARRING

David Boreanaz . . . . Angel

Charisma Carpenter . . . . Cordelia Chase

Glenn Quinn . . . . Allen Francis Doyle (through "Hero")

Alexis Denisof . . . . Wesley Wyndam-Pryce (beginning with "Parting Gifts")

"CITY OF"

FROM THE FILES OF ANGEL INVESTIGATIONS
CASE Nº: 1ADH01

ACTION TAKEN

It's night in Los Angeles, City of Broken Dreams. Time for trendy clubs, warp-speed hookups, and unfulfilled hopes.

Angel sits in a bar, empty shot glasses lined up, pretending to be drunk. But he's got prey to follow—three vampires on the prowl for California girls who have no idea what they've gotten themselves into.

Black coat swirling like shadows and fog, Angel trails them outside. The vamps throw off their human masks and sharpen up for the kill. Angel does the same, and the battle begins. Vampire #1 is taken out with ratcheted stakes telescoping from Angel's coat sleeves, and Angel slams the other two around, dusting the trio.

When the girls thank him, he smells the blood from their wounds, and the hunger rises inside him. He conquers the urge to drink—*this time*—and gets the hell away from them.

WRITTEN BY David Greenwalt & Joss Whedon
DIRECTED BY Joss Whedon
GUEST STARS: Tracy Middendorf (Tina), Vyto Ruginis (Russell Winters), Christian Kane (Lindsay McDonald)
CO-STARS: Jon Ingrassia (Stacy), Renee Ridgeley (Margo), Sam Pancake (Manager), Josh Holloway (Good Looking Guy), Gina McClain (Janice)

The sanctuary and loneliness of his new Los Angeles lair embrace the vampire—an unused office above, a brick basement apartment below. Weapons line the walls, as well as art objects that speak of his centuries of un-life—statues, paintings, and his own sketches. He unpacks tonight's portable arsenal and becomes aware that he is not alone.

His visitor is Doyle, a half-demon, who has been sent by The Powers That Be. Doyle has visions, and he's come to help Angel in his quest for atonement . . . and to save him from himself.

"Let me tell you something, pal. That craving is gonna grow. And one day soon one of those helpless victims you don't really care about is gonna look too appetizing to turn down. And you'll figure, 'What's one against all I've saved? I might as well eat them; I'm still ahead by the numbers.'" —*Doyle*

Doyle explains that he gets visions from The Powers That Be, who are "trying to make things right." These visions have told Doyle a lot about Angel, including his ill-fated romance with Buffy, and now have brought him to an initially reluctant Angel.

ANGEL: "Why me?"

DOYLE: "'Cause you got potential. And the balance sheet ain't exactly in your favor yet."

ANGEL: "Why you?"

DOYLE: "We all got something to atone for."

It's time for Angel to "mix" with the humans, and Doyle has brought Angel his first assignment from The Powers That Be: He is to help Tina, at the Coffee Spot in Santa Monica. A scrap of paper with that information is all Doyle can supply. Angel himself must solve the rest of the mystery—who she is and what she needs from the vampire with a soul.

Reluctantly, Angel accepts the case.

He drives to the Coffee Spot and locates Tina, who works there. He tries to strike up a conversation, but he could really use a set of cue cards. He's not so great with the small talk—or with any talk, for that matter. But his awkwardness actually charms the young woman, and she agrees to meet him after work.

He waits, and she shows, a knockout in her party dress and upswept hair, but wielding a can of Mace. Clearly terrified, she tells him to stay away from her. She orders him to tell Russell to leave her alone.

He tells her that he doesn't know Russell and he doesn't know what she's talking about. Somehow he connects; she believes him. He drives her to her "fabulous Hollywood party"—accent on sad irony—where she's hoping to collect her cleaning deposit money. She's trying to save up so she can go back home to Montana.

The party hostess is Margo, who merrily video-tapes Angel and Tina's arrival. Tina goes off with Margo to discuss the money, leaving Angel alone with "the beautiful people," including an agent named Oliver who immediately recognizes Angel's screen potential. Angel flounders, adrift in a sea of sharks, when he hears a very familiar voice. It belongs to Cordelia Chase, who has moved to Los Angeles from Sunnydale, aka Buffy Country.

Cordelia is all bright eyes and lies, as she assures Angel she's doing great in Los Angeles, with a wonderful career as an actress.

Stacey, a slimy thug, tries to strong-arm Tina when she rejoins the party scene—without her money, which Stacey seems to have some claim on. Angel intervenes, but Tina still won't level with him about what's going on. Finally, after she's accosted and he's attacked in the parking garage, he spirits her away to his apartment, and once there, she breaks down and spills about her mysterious benefactor, Russell.

As Tina sleeps, Angel uses the Los Angeles Public Library to do the research, and Denise comes up dead.

When he returns to his lair, Tina is waking from a nightmare. While he's telling her about Denise, she notices Doyle's note with her name and place of employment written on it. Positive now that Angel is working for Russell, she flees. When Angel reaches out to stop her, his arm reaches into the sunshine and bursts into flame. In agony, he vamps, and Tina escapes in terror.

She's almost finished packing her things at her apartment when Russell Winters himself arrives. She tries to fend him off with a gun, but he kills her. Russell Winters, it turns out, is a vampire.

Angel, having arrived too late, mourns, standing vigil from afar as Tina is bagged by the coroner's office and carted away. He assumes he has failed his first assignment from The Powers That Be.

At Winters's palatial estate, a handsome young attorney named Lindsey McDonald, from the firm of Wolfram & Hart, pays a call. Winters is bidding Tina adieu by watching her on videotape . . . the same video Margo shot at her party. While Lindsey calmly briefs Winters on the steps his firm has taken to shield the vampire from being implicated in Tina's murder, the demon zeroes in on Cordelia. His interest is piqued by this fresh face. He only wants something to eat.

After Lindsey leaves, Winters calls Margo so she can arrange a meeting with Cordelia. Margo does, interrupting Cordy's lonely soliloquy. Her stories to Angel are revealed to be lies as she suffers in squalor and unemployment. Cordelia happily accepts Margo's offer to introduce her to a rich and powerful man who might help her career and finances. At the appointed hour, the desperate Cinderella emerges from her dump of an apartment and is whisked off in a private limo to an audience with the powerful prince of stocks and bonds.

Meanwhile . . .

Tina is dead, but as Doyle reminds Angel, Russell Winters can still prey upon hundreds of young women. Realizing that Doyle has a point, Angel goes after the vampire. First he beats Winters's henchman, Stacey, to a pulp for Winters's address. Then he arms himself like a commando and Doyle drives him to the gates of Winters's compound, Angel unaware that Cordelia has arrived at the mansion and discovered Winters's secret.

She bolts, but Winters is right behind her. While Angel plants explosive charges to blow Winters to hell, Cordelia is running for her life down seemingly endless corridors and past grand staircases.

Angel enters the mansion, confronts the demon, and dedicates the impending kill to Tina. But in saving Cordelia, he lets Winters get away. Doyle, whose intention had been to drop Angel off and scram at the first sign of trouble, has actually suffered an attack of conscience and returns just in time to pick up Angel and Cordelia outside the house.

Angel needs no convincing to go after Winters again. Cordelia is in danger as long as the vampire is at large.

Angel lets nothing deter him, not even the light of day—and fortunately, a vamp who's also a captain of industry isn't hard to track down. In the luxury high-rise that houses Russell Winters Enterprises, Angel interrupts a meeting at which he is the main topic under discussion. Attorney Lindsey McDonald attempts to hold Angel at bay with vague threats of legal action, but Angel ignores him to focus on Winters. Winters tries a different approach to saving his own vampiric neck:

"We don't have to go around attacking each other. Look at me. I pay my taxes. I keep my name out of the paper. And I don't make waves. In return, I can do anything I want."   *—Russell Winters*

Angel, unimpressed, asks, "Can you fly?" He shoves the other vampire's wheeled office chair backward, through the tinted glass windows of his skyscraper, and out into the sun. Winters is reduced to a pile of cinders before the chair hits the ground.

As Angel strides out of the meeting room, Lindsey makes an urgent call on his cell phone.

"Set up an interoffice meeting at four. It seems we have a new player in town."*—Lindsey McDonald*

RESOLUTION

Lindsey isn't the only one making phone calls. Angel dials a number, but when Buffy's voice answers, he hangs up.

There is new life in Cordelia Chase's eyes, a purpose and direction she has lacked until now. She has decided to be Angel's office manager . . . if he'll have her. Angel Investigations—comprising Angel, Doyle, and Cordelia—is born.

Doyle is interested in Cordelia, although it remains to be seen if she will return his affections.

Wolfram & Hart are established as an enemy, and The Powers That Be are established as . . . The Powers That Be.

> **DOYLE:** "You know, there's a lot of people in this city need helping."
> **ANGEL:** "So I noticed."
> **DOYLE:** "You game?"
> **ANGEL:** "I'm game."

Case closed.

DOSSIERS

CLIENT Tina is the primary client in this case, as she's the woman to whom Doyle's vision referred. Hailing from Missoula, Montana, she was a former Girl Scout who could live out of her large black leather bag for days. She came to Los Angeles to become a movie star, but she was not prepared for the cruelty she would find there. (Deceased.)

Cordelia Chase is the secondary client of this case. Cordy's been on a downhill slide ever since she came to Los Angeles. Now she has a real purpose, an opportunity to grow as a person . . . and a salary, though as she puts it, only "until my inevitable stardom takes effect."

SUSPECTS Russell Winters is a wealthy international businessman and Hollywood power broker. He is also a vampire. (Deceased.) It's possible that **Margo** is aware of his double life, but, at the least, she acts as a procurer of playmates for him. (Remains at large.)

CONTINUITY

Doyle recaps a bunch of Angel's history, as seen on *Buffy*, when explaining his purpose for contacting Angel. Angel's temptation to drink from the girls in the alley is in part a consequence of his drinking Buffy's blood to save himself from Faith's poison in "Graduation Day, Part Two." Graduation day was also the last time Cordelia and Angel saw each other. While Cordelia is putting a bright facade on her life in L.A., she can't conceal her unhappiness about the IRS's interference in her family's finances, first mentioned in *Buffy* episode "The Prom." Angel's famous weapons cabinet is introduced in this episode. Hollywood agent Oliver Simon, who gives Angel his card, also represents Rebecca Lowell in "Eternity." Angel's abortive call to Buffy is symbolic of the difficulties they will experience trying to maintain a relationship, as seen in his visit to Sunnydale in "Pangs," and her visits to L.A.

QUOTE OF THE WEEK

CORDELIA: "So, are you still . . . grrr . . . ?"
ANGEL: "Yeah. There's not actually a cure for that."
Cordelia, having not seen Angel since her Sunnydale days, checks on his vampiric status.

THE DEVIL IS IN THE DETAILS

EXPENSES

2 plate glass windows
1 Mercedes Benz
The front end of Angel's 1967 Plymouth Belvedere GTX convertible

WEAPONRY

During this case, Angel uses double-ratcheted stakes, a broken piece of wood as a stake, a three-pronged gladiatorial hand trident, and plastic explosives. He threatens Stacey with a gun. Doyle uses Angel's car in his unsuccessful attempt to take down a security gate.

THE PLAN

Angel is not sure he is impressed with his new mission, having found Tina's corpse.

ANGEL: "She wanted to go home."

DOYLE: "Yeah."

ANGEL: "I'd like to compliment The Powers That Be on a terrific plan. I really saved the day."

DOYLE: "It didn't work out."

ANGEL: "It didn't work out? Tina died. A vampire ripped her throat out. Was that the grand scheme?"

DEMONS, DEMONS, DEMONS

THE VAMPIRE RULES

Vampires burst into flame when exposed to sunlight.

Vampires can eat, drink, and shoot pool. As dates, they generally suck.

They do not cast a reflection.

They can smell the difference between humans and nonhumans.

THE PEN IS MIGHTIER

"Wolfram" is actually a mineral, also called wolframite or, more commonly, tungsten.

FINAL CUT

In the original script, Angel was going to taste Tina's blood after her death, but the scene was cut. The intention was to show that Angel is really on the edge, really struggling, but the production team decided that it was enough that he wasn't able to save Tina.

Stage directions from the script:

A woman's laugh draws Angel's gaze to three GOOD-LOOKING GUYS shooting pool with TWO GOOD-LOOKING YOUNG WOMEN nearby. They're laughing, having a good time. One of the guys gets behind one of the women (JANICE, who may resemble Buffy) helping her line up a shot.

Stage directions:

Angel leaps over the last car and—cool action hero that he is—lands in a convertible. Problem is: it's the wrong convertible.

POP CULTURE

❇ **"You know, I'm parched from all this yakkin', man. Let's go treat me to a Billy D."** Doyle makes reference to the Billy Dee Williams (Lando Calrissian in Star Wars) commercials for Colt 45 Malt Liquor

OUR HEROES

"Given that you are kind of the Joss Whedon on Angel *with Joss on* Buffy, *what's the difference?*

DAVID GREENWALT, EXECUTIVE PRODUCER: "Well, first of all I have Joss, and secondly Joss eats, sleeps, and lives *Buffy* twenty-four hours a day and I eat, sleep, and live *Angel* seventeen hours a day."

And some further insight into the new show he shepherds . . .

DAVID GREENWALT: "The question arises, 'Are these shows for children or not and how scary are they?' And the WB gives a rating and some of the shows are for people fourteen and over and some of the shows are more for everyone. One of the things . . . that keeps the show alive and interesting for those of us who create it is that it's different week to week. One week it's a farce, one week it's a melodrama, and sometimes it's very, very scary. So it differs from week to week.

"My own son, who's nine, claims that *Angel* is his favorite show because his dad produces the show, but he's only seen a couple of them. I kind of sift carefully. And it's different for different kids because I have friends whose kids never miss one. It never bothers them. I think the shows can definitely have a shock to them, either in the horror or something in the story can turn very dark and you know one should look at that little guide I think, or watch one before you show them to your kids.

"Why did you pick a law firm as a haven for monsters?"

DAVID GREENWALT: "Joss came up with the idea [for] *Angel*, to say we need some overarching villainous group that is not, you know, a black ops group or not monstrous. And he had this idea of a law firm, Wolfram & Hart. What Joss loved about using a law firm is that they broker deals for people. In the first episode they just represent the bad guy. They are not per se evil themselves, they just represent, they make deals. I love writing Wolfram & Hart, and we have a number of terrific running characters."

"First question is, Angel's car, the Angelmobile: How many of them are there?"

ROBERT ELLIS, TRANSPORTATION COORDINATOR: "I love that car. There's three, actually. We purchased one and restored it about fifty percent capacity, because it didn't make sense to restore the car all the way, make it look perfect. Because that wasn't reality, we just had it so it was a nice car that he took care of. He took care of it, he liked it, it was part of his personality, pretty much. However, he wasn't obsessed with it. It was just a car. But then again, he wouldn't own something he didn't respect. It's the Batmobile, is what it is to a certain extent."

SIX DEGREES OF . . .

Christian Kane, who plays Wolfram & Hart attorney Lindsey McDonald, was Ryan (Flyboy) Legget in the series *Fame L.A.* The series was directed by Bruce Seth Green, who directed "In the Dark" on *Angel*. Kane appeared in *Summer Catch* with Marc Blucas, who plays Buffy Summers's boyfriend on *Buffy the Vampire Slayer* and Freddie Prinze, Jr., who is Sarah Michelle Gellar's (Buffy) real-life fiancé.

Tracy Middendorf (Tina) played Julie in *Wes Craven's New Nightmare*, the seventh film in the *Nightmare on Elm Street* franchise. One of the makeup crew was Douglas Noe, who is also one of the makeup artists on *Buffy*. Middendorf also appeared on a *Star Trek: Deep Space Nine* episode, where recurring *Buffy* guest star Armin Shimerman (Principal Snyder at Sunnydale High) was a regular cast member portraying Quark.

Michael Mantell (Oliver Simon) has appeared on *Roseanne*, on which Glenn Quinn (Doyle) was a regular as Mark Healy. Joss Whedon was a writer on *Roseanne* earlier in his career.

TRACKS

To get the haunting theme song for *Angel*, music coordinator John King put out the call to local bands who might be interested in having their music heard every week on national TV. He describes what he was asked for:

"I just quoted Joss. He said, 'I'm looking for Batman meets Smashing Pumpkins à la cello-rock.' A band by the name of Darling Violetta wrote a piece with Holly Knight that best fit the description and the rest is history." —**JOHN KING**

What Darling Violetta came up with is called "*Angel* Main Title Theme." The band, long associated with the *Buffy* series, explained what it was like to know their music would open the show every week:

JYMM THOMAS: "Our appearance on *Buffy* led directly to our landing the *Angel* theme. It's very cool to know that millions of people all over the world have been exposed to our music via the shows and the Internet."

STEVE MCMANUS: "We definitely get a lot more hits on our Web site! And I've noticed that because we've been on *Buffy* and *Angel*, people are more willing to investigate the rest of our catalog."

ATTO ATTIE: "So you could say some doors have opened for us . . ."

CAMI ELEN: "That were deadbolted and chained before!"

Also featured in this episode are "Right of Left Field" by Wellwater Conspiracy, from their *Brother-hood of Electric: Operational Directives* CD; Howie Beck's "Maybe I Belong," from *Hollow*; and two songs by Gus Gus from their *This Is Normal* CD, "Ladyshave" and "Teenage Sensation."

"LONELY HEART"

**FROM THE FILES OF ANGEL INVESTIGATIONS
CASE № 1ADH02**

ACTION TAKEN

It's a Friday night. Angel prods Doyle to ask Cordelia out, instead of pestering him to stop brooding alone in the dark "like a vampire." But the half-demon would prefer the cover of a staff celebration toasting the new business to asking Cordy directly.

Their conversation is interrupted by the arrival of Cordelia, who has brought Angel's new business cards. Miffed that the boys can't decipher her hand-drawn logo (an angel), she swats Doyle—just as he's having a vision attack.

Unlike Doyle's vision of Tina, which came complete with her name and the name of her workplace, this vision is far more cryptic. He sees a blurry montage of faces inside a bar he vaguely recognizes as, "one of those terminally stuck in the eighties places."

In a bar called D'Oblique, a plain-faced girl talks with a guy, another D'Oblique regular. Their poignant conversation pretty much sums up the dilemma of all the lonely people in the bar:

> **KEVIN:** "When I was a kid I thought, you grow up, you meet *her*, and then everything sort of falls in place."
>
> **SHARON:** "Yeah, I had that. Only I had a *him* where you had a *her*. . . . Actually I just had a Ken and a Barbie."

WRITTEN BY David Fury
DIRECTED BY James A. Contner
GUEST STARS: Elisabeth Rohm (Kate Lockley), Lillian Birdsell (Sharon), Obi Ndefo (Bartender)
CO-STARS: Derek Hughes (Neil), Johnny Messner (Kevin)

(213) 555-0162

KEVIN: "Ken and Barbie had it easy. They didn't have to come to places like this. But you gotta try. I mean, what if she was here and you missed her because you were, too, I don't know, burned out to still believe. . . . You know what I mean?"

SHARON: "I know exactly what you mean. You have to believe that someday, you'll meet someone special."

KEVIN: "I think I have. God, I can't believe I just said that. I mean I think you're special. It just sounded so . . ."

SHARON: "No. It sounded nice, Kevin."

Angel, Cordelia, and Doyle have found a bar matching Doyle's vision. They arrive at D'Oblique and begin looking for someone who looks like they need help. Cordelia passes out Angel's business cards to the assembled multitudes, until Doyle advises her to fly a little farther below the radar—Angel doesn't have a private investigator's license, so certain authorities might look upon his activities with disfavor.

During their assessment of the crowd, Cordelia scrutinizes Kevin and Sharon, who are leaving together. Unlike Sharon, Kevin is noticeably attractive. Unfortunately, the incongruity of the pairing doesn't set off any alarms for Cordy or Doyle.

Meanwhile, Angel gets to work talking to a young woman.

ANGEL: "No, I'm looking for someone to . . . rescue?"

KATE: "Well, that's the strangest line I'm gonna hear tonight."

Eventually Kate asks Angel if he'd like to go someplace quieter. Awkwardness ensues. Angel can't leave the bar until he has more clues about who, what, and why, and Kate figures she didn't pass inspection.

After it's all over, and the bartender's shutting down, the gang debriefs on how awful it is to date nowadays.

ANGEL: "This socializing thing is brutal. I mean, I was young once. I used to go to bars. It was never like this."

DOYLE: "I used to go to taverns, man. Small towns. Everybody used to know each other."

CORDELIA: "Like high school. It's easy to date there. We all had so much in common. Being monster food every other week, for instance."

Speaking of monster food, Kevin has become a desiccated corpse after hollow and disappointing sex with Sharon. The next morning, Sharon is no longer so plain—her makeup and her demeanor are much sexier—as she departs Kevin's bachelor pad without so much as a glance at the dead man.

That night, it's research time at the Angel Investigations office, and they hit pay dirt. According to a Net search, D'Oblique is the epicenter of a string of several recent murders. While Cordy and Doyle continue to look for other similarities to the homicides, Angel heads back out to the bar.

Kate's on her way into D'Oblique as well, and Angel manages to hurt her feelings again when he tries to talk her into finding a new place to party—even though he himself is going into D'Oblique. She's frosty, and he's frustrated that he can't explain that he's not brushing her off, just trying to protect her from harm.

Angel gets a tip from the bartender: One of the regulars, a guy named Kevin, was a no-show at work and hasn't come into the bar tonight. But Sharon Reichler, Kevin's most recent sack partner, is already back for more. Angel starts making connections . . . mental connections.

Sharon's hookup is more . . . visceral. She picks up a guy named Neil, takes him back to her place, and the demon inside her body rips out of her chest and burrows into Neil's back.

Having learned Sharon's address, Angel shows just after the gory transfer. He confronts the demon, who insists that it will continue to move from human host to human host until it finds one it can stay with. Angel fights it, trying to take down the human host to get at the demon within, but the demon inside Neil's body escapes.

Then Kate arrives on the scene. It turns out she's an undercover cop and has followed Angel because of his odd behavior. Suspecting that he's the killer she's been after, she reads him his rights. He leaps out of the second-story window of the apartment building. Kate takes note . . . this guy is no veterinarian, as he had informed her back in D'Oblique, the night before.

Angel tells Cordelia and Doyle to meet him at Cordelia's apartment, revealed to be an amazing pigpen. And she of the mile-high SAT scores shows once again that the line between humor and ignorance is not necessarily all that fine:

> **ANGEL:** "I saw it. It's a burrower demon."
>
> **CORDELIA:** "It's a donkey? Oh, we didn't see any donkey demons."
>
> **ANGEL:** "Burrow*er*. It eviscerates its victims as it goes from body to body."

The demon, one Talamour, is yearning to make a connection, just like the lonely people whose bodies it invades. But each time it moves into a new body, it fails to find what it's looking for. Just like all the lonely people in D'Oblique.

Armed with that knowledge, Angel phones Kate, who's still convinced that he's the psycho killer. She agrees to meet him at D'Oblique, and when she arrives, the bartender tells her that Angel's outside, in the alley.

Kate goes out into the alley, unaware that the demon Talamour has entered the bartender's body. It follows Kate out into the alley and bashes her over the head with a wine bottle. Angel arrives just in time to prevent Talamour from burrowing into Kate. The demon locks them both into the wine cellar, then staggers back inside, moving amongst the bar patrons, desperate to connect with a new life partner before it dies inside its current imperfect match. Its desperation echoes the awkward "lines" of so many:

"Hi. How's it going? I've been noticing how gracefully you move and was wondering if you were, like, a dancer or something, 'cause I wish I could move like— Hey, excuse me, that's a really beautiful dress you're wearing; it really brings out your skin tone. . . . Would you like a drink or something? Because I'm, like, the bartender here. . . . Just want to talk to somebody. Want to make a connection . . ."

—*Bartender (Talamour)*

Angel is forced to reveal some of his Batmanlike gadgetry to Kate as he attempts to hoist them both to freedom through a high window in the wine cellar. When that fails, Kate takes out her service revolver and simply shoots the lock on the door.

Inside, the bartender, Talamour is frantic to move into a new body as the bartender disintegrates. After a chase through the streets, Angel fends him off from a new intended target and sets him on fire. The demon attacks Angel in one last attempt at life, and Kate shoots the bartender dead, never comprehending the supernatural nature of the crimes.

> **KATE**: "It all seems to add up. The bartender was connected to everyone. I must have talked to him a dozen times. I never had a clue."
> **ANGEL**: "It's hard to get to know people."
> **KATE**: "Yes, it is."

RESOLUTION

Talamour is killed, and Kate comes clean with Angel. A relationship of some sort is growing between them.

> **KATE**: "I think you should know I searched your place. Illegally. No warrant."
> **ANGEL**: "Why are you telling me?"
> **KATE**: "I don't know. I guess so we can start fresh. No secrets. You've got some pretty weird stuff for a veterinarian."

Case Closed.

DOSSIERS

CLIENT It could be argued that **Kate Lockley** is the accidental client in this case, as Angel not only helps her solve the mystery of the D'Oblique murders, but also saves her from Talamour.

CIVILIAN SUPPORT The **bartender** is very helpful until he is burrowed by Talamour. A **bar regular** inadvertently alerts Angel to the fact that Kevin is missing, and also supplies Sharon's last name (Reichler), thus enabling Angel to find her address and confront Talamour.

VICTIMS Talamour's known victims include **Sharon Reichler, Kevin, Neil, the bartender, Heather Nolan,** and **Martin Haber.**

SUSPECTS Kevin, Sharon, Neil, and the bartender are all burrowed by **Talamour. Angel** is Kate's prime suspect.

CONTINUITY

Angel and Cordelia are privy to one of Doyle's vision attacks up close and personal for the first time. Kate, not knowing Angel's history, doesn't realize his "been there, done that" response to her suggestion that he visit Hell is entirely literal.

QUOTE OF THE WEEK

DOYLE: "Wait a minute, I don't know if she likes me unless you put in a good word for me. You know, just tell her what a great guy I am."
ANGEL: "I barely know you."
DOYLE: "Perfect, that should make it easier for you then."

Doyle wants to ask Cordelia out, but wants Angel to pave the way for him.

THE DEVIL IS IN THE DETAILS

EXPENSES

Angel's new business cards
Dented car hood

WEAPONRY

Kate uses her service revolver, and the D'Oblique tables and chairs serve during the free-for-all.

DEMONS, DEMONS, DEMONS

Talamour demon

A **Piasca** is a flesh-eating Indian demon that enters victims through the mouth and eviscerates from within.

Talamour is a burrower demon that has been around since the dawn of time, a parasite that moves from body to body. When it starts to leave one body for the next, the first one goes "gerploohy" pretty fast.

THE VAMPIRE RULES

If Angel has a moment of true happiness, he will lose his soul again.

AS SCENE IN L.A.

"I was brought back for a reason, Doyle, and as much as I would like to kid myself, I don't think it was for eighteen holes at Rancho." Angel might be referring to the Rancho Park golf course in Los Angeles.

THE PEN IS MIGHTIER

FINAL CUT

The set list includes: D'Oblique (Bar), Different Bar, and Yet Another Bar.

Also cut from the script:

> **DOYLE**: "Good. The two of you working separately, better the odds."
>
> **ANGEL**: "Not of her surviving if she finds this thing before I do."

Angel's logo is mistaken for a butterfly, a bird, and a lobster. His phone number is 213-555-0162. The 213 area code marks the location as central Los Angeles. 555 is a generic exchange used in drama and literature, but it only works for information.

POP CULTURE

❋ Cordelia says of Sharon as she leaves with Kevin: **"Check out Sarah Plain and Tall."** The Patricia MacLachlan novel *Sarah, Plain and Tall* was adapted for a TV movie starring Glenn Close.

❋ Cordelia also says of Sharon as she leaves with Kevin: **"Well, you gotta be rich to snag the Calvin Klein model she's leaving with."**

❋ **"Cagney and Lacy Kate?"** Cordelia identifies Kate with the famous female TV cops.

OUR HEROES

"There were two things you had to establish [about Angel's apartment]. One is, he's only about twenty-eight years old when he went vampire, which is a certain time in life. . . . I did a lot of research of what it was like in Ireland in the 1700s, when he was a kid, when he became changed. . . . Then we thought about the fact that he had a hundred years when he was pillaging, when he was Angelus. So I figured, in that time, he took a lot of stuff.

"We had a lot of pictures of castles and things, and we made sure they weren't too bright and sunny. Because that was just where he was at that point. He'd also just broken up with Buffy, so he had that horrible pain.

"When I actually finished the set I took [David Boreanaz] through it . . . and we talked about whether or not he would have weapons, because he's not violent right now. But he felt that it was a good thing to have, because they reminded him of his past.

"He collected masks. He collected books. He collected a lot of things that represented his passage of time. And I had a lot of nice things about London, because he had spent a lot of time in Europe. But then you've got to have stuff from the forties and fifties. Because he was alive then, or in the thirties. It really gave you freedom to pick up stuff that he just might like. And that was a lot of fun, because you wanted to give his history."

—SANDY STRUTH, SET DECORATOR

"The original script I wrote for two was not 'Lonely Hearts.' I'd written another script, called 'Corrupt,' which was based on a story that Joss and David and I broke. That was the original direction—the series was going to be a much darker, seedier, much more adult undertaking. There was no concession at that point to it being about twentysomethings. It wasn't going to be the metaphor that *Buffy* was. It was going to be strictly kind of a down and dirty sort of series, and sometimes shocking. That was the intent of 'Corrupt.'

"And it worked, because the network was shocked. They said, 'We can't shoot this show.' And this was merely days before production. 'This is way too dark. This is not what we signed on for.' So . . . we shut down production for two weeks. This is the script that shut down production on *Angel*. And we had to completely regroup and write a whole new episode.

"Very fortunately, we were able to break a new idea. Marti Noxon was a big part of the writing of the new number two. She did the third act. Because we had to turn it over in three days. So she wrote the third act and I wrote the rest of it. And again, fortunately, it all came together and it turned out pretty well.

"But while I was trying to write 'Corrupt,' I took my family for one last vacation in Hawaii, and I'm at the hotel registering. I'm thinking about *Angel*, all I have is *Angel* on the brain, knowing I have to write this, and then there's a guy standing next to me who's, like, looking at me. And I turn, and it's David Boreanaz standing there. I flipped out. It was like, 'I've manifested Angel, he's right there!' It was a very freakish experience. He was playing with me, he saw me there and he just came over. He stood there waiting for me to notice him. So I took that as a good omen."

—DAVID FURY

JAMES CONTNER, DIRECTOR: "'Lonely Hearts' was interesting, and a very difficult show, because it was a script that had gone through many, many changes. It was the second episode of the season, and it was really discovering the direction in which *Angel* was going to go. The type of humor, how dark were they going to go. How dark was dark as far as the tone and mood of the show. How far to take Angel, who has always been a broody kind of guy in the storylines. How deep would they go as far as the really dark subject matter.

"We were six days into preproduction and suddenly shut down. Two more days to prep and then we were supposed to start shooting. It was a meeting of the minds between the network, the WB and Fox and Joss and Greenwalt about what the direction of the show would be. They certainly toned back a lot, and they kept Angel slightly lighter. Not that they haven't taken him into darker realms, but they felt that they didn't want to have him in that place the whole time."

"So when they decided, essentially, to start over, was it hard for you to revise what you had already started on?"

JAMES CONTNER: "No, not at all. Because I did think it was sort of the wrong direction, and I had questioned some of it during the prep of it. They were establishing a new character, Kate, the cop that befriends Angel. They establish this character who nobody was really going to like or root for, and had no redeeming value. She was as bad as the people she was arresting and interrogating. So that had to change, and did, and Kate became still a hard-edged person but a lot more likeable as a person who is flawed, but not willing to sink herself into the depths of moral depravity."

"How did you feel when they stopped production and re-tooled and started over? Did it throw you in any way?"

DAVID BOREANAZ: "No, it didn't throw me because it's really not my job to be involved in that. I'm not paid to be a producer or a creator. I'm paid to know my words and go home. So it didn't really throw me. It was kind of a reassurance that they obviously were not on track with what the network wanted, and it gave the opportunity for the writers to explore more avenues. It was a minor glitch that kind of helped us look at the stories a little bit deeper."

"Who designed the Angel logo on the business cards?"

COURTNEY JACKSON, PROPERTY MASTER: "It was funny, because I made a lot of different passes at it, and we just kept showing Joss Whedon, and this ended up being something that our production designer drew. Just kind of quickly on the back of something. Which we sometimes refer to as the Ringo, because it looks a little bit like Ringo Starr with his nose and his hair. And it got approved, and then it became his business card."

"When Kate and Angel are talking in the bar, Kate seems to be a pretty tough person. How much of what she reveals to Angel in that first conversation is her genuinely being vulnerable, and how much do you think is her trying to do her job?"

ELISABETH ROHM: "It's not genuine. She's undercover, so she's playing somebody who's looking for friends, going out to a bar looking to meet a guy, or whatever. But when you're going through a situation, you're probably going to use things from your own experiences. So she's playing undercover, it's not genuine. But I think because she is very lonely, and doesn't have very many friends, and tends to feel somewhat isolated—not unlike Angel—she uses her experience from her own life to kind of explain what she feels about being out in that pickup world."

SIX DEGREES OF . . .

Obi Ndefo has appeared, as have many *Angel* actors, in *Star Trek* episodes, including the *Deep Space Nine* episode "The Way of the Warrior."

TRACKS

Much of this episode takes place in a nightclub, so there is a lot of music. Songs include "Dissonance" by Ultra-Electronic; "Girlflesh" by THC, from their *Adagio* CD; Kathy Soce's "Do You Want Me"; Sapien's "Neo-Climactic"; "Emily Says" by Chainsuck, from the CD *Angelscore*; and "Touched" by VAST, from a CD also called *VAST*.

"IN THE DARK"

FROM THE FILES OF ANGEL INVESTIGATIONS
CASE №: 1ADH03

ACTION TAKEN

Rachel has hired Angel Investigations to protect her from her violent boyfriend, whose name is Lenny. One night, Angel stops Lenny from shooting her on a deserted L.A. street. Angel is unaware that Spike, the vampire, observes from a rooftop, mocking his arch-nemesis:

"'How can I thank you, you mysterious black-clad hunk of a night thing?' 'No need, little lady. Your tears of gratitude are enough for me. You see, I was once a badass vampire. But love—and a pesky curse—defanged me, and now I'm just a big fluffy puppy with bad teeth. . . .' Go on with you, play the big strapping hero while you can. You have a few surprises coming your way—the Ring of Amarra, a visit from your old pal Spike . . . and, oh yeah, your gruesome, horrible death." —*Spike*

WRITTEN BY Douglas Petrie
DIRECTED BY Bruce Seth Green
GUEST STARS: Seth Green (Oz), James Marsters (Spike), Kevin West (Marcus), Malia Mathis (Rachel)
CO-STARS: Michael Yavnieli (Lenny), Ric Sarabia (Vendor), Tom Rosales (Manny the Pig), Gil Combs (Bouncer), Buck McDancer (Dealer), Jenni Blong (Young Woman)

Spike knows that Oz, a friend of Buffy's from Sunnydale, is bringing the Ring of Amarra to Angel. Spike and his current lust interest, Harmony, found the ring, but Buffy stole it from him. It will make any vampire who wears it invincible—and able to get a tan.

Sure enough, Oz shows.

ANGEL: "Hey, guys. Oz."

OZ: "Angel."

ANGEL: "Nice surprise."

OZ: "Thanks."

ANGEL: "Staying long?"

OZ: "Few days."

DOYLE: "They always like this?"

OZ: "No, we're usually laconic."

In Doyle's mind, the ring's a better treasure than the pot of gold at the end of the rainbow, but Angel's not so sure. He stays behind to hide the ring while Doyle, Oz, and Cordelia go off to celebrate Angel's good fortune.

Morning breaks, and poor Doyle has had too much fun—about which Cordelia can't resist teasing him.

Meanwhile, due to a technicality, Rachel's abusive boyfriend, Lenny, has been released from police custody and Rachel's in a blind panic. She calls Angel, who assures her that he's on his way to help her. In his parking garage, Angel runs into Spike, who greets his former mate with a two-by-four and a demand for the Ring of Amarra . . . or else.

But Angel thrashes the Big Bad, and Cordelia and Doyle show up just in time to witness Spike's hasty retreat. Angel tells Cordelia to hide out at Doyle's apartment, on the theory that Spike, who knows Cordy from Sunnydale, will be able to track her down at her own place. Doyle's housekeeping is pathetic but he gives good phone: soon enough, an informant named Manny the Pig all but admits he's in contact with Spike.

Angel calms Rachel down and visits Manny the Pig, who gives up Spike's location. Angel runs Spike to ground . . . not realizing he's just walked into a trap. Spike has help: A huge, powerful vampire named Marcus appears from the shadows. He takes Angel captive and chains him up in a warehouse.

"Marcus is an expert. Some say 'artist,' but I've never been comfortable with labels. He's a bloody king of torture, he is. Humans, demons, politicians, makes no difference. Some say he invented several of the classics, but he won't tell me which ones. Beneath the cool exterior, you'll find he's rather shy . . . except with kids. You like kids, don't you, Marcus?"   —*Spike*

Marcus also likes Mozart. To the dulcet melodies of "Symphony No. 41" he goes to work on Angel. It's not pretty.

Angel points out to Spike that hiring a vampire, who could use the Ring of Amarra himself, might not have been a good idea. But Spike sarcastically assures Angel he's thought of that. Marcus has no interest in the ring, or in anything but causing lots and lots of pain.

Growing bored with the torture session, Spike leaves the warehouse and ransacks Angel's apartment, looking for the Ring of Amarra. While he's there, Cordelia and Doyle show, and Spike offers them a trade—they find the ring, he'll give them back Angel. It's the best offer they have, so they agree to it.

But after they exhaust the obvious places, they decide the ring isn't in the apartment after all. Turning to the next most likely spot, they go to look for it in, as Cordelia puts it, "the rat-infested sewer tunnels he uses to get around in the daytime."

Eureka. The tunnels it is. Using his demonic nature, Doyle locates the ring under a brick. They reconnoiter with Spike, holding out on him until they can verify that their boss is still alive. Spike reluctantly takes them to the warehouse where they see that Angel is in really bad shape.

Spike being Spike, of course, has every intention of betraying them—keeping the ring *and*

Angel—but the timely appearance of Oz, crashing his van through the warehouse wall, puts a crimp in that scheme. As Angel, Cordelia, and Doyle escape in Oz's van, Marcus finds the ring and makes his exit, leaving Spike alone to throw a tantrum.

Angel's seriously messed up. Cordy and Doyle want Oz to take him to a hospital, but, as Oz points out, "Which one? They all tend to specialize in humans."

Angel doesn't have time for that anyway. Marcus is now unkillable, able to get around in sunlight, and not a nice guy, especially to children. Angel needs very badly to put this vampire away, permanently.

Marcus is strolling along a public pier jutting out into the Pacific Ocean. Families, fishermen, a scout troop—it's a lovely Southern California day, and the heavily trafficked pier is a virtual smorgasbord for Marcus. He is selecting his first victim from the menu when Oz's van roars up behind him and Angel leaps from it, bursting into flames as the sunlight strikes him. He smashes into Marcus and they crash through the rail and go over the side, into the water. Beneath the pier, they battle to the death—but since Marcus wears the ring, it looks like the death will be Angel's. He's weak, tiring quickly. Finally, he impales Marcus on a jutting section of pier. Marcus looks down at the wood sticking through his chest and just laughs at it.

Which is when Angel headbutts him and snatches the Ring of Amarra off Marcus's finger.

Marcus lives just long enough to realize his own fate, and then vanishes in a cloud of damp dust. Angel puts the ring on his own hand and walks out, blinking, into the California sunshine.

RESOLUTION

Later, on the rooftop of Angel's building, Angel and Doyle watch a sunset—the first one Angel has seen in two hundred years. Angel seems enraptured by it, but Doyle points out there'll be another one tomorrow. Angel explains that there won't be for him—that he's not going to keep the ring.

> **ANGEL:** "I've thought of it from every angle. And what I figure is, I did a lot damage in my day. More than you can imagine—"
>
> **DOYLE:** "So, what? You don't get the ring because your period of self-flagellation isn't over yet? Think of all the daytime people you could help from nine to five."
>
> **ANGEL:** "They have help. The whole world is designed for them. So much that they have no idea what goes on around them after dark. They don't see the weak ones lost in the night—or the things that prey on them. And if I joined them, maybe I'd stop seeing too."

As the sun drops behind the horizon Angel slips the ring from his finger and smashes it with a rock. Finally, in the gathering dark, Doyle remembers that Rachel called to tell Angel thanks, and that she'd be okay.

Case closed.

DOSSIERS

CLIENT Rachel, Angel's first paying client, is also the first "paying" client who stiffs him. She won't be the last.

CIVILIAN SUPPORT Oz, the werewolf from Sunnydale, brings Angel the ring and proves to be an intrepid wheelman.

INFORMANTS Frankie Tripod is mentioned in passing but never seen. Other sources of information for the gang include **Manny the Pig**, who actually directs Angel to Spike, an **unnamed dealer** at a card game Angel breaks up, and an **unnamed bouncer** at a strip club.

SUSPECTS Lenny is easily taken out by Angel at the beginning of the episode, but released by the police shortly thereafter. (Remains at large.)

Spike has been on the losing side of many encounters with Angel and Buffy (to the best of Angel's knowledge he remains at large). **Marcus** eventually succumbs to the temptation of the Ring of Amarra. (Deceased.)

CONTINUITY

Although Cordelia knows Doyle is "Vision Boy," he still hides his demonic family history from her, and will until "Hero." Angel and Spike last met in "Lovers Walk," before Spike made some cutting remarks about Angel and Buffy's doomed relationship and left Sunnydale to resume his torturous relationship with Drusilla. Cordelia's criticism of Doyle's messy living arrangements is a case of the pot calling the kettle black. Her living conditions will improve with Dennis's assistance after "Rm w/a Vu." When Cordelia is bringing Doyle up to date on Spike, she refers to the Judge, who Angel, Drusilla, and Spike set loose in Sunnydale in "Surprise" and "Innocence."

QUOTE OF THE WEEK

(damsel voice)
"But . . . there must be some way to show my appreciation. . . ."
(Angel voice)
"No, helping those in need's my job. And working up a load of sexual tension, and prancing away like a magnificent poof is truly thanks enough."
(damsel voice)
"I . . . understand. I have a nephew who's gay, so . . ."
(Angel voice)
"Say no more! Evil's still afoot, and I'm almost out of that Nancy-boy hair gel I like so much! Quickly! To the Angelmobile! Away!"

> Spike, too far away to hear a conversation between Angel and Rachel that he observes, provides his own imagined sound track

THE DEVIL IS IN THE DETAILS

EXPENSES

Bodywork on Oz's van
New duster for Angel after he is tortured and it is ruined

WEAPONRY

Marcus uses hot pokers, sunlight, and "The Pear" torture device on Angel. Cordelia and Doyle aim crossbows at Spike. Oz saves the day with his *deus ex* van-*icus*.

THE PLAN

Cordelia narrows their job down to the basics.

"This is so awesome. Our first walk-in client and everything is going according to plan. See girl in distress. . . . See Angel save girl from druggie stalker boyfriend. See boyfriend go to jail. And see invoice. Taa-daa!"

—Cordelia

Spike has a plan of his own.

> **ANGEL**: "So you and I duke it out, huh? This your big strategy for getting the ring back?"
>
> **SPIKE**: "I had a plan."
>
> **ANGEL**: "You? A plan?"
>
> **SPIKE**: "A good plan. Smart, carefully laid out . . . but I got bored. All that watching . . . waiting. My legs started to cramp."

DEMONS, DEMONS, DEMONS

THE VAMPIRE RULES

The Gem of Amarra renders any vamp who wears it invincible.

AS SCENE IN L.A.

"[The pier where the climactic battle between Angel and Marcus was filmed] is Paradise Cove. It's out towards Malibu, and it's north of Topanga Boulevard, it's almost up by Zuma Beach. That particular pier is a private beach that you can only get to by paying money. We bought access to the beach and the parking lot and everything so we were able to control it a lot more. They originally wanted to shoot that at Santa Monica Pier, but one of the things about locations is, sometimes you have to be realistic. Controlling Santa Monica Pier, and throwing someone off the pier, and shooting under the water, you have to work within a certain budget and time frame, so Santa Monica Pier was just going to be too much."

—KEVIN FUNSTON, LOCATIONS MANAGER

THE PEN IS MIGHTIER

FINAL CUT

Spike's first appearance in the script is described in the stage directions:

Now we see who this narrator is: It's SPIKE. Perched high overhead on a rooftop ledge, looking down on the alley like some living gargoyle. Having the time of his life.

Doyle's apartment is described in the script as:

It is, almost literally, the bachelor pad from hell. Piles of laundry, crushed beer cans, and take-out food cartons lie scattered about, mixed in with some supernatural knickknacks: a goat's skull, black candles, books.

We actually see a human skull, but not a goat's. And *Iberia* by James A. Michener, seen on Doyle's bookshelf, is a fine nonfiction book about Spain but possibly a little out of Doyle's usual range of reading material.

Spike's description of the torture expert Marcus includes this line, which was cut:

"Marcus was run out of Novi Grad by a pack of angry Howler demons for his antics with some local sprites—and you know Howler demons, they'll put up with anything."

Writer Doug Petrie included this line in the script's stage directions, describing Marcus's torture paraphernalia:

Marcus opens a battered old trunk filled with torture implements—among them we may see a cat's paw, a breast ripper, a heretic's fork, "the Pear," etc.

POP CULTURE

❋ **"It's daylight, you're ringless, and unless you're changing the act to Human Torch, I don't think so."** Cordelia says this to Angel, referencing the Marvel Comics superhero who has a habit of bursting into flames, when Angel insists on going after the now-invincible Marcus.

❋ **"Since when did you get all Versace about accessorizing?"** Cordelia asks Doyle about his sudden interest in the ring of Amarra. Versace is a famous fashion designer.

❋ Oz explains the recent history of the Ring of Amarra to Angel: **"Yeah, your old buddy Spike dug up Sunnydale looking for it—but he got a fistful of Buffy and left it behind."** A reference to the Sergio Leone spaghetti Western *A Fistful of Dollars,* starring Clint Eastwood.

❋ **CORDELIA: "I think the trick is laying off the ale before you start quoting *Angela's Ashes* and weeping like a baby man."**
DOYLE: "Hey, that's a good book."
CORDELIA: "So I've heard, but I doubt very much that the main characters are Betty and Barney Rubble—as you so vehemently insisted last night. Also, I don't think Oz appreciated being called 'my li'l Bam Bam' all night."
Angela's Ashes is an autobiographical work by Frank McCourt about his Irish heritage. Bam Bam is the offspring of cartoon characters Betty and Barney Rubble, neighbors of Fred and Wilma Flintstone of *The Flintstones.*

Who Let the Bats Out?

(References to another solitary figure who cuts a fine figure in a cape)

"Well, I like the place. Not much with the view, but it's got a nice Batcave sort of air to it."
—Doyle shares his first impressions of Angel's downstairs apartment. ("CITY OF")

"I mean, it's not like you got a signal folks can shine in the sky whenever they need help."
—Doyle explains the usefulness of his visions. ("LONELY HEART")

"Quickly! To the Angelmobile! Away!"
—Spike, in his soliloquy, likens Angel's convertible to the caped crusader's. ("IN THE DARK")

"She looked ridiculous, like Catwoman taking out the cat-trash."
—Cordelia is ticked off at the actress who wore a leather jumpsuit and landed a trash bag commercial she wanted. ("RM W/A VU")

ANGEL: "You look nice."
CORDELIA: "Bah! And now I look like the Joker."
—Angel startles Cordelia while she's making her finishing touches before a date, causing her to jump and smear lipstick across her cheek. ("EXPECTING")

After Trevor Lockley dies and Angel goes back to his place to arm himself before taking out the Head Demon Guy, the stage directions read: "A VARIETY OF SHOTS. Angel arming himself for bear. The big ol' *Batman* montage of gadgets, steely eyes, etc. Wrist stakes: check. Enchanted dagger: check."
("THE PRODIGAL")

"Fresh from a mountain spring. Delivered right to our door—then blessed every second Tuesday by Father Mackie, the local parish priest, while you're down there in your Bat Cave sleeping through the better part of the day." —Cordelia menaces the drugged Angel with her "holy water." ("ETERNITY")

52

OUR HEROES

In this episode, you spent quite a bit of screen time with your arms chained over your head, and also quite a lot of time outside in sunlight, neither of which are very standard. Was any part of that particularly challenging in any way?

DAVID BOREANAZ: "My arms were killing me. I'd just gotten into a car accident, going to work. I got hit from behind. So my back was pretty jolted up. And I went to work, and I had to hang on that stirrup, and my back was jolted so it was a pretty weird day. But I got through it."

"Dave Miller was the effects guy of record [for Season One]. We just helped out when we were called and asked. For 'In the Dark,' we just provided some vampire foreheads that had already been created for *Buffy*. I know that David Greenwalt wanted the vampire foreheads to be redesigned for *Angel*. He felt the ones on *Buffy* were a little bit too subtle, and he wanted something a little more monstrous."
—ANDY SANDS OF FX HOUSE OPTIC NERVE

TRACKS

The aforementioned "Symphony No. 41," by Wolfgang Amadeus Mozart, plays a prominent part in Marcus's torture scenario.

"I FALL TO PIECES"

**FROM THE FILES OF ANGEL INVESTIGATIONS
CASE Nº: 1ADH04**

ACTION TAKEN

Angel Investigations is developing a serious cash flow problem. Angel doesn't love to charge people for his help almost as much as he doesn't love Cordelia's truly atrocious coffee, which she makes from recycled grounds to cut down on expenses. Doyle saves Angel from a prolonged discussion on the subject by having a vision. And this vision has a name and an address: Melissa Burns, who works at Pardell Paper Products, 200 Wilshire Boulevard.

Melissa has been at her new job for only a month, but it's clear that she's a warm, caring, and creative person, as she presents one of her colleagues with a hand-painted pot for her birthday. The pleasure of the simple office party is turned into misery, however, when an ostentatious bouquet arrives for her—not the birthday girl. The flowers are from "Ronald," and their delivery is enough to drive Melissa into the bathroom to down some tranquilizers, then to leave work early.

Angel meets up with her in the parking garage, and as usual, he is very awkward at making that initial connection to offer help. Although Melissa does accept one of Angel's business cards, Angel figures he's blown it, frightened her off, and that he'll never see her again.

Then Ronald ambushes Melissa at an ATM. As he completely ignores her pleas to leave her alone, focusing instead on what he wants reality to be, it becomes obvious that Dr. Ronald Meltzer is pretty darn insane.

Apparently deciding that the broody guy in black is less frightening than Meltzer, Melissa goes to Angel's office and tells her story. Meltzer, her former neurosurgeon, has been stalking her for seven

STORY BY Joss Whedon & David Greenwalt
TELEPLAY BY David Greenwalt
DIRECTED BY Vern Gillum
GUEST STARS: Elisabeth Rohm (Kate Lockley), Tushka Bergen (Melissa Burns), Andy Umberger (Dr. Ronald Meltzer), Carlos Carrasco (Vinpur Natpudan)
CO-STARS: Brent Sexton (Beat Cop), Garikayi Mutambirwa (Intern), Kent Davis (John), Jan Bartlett (Penny), Patricia Gillum (Woman Patient), Hand Performance by Christopher Hart

months. The irony is that while he's a washout as a human being, he's actually a great doctor, and saved Melissa's sight. Since then, he's been spying on Melissa constantly, keeping tabs on her every move. As they begin their investigation, Angel and Cordelia ponder Meltzer's methods.

> **ANGEL:** "How's he doing it? How's he see her when she's alone, in private? Is he invisible, some kind of ghost? Maybe he can astral project."
>
> **CORDELIA:** "Or maybe he has an accomplice or he has a hidden camera . . . not everything has to be creepy and supernatural, you know."
>
> **ANGEL:** "Not everything, but Doyle had a vision. . . ."
>
> **CORDELIA:** "Which last time led to a sex-changing, body-switching, tear-out-your-innards demon. . . . Right. I guess they don't call you for the everyday cases."

Angel checks in with Kate at the police department, and she verifies that Melissa Burns filed a complaint about Ronald Meltzer. It turns out that Wolfram & Hart are Meltzer's attorneys, and they in turn filed a restraining order against her. Angel remembers that particular law firm very well.

Kate assigns a cop to watch Melissa's building. She also encourages Angel to help Melissa get angry so she can fight back.

"This guy could go to jail tomorrow, Angel, and still kill her in her dreams every night. I've put a few of these creeps away, and the hardest thing is knowing he's still winning. She's still afraid. He took the girl's power away, and nobody can get it back for her but her."   —*Kate*

Angel shows up in Meltzer's office, posing as Brian Jensen, a wealthy international businessman whose wife has a terminal tumor behind her eye. He offers to pay anything to save her life, even if it will mean an illegal operation. He pushes Meltzer's buttons by picking up the doctor's framed photo of Melissa and demanding, "What does she mean to you?"

He asks Meltzer to imagine how far he'd go for his own beloved.

When Meltzer leaves the room for a moment, Angel notices a book entitled *Anything's Possible* by a man named Vinpur Natpudan. It's inscribed "To Ronald, thanks for having the 'nerve' to believe. Fondly, Vin." Angel decides to check the book out of Meltzer's private library . . . for good.

Meanwhile, Cordelia is playing journalist and interviewing a physician who may be able to shed some light on the scary doctor. She learns that the good doctor is just as secretive as he is skilled, developing new and radical techniques that he keeps hidden from his peers.

Angel wonders if some of Meltzer's secrets have come to him courtesy of Vinpur Natpudan. Searching on the Net reveals that the author conducted an exclusive retreat for prominent physicians and Yogis, and shortly thereafter had a nervous breakdown. Ronald Meltzer was at the retreat.

Natpudan has gone into seclusion, but Angel manages to pique the man's interest by sending him an e-mail message: "I hope you'll have the nerve to believe I need help with Ronald Meltzer."

The two meet, and Natpudan explains his belief system to Angel: that our brains are the most powerful force in the universe, even when operating—as most do—at less than 20 percent of their capacity. We are all everywhere at once, since we're all made up of the same molecules.

> **NATPUDAN:** "I introduced Doctor Meltzer to psychic surgeons, Yogis who can shut down their somatic systems for days at a time. But he eclipsed us all. Until Doctor Meltzer, my studies had been based on hearsay and theory—but he exploded all that. That's when I stopped teaching."
>
> **ANGEL:** "Because you stopped believing."
>
> **NATPUDAN:** "No. Because I began to believe completely."

During Angel's meeting with Natpudan, Meltzer is standing outside Melissa's apartment building and has used his mind to detach his own hands and send them into her bedroom to caress her. Kate's beat cop sees him standing in the shadows and tells him to put his hands up. But Ronald Meltzer has no hands . . . The cop apologizes, and unknowingly allows Meltzer's remote-control attack to continue.

When Melissa awakens, screaming, the cop bursts in to save her, and Meltzer strangles him with the disconnected hands. Angel, who was on his way to Melissa's apartment after his meeting with Natpudan, appears and comforts her as the coroner takes away the body of the dead cop.

Ronald Meltzer's hair-trigger rage has a new target: another man has moved in on his dream girl.

Kate arrives to investigate the cop's death. The relationship between her and Angel is deepening—or rather, moving closer to the truth of the fact that he is a supernatural being dealing with supernatural problems.

> **KATE:** "Well, how could he do it? She's got bars on the windows, security cameras in the hall show our officer running in, nobody else suspicious all day—who is this guy, Houdini?"
>
> **ANGEL:** "Something like that."

Kate doesn't press, and tells Angel that she's having Meltzer's prints run through the computer. If they match the prints found at the murder scene, she'll bring him in. But Angel knows that prison bars can't contain a man who can turn himself into very small pieces.

Angel brings Melissa to his place so that he can protect her, but he, Cordelia, and Doyle realize that even there, they are in danger. They tape over every vent and block every threshold they can find. Angel talks to Melissa, pointing out to her that she's actually winning—that she's surviving while Meltzer is becoming unhinged because he can't control her. Melissa is the strong one, Angel says.

Then the "special line" rings on Angel's office phone—the one he's dedicated to "Brian Jensen," the fictitious businessman persona Angel adopted to explain his presence in Meltzer's office. Meltzer says he's decided to operate on "Jensen's" wife, but he'll need a hundred thousand dollars "to get things rolling."

Angel shows at Meltzer's office, carrying a safe-deposit box. But it's clear from the get-go that Meltzer has lured him into a trap and that he believes that Angel is his rival for Melissa's love.

Meltzer fires a hypodermic needle at Angel from a high-pressure injector, explaining that he's just given him a paralytic drug that will eventually stop his heart. The doctor selects a sharp scalpel, then leaves Angel, who has sunk to the floor.

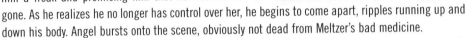

Meltzer shows up at Angel's apartment . . . in pieces. He grabs Cordelia from behind with his right hand over her mouth, slams her against a wall, and locks her in a closet. His left hand, which is detached, yanks Doyle into the entrance of an underground tunnel and locks him in.

This time Melissa stands up to her stalker, calling him a freak and promising him that her fear of him is gone. As he realizes he no longer has control over her, he begins to come apart, ripples running up and down his body. Angel bursts onto the scene, obviously not dead from Meltzer's bad medicine.

Meltzer fights back, flinging his teeth at Angel, who manages to grab the doctor's scalpel and pin his detached hand. Then the disembodied doc begins to disintegrate, ear falling off, parts dropping to the floor, and Angel uses a floor lamp to whack him so hard his head flies off.

RESOLUTION

Angel buries the bits and pieces of Dr. Ronald Meltzer "in twelve steel boxes buried in twenty cubic feet of concrete in L.A.'s newest subway stop." Melissa is free once more to enjoy life without constant fear and terror. Angel has learned a little more about how to connect with humans. He grasps that people need to be able to face and conquer their fears in order to feel whole. And he also learns how to charge money for his services.

Case closed.

DOSSIERS

CLIENT Melissa Burns, who went to Meltzer for an eye operation and had one drink with him. Before Meltzer started stalking her, she was a thrill seeker who liked to bungee jump. Now, liberated from fear, she becomes the firm's first actual paying client.

CIVILIAN SUPPORT Dr. Martha Tyson discusses Dr. Meltzer with Cordelia, who is posing as a journalist. She tells Cordelia about the doctor's radical work with reattaching severed limbs and nerves, also revealing that he's not very likable. **Vinpur Natpudan**, once a renowned New Age guru of mind power and author of *Anything's Possible*, became a recluse once Ronald Meltzer took his work past the theoretical and into the practical.

SUSPECTS Angel suspects **Dr. Meltzer** immediately, but wonders if he might be a ghost, or if he's using telekinesis to get what he wants. (Deceased.)

CONTINUITY

As if Dr. Meltzer weren't creepy enough in his own right, Kate mentions that he is represented by Wolfram & Hart, a sure sign that he is a black hat. "Protecting young women such as yourself? Yeah, there've been, ah four, and three of them are very much alive." Doyle somewhat weakly reassures

Melissa of Angel's ability to handle supernatural threats to young women, pointing out Angel has succeeded in keeping their clients alive—except for Tina in "City Of."

QUOTE OF THE WEEK

"I mean, it's just so unfair. This poor girl, she hooks up with a doctor! That should be a good thing. You should be able to call home and say, 'Mom, guess what, I met a doctor,' not, 'Guess what, I met a psycho who's stalking me and oh by the way his hands and feet come off and he's not even in the circus!'"

Cordelia expresses her empathy for Melissa's plight

THE DEVIL IS IN THE DETAILS

EXPENSES

Safe deposit box
12 steel boxes for storing body parts
Fake business cards for "Brian Jensen"

WEAPONRY

Ronald shoots Angel with a heart-stopping drug via high-pressure injector; Angel uses the doctor's own scalpel against him. Ronald uses mind games on Melissa . . . but they eventually backfire on him.

DEMONS, DEMONS, DEMONS

Dr. Ronald Meltzer is not a demon per se; he is actually a sort of psycho **astral-corporeal traveler**.

THE VAMPIRE RULES

It's impossible to kill a vampire by stopping his heart with drugs—it's already stopped.

AS SCENE IN L.A.

"The first season, [Angel's] office building and everything was actually the back lot of Paramount, and the building that you saw in the establishing shot was a building on the back lot. Second season, when he moved into the [Hyperion] hotel, that is the Los Altos apartments which is right there on the corner of Wilshire Boulevard and Norton. And it's funny, because we've had people call our department and ask where it is so they can go by and look at it. That particular building is a historical landmark, and we shot that for ["I Fall to Pieces"]. And they liked it, and they thought it would be a good location for Angel's home office."

—KEVIN FUNSTON, LOCATIONS MANAGER

THE PEN IS MIGHTIER

FINAL CUT

Cut due to length, this exchange in Melissa's office took place between two of her coworkers:

PENNY: "I sent my husband a bouquet the day the divorce was final."

JOHN: "And they say there's no romance left in the world."

Stage directions:

"BACK TO DOYLE. He's in pain but not a writhing, drooling kind of pain."

POP CULTURE

❊ The title of this episode, **"I Fall to Pieces,"** comes from a song popularized by Patsy Cline in 1961, written by Harlan Howard and Hank Cochran. Xander Harris listened to it on *Buffy the Vampire Slayer*'s "Prophecy Girl" after Buffy turned him down for the Spring Fling—i.e., Prom.

❊ **"And people who need people are the luckiest—"** Doyle recites lyrics from "People," written by Bob Merrill and Jule Styne, popularized by Barbra Streisand when she sang it in *Funny Girl* in 1968.

❊ **"I don't get it; this guy has a lot to lose. What is it about Melissa that's got him going all O.J. here?"** Cordelia makes a reference to O.J. Simpson, the actor and sports celebrity who was accused of killing his ex-wife, Nicole Brown Simpson, and Ronald Goldman in 1994. He was acquitted of criminal charges in 1995 after a long, spectacular trial, but found guilty for civil damages in a subsequent civil suit.

OUR HEROES

"When you do research, do you use forensics books?"

DAYNE JOHNSON, MAKEUP DEPARTMENT HEAD: "That's pretty much what you have to do. It can get pretty gross. They have a few books out there that they sell, like dermatology books, or those forensic-type books, you can find some pretty gnarly stuff. You can find some of that on the Internet."

"Have you ever had to do an effect or a makeup application that made you sick, or grossed you out too much?"

DAYNE JOHNSON: "Never. And it amazes me how people get grossed out. When I see somebody's head get cut off, or somebody slashed, or eye poked out or something [in a movie or TV show], I just go, oh, makeup. Because you know it's makeup. It's a television show, you know it's makeup. I mean, that's the way my mind thinks about it.

"It's like, Oh, here I am flinging blood. It's not gross, it's sticky, and somebody's got to clean it up. It doesn't gross me out at all, because it's just makeup. But then when the final look is done, I can see how it can gross somebody out. Which is good, I like to see somebody grossed out, because then I know my job's done. It's supposed to be gross."

SIX DEGREES OF . . .

Andy Umberger, who plays Ronald Meltzer, has also guest-starred on *Buffy* as the demon D'Hoffryn. D'Hoffryn was responsible for turning Anya into Anyanka the vengeance demon and offered Willow a chance to become a demon.

Director Vern Gillum has also directed *Bull*, a TV series in which Elisabeth Rohm (Kate Lockley) and Elizabeth Anne Allen (Witch Amy, on *Buffy the Vampire Slayer*) starred. Carlos Carrasco (Dr. Vinpur Natpudan) has appeared numerous times on *Star Trek: Voyager* and *Star Trek: Deep Space Nine*.

"RM W/A VU"

FROM THE FILES OF ANGEL INVESTIGATIONS
CASE №: 1ADH05

ACTION TAKEN

Cordelia's self-esteem is at an all-time low. Yet again, she has lost out at an audition, this one for a commercial about leaking trash bags, and as she says, "I was all about leaking." While she's telling Doyle about her disappointment, she ignores the ringing phone . . . and thank goodness, because it's Aura, one of her mucho-competitive girlfriends from Sunnydale High School. Cordelia blows off the call. She knows Aura is going to ask her how the acting is going and where she's living, and neither one is a question she wants to deal with.

Doyle can't do anything about the acting but offers to let her stay at his place once in a while, if she wants to get out of her own. He's rebuffed as well.

After she leaves, Doyle asks Angel for the back story on Cordelia. He genuinely likes her but he doesn't know very much about her. Angel fills him in:

> **ANGEL:** "Well, I know she can't type or file. Until today I had some hope regarding the phone."
>
> **DOYLE:** "Oh, yeah, who's Aura?"
>
> **ANGEL:** "Aura? Oh, I think she was one of Cordelia's group. People called them the Cordettes. Bunch of girls from wealthy families. They ruled the high school, decided what was in and who was popular. It was like the Soviet secret police if they cared a lot about shoes."
>
> **DOYLE:** "And she was the richest one of all? 'Cause she talks like she used to have servants made of solid gold or something."
>
> **ANGEL:** "Pretty much, until her parents lost it all. Riches to rags."
>
> **DOYLE:** "Hell of a come down."
>
> **ANGEL:** "Yeah. But she's doing all right."

She's really not. Her apartment is disgusting. The lights flicker; the faucet spews a single shot of rusty water at her, not her water glass. When she discovers dozens—if not hundreds—of roaches, both dead and alive, littering the carpet and crawling across the TV screen, she calls Doyle in desperation. But just as Doyle is entering his apartment door to grab the ringing phone, he's confronted by Griff, a muscle-bound Kailiff demon who's been hired to collect some money Doyle owes from gambling . . . or kill him. Doyle doesn't have the money, but he manages to escape . . . this time.

STORY BY David Greenwalt & Jane Espenson
TELEPLAY BY Jane Espenson
DIRECTED BY Scott McGinnis
GUEST STARS: Elisabeth Rohm (Kate Lockley), Beth Grant (Mom)
CO-STARS: Marcus Redmond (Griff), Denney Pierce (Vic), Greg Collins (Keith), Corey Klemow (Young Man), Lara McGrath (Manager), B. J. Porter (Dennis)

Cordelia tries the next name on her admittedly very short list, this time not bothering to call. She packs some bags and shows up on Angel's doorstep unannounced. In the morning, Doyle's shocked to see both Angel and Cordelia in bathrobes, Cordelia using the reflective surface of his teakettle to style her hair. Angel says to her, "You got peanut butter on the bed," and Doyle's demolished. He figures Cordelia's fallen for Angel's broody-guyness, but Angel assures him that he and Cordelia are still just friends.

Once all is set to rights, Cordelia shows her secretarial mettle once again. It turns out that she did answer at least one call the day before, from someone claiming to be Doyle's cousin—almost certainly Griff.

Shortly thereafter, as Cordelia shows Doyle some mementos of life in Sunnydale—"Your high school diploma is all . . . burned," he observes—Angel calls down to him that "a big guy" is waiting for him upstairs. Doyle replies cheerfully, then runs for his life . . . only to discover that Angel faked him out, in order to get him to talk about what's going on. Doyle spills, and Angel suggests they give each other a hand. Doyle can find Cordelia an apartment, and in return, Angel will help him deal with Griff.

Doyle takes Angel up on his offer, and soon he's accompanying Cordelia through a series of increasingly dreary and squalid apartments. One apartment is actually bed space in a religious commune; another is maintained by an *über*-creep landlord. Finally, Cordelia relents and lets Doyle contact his "guy." And the apartment he finds for her is exquisite. Other than a wall whose placement bugs her, the place couldn't be more perfect.

"Perfect" is in the eye of the beholder, though, and unseen by Cordelia and Doyle, a ghostly face bulges out of the oddly placed wall.

Meanwhile, Angel has ambushed Griff in Doyle's apartment. The vampire strong-arms the Kailiff demon into allowing Doyle to pay him, rather than killing the Irish half-demon as an example to other debtors.

Cordelia is spending the first night in her new place. A glass of water sloshes; invisible hands go through her dresser drawers; a radio turns itself on and locates an oldies station. There's whispering. Then a drawer slams shut, awakening her with a start.

Angel has told Doyle that he's gotten Griff to agree to spare his life in return for what he owes. Doyle's shocked and upset to learn that Griff wasn't even looking for money anymore. The demon was simply going to murder him.

Later, Cordelia's apartment is jumping: The water in her glass boils; the radio switches on and off; there's scraping, tapping, and pounding.

"It was too good. I just *knew* it. I'm from Sunnydale, you know. You're not scaring me." —*Cordelia*

As if in reply, her bed levitates.

She waits anxiously for the dawn, and when it comes, it seems the bad things are gone. But Cordelia's wrong; in her bathroom, an old, dead-looking woman stares at her in the mirror, but Cordelia doesn't see her reflection. A chair smashes against the wall so hard it breaks. The curtain and electric cords wrap around her. Cordelia puts on a brave front, but she's beginning to get scared.

Shortly thereafter, Angel and Doyle drop by with a housewarming gift. She tries to get them to leave as quickly as possible, but the flying scissors and toppling floor lamp are good indicators that something's amiss. The capper, however, is the word "DIE" written in blood across the wall.

> **CORDELIA:** "I'm not giving up the apartment."
>
> **ANGEL:** "It's haunted!"
>
> **CORDELIA:** "It's rent-controlled!"
>
> **ANGEL:** "Come *on*."
>
> **CORDELIA:** "I can deal. It's not so bad, with a ghost. It clearly brought the price down."
>
> **DOYLE:** "Cordy, it says 'die.'"
>
> **CORDELIA:** "Maybe it's not done. Maybe it's . . . 'diet.' That's friendly. A little judgmental, sure . . ."

Angel agrees that they can try to put the ghost to rest. At the office, they start searching on the Net for information about the apartment building. As they work, Angel once again tries to understand why this particular apartment is so important to Cordelia.

> **ANGEL:** "You know, this really is just a place to live."
>
> **CORDELIA:** "No. It's more. It's beautiful and if it goes away, it's like . . . like I'm still getting punished. For how I was. For everything I said in high school just 'cause I could get away with it. And then it all ended, and I had to pay. But the apartment . . . I could be me again . . . Like, like . . . I couldn't be that awful if I get to have a place like that. It's just like you."
>
> **ANGEL:** "Working for redemption."
>
> **CORDELIA:** "Um . . . I meant because you used to have that mansion."

Their computer search turns up a death. Mrs. Maude Pearson, the original owner of the Pearson Arms Apartments, had a heart attack in 1946 in Cordelia's living room. She was fifty-seven. Angel decides to check with Kate to see if she has any more information, leaving Cordelia alone at the office to sort through books and wait.

After a while, a call comes in on the machine. Apparently it's Angel, telling Cordelia to meet Doyle and him at the apartment.

But Angel's not making any calls. He's still with Kate, researching the Pearson Arms.

Eventually, Kate and Angel discover that Mrs. Pearson's death was investigated because her son apparently skipped town with his fiancée the same day. Then Angel asks Kate to check into suicides, explaining that there's a kind of killer that makes murders look like suicides. Bingo. Kate rattles off the names of three previous tenants before Angel goes to a phone. He calls his apartment. Shifting his sack of cleansing supplies, Doyle answers, and tells Angel about the message on the answering machine. The two figure out that Cordelia has been lured back to the apartment.

The ghost of Maude Pearson has materialized in the apartment, and she flings Cordelia across the room. She begins to berate Cordelia, pinpointing all Cordy's vulnerable spots—her damaged self-esteem, her sense of not belonging. A chain from the chandelier snakes around Cordelia's neck and draws her up, hanging her.

Angel and Doyle burst into the room and rescue Cordelia. They explain to her that on the drive over, they have figured out that Dennis Pearson, Maude's son, murdered her, and as a result, the ghost cannot rest. They begin the ritual, Doyle creating a binding circle while Angel reads a spell from an old book. The walls shake. While Angel chants, the ghost of the dead woman continues to whisper hatefully at Cordelia.

"They don't care about you. They want to see you fail. They know you're a tarted-up little whore with no money and no future and nothing going for you but painted good looks. And those aren't even enough to pull you out of the gutter."

                              —Maude Pearson

Angel and Doyle continue to work on the spell, but Cordelia is mesmerized by the terrible things Maude is whispering to her. Angel can't see the ghost, but he can see the effect she's having on Cordelia. Angel and Doyle decide to get her out of the apartment, but standing in the doorway is Griff, the Kailiff demon, and two minions. They're armed . . . and very dangerous. Gunshots and hand-to-hand fighting ensue. Maude Pearson is enraged when gunfire shatters her fireplace tile. She makes a kitchen drawer fly open, and knives catapult across the room, taking out one of Griff's minions.

Angel is fighting Griff. Using supernatural energy, Maude pulls Cordelia into her bedroom and begins to insult her again, urging her to pull the sheets off the bed and make a noose for herself.

Then the ghost says to her, "You better be sorry, you stupid little bitch."

That does it. Cordelia remembers who and what she is:

> **CORDELIA:** "I'm a bitch . . . I'm not a sniveling whiny little crybuffy. I'm the nastiest girl in Sunnydale history, and I take crap from *no one*. . . ."
>
> **MAUDE:** "You're going to make yourself a noose and put it around—"
>
> **CORDELIA:** "Back off, Polygrip. You think you're bad? All mean and haughty and picking on poor pathetic Cordy? Well, get ready to haul your wrinkly translucent ass out of this place 'cause, lady, *the bitch is back*."

The tide has turned. The fighting's over and the house goes silent. Then a possessed and purposeful Cordelia marches into the room, picks up the floor lamp, and bashes in the wall she's been planning to remove . . . revealing the corpse of Dennis Pearson. The trio are thrown into a flashback, wherein Maude actually bricked her own son—still alive at the time—into the wall to prevent him from marrying his fiancée, of whom she disapproved. After she had finished the job, she had a heart attack and died.

Then the energy of Dennis's ghost emerges from the wall and blasts his mother into ghost-atoms.

This apartment is clean.

RESOLUTION

Angel supervises Doyle while the Irishman installs a new deadbolt. Angel and he have a meaningful conversation.

> **ANGEL:** "You know I'll help you out."
> **DOYLE:** "For which I'm grateful."
> **ANGEL:** "But sooner or later I'm going to need to hear it."
> **DOYLE:** "Hear what?"
> **ANGEL:** "The story of your life."
> **DOYLE:** "And quite a tale it is, too; full of ribald adventures and beautiful damsels with loose morals—"
> **ANGEL:** "Doyle."
> **DOYLE:** "I will. Just give me time. The past don't let go, does she?"
> **ANGEL:** "She never does."

Cordelia finally calls Aura back in Sunnydale, chatting happily and cheerily dissing the fashion-challenged . . . all the while instructing Phantom Dennis, her new roommate, on the rules of their living arrangement—no touching her diet soda, and no TV when she's on the phone. . . .

Case closed.

DOSSIERS

CLIENT Cordelia, and indirectly, **Dennis Pearson**, who is finally able to rid himself of his mother's poisonous influence.

CIVILIAN SUPPORT Doyle's "guy" found Cordelia an apartment; **another of Doyle's guys** in Koreatown sold him the herbs (and bile) needed to cleanse the house. **Detective Randall** was the LAPD detective who originally investigated Maude Pearson's death in 1957. According to his notes, he thought the death was suspicious at the time.

SUSPECTS Dennis Pearson was suspected of killing his mother, Maude, but it turned out to be the other way around. **Maude** evolved from being controlling to homicidal, and Dennis paid the price. However, once the crime against him is revealed, Dennis summons the backbone to send his mother into the ether (or somewhere warmer, perhaps) and becomes a thoughtful and friendly ghost-roommate for Cordelia. (Both long deceased.)

VICTIMS Other women Maude talked into committing suicide: **Margo Dressner**, in 1959; **Jenny Kim**, 1965; **Natalie Davis**, "five years ago."

CONTINUITY

Cordelia's past as a Sunnydale student and leader of the Cordettes plays a large part in this episode. Doyle notices that her high school diploma was singed during "Graduation Day, Part Two." Her telephone call with Aura is also a link to her past, and the two discuss Harmony, who will visit Cordelia and Dennis's apartment in "Disharmony." Cordelia reminds Angel of the mansion he occupied in Sunnydale, which seems like really spacious living quarters, until compared to the Hyperion in "Are You Now or Have You Ever Been?" Griff is not the last demon who will seek out Doyle in search of monies owed.

QUOTE OF THE WEEK

"You know what? I get it. You're a ghost. You're dead, big accomplishment. Move on. You see a light anywhere? Go toward it, okay? Ooh, cold wind. Scary. What're you gonna do, chap me to death?"   Cordelia to Maude Pearson, on the occasion of their first meeting.

THE DEVIL IS IN THE DETAILS

EXPENSES

Cleansing spell supplies: lungwort, hawthorn berries, bile
Completion of demolition job on the murder wall, after Cordelia starts the job with a floor lamp
Broken lamp
Spackle for bullet holes
Payoff of Doyle's gambling debt
Deadbolt for Doyle's apartment

WEAPONRY

Doyle and Angel employ cleansing spell supplies; Griff and company employ guns; Cordelia employs a lamp; and Dennis employs ghostly power to send his mom to the cornfield.

DEMONS, DEMONS, DEMONS

Ghosts, while not actually demons, can move things, influence people, appear to the living, and be dispersed.

Kailiff demons such as Griff look rather . . . demonic, with ridges and bad 'tudes.

THE VAMPIRE RULES

A vampire can be "completely invited over" in the abstract and be able to cross the threshold of a private residence thereafter.

Griff, a Kailiff demon

THE PEN IS MIGHTIER

FINAL CUT

The set list includes:

BAD APARTMENT

VERY BAD APARTMENT

WORSE APARTMENT

The following was cut:

> **ANGEL:** "I should let you go ahead. Somehow I don't think you have wooden bullets."
>
> **GRIFF:** "Don't need 'em. Metal bullets coated with garlic work better. Lot more painful."

Also cut, as Angel and Kate look over the Pearson death case file:

> **KATE:** "Yikes. Handwritten notes by the original detective. Look at that. I thought everyone had beautiful penmanship back then."
>
> **ANGEL:** "Not really." (catches himself) "I suppose."

According to Loni Peristere, CGI effects for the appearance of Phantom Dennis were created by the Radium team as a deliberate homage to the scene in <u>Raiders of the Lost Ark</u> where a "beautiful woman" approaches evil Ark-thief, Rene Belloq, then turns into a demon.

POP CULTURE

❈ **"What about friendship and family, all those things that are priceless like they say in the credit card commercial?"** Doyle, referring to the MasterCard ads

❈ **"Listen good, Casper!"** Cordelia addresses the ghost in her apartment by evoking a gentler, friendly spirit from comic books and cartoons.

❈ **"Back off, Polygrip."** Cordelia insults the ghost of the elderly Maude Pearson; Polygrip is the name of a denture adhesive.

❈ **"Old lady ghost. How come Patrick Swayze's never dead when you need him?"** Cordelia is pining for the spirit of Sam Wheat in the 1990 film *Ghost*.

OUR HEROES

"How did you decide to take the 'bitch is back' attitude?"

CHARISMA CARPENTER: "That was David Greenwalt's doing. I think that came from just being so frustrated by doing it thirty times and feeling like I wasn't getting it the way that they wanted me to. The take they ended up using was when I didn't have anything left. And I knew David hated the take.

"He said, 'Well, that was good,' and I'm like, 'You hated it.' And he goes, 'Yeah, I can't lie to you, can I?' And I said, 'No.' And so I would do it again, and again, and there was always something, and then finally it was like, I wanted to be a bitch. So the line was just very fitting for the circumstance. Actually, that's a really convenient scenario to run across, as an actor. Having to be frustrated, or broken down, and then actually having an experience occur to you. Like maybe you're walking to the stage and you're on the phone and something really cruddy happens, or you didn't get a job you wanted, or your boyfriend pissed you off, or whatever. You can use that for the scene. But you don't count on that. You know, you do your preparation and your homework and stuff, but if that stuff happens, then you use it and you're lucky."

"A really interesting story from my standpoint, art department-wise, was the creation of Cordelia's apartment. It was to become a permanent set, but the whole idea was it was a story, it was a show that was going to take place in an apartment, all about Cordelia moving into an apartment that was such a great deal that she couldn't pass up. And the reason it was such a great deal is that it was haunted, and no one really knew it before then.

"So we had to create a set that not only came apart for the normal shooting needs—walls [that move, with] no ceiling attached. We had to create a wall that they could stick a wig through there, that they could levitate the bed so it was floating up and down, because the bed was possessed. We had to also create three or four different kinds of walls that would fill up one niche, where Phantom Dennis was inside. And Special Effects built a wall out of very tightly-stretched latex rubber that we painted to match the rest of our walls, and we put an actor behind, so he could push his face through there and make it look like his face was being pushed out through the impression in the plaster walls.

"Within that same episode, we had that same wall come out and we built another wall that went in there that looked like it was half-brick, and it was being bricked up as the mother in the flashback was bricking up her son. And another wall went in that was all bricked up, that she was just plastering over. So a challenge like that, I really thrive on. —STUART BLATT, PRODUCTION DESIGNER

SIX DEGREES OF . . .

Markus Redmond ("Griff") played Tom Cribb in "The Ring." Denny Pierce (Vic) did stunt work in *Wishmaster 2*, a movie that connects many *Angel* guest stars—for instance, Vyto Ruginis (Russell Winters in "City Of") who played Hosticka in the horror flick.

TRACKS

Music heard in this episode includes Ludwig van Beethoven's "Ode to Joy," the last movement of his Ninth Symphony, Op. 125; and "You Always Hurt the One You Love," performed by the Mills Brothers from the CD *Stardust: The Classic Decca Hits & Standards Collection*.

"SENSE AND SENSITIVITY"

FROM THE FILES OF ANGEL INVESTIGATIONS
CASE № : 1ADH06

ACTION TAKEN

Spivey, a small-time hood who has dealings with mob boss Little Tony Papazian, goes to great lengths to avoid meeting with detective Kate Lockley. But she spots him making his get-away and stops him. As she yanks him out of his car and kicks him in the back, she apologizes sarcastically.

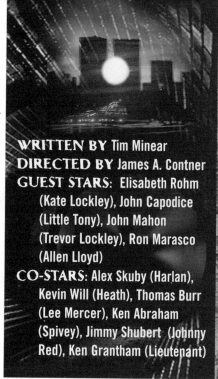

> "Gosh, Spivey, sorry. I guess I have a problem expressing myself verbally. It's something I struggle with."   —*Kate*

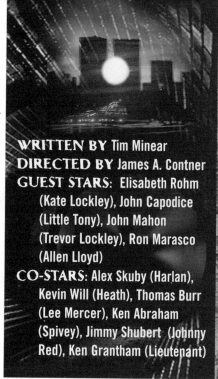

WRITTEN BY Tim Minear
DIRECTED BY James A. Contner
GUEST STARS: Elisabeth Rohm (Kate Lockley), John Capodice (Little Tony), John Mahon (Trevor Lockley), Ron Marasco (Allen Lloyd)
CO-STARS: Alex Skuby (Harlan), Kevin Will (Heath), Thomas Burr (Lee Mercer), Ken Abraham (Spivey), Jimmy Shubert (Johnny Red), Ken Grantham (Lieutenant)

Spivey appears to have a similar problem: Despite hours in a precinct interview room, he still won't divulge the where-abouts of Little Tony. Kate completely loses it and starts get-ting violent. Her fellow detective, Harlan, and some other plainclothes cops burst into the room and take over.

Meanwhile, Angel's in the sewers, battling a huge monster that has numerous tentacles and glow-ing green blood. Cordy and Doyle arrive in the nick with an enchanted sword. Angel dispatches the crea-ture, then barks at them to be sure to hack off all its limbs and both heads this time, and to bury all the pieces separately. While he strides off to clean out the nest, Cordelia expresses her ire over his cav-alier treatment of them:

> **CORDELIA:** "Okay, am I wrong in thinking that a 'please' and 'thank you' is generally considered good form when requesting a dismemberment?"
>
> **DOYLE:** "Well, he appreciates us in his own . . . unappreciative way."
>
> **CORDELIA:** "You know what I think? I think he uses his Tortured-Creature-of-the-Night status as a license to be rude and insensitive. Sure, he's polite to the helpless and the downtrodden. But he ignores the people closest to him . . . the people who matter the most, you know? Can you say 'clueless'?"

The fact that Cordelia's soliloquy takes place while Doyle is being strangled nearly to death by the still-living monster just makes it more ironic.

She confronts Angel when they reconvene at his office. He tries to defend himself, but Cordelia won't have it. She tells him to "spend a little time listening to how the living interact." But when Kate comes in, she and Angel speak in terse monosyllables.

Cordelia admits defeat.

Kate tells Angel about Little Tony and hires him to look for the thug. Angel tries to keep the matter on the level of a favor, but Kate insists on making it a formal job, for which she will pay. Furthermore, she puts limits on his involvement: As soon as he locates Little Tony, he is to notify her and leave the rest to her and the LAPD.

Perhaps Angel's people skills are not the best, but his deductive reasoning is sound. He asks Doyle to match tidal flow charts with where various body parts have been washing up on several Southern California beaches—Long Beach, San Pedro, and Carlsbad. They may be able to pinpoint Little Tony's primary dumping ground.

While the trio works on the case, Kate has her own issues to deal with: her father Trevor Lockley, a cop on the verge of retirement, and their disappointing relationship. They have very little to say to each other, and it's obvious that it Kate would like to be closer.

Angel's search strategy bears fruit. He locates Little Tony at the docks, calls Kate, and gives her a heads-up. As he prepares to leave per her request, a cabin cruiser is cutting through the harbor to pick up Little Tony and ferry him away.

To stall the mobster and his muscle, Angel puts on a loud Hawaiian shirt and a nerdy hat, performing a goofy charade as a confused tourist who thinks the cabin cruiser is the boat to Catalina Island. But Angel's bluff is called and he and Little Tony's two henchmen get into a fight. Little Tony flees the scene, only to be stopped dead in his tracks by Kate and some other squad cars. Kate is steamed, and unknowingly duplicates Angel's style of not thanking people for their efforts.

In custody, Little Tony makes his one phone call. His lawyers—no surprise here—are Wolfram & Hart. Lee Mercer, his personal attorney at the firm, assures him that they are aware of the thorn in his side—aka Kate—and assure him that "that thorn is about to be removed. Permanently."

Wolfram & Hart work for bad people, but they're good attorneys. Lee Mercer has brought all kinds of legal briefs stipulating that Wolfram & Hart's client is not safe in the precinct, and that he should be moved. He also demands that anything Little Tony says of a threatening nature be stricken from the record, while everything Kate says, including her loud sighs, be included.

Later, though, Kate goes to the local cop bar, shining like a Christmas tree as she gets high-fives and congrats from everyone—except her father. Trevor manages to throw cold water on her moment with a cynical hope that her arrest of Little Tony doesn't "fall apart" before she finishes filling out the paperwork.

Then fellow detective Harlan tells Kate that everyone is being ordered to take a sensitivity training seminar provided by the department, possibly because she strong-armed Little Tony. She's pissed off. Trevor speaks for many of the cops in the bar.

HARLAN: "You think they'll make us hug?"

KATE: "I'm not hugging you, sweatboy."

TREVOR: "Glad I'm getting out. In my day we didn't need any damn sensitivity."

Back at the station, the training begins. Kate is in a conference room with other cops, and everyone looks miserable. Their trainer is Allen Lloyd, the epitome of sanctimonious self-help gurus, and he's there to help them "experience the full range of human emotions." He shows them a talking stick, which they hold, one by one, as Lloyd begins to encourage them to express themselves. He's got Kate's number.

"Genuine emotion makes you uncomfortable. That's okay. Your inappropriate sarcasm masks anger. And do you know what anger is, Kate? It's just fear. Fear of being hurt. Fear of loss. You've been hurt, haven't you, Kate? And you're afraid of being hurt again. Who are you afraid is going to hurt you?"

—*Allen Lloyd*

Speaking of Kate and who might hurt her, Doyle has heard from one of his informants that Little Tony has put a contract out on her. Angel visits Kate at the precinct to warn her, and notices that she is acting very strangely—definitely not her usual hard-edged self. Kate, demonstrating her newfound sensitivity, apologizes to Angel for the way she treated him at the scene of Little Tony's arrest and invites him to her father's retirement party. "It'd be nice if there was at least one person there who wasn't . . . armed," she says. He agrees, and then tells her about Little Tony's contract.

KATE: "He's really acting out, isn't he?"

ANGEL: "Well, *yeah*. He wants you dead."

KATE: "Oh, I get that. I'm just saying he must be in some kind of pain, to have to strike out at others that way."

ANGEL: "Are you okay?"

KATE: "God, listen to me. Suddenly I'm Dr. Laura. Next thing you know I'll be talking about processing my inner child. I'm sure I'll be back to my usual level of cynicism in no time."

Lee Mercer drops in to visit Allen Lloyd, who, it turns out, has a fully stocked demonic altar in his private office. Wolfram & Hart hired Allen to work his juju on the police force, and Mercer's there to make sure he's getting the job done.

When Kate and Angel show up at Kate's father's retirement party, she's a bundle of emotion—not the least because she's supposed to make a speech. Her father, who has not touched the talking stick, remains his surly, insensitive self. The time arrives for Kate to say her thoughts . . . and she speaks from the heart, deeply and wrenchingly so.

KATE: "After Mom died, you stopped, you know. It was like you couldn't stand the sight of me. Her face, her eyes, looking up at you. But big girls don't cry, right? You said, gone's gone and there's no use wallowing. Worms and dirt and nothing forever. Not one word about a better place. You couldn't even tell a scared little girl a beautiful lie. God, I wanted to drink with you. I wanted you to laugh *once* with me the way you laughed with Jimmy here, or Frank. . . ."

TREVOR: "What the hell'd they do to her in that class?"

Soon, all the cops who have been through Lloyd's special brand of sensitivity training are spilling all over the place. Their emotion builds until they come to blows. Kate is in tears, and Angel ushers her out of there.

He takes her to his office and rouses Cordelia and Doyle to watch her. Angel phones the number on Kate's sensitivity training flyer, and gets Lloyd's address—The Institute for Self Awareness, 3322 Fletcher. When he takes off, Kate decides she needs to find her father. When she pulls out her gun, Cordelia and Doyle are persuaded to let her do just that.

Angel gets in contact with the demon-worshipping sensitivity trainer, but Lloyd recognizes Angel's antagonistic intent toward him. He hits Angel with the talking stick, and Angel grabs it. It doesn't appear to affect him as it did the humans who touched it.

At the precinct, the cops are out of control, all their emotions in overdrive. Officer Heath, feeling great compassion for the prisoners, lets them all out. Their gratitude is expressed by beating the crap out of him. And then Angel shows up, finding Cordelia and Doyle, who have followed Kate here. Unfortunately, the stick worked on Angel after all.

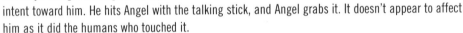

"Cordelia, do you have any idea just how precious you are?" —*Angel*

Despite his whacked-out condition, Angel explains that Wolfram & Hart hired Allen Lloyd to neutralize the police so Little Tony could escape. Cordelia and Doyle try to shake him out of his emotional overload, but he's become too sensitive for his own good.

CORDELIA: "It's time to go all vampy—grr! Kate needs you!"

DOYLE: "She's right."

ANGEL: "I don't want to. You both withdraw when I go vamp. I feel you judge me."

Little Tony has found Kate and is about to blow her away. Angel and Kate both appear completely incapacitated by their sensitivity, discussing his body language and his issues, until finally Angel—feeling "unheard" and dismayed by all the negativity in the room—moves into fighting mode.

The next day, Little Tony calls Wolfram and Hart, only to discover that they've abandoned him. He attempted to murder Kate in front of witnesses, and that's too much exposure even for such an evil firm. Besides, the Senior Partners feel the firm needs to spend its valuable energy on a more pressing matter . . . Angel.

RESOLUTION

The precinct is putting itself back together. Everyone's embarrassed, and Internal Affairs thinks the punch was spiked. Angel and Kate give each other some distance to get over their overemotional responses to each other.

Kate's father approaches her, but instead of being open to her emotional needs, he expresses shame at her public outburst at his retirement party, and turns his back on her. Angel has seen the entire hurtful exchange, but he moves quickly away, allowing Kate her dignity as she takes the wound.

Case closed.

DOSSIERS

CLIENT Kate Lockley, who wants to be a paying client, although it's unclear whether or not Angel actually invoices her.

CIVILIAN SUPPORT Johnny Red, a local thug, hears stuff at his gym and repeats it to Doyle. The gang manages to get the materials they need to slay the two-headed beast, even though, as Doyle explains, "Not a lot of enchanted swordsmiths open on Sunday."

SUSPECTS Little Tony Papazian is the prime suspect in this case, as it has been rumored that he's put a contract out on Kate. **Lee Mercer**, his attorney at Wolfram & Hart, hired **Allen Lloyd** on Little Tony's behalf.

CONTINUITY

Trevor Lockley's suspicions that Angel and Kate might be more than friends continues in "The Prodigal." He meets Angel in this episode and they run into one another at a crime scene in the latter.

QUOTE OF THE WEEK

"You know, Anthony, you could be a rainbow . . .
(Big ass punch!)
". . . and not a . . .
(does quotemarks)
". . . painbow." Angel demonstrates his sensitivity even as he takes Little Tony down.

THE DEVIL IS IN THE DETAILS

EXPENSES
Portion of Blue Moon repairs
New window in the police basement
Enchanted sword

WEAPONRY

Allen Lloyd and Angel use the talking stick; Kate and other officers (and jailbirds) use guns.

THE PLAN

Doyle's informants have provided him with vital information. Vital, but not extensive.

DOYLE: "So you were right. Papazian's planning something."

ANGEL: "What'd you hear?"

DOYLE: (didn't I just say this?) "Papazian's planning something."

ANGEL: "That's it?"

DOYLE: "Johnny Red says, quote: 'Papazian's planning something.'"

ANGEL: "I thought he might be planning something."

DOYLE: "See? You were right."

DEMONS, DEMONS, DEMONS

Allen Lloyd is a "polytheist," worshipping many demons.

THE VAMPIRE RULES

Apparently due to Angel's vampiric constitution, the talking stick whammy takes longer to work on him than it does on humans.

THE PEN IS MIGHTIER

FINAL CUT

An *Angel* key second assistant director is named Robert Papazian, Jr., sharing Little Tony's last name.

POP CULTURE

❋ The episode's title, **"Sense and Sensitivity,"** is a play on the title of *Sense and Sensibility,* a 1811 novel by Jane Austen that was made into a successful 1995 movie starring Kate Winslet and Emma Thompson.

❋ Spivey tells Kate that Little Tony's not around: **"Burbank. Stockholm. The planet Mongo."** Mongo is the home planet of Ming the Merciless, arch-nemesis of Flash Gordon.

❋ **"Jar Jar is getting his own talk show."** Still angry about Angel's dismissive behavior in the sewers, Cordelia describes a number of potential disasters that might be imminent, but which she doesn't want to hear about until Angel asks her and Doyle about their clean-up work. Jar Jar Binks is the annoying alien in *Star Wars: Episode One—The Phantom Menace.*

❋ Referring to Kate and Angel's monosyllabic conversation, Cordelia says, **"Mr. and Mrs. Spock need to mind meld, now."** Spock was the expressionless half-Vulcan science officer aboard the Enterprise on *Star Trek.*

❋ **"It means we will shine a light in the darkest corners of this precinct and give the people a view of the brutality and callousness of this police force that will make Mark Fuhrman look like Gentle Ben."** Attorney Lee Mercer threatens to take down the LAPD. Mark Fuhrman was a Los Angeles cop whose racist views were reported during the O. J. Simpson murder trial. Gentle Ben was a sweet, tame bear that starred in his own TV series in the sixties.

OUR HEROES

"In 'Sense and Sensitivity,' you got to do some funny comic bits, which you had far fewer of than in Season Two. Is humor becoming more acceptable and organic for your character?"

DAVID BOREANAZ: "I think that it's a slowly developing situation, especially at the end of [the second] season, where it's become so intrinsic. I think the environment and the situation will dictate his sarcasm and his sense of humor or his bitterness or his anger or his fear. I think that's really determined upon where we're heading with the stories, and what the story dictates. Now a lot of stories, we'll put him in a situation that makes him vulnerable, and any time there's egg on his face, it's funny."

"David has a wonderful goofy streak to him. He really does. It's not hard—sometimes, with certain things, he likes to protect his image, and there are certain things he doesn't want to go too far with. But you can draw it out of him. I learned a long time ago, if you really approach an actor in the right way, about getting him to do something that he doesn't want to do—and it varies depending on what you're asking him to do—it's all in the approach, and the sincerity and honesty with which you talk to him about it."
—JAMES CONTNER, DIRECTOR

"Kate really covers a wide emotional range. We've heard a lot about David's sense of humor. Did he help you or hinder you during the emotional scenes?"

ELISABETH ROHM: "Neither. He's a friend of mine, too, and we act really well together. So we feed off each other. But I definitely think when he and I work together it's like a chemistry set. So it works well. I don't know if he helped or didn't help, he was just there and the scene flew because we both showed up."

"So you guys weren't having to not crack up."

ELISABETH ROHM: "No, we definitely do that, but I would say when it's really emotional stuff, for either of us, we both are really—because we're quick studies, we always know our lines, we never go off. So we're pretty professional when we're together, unless it's something light. If he had to get very upset, I wouldn't be messing around with him."

"Did you have any sort of flavor for the sort of EST [Erhard Seminar Training, a very popular "human potential" movement of the seventies and eighties] background they were using for that, or are you way too young to have had any experience with that?"

ELISABETH ROHM: "No, I didn't know it was literally EST, but you grow up in this generation and everybody's parents, at least once, did something in self-help. It's that whole self-help generation, so it's all very familiar. And especially being in my generation, it's like I have a much more organic approach. So I really related to Kate. It's like, who are you? I'm not going to tell you my problems."

"Was it hard to do the scenes with David being 'sensitive Angel' with a straight face?"

CHARISMA CARPENTER: "It was frustrating for Cordelia to deal with Angel being so prissy. I think it was harder for David."

"After Kate reveals far more than she ordinarily would to her father, his response is to cut her off. When you were doing that, did you feel that came more from his inability to communicate with her since the loss of her mother, or that he just was such a complete tough guy that he wouldn't be able to communicate with anybody?"

JOHN MAHON: "Specifically in the script, what was there, I was directed and encouraged by the producers and directors to not show any sort of emotion, this guy was a hard nose. [I must say that I've worked] in close to a hundred and fifty episodic television shows . . . and I found working with Elisabeth—she's a delight—and David, both young, their work is very concentrated, they're very serious about their approach to the work, they're very professional, and I enjoyed meeting with both of them and working with them."

"The episode came in short . . . so I had to write additional material to sort of pad out the episode and make it long enough so we could air it. And the scene that I added turned out to be my favorite scene in the episode. It's a scene where Doyle and Angel and Cordelia are breaking into the police station, and I tried to write it so it would be easy to shoot. And if you look at the scene, for the most part there's no one in the scene. It's just the camera slowly creeping through this empty room, and we hear them outside arguing, until finally a window breaks. So my idea was just, we'll just play half this scene without any actors, and we won't have to stage anything, it'll just be this camera slowly creeping up to this window, and we'll just hear what's going on outside. Until finally the window breaks."   —TIM MINEAR

SIX DEGREES OF . . .

Thomas Burr (Lee Mercer) also appeared on *Fame L.A.*, with Christian Kane (fellow Wolfram & Hart lawyer Lindsey McDonald).

Alex Skuby (Harlan) played "Vincent" in the episode "Bad Girls," on *Buffy the Vampire Slayer*. Michael Beardsley, who plays an accident onlooker in this episode (uncredited), also played a U.C. Sunnydale student (again, uncredited) in *Buffy* episode "Beer Bad."

TRACKS

Heard in this episode are two songs by Solomon Burke, "Everybody Needs Somebody to Love" and "Baby (I Wanna Be Loved)" from the CD *Home in Your Heart: Best Of*.

"THE BACHELOR PARTY"

FROM THE FILES OF ANGEL INVESTIGATIONS
CASE № 1ADH07

WRITTEN BY Tracey Stern
DIRECTED BY David Straiton
GUEST STARS: Kristin Dattilo (Harry), Carlos Jacott (Richard Straley)
CO-STARS: Ted Kairys (Ben), Chris Tallman (Nick), Brad Blaisdell (Uncle John), Robert Hillis (Pierce), Lauri Johnson (Aunt Martha), Kristen Lowman (Mother Rachel), David Polcyn (Russ)

ACTION TAKEN

As usual, Angel's downtime consists of reading, while Doyle is restless for fun. Pierce, wealthy and handsome, comes to pick Cordelia up for a date, and Doyle sadly realizes that compared to Pierce, he's nowhere near the type of men Cordelia finds attractive.

While Doyle is absently flipping through the book Angel was reading, a picture of Buffy falls out. Doyle whistles appreciatively and asks Angel if this is "an old squeeze" of his. Finally Doyle catches on that this is Buffy. Deftly, he changes the subject—by having a vision of a guy in a vampire nest, about to be devoured.

Meanwhile, Cordelia is bored to tears at her fancy dinner with Pierce. He's going on and on about his fantastic pork belly trades, but it's obvious she wishes she were back on the job.

And work is definitely exciting as Doyle and Angel fight the vampires from Doyle's vision. At one point, Doyle morphs into his demon aspect, but he shakes it off. After the fight is won and the kid is freed, Angel asks Doyle about his choice.

ANGEL: "Doyle, you're stronger when you're a demon, right? Why'd you shake it off?"
DOYLE: "I don't like to fight that way."
ANGEL: "This isn't a spelling bee. Nobody expects you to play fair."

DOYLE: "It's not my style. That's all."

Pierce is *so* not Cordy's style, either, that she has asked him to take her back to the office early. He's total macho-gent as he escorts her to the main entrance, telling her he's not sure about the neighborhood, but he freaks out and abandons her when a vampire attacks.

Then Doyle appears and does battle, dusting the vamp and saving Cordy's life. Cordelia is one conflicted girl. She's become more interested in the type of guys who fight demons than in run-of-the-mill gorgeous millionaire bachelors. This leads to an admission that she's seeing Doyle in a different light, actually considering starting something with him.

"So I've gotta kill myself. I swore when I went down this road with Xander Harris, I'd rather be dead than date a fixer-upper again. Still, maybe you're right. Maybe Doyle does have hidden depths. I mean really, *really* hidden, but depths. And I kind of have to buy him a Mochaccino for saving my life. Don't you think?"   —*Cordelia*

She starts in with her pitch to Doyle, but she's interrupted by the arrival of a good-looking woman who smiles at Doyle and calls him Francis. And who turns out to be Harry. His *wife*.

They hug awkwardly, and it's clear Doyle is upset to see her. He makes more of himself than he is, telling Harry that Angel Investigations is his company and Cordelia and Angel are his helpers.

A few beats later, a big, friendly guy shows up in the doorway. He's a little goofy, but very kind. And when he lets slip that he's Harry's fiancé, Doyle is stunned. Harry has shown up unannounced because she's planning to marry Richard Straley, and she needs Doyle to sign the divorce papers.

Later that afternoon, Angel pours Doyle a whiskey in preparation for talking about Harry. Doyle slowly tells the tale. They were very young, and they fought badly. She was the one who left, but "she had reason." Doyle didn't know he was half-demon until after they got married.

"I never met my dad—he was the demon—and my mom, well, she figured she'd wait to see if I got his genes before she got all confessional."   —*Doyle*

Then he shifts gears, asking Angel to check out Straley for him. He wants to watch over Harry and make sure she's doing the right thing.

That night, Angel shadows Richard, soundlessly leaping off rooftops as he keeps track of Harry's intended. Angel watches him furtively accept a package from a man in a car, then give the man money in return. Richard walks into his family's steak house, and Harry's there with a bundle of packages. She wants to show him what she bought, but he leaves the room, admonishing her "not to move." He goes into the kitchen and pours himself a glass of wine. Then he morphs into a horrific demon and pulls a long, sharp knife out of a dishwashing rack.

As Richard approaches Harry from behind, Angel crashes through the plate-glass window and begins whaling on Richard. Harry yells at Angel to stop. It turns out that she knows Richard's a demon. The knife was to cut the strings on her packages. It takes less than a second for Harry to figure out who put Angel up to this—her first husband was always deciding what she needed.

But her kindly demon fiancé steps in and defends Doyle. It's good that Doyle wants to make sure she's in good hands.

> **HARRY**: "Tell Doyle I'm in the *best* hands. Richard and his family own this restaurant. They're Ano-Movic demons. A peaceful clan. Totally assimilated into our culture."
>
> **RICHARD**: "Harry's an ethnodemonologist. And a damn fine one, too. We met while she was scouting clans in North America."

It's true that Harry freaked out when Doyle went through his change. But after she adjusted, she became fascinated by his demonic heritage. She tried to get him to meet other demons and embrace that side of his heritage, but he couldn't handle it. His own anger and self-loathing were what drove her away.

Doyle's chagrined. During their marriage, he never believed that Harry was actually interested in and attracted to his demon side. He thought she was pitying him. Unhappily, he signs the divorce papers.

It's a tough moment for both of them when Doyle hands the papers to her. But her fiancé, who's very much of the big lug school, speaks from his heart, and then asks Doyle to his bachelor party. Harry invites Cordelia to her shower.

What neither Doyle nor Harry realizes is that the Straleys have not cast off their ancient traditions, as Harry believes. As they sit in their suburban home, eating take-out chicken, they discuss Richard's bachelor party.

"First we greet the man of the hour, drink, bring out the food, drink, then comes the stripper, darts, then we have the Ritual Eating of the First Husband's Brain."   —*Richard's Uncle John*

Doyle has asked Angel along to the bachelor party for moral support. The others seem surprised to see him when the two show, but greet him anyway and the party begins. As Angel saunters by Nick and Ben Straley, they are speaking demon-speak. As Angel passes, they both shut up and smile guiltily.

The shower and the bachelor party both progress—although the shower proves to be much more sedate than the bachelor party, at least until Pornographic Pictionary comes out. Finally, Richard asks Doyle for his blessing. He adds that without it, there won't be any wedding.

As Doyle takes this in, the stripper arrives. But Ben and Nick—the two Straley brothers Angel heard speaking demon, slink out. Angel starts looking for them and comes across Richard's Uncle John, holding an ornamental dagger over an open flame and chanting.

Angel calls Cordelia's cell phone and speaks to Harry, asking her to translate Uncle John's chant. As soon as he hangs up, four of the Straley clan take on Angel, overpower him, and dump him in the alley.

After the stripper finishes and leaves, Doyle gives Richard his blessing, unaware of what has happened to Angel. Richard announces this news to the rest of the partygoers. Everyone cheers, and then they slam Doyle into a sort of saunalike box with just his head protruding. Doyle is unnerved, but Richard has already progressed to thanking him deeply for his "incredible sacrifice." The Straley men all morph to demon face as Uncle John sticks Doyle in the temple with a hypo to numb his head before they cut into his skull.

Back at the Straley house, Harry does some field research:

> **HARRY:** "Excuse me, ladies . . ."
>
> **RACHAEL:** "What is it, honey?"
>
> **HARRY:** "It's about the bachelor party. Richard said something about having the former husband present was some sort of tradition. I was just wondering . . ."
>
> **AUNT MARTHA:** "Well, they're certainly not going to eat your ex-husband's brains! For instance . . . oops."

Cordelia and Harry are out the door.

Doyle is freaking out, asking for Angel. Richard tells him that his friend started a fight and had to be ejected. Meanwhile, the demon family is trying to get the details of the ritual ingestion correct, and Richard pouts a little when Doyle tries to take back his blessing. Then he quickly apologizes for being rude.

Just as they're about to cut into Doyle's head, Angel reappears in full vamp face. During the melee, Doyle's box is shunted about, rolling him around until he smacks into a wall and gets free. Everyone else has morphed into demon face, and now Doyle does too.

A wild brawl ensues, broken up by the entrance of Harry and Cordelia. Cordelia begins pounding on the nearest demon at hand, unaware that it's Doyle, until Angel pulls her off. When Cordelia looks away, Doyle morphs back to his human form. He allows Cordy to believe his injuries were caused by Richard and his kin, rather than letting her know that he was the demon she was hitting. Harry squares off with Richard. Richard tries to defend his actions, telling her he wanted to bless their marriage, "like in the ancient teaching." Harry scoffs; his family is not exactly observant. Uncle John protests, insisting that their beliefs are very dear to them.

> **HARRY**: "Oh, please, Uncle John. When's the last time you pried yourself away from ESPN long enough to spill the blood of a she-goat?"
>
> **NICK**: "Are you gonna let her talk to Uncle John like that?"
>
> **HARRY**: "You know how I feel about these barbaric Ano-Movician customs."
>
> **NICK**: "*Racist.* You're nothing but a racist!"
>
> **RICHARD**: "I should have told you. I'm sorry. But unless we complete the ritual, my family will never consent to the marriage."

RESOLUTION

Suffice to say, the marriage is off. Harry gives Richard back his ring and walks out of his life. Case closed.

But Doyle's pretty shaken up by seeing Harry again. Cordelia decides someone "with a pulse" should try to cheer him up, and makes a typically Cordelia-ish attempt.

> **CORDELIA**: "You can't live in the past. You've gotta move on. Let it go. Forget it. Tomorrow *is* another day. Did I mention letting it go?"
>
> **DOYLE**: "Twice."
>
> **CORDELIA**: "You'll get through this, Doyle. Nice guys don't always finish last."

The sweetness of the moment is interrupted by Doyle's intense vision . . . of Buffy, fighting for her life.

DOSSIERS

CLIENT Doyle is the client in this case, as Angel investigates his wife's soon-to-be new husband.

CIVILIAN SUPPORT Harry Doyle provides a translation for Uncle John's incantation. Aunt **Martha Straley** accidentally spills the beans about the Straley men's plan to eat Doyle's brains.

SUSPECTS Doyle was quite correct not to trust **Richard Straley.**

CONTINUITY

Doyle's former love returning sets the stage for Angel and Buffy's reunion in "Pangs" (glimpsed in Doyle's final vision) and "I Will Remember You." Cordelia mentions her romantic ties to Xander Harris during high school. They parted ways after Xander locked lips with Willow Rosenberg in "Lovers Walk," but Cordelia is still comfortable enough with Willow to call her when she is in need of computer expertise in "Blind Date."

QUOTE OF THE WEEK

"The whole night I'm bored silly. All I could think about is—if this wimp saw a monster he'd probably throw a shoe at it and run like a weasel. Turns out the shoe part was giving him too much credit."   Cordelia finds the uptight Pierce a highly disappointing date.

THE DEVIL IS IN THE DETAILS

EXPENSES
Shower gift for Harry
Two expensive windows at the Straley restaurant

WEAPONRY
Doyle's brain will be cut out with a ceremonial curved knife and devoured with a shrimp fork.

DEMONS, DEMONS, DEMONS

The Straley family are a clan of **Ano-Movic demons.** They were once a violent, nomadic tribe, but they reputedly gave up their orthodox traditions and language at the turn of the century. Now they own a number of restaurants "with pretty expensive windows," but still buy familiar-looking buckets of fried chicken for family get-togethers. Their native language is Aratuscan.

THE VAMPIRE RULES

Angel can drop off rooftops and land soundlessly.

THE PEN IS MIGHTIER

FINAL CUT

Cut due to length:

> **ANGEL:** "How common would you say it is for modern peaceful demon clans to retain the old languages?"
>
> **DOYLE:** "Huh?"
>
> **ANGEL:** "Harry said Richard's family was completely assimilated, but I've been getting a very nonassimilated vibe."
>
> **DOYLE:** "Oh, fine. Cultural prejudice from a vampire. It's not like they go to your family reunions and complain the dip needs garlic."
>
> **ANGEL:** "You okay?"
>
> **DOYLE:** "Do you think it's possible for somebody to love two people at the same time?"
>
> **ANGEL:** "Yeah. I think so . . . just maybe not in the same way."

Also cut:

Discussing Irish accents (which Angel also used to have), Doyle says: "'Cause some girls just think leprechaun, but others are all over you like white on a Republican."

Cut as well:

> **DOYLE:** "You're a lucky devil."
>
> **RICHARD:** "Yes, I— Hey that was clever! Lucky devil. Although, technically, I share no lineage with Satan per se."

Cordelia reports the location of Harry's wedding shower: "In the nether-world known as the 818 area code."–the San Fernando Valley, not the coolest part of L.A. (Native home of the Valley Girl).

POP CULTURE

❖ **"That's how he got the idea for that whole 'We Are the World' thing."** Harry, on Michael Jackson's inspiration to write an anthem encouraging people to unite and help the Third World.

❖ **"If I'm not here in the morning, you can just clear out my desk. I'll be moving on up."** Cordelia referring to the theme song from *The Jeffersons,* a TV series about an upwardly mobile couple who move into "a deluxe apartment in the sky."

SIX DEGREES OF . . .

Carlos Jacott (Richard Straley) played Ken in the *Buffy the Vampire Slayer* episode "Anne." He was also in *She's All That*, in which Sarah Michelle Gellar made an uncredited cameo.

"I WILL REMEMBER YOU"

FROM THE FILES OF ANGEL INVESTIGATIONS
CASE Nº: 1ADH08

ACTION TAKEN

Angel has returned from his Thanksgiving trip to Sunnydale, where he protected Buffy at a distance during her battle with the Indian revenge spirits. Cordelia, who's had experience with the bad things that usually happen after Angel has had an encounter with Buffy, braces for the aftermath.

Sure enough, as Cordelia and Doyle watch Angel through the window of his inner office, Angel pulls out a stake and examines it carefully. Assuming he's bent on committing suicide, the two burst into his office to stop him. He's amused, since he was just using the wood to fix his desk, which he noticed was off-level when he set a clock on it. The time is 8:53 A.M.

In addition to being amused, Angel is also touched by their concern, and he assures them that he's fine.

WRITTEN BY David Greenwalt & Jeannine Renshaw
DIRECTED BY David Grossman
GUEST STARS: Carey Cannon (Sister Oracle), Randall Slavin (Brother Oracle), and Sarah Michelle Gellar (Buffy Summers)
CO-STARS: David Wald (Mohra Demon #1), Chris Durand (Mohra Demon #2)

ANGEL: "Look, Buffy will always be a part of me, and that's never going to change. But she's human and I'm . . . not . . . and that's also never going to change. Look, we said our good-byes, no need to stir any of that up again."
CORDELIA: "You don't want to stir, but . . . if my ex came to town and was all stalking me in the shadows and then left and then he didn't even say hello, I'd be . . ."
BUFFY: ". . . a little upset. Wouldn't you?"
Uh-oh.

Buffy has officially come to town to see her father, but it's clear that she's found out about Angel's incognito visit to Sunnydale, and she's on a mission to find out what he was up to. Just as Angel and Buffy agree to stay out of each other's way, a Mohra demon crashes through Angel's window and attacks. They go after it into the sewer tunnels, Angel carrying a fighting ax and Buffy with a stake. They bicker a little, nervous about being around each other, but primed for battle. Angel finds traces of Mohra's blood and gets it on his fingers, which has an unexpected effect on him.

ANGEL: "I feel weird. . . ."

BUFFY: "I know . . . I do, too. I—I mean I only came so I could tell you face-to-face not to see *me* face-to-face anymore—and I know there's a fly in that logic ointment somewhere—the next thing I know we're being attacked by that mutant ninja demon thing, then we're on the floor on top of each other . . . it's just really confusing being around you."

ANGEL: "I meant I feel weird from the demon's blood. It's powerful."

But in actuality, Angel feels just as weird around Buffy as she does around him. "It's more than confusing," he says. "It's unbearable." They agree that their situation hasn't changed, that it's still impossible for them to be together—though neither can help feeling that old longing.

Angel guesses that the demon has gone topside, into daylight, where he can't follow. Buffy insists upon following it by herself, but once she's gone, it comes out of hiding and attacks Angel. They battle, and some of the Mohra's blood mixes with blood issuing from a cut in Angel's palm. The demon dies . . . and Angel lives. Literally. His heart starts to beat.

Doyle and Cordelia return to the office, surveying the upturned furniture and broken window . . . and a dust pile.

"She killed him. SHE KILLED HIM! Oops, my bad. That's just dust I forgot to sweep under the rug."

—*Cordelia*

Then Angel slowly approaches, walking out of the sunshine and into the office. He tells Doyle and Cordy that he's become mortal. He decides not to tell Buffy until he understands the implications, and whether it's temporary or permanent. While he's figuring things out, though, he seems intent on sampling every food substance that's not blood that he's been missing out on.

He and Doyle research the demon, and realize that by mixing Angel's blood with the Mohra's "blood of eternity," he has been made mortal. Doyle reveals that The Powers That Be—the same PTB who sent him to Angel and give him visions, can also make Angel mortal. Angel demands to speak to them—he needs to know if he's a "normal Joe" or what.

Doyle finally agrees to take Angel to the Oracles. He leads the vampire into a subterranean cave that's just underneath the post office and performs a ritual. After a blinding flash, Angel finds himself in a temple, facing the Oracles, a brother and sister with golden skin decorated in blue.

Doyle—who, as a lowly messenger, could not accompany Angel—forgot to tell Angel to bring an offering, so the vampire gives the Sister his wristwatch. Then he asks them to explain what's happened, and if it was The Powers That Be who arranged for his becoming mortal.

BROTHER: "*The Powers That Be?* Did you save humanity, avert the Apocalypse?"

SISTER: "You faced a Mohra demon. Life goes on."

ANGEL: "My life, as a human? I'm not poisoned, or under some spell?"

SISTER: "The auguries say no. If it has happened, it was meant to be."

BROTHER: "From this day you will live and die as any mortal man—"

SISTER: "—privy to all the attendant pains and pleasures."

BROTHER: "That which we serve is no longer that which you serve; you are released from your fealty."

With that, Angel is returned to the cave, standing beside Doyle. Angel has no idea where to go, what to do . . . until Doyle asks him what he wants.

What has Angel always wanted?

Angel immediately finds Buffy at the beach and walks toward her, from shadows into sunlight. Stunned, she moves into his arms, and they kiss.

They return to Angel's apartment. Over chaste tea and crackers, they agree to try to take things slowly, pondering the implications of Angel's transformation and what it means for them. But one mere touch and they're all over each other. Later, they're naked in bed, munching out—it's all like a wonderful dream.

Meanwhile, Doyle and Cordelia sit in a bar, reexamining the situation. Cordelia assumes

they're both out of a job; Doyle wonders if he's off the hook with The Powers That Be as well. As soon as the words are out of his mouth, though, Doyle has a vision: the Mohra demon is back, and he's bigger and stronger than ever.

He goes to tell Angel, who remembers that the demon needed a lot of salt to survive. He figures it might be headed for the saline plant in Redondo. Doyle suggests they send Buffy to fight it, but Angel demurs. He doesn't want to destroy her perfect day. He also wants to be able to handle his end of things; otherwise it can't work between him and the Slayer. As Buffy sleeps, Angel and Doyle track the Mohra, unaware that the demon is tracking them. Coming upon some dead workers, Angel feels sick to his stomach at the sight of blood. Another new sensation. The demon attacks, and Angel is not up to the battle. Things are looking very bad.

Buffy awakens to find Cordelia planning a going-out-of-business sale, tagging all the office equipment and weapons. She asks where Angel is, and Cordelia's miffed that Buffy doesn't care that she, Cordelia, is in a bit of real pain. As they spar, Cordelia blurts out that Angel has gone off to fight "that thing" by himself.

The Mohra is a relentless warrior, and without his vampiric powers, Angel is struggling. The demon exults over what appears to be his inevitable triumph. But his victory speech is cut short.

> **MOHRA:** "The End of Days has begun and cannot be stopped. For any one of us who falls, ten shall rise."
>
> **BUFFY:** "You hurt my boyfriend."
>
> **MOHRA:** "A great darkness is coming—"
>
> **BUFFY:** "You got that right."

Buffy and the Mohra fight, hard, and the demon is winning. Angel is able to help by throwing salt in the demon's face, but that only temporarily stops him. Then Angel mulls what Doyle had read in the Book of Kelsor about killing the demon: "To slay the beast, one must bring darkness to the thousand eyes."

There is a jewel in the center of the demon's forehead. Angel realizes that the prismatic jewel is the "thousand eyes" that must be destroyed, and yells to Buffy to smash it. She does so, and brilliant light consumes the demon.

Buffy and Angel are both still alive, and Buffy comforts Angel, who's hurt and winded. And who was worthless in battle.

RESOLUTION

Angel goes back to speak to the Oracles, who confirm that because he is no longer a warrior in the battle between good and evil, the End of Days has begun, and the Soldiers of Darkness are coming. The bottom line is when the Soldiers come, the Slayer will die, sooner than she otherwise would have, because Angel has been "decommissioned." He asks them to make him what he was again—a vampire with a soul. Unaccustomed as they are to accommodating the wishes of a "lower being," they agree, because as they explain:

"This one is willing to sacrifice every drop of human happiness and love he has ever known for another. *He is not a lower being.*"
—*Sister Oracle*

The Oracles tell Angel that they can "swallow this day, as though it never happened." Only Angel will remember the last twenty-four hours. Reluctantly, he agrees to these terms, and returns to his apartment. Buffy has been anxiously waiting for him, not knowing where he's been. He has to tell her the truth. As she panics, he reminds her that they don't belong just to each other.

Buffy is desperate for him, but she finally accepts what he's telling her. Their mutual yearning grows; Buffy clings to him; one last kiss . . . their last minute as mortals together is almost gone.

"I'll never forget . . . I'll never forget . . . I'll never forget . . . I'll never forget . . . I'll never forget."
—*Buffy*

But she does. She has no choice. In the next second, she resumes her speech from the day before, about keeping their distance from each other. The Mohra demon attacks. But this time, Angel knows how to deal with it. He whacks the demon on its crystal eye, dispatching it easily.

Buffy leaves Angel's offices. He looks down at his clock, and it's only 9:02.

He's in for a very long, lonely day.

Case closed.

DOSSIERS

CLIENT **Angel** and **Buffy**, soul mates doomed once again to remain apart.

SUSPECTS The **Mohra demon**, whose regenerative blood tips the scales of good and evil. (Deceased.)

CONTINUITY

Buffy and Angel have years of shared history and heartbreak, including a wrenching disagreement over the course of their relationship in the Sunnydale sewers in "The Prom." Buffy also told Angel jokingly she doesn't look that good in sunlight in "Some Assembly Required"—now he has a chance to find out for himself. Cordelia gives Doyle a brief recap of the Buffy and Angel romance in her typical dry fashion. Angel is the first vampire known to have become human again and then returned to his vampiric state, but he won't be the last.

QUOTE OF THE WEEK

"Let me explain the lore here, okay? They suffer, they fight, that's business as usual. They get groiny with one another, the world as we know it falls apart."

> Cordelia shares with Doyle her extensive experience with Buffy and Angel.

THE DEVIL IS IN THE DETAILS

EXPENSES

Angel's office window
Groceries (in Day 1.0, but not in Day 2.0)
Cordelia and Doyle's bar tab (in Day 1.0 but not in Day 2.0)

WEAPONRY

Angel goes after the Mohra demon with an ax and Buffy uses a stake. They temporarily stun the demon by throwing salt in its eyes. Cordy wields her sarcasm. The Mohra demon wields a spiked mace.

THE PLAN

Buffy has a plan for dealing with her relationship with Angel.

> **BUFFY:** "So let's just stick to the plan, we keep our distance until . . . a lot of time has passed. Given enough time we should be able to . . ."
> **ANGEL:** ". . . forget."
> **BUFFY:** "Yeah."

DEMONS, DEMONS, DEMONS

According to the *Book of Kelsor*, **Mohra demons** are assassins who take out warriors on the side of good. They need vast quantities of salt to live, and their "veins run with the blood of eternity." If they're killed, they regenerate and are bigger and stronger. "To slay the beast, one must bring darkness to the thousand eyes."

THE VAMPIRE RULES

The blood of a Mohra can make a vampire human again, heartbeat and taste buds fully operational.

THE POWERS THAT BE

Doyle tells Angel he can beseech the Oracles to explain what has happened to him. Later he asks them to take his life away again. They are golden twins, one male, one female, dressed in vaguely Grecian robes, their skin decorated with strange streaks of blue.

THE PEN IS MIGHTIER

FINAL CUT

Cut due to length:

> **DOYLE:** "So Buffy and Angel, it's always been pretty . . . (mimes fisticuffs) . . . volatile?"
>
> **CORDELIA:** "That was nothing. One time they kicked the daylights out of each other at the mall—I was too embarrassed to shop there for, like, weeks."
>
> **DOYLE:** "It must have been good *sometime* . . ."
>
> **CORDELIA:** "At first he was just hanging around in the shadows, spying on us—boy, a lot's changed there, huh?—I was seeing someone at the time so I guess he sort of fixated on her."
>
> **DOYLE:** "And eventually they got together."
>
> **CORDELIA:** "Did they ever, on her seventeenth birthday. Which kicked in his 'knowing a moment of true happiness' curse and then it really got ugly."
>
> **DOYLE:** "He went bad, tried to kill her."
>
> **CORDELIA:** "He tried to kill everybody. You weren't really goin' out much after dark in those days. . . . Then she ran him through with a sword, sent him to Hell. He popped out four months later which was like a hundred years of torment in demon time or something. . . . His hair's never really been the same."
>
> **DOYLE:** "And then?"
>
> **CORDELIA:** "Then they were on-again off-again—you sort of need a score card at this point—but finally they broke up for real last spring. That's when he took off for L.A. The story thus far."
>
> **DOYLE:** "Great. So what happens now?"

POP CULTURE

❖ **"Oh, yeah, the Buffy and Angel show."** Cordelia refers to "The Itchy and Scratchy Show" a cartoon-within-a-cartoon about a cat and mouse who continually physically assault each other, on the TV series *The Simpsons*.

❖ Doyle is trying to remind Angel to stay on target when he says, **"Orson, we're in a situation here."** Mork from the Planet Ork (played by Robin Williams) reported to his fearless leader, Orson, on *Mork and Mindy* (1978–1982).

❖ **"We have time for a cappuccino—and probably the director's cut of *Titanic*."** Cordelia gives Doyle some idea of how long it will take Buffy and Angel to have a really awesome argument. The James Cameron film (1997) lasted over three hours.

❋ When searching below-ground for the demon, Buffy says: **"Tunnel number one it is."** This is a reference to *Let's Make a Deal,* a show on which contestants choose Door #1, #2, or #3.

❋ **"The next thing I know we're being attacked by that mutant ninja demon thing. . . ."** Buffy recounts her experiences in a reference to the Teenage Mutant Ninja Turtles, characters created by Kevin Eastman and Peter Laird in the mid-eighties.

OUR HEROES

"When Sarah came to your show, in 'I Will Remember You,' how did that change the working dynamics between you?"

DAVID BOREANAZ: "Didn't change the working dynamics at all. It was pretty much what we had from the beginning, transformed just to another set. It was very easy, a simple walk and a nice dance. It just was a different call time, different set."

"We did a set last year for the Oracles; they were sort of a brother and sister act who lived in another dimension, and they would be visited for knowledge. On that set, we wanted to create something that looked like it went on forever, a hallway that looked like it just kept going and kept going and kept going. And for budgetary and for space constraints, we couldn't do that. So we tried a tried-and-true trick of forced perspective, we built a set with diminishing-size arches that, when you put the camera in the right position, it looks like they just go on."

—STUART BLATT, PRODUCTION DESIGNER

SIX DEGREES OF . . .

Randall Slavin, the male Oracle, appeared on *Roseanne* during the time that Glenn Quinn was on the show.

"HERO"

FROM THE FILES OF ANGEL INVESTIGATIONS
CASE № 1ADH09

ACTION TAKEN

Angel is suffering in silence over having given back his humanity to The Powers That Be. The business is sliding, and Cordelia is trying to save it by producing a TV commercial for Angel Investigations. It will star a "beautiful young actress" in danger, who will be saved by Angel.

But Angel is not thrilled with the concept and silently goes down to his apartment while Cordelia voices her concerns about the state of their business, which is dire. Doyle discusses the situation with Cordelia and tries to allay her concerns, and she decides to cast him instead of Angel for their commercial. Alas, Doyle's line reading is very sucky, and Cordelia is underwhelmed.

Doyle goes downstairs to Angel's apartment to have a heart-to-heart. Angel tells him about the day that everyone relived, but only he, Angel remembers. Doyle's awed by Angel's sacrifice.

WRITTEN BY Howard Gordon & Tim Minear
DIRECTED BY Tucker Gates
GUEST STARS: Tony Denman (Rieff), Anthony Cistaro (Trask), Michelle Horn (Rayna), Lee Arenberg (Tiernan), Sean Gunn (Lucas)
CO-STARS: James Henriksen (Elder Lister Demon), David Bickford (Cargo Inspector), Christopher Comes (Storm Trooper #2), Paul O'Brien (Captain), Ashley Taylor (First Mate)

DOYLE: "Human? You were a real live flesh-and-blood human being? And you and Buffy . . . You had the one thing you've wanted in your unnaturally long life . . . and you gave it back?"

ANGEL: "Maybe I was wrong."

DOYLE: "Or maybe Cordelia was right. About you being the real deal in the hero department. See, I woulda chose the pleasures of the flesh over duty and honor any day of the week. I just don't have that strength."

ANGEL: "You never know your strength till you're tested."

The Oracles told Angel that something bad was coming—Soldiers of Darkness ushering in the End of Days. Angel can feel it, and it is indeed something very bad. Doyle figures that for unfair; that not only does Angel have to do a lot of one-on-one saving of the helpless, now he has to fight the Apocalypse as well.

"It's all the same thing. You fight the good fight. Whichever way you can."   —*Angel*

Doyle tells Cordelia about Angel's heroic sacrifice of his regained humanity. Sitting in the lobby of Angel's building together, they share their amazement, and Cordelia says it was wrong of Angel not to tell them. That they can't keep secrets from each other.

Doyle is about to use that as his segue to revealing his half-demon heritage when he's interrupted by a vision. He sees about two dozen Lister demons huddled together in darkness, terrified. Angel and Doyle investigate. They locate the Lister clan, who are living on the run. Like Doyle, they are half-demons; as such, they are being hunted by a group of Nazilike, pure demons called the Scourge. The Listers are trying to get to Briole, a small island off the coast of Ecuador, where others of their kind have found sanctuary.

Two of the Lister youths, Rayna and Rieff, return while Doyle and Angel are being briefed, and they are told that Angel is the Promised One.

> **ANGEL:** "Ummm . . . I think there's been some kind of misunderstanding—"
>
> **ELDER:** "I don't think so. Many of our prophecies are cryptic but on one thing they're all clear: in the final days of this century the Promised One will appear and save us from the Scourge."

Doyle pales, and remembers his first encounter with the Scourge. He had just found out he was half demon. He wasn't dealing with it well, living in a flophouse and not taking care of himself. A Brachen demon—Doyle's race of demons—was hiding in his apartment and asked Doyle to help him and the rest of his clan. They were from Oregon, and the Scourge was pursuing them.

> **DOYLE:** "An army. Of pureblood demons. Got a big hate-on for us mixed-heritage types. Very into the pedigree. Hunt us down like animals."
>
> **ANGEL:** "No one fights back?"
>
> **DOYLE:** "Sure they do. All the time. You can kill 'em, but these guys believe in what they're doing. They're ready to die for the cause."

The Brachen demon had come under the assumption that Doyle would aid his own kind. Still over-whelmed with self-hatred and shame about his own heritage, Doyle refused him. Shortly after that, Doyle had his first vision, and he saw the Brachen demons in trouble.

"When I got the visions for the first time, I thought I was having a stroke. I didn't know what the images meant, but I had to know if what they showed me was a dream or real." —*Doyle*

He found the refugee encampment of the Brachen demons. They had all been massacred—from Lucas, the demon who had asked him for help, down to the tiniest child. Doyle was overwhelmed with guilt . . . and still is. This time, he's going to stand and fight.

Angel sends Cordelia with a van to pick up the Lister clan, with the plan to take them to a freighter and get them out of Los Angeles. He neglected to mention that they're demons, however, and Cordelia tries to hold them at bay. Doyle shows, and explains that this is the group they've been sent to help.

> **CORDELIA:** "You did notice that these folks are *demons*."
>
> **DOYLE:** "Yeah. I know that. That doesn't make them bad people."
>
> **CORDELIA:** "'Scuse us a sec. Okay, Mission Statement check. Aren't we supposed to be *battling* the forces of darkness?"
>
> **DOYLE:** "They're not forces of darkness. They're half human and they're in trouble. . . ."

Cordelia acquiesces. When all is said and done, she's a team player. Doyle tells her to make contact with the freighter captain, then to call him on the cell phone when it's safe to transport the Lister demons to the vessel. Angel is with the cargo inspector, forcing him to sign documents saying that the freighter is carrying medical waste.

While the Lister demons are waiting for Cordelia's call, Rieff, one of the younger male demons, takes off. He doesn't believe that Angel is the Promised One, and he doesn't want to be a sitting duck for the approaching Scourge. Doyle tells the leader of the Lister clan to wait for Cordelia's call, while he searches for Rieff. If he and the boy don't make it back before the others have to go to the ship, Doyle will rendezvous with them there later—he hopes—with Rieff in tow.

He locates the boy, whose bitterness at being a half-demon is an echo of Doyle's own.

> **RIEFF:** "You wouldn't get it. You're passing. My mother was the same way. Could walk down the street. She took me out with her one day. I was so excited. Just out in the neighborhood with all the other kids. You know what day it was? What day was it?"
>
> **DOYLE:** "It was Halloween."

As Doyle and Rieff head back to the Lister hideaway, the Scourge advances. The two hide while the stormtroopers begin a sweep, setting a car on fire, getting closer and closer to Doyle and Rieff. To draw them away from Rieff, Doyle assumes his Brachen visage and allows the stormtroopers to see him. They give chase; then Angel appears as if out of nowhere and yanks Doyle to safety.

Essentially cornered in one of the tenement buildings, Angel vamps out and pretends Doyle is his captive. He seemingly breaks Doyle's neck and throws him to the floor of the burned-out building. Then he tells Trask, one of the pureblood leaders, that he wants to join them. The leader agrees.

After Angel leaves with the others, Rieff creeps in to stare at Doyle's body . . . only to discover that Doyle is just pretending to be dead. He straightens out his neck and he and Rieff realize the rest of the family must have gone on to the ship.

The ship's captain wants to shove off. Cordelia's trying to make him wait a few more minutes—a feat which is accomplished by dickering over money, a topic near and dear to her. Cordelia reports her success to the elder of the clan, who spills the beans about Doyle, mentioning that the Irishman is also a half-demon. Cordelia is stunned at this revelation.

Angel has been given a Scourge uniform and stands with the others in a vaulted lair as Tiernan, their leader, whips up the troops. Then Tiernan calls for the freighter's first mate to be brought forward. The first mate is actually a traitor, having notified Tiernan of the presence of the Lister clan in the freighter, in return for money. But Tiernan has other plans for him.

Tiernan reveals a large metallic object that begins to pulse. The Beacon, as it is called, grows brighter and brighter. Tiernan explains that any creature contaminated by human blood will perish the instant the Beacon's light hits it. When the Beacon reaches full power, it will detonate, and all human life within a quarter mile in every direction will be extinguished.

The Beacon pulses, and the traitorous first mate shrieks as the light touches him. As he screams in agony, the light melts him away to nothing. As the exuberant crowd is swept up into bloodlust, Angel maneuvers his way into a side tunnel. There he knocks a demon off a motorcycle and makes his escape.

Aboard ship, Rieff is reunited with the clan. And Cordelia smacks Doyle.

> **CORDELIA:** Why didn't you tell me you were half demon? I thought we agreed secrets are bad."
>
> **DOYLE:** "I wanted to tell you. I was afraid . . . I thought if I did you'd reject me."
>
> **CORDELIA:** "I rejected you way before now! So you're half demon. Big whoop. I can't believe you think I'd even *care* about that. I mean, I work for a *vampire*! Hello!"
>
> **DOYLE:** "It's true. I just . . ."
>
> **CORDELIA:** "What do you think I am, *superficial*? I mean, you're *half* demon. That is so far down the list. Way under 'short' and 'poor.' Is there anything else I should know?"
>
> **DOYLE:** "The half-demon thing—pretty much my big secret."
>
> **CORDELIA:** "Good. That's out. It's done. Would you ask me out to dinner already?"

It's a sweet, wonderful moment, their smiles speaking volumes to one another. Then Angel arrives and shouts for the captain to get underway. The Scourge is following close behind.

Angel tries to hold off them off, but there are too many. The Lister demons, Doyle, and Cordelia huddle in the locked hold as the Scourge lowers the Beacon over their heads. Angel drops down to join them. No one can get back out; the doors have been locked from the outside.

As the glow begins, Angel realizes he's going to have to sacrifice himself to stop it. He'll have to cling to the Beacon in order to pull the power cables apart.

It's a suicide mission and they all realize it. Cordelia tries to talk Angel out of it. Then Doyle steps up, smiling at Angel. The two share a brief, comradely moment.

"You never know till you're tested. I get that now."   —*Doyle*

And then he slugs Angel with everything he's got, knocking the vampire off the catwalk and out of reach of the Beacon.

Doyle kisses Cordelia good-bye, a faint blue glow emanating from between their lips. He says gently, as he morphs into demon face:

"Too bad we'll never know if this is a face you could learn to love."   —*Doyle*

Doyle hurls himself at the Beacon, catching hold of the cables. He is in terrible pain as Cordelia and Angel shout his name. His flesh begins to burn away; he's in agony . . . but he manages to unplug the cables, moments before the light consumes him . . . and he is gone.

Doyle, not Angel, is the Promised One. He has saved the Lister clan, and atoned for deserting the Brachen demons years ago.

He is a true hero.

RESOLUTION

Later, Cordelia and Angel watch Cordelia's commercial video in silence. It is a fitting eulogy to their fallen comrade.

> **DOYLE**: "Angel Investigations is the best. Our rats are low—"
>
> **CORDELIA**: "Our rates . . ."
>
> **DOYLE**: "It says 'rats.' Our rates are low, but our standards are high. When the chips are down, and you're at the end of your rope, you need someone you can count on. And that's what you'll find here. Someone who'll go all the way, who'll protect you no matter what. Don't lose hope. Come on over to our offices, and you'll see there's still heroes in this world. Is that it? Am I done?"

Rest in peace, Allen Francis Doyle.

Case closed.

DOSSIERS

CLIENT Doyle has visions about the **Lister demons**, but is it they who are the clients in this case, or **Doyle** himself? He has finally found peace with his demon side, bonded with Cordelia, and atoned for his frailties. He has lived a full life.

CIVILIAN SUPPORT The **captain of the** *Quintessa* agrees to illegally transport the Lister demons in return for a sixty percent reduction in a debt he owes Angel—a debt which Angel was willing to forgive in full, but Cordelia drives a hard bargain. The **cargo inspector** agrees to forge documents stating that the *Quintessa* is carrying medical waste and should not be further inspected prior to departure, nor boarded while at sea.

SUSPECTS **Tiernan** is the leader of the Scourge. **Trask**, one of the Scourge, manages to slow Angel down, making it possible for Doyle to sacrifice himself instead. The **ship's mate** betrayed the Lister clan to the Scourge, and died from the Beacon's rays. (All deceased.)

CONTINUITY

Doyle recalls his ex-wife, Harry, visiting and causing him heartache (as well as endangering his life) during her new fiancé's "Bachelor Party." He attempts to console Angel for the sacrifice Angel made for the sake of Buffy and the innocents of the world in "I Will Remember You."

QUOTE OF THE WEEK

CORDELIA: "I don't know, I'm not getting Everyman, I'm getting weasel. We don't want weasel."

DOYLE: "I don't know, I think people'll be pouring in when they hear about our low rats. I can take another crack at it—"

CORDELIA: "I don't think so."

DOYLE: "Weasel factor, huh?"

> Cordelia critiques Doyle's performance in her commercial.

THE DEVIL IS IN THE DETAILS

EXPENSES

Video
Sixty percent of the debt due Angel
Doyle's life

WEAPONRY

Cordelia threatens the Lister clan with a can of Mace; the Beacon is the ultimate demon weapon to rid the planet of human contamination.

THE PLAN

Doyle is not a fan of Angel's improvised neck-snapping.

"I think I hated that plan." **—Doyle**

DEMONS, DEMONS, DEMONS

Brachen demons look like blue, pinheaded humans. One of the clans lived in the Oregon woods for a time. They're reputed to have great sense of direction.

Lister demons look vaguely like the zombies in Michael Jackson's "Thriller." The clan in Los Angeles is trying to get to Briole to join others of their kind. Their ancient prophecies foretell the coming of the Promised One who will save them from the Scourge in the final days of "this century." Some can pass for human and others can't.

The Scourge are a Nazilike army of purebred demons dedicated to wiping out all half-demons. They are led by Trask and Tiernan, who have devised the Beacon as the ultimate weapon.

THE VAMPIRE RULES

Vampires don't feed on demon blood.
Vampires are considered the lowest of all the half-breeds by certain other demons.

Demon Trooper Masks

AS SCENE IN L.A.

"Where is the pier where the ship that takes on the refugees is docked?"

KEVIN FUNSTON, LOCATIONS MANAGER: "That was at Southwest Marine, and that's down in San Pedro/Long Beach, the Port of Long Beach. As location managers, we have to build relationships with a lot of these different areas where we want to film, and we have a pretty good relationship with Southwest Marine. We rented the boat separately from a company that had it docked there."

THE PEN IS MIGHTIER

FINAL CUT

Cut for length:

CORDELIA: "Now, we'll have to do something with your hair."

DOYLE: "What's wrong with my—"

CORDELIA: "Nothing, you're right. That's dull, generic, real-life hair. Nobody's gonna be threatened by that hair. Take a step to the right . . . cock your head a little, chin up . . . boy, this could take a lot of makeup."

In the stage directions, an establishing shot of a faded sign identifies the tenement where the Lister clan is living as "The Brinks Hotel."

POP CULTURE

❖ **"Maybe that bald *Star Trek* guy or one of the cheaper Baldwins."** When casting her envisioned commercial, Cordelia suggests some actors for voice-over work. The bald *Star Trek* guy is Patrick

Stewart, who played Jean-Luc Picard on *Star Trek: The Next Generation.* The Baldwins are a family of actors which includes brothers Alec, Stephen, Daniel, and William.

❖ **"He's a larger-than-life character, way too *Braveheart* for Joe Couch-Potato to relate to."** Cordelia doesn't think Angel is right to play the hero in her commercial. *Braveheart* was a 1995 film about a legendary Scottish hero, directed by Mel Gibson, who also starred.

❖ **"Wait! I know this one. Uh, *Mask! Mask,* head . . . *The Man with Two Brains!* Wait . . ."** Cordelia is pretending to play charades with Doyle as he contorts with pain during a vision. *The Mask* was a 1994 film starring Jim Carrey; *Mask* was a 1985 film starring Cher. *The Man with Two Brains* was a 1983 film starring Steve Martin.

❖ Discussing "booking a cruise" to get the Lister clan out of L.A., Cordelia says: **"I'm guessing not Carnival—"** She is referring to a well-known cruise ship line.

❖ As Cordelia checks out the *Quintessa*, she says: **"Well, it's not exactly the Love Boat, is it?"** *The Love Boat,* a TV series about people finding love on a cruise ship, aired from 1977-1986, and has spawned a new series and several TV movies.

OUR HEROES

"How did you come up with the Beacon?"

COURTNEY JACKSON, PROPERTY MASTER: "The giant ball? Stuart Blatt, our production designer, designed the shape of it. And Lighting was involved with that, as well, because we had to put a giant light in it to make it actually shine. And then I believe Special Effects welded the giant box that it lived in, because it had to actually have a pick point where we could put it on a crane safely. And the little design, we knew we had a triangle and we wanted all the different buttons and stuff. And I did all of those, I did the control panels. So again, it was one where everything comes together. Then the scenics had to paint, to make it all look right. So between Special Effects, and Lighting, and me and the production designers, we ended up with that giant ball."

"In 'I Will Remember You' and 'Hero' we see characters making huge personal sacrifices for the greater good. Do you think it takes a larger-than-life, fictional character to do something like that?"

RANDALL SLAVIN (BROTHER ORACLE): "I think you see it all the time in random emergencies, and you see it in wartime, where people sacrifice their own safety for others. So I don't think it's that outlandish of an idea that people do this. It doesn't happen much, but it does happen and it's always the person you would least expect to do it, which is probably true of Doyle—the person you would least expect to be selfless."

"Do you have any special memories or stories about your time on the set, other than having your person painted by strangers?"

RANDALL SLAVIN: "Glenn and I met the day he got off the plane from Ireland. It was down in Long Beach, California. I was friends, completely randomly, friends with his cousin who he came here from Ireland to live with. So I met Glenn when he first got here, literally the day of. And we'd run into each other, and then I did *Roseanne*, and throughout the years we'd just sort of pop into each other's lives for a little while and catch up. So that was nice when I did it and got to spend time with Glenn again."

SIX DEGREES OF . . .

Lee Arenberg (Tiernan) has appeared on *Star Trek: Deep Space Nine*, with Armin Shimerman of Buffy fame. Anthony Cistaro (Trask) played the Ethros demon in "I've Got You Under My Skin." Sean Gunn (Demon Lucas) played Mars, the spa owner in "She." James Henriksen (Lister demon elder) was in *Flight of Black Angel*, a film about an Air Force pilot who decides God wants him to "cleanse" sinful cities with stolen nuclear weapons. Randy Ericksen was the art director on *Flight of Black Angel*, and assistant props on *Pleasantville*. Marc Blucas, Jason Behr, and Danny Strong, all appearing on *Buffy the Vampire Slayer*, appeared in *Pleasantville*. Jason Behr is Max Evans on *Roswell*. Julie Benz, who is Darla on *Angel*, is Kathleen Topolsky on *Roswell*. Julie Benz also appeared on *Sliders*. Reza Badiyi directed episodes of *Sliders* and *Buffy the Vampire Slayer*. Vern Gillum directed *Sliders* and *Angel* ("I Fall to Pieces"). Fernand Bos has served as music editor for both *Sliders* and *Buffy the Vampire Slayer*. Skip MacDonald was the assistant sound editor on *The Man with Two Brains*, referred to by Cordelia during this episode; he was an editor on the film *Buffy the Vampire Slayer* (1992).

TRACKS

"Doyle had a [musical] theme that was fleshed out in 'Hero.' We first hear it quietly, yet with a little impending weight, when Angel tells Doyle that there is a Darkness coming. My intention was for it to foreshadow Doyle's key involvement in that upcoming battle. We don't know it yet, but the music is telling us that Doyle will make the ultimate sacrifice. We later hear it over one of Doyle's flashbacks, hauntingly sung by Elin Carlson, when Doyle discovers brutally murdered bodies of those of his own race. The scene could be played horror or suspense, but we play this beautiful, ethereal sad melody, again grounding his theme in the importance of his place in the story. At the end, he sacrifices himself to save the Listers, with whom he shares blood, and we now hear his theme in full hero treatment with brass and huge bass drums, et cetera, then at the end of the show a solo flute plays his theme as slowly as humanly possible (my flute player was exhausted) as Angel and Cordy remember him." —ROBERT KRAL, COMPOSER

"PARTING GIFTS"

FROM THE FILES OF ANGEL INVESTIGATIONS
CASE Nº: 1ADH10

ACTION TAKEN

Angel visits the Oracles to ask them to restore Doyle to life. They refuse and the brother directs him not to come to them again on so self-serving a matter. Angel reminds them that Doyle was his contact to The Powers That Be. The Sister Oracle delivers that time-despised bromide, "For each door that closes, another opens," and they send Angel away.

Meanwhile, a short, elfin demon is running for his life from a figure in black leather motorcycle gear and a helmet while, in Angel's office, Cordelia is searching for Doyle's special coffee mug—or anything of Doyle's. It's almost as if he had never existed. She's mournful, and Angel suggests she take the day off—an offer she heroically refuses until her watch beeps, reminding her she's got an audition.

As Cordelia sails out the door, she nearly collides with the elfin demon. His name is Barney. He's a talkative guy, kind of a lounge-lizard type, and he's there to see Angel. Someone—or something—"unstoppable" is after him, always a step or two behind. Barney is convinced that his pursuer is an assassin.

When Angel asks him why he's being dogged, Barney tries to prevaricate. Finally, he comes clean.

WRITTEN BY David Fury and Jeannine Renshaw
DIRECTED BY James A. Contner
GUEST STARS: Maury Sterling (Barney), Carey Cannon (Sister Oracle), Randall Slavin (Brother Oracle), and Alexis Denisof (Wesley Wyndam-Pryce)
CO-STARS: Jayson Creek (Producer #1), Sean Smith (Producer #2), Sara Devlin (Producer #3), Jason Kim (Spon), Brett Gilbert (Reptilian Demon), Henry Kingi (Kungai Demon), Lawrence Turner (Hank)

NOTE: This is the first episode naming Alexis Denisof (Wesley Wyndam-Pryce) in the opening credits.

"Hey, I never said I was a boy scout. I'm an empath demon. I can read emotions. Gives me a slight advantage at cards. You know, blackjack, poker. Oh, it's also good for the fights."   —*Barney*

Meanwhile, Cordelia's having a trying time at her audition for a laundry detergent commercial. First, grief over Doyle's death has her weeping—rather than ecstatic—at the lack of a stain. Given a chance to "change her interpretation" by the producers, she is struck by a blinding migraine, accompanied by what has to be a vision. The producers are dumbfounded.

Cordelia returns to Angel's office, crosses to Angel, and takes him by surprise with a megawatt kiss.

ANGEL: "Um . . . Okay, Cordelia. That was . . . I think you're acting out of grief and you're confusing our friendship as something more than—"
CORDELIA: "I didn't feel anything. Did you feel anything?"
ANGEL: "No, see, that's what I'm trying—"

CORDELIA: "Arrgh! That means I still have it. I cannot believe he did this to me."

ANGEL: "Who did what?"

CORDELIA: "Doyle. I thought our kiss meant something. Instead, he used that moment to pass it on to me. Why couldn't it have been mono? Or herpes?"

ANGEL: "Cordelia—"

CORDELIA: "I didn't ask for this responsibility. Unlike some people who shall remain lifeless, I don't have anything to atone for. If they know what's good for them, The PTB better just stay out of my head."

ANGEL: "The Powers That Be. You had a vision."

CORDELIA: "Boy, howdy! And guess what? You know how they look painful? They feel a whole lot worse."

She tries to get rid of the gift by smooching Barney as well, but that doesn't work, either. When Angel asks her what she saw in her vision, she shrugs: some ugly, gray, blobby thing, who cares? Seemingly forgetting her indecipherable rendition of an angel on his business cards, Angel asks her to sketch it while he goes to check out Barney's apartment.

Angel arrives at the Regal Apartments, the flophouse where Barney is staying. As he enters the apartment, he's shoved into the room by the leather-clad figure, who is now pointing a loaded crossbow directly at his chest.

It's Wesley Wyndam-Pryce, who tells Angel that he left the Watchers Council because he had no one to watch, and has become a "rogue demon hunter." Angel guesses that he's the one who's been trailing Barney, and assures him that the empath demon is harmless. But as Wesley describes the trail of mutilated demon corpses he's been following, it's clear that whatever has been hunting the victims is collecting demonic powers. As they compare notes, a horrific demon drops from the ceiling. Angel battles it and Wesley shoots it with the crossbow. It crashes through the window, lands two stories below, and runs off.

Back at Angel's apartment, Cordelia is trying to sketch the strange object she saw in her vision. Barney kibitzes a little, and Cordelia begins to open up, talking about how much she misses Doyle. Then Wesley and Angel show up, and Barney freaks out—Wesley is his dark pursuer.

Cordelia tries to give Wesley the visioning gift with a huge, amazing kiss. She doesn't succeed, but sparkage occurs. They catch up, and Wesley explains he's a lone wolf, a rogue demon hunter. "Wow," Cordelia replies, "what's a rogue demon?"

Angel and Wesley in turn explain to Barney that Wesley has been hunting the thing that was stalking him, Barney. They assume that the other demon wanted to steal his empathic abilities. Using Angel's books, Wesley identifies the demon they fought at Barney's apartment. It's a Kungai, and its Tak horn is capable of consuming its opponent's life force. Angel announces he'll start looking for it at the last place Wesley tracked it—Koreatown.

WESLEY: "The hell you say. The demon is mine, Angel. I know how to track him. You're not catching him without me at your side."

ANGEL: "I had somebody at my side. He's dead now. I'm not going to let that happen again. I work alone."

Angel leaves by himself and finds the Kungai demon at the Lotus Spa, a demon hangout. Its horn has been ripped off, and it's dying. Wesley follows Angel there, and he translates the dying Kungai's last words. It reveals that it was attacked and its horn taken by a "demon heart reader." Which can only mean Barney, the empath demon.

Back at Angel's apartment, Cordelia is still working on trying to draw the blobby thing she saw in her vision. She's unaware that Barney is the bad guy. He hangs over her shoulder, watching, and asks her why she's so frustrated. As they chat, she tells him about inheriting the visioning gift from Doyle, which Barney points out was probably the most valuable thing he had to give. When she takes a break from the sketchpad to make coffee, Barney makes a furtive cell phone call to his partner, Hank. He reports that he has hidden the Tak horn in a safe place . . . but he's found an even better power to collect.

Cordelia finishes the coffee and Barney drops his act, taunting her and calling her a terrible actress. She now realizes he's not the friendly lunk he has been pretending to be.

He pins her down and starts to tie her up. When her "terrible acting" convinces him that she's having a vision, he lowers his guard. She almost makes a getaway, but he catches her and knocks her out.

Cordelia slowly wakes up from unconsciousness. Bound and gagged, she focuses in on the blobby, gray object of her vision. It's a piece of sculpture. As she takes in her surroundings, she sees a demon claw on a pillow, bits of demons in jars, containers filled with organs, etc. Clearly she's staring at some kind of collection, a veritable treasure trove of gross bits and pieces. Within her hearing, Barney and his partner, Hank, are discussing whether they should extract Cordelia's eyes or leave them "in the body." Hank's all for popping them out right now, but Barney thinks they'll get more money if they're fresh.

Terrified, Cordelia shuts them, pretending she's still asleep.

Meanwhile, Angel and Wesley burst into Angel's apartment, but they're too late. The signs of a struggle confirm that Barney is indeed their target, and he's taken Cordelia with him. Wesley blames himself.

"I'm a fraud. The Council was right to sack me. Yes, I was fired. I had two . . . *two* Slayers in my care. One turned evil and now vegetates in a coma. The other's a renegade. Fire me? I'm surprised they didn't cut my head off."

—Wesley

Angel finds the sketch Cordelia was working on, and recognizes it as a famous blobby sculpture. Using the computer, he tracks it down—it's in the lobby of a nearby hotel. Wesley manages to decipher a strange word the Kungai was saying as it lay near death: it's the Kungai word for "auction."

In the hotel's ballroom, the auction of powers is already underway. The Tak horn is the item up for bidding. In the audience sits Mac, an attorney from Wolfram & Hart.

Next up: Cordelia's vision power, "a rare and beautiful find." She tries to keep the bidding going in hopes of imminent rescue. Barney joins in and they work the room together, until one of the bidders reaches twenty thousand. Cordy's eyeballs are going once, going twice, when Mac, the lawyer from Wolfram & Hart, raises the bid to thirty thousand.

Fair warning: once, twice, sold.

Mac announces that Wolfram & Hart wants the eyes extracted, so Barney and Hank move in to rip them out of Cordelia's head with a device that looks like a torturous combination of a pair of tongs and a sawed-off eggbeater.

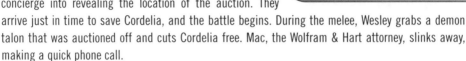

Angel and Wesley reach the hotel and intimidate the concierge into revealing the location of the auction. They arrive just in time to save Cordelia, and the battle begins. During the melee, Wesley grabs a demon talon that was auctioned off and cuts Cordelia free. Mac, the Wolfram & Hart attorney, slinks away, making a quick phone call.

"Our merchandise was just taken off the market. Three guesses by whom."　　　　　　*—Mac*

Fight, fight, fight: Wesley and Barney go at it, but Barney's the stronger. Things do not look hopeful for the rogue demon hunter until Cordelia grabs the Tak horn and plunges the business tip into Barney's back.

Barney dies, deflating weirdly.

Cordelia, Wesley, and Angel are the only ones left standing.

RESOLUTION

It's the morning after at Angel's apartment. Cordelia is ironing her sketch, while Wesley is packing to leave. Angel is scrambling eggs.

She finishes ironing the sketch and holds it up.

"This, I frame for saving my life, and as a reminder that something of Doyle's is here in our office."　　　　　　*—Cordelia*

Wesley prepares his dramatic exit, speaking of the lurking evil and the rogue demon hunting, and so on . . . protesting a bit:

"No rest for the wicked fighters. Through storm and rain, heat famine . . . deep, painful, gnawing
hunger . . . I go . . ."　　　　　　*—Wesley*

. . . Until Angel finally asks him if he'd like to stay for breakfast. It's clear he'll be staying on, at least for a while.

Case closed.

DOSSIERS

CLIENT Barney hires the firm, pretending to be a victim. However, it turns out that the **Kungai demon** is really the one being stalked. After the Kungai is killed, it is **Cordelia** whose life must be saved.

CIVILIAN SUPPORT **Wesley Wyndam-Pryce** helps to reveal Barney's deception by hounding him until he seeks help from Angel, translating the Kungai's deathbed statements, assisting with finding the sculpture, and fighting the good fight at the hotel. At the Lotus Spa, **Soon**, the desk clerk, tells Angel that the Kungai demon is in the back. The **concierge** at the Ramsey Hotel grudgingly informs Angel and Wesley that the auction is in the Tulip Room.

The Oracles refuse to restore Doyle's life.

SUSPECTS The **Kungai demon** is also a suspect, until it speaks to Wesley on its deathbed. **Barney** and his partner, **Hank**, are the diabolical forces behind the auction of demon powers. (Barney is deceased, Hank's fate remains uncertain.) **Mac** from Wolfram & Hart wants Cordelia's eyes . . . on a plate. (Remains at large.)

CONTINUITY

When Angel attempts to bargain with the Oracles to bring Doyle back, he reminds them that they altered time and consequences in the past, when they returned him to his unlife in "I Will Remember You." Evidently *everyone* knows the trick for public speaking is to picture one's audience in underwear. Barney gives this advice to Cordy. Angel gave it to Kate in "Sense and Sensitivity." And Giles gave it to Cordelia before she performed a Whitney Houston song at Sunnydale High's talent show in "Puppet Show."

QUOTE OF THE WEEK

BARNEY: "Sensing a little performance anxiety there. Little trick: picture everybody—"
CORDELIA: (anticipating) "In their underwear."
BARNEY: "I was gonna say dead, but hey, if that underwear thing works for you . . ."

Barney the empath demon demonstrates his ability.

THE DEVIL IS IN THE DETAILS

EXPENSES
$50 bribe for Soon

WEAPONRY
Wesley's crossbow staves off Angel; the Tak horn deflates Barney's ego . . . and his whole body.

Barney

DEMONS, DEMONS, DEMONS
Kungai demons are a powerful race of yellow-green, Asian demons whose Tak horns suck the life force out of an enemy.

Barney is an **empath demon** who can read people's emotions.

THE VAMPIRE RULES
Vampires don't really sleep in coffins. Angel attributes that misconception to "hack writers and an ignorant media."

Angel-ic Merchandise for the True Collector

Gotta have Faith? In fall 2001 Moore Action Collectibles introduced an action figure of the rogue Slayer in their *Angel* line. A special Slave Cordelia variant was released in early 2002. Angel, Cordelia, and Drusilla all have figures released under their Buffy line. Angel and Cordelia have already been released in MAC's *Buffy* line. Throughout 2002, M.A.C. will release figures of Wesley, the late Darla (presumably with<u>out</u> child), and the Host/Lorne.

Angel coffee mugs come in both ceramic and metal designs, for stationary or mobile caffeine infusions. Must be Cordelia's request.

An *Angel* cell phone faceplate? (Hello? Angel and cell phones?) Available for Nokia models.

Darkhorse's "Angel" comics line took a hiatus for Summer 2001, then relaunched in the fall with Joss Whedon cowriting.

Angel and his supporting team members are available as two different sets of Christmas ornaments.

Cordelia, Phantom Dennis, and some lingerie took center stage in disposing a demon in the Dark Horse Comics "Cordelia" one shot.

Busted! Cordelia, Angel, and the Host have received the three-dimensional bust treatment from Moore Creations.

Pocket Books' *Buffy the Vampire Slayer/Angel: Unseen* crossover trilogy is the only licensed fiction to cover the time period between *Angel's* Seasons One and Two.

Inkworks offered a special by-mail trading card from their Web site for Seasons One and Two, as well as foil and autographed bonus cards.

Angel is able to enter Barney's apartment because Barney is a demon.

AS SCENE IN L.A.

The Ramsey Hotel location is actually the Ambassador Hotel. In 1968, Robert Kennedy was assassinated in the kitchen en route to the ballroom to accept the Democratic Presidential nomination.

THE PEN IS MIGHTIER

FINAL CUT

The Ramsey Hotel was originally called the Tamarind in the script.

This was deleted from the script, because of length:

> HANK: "Can't we at least take off the tape? It's more fun when they scream."
> BARNEY: "You heartless bastard. There are people trying to sleep in this hotel."

This was also cut:

> BARNEY: "One small favor? Can I see you turn into a bat?"
> ANGEL: "You want to get to why you need my help, Barney?"
> BARNEY: "Oh, yeah. I'm being stalked . . . hunted. Like a dog. Not a dog. Dogs hunt. They don't get hunted. What's something that gets hunted?"
> ANGEL: "I get the pict—"
> BARNEY: "A deer! Hunted like a deer. A little fawn all alone in the—"

POP CULTURE

✣ Barney says of "the rogue demon hunter": **"I don't think he's tracking me down to tell me I won Publisher's Clearing House."** Barney's referring to the multimillion dollar Prize Patrol Ed McMahon made famous.

✣ **"Alrighty then . . . Hank?"** Comedian Jim Carrey made this phrase popular in *Ace Ventura, Pet Detective* (1994).

OUR HEROES

"Did Glenn's leaving and Alexis's coming present a difficult thing to work through?"

DAVID BOREANAZ: "Yeah, it was difficult. Anytime that a person who's number one, your friend, is put into a situation that that happens to, it makes it difficult. So it was very hard for me, but it was something that I worked through, and also used it to work through the character as well, accepting Wesley's character."

"When Cordelia gets the job of receiving the visions, from an audience viewpoint, we see what she's seeing. How do you prepare to show her being hit by the visions?"

CHARISMA CARPENTER: "The only thing that was explained to me about the visions was that it just hurt, it was really painful. I never saw what the visions were supposed to look like until the show aired. I do get a neckache. We don't do it too many times. And also, they can get kind of violent. I do my best to be as padded as possible, and do all I can. David [Boreanaz] always catches me."

The tattoo at the base of Charisma Carpenter's spine is visible when she's making coffee at Angel's stove.

"When you directed Cordelia doing her commercial, and she's sobbing over the death of Doyle, how did you do it?"

JAMES CONTNER: "Actually, there's one instance where we tried a bunch of different things, how far she should go. After the fact, I'll be honest with you, I think I had her peak too soon as far as crying, breaking down too soon rather than kind of building to it. So we actually went back and reshot a close-up of her. Sometimes you . . . look at the dailies and you think, I could have done that better. So that's one instance where we went back and just reshot her close-up, just to have her build into it a little more."

"Did Wesley showing up in 'Parting Gifts' affect you in any way you didn't expect? You directed him on Buffy."

JAMES CONTNER: "Yeah, actually, the Wesley character is, I always thought, the perfect foil for Angel, and I was delighted that they brought him into the show. First of all, it made perfect sense. Because last we saw him, he was carrying this torch for Cordelia. Wesley was a wonderful character on *Buffy*, sort of full of himself and pompous and always ended up kind of being the fool in the end, outsmarting himself, and being the butt of a bunch of jokes. So here he had a chance to come in and actually change his image, and develop this character into something more than just a bumbling smartass sophisticated guy. He had a chance to come in and try to be what Angel is. He wants to be the macho guy. He has such wonderful comic timing, and a sense of humor that just works so well for the show."

103

"SOMNAMBULIST"

FROM THE FILES OF ANGEL INVESTIGATIONS
CASE N⁰: 1ADH11

ACTION TAKEN

A frightened woman runs down a dark, lonely street as if the devil himself were at her heels. She runs straight into a black-clad figure, who catches her in one strong hand and brings the other—its thumb wearing a strange, sharpened metal cap, like a malevolent thimble—to her cheek. He punctures her cheek, drawing blood, and slices a thin line. When he finishes his carving, he bends forward and drinks her blood.

On her cheek he has incised a Christian cross.

Angel wakes up suddenly, wearing his vamp face. He's coming to after a vivid dream as sirens wail in the distance. His face morphs back to human form as he gets his bearings. He's lying on top of his bed sheets, fully dressed.

Elsewhere in the city, police cruisers close in on a crime scene. Kate Lockley emerges from a vehicle and looks at a body on the ground. Kate doesn't recognize the woman, but she just starred in Angel's nightmare. She's dead, a cross carved into her cheek. "It's the same guy," Kate says, familiar with the killer's trademark if not the victim. "This makes three. He's just getting started."

Wesley finds news about the killings in the paper, and he and Cordelia make a connection they are not liking—that this is the work of a vampire . . .

Meanwhile, Kate gives Angel the lowdown on the case while she's doing some off-the-record computer work for him. Angel's worried—the killings sound like his own work. Kate goes into a conference room to address a task force brought together to apprehend this killer. As she speaks, she could be describing Angel:

". . . to the observer he will not seem a monster. His victims put up little or no struggle, so it's likely he's charming, attractive. But at his core, he's a loner . . . Possibly a dual personality, who, once the crime has been committed, retains no memory of the act. He will not view his victims as subhuman, rather, it's himself he regards as something other than human. More than human. A superior species. Stalking his prey, getting to know them. It's unlikely he'll be married, though he may have recently come out of a bad relationship that ended badly. We look for a precipitating event in cases such as this, and a painful breakup is always at the top of our list."
—*Kate*

She closes with a warning: he's been doing this for a very long time, and he'll do it again.

WRITTEN BY Tim Minear
DIRECTED BY Winrich Kolbe
GUEST STARS: Elisabeth Rohm (Kate Lockley), Jeremy Renner (Penn)
CO-STARS: Nick McCallum (Skateboard Kid), Kimberliegh Aarn (Precinct Clerk), Paul Webster (Uniform #1), Brien DiRito (Task Force Member #1)

Angel returns to his office to discover that Cordelia and Wesley have made the same not-great conclusions he has, having read newspaper accounts of the killings and recognized the basic modus operandi, and they're ready to stake him. Angel tells them that he's been having dreams of killing people. And they're not nightmares, because he's been enjoying them. Wesley understands—Angel believes he's been sleepwalking in the predawn hours, committing the murders in his sleep. The only way to test the hypothesis

is to chain Angel to his bed and see what happens. Cordy makes sure the chains are good and tight, then bails, not wanting to be around for Angel's "nocturnal commissions."

Another dark street, another woman, but this one is dressed in Puritan garb, from 1786. She runs, she's caught, she's carved. As she dies, Angelus asks, "There, now, isn't that better?"

Angel wakes up, tugging at his chains, and awakening Wesley, who's fallen asleep on guard duty. It's the next day and Cordelia comes in, waving a newspaper triumphantly.

> **CORDELIA:** "Great news, sports fans! There's been another killing! Okay, maybe not-so-great-news for the, you know, dead person, but at least now we know Mr. I'm-So-Tortured didn't do it."
>
> **ANGEL:** "Yes I did."

Angelus, we learn, was talking to Penn in his dream. In 1786, Angelus had recently sired Penn and was showing him the bloodsucking ropes—which included an activity near and dear to Angelus's own heart, slaughtering and feasting on his own family. Penn's first kill was his sister, and Angelus prompted him to drop in on the rest of the clan, particularly his disapproving father.

But that was the Penn of long ago. The Penn of today tapes newspaper articles about a serial killer on the walls of his yuppie apartment. Angel reveals that he used to have a strong connection with the vampires he sired, so Penn must be close by for Angel to be sensing the murders. Even if the cops find him, which Angel is convinced they will, they won't know how to deal with him. The harder Kate looks for the killer, the more trouble she'll be in if she turns him up. He's got to help her.

Angel has proven to be a pretty good artist in the past, and he comes through this time with a reasonable likeness of his old friend. He delivers his sketch to Kate at the police precinct—and predicts the killer's next choice of victim—a young man. On his way out, Angel lifts a police radio from a police car, so they'll be able to keep tabs on the investigation.

Kate has taken Angel's warning seriously, and shared it with the rest of the task force. Cops all over the city will be watching for adolescent males near bars and liquor stores. That night, Penn finds a skateboarder hanging around looking for someone to buy him beer. He takes the kid around the corner and makes his move, chomping down on him—but then spotlights from several police cars pin him. He leaps high into the air, crashing through the second-story window of an abandoned warehouse. The call goes out over the police band, and Angel goes into the warehouse after Penn.

Kate has also gone in, service weapon in hand. When Penn ignores her orders to freeze, she fires several times, dropping him. Kneeling beside him, she checks his pulse, which is, of course, nonexistent.

Penn grabs Kate and hurls her across the room. He gets to his feet to finish her off, but Angel crashes through the ceiling and drops to the floor in front of him. Elated to see his sire, Penn gives Angel a crushing embrace.

Angel vamps out and attacks Penn, and Penn likewise morphs, defending himself. Kate is suddenly faced with something terrifying that she can't deny. Hearing Kate's backup approach, Penn takes off, leaving Angel alone with a very freaked-out Kate.

She sticks a gun into his chest, and asks, "What are you?"

He points out that she already knows the answer, and speculates that a small detail must have been left out of the press reports, the fact that all the killer's victims had puncture wounds in their necks, and were drained of their blood. She admits it, but the fact that Angel knows it certainly doesn't make her any more comfortable with him. He tries to tell her how to stop Penn, but Kate won't listen, doesn't want anything to do with it. Angel insists that she's going to lose because she won't face the truth.

Cordelia finally has someone to give her Angel Investigations sales pitch to—a new prospective client has come in the door. Unfortunately, she doesn't know that it's Penn, pumping her for information about both Angel and Kate. Finally, the light dawns. When she figures it out, he threatens her, but she's clever enough to open a window shade, admitting a shaft of sunlight bright and wide enough to keep him at bay. Angel enters.

> **PENN:** "What, you don't drink now so no one gets to?"
>
> **ANGEL:** "I don't expect you to understand."
>
> **PENN:** "Oh, I understand. I was a Puritan, remember?"

Angel insults Penn, calling him "a cheesy hack" who has been repeating the same crime, killing his father over and over for two hundred years. Penn is stung by his mentor's criticism. Then Wesley walks in and Penn grabs him, using him as a shield while he makes his escape, leaving one final hint as he goes.

"Just think of the worst possible thing you can imagine . . . and I'll see you there." —*Penn*

Kate continues her research, moving from police files to texts on vampirism and the occult, while Angel pounds the pavement looking for Penn. Finally, Angel goes to see Kate at her apartment, but she won't let him in the door. Her earlier warmth is gone. She knows vampire lore now, and she tells Angel about previous Penn visits, in 1929 and 1963. She's also found references to Angel himself.

"Angelus. I looked it up. It's all right there. The demon with the face of an angel. A particularly brutal bastard, by all accounts. Oh, and no. You can't come in." —*Kate*

He pleads for her to allow him to help find and kill Penn, but she refuses.

"Thanks for the offer, but I don't need your help. I know what to do. Drive a stake right through the sonofabitch's heart. And when that happens, I suggest you don't be there . . . because the next time we meet, I'll do the same to you." —*Kate*

Back at his office, Angel asks Cordelia to look up the dates of the crimes Kate listed. Two buildings that figure in the stories prove to be the same building with different names. It was a hotel, then an apartment building, and now it's a condo. Angel and Wesley go check it out.

Penn's not there, but it's obvious from the clippings on the wall that he has been. The vampire's photos of a school bus and a flyer announcing a school field trip chill Angel to the bone.

Kate passes out pictures of Penn and Angel to her task force. She tells them to be on the lookout for Angel, as he might lead them to Penn, or even be the next victim. She's wrong there—Penn himself is in the task force room. He complains loudly about Angel's drawing of him, then plows through a bunch of cops and grabs Kate.

By then, Angel has figured out that the bus was a ruse, and the real target was Kate. He goes after Penn in the sewer tunnels. Kate, who has armed herself with holy water, splashes it on Penn as he and Angel face off.

"You were right about one thing, Angelus. The last two hundred years has been about me sticking it to my father. But I've come to realize something—it's you. You made me! You taught me! You approved of me in ways my mortal father never did. You're my real father, Angel." —*Penn*

As they battle, Kate manages to raise a piece of old wood, three feet long and heavy. But Penn holds Angel from behind—to stake Penn, she's got to go through Angel. She hesitates. Angel looks at the wooden point aimed at him and nods, almost imperceptibly. And she lunges forward, driving the stake through Angel into Penn's heart. Penn—but not Angel—explodes in a cloud of dust.

ANGEL: "You missed."
KATE: "No. I didn't."

She tugs the wooden stake out of him and he collapses on the ground in agony. She has spared him by missing his heart, but she's no warmer than she was before.

RESOLUTION

Angel sits on his rooftop, looking out at the city. Cordelia joins him, and he wonders aloud if anything really changes. She assures him that he has. She points out that she got a vision, but it was for Angel, not for her. The Powers That Be trust him to help people, and they wouldn't if he was still the same old Angelus.

CORDELIA: "People really do change."
ANGEL: "Yes they do. And sometimes they change back . . . if the day ever comes that I . . ."
CORDELIA: "Oh, I'll kill you dead."
ANGEL: "Thanks."
CORDELIA: "What are friends for?"
Case closed.

DOSSIERS

CLIENT **Angel** works to solve the mystery of the serial killings, initially out of fear that he's committing the murders himself in what Wesley calls a "hypnogogic state"—sleepwalking, or, in the word from which the episode title derives, somnambulism.

VICTIMS According to Kate: "**Reggie Sparks**. Volunteered as a crossing guard. **Jinny Markem**. She'd just started the tenth grade. And **Jessica Halpren**, twenty-five. Worked as a waitress." We never learn the identity of the body found after Angel's slumber in chains.

SUSPECTS First, **Angel** is the most obvious suspect, and Wesley has a dossier on him, presumably from the Watchers Council. But the culprit turns out to be **Penn**, a Puritan turned by Angel in 1786. Penn follows in Angel's footsteps by killing his own family almost immediately upon reawakening as a vampire. (Deceased.)

CONTINUITY

Wesley cites his working with Angel to successfully rescue Cordelia from Barney in "Parting Gifts" as a reason they should continue to function as a team. Cordelia, who still has her eyes (and her visions), emphatically agrees. When Wesley mentions his extensive research into Angel's past and acquaintances, he fails to mention he also led Council members in an attack on Angel while in pursuit of Faith, who had gone rogue in "Consequences." These minor details will return to haunt him in "Five by Five" and "Sanctuary." Angel glosses over his time in Romania with Darla and the Gypsy girl when explaining to Penn why he isn't the demonic Angelus that Penn remembers. Wesley and Cordelia will need the chains on Angel's bed again in "Eternity." Although he sketches Penn in this episode, Angel's artistic work usually seems to involve petite blondes: He sketches Buffy in "Passion," and Darla in "Darla." Kate deliberately specifies that Angel is not welcome in her apartment, which will be significant in "Epiphany."

QUOTE OF THE WEEK

WESLEY: "You can't walk into a police precinct with intimate knowledge of these murders and claim a two-hundred-year-old Puritan's responsible. You'd be locked up faster than Lady Hamilton's virtue."
(to Cordy)
"My apologies."
CORDELIA: "That's okay, I don't know what that meant."

Wesley tries to dissuade Angel from taking his suspicions about Penn to Kate.

THE DEVIL IS IN THE DETAILS

EXPENSES

A new duster for Angel

WEAPONRY

Penn uses a wicked thumbnail-knife to carve his victims. Kate splashes Penn with holy water, then skewers Penn and Angel with a big piece of wood. Cordy uses a cross.

Penn's thumbnail knives

THE PLAN

Penn takes Kate into his confidences in his own special way.

KATE: "What are you going to do?"

PENN: "Well, first I thought I'd stop everything to tell you my plan—"

He shoves her against the tunnel wall, hard.

PENN: "Better yet, why don't I just show you?"

He morphs to vampface, bares his fangs, and moves toward her.

DEMONS, DEMONS, DEMONS

THE VAMPIRE RULES

Vampires sire other vampires and serve as mentors and parental figures for them.

Vampires linked by blood can sense each other's presence and may be psychically linked in dreams.

To dust a vampire, he/she/it must be skewered exactly through the heart.

THE PEN IS MIGHTIER

FINAL CUT

As Cordelia tries to persuade Angel to take a license plate problem to Kate, she offers this argument, cut for length before the episode aired: "Just remind her that if it wasn't for you she'd be the curdled gooey leftovers of a proto-Babylonian Burrower demon. Or words to that effect. You'll pretty it up."

When Kate goes into the abandoned warehouse in search of Penn, her journey is described this way in the stage directions: "It's all very tense and *Silence of the Lambsy* as Kate sweeps the room looking down the nose of her firearm."

POP CULTURE

- **"I thought maybe you could have Police Woman run it for us on the Q.T."** Cordelia refers to Police Woman, a TV series that aired in the mid-seventies, starring Angie Dickinson as "Pepper" Anderson.
- Cordelia describes Penn as **"A real Psycho-Wan-Kenobi,"** a reference to Luke Skywalker's mentor Obi-Wan-Kenobi from *Star Wars.*
- **CORDELIA: "No lie. Gallagher's changed his act more times than this dude has in the last two centuries. Why do you figure he's still doing the same old shtick?"**

  WESLEY: "Well, I mean it's a classic, isn't it? Every time he smashes that watermelon with a sledgehammer, I just . . ."

  Penn hasn't changed his routine for more than two hundred years, prompting Cordelia to draw an unlikely association with a certain comedian.

❖ **"Oh, crap. You're him. He. The guy. Apt Pupil boy."** Cordelia figures out that the potential client is really Penn. "Apt Pupil" was a novella in Stephen King's *Different Seasons* collection that became a 1998 film, starring Ian McKellan as an ex-Nazi and Brad Renfro as the boy who wants to learn his secrets.

OUR HEROES

"The first episode that I wrote was 'Somnambulist.' But it was not, however, my first episode that was produced. All the new writers that year came in and we all sort of picked an area that we liked, and then we broke everybody's story, and then everybody wrote a script that we put into the bank, because we had plenty of time before we even started shooting. So we wanted to stockpile some things, because there always comes that time when you run out of scripts and you get behind the eight ball. So we all had these scripts, so I wrote this script, and Doyle was in that episode, initially, so when I ended up doing the rewrite I had to rewrite it for Wesley, which made the script much more interesting, incidentally.

"He was a former Watcher, who did not necessarily trust Angel, and it just made sense that he would walk in with this dossier on Angel and say, 'Look, Cordelia, I must warn you, I think he might be doing horrible things again.' And suddenly that made it more interesting, and there was automatic tension built into the first act. It wasn't really there with Doyle. In the first version, it was structurally the same, but it was more like Angel comes back home and Doyle says, 'Is there something you want to tell me?'

"But with Wesley, not only did you have a whole interesting dynamic of conflict between the three characters, but it's also very good for the writer when exposition guy can come in and give exposition and there's a reason for it. So that worked really well.

In Jane Espenson's script for "Sense and Sensitivity," Kate teases Angel about having a single name, a conceit usually reserved for rock stars and popes. Angel ripostes, "You've got me. I'm the pope." In "Somnambulist," the media labels the serial killer "The Pope." After Tim Minear completed the script for "Somnambulist," he noticed the coincidence.

"It was originally titled 'The Killer I Created,' that was sort of the working title of it. And way before we ever shot a foot of film on that, I saw the entire plot spoiled on the Internet, under that title. And of course the plot was, Angel's protégé comes back, and he's killing, and blah blah blah, and the one thing I came up with when I was pitching my structure to Joss, was that for the first act Angel thinks he's committing these crimes. So that's really what the first act was about. And then the story becomes what it really is.

"So at that point I went on The Bronze and I talked about my next episode, and I gave it a new title, this obscure German word for sleepwalking. And teased the episode with the fact that Angel may be doing horrible things in his sleep. Which is really not what the story's about, but it seems to be for a minute. So people were expecting that episode, but they were also talking about this other episode, and they had no idea they were the same thing, even when it aired. And then they realized, 'Oh, this sounds like that thing we heard about before.' So that was my first attempt at thwarting the fans."

—TIM MINEAR, WRITER

"There were two things going on through the first season: making some changes to Wesley and having him evolve and grow into a character that could be around all the time. Because as he was on Buffy, that's not somebody that you would want to have around all the time.

"So, part of the process was finding the sides of him that needed to grow and come to the surface more in order for him to be able to be part of the team. And then the other thing was the growing relationship between the other characters, and how he was fitting in there, and what exactly his role would be. Not only his role, practically, as a member of the team, but also how he would emotionally relate to the others, and intellectually, and all of that was an ongoing process, and it still is. I mean, the whole nature of the show, both our show and Buffy, is that these are long-term relationships that have a lot of complex wrinkles and surprising turns. They're not static. I don't feel that that process ever ends.

"I think in those early episodes he went from being a very clear outsider to finding things that he could really offer that were needed by the group. And also finding qualities in himself that were much more durable as a character."

—ALEXIS DENISOF

ELISABETH ROHM: "There's a frustration for [Kate] in that she knows what [Angel] knows, but she is an outsider in that. So it's almost like being from a family in the business. You just have an inside step. So Angel, being a vampire, organically knows how to approach that world, whereas Kate doesn't.

"For Kate, now she's learned this information, she's completely convinced of it . . . for Christ's sake, she saw her best friend with a vampire face . . . and yet, at the same time, what do you do with that information? He's always ten steps ahead of her. And I'm sure that adds to the hostility. Yeah, she felt betrayed. But I think they're also competitive with each other."

"Kate, being a very pragmatic person, adjusts to Angel being a vampire pretty quickly. If something happened to you, where you were confronted with the supernatural, do you think you could be that rational?"

ELISABETH ROHM: "I actually think maybe that's part of why Kate became rational faster than you might have expected. Well, A, it's in the writing. But B, I really actually happen to believe in the supernatural—I know there's other stuff going on in this planet. Things we can't touch and see and feel and understand. And I definitely believe that . . .

"She's not hallucinating. She's pragmatic enough to know that. So you've got to take it for what you see. And then, on an instinctive level, with all great cops or detectives or undercover agents, they are extremely instinctive, you know, they can smell things out, and I'm sure she instinctively really felt, *this has got to be true*. And then you mix in the fact that I think that there is another layer of stuff, and you know she had to adjust."

SIX DEGREES OF...

Elizabeth Penn Payne, who plays a brief role in the teaser of the waitress who is killed by Penn, also played a waitress in the *Buffy* episode, "A New Man."

TRACKS

A transition from a flashback scene with Penn to the contemporary Penn in his condo is accompanied by music, described in the script this way:

And as they move off, WIPING FRAME: A THROBBING, bloodpulsing BEAT becomes TECHNO, or Garbage or something too cool for the CBS demographic.

Lunatic Calm's "Leave You Far Behind" is heard in this episode. The song is available on the *Metropol* CD or on the soundtrack to *The Matrix*.

"EXPECTING"

FROM THE FILES OF ANGEL INVESTIGATIONS
CASE № : 1ADH12

ACTION TAKEN

Cordelia is stepping out tonight. Her knockout girlfriends Serena and Emily come to pick her up.

As she's getting ready for her grand exit, Cordelia goes into vision mode, and Angel covers for her with her friends while she does a face-plant behind his desk. Hauling herself to her feet, she tells Angel, in code, what she saw—the birth of a clawed demon hatching from a big egg. "With really large hands, in need of a manicure." She scribbles an address on a piece of paper and leaves with her friends for Lounge LaBrea, where they're meeting their dates, including Cordelia's, a man named Wilson Christopher.

Angel allows Wesley to join him to slay the "baby," and they head to the address Cordelia has scrawled. But in her haste, the address, 25 Cabrillo, looks more like 23 Cabrillo. So when Wesley kicks in the door and charges inside, Bavarian fighting adz and crossbow in hand, he finds an elderly couple watching TV in their living room. Finally he and Angel get it right, just a little too late to stop the demon from hatching.

A ferocious battle ensues. When it's over, the newborn is dead, and Wesley's jacket is covered in demon blood and parts—a fashion statement that causes a pedestrian to back away from him in horror.

Meanwhile, at Lounge LaBrea, Cordelia talks with Wilson Christopher, who is proving to be real dream-date material. So it's not much of a surprise that, when he drops her off at her apartment, she invites him in. Of course, there's the issue of her spectral roommate Dennis to contend with.

> **WILSON:** "You live alone, right?"
>
> **CORDELIA:** "In the sense that I'm the only one living here who's actually alive."

Phantom Dennis, we learn, is more than a little possessive—or is it protective?—of Cordelia. When she dims the lights, he turns them up. When she switches on soft music, he changes the station to a jaunty polka. Cordelia explains the problems as "old wiring." Wilson, thoroughly entranced by Cordelia, seems willing to accept just about anything. He kisses her. The kissing moves from the kitchen to the bedroom.

The morning after, Cordelia wakes up alone. Her bedside digital clock reads 10:47. She's worried about being late for work, but as she pushes the covers away from her, she notices something new— a beach ball–size stomach she didn't have yesterday. Cordelia's very pregnant!

WRITTEN BY Howard Gordon
DIRECTED BY David Semel
GUEST STARS: Daphnee Duplaix (Serena), Ken Marino (Wilson Christopher), Josh Randall (Bartender)
CO-STARS: Doug Tompos (Dr. Wasserman), Louisette Geiss (Emily), Julie Quinn (Pregnant Woman), Maggie Connelly (Nurse), Steven Roy (Jason)

Angel and Wesley, concerned about Cordelia since she hasn't shown up for work, go to her apartment to check on her. They find her still in bed, in a state of shock. She believes she's dreaming and can't wake up, but Angel convinces her that it's not only real, but a real problem. She explains what happened.

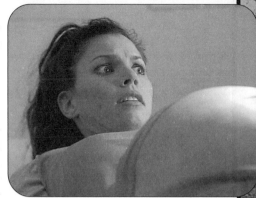

"He was really nice, and we, you know . . . it was normal and . . . he was normal . . . it was safe! It was all really . . . safe . . ." —*Cordelia*

Angel wants to talk to this Wilson, but his number is disconnected, and there's no forwarding number.

> **ANGEL:** "I'm guessing he's some sort of procreaparasitic demon."
> **WESLEY:** "A demon who can only reproduce by implanting a human woman with its seed . . . I've heard of such entities . . . the human mothers . . ."
> **ANGEL:** ". . . rarely survive labor. And the ones that do, wish they hadn't."

He assigns Wesley to take Cordelia for a prenatal exam while he works on tracking down Wilson Christopher. A bartender at Lounge LaBrea tells him Serena's name, giving him someplace to start, and opines about L.A. in the process. "They travel in packs, the guys have the money, the girls have the pretty. The girls decide what club's the flavor of the month, and Serena rules the girls."

"Mr. and Mrs. Pangborn," aka Cordelia and Wesley, visit one Dr. Wasserman for the prenatal exam. Dr. Wasserman and his nurse are goggle-eyed at the number of heartbeats they detect via Cordy's ultrasound. As the "Pangborns" look on, the doctor stops counting at six when something else on the monitor grabs his attention, and a looks of horror crosses his face. Dr. Wasserman declares that he'd like to draw some amniotic fluid for a test.

Angel has tracked down Serena's address. Calling through the door, she invites him in, and he enters only to find an apartment that's more than dark enough to make him feel at home. It's lit by candles—lots of candles—and Serena stands before them clutching a bottle of booze. She turns to Angel, revealing that she's every bit as pregnant as Cordelia.

Meanwhile, back at the ob-gyn, the amniotic fluid Dr. Wasserman draws from Cordy's abdomen eats through the hypo, and then dissolves the floor like hot water through sugar. Dr. Wasserman and the nurse bolt from the room in terror.

Cordelia is likewise freaked, but at the same time protective of what's growing inside her.

Serena expresses her concern to Angel. Her date was named Jason, and she can't find him. She says she thought something was strange about the guys, because their money smelled bad. "But, this town, you know, everything's fake, things are weird, and you stop asking questions," she says.

Wesley has helped Cordelia back to Angel's apartment and tries to make her comfortable. "There're seven of them," she says. "There's seven of his children. Growing inside of me." After a little back and forth, she comes to what seems to be a logical conclusion.

CORDELIA: "They're not human."

WESLEY: "I imagine that's true."

CORDELIA: "But, I mean, that could be okay, right? I mean, look at Angel. He's not human. And Doyle . . . he wasn't human, either. . . . I mean, not totally . . . he was good."

Angel arrives and tells Wesley about his conversation with Serena, explaining that there seem to be at least four guys involved. Multiple pregnancies, multiple heartbeats . . . Angel concludes, "Someone's raising an army."

Serena told Angel that the guys hang out at a private gun club, so Angel digs out the phone book and lets his fingers do the walking.

ANGEL: "While I find them, you should be narrowing down the species. Maybe you can figure out a way to terminate this without hurting her."

WESLEY: "And if we can't?"

ANGEL: "Then we'll need to know what to do once they're born."

As they talk, they round a corner and see Cordelia standing in front of the refrigerator, drinking some of Angel's bottled blood. She guzzles it, then replaces the container and closes the door. Turning, she wipes her mouth off with the back of her hand and goes back to bed. "I don't think I ever realized how disgusting that was," Angel admits.

At the Beverly Hills Gun Club, Angel finds Wilson Christopher engaging in some target practice. They chat.

WILSON: "This is a private club. Featured word 'private.'"

ANGEL: "You don't talk to me I'll kick your ass. Featured word 'ass.'"

Wilson shoves the gun in Angel's face, which only serves to anger the vampire. He knocks the gun away, spins Wilson around, and gets him in a chokehold. This close to Wilson, he realizes that the man is human, not a demon after all. When Wilson still refuses to talk, Angel begins to pound on him, brutally, all his emotion over Cordelia's condition coming through. Wilson is powerless against Angel's greater strength, and Angel would probably beat him to death if not for the sudden entry of Jason and two of Wilson's other friends. This being a gun club, they all have guns.

While Angel fights, Wesley studies. He inspects Cordy's ultrasound with a magnifying loupe, comparing the image to demons in his texts. He finds a scaly, horned creature that is uncomfortably similar to the ultrasound image. As he looks at it, Cordelia approaches, looking down at the page to see what he's unearthed. He tells her not to lose hope, that they'll figure out how to stop it, and she belts him with the heavy book. "You're not going to hurt my babies!" she shouts, hitting him a second time for emphasis. "No one's going to hurt my babies."

Surrounded by the party boys, Angel has figured out the scheme. In exchange for money, success, and all the dates they can handle, all they have to do is implant the demon's life force in the women they meet. Angel goes back to the pounding in an effort to get them to spill more important factoids . . . such as Big Daddy's address.

At an abandoned industrial plant, Cordelia walks through the shadows, her expression blank. Other women arrive—Serena, Emily, and three more. They're all equally far along in their demonic pregnancies.

Angel calls Wesley from a pay phone, rousing him from where Cordelia had left him unconscious on the floor. Wesley tells Angel that he's identified the father as a Haxil Beast—very enormous and very difficult to kill. Angel shares his own bit of information: that the Haxil's shrine is at the Millikan Industrial Park in Reseda. They assume that Cordelia is on her way there—a "psychic umbilical cord" connects the father to the offspring and controls her. All they have to do, Wesley realizes, is kill the demon and all the pregnancies will be terminated.

In front of a gigantic tunnel blasted into the wall of the industrial plant, the pregnant women, now dressed in white ceremonial robes, enter a foul, murky pool of some dark liquid to wait for the appearance of the Haxil Beast.

He is not the first visitor, though, as Wesley shows up, nervous and scared. He tries to coax Cordelia and the others out of the pond, but gets no takers. Cordelia only turns to him and says, "We serve our master."

And then the master appears from the tunnel—the Haxil Beast himself, twelve feet tall, with immense horns, dripping slime from his mouth and teeth.

> **HAXIL BEAST:** "To think you can disturb the birth of my children . . . who are you?"
>
> **WESLEY:** "Wesley Wyndam-Pryce. Rogue demon hunter. And I'm here to fight you, sir, to the death."

But before the fight—or should we say, the slaughter—can begin, a loud *thunk* announces the presence of Angel, rolling a large canister of some kind before him. He picks it up, spins like a discus thrower with it over his head, and hurls it at the demon. The Haxil Beast catches it and looks it over. It's liquid nitrogen, and while the demon inspects it, Wesley draws a gun and fires two shots into the side of the tank. The liquid nitrogen freezes the demon where he stands. As he becomes a giant ice sculpture, the women clutch their bellies in pain—the babies are leaving their wombs.

Climbing from the pool, a look of pure hatred on her face, Cordelia grabs a heavy pulley attached to a thick rope and draws it back. For one frozen moment of terror, it looks as if her target is Wesley. But she flings it past him, and it slams into the frozen Haxil Beast, shattering him into tiny ice crystals.

"I really hate dating," she says.

RESOLUTION

Cordelia comes back to work after resting for two days, only to find Angel and Wesley falling over each other to get the office spruced up for her. Angel tells her she could have taken off more time, but she reassures him that she's fine. In fact, she's just had a great audition for a cracker commercial, with a producer who really seems to like her.

> "He is so sweet. He says that all I have to do is let him impregnate me with his demon master's seed, and I've got the part."
> —*Cordelia*

It's a moment before Angel and Wesley realize that she's kidding. She tells them again that she really is okay, and that she learned something from the whole ordeal.

        CORDELIA: "I learned that men are evil? Uh, wait, I knew that. I learned that L.A. is full of self-serving phonies. Nope, had that one down, too. Uhh, sex is bad?"

        ANGEL: "We all knew that."

        CORDELIA: "Okay. I learned that I have two people I trust, absolutely, with my life. And that part's new."

Wesley finds himself tearing up over this admission, which he explains away as "Allergies." Case closed.

DOSSIERS

CLIENT **Cordelia** and the **other suddenly pregnant girls** are the "clients" in this case, though the demon's influence makes them very protective of their spawn.

SUSPECTS **Wilson Christopher** breaks through Cordelia's defenses in three dates and manages to implant the Haxil Beast's seed. **Jason**, Wilson's friend, is Serena's "date." The **Haxil Beast**, a pro-creaparasitic demon, shares much in common with L.A.'s everyday lounge lizards, except that he's about twice their size, horned as well as horny, and the money he gives them stinks. (Deceased.)

CONTINUITY

Cordelia compares her new digs to her old hovel of an apartment while talking to Wilson Christopher. She and Dennis the ghost are growing more comfortable as roommates. She conceals her date from Angel to avoid the interrogation techniques he displayed in "The Bachelor Party." Cordy will face issues of sexual relationships with demons again in Pylea. Fortunately for Angel, being shot is merely painful to vampires. Darla shot him in Sunnydale, just before he staked her in "Angel." And various L.A. thugs have tried gunfire as a defense against the Dark Avenger.

QUOTE OF THE WEEK

ANGEL: "I'm confused here, why is Mrs. Benson filed under 'P'?"
CORDELIA: "That's not a 'P,' that's an 'F.' Or is it an 'R'?"

ANGEL: "I don't know. Maybe we could be a little less young and carefree with the filing—"

CORDELIA: "Oh, it's an 'F,' I remember now."

ANGEL: "All right . . . so why is Mrs. Benson filed under 'F'?"

CORDELIA: "Because she's from France. Remember what a pain she was?"

ANGEL: "Yes . . . made me want to drink a lot."

CORDELIA: "Well, that's the French for ya."

Cordelia reveals why she gets paid the big bucks.

THE DEVIL IS IN THE DETAILS

EXPENSES

Front door at 23 Cabrillo

Doctor visit, possibly doctor floor

Can of frozen nitro

Extra O pos. for the young mother

WEAPONRY

Bavarian fighting adz, crossbow, and sword to battle the newly hatched Tarval demon. The guns at the shooting range, which Angel uses to threaten the Haxil Beast's surrogate fathers after they've unsuccessfully threatened him. Wesley's shootin' iron at the birthing place. Cordelia bashes Wesley over the head with a big, heavy reference book, and the liquid nitrogen freezes the Beast so that Cordelia can shatter it with the pulley.

DEMONS, DEMONS, DEMONS

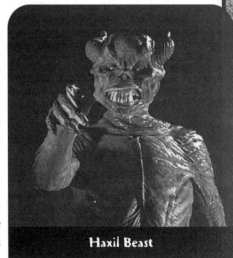

Haxil Beast

The **Haxil Beast**, "Haxil Daemonica" in Wesley's big book, written in the sixteenth century. It impregnates human women via human men, then telepathically controls the women via its link to its unborn children. It's huge, and neither fire nor decapitation will kill it.

Angel and Wesley kill a **Tarval hatchling** (at 25 Cabrillo Street). It gestates inside a large curved cocoon and claws its way out. Very slimy.

AS SCENE IN L.A.

Dr. Wasserman's office is located at Pershing Square in downtown Los Angeles. This is a public park bounded by Fifth, Sixth, Hill, and Olive Streets. The Biltmore Hotel faces onto the park, and L.A.'s jewelry district is at Sixth and Hill.

"Imagine Bonnie and Clyde if they'd had a hundred and fifty years to get it right."

—CORDELIA

"Batten down the hatches, here comes Hurricane Buffy."

—CORDELIA

ANGEL

"Well, hey, how 'bout that? A *performer*.
Why don't we just call him 'Angel: the
vampire *with* soul.'"
—THE HOST

CORDELIA

"I'll have to check—with *myself!* I mean,
am I not the princess?"
—CORDELIA

DOYLE

"I rejected you way before now! So you're half demon. Big whoop . . . I mean, I work for a *vampire!*"
—CORDELIA

WESLEY

"A lone wolf, such as myself, never works with anyone. . . . I'm a *rogue* demon hunter now."
—WESLEY

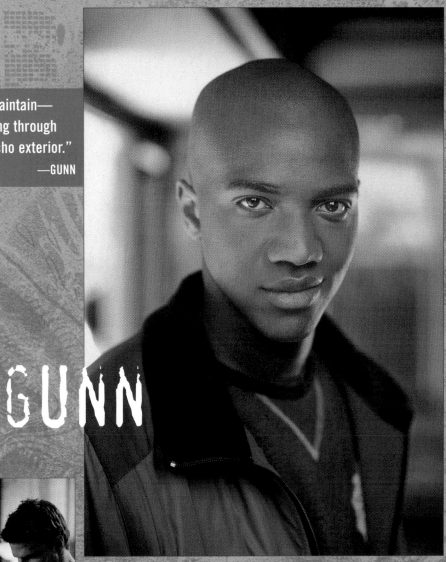

"Hey, I got a rep to maintain—
can't have y'all seeing through
my brusque and macho exterior."

—GUNN

GUNN

THE ORACLES

KATE

THE HOST

> "He's a demon. Better do what he says, or he might . . . talk your ears off."
> —ANGEL

ANNE

FRED

"If you take the collar off, bad things'll happen to your head, like it'll implode, so don't take the collar off, okay? I can't talk to you if you don't have a head, okay?"

—FRED

FAITH

> "The road to redemption is a rocky path."
> —FAITH

WOLFRAM & HART

Voice (213) 555-0044
Fax (213) 555-0133
Telex: 8XZ-BRB

New York • Los Angeles • Paris • London • Cairo

BOONE: "Wolfram and Hart.
Who are they?"
MERL: "Law firm. Technically.
More like Evil Incorporated."

LILAH

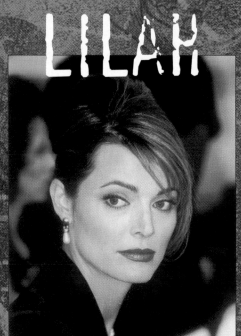

LINDSEY

DARLA

"It won't last. I give it a century. Tops." —THE MASTER

SPIKE & DRU

THE PEN IS MIGHTIER

FINAL CUT

Stage Directions from the script:

Wesley charges in, startling an ELDERLY COUPLE watching TV. Angel charges in behind him, SMACK! right into the "No Uninvited Vampires Allowed" threshold.

Cut for length:

When Dr. Wasserman sees all the heartbeats during the ultrasound: "Did you have fertility treatments?"

POP CULTURE

❋ **"All right, Dennis, knock it off. This is the one guy I've actually liked in a long time, and if you keep killing the mood I'll kill you—all right, empty threat, you being a ghost, but I'll do something worse. . . . I'll play Evita around the clock, the one with Madonna."** After inviting Wilson in, Cordelia excuses herself to go make tea, at least partly so she can threaten Dennis in private with Andrew Lloyd Webber's famous musical, filmed with the Material Girl in 1996.

Cordelia's apartment number is 212.

OUR HEROES

"I wore Julianne Moore's fake belly [from *Nine Months*, with Hugh Grant], the leotard with the cushion. That was a great, great time. Because I got to be evil, funny, scared, and vulnerable."

—CHARISMA CARPENTER

"Angel's office was downstairs and there's an elevator, and right next to the elevator, clearly, are cement stairs. But they're not cement. They're made of wood and they're covered to look like cement. Every time he came down the stairs, I had to change the sound."

—SKIP SKOOLNICK, COPRODUCER

TRACKS

In "Expecting" we hear the appropriately titled "Games You Play" by Splashdown, from the CD *Blueshift*.

"SHE"

FROM THE FILES OF ANGEL INVESTIGATIONS
CASE № 1ADH13

ACTION TAKEN

Cordelia throws a party in her apartment. The music's loud, the conversation shouted, the dancing frenetic. Diego, one of Cordelia's friends, arrives with a bag of ice to contribute to the cause (and this is not the last time we'll be seeing ice). Wesley hurls himself headlong into the beat, at one point throwing himself all the way to the floor, but Angel, brooding as usual, refuses to dance, mingle, or pretty much do any of the typical party things.

> CORDELIA: "Hi. You having fun?"
>
> ANGEL: "Sure . . . this is . . ."
>
> CORDELIA: "Your idea of Hell."
>
> ANGEL: "Actually in Hell you tend to know a lot of the people."

WRITTEN by David Greenwalt & Marti Noxon
DIRECTED BY David Greenwalt
SPECIAL GUEST STAR:
    Bai Ling (Jhiera)
GUEST STARS: Colby French
    (Tay), Heather Stephens (Shari),
    Sean Gunn (Mars)
CO-STARS: Tracey Costello
    (Laura), Andre L. Roberson
    (Diego), P. J. Marino (Peter
    Wilkers), Honor Bliss (Girl)

Wesley speaks briefly to a girl, who moves off in mortal terror at his reaction to her compliment of his sweater. Angel finds himself locked in conversation with Cordelia's friend Laura, but things don't go any better for him. A mental image of himself on the dance floor strikes fear into his heart, so he heads for the kitchen, where Phantom Dennis hands him a beer.

Drinking a beer of his own, at precisely this moment, is a private security consultant named Pete Wilkers. He's inside the Jerico Ice Factory in L.A., keeping an eye on a coffin-size box marked DANGER—HAZARDOUS MATERIALS, DO NOT OPEN! Naturally, with a label like that, he's curious, especially when the container starts making noise. He finds a crowbar and breaks off the lock, opening the heavy wooden lid, and what he sees inside fascinates him.

Briefly.

At Angel's office the next morning, Angel is looking for a cup of coffee instead of blood, but the beans came whole, and there's no grinder. Cordelia suggests that Angel use his vampire strength to "mush" the beans. He declines, and then compliments her on the previous night's party.

> CORDELIA: "I'm so glad you came. You know how parties are: you're always worried no one's going to suck the energy out of the room like a giant black hole of boring despair, but there you were, in the clinch."
>
> ANGEL: "I didn't . . . boring?"
>
> CORDELIA: "You used to be a person! Did you never party? Did people not gather in olden times?"
>
> ANGEL: "I talked to people . . . Laura . . ."
>
> CORDELIA: "Laura thought you hated her. I had to tell her you were challenged."

Wesley enters then, still energized and wondering if there are any appetizers left over from the soiree. Angel realizes the rogue demon hunter is broke, and offers him a job. When Cordelia learns that she doesn't have to take a pay cut in order to bring Wesley on board, she's all over the idea. Finally, after the exceptional way in which they worked as a team in "Expecting," they are one officially. Wesley tears up again—this time, instead of "allergies," he explains it as "something in my eye."

And at that, Cordelia suffers another of her excruciating visions, this one of the aforementioned Pete Wilkers, back at the ice company, being burned from the inside out. She tells Angel and Wesley that the guy's already dead, and they decide they need to go check it out anyway.

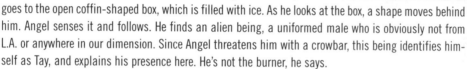

Wesley drives Angel's car to the factory, and Angel goes inside to check on the crispy corpse while Wesley waits by the car, his trusty Bavarian fighting adz in hand.

Angel inspects the body, finding a wallet that identifies the corpse as the former Pete Wilkers, Private Security. From there, he goes to the open coffin-shaped box, which is filled with ice. As he looks at the box, a shape moves behind him. Angel senses it and follows. He finds an alien being, a uniformed male who is obviously not from L.A. or anywhere in our dimension. Since Angel threatens him with a crowbar, this being identifies himself as Tay, and explains his presence here. He's not the burner, he says.

> **TAY**: "I was sent by my people to stop it."
>
> **ANGEL**: "Stop what?"
>
> **TAY**: "The bringer of chaos."
>
> **ANGEL**: "What is it? A demon?"
>
> **TAY**: "More than a mere demon. It is a vessel of pure rage. It has almost destroyed my
> world. And now it is loose in yours."

Angel puts down the crowbar—this sounds serious, and he wants to help. Tay uses this opportunity to slip away, onto a sunlit loading dock where Angel can't follow. He warns Angel to leave it alone and takes off.

That night, Angel assigns Wesley and Cordelia to try to figure out what kind of being Tay is while he investigates Pete Wilkers's office. He's examining a hidden wad of cash when he is suddenly attacked from behind—by something that burns through his coat and arm! Looking up, he sees an exotic and beautiful woman in a tight leather, revealing but combat-ready outfit . . . only this "woman" is no more human than Tay was.

This is Jhiera.

She believes that Angel is working for Tay, trying to track her people down. He denies it; they fight, and she proves to be more than Angel's equal. She knocks him through a door, and while he is regaining his equilibrium her cell phone rings. It doesn't sound like good news, and she takes off. He leaps down to his car and gives chase.

Jhiera drives to a downtown art museum. On the way in, she spots Angel following and points him out to a security guard, saying that he's been following her. The guard puts out an alert and other guards join him to catch the supposed stalker. Angel throws them off for a while by removing his coat and posing as a guide, giving the opening-night crowd a surprisingly personal look at Manet's painting, "La Musique aux Tuileries."

"On the left, one spies the painter himself. In the middle distance is the French poet and critic Baudelaire, a friend of the artist. Now Baudelaire, interesting fellow, in his poem, 'Le Vampyr,' he wrote, 'Thou who abruptly as a knife/Didst come into my heart'; he strongly believed that evil forces surrounded mankind, and some speculated the poem was about a real vampire. Oh, and Baudelaire was actually a little taller and a lot drunker than he's depicted here." —*Angel*

While Angel plays art historian, Wesley and Cordelia have been doing some digging of their own. They've discovered four other men who have been similarly burned to death from the inside in the last couple of years, and Wesley has found a race of beings that match the description Angel gave:

> WESLEY: "Oden Tal, the men are called Vigories, they have four distinct ridges on their foreheads, are said to be fierce warriors, and the women live enslaved to them."
>
> CORDELIA: "Way to go, Wes. Angel said the Tay guy could be the key—any way to find him here in town?"
>
> WESLEY: "It says that the men are herbivores. They eat a thick stew made from rotting plants and flowers—and they need to consume half their body weight a day."
>
> CORDELIA: "Whoa—so we're looking for, like, the biggest compost heap in L.A.?"

Back at the museum, Angel has eluded the guards and catches up to Jhiera in a storage room. He tries to question her, although forthcoming is not in her vocabulary. As they not-quite-talk, a strange ball of light appears above them—a portal to another dimension—and a naked woman drops from it to the floor. Named Shari, she is obviously from Jhiera's dimension. Gentleman that he is, Angel grabs a blanket and puts it over her. But before he can get any answers, Tay and four of his comrades enter the room.

They fight, Jhiera and Angel against the Vigories of Oden Tal. It's a fierce battle, during which some of the Vigories escape—with Shari. Angel asks what'll happen to her, to which Jhiera replies, "She'll be unmade."

Tay and his thugs take Shari to the Los Angeles Flower Mart, their temporary headquarters. Ignoring her screams, Tay says, "It has been recovered. It will now be restored." He pulls the blanket away from her back, revealing a series of very pronounced ridges running down her spine. He is handed a wicked-looking metallic device clearly made to fit these ridges—and extract them. He pushes it into place on Shari's back and goes to work.

Angel has taken Jhiera to his apartment to dress the wounds she suffered in the fight. As they work, she tries to explain what it means to be "unmade."

> JHIERA: "In Oden Tal, what you call personality—our passions—these impulses sit in an area of the body we call the Ko."
>
> ANGEL: "And your pursuers—they want to take this from you?"

JHIERA: "From the women, yes. Once females come of age, Ko controls our physical and sexual power—it even signals when we're aroused and have met desirable mates. But when it's removed—"

ANGEL: "You're more easily controlled."

JHIERA: "We marry who they command, serve without questioning. We leave behind dreaming . . ."

Jhiera reveals that her family rules Oden Tal, and Angel guesses that they didn't appreciate her skipping out of the dimension to avoid being unmade. As they talk about it, the heat in the room rises dramatically—Jhiera explains that when the Ko first matures, young women can't manage it, and it attracts men, even involuntarily. When the men try to force themselves upon the Oden Tal women, the heat is too much and they combust.

But the heat Angel and Jhiera feels is definitely two-way—her Ko is glowing red-hot, and they are drawn to each other by a powerful urge that neither is quite willing to give in to or to deny. They argue, Angel telling her that he won't allow her women to kill men in his world, and she claiming that if a few have to die to protect all the women of Oden Tal, then that's just the way it has to be. The heat of the disagreement overcomes the heat of passion, and she stalks out, leaving a bewildered Angel in her wake.

Wesley and Cordelia, meanwhile, have ascertained that the best place to find lots of compost is at the L.A. Flower Mart. Cordelia thinks maybe it was a bad idea to come here without Angel, but when they hear the voices of Tay and the Vigories coming from the compost room, they stay to listen.

Jhiera has gone to the Palm Ridge Spa, where a friendly and slightly flaky owner, Mars, has been keeping some of her women on ice—ice shipped in, naturally, from the Jerico Ice Factory. The women are maturing here, wearing little more than skimpy bits of cloth that cover the vital areas. Jhiera is upset that the woman she went to meet was taken, and realizes that this place is probably not safe anymore.

Cordelia and Wesley overhear the Vigories making a plan to capture Jhiera and the other women— they've learned that the ice factory has been shipping two tons of ice a week to a particular address. But they don't say the address out loud. When Wesley and Cordelia hook up with Angel at his apartment, they tell him about the ice shipments, which reminds him of the shipping order he took from the office of the deceased Pete Wilkers. Finding the order, he learns about the spa.

At the spa, Angel leaves Cordelia and Wesley at the car when the Vigories show, and he goes in to look for Jhiera. After convincing Mars that he's a friend of hers, Angel is shown in to the chamber where the women slumber in their ice baths. He tells Jhiera the Vigories are coming. While he tries to persuade her of the urgency, Cordelia and Wesley rush in to say that they're coming now. They help the women from their baths—and Wesley finds himself quite taken by them. Though it's against his will, a function of their maturing Kos, the fact remains that they're all quite fetching in their tiny bits of fabric.

With the women safely away, Angel and Jhiera once again battle the Vigories. It's a huge, perilous battle, but it seems like things might go our heroes' way—until Cordelia and Wesley return and are immediately captured and threatened with scythes held to their necks. Jhiera doesn't want to give up—she would rather see them dead than see her women captured and returned to Oden Tal. She leaves.

However, Cordelia and Wesley break free from their captors. Wesley in particular acquits himself quite well in the butt-kicking department, and they beat the Vigories. Angel holds Tay back and makes him let Jhiera and the women go free, then warns Tay not to pursue his quest on Angel's turf.

Back at his office, the three are attempting to make coffee when Jhiera enters. She tells Angel that the girls are safe outside the city. He's happy to hear it, but still not thrilled with the fact that she was willing to write off Wesley and Cordelia. She says that she had no choice, but Angel disagrees.

> **ANGEL:** "If you vowed to protect the innocent, Jhiera, it shouldn't matter what dimension they're from."
>
> **JHIERA:** "An easy sentiment, when your people are free."
>
> **ANGEL:** "I'm not saying you shouldn't fight—just know I'll be here to stop you if you cross the line."

That settled, she turns to go. Angel doesn't try to stop her.

As she walks past him, he notices that her Ko is glowing, red-hot. She's aroused.

Then she's gone.

Case closed . . . for now.

DOSSIERS

CLIENT Pete Wilkers, the deceased private security man, is the subject of Cordelia's vision. **Jhiera** and the newly arrived **women of Oden Tal** also become clients of sorts, since Angel employs his bodyguard capabilities on their behalf.

CIVILIAN SUPPORT Mars runs the Palm Ridge Spa. He seems very knowledgeable about the care and feeding of Oden Tal females and has earned Jhiera's complete trust.

SUSPECTS Tay and his **Vigories of Oden Tal** have pursued Jhiera and the other Oden Tal females to our dimension to remove their Kos and ensure their subservient positions back home. (Remain at large.)

CONTINUITY

Angel and Cordelia compare her party to his sojourn in Hell. Wesley finds himself quite drawn to the Oden Tal females, but it is not until he meets Virginia Bryce in "Guise Will Be Guise" that he finds any sort of lasting romance.

QUOTE OF THE WEEK

"Please don't fire me, what happened yesterday was an anomaly. I am very rarely taken hostage."

Having just been officially hired, Wesley still feels on thin ice in his job.

THE DEVIL IS IN THE DETAILS

EXPENSES

Angel needs a new duster and a shirt because his are burned up.

WEAPONRY

The extreme body heat of the Oden Tal women can kill; Angel does the bat-thing with grappling hooks. Angel packs lots of weapons in preparation for battle with whatever is burning men from the inside out. The Vigories use scythelike weapons to fight the women at arm's length.

THE PLAN

Angel believes in the tried and true.

> ANGEL: "We got an address. We're heading out."
>
> WESLEY: "That's it? They seemed . . . There were quite a few of them. Perhaps we need a plan?"
>
> ANGEL: "Here's the plan. We go in. I start hitting people hard in the face. See where it takes us."

Got Milk? During the initial airing of this episode, TV Guide magazine advertised an offer for a "WB Milk Mustache Poster, featuring Angel's David Boreanaz."

DEMONS, DEMONS, DEMONS

Kovitch demons: Wesley initially figures Tay for one but soon after discovers the truth. These beings hail from the Caucasus.

The **Oden Tal** are beings from another dimension. To keep the women subservient, the Vigories, a male contingent, amputate their Ko, which is a ridged back structure giving the individual personality and will. Female Oden Tal burn with desire and life force when they mature, and are extremely hazardous to be around until they learn to cool down.

THE VAMPIRE RULES

Apparently Baudelaire knew Angel (see Pop Culture.)
Vampires are known to the people of Oden Tal.

AS SCENE IN L.A.

The Jerico Ice Factory seems to be across a parking lot from the Southwestern Bag Company, a business that supplies sand bags to the City of Los Angeles Division of Flood Management, on East Sixth Street in L.A.

The L.A. Flower Mart is the largest flower district in the United States, spanning more than two city blocks of downtown L.A. near the Garment District, with more than eighty wholesale and retail growers exhibiting. If one were looking for compost, this would be a reasonable place to look.

THE PEN IS MIGHTIER

FINAL CUT

Cordelia's vision in this episode is particularly gruesome, described this way in the script's stage directions:

> A MAN—PETE WILKERS, IN FACT. Screaming, looking down at something on his chest. The camera cannot see that far down but there is smoke rising from his body. Then, FLASH, his face and neck are black and grimy as though being burned from within. Finally (this is the funny part) his eyes explode.

The scraps of clothing the Oden Tal women wear in their ice baths are described in the script as "small, *FIFTH ELEMENT*-LIKE coverings." Gaultier, known for Madonna's cone-bras, designed some of the costumes for this Luc Besson movie starring Bruce Willis, Chris Tucker, and Milla Jovovich (1997).

Cut from the script for length was this instant diagnosis Mars offers Angel: "When you're spiritually constipated? Gotta lose the black. Energy can't move through black. Try yellow, something with flow. Also, you need to spend a little time with the sun, bro."

The storage room inside where Shari falls from the portal is described in the script thusly:

As big and interesting as we can make it for $1.98. Stacked paintings, statuary, ancient artifacts (Spiro [Season One stunt coordinator Spiro Razatos], fun stuff to break!) in the process of being restored.

POP CULTURE

❋ **CORDELIA:** "A chick that burns? Are you okay? Did she . . . care . . . you?"
ANGEL: "Did she *care* about me?"
CORDELIA: "Did she Carrie you. Carrie? The movie? You know?"
Cordy's referring to Brian DePalma's film adaptation of Stephen King's first novel, *Carrie*. Carrie, played by Sissy Spacek, could maim and kill with telekinesis, and she set fire to her high school prom.

❋ Angel implies that French poet Charles Baudelaire wrote the poem "Le Vampyr," published in the 1857 collection *The Flowers of Evil,* from some actual knowledge of vampires. The book caused a sensation when it was published in France as Les Fleurs du Mal, catapulting Baudelaire to the forefront of a movement called the Decadents. They were interested in the collision between aestheticism and the macabre in human emotion—which makes them highly appropriate grist for Angel's mill.

OUR HEROES

"In 'She,' we get a glimpse of a previously unknown part of Angel's past. Would you like to see the character having more chances to reveal bits of his history?"

DAVID BOREANAZ: "Yeah, and I think that's pretty much a running theme for the show. He is so old that references are going to be made to his life, things that happened to him in the past. So it's important to have those."

"How do you feel about the lack of a sustained romantic interest? Would you like to have one, or do you think it's more interesting for Angel to be solo?"

DAVID BOREANAZ: "At this time, I think it's better for him to be solo. I kind of look at him as an only parent, so to speak. I kind of enjoy that, and I think it's an interesting way of looking at him."

Musical Angel: This episode was the source of a fan-favorite moment for Angel, affectionately called "the spaz dance." During Cordelia's party, when he's asked by Laura to dance, he sees a brief image of himself out on the dance floor, moving in a ridiculous fashion like someone with 50,000 watts of electricity running through his body. It's described in the stage directions: "And Angel is suddenly on the dance floor doing that crazy David Boreanaz dance. People give him a wide swath—Laura backs away in horror." The dance scene played over the closing credits for the episode, a first for Angel.

In addition to appearing in major motion pictures like The Wild Wild West, Anna and the King, Red Corner, and Goth fave The Crow, Bai Ling, who plays the stunning Jhiera, was one of People magazine's "Fifty Most Beautiful People in the World" for 1998, joining Buffy star Sarah Michelle Gellar (David Boreanaz made the list in 1999). The script describes her having "impossibly bright blue eyes, otherworldly ridges run down her cheeks, a ring or a couple of studs in one of the ridges. (She also has distinctive ridges on the back of her neck that run down her spine, but more on that later)." A later dialogue reference to her blue eyes was changed to purple after Bai Ling was cast.

"Do you see the sort of continued bickering Wesley and Cordelia them as more of a friends relationship, or more of almost a siblinglike relationship?"

ALEXIS DENISOF: "Well, I think they have an unusual bond and partially because they had a romance that never got started. In a sense, it's given them permission to bicker whilst being the greatest of friends, in the way that partners can. So I think the relationship they have is that they trust each other completely and have a deep sense of friendship and protectiveness over one another. And love. But at this point it's not sexual. So the other side of that is that they just irritate the hell out of each other from time to time, because they're from such opposite worlds. And that's what makes them fun together."

SIX DEGREES OF . . .

Sean Gunn, who plays spa owner Mars, also appeared in the *Angel* episode "Hero," as Demon Lucas.

Colby French, who plays Tay, was in the *Star Trek: Deep Space Nine* episode "When It Rains" with Armin Shimerman.

Cordelia, talking about her party guests, says: "Oh, Steve Paymer came. Can you believe that? David Paymer's brother, Steve." David Paymer is an acclaimed actor who, among many other roles, appeared in the 1997 movie *Amistad* with Harry Groener, who was the Mayor of Sunnydale in the days when Angel and Cordelia lived there. Steve Paymer isn't as busy as his brother, but he's appeared frequently in TV shows *Mad About You* and *Will & Grace*.

TRACKS

Another episode loaded with music from outside sources, including "Strange Love Addiction" by Supreme Beings of Leisure, from their eponymous CD; Freebie & The Bean's "Pure Roots," which has the distinction of being the song to which Angel dances; "Light Years On" by 60 Channels, from *Tuned In . . . Turned On*; and Morphic Field's "In Time," from the CD *Morphic Field*.

"I'VE GOT YOU UNDER MY SKIN"

FROM THE FILES OF ANGEL INVESTIGATIONS
CASE N⁰: 1ADH14

ACTION TAKEN

Cordelia and Wesley are quarreling like children over an ancient dagger that she tries to use to cut brownies when Angel, who's heard enough, accidentally calls Wesley "Doyle." Angel is clearly still shaken by Doyle's death. In fact, he believes that Doyle's death is somehow his fault, that he should have prevented it.

> **CORDELIA:** "You called him Doyle."
>
> **ANGEL:** "It just . . . happened. I hope Wesley's okay with it."
>
> **CORDELIA:** "Oh, who cares about him. This is about Doyle. You never say his name."
>
> **ANGEL:** "I say it."
>
> **CORDELIA:** "No you don't. Look, you don't have to be Joe Stoic about his dying. I mean, I know that you have this unflappable vibe working for you. But you don't have to do it for me."
>
> **ANGEL:** "I'm not unflappable."
>
> **CORDELIA:** "Great. So . . . flap."

STORY BY David Greenwalt & Jeannine Renshaw
TELEPLAY BY Jeannine Renshaw
DIRECTED BY R. D. Price
GUEST STARS: Elisabeth Rohm (Kate Lockley), Will Kempe (Seth Anderson), Katy Boyer (Paige Anderson), Anthony Cistaro (Ethros Demon), Jesse James (Ryan)
CO-STARS: Ashley Edner (Stephanie Anderson), Patience Cleveland (Nun), Jerry Lambert (Rick the Clerk)

At the same time, in the home of the Anderson family, recently moved to Los Angeles from Ohio, eight-year-old Ryan Anderson accuses his six-year-old sister Stephanie of taking one of his trading cards. Their shouting match is refereed by their mother, Paige. But even she can't bring things under control until their father, Seth, enters, telling them both it's time for bed. With the children tucked in, Paige reluctantly lets Seth lock both kids in their rooms with heavy-duty padlocks.

Cordy sees disjointed bits and pieces in a vision, and Angel and Wesley drive to the Anderson house—address provided by Cordelia. As they park, little Ryan starts across the street, directly into the path of an oncoming car. Angel dives from his car and snatches up the boy, saving him from certain death.

Ryan's parents run outside, and his mother, overcome with gratitude and seeing that Angel is hurt, invites him into their home. Paige rambles on, talking about how they've just moved to California, and it becomes clear that they've moved a lot. Her thankfulness borders on the psychotic, offering to pay Angel, or to have Seth, an investment counselor, give him investment advice. When she learns what Angel's name is she goes even further, bringing out some angel statuettes from her extensive collection.

Seth, having had enough of his wife's gushing over this handsome stranger, makes it clear that he'd like Angel to go. Paige, just as evidently, wants Angel to stay, and invites him for dinner the next night. Angel senses that Paige wants to talk, but is afraid to with Seth in the room. So he accepts the invitation and takes his leave.

Meanwhile, Wesley has been inspecting the outside of the house, and he's collected a vial of Plakticine, the bodily excretion of an Ethros demon. He and Angel both know what that means: some-one in the Anderson household is possessed.

The research begins. Cordy finds that in the past three years, the Andersons lived in Baton Rouge, Miami, and Akron. Further, Cordelia says, "Everywhere they go, there's been reports of dis-turbances, and—yuck—animal deaths. In Akron a friend of the family went missing. He's still missing." Apparently the Ethros demon possessing one of the Andersons is on the antisocial side of the scale.

When Angel says that they have to evict the demon, Wesley agrees, offering to look into finding a priest who does exorcisms. But the problem, as Cordelia points out, is that they don't know which Anderson is the one carrying an unwelcome visitor.

ANGEL: "The father seemed kind of off. They were afraid of him."

WESLEY: "A father doesn't have to be possessed to terrorize his children. He just has to . . ."

He cuts himself off without finishing the thought, having already revealed more than he wants to. He says the way to get the demon to show itself is to feed it some Psylis Eucalipsis powder.

When Angel shows up for dinner the next night, he brings some homemade brownies—laced with the powder—with him. But it's not Seth who's possessed: Ryan's face becomes semitransparent and extended, exposing the snarling demon within. Sister Stephanie announces, "Ryan's bad. Ryan's always been bad." Seth's strange behavior was just his way of being protective of his family, with this monster in their midst. Angel convinces the family to let him help.

Angel calls Wesley to let him know who the exorcist will be working on—but Wesley's been hav-ing some trouble actually rounding one up. He has a name, but he hasn't been able to locate the priest that goes with the name. For the immediate future, Angel instructs him to whip up a binding powder so they can contain Ryan while they work on tracking down the exorcist.

After arranging for a baby-sitter for Stephanie, the rest of the family accompanies Angel back to his place to meet Cordelia and Wesley. Ryan is parked in Angel's bed, and Cordy draws a circle around the bed with the binding powder. Angel instructs Paige and Seth to leave Ryan in the bed and not to break the circle while he and Wesley go in search of the priest. The demon, he warns, is angry at hav-ing been exposed and will kill them if it has a chance.

At the church, a praying nun is more than a little surprised to see Angel, detecting his vampiric nature right away in spite of the human face he wears. Wesley asks to see Father Fredricks, and is directed to go out behind the church . . . to the graveyard. Father Fredricks died performing an exorcism six months before.

Wesley and Angel realize they'll have to perform the exorcism without the benefit of clergy. Wesley volunteers, since he knows the ritual. Angel isn't loving that thought—and besides, he's still smarting from having allowed Doyle to sacrifice himself.

Wesley argues that their only other option is for Angel to do it. To demonstrate the inappropriateness of that, he tosses Angel a crucifix—standard equipment for exorcisms. Angel concedes the point, but insists that he will be present at all times.

Angel and Wesley arrive home as Wesley reads some last-minute instruction on exorcism, including an important note: "I believe I know how the priest was killed—when an Ethros is cast out, it immediately seeks another body to inhabit . . . but the demon is expelled with such force that the newly inhabited rarely survives."

Ryan—or the demon within him—has been working on Paige, pleading in his little-boy voice for her. She breaks from Seth and Cordelia and crosses the binding circle. Angel and Wesley, temporarily trapped by demonic forces inside the elevator, manage to reach the bedside in time, breaking out a crucifix and the Latin exorcism ritual. The demon releases Paige.

Cordelia, as research girl, has found that there is a way to contain an Ethros demon cast out of a human host—all one needs is a handy Ethros Box. Not something one would find at the corner store. Angel describes it and sends Cordy to Rick's Majick 'N' Stuff, at Melrose and Robertson. "Between the yogurt shop and the Doggie Dunk."

In Angel's bedroom, Wesley continues to speak the Latin words of the rite of exorcism as he sprinkles holy water on the bed in which Ryan sleeps. The lights flicker in reaction to this disturbance. Then, without warning, the boy is sitting up, fixing Wesley in a malevolent gaze. When he speaks, it's in a demon's voice.

> **RYAN:** "Your Latin sucks."
>
> **WESLEY:** "I know your tricks. You'll not deter me from doing what must be done."
>
> **RYAN:** "You? *Do* something? What makes you think you could *do* anything?"
>
> **WESLEY:** "In odorem suavitatis. Tu Autem effugare, diabole; appropinquat enim judicium Dei—"
>
> **RYAN:** "You couldn't even Watch."

Wesley reacts to this attack by brandishing a crucifix at the demon. But Ryan doesn't give up that easily.

"All those hours locked under the stairs and you still weren't good enough. Not good enough for Daddy, not good enough for the Council . . ." —*Ryan (in Wesley's own voice)*

130

As Angel tries to intervene, Ryan continues his attack:

  RYAN: "Go ahead, Wesley. Tell him why he's a fool to trust you."

  WESLEY: "... effugare, diabolo ..."

  RYAN: "Tell him how you plan to kill him—"

  WESLEY: "That's not true—"

  RYAN: "Oh no?" (To Angel) "He's more afraid of you than he is of me."

 Enraged, Wesley lunges for Ryan—and his foot breaks the circle. Ryan grabs him, yanking the crucifix from Wesley's hand and stabbing the ex-Watcher in the neck with it. Wesley falls away from the bed, and Angel hurries to save his friend.

 Around Angel's kitchen table, Angel and Wesley discuss Wesley's defeat at the hands of the demon. As they talk, a bag of Ryan's marbles opens and marbles spill out, spelling the words SAVE ME on the table. Suddenly, they hear Doyle's voice coming from the bedroom.

 The door opens on its own and Ryan glares at Angel. He plays upon Angel's guilt over Doyle's death, saying, "Doyle wants to know why you couldn't protect him."

 Furious, Angel wraps a kitchen towel around his fist so he can pick up a crucifix. Cordelia arrives with a Shorshack Box, which is not quite an Ethros Box, but the closest thing Rick had in stock. Without even looking at it, Angel orders her to get it ready.

 Crucifix in hand, Angel enters the bedroom. It's a mighty struggle, the demon battling to hold onto Ryan with everything it has, Angel holding the crucifix against Ryan's chest as he reads the Latin phrases, Wesley participating with alternate English ritual phrases. The stress causes Angel to change into vampface just as he shouts at the demon, "Now get the hell out!"

 And the demon does, bursting free from Ryan's body in a flash of light and slamming into the inferior Shorshack Box—smashing it to kindling. Ryan is a little boy once more, free of demonic influence . . . but the demon has escaped.

 From what he knows of Ethros demons, Angel deduces that it will have taken refuge in a sea cave while it recharges itself. He and Wesley track it down, finally finding Plakticine on the walls of a cave to let them know they're in the right place. As they track the Ethros, Wesley tries to explain to Angel about what the demon had said before, but he can't quite get the words out. Angel assures Wesley that he knows Wesley isn't planning to kill him. "But you're willing to," he says. "And that's good." Soon, they find the demon and confront it. It's far from repentant, though, and it has a surprise for Angel and Wesley.

  ETHROS DEMON: "I am Ethros! I corrupted the spirits of men before they had speech
   to name me. The child was but the last among tens of thousands. One more pure
   heart to corrupt. One more soul to suck dry."

  WESLEY: "Well, chalk up one exciting failure. You didn't get that boy's soul."

ETHROS DEMON: "What soul?" Do you know what the most frightening thing in the world is? Nothing. That's what I found in the boy. No conscience, no fear, no humanity. Just a black void. I couldn't wait to get out; I never even manifested until you brought me forth. I just sat in him and watched as he destroyed everything around him. Not from a belief in evil, not for any reason at all. That boy's mind was the blackest hell I've ever known."

The Ethros demon was the one who spelled out the message in the marbles. It also walked Ryan in front of a car, trying to free itself. The Ethros does not fear the death that it knows Angel must deliver—it feared only Ryan. Wesley urges Angel on, and Angel kills the Ethros with an ax.

And back at the Anderson house, everyone is asleep, peaceful for a change, believing Ryan to be free of the evil at last. But he's not, and in a fit of temper over marshmallow inequity with his sister, he jams blocks under his parents' door to wedge it shut, scatters gasoline around the house, and drops a match.

Angel and Wesley arrive at the house just in time to help the Andersons escape the blaze.

RESOLUTION

Later, police cars and firefighters surround the house. Kate Lockley talks to Paige and Seth, telling them that Social Services will take over with Ryan, and they won't know what to do with him until after he's evaluated. She takes Ryan away in her car, leaving Angel outside the house with Seth, a father who has gone to great lengths to protect his family as best he could.

Case closed.

DOSSIERS

CLIENT The **Anderson family** is the closest Angel has to a client in this case. **Paige** initially beseeches Angel, in her own troubled way, to help the family. Her husband **Seth**, while ultimately sympathetic, is at first reluctant to allow a stranger into their tight circle.

CIVILIAN SUPPORT An **unnamed nun** allows Angel into the church, even though she knows what he really is, and gives her blessings to their effort even though she can't help. She allows Wesley and Angel to load up on holy water, candles, and crucifixes, knowing these tools will be needed to exorcise the Ethros. **Rick**, owner of Rick's Majick Shop, turns out to be less than helpful, selling Cordelia a useless Shorshack Box that couldn't hope to contain an Ethros demon. At least she saved twenty bucks.

This episode owes much to _The Exorcist_, the groundbreaking horror novel by William Peter Blatty that became William Friedkin's Academy Award-winning 1973 screen blockbuster. In the movie, Linda Blair played twelve-year-old Regan, the girl who is possessed by a horrific demon. Blatty claimed that his 1971 novel was based on a true account of an exorcism that took place in the 1940s. In the book and movie, a Catholic priest dies in much the same manner as Angel's Father Fredricks.

SUSPECTS Ryan proves to be one of the most chilling adversaries to date. Any child who can terrorize an Ethros demon is someone to be feared. (In custody.)

CONTINUITY

Ryan is confined to Angel's bed through binding powder rather than chains (as in "Somnambulist" and "Eternity"). The Ethros demon torments Angel with his "failure" to protect Doyle in "Hero." We get the first suggestion of something very wrong in Wesley's family dynamics, and learn more in "Belonging."

QUOTE OF THE WEEK

"They're brownies. Full of nutty goodness, not red blood cells."

Cordelia explains to Wesley why he, not Angel, gets to be the guinea pig for her experimental brownie recipe.

THE DEVIL IS IN THE DETAILS

EXPENSES

Shorshack Box
Psylis Eucalipsis
Donation to Catholic Charities for exorcism supplies (candles, holy water, etc.)

WEAPONRY

Binding powder is spread in a circle around the possessed Ryan to keep him contained in Angel's bed. The exorcism supplies (holy water and a crucifix) successfully drive the Ethros demon out of Ryan; Angel then dispatches the demon with an ax. Ryan sets his house on fire.

Cordy and Wes holding
a Shorshack Box

DEMONS, DEMONS, DEMONS

An **Ethros demon** is a demon that inhabits humans and sends them on rampages. (According to Wesley's books, famous New England family killer Lizzie Borden was inhabited by an adolescent Ethros.) They excrete Plakticine, and by the amount of Plakticine present at a site, one can determine the approximate maturity of the possessing Ethros. Its presence can be revealed by feeding the demon's host some Psylis Eucalipsis powder. They can be contained within an Ethros Box, which is made of six hundred species of virgin woods and handcrafted by blind Tibetan monks.

A **Kek demon**, which the gang is discussing during the opening of the episode, was a type of hibernating demon, now extinct. A knife emblazoned with the Mark of Kekfadlorem was the only weapon that could kill them.

133

Shorshack demons are somewhat smaller than Ethros demons. They can be contained in a Shorshack Box, which is pieced together by mute Chinese nuns.

THE VAMPIRE RULES

Some people with a strong religious faith just "know" when they see a vampire—viz., the nun.

Angel can apparently cast out other demons through an exorcism. But he can't touch most of the elements used for the rite.

Vampires may set foot on holy ground, but they are uncomfortable.

THE PEN IS MIGHTIER

FINAL CUT

Script directions re: Cordelia's brownie baking efforts: "She tries cutting them. They fight back."

When Angel and Wesley are preparing to go Ethros-hunting in the sea caves, the script's stage directions call for this: "Angel moves to the weapons cabinet, starts selecting various very bitchin' and lethal-looking items (production note: that he will never use.)"

After Angel saves Ryan from the speeding car, the script's stage directions read: "Angel reaches out, awkwardly tousles Ryan's hair in an imitation of human behavior."

POP CULTURE

❊ **ANGEL: "How many Thigh Masters do you own?"**
  WESLEY: "The second one was a free gift with my Buns of Steel . . ."
  Angel reminds Wesley that he lacks the gift of sales resistance.

❊ **RYAN: "She has nine marshmallows and I only have seven."**
  PAIGE: "Well, we'll just have to write the Nestlé Bunny about that."
  Ryan's mad enough to kill over his hot chocolate. The Nestlé Bunny is the mascot of the chocolate company's chocolate milk products.

OUR HEROES

Appearing (uncredited) as a language lab director in The Exorcist is John Mahon, who shows up in Angel as Detective Kate Lockley's retired cop father, Trevor Lockley.

"In 'I've Got You Under My Skin,' there's a suggestion of something really dark in Wesley's past, with his father. Is it just lingering there to be a future storyline, maybe?"

ALEXIS DENISOF: "We talked a little about Wesley before coming to the show, and about fleshing him out prior to him joining *Angel*, and some of the themes that were part of the character's makeup. Some of which would be obvious initially, and some would be more gradual. One of the great qualities, of many that Joss and David Greenwalt have, is the ability to take a long time to develop a thread in a character.

"We had talked about some family issues for Wesley that would inform who he decided to become, and doing what he decided to do with his life. I don't think it's constructive to talk specifically about that, because it's background to the character, and if at some point in the future it's decided to explore that very deeply, then great, but if not, then I think it's just something that I use in my mind, that I have created and that I use when necessary, and is one of the foundations of the person. It's part of how he responds to the world and how he thinks of himself, but it doesn't need to be in the audience's face all the time. Some things are stronger left unsaid and just alluded to. You can leave it at that and have it be more powerful."

To seal the _Exorcist_ connection, when Cordelia is pouring binding powder around Angel's bed, she says, "I wonder if I should put plastic down. Angel, are we expecting any big vomiting here? 'Cause I saw the movie."

"When you're working on something like, say, 'I've Got You Under My Skin,' and it's supposed to be such a normal little house. . . ."

SANDY STRUTH, SET DECORATOR: "Then you're doing _Ozzie and Harriet_. You're doing a traditional home. And the contrast is the action that the little boy does. You're almost not sure you're watching an episode of _Angel_. Usually with _Angel_, because of the nature of the piece, when you're channel-surfing you know it's _Angel_ because something's off there, it's dark, it's nighttime. But with that [set], that's interesting because that's one of those ones where you might not know for a minute, except something's happening."

"Children. Children are very difficult [to find stunt doubles for]. We had to do a near-miss with a little boy that was demon-possessed, and I had to find a little person, actually someone who's under four foot tall, Larry Nicholas, but he's an adult, he's thirty-five years old. But finding a good little person double is tough. Easiest is six one, hundred and eighty-five pounds. Male."

—**MICHAEL VENDRELL, STUNT COORDINATOR**

SIX DEGREES OF . . .

Anthony Cistaro, who plays the Ethros demon in this episode, was also in the _Angel_ episode "Hero" as Trask.

"THE PRODIGAL"

FROM THE FILES OF ANGEL INVESTIGATIONS
CASE №: 1ADH15

ACTION TAKEN

The roots of this case reach back hundreds of years, to Galway, Ireland, in 1753. A young Liam, who we will come to know, in later years, as Angel, is flirting with Anna, his family's pretty young maid, unable to stand the sunlight . . . for no reason more sinister than a terrible hangover.

Liam's father interrupts the scene before it can go any further. His distrust and disgust for his son know no bounds.

"Out again all night, is it? Drinking and whoring! I can smell the stink of it on you!"
—Angel's father

WRITTEN BY Tim Minear
DIRECTED BY Bruce Seth Green
GUEST STARS: Elisabeth Rohm (Kate Lockley), Julie Benz (Darla), John Mahon (Trevor Lockley), J. Kenneth Campbell (Angel's father), Henri Lubatti (Suit)
CO-STARS: Frank Potter (Uniformed Delivery), Eliza Szonert (Chamber maid), Bob Fimiani (Groundkeeper), Christina Hendricks (Bar maid)

After a few more choice words, Liam's father backhands his good-for-nothing layabout of a son.

In present-day Los Angeles, Angel also takes a hit, this one from a powerful demon dressed in rags. Battling Angel in a subway tunnel, the thing is incredibly strong and impossibly vicious, getting the better of Angel at every turn. Finally, it suddenly stops, clutching at its chest as if for air.

At the other end of the tunnel, on a subway platform, Detective Kate Lockley gets information from a uniformed cop who was first on the scene of a crime. A "crazy homeless guy" tore up a subway car until a passenger pulled the emergency cord and the train stopped. But before it stopped, according to the witnesses, the "homeless guy" went out through the train's top vent, while the train was still moving. Or was pulled out. She leaves the uniformed cop to get more information, and she heads down the subway tunnel, where she comes upon Angel and the other demon, who is having some kind of seizure. It collapses and dies. Kate is still having some trouble coping with "all this otherworldly stuff," asking only, "So do I call the coroner or hazardous materials?"

She and Angel leave the tunnel. Then Angel notices her father, Trevor Lockley, on the platform talking to a uniformed officer. Trevor says that he was listening to his police scanner, heard there was a hostage situation, and came down. He won't admit that he knew Kate was the lead officer on the scene, but she suspects that is what it's about—he's checking up on his little girl. Revealing this to Angel leads to an intimate moment, but her mood changes suddenly.

> **KATE:** "No. You don't get to do that."
>
> **ANGEL:** "What?"
>
> **KATE:** "Kill a demon in front of me, then act like we're gonna have a cappuccino together. It doesn't work that way—"
>
> **ANGEL:** "How does it work?"
>
> **KATE:** "I'm not convinced it does. . . . Look, no offense, I think you're probably a pretty decent guy for a . . . you know what you are. But let's keep it strictly business, all right? We don't get personal. I'm not your girlfriend."

Once Angel's back at his office, Cordelia tries to get him to focus on the instructions for the alarm system that's just been installed in his office. Wesley has been doing the research and tells Angel that the demon he battled on the subway was a Kwaini demon. According to his big book, they're always female, and they're extremely gentle and peaceful. The facts are not adding up.

Angel goes to see Kate, telling her that he figures the Kwaini must have been attacking a particular individual. He eventually zeroes in on the delivery guy who pulled the subway's emergency brake.

Later, Angel waits outside the Blue Circle Delivery warehouse. Back in the subway tunnel, Cordelia hacks the body of the Kwaini into transportable bits while, on his cell phone, Wesley ponders Kate's lack of enthusiasm for the supernatural with Angel.

> **WESLEY:** "I suppose one can hardly blame her for being skittish about the topic."
>
> **ANGEL:** "I guess so. I don't know. Ever since she ran me through with a two-by-four things have been different."

Wesley assures Angel that some people just have a harder time accepting the "dark forces which surround us. Women, in particular, I think—"

Cordelia interrupts his train of thought with a victorious shout as she put the last chunk of Kwaini in a Tupperware container. Aboveground, the delivery guy from the subway is getting out of his van— prompting Angel to wonder why a delivery driver with a van would ride the subway in the middle of the day. When the guy heads out again, Angel follows. Eventually the driver stops at an apartment building and goes inside, slinging a bag over his shoulder. Angel goes inside, too, watching the man knock on an apartment door. He's surprised when, instead of making a delivery, the driver makes a pickup— a brown paper-wrapped package about the size of a book—from Trevor Lockley.

When the delivery guy leaves, Angel hangs behind, and he knocks on Trevor's door. It takes a moment for Trevor to remember him, and then his first concern is for Kate—as it would be for any relative of a police officer, when a friend comes unannounced to the door. Angel assures him that she's fine, and that while she doesn't know he's here, she'd be very interested to know what was in that package he just gave the deliveryman. Angel also accuses Trevor of having removed something from the scene of the crime—there's no other reasonable explanation for him having been down on the subway platform while the delivery guy was.

Trevor Lockley is unrepentant, though.

> **TREVOR**: "You got any kids, Angel?"
>
> **ANGEL**: "No."
>
> **TREVOR**: "Right. Then don't think you can know how a father feels—or why he does the things he does."

He shuts the door in Angel's face.

Back in 1753 Ireland, Liam's father throws him out of the house for the last time, telling him not to return. He warns Liam that if he goes looking for trouble, "you're sure to find it!" Which Liam does, in the enticing form of Darla, his vampiric sire.

Trevor Lockley takes his daughter to a public pier for a gourmet lunch of Manny's hot dogs ("the best there is," he proclaims). But the invitation seems to be less about eating together and spending time than about grilling her about Angel, a guy he claims to have only met once, at his retirement party. Obviously, the visit of the night before isn't mentioned. She denies that they ever "went out," saying, "Angel's just . . . not my type. There's definitely a type involved and it's the wrong one."

Wesley, meanwhile, has been busy performing a kind of autopsy on the Kwaini parts that Cordelia brought home—on Angel's kitchen table. He has found something odd—something that might be compared to a human adrenal gland. It should be the size of a walnut, but this one is enlarged to the size of a pear. He has also discovered a fluid that, he says, ". . . seems to contain properties not unlike street PCP, though more metaphysical in nature, of course." The Kwaini was hooked on drugs that dramatically altered its body chemistry, making it violent—and it attacked the train, probably looking for more.

Cordelia interrupts, having been hard at work following the Blue Circle Delivery driver on his appointed rounds. For the tailing work, she's donned a disguise: blond wig, sunglasses, pink coat, with a camera bag over one shoulder. Subtle as heck.

> **CORDELIA**: "Move your entrails."
>
> **ANGEL**: "So you're back—"
>
> **CORDELIA**: "Very good, Mr. I-Can't-Tail-the-Suspect-During-the-Day-Because-I-Might-Burst-into-Flames-Private-Eye."

Cordelia managed to take some digital photos of the delivery guy loading his van with brown packages like the one he took from Trevor Lockley. These he got at a business called "Kel's Exotic Auto."

At that moment, inside Kel's, Trevor Lockley converses with two men in suits. He wants to know what was inside the packages they've been moving—which he was told were untariffed auto parts. He complains that he never signed on to remove evidence from crime scenes or to pump his own daughter for information. One of the suits hands him an envelope stuffed with cash, as thanks for going beyond the boundaries of the original agreement.

After he leaves, the real head of the operation, a demon, comes into the room. One of the suits asks him how to deal with Angel, who came up in the conversation. The demon instructs the suit to kill him, adding, "Kill Lockley, too. God, do I have to think of everything around here? Get me an adrenal gland!"

And back again, to Ireland . . .

Liam's funeral, dead at age twenty-six, doesn't draw many sorrowful onlookers. About a dozen people gather around his grave. His mother and sister weep, but his father, grim and stoic, just watches his son be buried in Galway's rich earth. After the sun sets and everyone else is gone, Darla steps from the shadows to wait for her lover's emergence. It isn't a long wait—his hands thrust up through the freshly packed dirt and he drags himself from his grave. A groundskeeper sees them, spots the open grave, and accuses them of being grave robbers. But with Darla's encouragement, Liam attacks the groundskeeper, taking his first victim.

He likes it. A lot.

Back in Angel's Los Angels office, Kate brings Angel the list of names he asked for, the passengers from the subway. She's acting considerably warmer as she also tells him she'd like to be involved—in the case, she adds, dashing any other hopes. If he finds anything, he's to let her know. After all, she says, she's "gotta face those demons sometime, right?"

She leaves, and Angel heads out to talk to Trevor about the demon drugs. Cordelia's newly installed alarm system signals the arrival of some snarling Kwaini demons who attack Cordelia and Wesley. But the fighting comes to an abrupt halt when Angel returns, holding up a vial of the drug Wesley took from the first dead Kwaini. Angel gets one of the demons in a vise grip and demands information. Whatever the demon tells him prompts him to grab his cell phone and call Kate—getting only her answering machine. He tells her that if she picks up the message, she should get in touch with her father and get him out of his home—he's in danger.

While he's leaving the warning, the danger has already come to Trevor, in the form of the two suits we saw at the exotic car warehouse. They've come to Lockley's apartment to pay a little visit.

Back in old Ireland, Liam's father desperately tries to save himself from his son. Liam's little sister, Kathy, invited her big brother into the house, assuming that he was now an angel. He repaid her by savagely attacking and killing her.

Now it's Liam's father's turn . . .

In Trevor's apartment, the suits want to know if he's told his daughter anything about their association, however casually. He assures them that he hasn't—good news for them, bad for him.

As they talk, Angel pounds on the front door. Trevor opens it, sees Angel there—but Angel has never been invited inside the apartment, so he's stuck in the hallway. He pleads for Trevor to invite him in, but the gruff ex-cop refuses to do it. Angel, helpless, has to watch as the two men vamp out and kill Trevor.

Once Trevor is dead, though, the rules about entry change, so Angel charges in. He dusts one of the vampire suits, but the second one runs out the door. Angel turns to follow, but as he does, Kate appears in the doorway, seeing her father on the floor. Turning him over, she sees the bite marks on his neck and looks at Angel. He tries to explain—Trevor invited them in, he didn't know the danger, he was involved in something crooked . . . but Kate is having none of it. She sends Angel away.

Angel goes home, opens his weapons cabinet, and arms himself to the teeth. Axes, swords, daggers, spring-loaded stakes on both wrists—he's ready for anything. As he prepares, Kate remains in her father's apartment, trau-matized, hugging the wall. Finally, her gaze rests on an envelope of cash that has fallen open on the floor. This, combined with what Angel told her, triggers something, and she looks inside, discovering a business card from Kel's Exotic Auto.

Inside Kel's, the two suits stand around a desk with another one, as a fourth sits behind the desk looking through paperwork. Kate enters, gun blazing, and drops three of them instantly. The fourth—the one who actually killed her father—transforms into vampface and comes at her. Unknown to the vampire, she has learned a thing or two from her brief apprenticeship in darkness at Angel's hands. She knows her bul-lets won't kill this thing—but the stake she has hidden in her clothes will. As it approaches her she pulls the stake and dusts the suit-vamp.

But her victory is short-lived. The head demon comes out from another part of the warehouse, and the other vampires who were only shot get up. Her gun doesn't help anymore. But Angel walks in, twirling an ax in his hands.

The demons rush Angel, but he's ready for them. Kate dusts one of them. Angel performs a slick maneuver, hurling his ax into the air like a cheerleader's baton as two of them attack from the sides. He thrusts his arms out, activating the spring-loaded stakes up his sleeves, and dusts two at once, bringing his arms back together in time to catch the ax and behead the Head Demon Guy.

When the carnage is done, Angel tries to talk to Kate.

> ANGEL: "Kate, uh, I know what happened with your father . . ."
>
> KATE: "My father was human. And you don't know anything about that."

She stalks out, leaving him alone.

In Galway, Liam sits among carnage of his own making—his mother, father, and sister all dead at his hands—looking self-satisfied. Darla, having goaded him into this act, reveals herself to be the true victor . . . over Angel's will.

> DARLA: "Your victory over him took but moments—"
>
> ANGEL: "Yes."
>
> DARLA: "But his defeat of you will last lifetimes."
>
> ANGEL: "What are you talking about? He can't defeat me now."
>
> DARLA: "Nor can he ever approve of you . . . in this world, or any other. What we once were informs all that we have become. The same love will infect our hearts, even if they no longer beat. Simple death won't change that."

RESOLUTION

In a different cemetery, in a different time, Kate Lockley kneels at her father's graveside. From the shadows, unobserved, Angel watches her, knowing full well what it's like to lose a father, and more, and also knowing that whatever they might once have had together, there's no chance for it now. That nascent relationship is as buried as Trevor Lockley. As his headstone says:

TREVOR LOCKLEY

BORN 1938

AT REST 2000

BELOVED FATHER

DOSSIERS

CLIENT The **Kwaini demons** have become addicted to drugs. **Trevor Lockley**, caught up in a situation he can't control, is a client, albeit one that Angel cannot save.

SUSPECTS At first, Angel believes the **Kwaini demon** is a killer, but then he realizes the real baddie on the subway was the **delivery guy**. Angel knows that **Trevor Lockley**'s up to something illegal. The **Head Demon Guy** running the drug operation meets his end at Angel's hands.

CONTINUITY

The *Buffy* episode "Becoming, Part One" set up the basic structure for Darla and Angel's first meeting, expanded upon in "The Prodigal." Angel met Trevor Lockley in "Sense and Sensitivity," and remarks on Kate's killing Penn while sparing him in "Somnambulist." He also refers to the sewer system leading into the police precinct, although he entered through a basement window in "Sense and Sensitivity."

QUOTE OF THE WEEK

CORDELIA: "The installation guy said it should be something easy to remember. Like my birthday."

ANGEL: "I don't know your birthday."

CORDELIA: "Tell me something you don't know that I don't know. But after eleven and a half months of punching it into this, you won't have any excuses."

Cordelia has a self-serving reason for choosing a particular alarm code.

THE DEVIL IS IN THE DETAILS

EXPENSES

Tupperware

Angel Investigations security system

Undercover wear: blond wig, vinyl coat

WEAPONRY

Angel arms himself for bear (or rather, vamps) with his double-wrist stakes, a dagger, a battle-ax, and many other sharp and heavy objects, including a table leg used to stake a vamp. Kate uses her service revolver and a stake to take down her first vampire.

Angel's stake rachet

THE PLAN

WESLEY: "What happened to calmly, cautiously, and deliberately investigating before rushing in?"

ANGEL: "That was plan A. We've since moved on to plan B."

WESLEY: "And plan B is . . . ?"

He reaches over, hefts his battle-ax. This guy's ready to rock and roll.

ANGEL: "Do I *really* have to explain it to you, Wesley?"

DEMONS, DEMONS, DEMONS

Angel explains to Kate that demons were in this dimension before humans were.

Kwaini demons are generally peaceful, balancing demons. They're incredibly articulate, gentle, nonviolent, and always female. Their adrenal glands are usually the size of a walnut. The addictive drug the Kwaini were taking in Los Angeles contained Eye of Newt, probably added for taste. It had an effect on them similar to that of PCP on humans (increased strength and violent behavior). To dispose of them, they should be buried in virgin soil with a simple Latinate incantation.

THE VAMPIRE RULES

Vampires carry the human emotions and memories they had previously—love, hate, vengeance, and so on—into their new "lives."

THE PEN IS MIGHTIER

FINAL CUT

The first time we meet him, according to the stage directions,

"OUT OF THE SHADOWS waddles (or walks or skips or whatever Mister Miller is devising) HEAD DEMON GUY. And boy, is he ug-leeee."

His death is also detailed:

"He [Angel] snatches it [the ax] from the air and brings it around in a perfect arc—decapitating Head Demon Guy, whose name now takes on a nicely ironic meaning, for the reader, anyway."

When Kate mourns her father, the stage directions read:

"And off this urban Pieta . . ." referring to the statue of Mary holding the body of Jesus after he was taken off the cross.

As Liam menacingly approaches his terrified father, the stage directions read: "Angel looks, well, fabulous, actually. Reeking with taste, dripping with style."

Some of the footage used to show Angel's turning at the hands, or fangs, of Darla is lifted from the *Buffy the Vampire Slayer* episode "Becoming, Part One."

Cordelia's birthday is May 22.

POP CULTURE

❖ (from the stage directions)

[Kate's] father's dead body lies where it was. It's clear she hasn't picked up the phone, has done nothing. She's Ophelia.

Kate is likened to Hamlet's tragic love interest, from the Shakespearean play of the same name.

OUR HEROES

"In 'The Prodigal,' there's the scene where Kate and Trevor are sitting and eating hot dogs, and he's asking her questions—"

JOHN MAHON: "Oh, yeah, I call that the hot dog scene. It was fun. I think we did that in one take, and I think the director expected to have more difficulty. Well, they did coverage on the scene, but as I remember they liked the first take, and I think she and I had established, I call it an imaginary reality, or an imaginative reality. We got to know each other and talked to each other. We talked about where we're from, our families, so that we had established a relationship. I think that's very important to do. Otherwise, you're two actors speaking lines to each other. Acting, in my humble opinion, is living truthfully and honestly in an imaginary circumstance, and I think that's the way I approach the work and that's what we tried to do. And that scene, I think, was so well written, that scene was fun to do, and when I saw it, I thought it had a real sense of reality about it. You couldn't really see the technique, or the acting. And I think that's important, in the work that I strive to do."

"The idea for episode fifteen was . . . we knew we wanted to do a story about Kate and her relationship to her father, which was only marginally interesting to me. So I pitched to Joss, you know, what if we also do a story about Angel and his father, because to me that's slightly more interesting. Once he eats his family, very interesting.

"I had two images in my head that really sparked with Joss, and one was Angel clawing his way out of his grave, after he is reborn, and just this idea that [today's Angel] goes to save somebody who will not invite him into their house, and he has to stand there and watch them get eaten, and there's nothing he can do.

"And sort of the theme became about naïveté. His little sister is so naive, she invites him into her house and he kills his family, and Kate's father is so naive that he does not invite him in, and he ends up dying because of it. And that was also the beginning of Kate's descent, which I liked very much. People were very upset, they thought we were going to hook them up romantically, and that made them mad. So the minute I made her slightly unlikable, they started to like her. Because they felt safe, I think. She was gonna keep her blond paws off him."

—TIM MINEAR

"I used one [a lace wig] on David too, with his long hair, for all the periods that we go through with him. We use a lace wig as well. We had that made for him. It took about a week. A guy came in and measured his head, and used plaster of Paris, and that's how they do it. It came out very nice. We designed it. I wanted . . . lighter brown face-framing highlights, and a certain length I cut to create this look of sort of a rebel. You know, he's kind of wild throughout each period, nothing conservative for Angelus. It's all human hair that I set on rollers, and I use Marcel irons with it. It's braided pieces of hair, and you can take it apart and fill in areas, to make it appear fuller, and to give it height, or fullness, and it's all hidden inside."
                                                    —DIANA ACREY, HAIR DEPARTMENT HEAD

SIX DEGREES OF . . .

Michael Vendrell, who plays "Suit #2" in this episode, was Sean Connery's stunt double in *The Rock*, a 1996 film. Actors Anthony Guidera and Juan A. Riojas were in both *The Rock* and in the *Angel* episode "The Ring."

Mark Ginther (Head Demon Guy) also plays a demon in "The Ring."

TRACKS

ROBERT KRAL, COMPOSER: "[Darla's theme music] first appeared in 'The Prodigal,' when we see Darla seeing Angel for the very first time. He's fighting in the pub. We could've had fight music, but I really wanted *Darla* music and wanted it to say: she's sexy, she's crafty, she's stylish and smooth, and she's really dangerous! I've used that theme in so many different ways it's a fantasy of mine to release an album of just Darla's music!"

"What elements have you incorporated for scenes from different time periods or different settings?"

ROBERT KRAL: "In 'The Prodigal,' I introduced the viola into the Angel score. It instantly evokes a feeling of an older time period, as well as being both dark and graceful, and somewhat mournful. Also the Darla theme, which is used a lot in that episode, as well as the funeral theme, is written harmonically in a way to sound more 'classic.'"

What's in a name? He's been referred to as Angel, Angelus, and now, for the first time, Liam, with no last name given. His headstone reads: 1727–1753 Beloved Son

"THE RING"

**FROM THE FILES OF ANGEL INVESTIGATIONS
CASE Nº: 1ADH16**

ACTION TAKEN

Wesley and Cordelia are spatting—how new—until Angel points out that a client has arrived. The client, Darin MacNamara, looks like a man who's had a bad night—one which included a serious blow to the face. Angel and Wesley help him to the couch, and he tells them that his brother Jack was kidnapped the night before. He fishes a small white box from a pocket; Angel opens it to find a man's severed finger.

> **ANGEL:** "Do you know the people who did this?"
> **DARIN:** "That's why I came to you. They weren't people."

Darin shows Angel a picture of his brother, and describes their relationship. Darin has made something of his life and Jack hasn't. Jack gambles, and is in debt to one of his bookies. Darin went to Jack's place to look for him and encountered inhuman creatures dragging his brother away. He tried to stop them, which is when they roughed him up. Angel gets Darin a pad so he can write down everything he saw for Cordelia and Wesley. In the meantime, he'll start with the bookie, one Ernie Nellins.

WRITTEN BY Howard Gordon
DIRECTED BY Nick Marck
GUEST STARS: Markus Redmond (Tom Cribb), Douglas Roberts (Darin MacNamara), Scott William Winters (Jack MacNamara), Stephanie Romanov (Lilah Morgan)
CO-STARS: Anthony Guidera (Ernie Nellins), Chris Flanders (Mr. Winslow), Marc Rose (Mellish), David Kallaway (Doorman), Juan A. Riojas (Val Trepkos), Michael Philip (Announcer), Mark Ginther (Lasovic)

He finds Ernie Nellins playing poker in the back room of Shots, the bar he works out of. Ernie rebuffs Angel until he puts Darin's picture of Jack on the table. Ernie draws a gun but Angel catches his hand, holding it down. Angel persuades him that he's just looking for Jack, and they go out to an alley behind the bar to talk. It costs Angel a hundred dollar bill, but Ernie finally tells him. "There's a place in Beachwood Canyon . . ." he says. "Well, not exactly in Beachwood Canyon . . . under it, actually." Angel heads out there, finds a wide drainage pipe running under the canyon, and, using a flashlight, goes inside.

Meanwhile, the struggle between computers and books rages on at the office. Cordelia enters the details that Darin gave them in a demon database she has established.

> **CORDELIA:** "Claws or hands?"
> **WESLEY:** "He wrote 'clawlike hands.'"
> **CORDELIA:** "Hmm, could be a mixed-breed. Smell?"
> **WESLEY:** "Sulfuric."
> **CORDELIA:** "Add a Porsche and hair plugs and I've dated this guy, a lot."

Wesley insists that looking in a book is just as quick, but before he finishes his sentence, the database has come back with a match. Darin saw howler demons.

145

Angel, in the tunnels, is set upon by just that: white-skinned howler demons wearing red suits. They're good fighters and it's a real battle for Angel, but he finally takes them. He asks one where Jack MacNamara is, and the demon tells him they sold Jack.

Following this lead takes Angel to a warehouse in a desolate, industrial part of the beachfront community Venice—except that instead of being deserted on this night, the warehouse is the scene of lots of activity. Limos drop off well-dressed couples. Clearly affluent types who look as though they'd never be caught dead here stand in line, tickets in their manicured hands. A bouncer checks their tickets and admits them into the warehouse and down a set of stairs.

Angel finds a barred window, and a few minutes later he's inside, mingling with the moneyed. His first face-to-face is with a lovely young woman, Lilah Morgan, who drops one of her betting slips as she sips her drink at the bar. Angel catches it before it hits the ground, handing it back to her. She thanks him and moves on, but he notices her.

Angel continues on, eventually reaching a sunken amphitheater. The capacity crowd around it cheers on some kind of athletic event. He moves toward the front, where a railing holds back the audience. The top of the railing is painted red, with the message WARNING: DO NOT CROSS RED LINE painted in big white letters across it.

Finally, he gets to a position where he can see down into a gladiatorlike arena in which two demons are locked in a battle to the death. The bloodthirsty crowd chants "Killing blow! Killing blow!" as the match nears its inevitable conclusion. Angel notes that both demons wear a similar metal cuff on one wrist. Over the frenzied cheering after the downed demon is dispatched, an announcer says, "The winner, ladies and gentlemen, is Tom Cribb. Official time: six minutes and twenty-two seconds. The fight pays out at two to five. For those of you keeping track, that was Cribb's seventh career kill."

Sentries drag the loser's corpse away as the next contestant makes his entrance. The announcer brings him in with a flourish: "Let's give it up for the menace of Venice, the titan of terror, the emperor of agony, the one, the only, Val Trepkos!" Trepkos is huge, battle-hardened, and deadly looking, though not without a certain calm dignity. As Angel peruses the mob scene, he spots Jack MacNamara, being ushered through the crowd by a couple of sentries. Angel follows.

And on the other side of the curtain, he's confronted by Jack, with sentries by his side. As Angel and Jack face each other, Darin enters, and Angel realizes that Darin set him up from the beginning.

He tries to escape, but the sentries attack him with powerful electric prods, stunning him.

Angel wakes up in a cell underneath the old warehouse. He's been stripped of his shirt, wearing only his own sleeveless undershirt, and he has one of the metal bands on his wrist, with the roman numerals XXI emblazoned on it. His cellmate is a large but not talkative demon named Lasovic. Other cells line the walkway, with a now-familiar red line between the cages and the walk. Angel has become one of the gladiators, and it's obvious now that this was MacNamara's plan all along.

Jack comes in to explain to Angel and any other newbies what the rules are. They're to remain behind the red line—the wristband insures that they will—and the wristband only comes off when the wearer is dead, or after he makes his twenty-first kill.

Back at the office, Cordelia and Wesley are worried about Angel since he hasn't checked in. Wesley gets off the phone after calling Kate Lockley with no success. Cordelia points out that it's also strange that they can't reach the client, who should be waiting by the phone for news of his brother. Wesley tells her to keep trying—he's going to follow in Angel's footsteps, beginning with a visit to Shots, the sports bar.

Angel begins the life of a gladiator. The local bully is Tom Cribb, who steals food from a squirrely demon named Mellish. Angel steps in long enough to annoy Cribb and embarrass Mellish, who insists that he could have held his own against Cribb. Before they can go further, Jack comes in to read off the fight card for tonight's bouts. Angel's cellmate Lasovic will fight someone named Baker, and Mellish is up against Val Trepkos.

Instead of agreeing, Lasovic makes a run for it. As he crosses the red line, though, he's instantly incinerated, reduced to nothing but a handful of ashes and the metal cuff, which Darin picks up. Now Baker's in need of an opponent, so Angel is chosen.

Wesley encounters trouble at Shots. When he walks in, Ernie Nellins is in the process of delivering a beating to some other wayward gambler. Wesley orders him to stop. He introduces himself, and says that he's there looking for Angel.

> **ERNIE:** "Your boss? Gave me two hundred dollars to answer his questions. I'm a businessman, make an offer."
>
> **WESLEY:** "You should understand that the man I work for means a great deal to me and I will *not give you a single red cent*. What I *will*, do, sir, is beat it out of you if I have to."
>
> **ERNIE:** "You're from another country, right?"

Ernie advances with a gun in his hand, but Wesley pulls a crossbow and shoots. The bolt goes through Ernie's hand, pinning it to the wall. His gun hits the floor, and Wesley snatches it up, holding it on Ernie's pals before they can even get their own guns drawn. It's a remarkably smooth move, and it works. Wesley, pressing his advantage, goes to Ernie and leans on the bolt. This has to hurt. Ernie talks.

In the slave cells, Mellish tries to repay Angel's favor by giving him advice on dealing with Baker. But Angel continues to insist that he's not going to kill anyone. "You on drugs?" Mellish asks him. "It's not like you have a choice." Then the match begins. Baker and Angel are ushered into the amphitheater.

Outside, Cordelia and Wesley look for a way in—the place isn't exactly crawling with ticket scalpers. But Cordelia has an idea. She approaches a well-off young couple and identifies Wesley and herself as detectives. She informs the civilians that they're about to enter an unlicensed sporting event, and imply that there's a raid planned. The couple appreciate the tip-off and head home, leaving their tickets in Cordelia's hands.

Inside, the bout continues, with Angel refusing to engage Baker. He takes some hits, and he dodges, but he won't attack. Cordelia and Wesley make their way inside, spotting Darin on the other side of the arena. Cordelia is surprised by the match under way, but Wesley isn't.

He also knows many of the details, including the role the wrist cuffs play in keeping the slaves in line.

Cordelia, still watching Darin, sees him set one of the cuffs—presumably the one he took from the deceased Lasovic—down on the rail. Darin signals to one of the sentries, who tosses a wicked-looking knife to Baker.

In the arena, Baker manages to slice Angel, drawing blood. Angel reflexively morphs into a vampire and attacks, hard and fast. The crowd had been chanting "Killing blow!" but now the chant changes to "Angel! Angel! Angel!" Baker regains his feet after Angel's brutal assault and charges with the knife. But Angel catches his wrists and turns his hands, and Baker's own momentum drives the knife into him.

Accidental or not, Angel has made his first kill in the arena, and the crowd goes wild.

The night's main event, pitting Trepkos against Mellish, is about to begin. Angel stops Trepkos, suggesting that they're all fighting the wrong opponents. If they fight their captors, they can all live. But Trepkos, and Cribb, looking on, are having none of it. Trepkos goes out, and Mellish doesn't stand a chance.

Wesley and Cordelia have left the warehouse, trying desperately to come up with a plan to save Angel. Cordelia's for calling the cops, but Wesley points out that the bad guys would probably just destroy the evidence—meaning Angel and the other captives. He says they could fashion a key to remove Angel's cuff—if only they had a cuff to work with. Cordelia reveals hers—she stole the one Darin left on the rail.

Back in the captive quarters, Jack McNamara taunts Angel. "My favorite part," he claims, "was when you stuck Baker with the knife. Kinda put a damper on that whole brotherhood spiel." Enraged, Angel reaches through the electronic barrier, enduring the pain, and grabs Jack, pulling him onto the wrong side of the red line. Holding Jack hostage, he sends a guard for Darin. Darin arrives a few moments later, and Angel makes his demand—he wants all the prisoners freed, or Jack dies. Darin simply draws a gun and shoots his brother three times, killing him and defusing Angel's threat. Some of the shots passed through Jack and into Angel, and when the sentries move in with their cattle prods, they knock him out.

He wakes up later, in a plush office. Lilah Morgan is there—she's the woman whose betting slip he retrieved.

> ANGEL: "You're a fight fan . . . and a lawyer. Let me guess, Wolfram & Hart."
>
> LILAH: "I'm an associate here. It took some arm-twisting, but I convinced MacNamara to sell your contract to the partners."

His wrist cuff is gone. He's free. But there's a catch. He has to forget MacNamara and the whole demon-gladiator deal ever existed. But that's not a deal Angel is willing to take, and Wolfram & Hart is not a law firm he's interested in working with. Guards step from the shadows, prods in hand, to take him back.

In Angel's kitchen, Wesley experiments with the wrist cuff. He needs something that conducts electricity, but not too much of it, as the cuff is half magic and half medieval technology. He tries a new substance, and the resulting blast of electricity knocks him off his stool.

And at the demon quarters, Angel is led back into captivity as Trepkos, Cribb, and Darin watch.

"You think you're setting some kind of example by coming back here? They didn't help you before and they're not gonna help you now. Every one of them knows . . . the only way out of here is by himself. But you'll find that out soon enough. Because tonight you're going to fight Trepkos. Smart money says he's walking out the front door. You're his twenty-first kill."
—*Darin*

As Wesley continues to work on the cuff, Cordelia finally offers him some horsehair—a souvenir of Keanu, her palomino, confiscated by the IRS. Wesley tries the horsehair, and it works. The cuff opens.

In the ring, the announcer introduces the competitors, Angel and Val Trepkos. Angel tries one last time to reason with the demon, but without success. The match begins. Angel, once again, is dodging, or trying to, not throwing any punches of his own. But Trepkos is skilled and powerful, and he pummels Angel.

Elsewhere in the warehouse, Cordelia distracts a guard, allowing Wesley to slip past him into the demon quarters. He finds Cribb, tells him he's looking for Angel. Cribb tells Wesley Angel is already dead, or will be in about twenty seconds. Wesley explains that he has a key to open the cuffs—and Cribb, using his frog tongue, snatches it from Wesley's hands.

In the arena, Trepkos is slaughtering Angel. The vampire remains upright, but barely, under the demon's relentless assault. Finally, at Darin's signal, both fighters are given wooden staffs to battle with. They go back and forth with these for a moment, and then Trepkos spins one around and rams it through Angel's torso—too low to hit his heart. Angel snaps the staff in half. When Trepkos attacks, Angel throws him to the ground and shoves the broken staff against his neck.

Cribb, testing Wesley's key, gets his cuff unlocked. He pushes through the other combatants, huddled at the door watching the action, and sees what is occurring in the ring.

Angel, with Trepkos pinned and shouts of "Killing blow!" ringing in his ears, backs away from the demon, refusing to finish him off. Trepkos has no such compunctions, and he resumes beating mercilessly on Angel. Angel is really unsteady now, barely able to defend himself. Trepkos closes on him, and the crowd's chanting grows even louder. Trepkos prepares to deliver what will surely be the killing blow—but then he changes his mind and lowers his fists. He won't do it.

The guards, unsure of what to do, look to Darin, who orders both fighters killed. Before anything can happen, though, Wesley draws a gun on Darin and tells him to call off the guards. Darin refuses. Suddenly, the doors into the ring crash open and the demon gladiators flood the arena, free of their cuffs. Darin takes advantage of the distraction and grabs the gun away from Wesley. Most of the crowd heads for the exits, Lilah Morgan included, but angry demons kill the spectators they can catch.

In the ring, Cribb kneels at Angel's side and unlocks his cuff.

Darin holds the gun on Wesley now, but he doesn't get a chance to use it, because Cordelia comes up from behind him with a pole and bashes him over the railing, into the arena. Darin manages to keep a grip on the gun, and he turns it on Trepkos. He fires, but Angel catches his wrist, turning the gun away. Cribb joins in, and when he slaps a cuff on Darin's wrist, Angel and Trepkos together hurl Darin into the air—straight at the red line. The man is incinerated, a rain of ash falling back into the ring.

As they head for an exit, Angel stumbles and Trepkos catches him, supporting him.

> **TREPKOS:** "It was a good fight."
>
> **ANGEL:** "Yeah . . . I could've taken you . . ."

But in fact, he can barely walk.

RESOLUTION

Outside, Angel thanks Cordelia and Wesley for saving the day as the demons scatter in every direction. It's a little late in the game for it to occur to them that they've just set a bunch of demons loose on the city . . . but that's exactly what they've done.

Oops.

Case closed.

DOSSIERS

CLIENT It's been a while since Angel Investigations has had a paying client, and **Darin MacNamara** turns out to be less than up-front with them—he isn't really looking for a detective, he's looking for the vampire he's heard about, to be another gladiator in his pen.

CIVILIAN SUPPORT Though they're tricked into cooperating, **the Winslows** give Cordelia and Wesley their tickets to get into the arena.

INFORMANTS Ernie Nellins, the bookie, turns out to be another part of the trap that snares Angel, but he also—thanks to Wesley's skill with a crossbow—gives Wesley the information that leads to Angel's rescue.

SUSPECTS He looks like a victim at first, but **Jack MacNamara**, in league with his brother **Darin**, runs the whole Octavian match operation, undoubtedly drawing in a huge profit from the wealthy, bloodthirsty spectators, even after subtracting expenses like ancient wrist cuffs and gruel. (Both deceased.) **Lilah Morgan** of Wolfram & Hart is also not of the good.

CONTINUITY

Cordelia bemoans her family fortune's fate at the hands of IRS auditors, first established in "The Prom." Angel is shot . . . again. Wesley asks if the Demons, Demons, Demons! database that Cordelia consults includes the Vigories of Oden Tal, referring to their opponents in "She."

QUOTE OF THE WEEK

WESLEY: "I don't know why you take everything so personally."

CORDELIA: "Me? This is rich coming from Mr. Don't talk to me before I've had my flagon of Oat Bran in the morning."
Cordelia and Wesley continue their eternal sparring match.

THE DEVIL IS IN THE DETAILS

EXPENSES

Bribe for Ernie Nellins

Everything Wesley blows up testing the cuff

WEAPONRY

Guns, "claw-like hands," a flashlight, cattle prods, hunting knives, crossbows, wrist cuff and the thick red line, and hardwood staffs.

DEMONS, DEMONS, DEMONS

While Cordelia searches the Demons, Demons, Demons! database, Wesley tests this newfangled approach: "Do they have the Vigories of Oden Tal?" They don't—but after all, they weren't technically demons, just beings from another dimension.

Howler demons are bald, have ultra-white skin, slime, and smell sulfuric. Their hands are clawlike and they emit an eerie high-pitched howl or wail, probably in preparation for fighting or mating.

The gladiator demons are a varied lot. **Tom Cribb** has green skin and amphibianlike features, including a tongue that works like a frog's. **Val Trepkos** is very strong and muscular, with a bony crest on his head. **Lasovic**, who shares a cell with Angel, is most notable for his unwillingness to converse, though like most of the others he is large and powerful. **Mellish** appears to be the weakest of the lot, and is fairly humanoid except for some horns projecting from his forehead. **Baker**, whom Angel fights, might be the same kind of demon as Mellish.

THE PEN IS MIGHTIER

FINAL CUT

Cut from the script for length was this exchange, continuing the Cordy/Wesley bickering that runs throughout. As they're heading back into the warehouse after having come up with the horsehair solution to the cuffs:

> **WESLEY:** "All I'm saying is you might have thought of the horsehair sooner, not that being flung repeatedly across a room isn't jolly good exercise."
>
> **CORDELIA:** "Speaking of horsehair, where did you find that jacket?"
>
> **GUARD:** "Mr. and Mrs. Winslow, good to see you again."
>
> **WESLEY:** "Don't touch me."
>
> **GUARD:** "Remind me never to get married."

"Do you speak Spanish? Are you from Belarus? Maybe you're Italian?"
—Angel

Howler demons were mentioned in the script of the earlier episode "In the Dark," but that scene didn't make it to broadcast.

The makeup team for "The Ring" was nominated for an Emmy in 2000, mostly on the strength of the numerous demons populating the captive cells.

Language lesson: Awakening inside his cell for the first time, Angel tries to communicate with Lasovic, his cellmate. Lasovic only grunts in return, so Angel tries a variety of human languages. In the episode, he speaks the given languages, so here are the translations.

POP CULTURE

❊ **"What about Captain America here?"** Jack describes Angel in superhero terms when he is tapped to battle Baker in the dead Lasovic's place.

❊ **"Oh, I know, every night it's Jeopardy, followed by *Wheel of Fortune* and a cup of hot cocoa. Look out girls, this one can't be tamed."** Cordelia comments on Wesley's busy social life.

❊ **"There's always slime . . . this is why I don't gamble, you make a small wager one day, a bigger one the next and before you know it Beetlejuice the Albino comes a knockin'."** Cordy finds similarities between demons and L.A. men. *Beetlejuice* is Tim Burton's 1998 film about a crude ghost helping a newly deceased couple learn their way around the afterlife.

❊ **"Couldn't they have just done *West Side Story*?"** Cordelia's response when Wesley identifies the combat as an "Octavian match." Arthur Laurents wrote the play that updates the Romeo and Juliet story into the era of 1950s youth gangs. The 1961 movie, with music by Leonard Bernstein and Stephen Sondheim, won ten Academy Awards.

❊ **"You'd think people'd get enough gratuitous violence watching *Jerry Springer*."** Shaken by the sight of the arena combat, Cordelia interrupts Wesley as he tries to figure out the wrist cuffs. Jerry Springer's TV talk show is famous for its fights.

OUR HEROES

"[Lilah Morgan] is just such a beautiful character to dress. She's in a man's world, she is in a demon world, she is beautiful, she's sexy, and she's in authority. I just love doing a person like that.

"I like to buy stretchy kind of suits for her, with a lot of Lycra and wool mixed together, and silk. Hepburns [a store in Sherman Oaks, CA], is a good place for suits for her, because they have that odd suit. Bloomingdales, Saks, anything that has a little stretch to it that has a great jacket, short skirts. I really wanted to start putting her in something other than the suits, so I got her a black cashmere crewneck short-sleeve sweater and a tight black wool skirt with a little slit that went all the way to her knee. Not short and sexy, classy. Like a little necklace. I love everything sharp. I just love that sleek look. And you can do that, even if it's colorful."
—CHIC GENNARELLI, COSTUME DEPARTMENT HEAD

DAYNE JOHNSON, MAKEUP DEPARTMENT HEAD: "One of our biggest episodes [first season] was 'The Ring.' It had the Cribb character, the Trepkos character, and Baker, and a bunch of background demons, and stuff like that. It was a lot of work. I had sixteen extra makeup artists one day, and I carried eight or ten makeup artists almost all the way through that episode. I had to have somebody to do each of those background [characters], they worked every day. I'm proud of a lot of the work, but as far as a body of work for one episode, that was the biggest one that we had last year."

"How do you make a bruise?"

DAYNE JOHNSON,: "Well, there's a lot of different ways, a lot of different products that we have out there now. Everybody's got some kind of a product. I'll say for instance, on David Boreanaz, I'll just use a Ben Nye bruise wheel, they call it. It's got four different colors in it, a red, a blue, a yellow, and a purple. It has those colors in four little spots. Old bruise, new bruise, fresh cuts, old cuts, whatever. They have it all made up for you. But that's just buying the color. And then after that, you have to take it and stipple it on, and get creative with the intensity. What day it is, is it a new bruise, an old bruise, how many days old is it, you really want to carry it along. Is it five days old, has the red gone, the purple set in, and some of the green is starting to happen, the yellow? Something else to research. There are other products you can use that are alcohol-based inks, that don't come off near as easy as that. Because the Ben Nye bruise wheel are oil-based colors, you can just take your finger and run right through them and you'll smudge the whole thing."

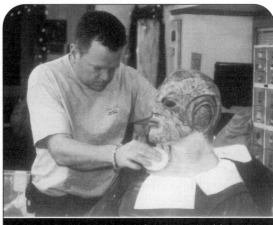

Dayne Johnson finishing Cribb

SIX DEGREES OF . . .

Douglas Roberts, who plays Darin MacNamara in this episode, appeared in the 1998 Robin Williams movie *Patch Adams* as Lawrence Silver. Also in *Patch Adams* was Harry Groener, alias Richard Wilkins III, the Mayor of Sunnydale.

Markus Redmond, who plays the demon Tom Cribb, also played Griff in "Rm w/a Vu."

Anthony Guidera, the bookie Ernie Nellins, appeared as a Cardassian in an episode of *Star Trek: Deep Space Nine* called "The Circle."

TRACKS

We hear "Consciousness (Aware of You)" by Morphic Field, from their eponymous CD. Morphic Field was also heard in the episode "She."

"ETERNITY"

FROM THE FILES OF ANGEL INVESTIGATIONS
CASE Nº: 1ADH17

ACTION TAKEN

Angel and Wesley are manfully—and barely—enduring Cordelia's star turn as Nora in Ibsen's *A Doll's House*. When the curtain falls at last, and the trio leaves the scene of the crime, Cordelia spots Oliver Simon, manager to the stars, across the street. Cordelia's excitement mounts when she realizes Simon is escorting actress Rebecca Lowell, whose devoted fan following has not been diminished by the cancellation of her show, *On Your Own*.

WRITTEN BY Tracey Stern
DIRECTED BY Regis B. Kimble
GUEST STARS: Tamara Gorski (Rebecca Lowell), Michael Mantell (Oliver)
CO-STARS: Robin Meyers (Masseuse)

Angel's offhand interest in Rebecca sharpens into focus as he notices an idling car speed up and aiming at her. Angel saves Rebecca, and his casual acceptance of her gratitude and his dark charm intrigue her, despite Cordelia's intrusive gushing. Cordelia manages to put one of Angel's business cards in Rebecca's hand as the "Dark Revenger" disappears into the darkness, away from the lights and commotion of the television crew who have just arrived on the scene.

Rebecca comes to the office the next day. She has been having problems with a stalker but has not sought outside help before because she doesn't want her difficulties made public. In addition to the attempt of the previous night, she has received letters written in what she believes to be blood. Angel assures her that they are not. But when she asks Angel to help her, he declines.

Cordelia's very bummed and tries to change Angel's mind, even channeling a pretend vision, her acting as stiff as it was on stage the night before. Angel is adamantly opposed to taking the case, and Wesley is perceptive enough to understand why: Angel is actually attracted to Rebecca.

> **CORDELIA:** "Great, just great. Because Mr. Distant has intimacy issues I lose my brush with fame."
>
> **ANGEL:** "Cordelia, she's just a person."
>
> **CORDELIA:** "Spoken like a true nonperson. Just *knowing* a star makes your life better. I'd do anything to live in her world."

Cordelia wishes she were living the life of a star, but Rebecca's life isn't that great. She has paid staff to care for her and to make her paranoid about losing her physical assets at her advanced age (late twenties), but no one to stand by her. And so she is alone that evening when an intruder attacks her in her home. Angel—who was keeping watch in spite of his refusal to take her case—crashes through a window to rescue her, but the intruder dumps a bookshelf on Angel and escapes through the newly created exit. As she thanks him, she realizes he's casting no reflection in her huge mirror.

ANGEL: "I'm not what you think."

REBECCA: "You're not? Because . . . no reflection . . . dark, private office . . . instantly knowing those letters weren't written in blood. I guess what I would think is, vampire."

ANGEL: "Then again . . ."

Now impressed by her casual acceptance of him, Angel takes the case.

Wesley tells Cordelia about their boss's change of heart and she heads for Rebecca's house to assess the situation. If he's gotten fleshy with Rebecca, she's probably out of a job because he's evil. But when she sees Angel, she's reassured. "Evil Angel never would've worn those pants," she says.

Unfortunately, Cordelia gets no chance to schmooze with Rebecca, who is having lunch with Oliver. Later, Rebecca vents about her circumstances to Angel. As someone who hasn't had a show for more than a television season, despite her popularity and talent, she is being asked to "read" for parts she once would have been handed. The tabloids are featuring "where are they now" stories on her, and she is getting a little shaky about her future. However, for the immediate future, she has had a very sexy suit and tie delivered for Angel to wear as he accompanies her to a premiere.

They arrive at the premiere uneventfully, enter, and immediately exit to an alley as Rebecca explains that she rarely actually stays beyond the photo ops at such events. A gunman attacks, and Angel performs his bodyguard duties well. Rebecca recognizes her assailant as another client of Oliver's, and realizes that her manager has staged the attacks to generate publicity.

Oliver admits to the ruse, breaking the news that she didn't get a part she'd been hoping for. When Rebecca remarks on the difficulty of forever being in competition with her character, eternally younger in syndication, Oliver points out that "nobody stays young forever." Rebecca's gaze turns to Angel, a walking contradiction of that truth. Later, Rebecca invites Cordelia to go shopping. Cordy is so delirious to be Rebecca's chosen companion, she is oblivious to Rebecca's subtle interrogation into Angel's background.

That evening, a stunning Rebecca clad in a sexy black slip-dress descends Angel's stairs, champagne bottle in hand that she's brought Angel as a thank-you gift. She reveals that she has figured out the stalker set-up, relieving Angel of that burden. They pour the champagne, and Rebecca persuades Angel to try to drink it with linked arms, "accidentally" pouring hers down his shirtfront. When he retires to his bedroom for a clean shirt, she adds something to his glass, then tops it off. Upon his return, they lift the glasses and drink.

Cordelia pages Wesley to meet her at her apartment, and when he gets there, tells him she has finally emerged from her starry-eyed haze and is alarmed when she revisits her conversation with Rebecca, especially the questions about Angel and how one might become a vampire.

Back in Angel's apartment, the mood has shifted. Whether it's the champagne or the added drug, Rebecca can't tell, but Angel's become sullen and moody in a manner unlike his usual state. Rebecca offers him comfort, first subtly, then directly, offering him her neck and inviting him to choose her as an eternal companion. Angel drags her to the kitchen and dumps some of his stored blood from the fridge into her mouth, daring her to taste eternity. Recognizing the inappropriateness of his behavior, he deduces she has drugged him. She reveals that she gave him a little dose of chemical happiness.

REBECCA: "I just . . . wanted us both to be happy."

ANGEL: "But I am happy . . . perfectly happy."

Angelus is back!

The vampire toys with her using his trademark cruelty, but she manages to stun him long enough to try to escape. She runs to Angel's elevator, but it's not working well, and is just as likely to be a trap as an escape. Fortunately for her, Wesley and Cordelia arrive and rescue her, and they quickly determine that while Rebecca and Angel have not done the dirty deed, the drug Rebecca administered *has* created the monster they feared. Wesley explains that Doximal is a powerful, bliss-inducing tranquilizer.

CORDELIA: "Bliss?! Bliss? As in SHEER CONTENTMENT? PERFECT HAPPINESS?"

WESLEY: "It's synthetic. Not true happiness."

REBECCA: "It's really good stuff—"

The lights in the office go out, and Angelus is at the door in the dark. Wesley tries to reason with him, pointing out he is experiencing a "chemical suggestion" rather than a true emotion, but Angelus rounds on him, sending him crashing across the room. Cordelia steps forward to defend Wesley, and when she is at a loss for words, Angelus mocks her with a cruel impersonation of her Nora, a dig at Rebecca/Raven thrown in for good measure. An enraged Cordelia reaches into her gym bag and pulls out a sports-bottle of water. She explains that like a good Girl Scout, she believes in being prepared, and the holy water in the bottle is part of her personal arsenal that she keeps on hand these days, just in case.

ANGEL: "You're bluffing."

CORDELIA: "Am I? You don't think I wasn't *ready* for this, do you? That I haven't planned for it? Why do you think I've got a stake stashed in my desk, a cross in my bag—I think about this happening <u>every single day</u>!"

Angel buys into the story for just a moment, long enough for her to douse him—with regular old water—and delight in her ability to convince him. As he readies himself to attack her, a recovered Wesley knocks him across the room and through the elevator shaft to the floor below.

RESOLUTION

The following morning Angel awakens to find himself haphazardly but sturdily bound to his bed with chains. Looks like the work of two people who suddenly found themselves facing death, and worse, at the hands of one of their best friends. He raises his head to find Cordy sitting beside the bed, waiting to see who awakens: Angel or Angelus. It's a contrite Angel, who apologizes and asks after Rebecca.

ANGEL: "Rebecca. Is she—?"

CORDELIA: "Gone. Oh, and no. She won't be keeping you on retainer as her bodyguard. I think it was the trying to *murder* her that lost you the gig."

Angel continues to apologize, and Wesley reassures him that apologies aren't necessary, as their friend Angel shouldn't be held responsible for the chemically induced Angelus's deeds. Angel compliments the departing Wesley on his fighting performance, then is left in awkwardness with Cordelia. Cordelia applies the directness she is known for to their situation.

CORDELIA: "Okay, here's something I never thought I would say to you: Wesley's right. Forget about it."

ANGEL: "But I really didn't mean . . ."

[re: the unkind comments about her acting]

CORDELIA: "Yes, you did. And I'd appreciate it if you didn't try to weasel out of it. Angelus may not be the most relaxing company, but at least he's honest. Shouldn't I expect the same from the not-evil version of my friends?"

They come to terms, then she leaves the bedroom, with Angel still bound. Just because Wesley and Cordelia are willing to forgive him doesn't mean they aren't willing to extract just a little more justice. After all, they won't leave him there for eternity.

DOSSIERS

CLIENT Rebecca Lowell is Angel's first strictly human potential romantic interest we've seen. Too bad her ambition to live forever in flesh as well as celluloid got in the way.

SUSPECTS Oliver Simon is the manager willing to do just a little extra for his clients, even if it's a bit beyond the usual scope. **Angelus** makes a temporary comeback when Rebecca slips Angel drugged champagne.

CONTINUITY

Angel favorably compares his stint in Hell to being trapped in the theater watching Cordy's performance. Oliver Simon gave Angel a business card in "City Of." Cordelia refers to the Burrower demon from "Lonely Hearts" while attempting to persuade Angel to take Rebecca's job. Although Wesley was not yet in Sunnydale, he is familiar with the consequences of Angel's finding perfect happiness in Buffy's arms in "Innocence" and "Surprise." Cordelia, who knew Jenny Calendar as well as other innocents, was on the scene. Rebecca discovers from Cordelia that Angel has helped avert the end of the world more than once, including in "The Harvest," "Prophecy Girl," and "The Zeppo."

QUOTE OF THE WEEK

"Oh, it's only like his purpose in life. Angel's the Dark Revenger. Only not too dark. Happy dark. I have a card in here somewhere." Cordelia's sales pitch to Rebecca.

THE DEVIL IS IN THE DETAILS

EXPENSES

More chains and padlocks for Angel

Replacements for the items Angelus breaks in Angel's apartment

Elevator repairs

WEAPONRY

A car rushes Rebecca; Angel pushes over a bookcase to try to trap her assailant; a gun loaded with blanks provides realism for the scheme to generate publicity; Rebecca gives Angel a "fake happiness" pill; Cordy tricks Angelus with an ersatz holy water bottle; and the elevator pins him.

DEMONS, DEMONS, DEMONS

THE VAMPIRE RULES

If Angel's moment of true happiness is artificially induced (i.e., by a drug), his stint as Angelus only lasts as long as the drug remains in his system.

This exchange between Angel and Rebecca at the premiere was cut due to length.

> **REBECCA:** "I take it you've never actually seen *The Bodyguard*? (then, re: photogs) Say—when they develop these pictures—"
>
> **ANGEL:** "You won't be walking by yourself. The 'we don't photograph' thing's a myth. I think it comes from the truth about us not reflecting in mirrors. It's not about physics. It's metaphysics."

AS SCENE IN L.A.

"In this episode, the script calls for a shopping scene on Melrose. Were you able to shoot it there?"

KEVIN FUNSTON, LOCATIONS MANAGER: "That was not actually Melrose. That was on Hollywood Boulevard. Cordelia's walking down the street with the girl who's the actress. We actually filmed that by the Pacific Theater, where we ended up filming the exterior and the interior for the arrival, when Angel pulls up for the premiere. We combined it because you lose a lot of time if you make a lot of moves. In television you have to be very efficient as far as getting things shot and done. You only have a certain amount of time that you can shoot in, per day, and we usually have a pretty full day."

THE PEN IS MIGHTIER

FINAL CUT

Cordelia and Wesley deconstructed Cordelia's destruction of the part of Nora, in this exchange cut due to length:

> **WESLEY:** "I've always regarded Nora as one of the seminal characters of late-nineteenth, early-twentieth-century literature."
>
> **CORDELIA:** "Yeah, but I thought I managed to breathe a little life into her, anyway—" (drinks) "—you have to train for a tour de force like this, lots of water, lots of power walking."
>
> **WESLEY:** "Yes, I, uh, don't recall seeing Ibsen's Nora portrayed as a power-walker before."
>
> **CORDELIA:** "I brought that to the part, the director was, like, clueless."

POP CULTURE

❋ **"We have to use this now, before she's just another *E! True Hollywood Story*!"** Cordelia refers to the biographical E! TV series that often chronicles the downfall of famous Hollywood stars.

* **REBECCA: "Which is impossible. Bela Lugosi, Gary Oldman—they're vampires."**
  ANGEL: "Frank Langella was the only performance I believed, but . . ."
  When Rebecca figures out that Angel is a vampire, she questions her own deduction for a moment. *The Prince of Darkness,* Vlad Dracula, was portrayed by Lugosi in 1931, Langella in 1979, and Oldman in 1992.
* Several movies have been made dealing with actors seeking eternal youth and beauty; *Death Becomes Her* is probably the best known of these.

OUR HEROES

"When Cordelia is on stage doing some really bad acting, how hard is it for you to portray bad acting?"

CHARISMA CARPENTER: "That's a really flattering question. I could have been funnier. I was kind of disappointed when I saw it. It wasn't my best performance. But I had to do what I had to do, you know, what I was directed to do and stuff. But just do everything over the top, and I guess that's bad. You know, big swooping gestures, that kind of stuff."

"Is it ever hard to do some of the little scenes with a straight face? For example, in 'Eternity,' when Wesley and Angel are saying the cliched, "We're trapped. There's no way out," and you have to do it with a straight face?"

ALEXIS DENISOF: "Well, they just don't print the first three takes where we're laughing."

"In episode seventeen we had a scene where Angel was supposed to jump through a sliding glass door. We put a charge on the sliding glass door, and the stuntman hits it and the effects man blows it. So Mike Massa came running at the sliding glass door, and the charge didn't go off. I mean, it was like a Road Runner cartoon. 'Cause the glass just boomed and blew Mike back, and fortunately he wasn't hurt."

—KELLY A. MANNERS, PRODUCER

"When you dress David, what do you look for, where do you shop for him?"

BILLY MCKENNA, COSTUME DEPARTMENT: "Because he wears long, leather, sometimes fabric coats, a lot of the shirts that we like to either make for him or buy for him are ones that have higher collars, such as Hugo Boss, Costume National, and we use a lot of Comme des Garçons. French designers, because they tend to do a higher collar, look better up underneath jackets and things of that nature, but not high enough to where it looks like 'Vladimir,' if you know what I'm saying.

"In his closet there must be twenty [dusters]. He has a stunt double, so of course everything we buy is in duplicates, sometimes even in triplicates. Everything just gets destroyed. If you could see some of these clothes with the holes and the rips and the fake blood. We stab Angel a lot. Or he gets shot. He just magically heals, but his clothes don't.

"His most expensive duster would probably have to be one of his Guccis that was ranging around two thousand. And for the stunt double, a lot of times we can do a knockoff for that. Mike Massa, the normal stunt double for him, is hard on the clothes. These stuntmen, they are tough on clothes. They're out there to make the shot look good, they don't think twice about ruining a two thousand dollar coat. So a lot of times we'll knock off the leather coats and things like that, for the stuntpeople to wear."

"FIVE BY FIVE"

FROM THE FILES OF ANGEL INVESTIGATIONS
CASE N⁰: 1ADH18

ACTION TAKEN

The Angelmobile emerges from out of the shadows, Wesley at the wheel, Angel wielding a sword in the passenger seat. Three demons are menacing a human gangbanger, and Angel disposes of the three by whacking off their heads.

Meanwhile, down at the bus depot, a beautiful young woman with a battered bag, a tired, too-much-coffee-and-not-enough-rest look, and a dingy football jersey steps off the bus and immediately attracts the attention of a human predator. Dick "helpfully" offers the young woman assistance.

Faith, in town on the run after her most recent encounter with Buffy, responds in classic Faith style—she kicks Dick's ass and helps herself to his jacket, wallet, and apartment. She approves of L.A. immediately, saying, "Now I got money. And a place to stay. I think I'm gonna like it here."

WRITTEN BY Jim Kouf
DIRECTED BY James A. Contner
GUEST STARS: Julie Benz (Darla), Christian Kane (Lindsey McDonald), Thomas Burr (Lee Mercer), Tyler Christopher (Bret Folger), Stephanie Romanov (Lilah Morgan), Eliza Dushku (Faith)
CO-STARS: Rainbow Borden (Gangbanger), Francis Fallon (Dick), Rodrick Fox (Assistant DA)

Back in L.A., Angel saved the gangbanger—one Marquez—so he could testify in a court case. But the smarmy creep has no interest in doing his civic duty. Still, Wesley holds out hope.

> **CORDELIA:** "Wesley, you don't change a guy like that. In fact, generally speaking, you don't change a guy. What you see is what you get. Scratch the surface and what do you find? More surface."
>
> **WESLEY:** "I suppose one could have said that about . . . Angel."
>
> **CORDELIA:** "Oh, please, he was cursed by Gypsies. What's Angel going to do, drag a bunch of them in here to shove a soul down this guy's throat?"
>
> **WESLEY:** "He may be a ruffian, but he's already got a soul—and therefore, somewhere deep down inside, an urge to do what's right."

Ultimately, Wesley's vindicated. Marquez does indeed do the right thing and show up in court—much to the vast disappointment of Lindsey McDonald of Wolfram & Hart.

Meanwhile, Faith has made her mark on a downtown bar, dancing and fighting. Another Wolfram & Hart attorney, Lee Mercer (who once represented Little Tony Papazian) suggests her to Lindsey and Lilah Morgan as a solution to the problem of the annoying thorn in their side known as Angel. Lilah connects with Faith at another bar and introduces herself as more than a target for Faith's quick gratification.

> **FAITH:** "I guess we could go somewhere and talk . . . although I'm not much of a talker, I'm more of a doer."

LILAH: "I think you might've misunderstood my intentions."

FAITH: "No. I think you misunderstood mine. I like that watch. Diamonds, right?"

Lilah lets Faith know what's what—Wolfram & Hart wants to hire her to take out Angel. Faith is absolutely delighted.

Meanwhile, talk of souls and redemption has sent Angel down memory lane, remembering the fateful gift he received from Darla one night in 1898. It was a beautiful Gypsy girl, and when he killed her, he drew the wrath of the Gypsy clan on himself. They gave him back his soul . . . and he lost Darla.

Later, Angel, Cordelia, and Wesley are in the rotunda of a government building, with Cordelia trying to sell the guys on taking a divorce case.

CORDELIA: "According to the husband . . . the wife's a real witch!"

WESLEY: "It seems a bit on the seedy side."

CORDELIA: "This is not seedy. He's in the government! Just talk to him. Oh, and we should pick up the tab for lunch. Nothing says success less than splitting the bill."

As their financial/business debate continues, Faith enters the rotunda, unseen by any of them. She fires a crossbow at Angel, who stops the arrow mere centimeters from his chest. Faith, undeterred, grins at him. Then she is gone, leaving a stunned trio behind.

Back at the office, Angel calls Giles to get the lowdown on Faith—who is clearly no longer in a coma. Wesley is affronted that Giles didn't immediately contact *him*, as Faith's former Watcher, and Angel reminds him not unkindly, but not gently, that his track record with Faith is not the best. He assigns Wesley and Cordelia the task of discovering Faith's likely whereabouts by tracking recent crimes.

Angel goes to his apartment to review his weapon options, then returns to the office. A sound in the outer office causes him to hesitate. Faith is there, standing in the sunlight and holding a revolver. She tosses it to Angel, daring him to take her out. He fires at her leg, but it's a blank, and he returns the revolver to her. She reveals that not only is she committed to assassinate him for her personal pleasure, but she is being paid to do so! She taunts him for his reformed outlook on life, apparently having gained nothing from their heart-to-heart talks in the past—when he tried to save her from herself (and the Mayor) in Sunnydale.

"Jeez, you're pathetic, you and your little tortured soul, gotta think everything through—well, think fast, lover, you don't do me, you know I'm gonna do you." —*Faith*

And she fires the next round at him—a real bullet, this time—and leaps out through the window into the sunlight. If he were human instead of vampire, he'd be dead.

Later Angel, in a suit and tie, carrying his beloved cell phone, enters Wolfram & Hart. He is on a beeline for the elevators when he is hailed by a random W&H drone who thinks he recognizes Angel from an earlier meeting. Angel manages to bluff his way through the encounter, then ascends to Lindsey's office. He is rifling through Lindsey's desk when the rightful owner enters, tie loosened and irony fully in place. Angel tries to pry information about Faith out of Lindsey, who is not forthcoming, but does impart one important tidbit for future reference:

> ANGEL: "So how's it work for a guy like you? Successful lawyer in a big law firm. Company car, nice office, bonus, can hire a killing whenever you want. Kind of got it made, right?"
>
> LINDSEY: "Well, we'll just add slander to breaking and entering. And while we're on the subject, I remember you throwing one of my clients through a window. Killed him if I'm not mistaken."
>
> ANGEL: ". . . Yes, I seem to remember . . . the window was just about that size. Too bad the body burned up before it hit the ground. I might have needed a good lawyer."
>
> LINDSEY: "I'm sorry, we only handle a certain class of clientele."
>
> ANGEL: "I'm sure I've killed enough people to qualify."

Angel leaves with no better sense of where Faith is than when he first broke in. Meanwhile, Cordelia and Wesley take the evidence they have gathered of suspected Faith sightings back to her apartment. Phantom Dennis doesn't want to let them in, and Cordy figures he's jealous of Wesley. But after they enter, Faith steps out of the bedroom, her very presence filling the air with menace.

> WESLEY: "Listen to me. It's not too late."
>
> FAITH: "For cappuccino? 'Cause it just keeps me up."
>
> WESLEY: "It's not too late to let me help you."

Faith isn't interested. She knocks Cordelia to the floor with an elbow to her face. When an outraged Wesley strikes her in retaliation, she laughs admiringly before flinging him across the room with the first blow of a brutal attack.

Unaware of what's gone on, Angel is thinking of Darla again, recalling the desperation of his hunger after she rejected him, back in their past: He attacked a woman but managed to let her go without drinking of her, and staggered off down the dark streets, facing an uncertain future.

Angel arrives at Cordelia's apartment and finds a battered and shaken Cordelia emerging from the debris and Wesley gone. Angel and Cordelia piece together Faith's likely whereabouts based on the police report of Dick's stolen wallet and keys. Faith has taken Wesley to her new lair and bound him to a chair, where he is a captive target for her sadistic games.

"Now we've only done one of the five basic torture groups. We've done Blunt, but that still leaves Sharp, Cold, Hot, and Loud. Have a preference?"   —*Faith*

She's about to start scorching various bits of Wesley when Angel slams through the door. Dropping the other stuff, she holds a knife to Wesley's throat, delighted that Angel is indeed playing her game. Faith is distracted enough that Wesley is able to plant his bound feet and kick back in the chair, temporarily knocking Faith down and causing her to drop the knife.

Immediately she and Angel fall upon each other in a fierce battle, Rogue Slayer vs. 244-year-old vampire. The battle rages all over the apartment, as a grimly determined Wesley makes his way to the knife and works to free himself. Faith's first few attempts at staking Angel fail, but she still seems to be holding the upper hand, much to Wesley's dismay.

Then Angel charges her as she attempts to stake him again, driving both of them out of a window. They ricochet off the top of a Dumpster and scramble to their feet in the alley below. Wesley manages to free himself and gathers up the knife, hurrying downstairs to Angel's aid.

Faith continues to attack Angel as ferociously as ever, but Angel seems to have switched to defensive mode, much to her fury. As rain pours down around them, she shrieks:

> **FAITH:** "I'M BAD! Fight back! You are going to die!"
> **ANGEL:** "Nice try, Faith. I know what you want. And I'm not gonna do it."

RESOLUTION

Angel allows Faith to fight herself into exhaustion and emotional defeat when she realizes he is *not* going to release her from her conscience by killing her. As he gathers her to his chest in empathy, perhaps the only person in the world who can appreciate what she is going through, a stunned and uncomprehending Wesley enters the street behind them. Wesley, shocked, drops the knife. And Angel supports Faith in the rain that washes over them.

Case to be continued.

DOSSIERS

CLIENT **Faith**'s life and soul hang in the balance again, as Angel tries again to get through to her before she can kill him.

SUSPECTS **Faith** arrives in L.A. ready to cause some havoc, and she does just that to Cordelia, Wesley, and Angel. **Lindsey McDonald**, **Lilah Morgan**, and **Lee Mercer** hire Faith to eliminate the soulful vamp. (All remain at large.)

CONTINUITY

Angel invested a great deal of time in trying to redeem Faith in the past in "Consequences"; his efforts were thwarted in part by Wesley's intervention, along with the Council Gang. Faith's first move in her game is firing an arrow at Angel, a move that served her well in "Graduation Day, Part One." "This Year's Girl" and "Who Are You?" involve Faith waking from the coma she fell into following her battle with Buffy in "Graduation Day, Part One" and exchanging bodies with Buffy temporarily through a device left by the Mayor. She disrupted nearly everyone in Sunnydale's life, and Buffy, in Faith's body, was hunted by the Watchers Council assassins. Eventually Faith was forced back into her own body by Buffy, then left town.

QUOTE OF THE WEEK

WESLEY: "—there's another assault just two blocks away. A fight in a bar. Several arrests made. And a woman fitting Faith's description was involved. However not arrested."

CORDELIA: "She charm her way out?"

WESLEY: "No, apparently she managed to break a policeman's jaw with his own handcuffs before she disappeared into the night."

CORDELIA: "For Faith, that is charm."

It doesn't take long for Faith to get into the papers after arriving in L.A.

THE DEVIL IS IN THE DETAILS

EXPENSES

Broken window in Faith's apartment hideout

New clothes for Wesley, Faith, and (sigh) at least a new duster for Angel.

WEAPONRY

Angel kills demons with a sword to save a gangbanger; Faith rams her dancin' elbows into various mortals who happen to be in the way. Darla and Faith—in different eras—both try to use stakes of various sorts against Angel. Faith slams Lee Mercer's face into a conference table, "misses" Angel with a crossbow and threatens him with a gun, as do guards at Wolfram & Hart. Faith employs many kitchen implements of torture, including big-ass knives, a shard of glass, and a cooking oil flamethrower.

THE PEN IS MIGHTIER

FINAL CUT

Angel's taking of the young Gypsy woman is described this way in the script:

Angel sensuously moves a hand up her bare leg, slowly pushing her skirt above her knee, up her thigh. Angel smiles at her. Then he slowly moves down to her leg and sinks his teeth into the inside of her thigh . . . just above the knee, get your mind out of the gutter.

In the original script, the gangbanger Angel saves is named Martinez. For broadcast, his name was changed to Marquez.

Cut from the final episode, for length. Angel initially resists Wesley's idea to help Faith:

> **ANGEL:** "I seem to remember trying with Faith once . . . I had her in a safe place, on the verge of facing herself and what she'd done. Then her Watcher knocked me unconscious with a tire iron, took her away, and let her escape. Which gave her the opportunity to put a poison arrow in my back." (stares at Wesley for a moment)
> "Then I nearly killed Buffy. Not that one should ever learn from mistakes."

❊ **"Okay, Elvis, when you're a big star you can get away without carrying cash."** Cordelia is annoyed that Angel doesn't have the dough to cover a lunch with a potential client.

OUR HEROES

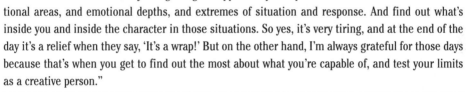

"For 'Five by Five,' how did you work with Eliza on the torture scenes?"

   ALEXIS DENISOF: "It was very simple. I told her to go for it, and don't hold back. And she made it very easy for me to play those scenes. She gave it all, and I gave it all, and I think those scenes read very much as what they were, which is people in a very extreme situation. I mean, the blood isn't real. Well, most of the time. But otherwise . . ."

"Is it hard on you to go through a scene with that many emotions?"

   ALEXIS DENISOF: "Yes, but it's also what you enjoy, as an actor. Part of the satisfaction of the job is getting the opportunity to explore emotional areas, and emotional depths, and extremes of situation and response. And find out what's inside you and inside the character in those situations. So yes, it's very tiring, and at the end of the day it's a relief when they say, 'It's a wrap!' But on the other hand, I'm always grateful for those days because that's when you get to find out the most about what you're capable of, and test your limits as a creative person."

   Michael Vendrell, Kelly A. Manners, and James Contner on the climatic fight scene:

"That was my favorite fight that I've ever done in my life. This was magical, with the rain and everything. You couldn't plan it, it just started raining at the right time, when they came out the window, bam as soon as they hit the trash can, they get up, it started raining. By the climax of the fight it was pouring rain. Real rain. There was nothing fake about that."   —MICHAEL VENDRELL, STUNT COORDINATOR

"They had written [the] big fight, between Faith and Angel, in an alley, with a high fall into the alley and a huge fight, and it was written for rain. And I fought Jim Kouf and David Greenwalt for a solid week. I did not want to shoot it in the rain because it would take too much time, it would be too much money, and there was just too much work to be done. And I finally won the battle, and we went out that night, and it poured like a son of a bitch. And we shot the whole thing in . . . actual rain. And I gotta tell you what, I realized right then what a mistake it would have been not to shoot it in the rain, because it made the episode. But I want to tell you what, that wasn't us. I talked them out of the rain, and God provided that rain."   —KELLY A. MANNERS, PRODUCER

   JAMES CONTNER, DIRECTOR: "That's probably my favorite episode. Eliza just had grown so much as an actress during her days on *Buffy*. And the culmination of where 'Five by Five' ended up with her breaking down, such emotion, having put up a tough facade for quite a few episodes now on *Buffy*. It was such a well-written show. I think all the actors did a great job, and Eliza especially. She really nailed that. The scene in the end, where she just breaks down after fighting with Angel and lets loose this totally raw emotion was just somehow moving to me. I was in tears, literally. You could just feel her pain. It was beautifully acted."

"How many takes were there of that?"

JAMES CONTNER: "I don't think we did too many. We had one of the biggest nights of shooting I've ever had. We did sixty-five set-ups. Including a fight, and dialogue, and all this emotional stuff, and in the rain. Luckily, knowing we were forecast for rain, we did bring the rain towers, because it stopped raining before we were finished shooting, so we did have to make [some] rain."

"What is an average amount of set-ups a night?"

JAMES CONTNER: "Well, whether it's night or day, I think we average about twenty-five to thirty set-ups a day. Some days better than others. A real good day is forty set-ups. But we're shooting two cameras, so that helps. We shoot multiple cameras a lot on this show. Because the shows are very ambitious, and you want to get as much coverage as possible. Especially with emotional scenes, you don't want to have the actors doing them over and over, because they do lose their spontaneity and their freshness. You can only ask an actor to cry so many times and have it feel real. So you really hope you get it in the first take or two. Usually in a big emotional scene like that, even if something goes wrong technically, or it's not quite right, I usually print it anyway, because sometimes you're never going to get a certain piece of that performance as good on a second take."

SIX DEGREES OF . . .

Stuntman Keith Campbell was also in *City of Angels*, in *Dead Man on Campus* with Alyson Hannigan (*Buffy*'s Willow), and played a werewolf in the *Buffy* episode "Phases." Camera Operator David Emmerichs worked on *Alien Resurrection*, written by Joss Whedon, and *Jason Goes to Hell: Final Friday*, in which Keith Campbell also worked as a stuntman.

TRACKS

Scary rocker-turned-filmmaker Rob Zombie has a song in this episode, "Living Dead Girl," from his CD *American Made Music to Strip By*.

"SANCTUARY"

**FROM THE FILES OF ANGEL INVESTIGATIONS
CASE № 1ADH19**

ACTION TAKEN

After Faith collapses against Angel in the alley, the two come in out of the rain and ride the elevator down to his apartment. He is concerned; she has nearly reverted to her comatose state. They enter his place of refuge, and he leads her to his bedroom and tells her she is safe, she can rest. Faith wearily accepts, then has an internal vision of herself armed and attacking Angel with a knife. A beat, and then she dismisses the vision.

When Wesley enters the office the next morning, a battered and bruised Cordelia greets him with the news that Faith slept at Angel's all night. Their mutual dismay is heightened when Angel enters the office in search of donuts for Faith.

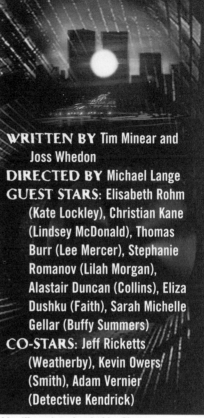

WRITTEN BY Tim Minear and Joss Whedon
DIRECTED BY Michael Lange
GUEST STARS: Elisabeth Rohm (Kate Lockley), Christian Kane (Lindsey McDonald), Thomas Burr (Lee Mercer), Stephanie Romanov (Lilah Morgan), Alastair Duncan (Collins), Eliza Dushku (Faith), Sarah Michelle Gellar (Buffy Summers)
CO-STARS: Jeff Ricketts (Weatherby), Kevin Owers (Smith), Adam Vernier (Detective Kendrick)

> **WESLEY:** "Won't she have trouble enjoying delicious jelly filled donuts if she is, one assumes, bound and gagged?"
>
> **ANGEL:** "Wesley, we went through all this last night. . . ."
>
> **WESLEY:** "Yes. And you were right. The police <u>would</u> be ill equipped to hold a Slayer against her will. . . . I understand why you chose not to turn her over to them. I do not, however, understand why the woman who brutally tortured me last night, this morning . . . gets pastries."

Angel and Wesley engage in a brief but fierce debate over the wisdom of even trying to reach Faith in hopes of redemption, and Wesley grabs his jacket and leaves. Angel turns to Cordy for reassurance, but Cordelia, expecting disaster, collects three checks' worth of paid vacation time and departs, leaving an office clouded with her anger. Meanwhile, the LAPD has found the apartment where Faith tortured Wesley, and Kate Lockley is on the case.

Angel takes donuts downstairs for Faith and realizes what a very long road they are facing when he encounters her standing in the shadows holding one of his kitchen knives. When a concerned Angel suggests that perhaps she should rest, she reminds him she has been resting—she was in a coma for eight months.

Lindsey McDonald sits in his office at Wolfram & Hart, commiserating with Lilah Morgan. Angel is still undead and seems to have persuaded Faith to blow off her assignment. When he expresses his amazement at Angel's continued existence, Lilah reminds him of Angel's track record, pointing out that not only hasn't he been killed by a Vampire Slayer, but he in fact used to date one. Lindsey dismisses this as an urban legend, little knowing the Slayer in question is about to arrive in L.A. As they plan their next step, Lee Mercer, still recuperating from a close encounter with Faith and a conference table, suggests they just kill her.

Faith just may beat them to the punch of this plan. While obviously in no condition to fend for herself, she moves into Angel's bedroom and begins packing. She needs to flee her ghosts so the consequences of her past choices can't catch up with her—and some of those consequences are very real, since she's still being sought in connection with the deputy Mayor's murder, back in Sunnydale. Angel points out all the reasons she shouldn't be on her own.

"Where are you gonna go? Back out into the darkness? I once told you you didn't have to go out into that darkness. Remember? That it was your choice. Well, you chose."   *—Angel*

She is still going through the motions of leaving, in some ways even less able to bear his sympathy than she would his anger, but as he continues to talk, she spins and strikes at him. He absorbs the blow, and waits for her to say the two important words: "Help me."

Wesley is taking out his frustration over a solitary game of darts. He has just stepped to the board to retrieve his handful of darts when one sails past his ear into the target. He looks across the pub to see Watchers Council representatives Collins, Weatherby, and Smith regarding him with speculation, having tracked Faith to L.A. The four of them retire to a table, and they order a round of drinks. They make small talk for a few minutes, then Collins moves to the meat of the matter, extending an invitation to Wesley to rejoin the folds of the Watchers Council. Wes had been fired after failing to keep not one but two Slayers reined in, Buffy and Faith. But the Council is ready to forgive and forget past events, for a price: Wesley's participation in the recapture of Faith. Wesley delightedly realizes that they really need him . . . Faith cleaned their clocks.

Angel and Faith have moved back into his kitchen, and he sits at the table while she leans on the counter, her back to him.

FAITH: "So, how does this work?"

ANGEL: "There's really no simple answer to that. I won't lie to you and say it'll be easy.

It won't be. Just because you've decided to change doesn't mean the world's ready for you to. And the truth is, no matter how much you suffer, no matter how many good deeds you do to try and make up for the past—you may never balance out the cosmic scale. The only thing I can promise you . . . is that you'll probably be haunted. And maybe for the rest of your life."

Faith's question, however, was less cosmic and more pragmatic. She wants to know how to operate the microwave to make popcorn.

She also expresses her admiration at Angel's ability to deal with his guilt and remorse, and wonders if she will be able to do the same. Angel informs her the first step in her twelve-step program toward redemption is feeling all the pain she has caused others.

FAITH: "I gotta be the first Slayer in history to be sponsored by a vampire."

ANGEL: "Yeah, well, I've got some experience in that area, too."

FAITH: "Oh, God— B. How am I ever going to make things right with her?"

ANGEL: "Faith, this isn't about Buffy."

FAITH: "All my life there was only one person that tried to be my friend, went out of her way when I had no right or reason to expect her to, and I screwed her. Not to mention her boyfriend, only, him literally."

ANGEL: "Faith, you and I never actually . . ."

FAITH: "No, not you. The new one. Oh, my God. Angel, I'm so sorry I . . ."

Thus Angel is introduced to the idea that there's a new guy in Buffy's life.

At Wolfram & Hart, Lindsey, Lilah, and Lee are briefing a murderous bug demon on its new target: Faith. Lee in particular—wearing a neck brace, his jaw wired shut—is very emphatic on how very dead he wants the Slayer.

In the pub, the Watchers Council assassins are eager to close their deal with Wesley. Collins slides a napkin across the table to Wesley, with a hypodermic needle hidden inside. They assure him, fairly convincingly, that they intend to capture Faith alive and take her back to the Council for rehabilitation. Wesley just has to inject Faith, then signal them to come get her.

WESLEY: "I have some conditions of my own. Just one actually. No harm must come to the vampire."

WEATHERBY: "Oh, don't be a ponce."

At Angel's apartment, Faith's listless television watching suddenly sharpens into personal interest. Angel joins her in time to see and hear Kate onscreen, warning the citizens of L.A. to be wary of Faith. Angel is beginning to calm her down when the bug demon drops from the ceiling.

The two pound the creature. Faith is all instinctual savagery, but once the demon is dead, she starts to break down again. Angel gathers her close, and they are embracing when a sound draws their attention to another unannounced guest: Buffy Summers. No one is sure what to make of this unexpected situation, and Angel moves to defuse Buffy before any misunderstandings can grow.

It doesn't go very well.

Angel questions Buffy's motivation for coming to L.A.—she states it was just concern for him, but he wonders if a chance for revenge on Faith wasn't a stronger factor. Faith starts to apologize to Buffy, but Buffy threatens to beat Faith to death if she doesn't shut up. Angel urges Faith up to the office over Buffy's objections. Buffy moves to physically restrain Faith, and Angel stops her with a hand on her arm. Buffy strikes out at him to free herself, and he hits her back. She stares at him in disbelief, unable to absorb this injury added to insult.

Faith makes it to the office, where she runs into another figure in the dark. It's Wesley, who asks her about Angel's whereabouts. Downstairs Angel and Buffy are talking across a chasm of completely different intentions. Angel is dedicated to redeeming Faith, leading her down the path he is oh-so-familiar with.

> **ANGEL:** "I know Faith did some bad things to you."
> **BUFFY:** "You can't possibly know."
> **ANGEL:** "You can't possibly know what she's going through."
> **BUFFY:** "But of course, you do. I'm sorry. I can't be in your club. I've never murdered anybody."

Hurried footsteps on the stairs prevent the debate from deteriorating any farther, as Wesley escorts Faith down with a hand on her back, instructing her to get her coat from Angel's bedroom. Wesley shows the syringe to Angel and warns him the Council members will arrive in about twenty minutes. Buffy is fully aware of how skilled the operatives are, having been captured by them while in Sunnydale. The three realize Faith has somehow slipped past them.

Wesley explains to Angel why he is protecting the woman who brutally tortured him the previous evening.

> **WESLEY:** "It wasn't for her."
> **ANGEL:** "I know."
> **WESLEY:** "It's because I trust *you*. More than three gun-toting maniacs, at any rate."

Lindsey, meanwhile, has decided to use old-fashioned legal intervention to stop Angel and Faith. He goes to the police station and tells Kate that Angel is harboring Faith, and that gets her attention. Except Faith isn't actually technically with Angel anymore. She is on the rooftop, with Buffy close behind. Faith is willing to accept blame for her misdeeds, but she doesn't think that Buffy will be satisfied with anything less than her death. Their argument is interrupted by the sudden spraying of machine-gun fire—the Watchers Council has arrived. Buffy dives for cover, instinctively taking Faith with her.

Angel and Wesley are intercepted en route to the roof by a little bullet action of their own, courtesy of Weatherby. When Wesley protests that he has not given the signal, Weatherby dismisses him and turns on Angel with an evil, delirious grin, crossbow and cross in hand.

Buffy and Faith are pinned by gunfire, but Wesley manages to throw the syringe at Weatherby, making a perfect dart toss into the man's neck. As Weatherby staggers under the influence of a sedative strong enough for a Slayer, Wesley assists him to the ground via a fist to the face while Angel goes to help Buffy and Faith.

Buffy leaps from behind the barricade and attacks Collins. He fails to hold his own against the Slayer and goes down for the count just as an approaching helicopter hovers to give the operative Smith a clear shot. Time is suspended for a moment before Angel achieves his rooftop goal and leaps at the helicopter, which rocks under the impact. In one continuous motion, Angel takes out Smith, morphs into vamp face, and orders the stunned pilot to take the helicopter down. The immediate threats gone, Buffy looks for Faith, who has gone AWOL.

As the helicopter reaches a nearby parking lot, several police cars pull up. Kate gets out of her unmarked car and confronts Angel with Faith's photograph, demanding to know her whereabouts. When Angel is nonresponsive, Kate barks an order to one of the officers to arrest him.

Wesley and Buffy arrive at the precinct in the Angelmobile mere moments behind Kate and the handcuffed vampire.

> **KATE:** "I think you're going to like the cell we have for you, Angel. Faces east. Give you a great view of the sunrise in about . . . four hours."
> **BUFFY:** "What?"
> **ANGEL:** "It's okay."
> **BUFFY:** "You know what he is?"
> **KATE:** "Who are you?"
> **ANGEL:** "She's nobody."

Buffy, who's been feeling exactly like she's "nobody" where Angel is concerned, doesn't appreciate that at all, but it doesn't stop her from protesting that Angel shouldn't be endangering himself on Faith's behalf. They argue all the way down the hall into the squad room, where they fall silent. Faith is seated at Kate's desk, with an officer standing over her, starting her paperwork. She stands, and when Kate reaches her, says, "I'd like to make a confession."

RESOLUTION

With Faith in custody, Kate is forced to set Angel free. He and Buffy head out of the precinct, resuming their unfinished disagreement. Buffy slams him for not being more forthcoming with her about what was happening, and he counters that it was none of her business.

> **ANGEL:** "Buffy, this wasn't about you! This was about saving someone's soul. That's what I do here and you're not a part of it. That was your idea, remember. We stay away from each other."
> **BUFFY:** "I came here because you were in danger."
> **ANGEL:** "I'm in danger every day. You came because of Faith. You were looking for vengeance."
> **BUFFY:** "I have a right to it."
> **ANGEL:** "Not in my city."

Stung, Buffy attacks again.

> **BUFFY:** "You know, I have someone in my life now. That I love. It's not what we had; it's very new. You know what makes it new? I trust him. I know him."
> **ANGEL:** "That's great. That's nice. You've moved on. I can't. You've found someone new.

I'm not allowed to. Remember? I see you again it cuts me up inside and the person I share that with is me. You don't know me anymore so don't come down here with your great new life and expect me to do things your way. Go home."

Buffy fires a parting shot about Faith winning again after all. After she leaves, Angel punches a wall in frustration.

Wesley compliments him on believing in Faith, and they share the hope that the inner strength that got Faith into the police station will hold strong and enable her to find peace.

As the sun rises, Faith sits quietly in her cell.

Case closed.

DOSSIERS

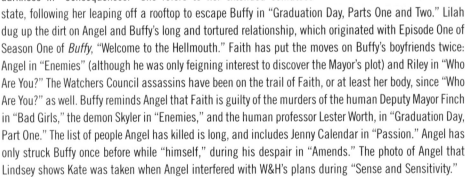

SUSPECTS Collins, Weatherby, and **Smith** plan to take out the rogue Slayer and "the vampire" by enlisting Wesley's help. **Lindsey, Lilah,** and **Lee** finally try to make the letter of the law work for them.

CONTINUITY

Angel reminds Faith of his previous attempt at reaching her in the darkness in "Consequences." She refers to her extended comatose state, following her leaping off a rooftop to escape Buffy in "Graduation Day, Parts One and Two." Lilah dug up the dirt on Angel and Buffy's long and tortured relationship, which originated with Episode One of Season One of *Buffy*, "Welcome to the Hellmouth." Faith has put the moves on Buffy's boyfriends twice: Angel in "Enemies" (although he was only feigning interest to discover the Mayor's plot) and Riley in "Who Are You?" The Watchers Council assassins have been on the trail of Faith, or at least her body, since "Who Are You?" as well. Buffy reminds Angel that Faith is guilty of the murders of the human Deputy Mayor Finch in "Bad Girls," the demon Skyler in "Enemies," and the human professor Lester Worth, in "Graduation Day, Part One." The list of people Angel has killed is long, and includes Jenny Calendar in "Passion." Angel has only struck Buffy once before while "himself," during his despair in "Amends." The photo of Angel that Lindsey shows Kate was taken when Angel interfered with W&H's plans during "Sense and Sensitivity."

QUOTE OF THE WEEK

"Well, if it's any consolation, it really does look like you were tortured by a much larger woman."

Cordelia tries to smooth Wesley's ruffled ego.

THE DEVIL IS IN THE DETAILS

WEAPONRY

In a vision, Faith wields a bowie knife, and later keeps a tight grip on a real kitchen knife. Wesley wields a syringe loaded with knockout drugs. Police cars with weapons come at the Slayers, as do Council operatives with machine guns.

DEMONS, DEMONS, DEMONS

Wolfram & Hart sends a **killer bug demon** after Faith and Angel, but it's not up to the task.

THE PEN IS MIGHTIER

POP CULTURE

❋ KENDRICK: "Come on, Kate. Everyone knows you've gone all Scully. Anytime one of these weird cases crosses anyone's desk, you're always there. We used to be friends—what's going on with you?"

KATE: "Scully's the skeptic."

KENDRICK: "Hunh?"

KATE: "Mulder's the believer. Scully's the skeptic."

Down at the precinct, Kate gets hassled by a fellow officer, but she corrects his *X-Files* reference.

OUR HEROES

"There was a scene where it starts with Faith asking about how to work the microwave oven, and then Angel explaining, basically giving this big AA sponsor speech to her. We shot that scene twice, and we did not change a word of it. But we just wanted them to play it differently. The one that we ended up putting in the show is entirely different from the first version that we shot of that scene. Without having changed a word.

"We just weren't getting the pain in the first version. It was a little too glib. And we lost the glibness and played the pain, and suddenly the scene worked.

"That show [was] also, incredibly short. So in order to make it long enough to air, I wrote three Wolfram & Hart scenes—where they hire a demon, where they regroup, pretty funny scenes with the three lawyers."

—TIM MINEAR

"We had prepped the entire show, and the great big finale scene was to take place on a rooftop with a helicopter. We had found our rooftop, we were all set to go, and two days before we started shooting we found out it wouldn't work after all [for some of the shots]. So we had to build a copy of the rooftop . . . in about three days, which was pretty amazing. And then Herb Davis, our DP, with his photography, was amazing. You really never knew when you were onstage or the rooftop. We did that with some visual effects tricks, where we had Sarah [Michelle Gellar] and Eliza Dushku on the fake rooftop, and with green screen we had the helicopter flying around. So that was pretty amazing."

—KELLY A. MANNERS, PRODUCER

"We figured out a way to shoot everything that involved the stunt with the real helicopter and the stunt-people on the rooftop in downtown Los Angeles, overlooking the city, and everything we shot there was going to be mostly looking away from the building, looking at the skyline of Los Angeles, and seeing the helicopter flying around firing down at the characters on the rooftop. And on stage we re-created it full scale, about a seventy-five-, eighty-foot-long rooftop on our stage, that we could put our actors

173

on and not have the challenge of being near the helicopter. And we were able to shoot both nights and marry the two together, and even on stage bring in helicopter skids attached to a crane and lower them down into frame. We used a big fan to simulate the helicopter wash from the blades, and it came out great. Much to everyone's surprise, it was fairly seamless."

—STUART BLATT, PRODUCTION DESIGNER

"Kate seems overly eager to get Angel into the system. For holding him accountable through her system, even threatening to put him in a cell facing the morning sun."

ELISABETH ROHM: "She adjusts to the knowledge that she's been imparted, but I think also when something comes into our lives and completely shakes our foundations . . . we can't do anything but accept it unless we're delusional, but then what do we do to get our footing back? We take control. We either become workaholics, or we take control of our life in some way. It's like, she lost her father, she lost her best friend, and now she's dealing with the fact that there's this whole supernatural world, and I think Kate's way of dealing with it is saying, 'Well, guess what, guys? You're still playing by my rules. Because, otherwise, what's the point of me even being here.' And that's her way of taking control and making things grounded again."

SIX DEGREES OF . . .

Eliza Dushku appeared in *Bring It On* with Clare Kramer, who played "Glory" on *Buffy the Vampire Slayer*, and with Nicole Bilderback, who played "Cordette #1" in "The Wish" on *Buffy*.

TRACKS

"When you have a scene with a character who appeared on Buffy, do you try to incorporate their established theme music, or compose something original?"

ROBERT KRAL: "'Sanctuary' was a new place for Faith. There was no looking at older themes for example. In fact the end of 'Five by Five' where Faith breaks down during a fight, into Angel's arms, we stop the fight music and the music disappears for the rest of the show. I felt that it was too huge a turning point to play music, that we needed to sit back and be totally stunned by what had happened. All this battle music, then nothing, just rain and tears. Faith has come to a new place, as Angel insisted she had good in her. For 'Sanctuary' there is a hint of a new [musical] theme for Faith, but it's very elementary, not developed, just in its beginnings if you will."

"WAR ZONE"

**FROM THE FILES OF ANGEL INVESTIGATIONS
CASE N°: 1ADH20**

ACTION TAKEN

A pretty young woman walks down an alley in one of the many bad parts of Los Angeles. Beverly Hills this ain't. When she turns to retrace her steps at the alley's dead end, three vampires stand in her path. They gaze upon their prey, ready to begin their meal, when footsteps behind them distract them. They turn, and one vampire says, "You," with no surprise but an element of worry.

Charles Gunn bars their way. He is dressed for battle, armed with a sword. Several other youths stand behind him, also bearing weaponry that's unconventional for the street, but just what the Slayer ordered for vampires. Behind them is a massive truck that has seen better days but is built to last. The truck is also armed with a gun and long stakes.

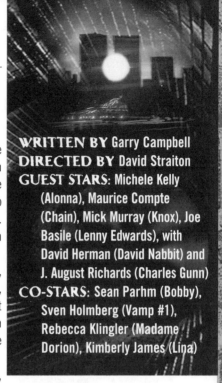

WRITTEN BY Garry Campbell
DIRECTED BY David Straiton
GUEST STARS: Michele Kelly (Alonna), Maurice Compte (Chain), Mick Murray (Knox), Joe Basile (Lenny Edwards), with David Herman (David Nabbit) and J. August Richards (Charles Gunn)
CO-STARS: Sean Parhm (Bobby), Sven Holmberg (Vamp #1), Rebecca Klingler (Madame Dorion), Kimberly James (Lina)

In an entirely different, more upscale part of town, Cordelia is in her element as she leads Angel and Wesley through a penthouse party crowd to meet their new client, David Nabbit. Nabbit, a software billionaire and a complete social geek, is at ease with the knowledge that most of his guests are there because of his funds, not his sense of fun. It turns out Nabbit is being blackmailed, and Angel is probably the best-equipped detective in Los Angeles for the particular problem that his role-playing-game habit has landed him in.

> **NABBIT**: "I used to play a lot in high school. It's . . . It's pretty cool, you know, you . . . get to be someone else for a while. A wizard, a warrior . . . and the whole world is majick. Fighting troglodytes, romancing exotic demon princesses . . . it's a rush."
>
> **CORDELIA**: (sincerely) "Did someone find out you're a big nerd?"
>
> **NABBIT**: That's actually public record. But . . . some of us got really into it. Especially the demon romance part. Then we heard about this place where the real . . . the guys were joking about getting some 'tail.'"
>
> **WESLEY**: "You went to Madame Dorion's."
>
> **NABBIT**: "Just once."
>
> **WESLEY**: (to the others) "It's a demon brothel."
>
> **NABBIT**: "Or twice."

Wesley knows Madame Dorion's is in Bel Air, but swears he knows it only by repute through the Watchers Council. Nabbit produces a photograph of one Lenny Edwards, the blackmailer. Nabbit's people have been unable to locate him, and that's where Angel comes in.

Meanwhile, the encounter between Gunn's gang and the vampires has blown into an all-out brawl. The street kids try to avoid battling the vampires one-on-one, fighting several humans to a vamp whenever possible. Gunn's sister Alonna moves close to the "War Wagon" during the fighting. Bobby handles the gun on the War Wagon, providing backup to those on the ground and firing stakes when necessary. Unfortunately, while he is providing protection, he forgets to watch for attacks himself, and a vampire uses its supernatural strength to pull him from the wagon and fling him into a wall with a sickening impact. Alonna rushes to her fallen comrade, and the rest of Gunn's team gathers, allowing the surviving vamp to retreat quickly from the battlefield. Gunn's deputy, Chain, follows the vampire as the rest of them gather up their casualties and head home.

After stashing the War Wagon in a concealed location, the troops carry Bobby into the deserted industrial building they call home. Alonna stays at Bobby's side, offering what comfort she can, but Bobby dies.

Angel shows at Madame Dorion's, where human men mix with lingerie-clad female demons of all sorts. Madame Dorion is uninterested in giving Angel any information about Lenny Edwards, though, until Angel points out that if word got out Edwards is blackmailing one of her clients, it would likely have a negative effect on business. Her civic nature suddenly inspired, she directs Angel to a particular call demon, Lina.

Lina, an attractive demon with a head of porcupinelike quills rather than hair, takes an immediate professional interest in Angel. Her prehensile tail caresses him sensuously, going limp when he shows her the photo of Edwards.

Meanwhile, Alonna tries to talk to her brother about the chances the group has been taking. She's worried that Gunn's playing with fire, cheating death because he likes it, and she doesn't want to lose him.

They share a quick hug before Chain returns with the news that he has successfully tracked to its nest the vampire who killed Bobby. Gunn's eager response to the news suggests he hasn't taken Alonna's worries to heart, but there is no time for them to continue their talk, as another sentry brings news of an impending attack and Gunn moves to marshal the troops. Coincidentally, Gunn's neighborhood is Lenny Edwards's chosen hangout as well. Edwards is initially unimpressed by Angel, and shows little interest in cooperating in the matter of David Nabbit's photos. He warns Angel to back off. Angel vamps out to intimidate him, not realizing that Gunn and Chain are observing as he threatens to move into Edwards's neighborhood and take it over. The two vigilantes take note. . . .

Angel and Edwards meet at the arranged time, but Edwards has arrived with more than just photographs. He has enlisted the aid of a particularly large and unpleasant Mofo demon to eliminate Angel.

Angel and the demon fight, not using weapons, just punishing each other with supernatural brute strength. Edwards gets a nasty surprise when the demon flings Angel into *him*, sending him unconscious to the ground and allowing Angel to retrieve the photos. Angel finally manages to break the demon's neck, and then he wearily drops to his knees in the street.

A stake slams through Angel's shoulder from behind, and he is on his feet and on the run instantly, the War Wagon in close pursuit. Angel's evasive maneuvers successfully prevent Gunn and Chain from staking him with the War Wagon's guns, but they prod him into a warehouse filled with deadly traps, all set with the dusting of vampires in mind. Members of Gunn's gang attack, and Angel responds defensively, rather than counterattacking.

At the end of the gauntlet he literally runs into Alonna, and hangs on to her. As soon as Alonna breaks free, Angel is fair game again, and the members of the gang gather for the dusting. As Alonna steps back to give Gunn a clear line of fire, she triggers another hidden trap, and a silver spike shoots out, lethally fast, aimed for her head. Angel intercepts the spike, which lodges most of the way through his palm.

As Gunn and the others absorb the improbable fact that a vampire has just acted to save the life of one of their own, Angel takes advantage of their confusion to try to clarify that they are on the same side.

> **GUNN:** "What, you gonna pretend you're different from the rest of 'em?"
>
> **ANGEL:** "Yeah, then I'll just pretend I just saved her life."

Angel admires their handiwork and offers to give them some pointers, but a wary Gunn isn't interested. He warns Angel that while his life is spared this time, it won't happen if he is seen in the neighborhood again. Then he and his posse split.

A battered and bruised Angel returns to the office to hand over Nabbit's photos to Cordelia. Wesley examines them, turning them around to determine the best angle, while Cordy administers first aid to Angel, in bad shape but determined to find out more about the street kids he encountered.

While the local vamps work themselves up over the change in the playing field, in Gunn's crib, Alonna wonders if they shouldn't take Angel up on his offer of assistance. But Gunn isn't about to trust Angel, or treat him any differently than any other vampire, even at his beloved sister's request.

Angel makes his way through the all-important sewer access to discover the vampires' hideout. When he enters, it appears deserted. A lone sentry attacks Angel from above, but he shrugs off the attack and turns the tables, demanding to know the whereabouts of the rest of the nest.

The vampires have launched an unexpected daytime assault on Gunn's group. Smoke bombs throw the street kids into confusion and Gunn charges out of the hideout to the street, just as a van, blacked out vamp-style, pulls up behind the fleeing kids. The van's door opens, and vamps wearing serious protective sun gear grab Alonna and pull her in. As she screams her brother's name, the door slams and the van pulls away. Gunn catches up to it briefly, just long enough to get one last look at Alonna's face as the vampires bite into her.

Angel has located Gunn's hideout, and encourages him to take a moment to plan some strategy before he races after his sister. But Gunn's not having any of it.

> "I don't need advice from some middle-class white dude that's dead! You don't know what my life is. You got no idea what it's like down here."
>
> —*Gunn*

When Angel pushes the point, Gunn yanks on a rope that opens a window, sending a burst of sunlight striking at Angel. Angel jumps back from the direct sunlight, and Gunn and Chain follow up on their advantage, shoving him into an old meat locker and securing the door. Gunn grabs his weapon and marches out to battle.

Arriving at the vampires' nest, though, Gunn uncharacteristically tells the rest of his crew to hold back from their initial assault. He instructs Chain to wait ten minutes for him to scout ahead. When Gunn enters the vamp hideout, nothing moves at first. Then his sister steps into a patch of moonlight. His initial relief at seeing her deflates as he realizes she has been turned. Alonna tries to persuade Gunn to set down his burdens and join her in the war—from the other side. Gunn is dismayed at his ultimate failure to protect his sister from a fate worse than death. Alonna challenges him to kill her, but he can't bring himself to do it.

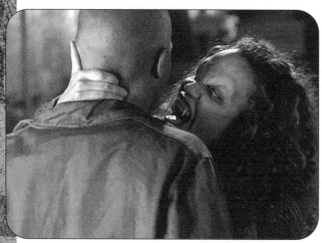

Angel has made painfully slow progress in escaping from the meat locker. Just as the door latch is finally within his grasp, Cordelia pulls it open for him and reminds him to use his cell phone more often. He takes off after Gunn.

Alonna uses her shared past with Gunn to tug at his heartstrings in the way only family can. She reminds him of foolish childhood stunts, and how he was always there to be the leader and to rescue her whenever she needed it. She tells him now she is the one in the leader's position, ready to come to his assistance. Gunn seems to have lost his hard edge, standing quietly as she morphs and moves in to bite him. Then he bids her a quiet good-bye and stakes her.

As the Alonna dust clears, Gunn sees Angel watching him commit his painful duty. All at once the hideout is filled with bodies as first Chain and the gang come in after Gunn, whose ten minutes are up, and then vamp leader Knox and the rest of his vamps converge. Knox focuses on Gunn and taunts him.

For a moment the warehouse breaks out into a full-on gang war face-off. Then Angel steps forward and announces the vamps have a choice: leave his town for the rest of their existence and survive, or else. Knox mocks him, so Angel stakes him and turns to the rest of the vamps, most of whom stare at him with a mixture of awe and fear. He offers them the choice again: truce or death. Chain objects, encouraging Gunn to rally the troops and fight, but Gunn is done for the evening.

Chain: "Gunn? You come all this way, you're not gonna kill any vamps?"

Gunn: "I already did."

And with that, Gunn departs, a reluctant Chain and the rest behind him. The vamps exit quickly as well.

RESOLUTION

Wesley and Cordelia enjoy a break from the office in one of Los Angeles's nicer outdoor locations and chat as Wesley tries to locate the actual coffee content in the foamy, creamy beverage he bought from a vendor. Cordelia comments on the sadness of people living in such dire circumstances, then suggests perhaps she will improve her own living conditions by prostituting herself to David Nabbit. Wesley chokes and says her name reprovingly, almost sure she isn't serious. She admits that even her financially oriented ethics wouldn't allow her to enter into such a relationship, since she's not big on overlooking what's on the surface of a person.

A few nights later, Gunn contemplates the L.A. skyline from a rooftop. When Angel joins him, they look silently out at the city for a moment.

GUNN: "She was the reason, man . . . How come you do it? How come you're out here?"

ANGEL: "What else are we gonna do?"

Another moment of silent gazing at the city, filled with demons.

ANGEL: "I'll be around."

GUNN: "I don't need no help."

ANGEL: "I might."

With that, Angel departs, leaving Gunn to the night and his thoughts.

Case closed.

DOSSIERS

CLIENT David Nabbit is a Bill Gates type—he has lots of brilliant ideas, but he's a nerd to the core. **Charles Gunn** regains his humanity as he looks for a new reason to go on.

CIVILIAN SUPPORT Chain is Gunn's right-hand man, an eager combatant in their battles against the undead. **Gunn's crew** fights vampires on the mean streets. **Lina**, one of Madame Dorion's girls, gives Angel some info on Lenny Edwards.

VICTIMS Alonna Gunn and **Bobby** fall prey to the vampires.

SUSPECTS Lenny Edwards is a two-bit hood who has discovered some of L.A.'s special inhabitants and only cares about their usefulness in his criminal activities. **Knox** and **his vampire gang** have enjoyed an extended reign as the top predators in their neighborhood until Gunn and Co. started fighting back.

CONTINUITY

Angel followed Buffy back to Sunnydale after "Sanctuary" and confronted her and Riley in "The Yoko Factor." Angel and Buffy reached a resolution in their relationship, acknowledging their existences are no longer tied together, and Angel has returned to L.A. Cordelia compares her first rathole apartment from "City Of" to Gunn's crew's neighborhood.

QUOTE OF THE WEEK

WESLEY: "You should have tried to call us on your cell phone. You probably forgot you had it."

ANGEL: "Those things hardly ever work. Besides, it was actually a lot easier and quicker to just . . ."

(mimes "punching," feels his wounded hand)

". . . look, I'm the boss here, I say when we use the cell phones and people are going to die and I have to go."

Wesley and Cordelia free Angel from his meat locker prison.

THE DEVIL IS IN THE DETAILS

WEAPONRY

The War Wagon, created by Gunn and his group, is tricked out with pneumatic stake-firing cannons. The posse also employs swords, crossbows, pikes, ball and chains, Gatling guns, and flamethrowers. They've set up tripwires with metal stakes. The vampires use tear gas and smoke bombs to confuse Gunn's people.

DEMONS, DEMONS, DEMONS

Madame Dorion's is a brothel staffed by **demon prostitutes**, mainly for the pleasure of human males. It's located in Bel Air, an upscale area of Los Angeles. One of its denizens, **Lina**, is a demon with quills for hair and a very talented tail. Most of the demons are reasonably humanoid, all are lithe and clad only in lingerie.

The **Mofo demon** Lenny Edwards brings along to his meeting with Angel is huge and silent, strong enough to stand up to Angel's best shots. He even manages to crack a few of Angel's ribs before he's finally brought down.

THE VAMPIRE RULES

As has been previously noted, vampires are looked down upon by other types of demons. They're not even welcome at demon-run brothels.

> **MADAME DORION:** "We don't do vampires. Sorry."
> **ANGEL:** "I just came to talk."
> **MADAME DORION:** "We don't do that, either."

THE PEN IS MIGHTIER

FINAL CUT

Gunn is introduced this way in the script:

We start in low and see a pair of black leather boots walk into frame. We move up to reveal black leather pants and the bottom of a long black coat.

We move up further to reveal a gloved hand holding a drawn sword. The camera moves all the way up to reveal, not Angel, but a YOUNG MAN. Hard beyond his years. This is CHARLES GUNN. Standing behind and to the sides of him now are FOUR SIMILARLY HARD LOOKING YOUTHS. One holds a crossbow, two are holding nasty looking pikes, and the fifth, CHAIN, holds a nasty length of chain with a spiked ball on it.

Idling behind them is a crappy but tricked out, old pickup truck with a Gatling gun on the bed, aimed over the cab, and stake pikes on either side. Off this stand off of the Mexican variety . . .

POP CULTURE

❋ **NABBIT:** "Are you familiar with Dungeons and Dragons?"
ANGEL: "I've seen a few."
WESLEY: "You mean the role-playing game."
ANGEL: "Oh. Game. Right. Heh."

David Nabbit refers to the extremely popular role-playing game.

OUR HEROES

"What was the most challenging scene for you so far?"

J. AUGUST RICHARDS: "The scene where I had to kill my sister. That was the most challenging scene. Because it was my first day, it was the first thing I had ever shot on this show. And the pressure was just so great, in terms of what the character was going through. It was so hard. I think it

was a great moment for me, because right before I did it, I discovered that my objective throughout the whole piece was to protect my sister. And in killing her, I think he felt that that was the last act of protection. So that's how I looked at it. So he was still doing something very heroic. It was still a positive thing, because in his framework, her being a vampire is just about as bad as it gets. So he had to do it."

"Do you think there was any waffling, where he tried to figure out how to spare her?"

J. AUGUST RICHARDS: "Absolutely. I think that whole scene, I was spending the whole scene trying to figure out. Eriq La Salle told me, he said 'You can never reach the climax until you've exhausted every other possibility.' So throughout the scene, I think I was looking for things to see that my sister was still there. But when I saw that face, that's when I realized she was gone, and that's when I realized I had to kill her."

Transportation coordinator Robert Ellis talks about creating the War Wagon:

"They picked a common truck that everybody from eight to eighty could identify with and not go too far back in the past. They didn't want too much of a character vehicle. They wanted to give it character by the people and the instruments they put on it. Then, we got a little sketch of what they wanted to do. So the effects and property departments put the instruments together to attach to the vehicle. The only thing we had to do with that was make sure that they weren't drilling through any wires or anything that was going to impair the use of the vehicle. And we put our practical knowledge into that too, and said, 'Don't mount a stake right here, because you won't be able to see.' The Gunn truck we ended up using without a windshield and without a door on its first appearance. As the series went on, the windshield came back and the door came back, for practical reasons and safety reasons. The more action they use, the more doors and windows were applied again. So the people weren't strewn all over."

—ROBERT ELLIS

TRACKS

The song "Para Lennon y McCartney," by A Friend From Rio, is heard in this episode. It can be found on the Guidance Recordings compilation CD *Hi-Fidelity Lounge*.

"BLIND DATE"

FROM THE FILES OF ANGEL INVESTIGATIONS
CASE Nº: 1ADH21

ACTION TAKEN

A blind woman walks down a busy city street, tapping her traditional red-tipped white cane before her. A street merchant hustles his wares out of her way to let her pass. In a nearby building, a major battle rages between Angel and two other vampires. They're tough; he's tougher. He manages to stake one of them the traditional way, dusting him. The second, he catches up in a chain and pulley system. Angel hoists the struggling vampire into the air and across the warehouse, ramming him into a protruding wooden beam. Before Angel can appreciate his victory, though, he hears a human scream from nearby.

WRITTEN by Jeannine Renshaw
DIRECTED BY Thomas J. Wright
GUEST STARS: Christian Kane (Lindsey McDonald), Thomas Burr (Lee Mercer), Stephanie Romanov (Lilah Morgan), Sam Anderson (Holland Manners), and J. August Richards (Charles Gunn)
CO-STARS: Jennifer Badger Martin (Vanessa Weeks), Keilana Smith (Mind Reader #1), Dawn Suggs (Mind Reader #2)

He rushes to help—and sees an injured man stumbling down some stairs. Angel goes to the man's side, just in time to see him die. Before Angel can really react, someone attacks him from behind—it's the blind woman from the street. She's remarkably powerful, fast, and skilled. And at one point, when she ducks a kick, her dark glasses fall off and Angel sees her eyes—milky white, glowing, almost luminous. She really is blind. So how can she fight like that?

She throws him across the room, and when he gets up, she's gone.

Back at the office, Wesley and Cordelia throw around some theories.

> **WESLEY:** "Of course . . . it's possible she's not a demon at all."
> **CORDELIA:** "You think?"
> **WESLEY:** "Perhaps she's simply learned to hone her senses around her disability. . . .
>   Angel said it was as if she anticipated his actions before he carried them out."
> **CORDELIA:** "A handy skill—in a fight or on a date."

Cordelia accesses the LAPD's online files and finds a criminal record for the mystery assailant. Her name is Vanessa Brewer. She has been arrested several times for a variety of crimes ranging from simple misdemeanor to aggravated assault, and she's currently standing trial for a double homicide, though she's apparently out on bail at this time.

Her lawyers—a surprise to no one—are Wolfram & Hart. Specifically, Angel's old adversary Lindsey McDonald is handling her case. His defense seems to be unbeatable—she's blind and helpless.

But during the trial, Angel walks through the courtroom door and hurls something at her. She doesn't even turn, just shoots her arm into the air and snags it. Clearly, she possesses special abilities. Nevertheless, Lindsey manages to get her off. When Angel discovers that the firm represented her for free, he figures she's working for them. She's not just a blind killer, she's a blind killer for hire.

In Wolfram & Hart's plush office building, attorney Lee Mercer teases Lindsey about his victory in court. Vanessa has been cleared of all charges and Lindsey's suddenly the golden boy of the firm. They both watch her in a discussion with Holland Manners and some of the other W&H brass. Then Holland calls Lindsey into the conference room. Vanessa thanks Lindsey, shaking his hand and holding it for a beat or two longer than is strictly necessary. When she and the other attorneys have left, Holland asks Lindsey to hang back.

He tells Lindsey that he's concerned about the young lawyer. He's been working hard, putting in hours, but his performance hasn't been everything that it should be, the Vanessa Brewer case notwithstanding. And he's noticed that Lindsey hasn't seemed happy lately. He doesn't think Lindsey will be happy until he's found his "place in the scheme of things." Lecture finished, he gets down to business.

HOLLAND: "I don't think she had a very happy childhood."

LINDSEY: "Sir?"

HOLLAND: "Our blind friend, Vanessa. I think she was terribly abused growing up. I
     think the details of that are tragic and shockingly specific, and I think you should
     create them, sooner rather than later."

Lindsey figures out where Holland's going with this.

LINDSEY: "She's going to do something else that may require a strong defense."

HOLLAND: "A strong defense, alibis, creative alternatives to incarceration. She's an
     invaluable tool to some of our most important clients, so we can't risk losing her."

LINDSEY: "What's she going to do?"

HOLLAND: "There are some children arriving . . . they pose a threat."

Lindsey is taken aback, but Holland refuses to elaborate on the plan. Back at his office, Angel is furious, raging. The Wolfram & Hart types, the lawyers, run the courts. That isn't a world in which he can move, or over which he has any sway. He can work the streets, but he can't affect the justice system. Lindsey McDonald enters the office, interrupting his rant. He tells Angel he needs his help: he wants out.

Angel, of course, doesn't believe him for a second. Lindsey launches into a soliloquy about his background, how poor his family was.

LINDSEY: "I'm talking dirt poor, no shoes, no toilet, six of us kids in a room and come
     flu season that went down to four. I was seven when they took the house, they just
     came right in and took it. My daddy's being nice, you know, joking with the bastards
     while he signs the deed. Yeah, we had a choice: you got stepped on or you got to
     steppin'. I swore to myself I wouldn't be the guy standing there with a stupid grin on
     my face while my life got dribbled out—"

ANGEL: "I nodded off. Did you get to the part where you're evil?"

Lindsey changes tactics. He tells Angel about the new target Vanessa's been given—the children.

But he's short on details. "Some kids from overseas," he says. "Job's in a couple of days." He tells Angel that there should be files, in a vault at Wolfram & Hart, but nothing to which he'd have easy access.

> **LINDSEY**: "They are constantly watching you. Other companies have drug testing; they have mind readers. I go back there they're gonna kill me."
>
> **ANGEL**: "That's what we call an acceptable risk."

Together they develop a plan to get past the W&H security. Lindsey's pass will get Angel into the vault, but there's no sewer access to the building, so Angel will have to cut his way through from the tunnels. Once he's in the vault, there's a Pregotthian demon to contend with. And to top it off, Security has a shaman who can sense the moment a vampire crosses the threshold.

Angel tells him not to worry about that.

Later, Angel pays a visit to Gunn, and manages to talk Gunn into doing him a favor by promising that it'll be extremely dangerous. Gunn's face lights up at the news, and he agrees.

The next day, Lindsey strides through the luxurious Wolfram & Hart lobby, passing fellow attorneys and uniformed security guards. He's nervous but tries to maintain his cool. He heads for the elevators, but instead of going up as he usually does, he pushes the down button. Below, in a sewer tunnel, Angel works with a welding torch, cutting a passage from the sewers into the W&H boiler room, which is opposite the vault.

In the hallway downstairs, Lindsey—clearly feeling under some pressure, skulking about in areas he doesn't usually frequent—is surprised by Lilah Morgan's emergence from a door marked BACK RECORDS. She's as startled as he is, and they both make nervous small talk for a moment before she hurries on her way. He goes into the records office for long enough to throw her off the track, and then comes out again. Passing a wall-mounted fire extinguisher, he removes his badge and sticks it on the bottom of the extinguisher unit.

Back in the tunnel, Angel cuts all the way through, grasps the piece he's cut out with a suction device, and prepares to remove it.

Lindsey heads back up to an upper floor, beginning to sweat from the stress.

And Angel removes his coveralls. Underneath, he's dressed like a lawyer. He's even brought a briefcase, though it's empty. He checks his watch. It's 12:15.

Lindsey walks into the security office to ask a guard some questions about a home security system. The shaman, a hooded, white-skinned demon, sits silently in a nearby chair. The guard can watch events all over the building on his bank of security monitors, and a computerized voice alerts him to various events. As they talk, Lindsey looks at his watch. 12:16.

At that moment, he sees, on one of the guard's monitors, the front door to the building open up and Gunn walks though, whooping and shouting noisily, a one-man distraction. "Oh, I get it," he shouts. "You'll cater to the demon, cater to the dead man, but <u>what about the black man</u>?"

It's 12:17. Angel climbs through the hole he's cut, into Wolfram & Hart territory. At the same moment, two men from Gunn's crew carry a bundle in the front door.

In the security office, the demonic shaman emits bizarre squealing noises that the guard interprets as meaning there's a vampire on the premises. He telephones an alert.

And in the lobby, Gunn cuts away the ropes on the blanket-wrapped bundle. A vampire scrambles out, wild-eyed. Guards draw stakes and chase him. Lindsey, monitoring things from the security office, manages to change the channel on the screen that shows Angel picking up his badge from the fire extinguisher, then leaves the guard to do his job.

The guards in the lobby dust the vampire. But there's still one more in the building, unknown to anyone. Angel opens the vault, and the Pregotthian demon guard rushes him. He punches it once, but it gets back up for more. When it comes at Angel this time, he blows a powder off the palm of his hand, paralyzing the thing. Then he pushes it over backward with a gentle shove, saying, "Thank you, Wesley." He goes into the vault, filled with all sorts of strange artifacts.

Upstairs, Lindsey has reached his usual stomping grounds. As he heads for his office, he feels a hand grabbing his shoulder—Lee Mercer. Mercer has heard about the commotion downstairs, and they chat for a moment before parting.

Angel has found what he's looking for, an array of computer disks. Rather than search through them looking for the right one, he just takes them all, tossing them into his empty briefcase. But on his way out, his gaze is caught by an unusual, ornately decorated metal tube, resting alone on a wooden stand. He looks at it for a moment, strangely drawn to it. Then, unable to resist, he picks it up from the stand.

Sirens blare. A metal grate begins to drop from the ceiling. Indiana Jones-style, Angel throws himself to the floor, sliding beneath the grate just before it clangs to the floor.

On his way out of the building, Angel calls Lindsey's cell phone with a simple message. "We're done," he says. "Get out now."

Lindsey tries to do just that, but the way is blocked by uniformed security. They knock on doors, bringing lawyers out into the office. Lindsey runs into Lilah, who says, "Can you believe this? It's a sweep." They're joined by Mercer, and the three of them see Holland Manners escort two mind readers into a conference room.

The attorneys of Wolfram & Hart are being subjected to surprise mind readings. Lilah, Lee, and Lindsey line up, and the mind readers step from person to person, scrutinizing each. Finishing the group, they talk briefly with Holland Manners. Then he turns away from them, toward the assembled lawyers, and expresses his profound disappointment at being betrayed by one of them. As he speaks, he stands before Lindsey, but then he moves at the last moment and finishes in front of Lee Mercer. Mercer, it seems, has been in secret negotiations with a rival law firm. He protests, but to no avail. Holland nods to an armed guard who has stepped up behind Lee, and the guard shoots him in the head. Blood splashes onto Lindsey's face and suit.

Holland dismisses the rest of them, but asks Lindsey to stay behind.

Angel makes it back to his office, a little surprised that Lindsey isn't already there. He doesn't waste time worrying about him, though. If he makes it out, okay, if he doesn't, that's okay too. He got the files, which is the important thing. He dumps all the disks onto Cordy's desk, and she starts going through them, looking for the one out of all of them that is germane to the case.

Wesley sees the tube that Angel has also acquired. He opens the tube and removes an ancient scroll. He gives it a quick once-over.

WESLEY: "Was there a reason you took this?"

ANGEL: "Yeah."

WESLEY: "And that would be . . . ?"

ANGEL: "I . . . I don't really know."

Wesley announces that he'll begin translating it, but before he can start Cordelia wants some help translating files—they're all encrypted.

In the Wolfram & Hart conference room, Holland reveals that he knows what Lindsey has been up to, and he's not happy about it. But he's not going to have Lindsey killed, at least not just now. He's going to give Lindsey a few days to think about what he's done, and he believes that Lindsey will do what's right. Lindsey is amazed that his life is being spared, after what happened to Lee Mercer for a much lesser transgression. Holland explains that he believes in Lindsey.

Cordelia is on the phone with Willow Rosenberg, back in Sunnydale, picking her brain for decryption advice. And it works—even long distance, Willow knows her way around a PC. Cordelia finds a personnel file for Vanessa Brewer, and reports on it. The woman blinded herself at age twenty-five. She spent five years in Pajaur, studying with the monks of the order of the Nanjin. Wesley knows who they are: "Cave dwelling monks. They believe enlightenment is seeing with the heart, not the mind."

Then they find the details of Vanessa's current target: three blind children, seers, each found in a different remote location and brought together in Los Angeles for the first time.

Lindsey walks in. He's greeted coolly by the others, and then it's back to business. The children have already arrived in the city. They're being kept in a safe house until a mentor arrives for them, and he's scheduled to show up that night. But Wolfram & Hart knows the address of the safe house, which makes it not safe at all. Angel instructs Wesley and Cordelia to find a way to stall the mentor, while he and Lindsey collect the kids.

But he may be a little late. The guardian taking care of the kids in the safe house is unexpectedly run through—with a red-tipped white cane—and killed. Vanessa Brewer has come to visit.

Angel and Lindsey show up before she can do any more damage, and there's another fight. As before, she can anticipate Angel's moves. The kids are terrified, and Lindsey tries to work his way to them, to calm them or get them to safety. Then Angel rushes her and she slams him into a wall, and he goes down.

And she can't "see" him while he's not moving. He sees the panic on her face when she "loses" him. So he uses that to his advantage, attacking and then freezing. With no heartbeat, no breath, to give him away, when he freezes he's completely invisible to her. Vanessa begins to panic, waving her cane around.

And this time, when she thrusts it out, Angel catches it, turns it around on her, and shoves it through her. She collapses, dead, to the floor.

Lindsey reaches the kids, reassuring them.

RESOLUTION

In his office, Wesley tells Angel that the kids are safe with their mentor. He's glad to hear it. Wesley also shows Angel the scroll, telling him that this is how Wolfram & Hart knew of the children's coming. Angel asks what it is.

> "If I'm right . . . it's the Prophecies of Aberjian. For centuries thought lost. I've translated some of the text. As I said, it mentions the children you saved today. But that's not all . . . I also believe I know why you were drawn to it. There's an entire passage. About you. It doesn't call you by name, but it tells of a vampire with a soul."
> — *Wesley*

Angel doesn't seem particularly surprised by this. He didn't know . . . but somehow he did.

At Wolfram & Hart, Lindsey walks into Holland Manners's office as a crew of movers take boxes out of it. Only a desk, chair, and telephone remain—and Holland Manners. Holland understands that Lindsey did the noble thing by saving the children—though the noble thing, of course, is not in Wolfram & Hart's best financial interests. He is also certain that, while Lindsey brought back the disks Angel stole, Lindsey kept copies of them. "Just enough to keep me safe," Lindsey confirms.

Holland understands that Lindsey has changed, although not necessarily in the way that he would have liked to have seen.

> "I hand picked you when you were a sophomore at Hastings. Not because you were smart, not because you were a poor kid who had to do better than everyone else—because you had potential— potential for seeing things as they are. It's not about good or evil, it's about who wields the power, and we wield a lot of it here and you know what? I think the world's better for it."
> — *Holland*

Then Holland offers him a new job—Holland's own job, in fact, as Holland's also being promoted. He leaves Lindsey alone in the office to think about it. Lindsey looks out the expansive windows at the glittering city below, looks at the doorway that leads out, to a different kind of life, looks at the broad desk and plush chair. And he makes his choice. He sits down.

In another part of the city, Angel looks out at a similar view, with an entirely different sense of purpose. Case closed.

DOSSIERS

CLIENT Lindsey McDonald comes to Angel to enlist the vampire's help getting out of Wolfram & Hart. His employers have finally gone over the line—even for him—with their plot to kill three innocent children. Angel has a hard time believing that Lindsey is ready to change—and his skepticism is prophetic in the end.

CIVILIAN SUPPORT Gunn is unwilling to help Angel at first, when he knows Angel is working with Lindsey. But upon hearing the news that the job will be dangerous, he's on board 100 percent.

SUSPECTS Vanessa Brewer is blind but obviously quite capable of death and destruction. (Deceased.) She's only a weapon, though, aimed and launched by the machinations of **Holland Manners**, who shows here that he's an astute judge of character as well as being exceedingly sinister. (Remains at large.)

CONTINUITY

Cordelia and Willow's techie exchange includes Cordelia's discovery that Willow has been decrypting the disks Adam fed to the Sunnydale Scoobies, via Spike, in "The Yoko Factor" and "Primeval." Lee Mercer seems to have recovered nicely from Faith's beating in "Five by Five," for all the good it does him. Angel's impulse to relieve W&H of the Scroll of Aberjian as well as the disks Lindsey stipulated will have far-reaching consequences, beginning in "To Shanshu in L.A."

QUOTE OF THE WEEK

"Well, my God. They told me it was true—I didn't believe 'em—but damn, here it is. Evil white folks really DO have a Mecca!"

Gunn's job is to create a distraction and to bring a vampire into \Wolfram & Hart to throw off the vampire-detecting shaman. He succeeds admirably.

THE DEVIL IS IN THE DETAILS

EXPENSES

Welding torch
Lawyer-looking suit and briefcase

WEAPONRY

Gunn has his stakes, his hydraulic stake gun, and billy clubs with stake inserts. Chain, pulley, and a wooden beam are in the game while Angel and Vanessa battle. Wesley gives Angel some red demon-paralyzing powder to use on the guard at W&H. Gunn's got a gun. Vanessa has a white cane, sharpened to a death-dealing point.

THE PLAN

"There is a design, Angel. Hidden in the chaos as it may be. But it's there. And you have your place in it." Wesley tells Angel about the discovery he's made in the scroll, and Angel's apparent place in the prophecy.

DEMONS, DEMONS, DEMONS

A **Pregotthian demon** guards the vault at Wolfram & Hart.
Wolfram & Hart have a **shaman** who can tell when a vampire enters the premises.

THE VAMPIRE RULES

Angel can smell fear on people.

THE PEN IS MIGHTIER

FINAL CUT

The initial fight between Angel and two vampires was written in the script as ending in a fiery conflagration of sparks, as Angel snaps a power line while the two vamps stand in puddles. Following the description of this elaborate fight is this note:

(NOTE TO PRODUCTION: If the vamp-b-que is too expensive or a massive pain in the ass, please have Spiro create a badass Angel vs. The Two Vamps fight.)

It apparently was, but Season One stunt coordinator Spiro Razatos came through.

When Vanessa sees, the effect is described in the script as ". . . like Kurlian photography. Videolike, brilliant fluorescent-colored outlines with people more bright and vivid than objects. Angel's movement sends a tail of light, like a comet."

POP CULTURE

❅ Discussing Vanessa's superhuman skills, Wesley tries to explain how it might work.

> **WESLEY:** "The human eye is only capable of registering a small portion of the electromagnetic spectrum. But if Brewer were somehow equipped to see outside that range . . ."
>
> **CORDELIA:** "She'd be Superman."

Not really—as described, Vanessa's powers much more closely resemble those of Daredevil, the Marvel Comics character known as The Man Without Fear. His secret identity is Matt Murdock, blind lawyer, and what the bad guys don't know is that he really is blind, but his other senses—as Wesley speculates at one point—have become superhumanly sharpened to make up for the loss of his sight.

OUR HEROES

"David's got the cool role, let's be honest. It's his show and he's a badass, but . . . he doesn't get to have the range that Lindsey does, because Lindsey's human, and he's got all this stuff. He does get to play it, but he can't really show a weak side. But I can do that all in one episode, and that's what's so fun about my character that I get to play. There's so much stuff that happens to Lindsey when he's by himself, so he gets to play that without even saying any words. It's the writing. I think my character's popular because of . . . Tim Minear's writing. I think a lot of it has to do with the episode 'Blind Date' last year . . . because . . . he joined the good side, so you're always rooting for him. And then a lot of people still want him bad. So it's kind of cool. What I like about this episode [was that] he's on the good side now, but he's still bad."

—CHRISTIAN KANE

"I was sort of a little character, and they didn't really sign me on long term. So nobody really knew what was coming next. It was sort of week to week. And I remember thinking that when I got smashed by Faith, I kind of thought that was the end. And then, while we were rehearsing, I think David mentioned something that happened in the next episode with me in a neck brace, and I was like, oh, I guess I'm gonna be around next week. And it was kind of like that. So when I finally died—you also figure, hey, it's a vampire show. I can always show up in Hell."

—THOMAS BURR

Property master Courtney Jackson described what went into creating the Scroll of Aberjian, which Angel stole from Wolfram & Hart:

"This is actually in Aramaic. We did a little research on the Internet and we got some examples of what Aramaic looked like, and this is more or less the Lord's Prayer over and over and over. Maxine Miller, who's this incredible illustration artist, does a lot of illustrations for us. So we'll sort of sit down and design together based on what the director wants, and what they're going to shoot. I picked out these different symbols from things that I've seen, or we created them together, and we sort of figured out the layout of what it would be like. Usually I'll come up with sort of a concept and run it by David Greenwalt or Joss Whedon or one of our directors and make sure that everybody's on the same page. It's just a lot of handwork.

"At one point in the script, it was torn in half. And they took that out, and instead it got lit on fire slightly. So it got singed a little. But we made these ourselves. And what I did was, I actually scanned parts of this into the computer and then printed them out on parchment. And then we took a scroll of paper, and just distressed that, and just the edge, then, would have this on it. But there is only one, and we just coffee-stain it and age it until it looks old. Rumpling it, and tearing pieces out of it, even though it kills you. And then it becomes this very delicate thing." —COURTNEY JACKSON, PROPERTY MASTER

"Lindsey, I love to dress. He's the guy. He is the total player of the show. So I have suits made for him from Italy. And I have this company in Beverly Hills called Rigatti, and they make me the most beautiful, hand-made Italian suits that I get for seven hundred dollars. An amazing price, and they're perfect for him. Stature wise, he's not real tall, and he's got a great body. He wants to show it off, even in the suits. So my cutter/fitter, Wendy, who is fabulous, recuts all of his shirts, even though you don't see them under the suit unless he takes his jacket off, and makes them fit him perfect. That's what our job is. I like a complete look. Don't just put a suit on, I want that suit to look phenomenal on you."

—CHIC GENNARELLI, COSTUME DESIGNER

SIX DEGREES OF . . .

Jennifer Badger Martin, who plays Vanessa—and more than holds her own in combat against Angel—is a stuntwoman as well as an actress. She is often credited as Jennifer Badger. She has worked as a stunt double for Cordelia, Jenny Calendar, and Drusilla on *Buffy* as well as doing stunts on *Angel*. She also did stunts in the 1997 horror hit *Scream 2*, in which Sarah Michelle Gellar played a featured role.

Derek Anthony, the man Vanessa Brewer kills in the beginning (credited in the cast list as "Dying Black Man,") comes back to life in Season Two to play a hotel security guard in the episode "Dear Boy."

"TO SHANSHU IN L.A."

FROM THE FILES OF ANGEL INVESTIGATIONS
CASE № 1ADH22

ACTION TAKEN

Angel, Cordelia, and Wesley are in the office, each bent over different reading material. Cordy has a newspaper, Angel has a book, and Wesley is straining his eyes and mind over the nearly incomprehensible Scroll of Aberjian. The term "shanshu" seems to be proving to be his Waterloo of translations. Wesley is concerned, because "shanshu" is the pivotal word in the part of the prophecies related to the fate of the vampire with a soul, as Angel is referred to in the prophecies. When Cordy asks what's taking him so long, he snaps at her.

WRITTEN AND DIRECTED BY David Greenwalt
GUEST STARS: Elisabeth Rohm (Kate Lockley), Christian Kane (Lindsey McDonald), Stephanie Romanov (Lilah Morgan), Sam Anderson (Holland Manners), Todd Stashwick (Vocah), Carey Cannon (Sister Oracle), Randall Slavin (Brother Oracle), Julie Benz (Darla), with David Herman (David Nabbit) and J. August Richards (Charles Gunn)

"Gee, I don't know, Cordelia, the Prophecies of Aberjian were only written over the last four thousand years in a dozen different languages, some of which aren't even human. Why don't we just get a Falanjoid demon in here, suck the brain out of my skull? Maybe that would speed things up."   —*Wesley*

Wesley returns to the puzzle. Cordelia finds a fascinating article in the paper, and shares with them the news that Lindsey McDonald's desire to climb the corporate ladder has triumphed over the pangs of conscience he recently suffered. Angel doesn't seem to have any lingering disappointment over his failure to reach Lindsey. He starts to return to his reading, but pauses at the sound of furtive movement in the outer office. The three of them grab weapons and investigate. Angel prods a mysterious cloaked figure in the shoulder with the business end of his battle-ax, nearly giving billionaire David Nabbit a heart attack. The adrenaline rush thrills Nabbit. He has just come by to hang out, to get a thrill from being in the company of the mighty demon fighters.

Meanwhile, Holland, Lilah, and Lindsey stand patiently as hooded monks chant, summoning Vocah, "he of pure darkness." As such, of course, he is welcome at the Wolfram & Hart offices. Vocah appears, wearing a cloak with far more menace than Nabbit, his facial features concealed under a brass mask.

Wesley begins to decipher "shanshu"; his elation quickly turning to dismay when he tracks down the "Proto-Ugaric" root, translating "shanshu" as "death." Angel's reaction is not as passionate as his cohorts might have expected.

CORDELIA: "But you said it was all about the vampire with the soul. Angel's going to die?"

ANGEL: "Oh. Anything else?"

Wesley speculates that the foretold death is undoubtedly years off, and there is no cause for worry. Which is great, since Angel doesn't seem concerned at all.

Then Cordelia has a full-on "scratch and sniff" edition of a vision, this one involving a homeless woman under attack by a slime demon, behind the waste treatment plant in El Segundo.

Angel wastes no time rushing to the woman's aid.

Holland and Lindsey sheepishly inform an enraged Vocah that exactly the wrong person has stolen the Scroll of Aberjian from their vault: Angel. They ask what they can do to make amends, but Vocah stalks out, accompanied by two priests, intent on recovering the scroll and contributing to Angel's undoing without further help in this matter from lawyers.

The slime demon's attack has been reported to the regular authorities, and several uniformed officers are on the scene at the sewage plant when a harried-looking Kate Lockley pulls up. She is not amused by the harassment she receives from them, nor does she appear pleased when she runs into Angel, murmuring reassurances to a homeless woman as he escorts her away from the slime demon's corpse. Kate is beyond brusque with him, spoiling for a fight. He lets her anger slide off him, although it takes effort.

The next morning, Wesley explains to Cordelia that a large source of his concern over Angel stems not from the prophecy of death, but from Angel's nonreaction to it. Wesley speculates that Angel has no raison d'être, no hunger for life.

Angel walks in, and Cordelia tries to excite him with donuts.

ANGEL: "Am I supposed to know what this is about?"

WESLEY: "We . . . were just discussing how . . . you don't . . . want that many things."

CORDELIA: "You're cut off from life. But don't worry, I'm gonna help you with that."

ANGEL: "Oh. Good."

CORDELIA: "We'll start small. Keep it simple. How would you like a puppy? Right. A ficus, they're low maintenance . . . ant farm?"

Wesley can't bear to watch her in action anymore. He departs for the rare book shops, leaving the scroll with Angel. As he leaves, he suggests to a resistant Angel that he might pay a visit to the Oracles.

The Oracles stand facing their guest, "cordial" as always. They demand to know what makes a "lower being" believe they can be summoned "on a whim." But this guest is Vocah, not Angel, and he explains that it is not whimsy that has brought him. The Oracles don't council the powers of darkness and demand to know how Vocah came to them. "The old order passes away and the new order's come. He that was first shall now be last and he that was dead shall now arise," he says, reaching behind his back and magically manifesting a nasty, sharp-bladed scythe.

Elsewhere, Cordelia strolls down the Venice Boardwalk in the sunlight, taking in the sights of performers and a variety of purchase options. A friendly woman staffing the "Art Attack!" table helps her make a selection of two bags worth of art supplies as a healing gift for Angel. She has just completed the transaction when Vocah approaches, a cold force moving unseen through the crowd around her. Vocah has removed his glove and, as he comes abreast of Cordy, he allows the back of his bare hand to come into contact with hers. She reacts slightly to the unseen touch, and then is hit by a vision, dropping her bags to the sidewalk. A little embarrassed, she opens her cell phone to call the guys with her vision info, when vision after vision cascades over her, each image more horrifying and heart-wrenching than the last, and she falls to the sidewalk. She lies there between the screens of art she took down with her, as the frightened art vendor shouts for someone to call 911.

Angel moves quietly downstairs to his apartment and places the Scroll of Aberjian securely in his weapons cabinet, locking it. He keeps sensing Vocah's presence in the apartment but gets no confir-

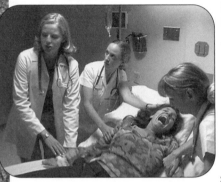

mation. The phone rings in the stillness, summoning him to St. Matthew's Hospital, where Cordelia has been taken. As soon as Angel is out of sight, Vocah emerges from the shadows in the apartment. The lock on the cabinet barely gives him pause as he opens it and removes the scroll. He reaches into his cloak and leaves some heavy, strangely humming device in the scroll's place.

Angel reaches the hospital and is asking for Cordelia's location when her frantic screams draw him to her bedside. A concerned doctor quizzes him on Cordy's mental state and possible drug use. Angel can't possibly know, but the visions are continuing to pour into Cordy's tortured mind. Her doctor gravely informs him there could be dire consequences if they can't stop the "psychotic episode."

Wesley returns to the office, tomes in hand. He goes down the stairs to Angel's apartment and notices the damage Vocah caused the cabinet. As he pulls the door open, the humming sound becomes ominously loud.

Angel has arrived back at the office as well, although he is just pulling up in the car outside. Angel is walking to the building's entrance when there is an explosion, and Angel is blown off of his feet.

Regaining his footing, he charges inside. He finds Wesley on the stairs, badly injured. He carries Wesley out of the death trap to meet the paramedics.

Kate and other police officers have arrived on the scene as well. Kate gets in Angel's face as Wesley is relocated to the hospital by an ambulance.

          KATE: "Never a dull moment when you're around, is there?"

          ANGEL: "I have to go."

          KATE: "Who the hell do you think you are? You're a major witness at a major crime scene—you are not going anywhere."

          ANGEL: "You want to try and stop me, Kate?"

          KATE: "I'm glad we are not playing friends anymore. I am real sick and tired of your attitude. There's a little thing called the law—"

          ANGEL: "This isn't about the law, this is about a little thing called life. Now I'm sorry about your father. But I didn't kill your father. And I'm sick and tired of you blaming me for everything you can't handle! You want to be enemies? Try me."

And he pushes past her, determined to do his damnedest for his friends.

In the hospital he checks first on an unconscious Wesley, then takes the stairway up to where

Cordelia lies, more quietly now, but with a terribly sad, far-off look on her face that tells him she has mentally retreated. He quietly promises her he will fix things. On the verge of tears, he gives her his pledge; holding her hand, he notices Vocah's mark.

Angel makes a copy of the mark (the first time he's used his artistic talents in a while) and journeys to the Oracle's chamber. There he is greeted by the ghost of Sister Oracle, hovering above the bloody corpses of her brother and herself. She offers him Vocah's name and the information that the help he seeks lies in the text of the scroll.

"The words of Anatole—only they can remove the mark and save your friend."   —*Sister Oracle*

She directs him to search for Vocah at "The Raising," and disappears. Angel arms himself with Vocah's discarded scythe, left beside the Oracles' bodies.

Angel is now a vampire with a mission, but he has learned from the events of the recent past to take precautions for his friends. He finds Gunn and crew loading food from the back of an Italian restaurant into the War Wagon. Gunn initially is in a good mood, giving Angel grief about his social skills, and game for an adventure. But Angel wants Cordelia and Wesley protected while he goes after Vocah. He makes it clear to Gunn how much they mean to him, emphasizing the importance of the task.

Lilah Morgan, Lindsey McDonald, and Holland Manners exit Wolfram & Hart, moving toward a waiting limo. A second limo and a moving van are also running and ready to go. As Angel watches from the shadows, Holland asks Lindsey for reassurance that all will go smoothly and the Senior Partners will not be disappointed. Lindsey responds in the affirmative, and Holland gets in the limo. It glides off into the night, and Angel joins the end of the convoy, unnoticed.

The Wolfram & Hart contingent arrives at a mausoleum where Vocah leads a group of monks in the words of the ritual. They are focused on a large crate, which has five vampires chained to it. Like most rituals, this one happens at a measured pace, and the lawyers are just a bit bored by the routine.

But Vocah pauses, breaking the rhythm of the summoning. He listens to something no one else can discern, then sets the scroll down. He moves toward a window, doing his magical scythe-summoning trick again, and has his weapon in his hand when Angel crashes through, also armed with one of Vocah's scythes. While the two of them engage in battle, the monks pause, having lost their leader. Lindsey isn't going to allow Angel to upset the process, and he grabs the scroll and uses all the law-school Latin he knows to continue. Holland, pleased at Lindsey's initiative, sends Lilah to summon the movers.

In response to Lindsey's words, the vampires chained to the box dust and their remains spin around the crate in a mystic whirlwind until they are sucked inside. The resulting explosion knocks Lindsey to the ground, stunned. Angel and Vocah continue their battle, oblivious to the monks they careen into, or the movers who hustle the crate out of the mausoleum. Angel executes some of his patented fancy moves, and knocks Vocah's scythe from his grasp. He follows this by inserting the handle of his scythe into Vocah's mouth, then using it to pry the demon's brass mask free. It falls away to reveal a writhing mass of maggots in the nasal cavity, spreading over the rest of the face. As Angel observes sarcastically, "Nice." Vocah is spared any further comments on his appearance by the fatal insertion of his own scythe.

Lindsey has recovered enough to start to leave. When he sees Angel triumph over Vocah, he grabs a cross to defend himself from attack. Angel asks Lindsey to hand over the scroll, but the lawyer refuses. Feeling his power, Lindsey says it's been foretold that Angel needs the scroll to save Cordelia and maintain his connection to The Powers That Be. Then he deliberately holds the scroll in the fire in the nearby brazier.

Angel has had enough. He throws the scythe, knocking the scroll clear of the flames—and taking Lindsey's right hand along with it. He moves to retrieve the scroll, leaving Lindsey on the floor in agony with the brief message, "Don't believe everything you're foretold."

Wesley has recovered enough to join Angel at Cordy's bedside, although he is in a wheelchair, with an IV stand and many bandages. He reads the words of Anatole from the scroll while Angel holds Cordelia's hand and watches her face for signs of recovery. As Wesley reaches the end of a long passage and utters "unbind" three times, a flash of healing light radiates through the room into the hall. Angel checks, and Cordy is free of Vocah's mark. But her experience has left her with a newfound resolve.

CORDELIA: "I saw them all . . . there's so much pain . . . we have to help them."

ANGEL: "We will. We will."

RESOLUTION

Angel and Wesley are seated in the dining room of Cordelia's (and Phantom Dennis's) apartment, while she putters domestically in the kitchen. Wesley still shows signs of the healing process. He remains undeterred in his quest to determine the meaning of the scroll.

WESLEY: "Here is something, the beast of Amalfie . . ."

ANGEL: "What is it?"

WESLEY: ". . . razor-toothed six-eyed harbinger of death. No, wait, that's due to rise in 2003 . . . in Reseda."

ANGEL: "I would've guessed Tarzana."

Cordy emerges with a sandwich and juice for Wesley and a cup o' blood for Angel. She encourages both of them to consume their nutrients, assuring a somewhat hesitant Angel that he can drink in front of them. "We're family." Wesley and Angel regard her with admiration and a little surprise at her new attitude. Then:

WESLEY: "Uh, oops. I may have made a tiny mistake . . . The word 'shanshu' that I said meant you were going to die? Actually I think it means that you are going to live."

CORDELIA: "Okay, as tiny mistakes go—that's not one!"

Wesley shares some of the etymology that has helped him get a better grip on the prophecy and determines that what is actually predicted is a change in Angel's state of being. In other words:

WESLEY: "A thing that's not alive never dies. It's . . . it's saying . . . that you get to live until you die. It's saying . . . it's saying you become human."

CORDELIA: "That's the prophecy?"

WESLEY: "Uh, the vampire with a soul, once he fulfills his destiny, will shanshu . . . become human. It's his reward."

CORDELIA: "Wow. Angel, human."

ANGEL: "That'd be nice."

The three of them start trying to decipher the small print, such as exactly what will be involved in Angel fulfilling his destiny. Angel cautions against premature celebration, but Cordelia is convinced even just knowing the future may hold this is cause for celebration.

At Wolfram & Hart, Holland, Lilah, and the wounded Lindsey, arm stump bandaged and cradled to his chest, enter the room containing the mysterious crate. The sound of rapid breathing fills the room, and Holland assures Lindsey they will achieve revenge on Angel, and that what's in the box is key to that revenge. Lilah approaches the box, speaking in the soothing tones one uses with a wild creature.

"We're all very pleased that you're here. . . . I know it's a bit confusing now, but it's going to be better soon . . . a lot better . . . Darla."

—Lilah

And a wild-eyed Darla, back from whatever Hell she's been in since Angel staked her four years ago in Sunnydale, gazes out at her surroundings.

Case . . . closed?

DOSSIERS

CLIENT The **homeless woman** was originally suffering from paranoia about the telephone company, rather than dentists. In either event, she took the appearance of the slime demon and Angel's dispatching the same well in stride.

CIVILIAN SUPPORT David Nabbit's fascination with the supernatural, what seems like a live version of his beloved role-playing games, will continue. Angel will call upon his financial expertise in the future.

The **doctor, nurse,** and **other medical staff** of St. Matthew's do their best for Cordelia and Wesley, although the mystical source of Cordy's problem is a bit beyond their skills. **Gunn** looks after Cordy and Wesley in the hospital.

The **art vendor** goes far beyond the call of retail when she tries to come to Cordelia's assistance.

SUSPECTS Vocah is a serious badass demon, able to take out the Oracles, the representation of The Powers That Be. He is summoned and assisted in his later spells by **two monks**. (Deceased.) It's business as usual for **Holland Manners, Lilah Morgan,** and **Lindsey McDonald.**

CONTINUITY

David Nabbit continues to be an übergeek, visiting the Angel Investigations offices on a break from his stint as Dungeon Master, as revealed in "War Zone." Angel hasn't paid a visit to the Oracles since his disappointing conversation with them in "Parting Gifts." He probably won't get another opportunity. Cordelia's comfort level with Angel's blood consumption may be related to her partaking of his supply in "Expecting." Gunn remembers with pleasure his "gifting" Wolfram & Hart with a vampire in "Blind Date." Although resurrecting a vampire was discussed in "When She Was Bad," the circumstances were different—the Master left a skeleton behind when Buffy dusted him.

QUOTE OF THE WEEK

CORDELIA: "Well, hurry up and figure out what it says about Angel 'cause I want to know what it says about me. If there's torrid romance in my future, massive wealth? If I have to I'll settle for enviable fame."

WESLEY: "It's an ancient sacred text, not a Magic Eight Ball."

Cordelia shows her impatience with the slow translation of the Scroll.

THE DEVIL IS IN THE DETAILS

EXPENSES

Hospital stays for Wesley and Cordelia

WEAPONRY

There are many, including stakes, daggers, swords, a battle-ax, Vocah's scythe, and a bomb planted in Angel's apartment that nearly kills Wesley.

DEMONS, DEMONS, DEMONS

Vocah is a Darth Maul-like being, a warrior of the underworld. He is capable of great harm with just a single touch . . . or a swipe of his scythe. The Scroll of Aberjian can stop him, when the words of Anatole are read from it.

THE VAMPIRE RULES

Certain vampires can be given a second shot at human life through redemptive acts.

AS SCENE IN L.A.

El Segundo actually contains the only sewage treatment plant for all of L.A. The sewage is turned into a combustible and used to generate power for the ever resource-hungry city.

The Venice Boardwalk is home to vendors and all sorts of eclectic Southern California oddities. A great place to shop for the vampire who doesn't want anything.

Milano's Italian Kitchen, where Gunn is loading the War Wagon with leftovers, is an actual chain restaurant specializing in Northern Italian cuisine

Reseda and Tarzana are subsections of greater Los Angeles.

THE PEN IS MIGHTIER

FINAL CUT

Many changes were made to the scene with Cordelia, Wesley, and the donut, including cutting this exchange:

> **WESLEY:** "'The end . . . death . . .' what if the root was proto-Anatolian, say from the Hittite . . . if it's Hittite, the root is really more like . . . close."
>
> **CORDELIA:** "Clothes? As in Armani the Hittite?"
>
> Wesley shoots her a look.
>
> **CORDELIA:** "I try to cheer people up and they give me that look."

POP CULTURE

❖ **"They bought another soul for twelve pieces of silver."** When Wesley hears of Lindsey's promotion at Wolfram & Hart, he refers to the thirty pieces of silver Judas, whose name became synonymous with "traitor," accepted for his betrayal of Jesus.

❖ "To Shanshu in L.A." is a play on *To Live and Die in L.A.*, a 1985 film directed by William Friedkin, director of *The Exorcist*.

OUR HEROES

"When the Oracles were killed, it took viewers by surprise. Did you know that was coming before you got the script?'"

CAREY CANNON: "Actually, Amy [Britt, casting director] did call and say, 'You know, I'm not really sure yet, but I think you may be dying,' and I said, 'o-kay.' And then I flipped through the script immediately. They have it messengered to you, so it's always exciting getting a new script, and you flip through it looking for your name, or the name of your character. And I missed the first scene and in the second scene, the first thing I read was, 'Sister Oracle, in a pool of her own blood . . .' Okay. I was stalking around my apartment, screaming at my husband, 'What do they mean, a pool of my own blood?' So it was somewhat surprising."

"Well, in this particular universe, being dead doesn't mean that you're necessarily off the show for very long."

CAREY CANNON: "That's what I understand. And in that same episode, I had a little ghost scene. So I thought, well, you know, that's something."

RANDALL SLAVIN: "You know, she was a great Oracle. She was a much better Oracle than I was. I was quite a little pissy brother. She was quite good and serious about it. I wasn't surprised when I got killed off, I thought I was gonna get killed off much earlier.

"It was an abrupt end to the cushiest job I ever had. I was happy because I didn't have to get painted up by strangers anymore, which was a nominal pain in the ass and a bit humiliating. But I was very disappointed because it was, like I said, the cushiest job I've ever walked into. They call you up and say, 'Hey, we need you.' I'm like, 'All right, I'll be there.' But if they called me again, I would still do it. But I was very surprised. I kept thinking, wait a minute, if this person can fold time, when you were wasting away there on the ground, fold some shit."

"The only time that I think I did a lot of research for what I saw, was for episode twenty-two. That's when I did a lot of research to make that excruciating pain very visual in my mind."

—CHARISMA CARPENTER

"We've lit a few [vehicles] on fire last year, when the apartment blew up. See that picture right there? See that flame in the top left-hand corner of the ball, there's a little thing sticking out? Well, that ended flying out across the street and landing in the back of the Angel car and burning the backseat. It was parked all the way across the street."

—ROBERT ELLIS, TRANSPORTATION COORDINATOR

"And then the way we ended the season, bringing Darla back, was interesting because we hadn't really planned that too early on. Joss had been saying, 'I'd love to bring Julie Benz back; I don't know how we'd bring her back but I'd love to bring her back.' And so I brought her back but in the form of these flashbacks, initially, in episode fifteen, and then in 'Five by Five,' she appears in that too. So we'd been setting it up—and my episode was really an origins piece, you know, how he became who he was, and she makes him into a vampire.

"And just jumping back to fifteen, I also knew that I wanted to take footage from Joss's *Buffy* episode 'Becoming' where we see Darla and Angel in the alley, and I wanted to write a scene that took place before that and a scene that took place after that. So there's a scene where he's in this tavern and she sees him, and then we see him outside the tavern getting bit by her, and then we see him clawing his way out, we see his funeral. I just wanted to play what happened before and after that moment in that *Buffy* episode.

"So we actually used some of the footage from that. I just thought it would be cool. I've sort of been accused a little bit on the Internet, you know, boy, they're so cheap, they're reusing footage, and to me that was the cool thing. He literally walks out of this scene in an *Angel* episode into a scene in a *Buffy* episode that you saw a year before, and then he walks out of that scene. I thought it was cool. So what I liked was at the end of this season, when we brought her back, we had inadvertently been preparing the way for that by introducing her in flashbacks.'"

—TIM MINEAR

"Were you surprised to learn that Darla would return to Angel's present, since we've never seen a dusted vampire resurrected?"

JULIE BENZ: "I was very surprised. I think I was more surprised than anybody else. Because, in keeping with the reality of the show, that's never happened before. When a vampire is dusted, that's it, and I didn't think that they would break that reality. Because then anything can happen, really. So I never thought that they would raise me from the dead."

"Did you use some of that surprise for Darla's reaction when she shows up in the crate at the end of 'Shanshu'?"

JULIE BENZ: "No, that was acting. The surprise came when I finally got the script. I knew I was in the season finale, and I knew something big was going to happen and it was going to set me up for the following year. But I didn't know what. So when I got the script and I got halfway through it and I hadn't shown up, it was like, 'Okay, what's going on?' And then I got three-quarters of the way through it, and I'm like, 'I am not in this script.' And then I got to the end, and I was like, 'God.' I was really surprised because I didn't realize they were raising me from the dead the whole time I was reading the script."

TRACKS

The acoustic "Time of Day" from Grant Langston's *All This and Pecan Pie* CD is heard during this episode.

Angel Episode Guide

SEASON TWO

EPISODE NUMBER	EPISODE NAME	ORIGINAL U.S. AIR DATE
2ADH01	"Judgement"	September 26, 2000
2ADH02	"Are You Now or Have You Ever Been?"	October 3, 2000
2ADH03	"First Impressions"	October 10, 2000
2ADH04	"Untouched"	October 17, 2000
2ADH05	"Dear Boy"	October 24, 2000
2ADH06	"Guise Will Be Guise"	November 7, 2000
2ADH07	"Darla"	November 14, 2000
2ADH08	"The Shroud of Rahmon"	November 21, 2000
2ADH09	"The Trial"	November 28, 2000
2ADH10	"Reunion"	December 19, 2000
2ADH11	"Redefinition"	January 16, 2001
2ADH12	"Blood Money"	January 23, 2001
2ADH13	"Happy Anniversary"	February 6, 2001
2ADH14	"The Thin Dead Line"	February 13, 2001
2ADH15	"Reprise"	February 20, 2001
2ADH16	"Epiphany"	February 27, 2001
2ADH17	"Disharmony"	April 17, 2001
2ADH18	"Dead End"	April 24, 2001
2ADH19	"Belonging"	May 1, 2001
2ADH20	"Over the Rainbow"	May 8, 2001
2ADH21	"Through the Looking Glass"	May 15, 2001
2ADH22	"There's No Place Like Plrtz Glrb"	May 22, 2001

STARRING

David Boreanaz . . . . Angel

Charisma Carpenter . . . . .Cordelia Chase

Alexis Denisof . . . . .Wesley Wyndam-Pryce

J. August Richards . . . . .Charles Gunn

"JUDGEMENT"

FROM THE FILES OF ANGEL INVESTIGATIONS
CASE N°: 2ADH01

ACTION TAKEN

A demon with a green-skinned face, Jay Leno chin, nose like a hooked beak, red eyes, red lips, and red horns casts a sinister look around—then raises a microphone to those red lips and launches into "I Will Survive." The demon is dressed to the nines: white dinner jacket, black pants, neatly coifed blond hair. This is the Host, in his karaoke bar, Caritas, in Los Angeles. Cutting off the song, he goes into monologue mode, describing the City of Angels.

"Oh, you know what I'm talking about: in this city, you better learn to get along—cause L.A.'s got it all, the glamour and the grit, the big breaks and the heartaches, the sweet young lovers and the nasty ugly hairy fiends that suck your brain out through your face—it's all part of the big wacky variety show we call Los Angeles. You never know what's coming next. And let's admit it, folks—isn't that why we love it?" —*Host*

STORY BY Joss Whedon & David Greenwalt
TELEPLAY BY David Greenwalt
DIRECTED BY Michael Lange
GUEST STARS: Christian Kane (Lindsey McDonald), Stephanie Romanov (Lilah Morgan), Andy Hallett (Host), Justina Machado (Jo), Julie Benz (Darla)
CO-STARS: Rob Bolton (Johnny Fontaine), Iris Fields (Acting Teacher), Keith Campbell (Club Manager), Matthew James (Merl), Glenn David Calloway (Judge)

Elsewhere, Cordelia Chase is paged during an acting workshop in which she's doing surprisingly well, and Wesley Wyndam-Pryce receives his summons while showing off at the dartboard in a pub. Angel, Wesley, and Cordelia, reunited and on the case, enter a gym. The manager tries to stop them, but this trio means business. On the other side of a mirror, a Carnyss demon and his human henchman prepare a ritual sacrifice. Angel and the others, working as a cohesive team now, save the teens and kill the Carnyss.

The next day the team enters the Carnyss information onto a large whiteboard they've set up in Cordelia's apartment. They've decided to get organized, primarily because they're still trying to figure out what was in the crate, what Wolfram & Hart raised with Vocah's help. Their brainstorming session is interrupted by a vision that comes upon Cordelia with such violence that Angel drops and breaks one of her little glass unicorns.

At Wolfram & Hart, Lilah pays a visit to Lindsey's office, arriving just in time to see the lawyer struggling to open a CD case with his new prosthetic right hand. He's putting on Chopin for Darla, who, having been dead and in Hell, is still a bit on the fried side. Suddenly, though, she brightens, sensing Angel somewhere in the city. "He killed me," she says. "I remember now . . . with a soul in his heart." Lindsey, still smarting about the hand, suggests that they both owe Angel a little something.

"Angel. It's been a long time. . . . I'd love to see that boy."   —*Darla*

She doesn't look as though she means it in a nice way.

Back at Cordelia's apartment, Wesley manages to find a picture of the demon from Cordy's vision in one of his many reference books. It's a Prio Motu, a killer. Now they know what it is, but they still don't know where. Wesley says that he might be able to help, that he's got a stool pigeon, a parasite demon named Merl, who hangs out at a safe haven for demons—Caritas, a karaoke joint.

Merl wants nothing to do with Angel, but an envelope full of cash helps calm his nerves. Once he hears the name Prio Motu, though, the cash is no longer enough. He demands more, gets it, and in return directs them to a likely spot.

As Angel turns to leave, he finds himself face-to-face with the Host, who seems to have taken an immediate liking to the vampire.

> **HOST**: "Love the coat. It's all about the coat. Welcome to Caritas. You know what that
>   means?"
> **ANGEL**: "It's Latin for mercy."
> **HOST**: "Smart *and* cute. How 'bout gracing us with a number."
> **ANGEL**: "I don't sing."

The Host, it turns out, is anagogic—which means, Wesley explains, "Psychic. Connected to the mystic. When you sing, you bare your soul and he sees into it."

Angel gets some direction from the Host and finds the Prio Motu, encountering him at the same time that he runs across a frightened-looking pregnant woman named Jo. The Prio attacks Angel, and they fight. Angel finally breaks its neck—and Jo drops to its side, in tears. Angel has just killed her protector, the one friend she had in the world. She orders Angel away from her, and he goes.

Angel finds himself truly distressed by his accidental killing of an innocent being, a soldier like himself. He has learned that the Prio Motu was supposed to be protecting Jo from something called the Tribunal. He sets Wesley and Cordelia to work on finding out what the Tribunal is, while he takes over the Prio's mission himself.

Tracking down Merl, he gets a little more information. The woman's daughter, Merl says, is supposed to become a powerful, benevolent being. So the Dark Ones want to take her out now, in utero, and if that means killing the mother, too, no great loss. After being slammed against a fence a few times, Merl reluctantly tells Angel where Jo is most likely hiding out.

Angel knows he's not familiar enough with the neighborhood to find the woman quickly—but he knows who is. Charles Gunn is happy to help out, and together they manage to locate the demon's lair. Inside, Angel learns that the Prio's name was Kamal, and he finds a hidden talisman, a disk engraved with a coat of arms. Thinking this might have something to do with the Tribunal, he sends Gunn to deliver the disk to Wesley and Cordelia. Angel stays behind, which turns out to be a good thing, since Jo shows up a few minutes later, and a talon demon arrives right behind her. Ascertaining from Jo that it's okay to kill *this* demon, Angel does so, but not without suffering some wounds of his own as the thing's claws rake his chest. And the talon demon has friends. Angel and Jo run through the tunnels, eventually coming up inside an old, abandoned, and quite lovely hotel. Which Angel recognizes . . .

The demons arrive, and Angel sends Jo to Cordy's place to wait for him.

Gunn delivers the talisman, finally meeting Cordelia and Wesley conscious for the first time (he had seen them in the hospital, after the explosion at Angel's office). By the time Angel gets back to Cordy's, though, Gunn is gone, and Jo has never shown up. He's lost her again.

And he can only think of one way to find her.

He returns to Caritas and sings "Mandy." And he's no Barry Manilow.

Jo runs through dark city streets, alone and scared. But there's no escaping the Tribunal. If they want you, they come to you, and now they appear suddenly at Fourth and Spring in downtown L.A., right behind Jo. An armored demon materializes on the street, mounted on a horse and carrying a lance. He throws down his talisman. But Jo has no talisman anymore, and no champion, now that Kamal is dead. One of the three judges tells her that without a coat of arms and a champion, her life is forfeit. Before he can do anything about it, though, Angel shows up, throwing down the second talisman. Now she *does* have a champion.

Jo is not convinced. So far, Angel has not exactly demonstrated great ability to do anything right where she's concerned. But he's Angel, so he's going to give it his best shot. He mounts up on another horse, lifts his lance, and the first jousting match in downtown L.A. in probably forever is under way. Angel gets in the first shot, but the demon takes the next one and knocks Angel off his steed. After some hand-to-hand, the more practiced knight manages to run Angel through with his own sword. Angel falls in the street. The judges award Jo to the knight, who draws a dagger with which to slit her throat.

And from behind him, Angel returns—and slices the knight's head off with the sword. Her champion victorious, Jo is under the Tribunal's protection, as is her daughter, "until she comes of age."

RESOLUTION

Angel realizes he should pay a visit to an old friend—Faith. Considering that she's in jail, having turned herself in voluntarily, she could be worse. She found herself on the wrong side of someone trying to make a reputation and earned a beating from the guards for her trouble. But she downplays it, and Angel trumps her by confessing that he sang a Barry Manilow song in public. "The road to redemption is a rocky path," Faith says. The subject is one Slayer and vampire both know more than a little about.

Case closed.

DOSSIERS

CLIENT Jo is a young pregnant woman who finds herself in an exceedingly unusual situation. Fortunately, she had found herself a champion, Kamal, except that Angel killed him.

INFORMANTS Merl, the weasely stool pigeon, has his ear to the ground and is always willing to share what he knows with the right persuasion—sometimes money, sometimes physical violence or the threat of it. He prefers the former, given a choice.

SUSPECTS We never really learn what the **Tribunal**'s agenda is. They seem not to have any particular stake in how things turn out, they just have procedures that have to be followed, and they make their judgment accordingly. (Remain at large.)

CONTINUITY

Angel refers to the destruction of the original office and "batcave" in "To Shanshu in L.A." He also reminds Cordelia of the terms of the prophecy when she points out that working out seems redundant for the immortally buff. The Angel Investigations scoreboard is a visual reminder of their goal—to achieve Angel's redemption and his return to a mortal state. In the same episode, Wesley speculates on what Wolfram & Hart raised in their ceremony. His guess is wrong. Although Gunn stood guard over Wesley and Cordelia in "To Shanshu in L.A.," this is their first face-to-face meeting. When he announces his name through Cordelia's apartment door, they think he is speaking of a "gun," like the armed demons who followed Doyle to the apartment in "Rm w/a Vu." Darla recalls being dusted at Angel's hands in Sunnydale in the *Buffy* episode "Angel." Faith's stint in jail is the result of her turning herself in to the police in "Sanctuary." Angel reenters the Hyperion for the first time in decades, setting up the opportunity for Angel Investigations to move out of Cordy's apartment and into the hotel after "Are You Now or Have You Ever Been?"

QUOTE OF THE WEEK

ANGEL: "You got your steam, your sauna, fresh towels . . . where's the down side?"
CORDELIA: "You shower with a lot of men."
ANGEL: (instantly) "I'll always be a loner."

Visiting the gym in search of a Carnyss demon inspires Angel, but Cordelia quickly deflates his dreams.

THE DEVIL IS IN THE DETAILS

EXPENSES

Whiteboard and markers
Cordelia's glass unicorn

WEAPONRY

Cordy clobbers a demon's henchman with a free weight in the gym. Angel and the Tribunal's champion joust with lances, in proper medieval fashion. When they dismount, they continue the battle with swords.

DEMONS, DEMONS, DEMONS

The Host, with his green skin, blond hair, and flashy clothes, will become an invaluable aid and friend to Angel and the others, helping them find their paths, as well as keeping his ear to the demonic ground for information.

Prio Motu demons, we learn, are ancient Ofga-beasts "bred to maim and massacre." Kamal was a rare exception to this rule, which is what made him a good champion for Jo until Angel killed him. Information about Prio Motu demons can be found in the book *Suleman's Compendium*.

The demon encountered in the gym is identified as a **Carnyss demon** at Cordelia's apartment, but Angel mistakenly calls it a Kwaini demon when they're storming through the gym to find it. The Carnyss is horned and enjoys beheading humans.

Caritas is a haven for demons, where they coexist in peace, whatever their personal habits may be. As the Host says to a lizard demon:

"Liz, I know it's hatching time and you're looking forward to that, but there's more to life than eating your young."

—Host

Merl, the stool pigeon, is a tongueless parasite demon with green, scaly skin, and a bald head.

AS SCENE IN L.A.

"We ended up closing down Hill Street in downtown L.A. between Fourth and Fifth, so Angel could do his jousting in the middle of the street in front of the Tribunal. *Angel* is a big show when it comes to locations. We usually end up closing down streets and putting lights down either end of the street and around the corners, things like that. It's very challenging and very exciting just to be able to do that. Also in that episode we shot in the old Red Car tunnel, which is in that building right next to Hill and Fourth. That's where the old Red Cars used to come into L.A., and that was their main terminal. And there's a tunnel down there that still exists. When [Angel]'s walking into the tunnel and he thinks the girl is being attacked by the demon . . . that is in the Red Car tunnels. It's a pretty neat location, really. I even remember David Boreanaz saying that this was the best location he's been at so far."

—KEVIN FUNSTON, LOCATIONS MANAGER

THE PEN IS MIGHTIER

FINAL CUT

The script's stage directions explain how the mirrored walls of the health club should be effected:

We see Wes and Cor and the manager moving toward us, people working out, etc., but no Angel. SWISH PAN away from this reflection (and hide the cut in the swish pan) and DISCOVER Angel where he belongs, in front of Wes and Cor, stopping a few feet in front of the mirror.

When Angel breaks one of Cordelia's glass animals, she complains about the agency using her place for their headquarters. Her line changed between original script and final airing.

The original version was:

"My landlady keeps saying, 'you better not be running a business up there, I hear a lot of noise' and I keep telling her, 'no business, just wild orgies.'"

But the line was changed to:

"Why can't we work out of Wes's?"

In the original script, but cut from the episode, is this exchange when Wesley tells Angel and Cordelia about Caritas and Merl.

> **WESLEY**: "I think I can help us with that. I've been working the street—"
>
> **CORDELIA**: "You're a prostitute? It's always the quiet British ones. . . ."

POP CULTURE

❖ **"Well, who's a little curt? Who's a little Curt Jurgens in *The Enemy Below*?"** When Angel snaps at the Host, the demon's response recalls *The Enemy Below*, a 1957 submarine action movie starring the aforementioned actor.

❖ **"Maybe it's time we pay your stoolie a little visit . . . and make with the chin music until he canaries. . . . I've been watching a Noir festival on Bravo."** Cordelia's been getting a little *too* into gangster flicks on the Bravo cable channel, which is known for its themed film festivals.

OUR HEROES

"When David Boreanaz sang 'Mandy' on the first show, (which, by the way, was hysterical, he can . . . sing better), he sang it once, pretty good, and then they said, 'No no no, it's got to be much worse.' So then he sang it and destroyed the song, and they said, 'Okay, not *that* bad.' So then after four takes we got a happy medium. And we have so many cuts from that, you know, the little bloopers? Oh my God, they're hilarious, of him doing that." —ANDY HALLETT

The "bloopers" Andy mentions of David singing were shown over the closing credits to this episode.

"I just tried to play [Darla] using her senses. She's very animalistic, and so the sound of the music is very sensory for her. I believe she can smell Angel miles away. I think her senses were on overdrive at that point. At that point, too, I didn't know she was human. So I was still playing her like she was a vampire. I didn't know, and I don't think they were a hundred percent sure what they were going to do either. I did make a specific choice that she keys into Lindsey and totally ignores Lilah. It's the male presence for her that's very strong. She doesn't play well with women. She doesn't have girlfriends. She tolerates them and uses them for whatever they're worth, but she's really keyed into the male in the room. And I think she also sensed in Lindsay that there was something that she knew she could manipulate." —JULIE BENZ

ANDY HALLETT: "[Getting into the Host makeup takes] a full three hours, it's a full prosthetic piece that goes over my entire face, with the exception of my ears. Then after they do the makeup, they glue it on and do lots of airbrushing and detailing. Then after that they color my hair with a spray. Because my hair's really dark brown, almost black. They put in a spray that makes it the blondish-goldish. Then after that come the contacts. And that's the part that I usually dread the most. So usually the lens technician puts them in, and then Dayne ends up having to touch up my eyes again after she does it. Once the makeup is on, it's fine, it doesn't irritate me or anything. But it's the lenses that keep me complaining all day."

"Do they alter your view, looking out?"

ANDY HALLETT: "Surprisingly not. If you look out of the perimeter you do see a little bit of red. But for the most part it just blurs my vision. Not to the point where I can't see where I'm going. But it definitely impairs my vision quite a bit."

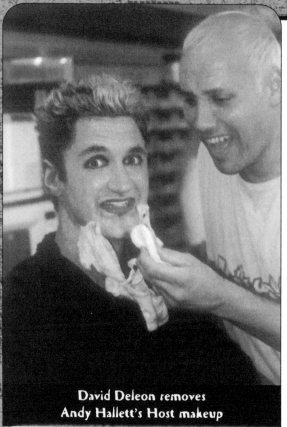

David Deleon removes
Andy Hallett's Host makeup

Stunt coordinator Michael Vendrell spoke about the jousting scene, which he said was his single favorite stunt of the season:

"I think Mike Massa [David Boreanaz's stunt double] is probably the greatest stuntman who's ever lived. I called him up and I asked him, 'Mike, have you ever jousted before?' and he says, 'Well, I've ridden a horse.' I said, 'Do you think you can do it holding a telephone pole?' He said, 'I'll try.' So we went out to the horse ranch, and he got on a horse and he just looked beautiful on it. Same with David Boreanaz, he climbed right up on the horse and he carried the lance like a pro. They both did really well. My job is to figure out how to put our star on a horse in the middle of downtown Los Angeles without killing himself." —MICHAEL VENDRELL

"Joss wanted to introduce a fun element of a karaoke bar to our show. His jumping-off point for us was he wanted some kind of place that maybe Dean Martin would have hung out in. So we were able to do some research and show him some sketches we came up with of something that would look like a swanky Las Vegas lounge from maybe like the seventies. And he has to have some more radius walls, he likes the idea of no sharp edges, he wants some more curves to it. And we came up with some really beautiful deep blue neon, and we had some booths custom-made for us, and we kept the tones in there very dark, but dark on the very lush and sexy side. I think the whole idea was that it had a little bit of a sexy feel to it, because it is a nightclub." —STUART BLATT, PRODUCTION DESIGNER

SIX DEGREES OF . . .

Keith Campbell, the manager of the health club in which the Carnyss demon is killed, played the werewolf alter ago of Seth Green's Oz in the *Buffy* episode "Phases."

Mordar the Bentback was played by E. J. Gage, who also appeared as Mover #1 in the *Buffy* episode "Buffy vs. Dracula," the *Buffy* Season Five opener which first aired the same night as "Judgement."

The glass unicorn that Angel breaks is a reference to the Tennessee Williams play The Glass Menagerie.

TRACKS

Songs performed in Caritas in this episode include Gloria Gaynor's 1979 disco legend and feminist anthem, "I Will Survive," written by Dino Fekaris and Freddie Perren and sung by the Host, and "I'm So Excited," sung by Liz, a lizard demon. This song was recorded by the Pointer Sisters and written by them with producer and horn player Trevor Lawrence. In the script, Mordar the Bentback sings Marvin Gaye's "Sexual Healing," but on stage it's barely recognizable as anything. The Host describes Mordar as "a foghorn on two legs." Angel, of course, sings the Barry Manilow hit "Mandy," written by Scott English and Richard Kerr. Horribly. Durthock the Child Eater sings "Achy, Breaky Heart," the 1992 song, written by guitarist Don Von Tress, that made a career for country singer Billy Ray Cyrus.

In his office, Lindsey plays Chopin's Prelude in C minor for Darla.

"ARE YOU NOW OR HAVE YOU EVER BEEN?"

FROM THE FILES OF ANGEL INVESTIGATIONS CASE Nº: 2ADH02

ACTION TAKEN

Cordelia serves drinks for Wesley, herself, and Angel: "English Breakfast Tea. Coffee. O pos." But Angel doesn't like his. He thinks it's starting to coagulate, but in fact, Cordy added some cinnamon, for flavor. As they imbibe, Angel shows Cordelia and Wesley a photograph of the Hyperion Hotel, his interest in it apparently sparked by a brief visit there with the pregnant Jo, while escaping some talon demons. The Hyperion, he tells them, is in the heart of Hollywood, and it's been deserted for years—"Sixty-eight rooms, sixty-eight vacancies." He instructs them to look into its history, to find out who owns it now and why it's been vacant for so long. He refuses to explain his interest and leaves while they're still trying to figure out what this new, sudden passion is all about.

WRITTEN BY Tim Minear
DIRECTED BY David Semel
GUEST STARS: Melissa Marsala (Judy Kovacs), John Kapelos (Manager), Tommy Hinkley (Goon), Brett Rickaby (Denver), Scott Thompson Baker (Rock Hudson Guy), J. P. Manoux (Bellhop)
CO-STARS: David Kagen (Salesman), Terrence Beasor (Older Man), Julie Araskog (Over the Hill Whore), Tom Beyer (Blacklisted Writer), Eve Sigall (Old Judy)

And then we flashback to 1952, in the lobby of the Hyperion Hotel, before it was abandoned. The hotel manager and a bellhop are engaged in a conversation about the mysterious occupant of room 217, who the bellhop complains gives him the "heebie-jeebies." "You ever look into his eyes?" he asks the manager. "There's nothing there."

Overruled, the bellhop is sent to deliver the weekly bill to that room. He knocks at the door, muttering, and scurries back to the elevator in hopes of being long gone by the time 217's occupant opens his door. When the door does open, the occupant is Angel.

The Angel of 1952 doesn't have much contact with the other guests in the hotel, which is the way he likes it. Other regulars include a "Rock Hudson-ish Matinee Idol" who uses the place for his peccadilloes with younger men, a "Salesman Type" who hears and obeys whispered voices, an "Over the Hill Whore," and a "Blacklisted Screenwriter." And a young lady named Judy Kovacs, whose room is right down the hall from 217. Many of the guests hang around in the hotel's lobby, where a TV seems perpetually tuned to the McCarthy Congressional hearings.

Returning to his room after filling an ice bucket at the hallway ice machine (and noticing a "goon" wandering around the halls), Angel finds Judy in his room. She claims to be the maid, a ruse that Angel doesn't believe for a second. "You're not a maid in this hotel. There's no cleaning trolley outside the door . . . those sheets are dirty . . . and you're the wrong color."

But she claims that she's hiding from her boyfriend. As they speak, someone tries to pick the lock to Angel's room, so Angel opens the door and finds the goon outside. The guy tells Angel to turn over the girl, and Angel refuses. When the guy shows a gun and tries to come in to look for himself, Angel slams the door on his face, probably breaking his nose. Reopening the door, Angel grabs the guy, hauls him to the elevator, and tosses him in, much to the dismay of the bellhop inside it. Back inside the room, Judy finally introduces herself.

In the present, Wesley has discovered that the hotel officially closed its doors in 1979, when a concierge went mad and shot all the guests. Cordelia adds what she's found, which is that the company that owns the property has been trying, without success, to sell it for years. Wesley is not surprised, considering what he's been learning of its past. But what still has them both stumped is why they're doing all this research. Finally, Cordelia uncovers a photo of the place in 1952. One of the guests visible in the photo is Angel.

In his room, back in 1952, Angel peacefully sips blood from a glass when he hears the Salesman Type, in the room next door, kill himself with a single shot from a handgun. Angel barely pauses before taking another sip.

The hotel manager is distressed by the suicide, particularly since it's the third one in the hotel in as many months, and they're never good for business. While he's complaining about it, though, he hears a demonic voice much like the one that instructed the salesman to kill himself. This voice tells the manager that the hotel will be shut down if people find out about the suicide. Instead of calling the police, the manager tells the bellhop to store the salesman's body in the meat locker. The other guests more or less approve of this plan of action—they've all got their own reasons why they don't want to answer any official questions.

But later, speculation turns to the rampant paranoia so common to the era, as many of the guests decide suicide is too simple an explanation—after all, the guy was found locked in his room with his gun in his hand, so he must have been murdered.

Angel, hanging around outside the Griffith Park Observatory, is told about the suicide by Judy, who doesn't know that Angel heard the whole thing. She invites him to watch the Observatory program—"the end of the world"—with her, but he declines.

Wesley and Cordelia, in the present, are putting pieces together like a jigsaw puzzle. They've learned of a bellhop named Frank Gilnitz who was executed in 1954 for storing, in 1952, a corpse in the hotel meat locker. Cordelia, ever sensitive, describes the process as the "Who Died Horribly Because Angel Screwed Up Fifty Years Ago" game.

In the past, Judy, who has been making friendly overtures toward Angel (and finding them rebuffed, but is apparently a persistent sort), invites him into her room. Realizing that he knew all along the goon looking for her was a private eye and not a jealous boyfriend, she breaks down and tells him what she's hiding out from. After being fired, she stole money from the bank she had worked for in

Kansas. She was fired because her mother was black. She's been passing for white since she was fifteen, but the bank found out her secret and let her go. She's been too ashamed of her action to even spend any of the money—which appears to be a considerable amount. Now she's afraid that if the police come in to investigate the apparent suicide, they'll find the money.

Angel, who has been around long enough to see almost everything, doesn't really get human prejudice.

JUDY: "My blood isn't pure. It's tainted."

ANGEL: "It's just blood, Judy. It's all just blood."

He should know.

And now, Wesley and Cordelia find a clipping about Judy Kovacs, headlined, FUGITIVE WOMAN BELIEVED DEAD. Apparently she was never heard from again after she ran off with the bank's money.

In the flashback, Angel helps Judy hide her suitcase full of money in the hotel's basement, near the boiler room. There are noises down here—strange whisperings—not boiler noises. Angel tells Judy to ignore anything she hears. She's terrified of prison, or of any kind of confinement, it seems. She asks Angel if he thinks the bank would call off the dogs if she just gave the money back. He's not convinced. "I mean," Judy asks, "there is such a thing as forgiveness, right?"

In the present, Angel returns to the hotel's basement, and finds the suitcase of money, still where they left it in 1952. And while he's doing it, he hears the whisperings again. Then he makes a phone call to Cordelia's apartment, still temporary headquarters for Angel Investigations, telling Cordy and Wesley that they're dealing with a paranoia demon called a Thesulac, and to bring Gunn. He had hoped that by researching the hotel's history, Wesley and Cordelia might have been able to figure out how to locate the Thesulac. But now it's clear that the demon has never left the premises. "We'll need all the muscle we can get when we raise this thing," Angel says. No one is very delighted to hear that idea.

The Angel of 1952 visits a rare book store, run by a beatnik named Denver. Denver knows quite a bit about the occult—enough to recognize Angel right off the bat as a vampire. But Angel dodges his attacks and threatens Denver into cooperation.

Back in the hotel, the guests have managed to work themselves into a frenzy over the "murder" of the salesman. And in her room, trying to ignore everything, Judy hears a voice that feeds into her fear of discovery and prison.

Denver explains that the only way Angel can fight the Thesulac demon is to make it corporeal, and that only happens when it's fed or if it's raised. But raising one is dangerous. He gives Angel an Orb of Ramjarin to raise it with, and a big ax to fight it with, should it come to that.

As the hotel guests turn from paranoid freaks into an unruly mob, the goon returns, introducing himself as C. Mulvihill, P.I. He shows a photograph of Judy to the others. And when Angel enters a few moments later, ax in hand, the lobby is strangely empty.

In the present, Angel, Cordelia, Wesley, and Gunn are all in the lobby, performing the raising ritual with the Orb.

But in the past, Angel gets upstairs just in time to see the mob dragging Judy from her room. They've discovered that she's registered under a fake name, and that's enough to make her guilty, in their book. She's apologizing, trying to get them to let her go—but then she sees Angel. Panicked, she points at him and tells the mob that he's the monster, that he has blood in his room.

The mob descends on Angel, Mulvihill knocking him down with the handle of the Denver's ax. They get into Angel's room and find his stash of blood, and considering that evidence enough to convict, they haul him out to the balcony overlooking the lobby, put a noose around his neck and throw the rope over a beam. He's pushed off the balcony, and he drops. As Angel's body swings from the rope, the roar of the mob quiets and everyone slinks away, ashamed of their lynch-mob mentality, except Frank the bellhop, gleeful till the bitter end.

Once everyone's gone, Angel stops playing dead.

But, getting himself down, he encounters the Thesulac demon, who's in a very cheery mood indeed.

"Well, I don't know about you, but I'm stuffed! God, I love people, don't you? They feed me their worst, and I kind of serve it right back to them. And the fear and the prejudice turn to certainty and hate— and I take another bite and mmmm! What a beautiful, beautiful dance!" —*Thesulac*

He tells Angel that this was especially good for him because Angel had really reached Judy, restoring her faith in people. "Now, she's a meal that's going to last me a lifetime!" he gloats. Then he grows serious. "You know what, there's an entire hotel here just full of tortured souls who could really use your help. Whaddaya say?"

Angel looks at him for a moment, and replies simply, "Take 'em all." He leaves, the Thesulac roaring with laughter behind him.

In the present, the Thesulac roars, but not with glee. Not happy about being raised, the Thesulac remembers Angel as if they had last seen each other yesterday. He appreciates the meal Angel has brought him now, full of tasty paranoia, especially Wesley. As they speak, it dawns on Angel that the Thesulac has been feeding on something . . . or someone, since the time of their last meeting. The realization spurs him to action and he grabs one of the demon's whipping tentacles and shoves it into an electrical box. The Thesulac smokes, pops, and explodes, finally freeing the Hyperion Hotel of its malevolent presence.

RESOLUTION

Without wasting any time, Angel hurries upstairs. He finds Judy's old room and goes in. An old woman waits inside. She recognizes Angel.

> **JUDY**: "You look . . . the same."
> **ANGEL**: "I'm not."

Which is correct. The Angel of 1952 was willing to walk out on a hotel full of people in danger. Today's Angel would never do that. She asks his forgiveness for fingering him, and, pleased to even be asked, he extends it. Finally at peace, Judy lays down and dies.

Downstairs, Angel surprises the others by announcing that Angel Investigations is moving in. Case closed.

DOSSIERS

CLIENT Judy Kovacs, like virtually everyone else in the Hyperion, including Angel himself, is hiding from her own past. In the end, before the old Judy dies, he manages to give her peace through the simple act of forgiveness. (Deceased.)

CIVILIAN SUPPORT Denver, the beatnik bookseller, is well-versed in the occult and well-equipped to battle it. After some not-so-gentle nudging from Angel, he provides an ax that might have slain the Thesulac—if it hadn't been used on Angel by Mulvihill instead—as well as the Orb of Ramjarin necessary to raise the demon and some other supplies for the raising ritual.

SUSPECTS Nearly everyone in the hotel is guilty of something, and, having banded together as a lynch mob, they'd be guilty of murder if Angel hadn't already been dead. The **Thesulac**, whispers his secret messages into people's ears in order to heighten their insecurities and stoke their paranoia, the better for him to feed on. (Deceased.)

CONTINUITY

Denver will resurface, still in the same occult occupation, in "Reprise." The Hyperion Hotel will see a lot more of Angel than it has in the past fifty years or so.

QUOTE OF THE WEEK

"It's not that vampires don't photograph—it's just that they don't photograph well."

Cordelia discovers a photograph of Angel from 1952, but not a flattering one.

THE DEVIL IS IN THE DETAILS

EXPENSES

Rewiring the hotel after shorting it out by inserting the Thesulac's tentacle into the electrical system

WEAPONRY

The Orb of Ramjarin does its thing, and the electricity helps. The ax was acquired by Angel to use on the Thesulac, but it was used against him instead.

DEMONS, DEMONS, DEMONS

A **Thesulac demon** is a paranoia demon with chalky skin, wearing a dark hooded cloak. It whispers to its victims, feeding on their innate insecurities. The one haunting the Hyperion Hotel had claimed the land even before the original building was constructed.

THE VAMPIRE RULES

A vampire occasionally likes his blood chilled. But no spices.
A vampire can't die from being hanged.

AS SCENE IN L.A.

A scene where Judy and Angel share a quiet moment away from the hotel was shot at the Griffith

Park Observatory, made famous in the 1955 teen classic *Rebel Without a Cause*. Angel, in this scene, is even dressed in a red jacket like the one James Dean wore at the Observatory.

"The [main] reason I wanted the Observatory was not because it was in a movie, although that's actually part of the reason. It was because I was looking for some period, iconic Los Angeles image, and there are very few. There are a few iconic things that tell you, I believe, it is the summer of 1952 in Los Angeles, and that particular place happened to be [one of them]. And it was magic, that night. It was about sixty-five degrees, all night, until the sun came up. And we shot till the sun came up. It was balmy. You walked around in your shirtsleeves. Stars were out. It was just unbelievable that night." —TIM MINEAR

"[The Hyperion Hotel location] is the Los Altos Apartments, which is on the corner of Wilshire Boulevard and Norton. That particular building is a historical landmark, and we shot that for an episode on the first season ["I Fall to Pieces"]. And they liked it, and they thought it would be a good location for Angel's home office kind of thing. [The owner] bought this old hotel . . . I think back seven years ago, it was a pretty dilapidated hotel. The owner bought it and got some funds from the state to fix it up, and he has a certain amount of controlled rent in there. And it's got quite a history because it had a lot of celebrities that lived there, like Bette Davis."

—KEVIN FUNSTON, LOCATIONS MANAGER

THE PEN IS MIGHTIER

FINAL CUT

The script describes the first appearance onscreen of the 1952 Angel:
LOW ON BILL TRAY as the door to Room 217 opens. A hand reaches down and picks up the tray. We follow it up to a face—
ANGEL
No light in that face. He's 1950s I-don't-get-involved-guy Angel. And frankly, he <u>is</u> kinda creepy.

In a scene that didn't air, Wesley and Cordelia, tracing the history of the hotel, have come across news clippings about a murderer who killed there in 1935.

CORDELIA: "So what horrible thing do you suppose he did?"

WESLEY: "Other than using the heads of his victims as decorative planters?"

CORDELIA: "What? No, not psycho slasher 1935. *Angel*. I mean, he woulda had a soul back then, right? So he probably wasn't *eating* people. So what's with the big guilt? He forgot to tip the doorman?"

WESLEY: "You must keep in mind that this was during a period in Angel's life when he wasn't *Angel*. At least not the Angel we know."

CORDELIA: "You mean before Buffy. Before all his trying to atone."

WESLEY: "Precisely."

CORDELIA: "So what kind of plants you gonna keep in a human head?"

WESLEY: "Well, ferns, one assumes."

POP CULTURE

✷ Room 217 is the same room number in Stephen King's 1977 novel *The Shining,* in which young Danny Torrance finds a dead woman in the bathtub.

✷ Judy Kovacs, the woman on the run, has a couple of pop-cultural antecedents. "Judy" was the name of Kim Novak's character in Alfred Hitchcock's *Vertigo*, which Tim Minear has said was a major source of inspiration to him. And Judy was on the run with stolen money, as was Janet Leigh's character in Hitchcock's *Psycho*.

✷ Mulvihill, the P.I., was named after a private eye rival to Jack Nicholson's Jake Gittes character in *Chinatown*. Like Gittes, this episode's Mulvihill ends up with a bandage on his nose, the result of Angel's having slammed a door on his face.

✷ When Angel drops in on Denver's bookstore, looking for information on the Thesulac, Denver slips a Bible into Angel's hands, burning them, and then pulls out a cross and a stake. But Angel gets behind him and takes control of the situation, warning, **"Now, it's been a long time since I opened a vein, but I'll do it if you pull any more of that Van Helsing Jr. crap with me."** Professor Abraham Van Helsing, of course, is a vampire hunter and Dracula's old nemesis in the Bram Stoker classic *Dracula*.

OUR HEROES

"In 'Are You Now or Have You Ever Been?' Angel reassures Judy he doesn't care about her being of mixed blood, saying 'It's all just blood.' Did that line have any special resonance for you?"

DAVID BOREANAZ: "That was a very racially oriented time period. So for him . . . it really is just blood, because he's been there, done it. He kind of has an understanding about it. It's pretty much an underlying theme for the whole show.

"We knew we wanted to do a story about the hotel, and that Angel had lived there. Initially we were going to set it in the forties, you know, Nazis and all that. It just seemed very romantic to all of us. And then at some point Joss said, 'You know, this should be the fifties.' And suddenly it was like, boom, it was about paranoia. It just made so much more sense to set it in the fifties. The cold war. Angel's personal cold war. It just made perfect sense."

"That just really fell together for me. It was the first time, I think, where I felt like pretty much exactly what I wrote ended up on the screen. That's what I wanted it to be, that's what I wanted it to look like, all the characters, all those little bits, those little character bits. I thought every actor was perfect.

"And I thought the director did a great job, and Herb Davis, who was our cinematographer, just made a movie. It did not look like a TV show. The way he filtered it, and gave everything a certain glow, and the fifties look. There's a shot . . . where Angel walks past Judy in the hallway, slams the door in her face, and without cutting the camera pans off the door, back to where you expect to see her standing there looking all dejected, and instead he's standing there and it's the year 2000 again—and also, the shot where Angel walks through the door, it's night. The door slams, and pans over to Angel standing there, and it's day.

"There was a lot of conversation about how to do this, how to accomplish this, in this small set, and we just insisted. Eventually we figured it out. Herb, who was using a different filter scheme between the fifties and the present day . . . was pulling filters out of the camera and changing the lighting, just as the camera is doing this. There's no [noticeable] cut. The door slams. There is a cut, the cut is this: David Boreanaz is walking toward the camera, we cut around onto David's back as he passes the girl.

"But as we cut around, that's not David anymore, that's a photo double going in through the door. The door slams, and then the camera, without cutting, pans over to David Boreanaz in his black. But also, as the camera's panning, if you'll notice, it goes by Judy, the door slams, and then the camera pans and now it catches a piece of the wall and the wallpaper's all peeled off. It's all peeling. The lighting is different, and David's standing there in present day. And that was just a bunch of people doing a bunch of stuff really fast." —TIM MINEAR

"'Are You Now or Have You Ever Been?,' with the introduction of our new hotel, was a really great and fun episode for the art department, because it really showcased the beautiful new set we did. But the challenge it created for us was, we had to present the hotel in its present-day, somewhat derelict condition, and in the flashbacks to 1952, when it was a sort of an ongoing, working concern of a hotel. And still do it all within eight days. So we swapped back and forth between wallpaper that had rips on it and graffiti on it, to wallpaper that was new. We brought in a lot of old dressing and sort of marred up a lot of the hallways, and had Angel walking through some parts of the hallways that had old bed frames and mattresses strewn about, and then he would turn a corner and all of a sudden he would be back in 1952. And we got a lot of help there from the DP being able to light it differently, create it moody in one aspect and a lot more saturated colors and a sense of life in the other."

—STUART BLATT, PRODUCTION DESIGNER

"Tim Minear . . . wanted this paranoia demon to kind of literally live within the walls of this hotel. And I wanted to kind of reinvent the way the demon might appear on stag. As well as having a traditional reveal, I wanted to invent how the whole paranoia thing might creep out, or how it might evolve. So Tim was really interested in seeing a squidlike, waterlike effect. That was a big breakthrough, because it was a three-dimensional approach to a portal instead of a two-dimensional approach to a portal, which means that when we used those elements we shot at Jex FX to create layers of depth from which I could bring in the Thesulac.

"On stage, we were able to shoot, untraditionally, multiple passes of the set, the set with people, and then the Thesulac against a green screen on this enormous parallelogram that Mike Gaspar built, that we were able to maneuver about the set without actually having the demon walk. So we gave this illusion that the demon was kind of floating or gliding through space, which we enhanced by distorting the environment."

—LONI PERISTERE, VISUAL EFFECTS SUPERVISOR

217

SIX DEGREES OF . . .

J. P. Manoux, who played Frank Gilnitz, the bellhop, appeared in the 2001 comedy *Beer Money* with Mercedes McNabb (Cordelia's friend from Sunnydale High, Harmony). In the science fiction comedy *Galaxy Quest,* he played a character called Excited Alien. Robin Sachs, *Buffy*'s Ethan Rayne, also appeared in that film, as Sarris. Manoux read twice for the role of Doyle on *Angel*, though the role ultimately went to Glenn Quinn. Manoux got a promotion on the WB's hit comedy *Nikki*, where he was upgraded to hotel manager. Nikki Cox's father on that show is Art LaFleur, the T'ish Magev in the *Angel* episode "Guise Will Be Guise."

TRACKS

"I took this Bernard Hermann score from *Vertigo*, plastered it all over the episode. And then Joss saw it and said, 'That *Vertigo* music is very important and we must have the *Vertigo* music.' And so I had Rob Kral just really try to get the flavor of that music, and if you look at the episode and listen for it, you can really get the feel. It feels like something Bernard Hermann would have scored in the fifties."

—TIM MINEAR

The tune to which the Salesman Type commits suicide is Perry Como's version of the polka standard "Hoop-Dee-Doo," by Milton DeLugg and Frank Loesser. Music coordinator John King talked about getting the clearance to use that song:

JOHN KING: "That was cool. That was a challenge. That was a bear to find. Because it was the only source cue, I wanted it to be relative to what somebody would be listening to before they blew their brains out.

"First we came up with Rosemary Clooney, which was 'Botch-a-Me.' And that was a quirky, funny tune; at the same time, it kind of worked against the scene. And it was all very fun and kind of eerie at the same time. So after spending weeks and weeks searching the Internet for hits of 1952, and prior to that, because it could have been anywhere before that time—and the thing about Rosemary Clooney was, they wouldn't let us have it because of the usage.

"That was another difficult problem. Publishers, when they have old songs, they're very protective of their material, particularly of people like Rosemary. So they wouldn't let us have it because the scene required some guy blowing his brains out while listening to it, and they felt that that didn't really do the song justice."

"You explained it was there for contrast?"

JOHN KING: "Yeah. You can explain, you can even try to fix the script so it's not so bad. I put in the clearance, 'Guy becomes possessed by self-destructive demon.' Got me Perry Como, and sometimes it shocks me. You'd be amazed at what you get."

"FIRST IMPRESSIONS"

FROM THE FILES OF ANGEL INVESTIGATIONS
CASE № 2ADH03

ACTION TAKEN

The Host compliments Angel on his most recent karaoke performance at Caritas, combining "Send in the Clowns" and "Tears of a Clown" in what Angel calls a "medley" and the Host calls "more of a duodely." When the Host turns away to sing a song of his own, Angel walks back toward the bar—where Darla waits for him, ravishing in a glamorous red dress. She leads him toward the dance floor. All the tables that were occupied when Angel just walked past are empty now, and the Host, up on stage, sings for Angel and Darla alone. They dance, holding each other close, and start to kiss. Finally, the Host interrupts his song, saying, "Someone get these two love vamps a room."

WRITTEN BY Shawn Ryan
DIRECTED BY James A. Contner
GUEST STARS: David Herman (David Nabbit), Andy Hallett (Host), Chris Babers (Jameel), Cedrick Terrell (Henry), Julie Benz (Darla)
CO-STARS: Edwin Hodge (Keenan), Lucas Babin (Joey), Alan Shaw (Deevak), Angel Parker (Veronica)

But none of this is really happening. It's a dream—one that Angel is *really* enjoying.

Cordelia and Wesley work on cleaning up the long-empty Hyperion Hotel's lobby. Gunn barges in, looking for Angel. Apparently Angel had promised to back Gunn up at a four o'clock appointment with an informant. It's now three-thirty and Angel's still asleep, much to Gunn's chagrin. This stool pigeon was supposed to direct Gunn to Deevak, a demon who has put two of Gunn's crew in the hospital. Cordelia offers her services and Wesley's, but Gunn isn't impressed with the suggestion.

Then another visitor appears—billionaire David Nabbit, clad in a long purple cape, armed with a sword. He was paged two days ago, while he was in Kuala Lumpur, so he's been delayed, but he's ready to slay demons now.

Finally, Angel comes down from his room. He had called Nabbit for financial advice, not demon-fighting assistance.

ANGEL: "We're making this hotel our new base of operations. Right now we're leasing it for six months with an option to buy."

NABBIT: "How much are you willing to put down?"

CORDELIA: "Nothing would be good."

NABBIT: "Oh, that's easy. You could look into seller financing, take over the owner's payments and skip a bank completely. Or you could make a play for a preservation grant. Offer to restore the original decor, get the city and feds to give you tax breaks and a loan at a sweetheart rate. Or you could apply for an F.H.A., get a P.M.I. in lieu of a down payment."

CORDELIA: "Is anybody else getting warm?"

Cordelia's attention flusters Nabbit, and he leaves, promising to have his money guy run some numbers for Angel. Gunn impresses upon Angel the urgency of the mission, so Angel tosses his car keys to Cordelia. When Gunn questions this, Angel observes that if they find Deevak they'll need the entire team.

They go to a covered parking garage for the meet. Jameel, the young man Gunn was looking for, is there, but he turns down the money offered to him. It turns out that he's more afraid of Deevak than he is of Gunn, and while he's come out of respect for Gunn, he's not going to rat out the demon. Gunn, concerned about his own soldiers, gets violent with Jameel. Angel grabs Gunn, trying to pull him off Jameel. Neither one is likely to back off . . . but before they can settle things, three vamps attack.

The fight is much longer and harder than it should be, considering that Angel is involved and there are only three vamps on the other side. Angel's disrupted sleep seems to be having unwanted consequences. Angel suggests that they need to regroup, but Gunn wants none of it. He goes off by himself to track down Jameel.

Later, Cordy drops an exhausted Angel off at the hotel. He tells her to bring the car back in the morning. So she heads back to her apartment, where she settles down with a book and a cup of tea—only to be racked by a typically excruciating vision. She sees Gunn, fighting for his life against an unseen foe and frightened out of his wits. She tries to phone Angel, but he's deeply asleep, lost in another of his Darla dreams. In the dream, he and Darla are on chairs by a pool, talking and flirting, playing with ice cubes from a drink. There's a distant phone ringing, but Darla tells Angel to ignore it.

When she can't raise Angel, Cordelia tries Wesley. She gets his machine and leaves a message, telling him to find Angel and meet her at Gunn's. Then she digs out a battle-ax from her closet and takes Angel's car.

At Gunn's place, a dingy, low-rent apartment building, she hears the sounds of combat. Convinced that her vision was right, she charges in and sees Gunn battling a young man with quarterstaves. She smacks him in the head with the flat of the ax.

But he's not a demon. Instead, he's Joey, one of Gunn's crew, and they've been performing an educational demonstration for the rest of Gunn's crew, which Cordelia, much to Gunn's embarrassment, has broken up with her assault.

Back in Angel's dream, Darla sadly tells Angel that she has to go away. Angel doesn't understand why he can't go with her, to protect her, but she tells him that he's too busy protecting everybody else. As they talk, there's a pounding noise. Angel looks to see what it is, and there's Wesley, hammering nails into a coffin. Angel tells him to stop, and looks back to see that Darla has disappeared. Enraged, he attacks Wesley, jumps on top of him, one hand clutching Wesley's throat.

Only this isn't the dream Angel, it's the real one, and the Wesley he's choking is also real. When Angel comes to, he's disoriented.

ANGEL: "What are you doing here?"

WESLEY: "Gunn's in trouble. Can't breathe."

ANGEL: "Gunn can't breathe?"

WESLEY: "*I* can't breathe."

ANGEL: "Oh, sorry."

WESLEY: (big gulp of air) "Quite all right. Now about the naked thing."

Angel, still naked from his sleepwalking incident, hurries off to get dressed.

Gunn starts to walk Cordelia to her car. But she insists that she's not leaving him unprotected. She had the vision, she knows he's in grave danger. Arguing, they head outside . . .

Where Angel's car is gone. Stolen.

Gunn puts Cordy into his truck and they drive off in search of the car. He knows the car thieves who work in this neighborhood, so he says they'll just work their way down the list until they find it. And then she'll leave him alone.

But she's still not going along with that plan. Besides the ax, she has Mace, and he needs protection.

Meanwhile, at the hotel, Wesley and Angel have just discovered that Angel's car is gone, Angel having forgotten that he loaned it to Cordelia in his rush to get more dream time. Fortunately, Wesley still has the motorcycle on which he arrived from Sunnydale. And he has a cool black helmet, which he's wearing. Which leaves a somewhat less cool pink helmet for Angel.

Gunn and Cordelia drop in on one of the local chop shops, where a young man tells them that he doesn't have the car, but that someone named Desmond specializes in convertibles. Gunn warns the young man about stealing cars from the neighborhood—he doesn't care if they go to more upscale areas to steal them, but he, as neighborhood protector, wants to keep the locals safe from car theft as well as from vampires.

When they leave, Deevak comes out of the shadows, having had a good close look at Gunn. He tells the young car thief that Gunn won't be a problem after tonight.

In quest of Desmond, Gunn and Cordelia go to a wild party. Cordelia insists that she knows how to blend, but when she goes inside and she's the only white person in the room, she suddenly feels a bit conspicuous. Gunn seems to know almost everyone, though, and the warmth of their feelings for him is obvious. When he finally spots Desmond, though, vampires attack the party. Gunn is held and beaten by some of the vamps, and a friend of his, Veronica, is slammed into a set of glass shelves in an alcove. A shard of glass slices open her neck. Falling to the ground, she pulls the glass out. Cordelia rushes over and applies what pressure she can. As soon as Gunn is freed from the vampires, Cordy tells him that Veronica needs a doctor. Gunn scoops her into his arms and they rush to the nearest E.R.

Veronica will be okay, thanks to Cordelia's quick thinking. But Gunn blames himself, believing that the vampires were after him and his friends were just trapped in the crossfire.

Desmond has also been brought to the hospital, and Cordy spots him there. She buttonholes him, demanding Angel's car.

Angel and Wesley have arrived at the remains of the party—ambulances and police cars, people rushing from the house. Angel stops a young woman on her way out, asking her questions about Gunn. She says she doesn't know him, but suggests that maybe he was one of the people taken to the hospital. Then, out of nowhere, Angel headbutts her—and she vamps out. "Now start talking," Angel snarls.

At another chop shop, Cordelia and Gunn find Angel's car. Not the keys, just the car. But Deevak shows up, dangling the keys. He's huge, seven feet tall, and hideously ugly, and he's accompanied by three vampire soldiers. He picks up Gunn by the throat. When Cordelia swings her ax at him, Deevak catches it, hurling it away, as Gunn dangles helplessly in his grip. Then Deevak morphs, becoming smaller—and turns into Jameel, the stool pigeon.

Once he's Jameel, and a little more reasonably sized, Cordelia hauls the Mace from her purse and squirts him in the face. His face begins to burn and smoke, and he releases Gunn, clawing at his own flesh and morphing back into Deevak. Two vamps attack Cordelia as the third goes to close the garage door. But Angel and Wesley arrive on the motorcycle, sliding just under the door. A furious battle ensues, and it's looking bad for Gunn as Deevak holds a ceremonial knife high, poised to strike him with it. But Angel leaps into the air, performing a flip. In the middle of his leap, Cordy throws him the battle-ax, and Angel buries it in Deevak's skull.

RESOLUTION

Wesley locates the keys to Angel's car, covered in demon blood, demon pus, or a combination of both. Gunn and Cordelia talk, and Cordelia tells him that Deevak wasn't the danger she was supposed to save him from. It's the way he lives his life, "on a self-destruct mission."

He can't quite bring himself to say "thank you," but he's touched by Cordelia's concern. And she's given him some things to think about.

When Angel gets back to the hotel, Darla's waiting for him. She tells him how unfair the others are, never thanking him, always making him be the protector but never letting him be protected. But Darla promises that she'll take care of him.

And it's another dream. Angel's asleep in his bed. Alone.

Only, not alone. Darla reaches out, touching his chest, rubbing it, climbing on top of him.

And this time, it's no dream.

Case closed.

DOSSIERS

CLIENT Charles Gunn is the client in need of saving. Except that what is endangering him isn't something from which Angel and company can save him with traditional weapons. He's putting himself in danger, every day and every night, by the way he's chosen to live his life. Guilt over the death of his sister Alonna at his own hands, and a driving compulsion to keep his neighbors safe from all harm, works on him to make him throw his own safety to the winds. There is no caution, there is only his urge to protect, no matter the cost to himself.

CIVILIAN SUPPORT David Nabbit is perfectly willing to fight demons, but is more in his element discussing finances.

SUSPECTS Deevak, the demon who made the mistake of moving into Gunn's neighborhood, is the case's prime suspect. Bigger and stronger and tougher than Gunn, he still isn't tough enough to take on Gunn and all his friends. (Deceased.)

CONTINUITY

Wesley's motorcycle makes its first appearance since the rogue demon hunter rode into L.A. on it in "Parting Gifts." Angel is confused by Darla's appearance in his dream, as he remembers dusting her in the *Buffy* episode "Angel." Wesley reminds Cordelia that she could be hosting Angel Investigations in her apartment again ("Judgement"), rather than helping dust the lobby of the Hyperion. David Nabbit was introduced in "War Zone" and reappeared briefly in "To Shanshu in L.A." Gunn refers both to his staking the vampire formerly known as his sister Alonna in "War Zone," and to the times he has assisted Angel since.

QUOTE OF THE WEEK

"It's just . . . you know . . . the whole visibility issue . . . not to mention the whole hat head thing . . . and you know, really, when you think about it . . . how come I have to wear the ladies' helmet?"

Angel tries desperately to avoid putting on Wesley's pink helmet.

THE DEVIL IS IN THE DETAILS

EXPENSES

New pager for Wesley, smashed in the garage fight
Dry cleaning, for bloodstains on Cordy's sweater after playing nurse to Gunn's friend Veronica
Repainting and maybe some bodywork on Wesley's motorcycle after Wesley and Angel lay it down

WEAPONRY

There's typical evil-battling stuff: stakes, a battle-ax, quarterstaves, and Mace

THE PLAN

When Angel's car is stolen, Gunn comes up with a way to find it.

> GUNN: "There's only a couple of guys in this part of town who jack vintage cars. We'll run down the list till we find Angel's ride."
> CORDELIA: "And then what? You're just going to ask them to give it back?"
> GUNN: "I'll say 'please.'"

THE PEN IS MIGHTIER

FINAL CUT

After the garage battle, the script sets the scene:

What's left of the attacking vamps. Not three neat little piles, nothing too cutesy, but clearly dead dusty chunky vamp dust.

POP CULTURE

- Gunn isn't impressed when Wesley and Cordelia offer to back him up.

  GUNN: "You two? I find Deevak, I'm gonna need something more than C-3PO and Stick Figure Barbie backing me up. No offense."

  CORDELIA: "When you do find him, you might want to be a little more Guy Pearce in *L.A. Confidential* and a little less Michael Madsen in *Reservoir Dogs*."

  GUNN: "I haven't bothered to see a movie since Denzel got robbed of the Oscar for *Malcolm X*. Later."

  Gunn stalks off, leaving Cordy, Wesley, and Angel recuperating against a car. After a moment, Wesley speaks up.

  WESLEY: "That was quite a performance."

  CORDELIA: "I know. Talk about wound up too tight."

  WESLEY: "No, I mean Denzel."

  CORDELIA: "Oh. Well, he's always great."

  WESLEY: (to Angel) "What about you?"

  ANGEL: "Who doesn't love Denzel?"

  Guy Pearce played Ed Exley, a cop who tries to rise above the corruption and violence that permeates the LAPD, in 1997's *L.A. Confidential,* adapted from the brilliant James Ellroy novel. In the 1992 Quentin Tarantino violence-fest *Reservoir Dogs,* Michael Madsen, as Mr. Blonde, performs a brutal torture scene that had audiences walking out of theaters. The Oscar that Gunn feels should have gone to Denzel Washington (and he's not alone in that belief) instead went to Al Pacino for his role in *Scent of a Woman.*
- **"And how exactly do you plan on protecting me? With some weak-ass Ladysmith Battle-ax?"** Gunn—stretching a bit for this one—is making a reference to the African vocal group Ladysmith Black Mambazo, popularized in the U.S. when they appeared on Paul Simon's *Graceland* album, as he questions Cordy's ability to keep him safe.
- **"I ain't buying none of this Dionne Warwick crap."** Scoffing at Cordy's psychic gifts, Gunn refers to singer Dionne Warwick, host of the Psychic Friends Network infomercials and an early advocate of numerology.

OUR HEROES

"I love [this] episode, because [it's] about making snap judgments on everything. Like I think that [Cordelia] has absolutely nothing to offer, I think she's a little model, waif, pretty girl who's not going

to get her fingernails dirty, and that's how I see her. And I think she has nothing to contribute. Obviously I learn the converse at the end.

"She thinks that I am just this angry street guy with no type of heart, and then she discovers that I have a heart because of the situation that I've been in with my sister.

"Then there's the Jameel character, who turns out to be Deevak. He's this little guy you see me bullying, but it turns out he's the arch-villain. So everything about that episode is not what it seems.

"Even Angel seeing the pretty girl leaving the party, it turns out she's a vampire. It's all about that judgment, that's what the whole episode is about. If you look at it, everything that's introduced is actually something different. When we walk into the party, I say hi to these two gangbangers. And Cordelia's all, oh, they're car thieves or whatever. And then it turns out that they actually save us. So everything is switched. It's a subtlety that I don't think everybody grasped from seeing the episode."

—J. AUGUST RICHARDS

"I think J. and I really bonded on that episode. We had a lot of late nights, and it was just the two of us, and—this is really funny, but that guy has got music in his head twenty-four/seven. He's always got a beat, he's always got a song, he's always hearing something. Like, he was singing 'Faith,' that song by George Michael, and I'd pick up on it. And we'd start boogying. And then we made up a routine. Like a Michael Jackson video or something. I really had a good time with him on that."

—CHARISMA CARPENTER

"The Hyperion Hotel set came about by a meeting that we had after the first season, with David Greenwalt and Joss Whedon and Kelly Manners and myself. And David and Joss wanted to give Angel a new place of residence, and a new place to work out of for Angel Investigations, because in the last episode of the first season, [his apartment] was blown up. So they debated for a while about putting him into a mansion, but that seemed a little Batmanlike, and they debated about putting him into a couple of other scenarios that didn't pan out to be as interesting, and one day Joss said, 'I'd like to put him into a hotel. Kind of like a creepy, abandoned hotel.'

"And I said, 'That sounds intriguing, are you thinking something along the lines of *The Shining*?' And he said, 'No, I'm thinking along the lines of *Barton Fink*.' And right then, right there, that gave me a really great jumping-off point that myself and my art director, Leonard Harmon, were able to go do some research, and use as a reference. We presented some ideas, and they said, 'Why don't we tone it down, why don't we make it look a little more like a standard hotel, nothing too creepy, nothing over the top. We don't want the hotel to be that much of a character, just from looking at it. We want that character to come out from the stories that they place in the hotel.

"We had an exterior of a building that was an abandoned apartment building years ago on Wilshire Boulevard, that's now being refurbished to residential apartments. We shot . . . the episode about the woman named Melissa Burns, with the doctor whose fingers came off. 'I Fall to Pieces.' We used that as the exterior of the apartment building, and we liked it so much David Greenwalt said, 'I wouldn't mind using that as the exterior of the hotel.' So we knew that would be a good jumping-off point, and then we took another week or so to do some drawings and start working on a

model. We built a scale model of exactly what we were planning to build, and went to present that to them.

"And they said, 'Okay, now this makes sense, we like this. Could you add some curves here? Could you get this grand staircase a little more grand? Could we have the elevators on this side as opposed to that side? Could we put the reception desk here, as opposed to there?'

"They decided they wanted to add an exterior garden to the hotel, but have it on stage so Angel could spend time outside during the day, but it would be a covered garden so he wouldn't be prone to burst[ing] into flames. We wanted a doorway that led to a basement, and then we built another set as the basement of the hotel.

"And once we had full approval from them as to design, and what all was going to go into the set, we put together a budget and they gave us the go-ahead, and from there it was a horserace of about six weeks to get it pretty much from start to finish. To where the crew could walk in there and start to film in there. It's the biggest thing I've ever built, and I'm completely pleased and blown away by how great it came out."
—STUART BLATT, PRODUCTION DESIGNER

"We went to the thirties [for Angel's new digs], and Angel's apartment has all this wonderful thirties furniture, and it's a little lighter. And his art has gotten a little brighter, but it still has a sense of a lonely person in it. He's someone who's still searching. We weren't able to have as many pieces, because the other place burned up, and I guess he didn't get into vampire storage much this year. But we kept a lot of the pieces from the building, we let the building have history.

"So our storage for this year was the hotel storage, so he got to furnish his room from the other rooms. And the same thing with his office, same thing happened. We assumed that the building had been going very successfully for many years, and then it was shut down like that. So everything was in there.

"So the building had its history, and . . . Stuart and I and the other powers that be established that there was a lot of history to the building, it had been very successful over the years. So that gave us a chance to have photos of false celebrities. It gave us a chance to have an old football with a nice statue. And I went and did a lot of antiquating for that, for little pieces that showed time again. But not Angel's time, the hotel's time. And then once he moved in, we got to pick the better pieces that we knew we were going to keep, and take away the junk. And so he had another, classier place."
—SANDY STRUTH, SET DECORATOR

"We ended up buying two other motorcycles and doctoring them up to look like [Wesley's] Triumph. And the stunt guys were great. They made those bikes slide and do everything the same, and we didn't have to lay the Triumph down. We shot that down at the Ambassador Hotel, on Wilshire. We got one of the *Dukes of Hazzard* cars in there, if you look at that episode. You'll see an orange car with a white stripe on its side. The General Lee. It's an old one. It's not necessarily one of the original ones, but it's one that somebody had made when they did a remake of the show."

—ROBERT ELLIS, TRANSPORTATION COORDINATOR

TRACKS

The Host, in the teaser, sings "Get Here," a song written by Brenda Russell and recorded by Oleta Adams.

Playing at the party Gunn and Cordelia crash is "Who Ride Wit' Us," by Kurupt.

"UNTOUCHED"

FROM THE FILES OF ANGEL INVESTIGATIONS
CASE № 2ADH04

ACTION TAKEN

Darla catches Lilah rifling Lindsey's desk after hours. Neither Lilah nor Darla has a lot of moral ground for outrage at finding the other in someone else's office—Lilah explains that it's just how things are done at Wolfram & Hart. As they talk, Lilah realizes that Darla is holding Calynthia powder, the substance that keeps Angel sleeping when Darla visits him.

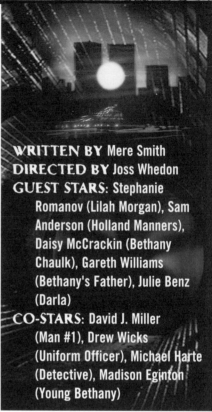

Angel wakes up from yet another in a long string of bad nights and heads downstairs, only to hear Cordelia and Wesley engaged in yet another in a long string of childish spats. They've been arguing about whether or not to pay Gunn for helping them out. Angel agrees to think about it, and asks if there's coffee. "There was, in the morning . . . it's ten o'clock at night," she says. But then she curtails the conversation with another vision—a girl in an alley, in trouble. Angel runs out the door, but Cordelia fears he'll be too late.

WRITTEN BY Mere Smith
DIRECTED BY Joss Whedon
GUEST STARS: Stephanie Romanov (Lilah Morgan), Sam Anderson (Holland Manners), Daisy McCrackin (Bethany Chaulk), Gareth Williams (Bethany's Father), Julie Benz (Darla)
CO-STARS: David J. Miller (Man #1), Drew Wicks (Uniform Officer), Michael Harte (Detective), Madison Eginton (Young Bethany)

Which, it appears, is the case. Bethany Chaulk is being menaced by two men with knives and unpleasant ideas. She's already hurt, bleeding from a cut on her forehead. Just when it seems that Bethany is out of luck, a heavy trash Dumpster lurches—seemingly under its own power—smashing the two thugs against a wall.

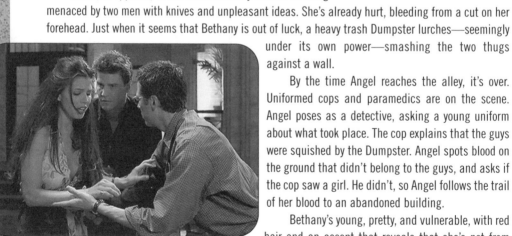

By the time Angel reaches the alley, it's over. Uniformed cops and paramedics are on the scene. Angel poses as a detective, asking a young uniform about what took place. The cop explains that the guys were squished by the Dumpster. Angel spots blood on the ground that didn't belong to the guys, and asks if the cop saw a girl. He didn't, so Angel follows the trail of her blood to an abandoned building.

Bethany's young, pretty, and vulnerable, with red hair and an accent that reveals that she's not from L.A. She's also terrified. She tries to warn Angel to keep away from her—and when Angel tries to put a hand on her arm to calm her, a rod of steel rebar shoots through the air and impales him.

Fortunately, it's steel and not wood. She panics, but Angel—as calmly as he can manage—

wrenches it from his chest. Now she knows there's something not-normal about him. He introduces himself, and she giggles a little hysterically.

"Great, I stabbed an angel. Now I'm really never getting into heaven."   *—Bethany*

He reassures her that it's just a name, and she begins to trust him a little, explaining that she didn't mean to hurt the men in the alley. She doesn't have any family in town, she admits under his questioning, but she's staying with a friend. Angel persuades her to take a business card, since she won't stick around to talk, and she leaves to go back to her friend's place.

Once she's gone, Angel drops to the floor, in real pain.

And Bethany makes it back to her friend's apartment—and the "friend" is Lilah Morgan, who has recognized Bethany's special powers and brought her to town.

Back at the hotel, as Cordelia dresses Angel's wound, Wesley points out that the girl is plainly dangerous and should be approached with caution. Angel agrees that she's powerful and that they should find out everything they can about her, to which Cordelia responds by reminding him that he didn't even find out her name.

Angel asks if she knows "how hard it is to think straight with a rebar through your torso?"

Which, of course, Cordelia does, having been through exactly that experience back in her Scooby days in Sunnydale.

But they don't have much to go on. Wesley's going to research telekinesis. Gunn shows up, bearing an ax made for him by some of the kids in his crew, and Angel assigns him to find out what he can about the thugs from the alley. Meanwhile, Angel's going to bed. Even though, as Cordelia observes, he's only been up for three hours.

Back at Lilah's place, Bethany has also gone to bed. As she sleeps, she dreams, a disturbing dream about her childhood in which her father, calling her "Rabbit," has clearly been behaving in an inappropriate fashion with his young daughter. Watching, even though she can't see Bethany's dream, Lilah seems to be enjoying a display of psychic power as a bedside lamp begins to vibrate. But before she can shield herself, Bethany awakes and the lamp goes flying, smashing into Lilah's face. Bethany screams and runs out the door.

Angel's dreams are of his own early life. He dreams of the night Darla brought him a young Gypsy woman, and of the passion with which he and Darla enjoyed each other. As he dreams, the real Darla is in the room with him, though thanks to the Calynthia powder, he doesn't know she's really there.

When he awakens, he goes downstairs to learn that there's been very little progress on finding out anything about Bethany. Wesley has learned that "telekinesis is a psychic phenomenon that occurs during periods of extreme emotional distress." Then Cordelia announces that she may have a lead—because Bethany has just let herself in the front door.

Angel introduces her to Wesley and Cordelia. "So it's a family business, huh?" Bethany asks, distaste evident in her tone.

At the Wolfram & Hart offices, Lilah confesses the events of the night before to Holland Manners. He's concerned that Lilah has lost control of Bethany. Lilah insists that she'll find Bethany, and as they talk her cell phone rings. It's Bethany, calling her to say she's okay.

Having reached her "friend" to check in, Bethany talks to Angel about what it's like when she has her telekinetic episodes. She has no control over it, she says. It's not a parlor trick. But she doesn't seem to want to delve too deeply into things. While they're talking, Wesley joins them, his tone stern. Tipped off by her comment about family and her youthfulness, he suggests that she doesn't seem to want their help, so they might as well send her home to her father.

At the mention of that word, Wesley is slammed into a wall and Angel is accidentally hurled into a patch of sunlight. He rolls into the shade, smoldering a little. Bethany runs away.

Cordelia, playing nurse again, tends to Wesley's bruises and wants to know why he forgot all about his own "approach with caution" idea. Left unsaid is the fact that Wesley knows a little something about dysfunctional father-child relationships from personal experience. Angel sends Wesley home, knowing that Bethany won't trust him if Wes hangs around.

He finds Bethany in a top-floor room in the hotel. She tells Angel that the worst thing about her experience is that she's embarrassed—she's killed people, and she's embarrassed.

After their conversation, they both go to separate bedrooms. Before long, Angel is dreaming, once again of the night with the Gypsy girl, and some heavy simultaneous chomping on his and Darla's parts.

When he wakes up, there's a woman in his room—but it's Bethany, not Darla. She suggests that Angel "do stuff" to her, have some fun. From the tone of her voice, it doesn't sound as though she's talking about fun. She puts a hand on Angel, through the covers, but when he touches her to move it away, she says "Get off of me!" and the bed shakes.

If her opinion of herself is pretty low, her opinion of men is microscopic, and probably with good reason. She describes the same sort of thing she talked about before—when she's with a man, she goes away, and comes back when he's done. Finally, she goes back to her own room, leaving Angel alone in his . . . except that Darla lurks in the shadows.

At the Wolfram & Hart offices, Holland Manners explains to Lilah why her project is putting a crimp in Lindsey's. If Angel doesn't sleep, Darla can't accomplish whatever it is she's trying to do. And that has a higher priority than Lilah's experiment with Bethany. He tells her to get Bethany out.

That afternoon Angel works with Bethany, demonstrating to her that she can control her powers. As they work, Cordelia comes in with an urgent request from Gunn. He needs Angel to meet him at a Brentwood address—more upscale than Gunn's normal stomping grounds. Angel leaves Bethany in Cordelia's hands.

In Brentwood, Angel breaks down the door of a luxury apartment. Gunn can enter, but Angel can't, which means the occupant, while not currently on premises, is alive. This is the home of one of the two thugs who attacked Bethany in the alley—not a cheap mugger or rapist after all, but high-priced muscle for hire. As Gunn searches the place, Angel falls through the doorway—which means the guy has died. Angel punches the redial button on the guy's phone, and it calls Wolfram & Hart.

Bethany has gone out with Cordelia. They're sipping coffee, talking, on a street near a carousel. Cordelia surprises Bethany by warning her away from sex with Angel, with an abrupt "Don't bone my boss." She points out that Bethany could have floated her attackers away, spun them around until they were sick—killing them was a choice. Maybe not a bad one, but a choice nonetheless, and she doesn't want any harm to come to Angel. As they're talking, a man bumps into them, surreptitiously shooting a tranquilizer dart into Bethany's neck. She starts to droop, and two other men grab her, muscling her into a waiting van.

Angel and Gunn come screeching around the corner in the Angelmobile. Cordy sends them after the van. Angel drives close to it, then hands off the wheel to Gunn. Angel climbs onto the hood of his own car and jumps to the back of the van, where he wrenches the door open and gets inside.

A furious Lilah is told, by phone, of the kidnap attempt's failure. But whomever she's talking to at least knows where Angel took Bethany.

"He took her to the hotel? Great. He wants to play with little miss time bomb, I say we let him. Pull the trigger."
—Lilah

And at the hotel, Angel argues with Bethany about Lilah, who Bethany still believes to be her friend. Things are flying all over the upstairs room Bethany has chosen as her refuge—her emotions getting out of control again, in spite of Angel's urgings to rein them in. Finally, she brings herself under control and opens the door to leave.

Only to find her father—the "trigger"—standing there. "Hello, Rabbit," he says. Every window on the hotel's top floor explodes.

Bethany's father explains that Lilah told him where to find her. He wants Bethany to come home with him. Bethany, meanwhile, is losing it again. The hotel literally tears itself apart—plaster flying from the walls and ceiling, floorboards prying themselves up. Bethany has surrounded herself with a psychic wall that not even Angel can penetrate. Bethany's father continues talking to her, using the pet name "Rabbit" that she has grown to hate, until finally she psychically lifts him into the air and hurls him through the upper-floor window.

Outside, he plummets, coming to a sudden stop four feet from the street, then drops the rest of the way, landing physically unharmed.

RESOLUTION

Bethany goes to Lilah's apartment to get her suitcase and clothes. Lilah tries to convince her that she's not cured, that she will get out of control again and need a friend. "My friends don't hire men to rape and kidnap me," Bethany replies. When Lilah says she was just trying to make Bethany stronger, Bethany's response is to telekinetically close her suitcase and fly it across the room into her hand. Mission Accomplished.

Angel waits for Bethany in the hall. Lilah, making a last-ditch stab, points out that Angel's a vampire. Bethany is not fazed by this news.

> **ANGEL:** "Looks like you're going to have to find somebody else's brain to play with."
> **LILAH:** "Yeah, we have someone in mind."

From the way Lilah looks at Angel, it's all too clear exactly who that someone is. . . .
Case closed.

DOSSIERS

CLIENT Bethany Chaulk is an abused young woman who seems to be afraid of her own power, but more than willing to use it when she believes herself to be under attack in any way.

SUSPECTS Bethany's father seems to underestimate the impact that his long pattern of abuse has had on his daughter. In the end, he finds out the hard way just how she really feels about him. (Remains at large.) **Lilah Morgan** hopes to use Bethany's power as a psychic weapon. **Wolfram & Hart** is successfully using Darla as a weapon, pointed straight at Angel's heart. But Darla seems to be a very willing tool.

CONTINUITY

Cordelia was impaled on construction materials in the *Buffy* episode "Lovers Walk." Angel warns Bethany she would not like a "happy" Angel, but does not elaborate on the curse. He recalls "getting happy" with Darla in the past. Gunn remarks fondly on Cordy's determination to save him from himself, as seen in "First Impressions."

QUOTE OF THE WEEK

WESLEY: "At least I've opened a book—"
CORDELIA: "Oh, don't even *try* with the snooty, Woolly Boy. I was top ten percent of my class."
WESLEY: "What class? Advanced Bosoms?"

Cordelia and Wesley engage in spirited intellectual debate.

THE DEVIL IS IN THE DETAILS

EXPENSES

Angel needs to replace the shirt Bethany drove a rebar through
And pants scorched when Bethany telekinetically hurls him into the sunlight
All the windows on the top floor of the Hyperion Hotel

WEAPONRY

"We made Gunn's ax out of hubcaps. They wanted to have something that looked a little different. So I went to the junkyard and kind of picked through old hubcaps and different things, and then went to the drawing board and drew up some different designs, got some things approved, and then went to Tony over at The Sword in the Stone, and he helped throw that together. And then in order for us to be able to do fights with it, we took it to Neotek later in the season, and had it vacuformed, so we could have a softer rubber one."

—COURTNEY JACKSON, PROPERTY MASTER

DEMONS, DEMONS, DEMONS

THE VAMPIRE RULES

Caffeine has the same effect on vampires as it does on humans.

THE PEN IS MIGHTIER

FINAL CUT

In the script, when Bethany comes into Angel's room while he's having his Darla dream, "she slips her hand under the covers and runs it up his thigh . . ." In the aired version, her hand remains discreetly outside the covers.

POP CULTURE

❖ **"Hey, you wanna get behind the tape? You gotta gawk, go home and watch a high-speed chase on Fox."** When Angel goes to the alley Cordelia saw in her vision, he pretends to be a police detective and pushes through the bystanders, making this reference to *Cops*, a long-running reality show on the Fox network.

❖ **"Nobody but our Mr. Bills."** Mr. Bill was a claymation puppet on early seasons of the *Saturday Night Live* TV show who was constantly being smashed, flattened, or otherwise mangled. A uniformed cop uses the phrase to describe the two guys Bethany crushed with the Dumpster.

OUR HEROES

"Untouched" is the first episode written by staff writer Mere Smith, after starting out as a *Buffy* fan and then working on *Angel* as a script coordinator. She spoke about the day her job description changed:

"I did that for a year, and then I got an opportunity to at least have a little creative input with the scripts sometimes, and they read my *Sopranos* spec and a couple of other specs that I had written, and this person came in to interview for the staff writer job, and I'm sitting at the desk out there going, oh God, there goes my last chance. That's it. I'm done. I'm never going to write on this show. They're going to hire this person, and I'm screwed, and I'm going be script coordinator for another year, and my head's going to implode.

"And when this person left, David called me in and he said, 'We're really disappointed with your script coordinating duties,' and I thought, not only am I not getting this job, I'm getting fired! And then he invited me to join staff, and I looked around the room, and I was like, 'If this is a joke, I'm going to be really pissed.' They all said, 'No, no, it's not a joke.'

"And one of the things that Joss said to me, which was just the most incredible thing, is when he hired me, he said, 'You know, we're not doing you any favors by hiring you.' And I was thinking along the lines of, you know, it's going to be tough, it's going to be like boot camp, okay. And he said, 'No, this isn't a favor that we're doing you by hiring you. We believe you can write the show.'

"And I was like, whoaaa . . . to have your Yoda say that to you. I walked out of the office and just burst into tears. I'm bursting into tears constantly, apparently. It was just amazing. And this year has been fabulous. I can't believe they pay me to do this. I show up to work every day, and it's like, I'm gonna get a check for coming here! It's so fantastic. There is no better job." —MERE SMITH

Julie Benz has her own unique take on the psychology of the interplay between Angel and Darla in this and the next few episodes, when Angel strays from the path that he's supposed to be on, the path of redemption, because he gets so pulled into dealing with Darla and being obsessed by her.

"Yeah, I think when you make that transition from teenager to adult, I think that happens. Growing up, you're told what you're going to do, and you rebel, and then you realize that it *is* what you want to do so you come back to it on your own terms. And having it be what you really want to do and not what people are telling you what you want to do. I think that's what makes you an adult. So I think every person goes through that. I know specifically I did. I was living in New York and partying a little too hard, having a little too much fun, and then one day I went, whoa, what am I doing here, what do I really want to do? I want to act, but I want to do it for my own reasons." —JULIE BENZ

Visual effects supervisor Loni Peristere from Radium described how Bethany's father's ninety-foot fall was done.

"Joss asked us to do a high fall that had a direct overhead shot of this character falling straight down. He wanted to see straight down, but actually a guy can't drop straight down without an airbag. So we made a green-screen airbag, and we put the floor back. We basically cut him out, and then Joss could have the illusion of a stuntman jumping right onto the pavement, which kind of enhanced the anxiety of that show." —LONI PERISTERE

SIX DEGREES OF . . .

Julie Benz and David J. Miller (Man #1, one of the thugs who threatened Bethany in the alley) both appeared in horror spoof *Shriek If You Know What I Did Last Friday the 13th*, along with recurring *Angel* actor David Herman (David Nabbit) and *Buffy* alum Danny Strong (Jonathon).

Madison Eginton (young Bethany) appeared as young Florence, uncredited, in another horror spoof, *Psycho Beach Party*, which costarred Nicholas Brendon (*Buffy*'s Xander Harris).

TRACKS

Composer Robert Kral describes his intentions in scoring the episode:

"Bethany in 'Untouched' was an abused, fragile, lonely soul, though she could kill just by thinking about it. I wanted to transport the audience to her inner little girl, an innocent child in need of loving." —ROBERT KRAL

While Cordelia and Bethany walk near a carousel, we hear "At the Fairground" by Pinelli and Thomas, from the 1970 musical adaptation of Harriet Beecher Stowe's novel *Uncle Tom's Cabin*.

"DEAR BOY"

FROM THE FILES OF ANGEL INVESTIGATIONS
CASE Nº: 2ADH05

ACTION TAKEN

Angel comes into the hotel lobby, looking barely alive. Plopping down onto a sofa, he ignores the tea he's offered. Cordelia remarks that he must be all worn out from having slept for the last three days. She's been doing some bookkeeping and has determined that Angel Investigations is out of money. They need a paying client, now. Wesley suggests she just have a vision. As they bicker, she in fact *has* a vision—a battle royal between a bunch of men in robes and a huge, slimy monster that seems to grow out of a wall, all in a strange, vast room full of pillars.

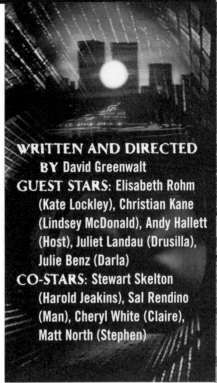

WRITTEN AND DIRECTED
BY David Greenwalt
GUEST STARS: Elisabeth Rohm
(Kate Lockley), Christian Kane
(Lindsey McDonald), Andy Hallett
(Host), Juliet Landau (Drusilla),
Julie Benz (Darla)
CO-STARS: Stewart Skelton
(Harold Jeakins), Sal Rendino
(Man), Cheryl White (Claire),
Matt North (Stephen)

Once he stops daydreaming about Darla and gets with the program, Angel realizes that the place Cordelia saw is a water tank built on the grounds of a cursed former convent. "I have a thing about convents," he explains.

He instructs Wesley to call in Gunn, and the four of them visit the enormous water tank. When they arrive, the battle still rages, the black- and red-robed combatants going at it with swords and axes. Growing between some of the tank's pillars is Turfog, the moldy, mushy monster Cordelia saw in her vision. Angel and Wesley recognize Turfog as a Thrall demon. The way to stop the battle is to kill the demon, at which point the acolytes will stop fighting.

Easier said than done, though, as Turfog sees them and shouts a warning. Now, allied against a common enemy, all the acolytes attack our heroes. During the battle, Angel knocks one of the acolytes down and keeps punching him, ignoring the rest of the fight. Gunn, using his hubcap ax, kills Turfog, after which they finally manage to pull Angel off his battered opponent.

Gunn, not happy with Angel's unwillingness to be a team player, brushes off the excuses Wesley and Cordelia offer.

Angel leaves by himself, going to Santa Monica's Third Street Promenade for some private, broody time amongst the hundreds of shoppers gathered there. As he walks, he sees Darla, meandering through the crowd in a tight red dress.

The sight reminds him of London in 1860, when Darla, still showing her dear boy the ropes, points out a special prize for him. A family with three daughters goes past, and in the middle daughter Angel can

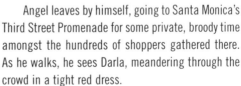

smell something unique. Darla tells him that she has the Sight. This intrigues Angel—she can see the future, she knows what he's going to do to her . . . this makes her a special prize indeed.

He doesn't know it yet, but this daughter is named Drusilla.

The present Angel snaps out of his reverie and tries to catch up with Darla. But he's jostled by a guy wearing a giant hot dog suit, and when he makes his way past the big frankfurter, she's gone.

Meanwhile, back at the hotel, Angel Investigations has a new paying client. Harold Jeakins has heard that Angel handles unusual cases, and his certainly qualifies. His wife, Claire, he explains, seems to be frequently abducted by aliens. But he found a receipt from the Franklin Hotel, at a time when she was supposedly in the Trifid Nebula, so now he wants to know if she's having affairs instead of being abducted.

Angel walks in from his window-shopping trip, totally ignoring the customer-to-be, and goes into his office. Cordelia and Wesley assure Harold that Angel is on the case. When Harold's gone, Angel tells them that he saw Darla. Wesley points out that Angel dusted her, three-and-a-half years earlier. Convinced he saw her, Angel dismisses their rationalizations.

And, in Lindsey's office at Wolfram & Hart, Lindsey and Darla celebrate the effect she's having on Angel—in Lindsey's words, "Unhinging him." Lindsey reveals that Wolfram & Hart doesn't want Angel dead, they want him dark. Darla's happy to help. As they talk, Lindsey prepares a special envelope for delivery.

At her police precinct desk, Kate Lockley is handed an envelope from a "friend of a friend." Inside is a photo of the Hyperion Hotel and one of Angel's business cards, with a note reading, "He's moved."

The next day finds Cordelia dressed in a skimpy cocktail waitress's outfit, making herself busy at the Franklin Hotel. Hidden within a stack of cocktail napkins is a tiny microphone, and Angel listens from a nearby hiding place while Wesley takes pictures with a miniature camera. They overhear "abductee" Claire Jeakins making arrangements to be "abducted" by a hotel repairman up to one of the rooms. They've got the goods on Claire—but instead of taking the evidence of his wife's behavior to Harold, Angel goes to Claire, advising her that Harold knows and that she should go home and tell him the truth.

Another client down the tubes, and before he's even been billed. As Wesley and Cordelia debate the point with Angel, he interrupts them because he spots Darla across the lobby. He confronts her—but this woman doesn't recognize him. He presses, scaring her, and a hotel security guard comes over. Angel knows that this is Darla, he can smell her. But she tells the guard her name is DeEtta Kramer. Then she sees her husband heading for the door, and she runs to him—and into bright sunlight, where Darla the vampire could never go.

Back at their own hotel, Angel tells Cordelia and Wesley to find DeEtta Kramer, if she really exists. He's going to try some other avenues. But before he can do that, he has to borrow some cash for the cover charge.

Which means he's going to Caritas.

Angel sings—atrociously—and then asks the Host about Darla. But the Host isn't having any. He tells Angel that he sets people on their path, but Angel is headed way off his path if he pursues the Darla angle. He offers to buy Angel a drink, but that's all he'll do.

Instead, Angel calls the hotel and gets the address Cordelia's turned up. Cordelia and Wesley start to prepare for the worst—Angel's mood has become so sour, they're worried that he might go bad again, and they decide to call Gunn to warn him of the possibility.

Angel goes to the Kramers' house and watches through the windows as a woman who looks decidedly like Darla enjoys dinner with Stephen Kramer. What he can't hear is the discussion going on inside—where "Stephen Kramer" reveals himself to be an actor, trying to get the part right and *really* getting on Darla's nerves in the process. Lindsey is plugged in, remotely, listening to everything and keeping an eye on Angel outside.

Gunn has come over to the Hyperion, more than a tad disturbed at the warning of what Angel might become.

And Angel's thoughts, outside Darla's house, seem to be running along similar lines. He remembers another convent, back in 1860, where, in spite of Darla's wishes, he sired Drusilla instead of killing her.

Inside the house, Lindsey gives Darla a signal and she goes into action, grabbing a phone and calling 911. She gives her false name and address and shouts that there's a man outside breaking into her house. Then she breaks down into terrified screaming and tears the phone from the wall. The actor playing Stephen objects—this is not what he signed on for. But before he can do anything, a vampire who's been hiding in the house kills him. Meanwhile, hearing Darla's cries for help, Angel charges through the door. He sees "Stephen" dead on the floor, sees Darla, hears police cars surrounding the house, and understands. His understanding comes just in time for the cops to come in and aim their guns at him.

Angel runs. The cops give chase, but he's gone.

Outside the house, Kate Lockley talks to "DeEtta Kramer" about the man who attacked her, whom Darla says has been stalking her for weeks and gave his name as Angel. Kate promises Darla that she'll make him pay for what he did. Then, as she issues instructions to the officers on the scene, strong arms reach down from above, clamping over Darla's mouth and lifting her away.

At the Hyperion, Gunn discusses strategy with Cordelia and Wesley.

> **CORDELIA:** "Ninety-nine percent of the time, good, and he's done a lot for us."
> **GUNN:** "There's nothing I respect more than loyalty."
> **CORDELIA:** "That's good to hear."
> **GUNN:** "But if the bad Angel walks in that door I will kill him in two seconds flat."

But there's someone at the door, and it isn't either version of Angel—it's Kate and her SWAT team. They begin to search the hotel. Kate, having never met Gunn before, takes his name and demands that his record be searched. He turns out to have a fairly impressive rap sheet—some from when he was a minor, but some from the last couple of weeks.

Angel's not there, though—he's back at the water tank, with Darla, demanding to know what her plan is. He reveals that he knows that she's been brought back by Wolfram & Hart—and as a human.

She seems scared at first, but then, when he morphs into a vampire and grazes her neck, her fear gives way to excitement and renewed lust.

At the hotel, Kate tells the Angel Investigations crew about Angel's attack on DeEtta Kramer. Gunn points out the fallacy in that argument—being a vampire, Angel could not have entered the house without an invitation, unless its owners, the *real* Kramers, were dead.

While Kate mulls that over, Wesley shows her a picture in one of his books—a daguerreotype, taken more than a hundred years earlier—of Darla.

And in the water tank, Angel explains to a reluctant Darla that her newfound humanity comes with a price. Along with a soul, she now has a conscience, and it's going to start weighing on her, especially the murder of the actor playing her husband, since it was done while she was human and not a vampire.

She tries to persuade Angel to let her give him his one moment of happiness, to bring back the dark Angel she knows and loves so well, and she figures that the dark Angel will happily turn her back into a vampire. But he tells her that, in spite of all they shared, she never made him happy. She, of course, disputes his memory of things, and compares herself to Buffy.

> **DARLA:** "There was a time, in the early years, when you would have said I was the *definition* of bliss. Buffy wasn't happiness. She was just new."
>
> **ANGEL:** "You know, you're getting awfully bent over this, Darla. I couldn't feel that with you because I didn't have a soul. But then I got a second chance. Just like you have."
>
> **DARLA:** "And what a poster child for soulfulness you are. . . . This is no life, Angel. Before you were neutered you weren't just any vampire, you were a legend. Nobody could keep up with you—not even me. You don't learn that kind of darkness—it's innate. It was in you before we ever met. You said you can smell me? Well I can smell you, too. My boy's still in there, and he wants out."

Angel is shaken by these words—as much as he believes in redemption, there's some truth to what Darla says.

The SWAT team can't find Angel at the hotel, of course. Kate expresses her concern for the innocents caught in the crossfire during Angel's seemingly perpetual quest against the forces of evil, and leaves the Angel Investigations team to think about her words.

Meanwhile, Darla continues prodding at Angel, telling him he's going to miss the dreams he's been having. Finally, she walks away from him, into the sunlight, and all he can do is watch her go.

RESOLUTION

Angel sits alone in his hotel suite, brooding as only he can brood. He's interrupted by a knock on his door. Opening it, he finds Wesley and Cordelia, the latter with her hands behind her back. She says because they hadn't seen him all day, they were wondering if everything was copacetic, and he assures them that he hasn't gone bad. Upon which Cordy shoves the tranquilizer gun she's been carrying into Wesley's hands. Wesley warns Angel to be careful—with Darla back, teamed up with Wolfram & Hart, he says, there's going to be trouble.

Case closed.

DOSSIERS

CLIENT Harold Jeakins, a husband who has come to believe that not all of his wife's alien abductions are real. But the Angel Investigations team's surveillance of Claire Jeakins leads them to an encounter with Darla.

CIVILIAN SUPPORT The Host tries to warn Angel away from Darla, but to no avail.

VICTIMS The unnamed actor who plays Stephen Kramer gives the performance of a lifetime—or the last performance of a lifetime, anyway—when he portrays DeEtta Kramer's husband opposite the murderous Darla. **The real Kramers** are presumably victims of Wolfram & Hart's machinations.

SUSPECTS Darla, after having played Angel in his sleep, now takes over his waking life as well.

CONTINUITY

When Angel protests taking on Harold Jeakins's case, Cordelia points out that Angel is the head of Angel Investigations. Not for long . . . Gunn demonstrates that, like the other members of Team Angel, he is willing to kill Angel if the vampire succumbs to his demonic nature (Cordelia demonstrated this in "Eternity," and Wesley in "I've Got You Under My Skin"). When Angel is describing his glimpse of the woman from his past to Cordy and Wes, at first Cordy thinks Buffy has returned to L.A. Upon learning that he means Darla, Wes reminds him that he dusted her more than three years ago in the *Buffy* episode "Angel." Angel remembers when he and Darla discovered Drusilla and turned her into a vampire. Dru will return the favor to Darla in "The Trial." The Host warns Angel to steer clear of Darla, and Angel storms out of Caritas, perhaps never to return.

QUOTE OF THE WEEK

"What if . . . every time you identified a demon on one of your old books we gave you ten bucks . . . or a chicken pot pie."

Cordelia looks for money-saving ideas to stave off bankruptcy, including cutting Wesley's pay.

THE DEVIL IS IN THE DETAILS

EXPENSES

Costume rental for Cordy's cocktail waitress outfit
Recording equipment for getting the goods on Claire Jeakins
The front door to the Kramers' house

WEAPONRY

Charging into the underground tank, Angel carries a sword, Gunn his hubcap-ax, Wesley a mace, and Cordelia an ax.

DEMONS, DEMONS, DEMONS

Cordelia describes **Turfog** as a "mush monster," and that's fairly accurate. He grows between pillars like a giant spider in a web and is repulsively slimy. His acolytes battle furiously over how best to worship him.

Steve Fink of special effects house Optic Nerve shared this about creating Turfog, the demon in the water tank:

"It's a challenge also if you have a creature that is not human form, but you still have to have a human performer inside of it. There was a character named Turfog and he was a big blob-monster thing. It was just this big blob thing, and we had four or five guys inside of that thing, articulating the face, which is mostly remote control. But then we had people moving the arms around and stuff. And eventually he gets an ax in the head and falls back. That's the largest thing we've done for Angel as far as size." —STEVE FINK

THE VAMPIRE RULES

Vampire senses are highly attuned in ways humans can't even begin to equal. Looking at Drusilla and her family, Angelus can sense that there's something unusual about Dru, which Darla confirms.

AS SCENE IN L.A.

"[The water tank] was something that we found, I believe it was the first episode, when we were looking for tunnels. I was on location and I was talking to the plant manager, and I asked, 'Do you have anything else around here that would be interesting to shoot in?' And this was the Jensen Water Plant. And he said that they had a huge [fifty-five million gallon] water tank that was empty, and there was only one way to get in and that was through this door at the top. He went over and showed it to me, we shot it and showed it to the producers, and they really liked it. So they wrote the script to that location. It was empty because they were repairing it. There was one other music video that shot up there, but I think once they fill it back up it won't be available again, so it was kind of an unusual location. It was difficult to get all the equipment in, because we had to rent a crane and have everything lowered down into the tank. And there's just one way in, and you go down the stairs into the tank." —KEVIN FUNSTON, LOCATIONS MANAGER

THE PEN IS MIGHTIER

FINAL CUT

In the script, Lindsey compliments Darla on her ability to manipulate Angel with this exchange, some of which was cut from the final episode due to length.

> **LINDSEY:** "We're counting on that. You've given us more information on Angel than we had when he first got here. Nobody knows him like you do, especially the side we're interested in."
>
> **DARLA:** "Which is—?"
>
> **LINDSEY:** "The particular set of hairs you have the boy by. Angel may be a vampire, but he's still a man."

POP CULTURE

❋ "**Imagine Bonnie and Clyde if they had a hundred and fifty years to get it right.**" Cordelia describes what Angelus and Darla were like when they rampaged the Earth together, likening them to the famous crime-loving couple.

❋ **WESLEY: "Oh, he's an eccentric, all the great ones are. Sherlock Holmes, Phillip Marlowe . . ."**
   HAROLD: "Those are fictional characters."
   WESLEY: "Yes, right you are! Which gives Angel rather a leg up when you come to think of it."

Wesley tries to explain Angel's distance to a client, referring to Holmes and Marlowe, both classics of detective fiction. Holmes was created by Sir Arthur Conan Doyle, and Marlowe by Raymond Chandler.

Angel reveals his special love for convents:
DARLA: "You made quite a mess out there."
ANGEL: "Convents. They're just a big cookie jar."

OUR HEROES

JULIE BENZ: "It was [strange to get to go outside on this show]. We don't do very many day exteriors, so it was a little weird. It was really hot that day, too. [Normally I wouldn't think that,] but I totally forgot we were shooting during the daytime outside. It's not something we're used to on the show."

"And then, the end scene in the water tank, how did you work with the parts where Darla's trying to get Angel to recognize who he is? Do you feel that that's her really asking him to become the Angel she wants again, or is she just trying to do her part for Wolfram & Hart and the powers of darkness?"

JULIE BENZ: "Oh, no, I think that's all her. [Darla] was brought back as a tool for Wolfram & Hart to use to try and get him to do whatever it was that they wanted. But ultimately, her mission was to get him to be the Angel that he was, the Angel that she made. That overrides anything. Darla is not one to really allow herself to be manipulated. Even in human form, she'll play the game but she's going to do it for her own motivations.

"I think the scenes in the water tank reveal how she really is the ex-wife, the scorned lover who can't get over him. And they were together for a hundred and fifty years. It was a long time, and she can't even grasp the idea of Buffy. She says, 'He thinks he's touching God.' It's that whole, I thought we were in this long haul thing, and you go out and have this affair. That's her opinion of it. Buffy only has three years on him, whereas she has a hundred and fifty. But I think it really sets up the whole scorned ex-wife thing. He was her true love. She was not his, but he was hers. And it devastates her, in a way, to think that she never gave him true happiness."

"The reason that Angel and Darla picked Drusilla was because of her extrasensory perception and ability to have visions. That was definitely a part of Drusilla *prior* to becoming a vampire. However, being tortured by Angel, the terrible things he did to her family, and what happened in the convent were huge in shaping who she is as well. So all of those components definitely figure in together. In the back story Joss filled in for us, Angel tortured and killed Drusilla's entire family in front of her. She fled to the convent as a means of seeking refuge. What then transpires with Angel has a darkly incestuous element because he's the father figure, he "makes" her who she is. There's that thread and she gets turned around, and her sensuality and sexuality got released in this unusual way. I don't think she would have been the same person in that realm, without that having happened." —JULIET LANDAU

"So, when we were talking about Season Two, we sort of didn't know what we were going to do with [Darla]. It's like, okay, so she's back, what does that mean? Does it mean that they're gonna try to get him to sleep with her? Is she gonna try to kill him? And . . . I pitched to Joss the idea that perhaps she was brought back as human. It just clicked with him immediately, and he saw all the possibilities. And it also changed everything, 'cause once he realized she was human, it just added this entire interesting . . . first of all, he couldn't just kill her. But if she were a vampire still, for sure he could. There would be no moral ambiguity there whatsoever. She's just a bad vampire, I will kill her.

"Also since we ended Season One with this promise of humanity for him, that at the end of the day, after he atones, he will get this reward, then for this creature to be brought back with the exact thing that he has been promised without having to work at all for it, without deserving it for a moment, and then not wanting it. Also, I think it's unbelievably Oedipal. She's his mother, she's his lover, she made him what he is, she's his ex-wife. They were together for a hundred and fifty years. She is the absolute reason he's having to atone for everything he's having to atone for." —TIM MINEAR

SIX DEGREES OF . . .

Actor Derek Anthony, who plays the hotel security guard who protects "DeEtta Kramer" (Darla) from Angel the stalker, also appeared in the Season One episode "Blind Date" as "Dying Black Man," Vanessa's victim.

TRACKS

In Caritas, Angel sings—badly—"Everybody Have Fun Tonight," the hit song by Wang Chung. When Angel sees Darla, we hear "Stinky Stinky Ashtray," by Damn!

"GUISE WILL BE GUISE"

FROM THE FILES OF ANGEL INVESTIGATIONS
CASE № 2ADH06

ACTION TAKEN

Working on files at Angel Investigations one night, Wesley is surprised by a potential client. His surprise comes across—reasonably, as he keeps falling down, dropping things, and bonking himself in the head—as clumsiness, not exactly confidence-inspiring. When Wesley reveals that he doesn't know where Angel is or when he'll return, the client leaves. Cordelia comes down from upstairs to find Wesley sitting on the floor in the midst of a stack of papers he's strewn everywhere.

At the Wolfram & Hart office building, Angel and Gunn emerge from a vent in the floor, having arrived via Angel's usual subterranean expressway. They get onto an elevator to go upstairs, but the elevator is blocked by a man's briefcase. When the doors open again, Cordelia and Wesley are there, dressed like lawyers. They enter, and Cordelia tries to persuade Angel not to go up, reminding him that Wolfram & Hart has vampire detectors and it's not safe for him to be in the building. But Angel wants to find Darla and, knowing Wolfram & Hart brought her back to life, figures this

WRITTEN BY Jane Espenson
DIRECTED BY Krishna Rao
GUEST STARS: Andy Hallett (Host), Art LeFleur (T'ish Magev), Brigid Brannagh (Virginia Bryce), Patrick Kilpatrick (Paul Lanier), Todd Susman (Magnus Bryce)
CO-STARS: Danica Sheridan (Yeska), Saul Stein (Benny)

is the place to do it. As they argue—Cordy punching the DOOR OPEN button repeatedly to keep the elevator on the ground floor—a uniformed security guard shows up, raising his nightstick and pressing a button that causes a stake to emerge from its end. Angel takes the nightstick away from him and drives the stake through the guard's shoe, pinning his foot to the elevator floor.

Recognizing that he's losing control over himself, Angel returns to Caritas for another session with the Host. It's Gunn's first visit.

> **GUNN:** "Okay, what I want to know is . . . is how I live in L.A. my whole life and never knew this weird-ass stuff was going on?"
>
> **CORDELIA:** "Oh, the ass is even weirder than you think."

243

WESLEY: "The Host, the fellow talking to Angel over there? He helps demons, reads their souls, senses their futures. . . ."

CORDELIA: "Yes, but he can only do it when they sing karaoke."

GUNN: "Wait. Are you saying . . . Is he gonna sing? Oh God, is Angel gonna sing?"

But the Host—knowing how Angel sings—relieves him of that nightmare this time. He gives Angel the address of the T'ish Magev, a sort of swami who will, in the Host's words, "shock your chakras, fillet your soul . . . whatever you need."

Angel drives off to Ojai that night to meet with the promised healer. At a rustic cabin by a lake he meets a beefy-looking guy in a flannel shirt, wiping his hands on a dish towel, not looking at all like Angel's expectation of a shaman. This is the T'ish Magev, and he's expecting Angel.

Back at the Hyperion, Cordelia is alone, closing up the office for the night, when she's grabbed from behind by a thug named Benny. He asks for Angel, to which she truthfully responds that he's not around. Benny doesn't like hearing that. He pulls a gun, saying that his boss needs Cordy's boss, so either she gets Angel or Benny blows her head off.

Wesley, passing by, hears this. Donning one of Angel's many black dusters, he strides confidently into the room, introducing himself as Angel.

At the cabin, the T'ish Magev questions Angel about his car.

ANGEL: "I thought we were going to talk about my problems?"

T'ISH MAGEV: "That car is your problem, pal. It says everything about you."

ANGEL: "The car?"

T'ISH MAGEV: "Yes, the car. You live in L.A. It's all about the car you drive."

ANGEL: "I really don't think . . ."

T'ISH MAGEV: "Vampire living in a city known for its sun, driving a convertible . . . Why do you hate yourself?"

ANGEL: "I don't . . . I got a deal."

T'ISH MAGEV: "You got a deal. Why not a personalized license plate that says 'irony'?"

Wesley, meanwhile, tries to be brave when Benny points the gun his way. The gun, Wesley assures Benny, is no threat because he's Angel, a vampire. Benny follows the reasoning and puts it away, telling Wesley to go with him. When Wesley objects, Benny points out that the gun will still hurt Cordelia. Following that logic, Wesley agrees to go.

Benny takes him to an imposing, and well-guarded, mansion. When they reach the door, Benny invites Wesley in—vampire protocol is obviously familiar here. As he leads Wesley deeper into the house, they encounter a man named Paul Lanier having a confrontational business discussion with Magnus Bryce, the owner of the house and Benny's employer. When Lanier leaves, Benny introduces his boss to "Angel."

Bryce apologizes to Wesley for the lateness of the hour, and dispatches Benny to get him a drink. He launches into an explanation—he needs protection for someone very dear to him—and then Benny returns with a nice fresh glass of blood. Wesley tries to refuse, but Bryce insists, and Wesley takes a drink, fighting to hold it down. As he does, Bryce explains that his family's fortune comes from wizardry, what he calls "custom-design work for people with the right money."

But, it turns out, he has a lot of business rivals, and they're not nice people. He has protection spells, but others in the same business know all the tricks to get around them. And someone's been threatening his only daughter. He wants Angel to protect her. He's very insistent—he'll pay well, but he won't take no for an answer.

The T'ish Magev tells Angel that there are two of him—more true than either of them know, at this moment.

ANGEL: "Two me's?"

T'ISH MAGEV: "This image you've worked so hard to create and the real you—"

ANGEL: "Well, maybe my persona is a little affected."

T'ISH MAGEV: "A little affected? Come on. How many warriors slated for the coming Apocalypse are gonna be using that hair gel?"

He pulls some sparring sticks from a wall holder, tosses one to Angel, and challenges him to fight, in order to test his theory that Angel is really fighting himself.

Wesley is introduced—as "Angel," of course—to Virginia Bryce, the daughter in question. Twenty-four, beautiful, with tight copper curls, she's more than a little snotty with him at first. Finally, asserting himself for the first time, Wesley sends everyone out of the room so he can talk privately with her. He proves to be both sensitive to her situation—observing that, because there are so many bookshelves in the room it is apparent that she spends a lot of time in it—and willing to do what he can to help. She needs protection and he wants to protect her, if she won't fight it. She agrees, saying that she wants to go shopping. He's surprised, since it's so late, but then he remembers that he's supposed to be a vampire, and couldn't really be expected to take her shopping during daylight hours.

Cordelia has called Gunn to the hotel and told him about Wesley's abduction. She sends Gunn to get Angel from the T'ish Magev while she looks through mug shots online, hoping to find a lead on Benny.

Wesley, meanwhile, is not quite as bad off as they think. He and Virginia have gone to a very upscale wizard supply shop, looking for a fiftieth birthday gift for Magnus Bryce. As they shop, some thugs try to grab Virginia. But when she identifies Wesley as Angel, they think twice. Wesley gets into the role, threatening them and touching his forehead as if he might morph. They let her go and, before they hurry away, let spill the fact that they work for Lanier.

Angel battles the T'ish Magev, who accuses Angel of holding back. Angel denies it at first, finally admitting that he can't let go because if he does, "it" will kill the T'ish Magev.

T'ISH MAGEV: "It?"

ANGEL: "The demon."

T'ISH MAGEV: "Ahh. But the demon is you."

With that insight, he launches into a move that knocks Angel to the ground, and leaves Angel with a few things to think about. Later, alone and clearly in pain, the T'ish Magev talks to Paul Lanier on the phone. He reveals that he's worried about Angel—the vampire can smell blood, and will soon figure out where the real T'ish Magev's body is stashed. Lanier is concerned for a different reason . . . if Angel is at the cabin, then who's guarding Virginia Bryce?

Cordelia, still looking for a mug shot of Benny, finds herself drawn to a celebrity magazine. She turns to the photo pages, and it isn't long before her eye is drawn to a shot of "Millionaire CEO Magnus Bryce and daughter Virginia." And, perfectly recognizable in the background, is Benny.

Wesley and Virginia are back at the mansion, walking toward her room. Two hooded guards in the hallway turn out to be not really guards at all, but more of Lanier's minions, making another attempt to snatch her. Wesley fights them off, solo—not just scaring them this time, but really performing, putting everything he's learned to use. He even impresses himself, and Virginia is awed.

The fake T'ish Magev is back with Angel, talking about Darla. He speculates that it was her return that triggered Angel's inner struggle, because she was the one who made him what he is. But his prescription takes Angel by surprise.

> **T'ISH MAGEV:** "You're deeply ambivalent."
>
> **ANGEL:** "Well . . . I am and I'm not."
>
> **T'ISH MAGEV:** "You need to get over her. Okay, what does she look like?"
>
> **ANGEL:** "She's beautiful . . . small, blond . . ."
>
> **T'ISH MAGEV:** "Right. So here's what you do—you go out and you find yourself some small, blond thing. You bed her. You love her. You treat her like crap. You break her heart. You and your inner demon'll thank me, I promise."

Of course, Angel's already been through his share of "small blond things." And he's still here. But a phony T'ish Magev can't know everything.

Back in Virginia's room, the girl opens up to Wesley, and his sensitivity to her plight proves to be irresistible. They begin to kiss. Then she tries to stop, explaining that she knows all about the Gypsy curse. He tells her that "curse" is too strong a word, that's it's more of a "hex," or a "recommendation." Before long, they're lost in passion.

The next morning, Gunn shows up at the cabin. The T'ish Magev goes out to meet him. When Gunn says he's come to get Angel, the T'ish Magev slugs him twice, knocking him down.

But Angel has seen the whole thing, and demands to know where the real T'ish Magev is. The phony just laughs—he's standing out in the sunshine, where Angel can't get him.

Except that there's a fishing rod on the porch, and Angel proves to be a surprisingly adept caster. He hooks the T'ish Magev's lip and reels him in, looking for answers.

Having slept with the boss's daughter, Wesley tries to sneak back to his own room. But Cordelia, of all people, stops him in the hall. She's come to rescue Wesley, who definitely doesn't want to be rescued. Virginia is still in trouble, and he's still her bodyguard as well as her lover. While they argue, Bryce approaches with Benny and another thug. Wesley tries to explain Cordelia's presence by saying she's an associate sent in to test their defenses. But Bryce explains that he allowed her in because he wanted his daughter to hear someone call Wesley by his real name. Benny shoves Wesley into a shaft of sunshine, where he, of course, fails to burn up.

Virginia is crushed. Not only did he lie, and not only is he not the friend she thought he was, but when she allowed him to take her shopping, he was putting her life in danger. She walks out, and Wesley and Cordelia are allowed to leave.

Benny is surprised that Bryce just let them go, but Bryce is furious with Benny for bringing the

WESLEY: "What happened to your head?"
CORDELIA: "Excuse me?"
WESLEY: "Your hair, it's new—it's
  great—when did this happen?"
CORDELIA: "Ten days ago."

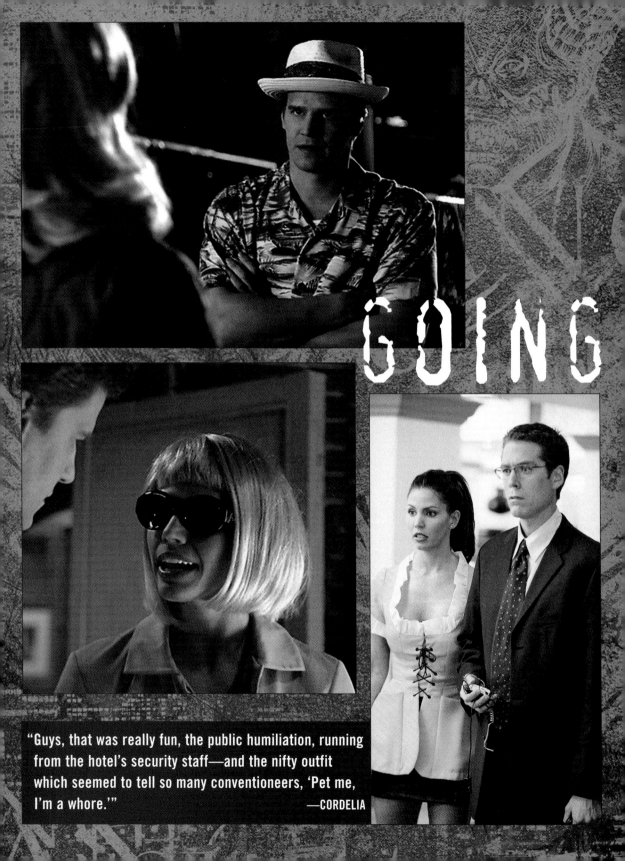

GOING

"Guys, that was really fun, the public humiliation, running from the hotel's security staff—and the nifty outfit which seemed to tell so many conventioneers, 'Pet me, I'm a whore.'"
—CORDELIA

UNDERCOVER

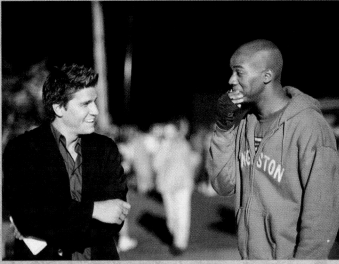

David Greenwalt directing "Dear Boy"

Tim Minear, David Boreanaz, and Joss Whedon, with Andy Hallett in the background

CREATING THE

ANGEL BEAST

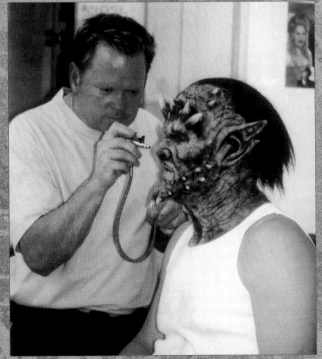

THE HOST

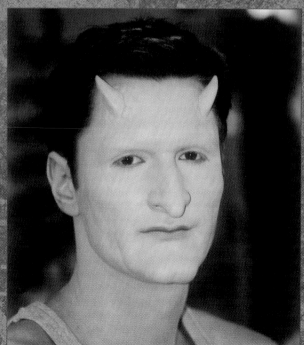

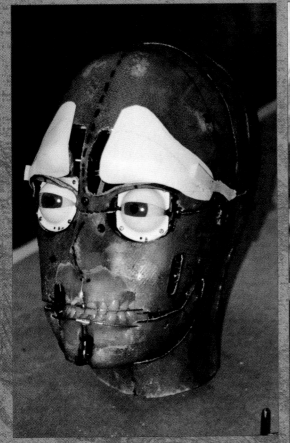

FROM CONCEPT TO DECAPITATION

TURFOG

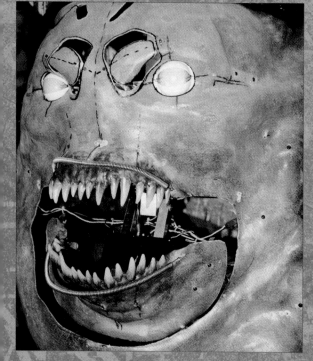

"A Torto demon and his parasite were murdering the Everly Brothers. . . ." —THE HOST

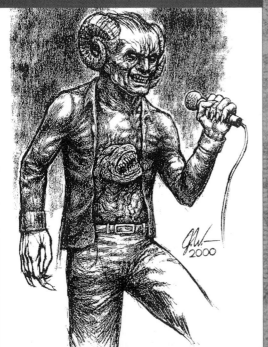

RESIDENTS OF PYLEA

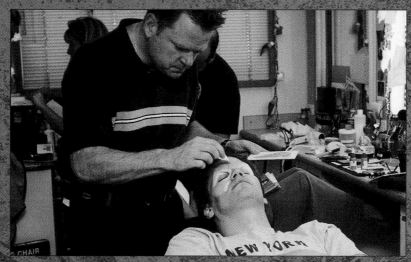

"Here's the plan. We go in. I start hitting people hard in the face. See where it takes us." —ANGEL

wrong guy. As they talk, Bryce checks out his sacrificial altar. It's only a few hours to the sacrifice, he says. The party of his life, and obviously Virginia's too.

Angel and Gunn return to the hotel to find Cordy and Wesley there—Wesley still wearing Angel's coat. Angel tells them about the fake T'ish Magev, and reasons that they had set the whole thing up to get Angel out of the way. Wesley speculates that the culprit must be Paul Lanier, thinking that getting Angel to the cabin would leave Virginia unprotected.

Cordelia explains to Angel that Wesley was posing as him. Wesley worries that Virginia might be in danger right now, at her father's big party. When Gunn asks about the party, Wesley tells him what it'll entail: "Cake, ice cream, tributes to the Goddess Yeska."

Angel interrupts. Yeska is a Davric demon, he says. Wesley knows that Davric demons don't serve humans—unless they're given live human sacrifices, usually girls. Then they'll grant immense power to the one who offers the sacrifice, on his fiftieth birthday.

Which, he realizes, is what Bryce is celebrating. Which spells trouble for Virginia.

The four of them crash the party. They take out the guards quickly—but not quickly enough to prevent Bryce from summoning Yeska. She arrives, and turns to take Virginia, who is shackled to Bryce's altar. But at the last second she won't accept the sacrifice, because it is impure.

When Yeska leaves, Wesley frees Virginia from the shackles. She asks him why he came back, and he says simply that he said he'd protect her.

Bryce blames Wesley for his daughter not being a virgin anymore. He wanted Angel, because Angel, he says, is a eunuch. Angel, of course, denies that. Wesley is a little concerned, himself, but Virginia says that she hasn't been a virgin for a long time, running off a list of chauffeurs and others. Finally, she punches her father and storms out.

RESOLUTION

Cordelia, having been reading the celebrity magazines again, shows Angel a photo of Wesley and Virginia at a society function. She's upset because Wesley's getting famous from his association with Virginia,

entertaining with style

Virginia Bryce, squired by Mr. Wesley Wyndam-Pryce, private detective and bodyguard to the stars.

an evening affair to remember

Everything was perfect - the food, the flowers, the fashions. The weather was perfect - a beautiful balmy evening with so many stars, they seemed to overlap. Inside, there were almost as many stars. The casts from *Where's Grandma*, *Sepulveda Place* and *Shopping for Sophie* were all in attendance, as well as the director of photography from *Yosemite* and the whole writing staff from the hit new reality show *Trapped in an Elevator.*

Things really got interesting when soap star Tripp Von Weisling from *Morning Light* tried to make off with an ice sculpture of supermodel Lula Gabrielle. We know she's an ice princess, Tripp, but really…

The happy couple enjoys a perfect evening

celebrity|86

247

when, clearly, fame is her thing. Angel's just upset because Wesley is described as a "bodyguard to the stars." "There's no Wyndam-Pryce Agency," he says.

Case closed.

DOSSIERS

CLIENT/VICTIM Magnus Bryce hires "Angel" to protect his daughter, **Virginia Bryce,** from threats theoretically made by business rivals. In fact, he's only concerned about keeping her alive long enough to sacrifice her on his fiftieth birthday, to increase his own power.

CIVILIAN SUPPORT The Host sends Angel to the **T'ish Magev,** but it turns out that the real shaman is already dead.

SUSPECTS Paul Lanier, Bryce's main rival. He really is trying to get to Virginia—because he knows what Bryce has in store for her, and he knows that if the sacrifice is successful, Bryce's power will far outstrip his own. **Benny** is a thug working for **Magnus Bryce**. **The fake T'ish Magev** is remarkably insightful for a phony swami, and his suggestions to Angel—except for the one about how to get over Darla—are mostly reasonably good advice. Most of which Angel will ultimately ignore.

CONTINUITY

The Host gives Angel guidance without Angel's needing to sing, and mentions Angel's choice of Barry Manilow's "Mandy" in "Judgement." Wesley's impersonation of Angel is a nice foreshadowing of his assuming leadership of the team in "Reprise."

QUOTE OF THE WEEK

"Yes! The point of a gun! He just walked Wesley right out of here. And this whole 'I'm Angel' thing is a very, very bad idea. I mean, if I thought that would work, I could've been Angel, because, guess what, pretty much a girly name."

Cordelia describes Wesley's kidnapping at Benny's hands.

THE DEVIL IS IN THE DETAILS

EXPENSES
New filing cabinet to replace the one Wesley breaks in the hotel office
Wall sculpture to replace the one Wesley breaks in Virginia's room

The first half of the teaser, with Wesley and the potential client, wasn't in the original draft of the script.

WEAPONRY
Fairly simple: a stake baton and a champagne bottle.

THE PLAN
Gunn accompanies Angel to the Wolfram & Hart offices because he believes that Angel has a plan. Bad call.

CORDELIA: "Gonna be a pretty short ride. They have vampire detectors!"
GUNN: "We know. It's okay. He's got a plan."

WESLEY: "A plan?"

ANGEL: "Yes. I get to the offices before they stop me."

GUNN: "See? What? That was the plan? Walking real quick was the plan?"

DEMONS, DEMONS, DEMONS

Yeska is a Davric demon, demanding a virgin sacrifice in return for granting power to the one offering the sacrifice on his/her fiftieth birthday. She's a heavyset demon with blue skin and a wild shock of white hair.

THE PEN IS MIGHTIER

FINAL CUT

Cut due to length is this scene in which Wesley meets a woman at Caritas and tries to impress her with his understanding of the demonic world.

WESLEY: ". . . might seem bizarre due to their very demonogenesis, by which I mean that they originate in a culture that stands outside and yet—"

Cordelia tugs him away from the woman, toward the door.

WESLEY: "I was having a conversation!"

ANGEL: "Wes, that was a Tarbo demon who was about a minute from plunging an ovipostor into your navel and spitting a larva into your colon."

WESLEY: "Oh. Heading home, are we?"

POP CULTURE

✳ ANGEL: "I guess, I'm a little rocky."

HOST: "Hmm. You're *Rocky* and *Rocky II* and half of the one with Mister T."

Sylvester Stallone played Rocky Balboa in the popular series of boxing films. Mr. T was Rocky's opponent, the aptly named Clubber Lang, in *Rocky III*.

✳ "You've got everyone scared around here, I'll tell you that. It's like they don't even know you're a Shemp." Cordelia to Wesley, surprised at how respectfully Bryce's people act toward him. Shemp was one of The Three Stooges of motion picture and television immortality.

✳ "I don't know how long I can keep up this Yoda gag." The fake T'ish Magev gives himself away as he talks to a compatriot on the phone. Yoda was Luke Skywalker's real "T'ish Magev" in the first *Star Wars* trilogy.

OUR HEROES

Alexis Denisof gave some insight into the relationship that begins between Wesley and Virginia:

"I really liked that arc. Because it was so unspectacular. Again, I felt like it was treated in a very human way. These two people, Wesley and Virginia, met in extraordinary circumstances, Wesley pretending to be a vampire and she's under lock and key in the midst of a wizard empire, and out of that they made what seemed to me a very comfortable, nurturing, domestic situation. And I liked that for the character. For all his eccentricity, I think it's good that he displays the ability to manage close to normal relationships and does some of the things that we all do. You know, if he had remained celibate forever, it would just ask too many questions about how bizarre he is."

—ALEXIS DENISOF

"The mansion was nice, for Wesley's girlfriend Virginia. She was sort of caught, she stayed in her room all the time, she was very book-read but she was an adult, so you got to have a little bit of her youth in there, but how she had done things to make it almost like a single apartment. But she wasn't stuck in time. That was nice, we don't get to do that a lot. It's nice when people have been there for a little while, because you get to say things about them. Even if nobody sees it, you get to say it. The actors are wonderful, they almost always notice and appreciate the little details. I love the things like the wizard's shop, because then you get to figure out, what do wizards sell?"

—SANDY STRUTH, SET DECORATOR

Yeska

"For Yeska, initially we were going to create the wig for her. And then as we were doing fittings for the actress, someone on their end said, 'Don't do a wig, we can do something with her hair.' And that is her actual hair." —ANDY SANDS, OF SPECIAL EFFECTS HOUSE OPTIC NERVE

SIX DEGREES OF . . .

Art LaFleur, who plays the phony T'ish Magev, and Brigid Brannagh (credited as Brigid Conley Walsh), who plays Virginia Bryce, both appeared in the 1988 comedy film *The Wrong Guys*.

TRACKS

Two Japanese tourists in Caritas sing "I Got You Babe," a hit record for Sonny and Cher in 1965, written by Sonny Bono. When they finish, the Host compliments their performance by saying, "Lovely! That was Cher-riffic, boys!"

Also heard in the episode are "Vedrai, carino" from Wolfgang Amadeus Mozart's opera *Don Giovanni*, and one of Franz Joseph Haydn's quartets.

"DARLA"

FROM THE FILES OF ANGEL INVESTIGATIONS
CASE NO: 2ADH07

ACTION TAKEN

Wesley enters Angel's apartment at the Hyperion Hotel to find Angel sketching a picture of Darla. Angel claims that he's fine and says good night, trying to get rid of Wesley. But "fine" is not what it looks like—surrounding Angel, dozens of other drawings are strewn around the room, all of Darla, in various stages of her life.

Darla herself, meanwhile, sits in the dark in her condo, glass all over the floor from mirrors that she's shattered. Her hands bleed from the destruction. Lindsey McDonald lets himself in and sees that she's in pain—not physical pain, but pain from deep down inside her newfound soul.

She tells Lindsey that now she and Angel have become something else, something they never were before—soul mates. She laughs when she says it, but the laughter is full of pain and irony.

WRITTEN AND DIRECTED BY Tim Minear
GUEST STARS: Mark Metcalf (the Master), Christian Kane (Lindsey McDonald), Sam Anderson (Holland Manners), Julie Benz (Darla), Juliet Landau (Drusilla), and James Marsters (Spike)
CO-STARS: Zitto Kazann (Gypsy Man), Bart Petty (Security Guard)

And in the Virginia Colony, in 1609, the human who would become Darla lives her last day as a prostitute dying of syphilis. A surgeon tries to save her by bleeding her with leeches as the nuns watch over. But a robed and hooded priest comes in, claiming that she invited him during the night, in her delirium. He knows who she is, and what she is, and he asks the doctor and nuns to leave them so that he might save her soul, since they clearly can't save her body.

But she doesn't want any of it. Her soul, she believes, is past saving. It turns out the priest is not exactly what he has passed himself off as. He lowers his hood and reveals himself to be the Master. He has no intention of saving her soul, but he intends to make sure that she can live forever without it— as a vampire. He bends forward to take her.

Back at the hotel, there's a meeting of the Angel Investigations team. Angel wants to find Darla, and the others are not so sure that's a good plan. Cordelia points out that, for weeks, she was in Angel's bedroom with him every night. Now that she's no longer paying her nocturnal visits, she might be a little tougher to locate. It takes Gunn to figure out that since Wolfram & Hart brought her, they probably have her stashed someplace. And since they're a law firm, there would be records, so they can write off the expense. Angel tells them wherever she is, she'll have a view.

Which is precisely what the Master's catacomb hideout, circa 1760, lacks, unless one's idea of "view" includes sewage and rodents. Having arrived back from the trip on which she met and turned Angelus, Darla introduces the new vampire to the Master. But Angelus doesn't treat the Master with the

same respect that Darla does, and he has some harsh words for the underground lair and the Master's facial features as well. Angelus wants to live among humans, on the surface, and he wants Darla to stay with him. Swayed by her love for him, she agrees and they leave together. The Master watches them go, predicting that the relationship will only last "a century, tops."

At the hotel, Angel has been looking up the origins of Darla's name, and he learns that it didn't come into common usage until more than a hundred years after she was born—which means he never even knew her human name. The Master must have been the one to christen her Darla. Wesley suggests that Wolfram & Hart may have brought her back precisely for the purpose of distracting him.

Lindsey has brought Darla to the Wolfram & Hart offices, against orders from Holland Manners. Holland observes that she's cracking up—ahead of schedule. Lindsey isn't quite sure what he means by this, but Holland advises that he remove anything with a sharp point from his office, just in case.

By 1880, in London, Darla and Angelus have picked up a third member of the family, Angelus's mad "daughter" Drusilla. Dru, though, is feeling a bit lonely. Darla and Angelus have each other, but she doesn't have anyone in the same way. Darla suggests that she could, if she wanted. All Dru has to do is pick one. As Darla says this, a young bespectacled man carrying a stack of papers runs into them, snarling as he does so. Drusilla looks after him as he hurries off. This young man will come to be known as "Spike."

Cordelia's found something. A property, owned by Wolfram & Hart, with a view. Further, she's posed as Darla's sister to the property manager and determined which apartment Darla is in. Angel is ready to go. Wesley stops him, recommending—very firmly—that Wes and Gunn check it out first. Angel reluctantly agrees.

In Lindsey's office, the young attorney enters bearing sandwiches from a vending machine, calling Darla's name. She wants to hear it again. She doesn't even remember what her name was when she was human. But she isn't sure what Wolfram & Hart brought back. A human? A vampire? She isn't quite either of those things now. She invites Lindsey to kiss her—which he's been aching to do. She seems to enjoy it, remembering that it's how humans get what they want. Then she bites Lindsey's neck—that, she says, is how vampires get what they want. If she was Darla she could snap him in half. He tells her he understands what she's going through, but of course he doesn't.

"No. Nobody understands! Nobody can understand! I can feel this body dying, Lindsey! I can feel it decaying moment by moment! It's being eaten away by the thing inside of it. It's a cancer, this soul . . ."

—*Darla*

Another time, another place: 1898, in a Gypsy village. Angelus has just had his soul restored by a Gypsy's curse, and Darla tries to get the gypsy to undo his damage. She threatens his family if he doesn't cooperate—but when it looks like he might, Spike, Drusilla's new beau, emerges from the man's trailer, belching after a big meal. Her last threat defanged, Darla simply snaps the man's neck.

Wesley and Gunn report back to Angel and Cordelia. They shot video footage inside Darla's wreck of an apartment. Angel understands why she shattered the mirrors. Now that she has a soul and remembers all she's done, she doesn't want to see herself.

Angel's urge to find her is only strengthened by this report. Wesley is just as adamant that she might just be a trap. As they argue, the phone rings, and Cordy answers it. It's Darla.

Angel takes the phone. Darla sounds awful—she's scared, an unfamiliar sensation to her. She asks Angel for help. Then, while they talk, Lindsey comes back into his office and finds her. He insists that she hang up the phone. She refuses, so Angel hears the whole exchange—including, when she holds the phone to her breast, her heart beating. A Wolfram & Hart security guard comes in, saying Holland Manners sent him. He tries to grab Darla but she slams him with the phone. Angel hears more struggle, and then a gunshot.

Later, Holland shows Lindsey video footage of the fight, including the struggle for the gun and Darla shooting the guard, then Lindsey helping her from the room. Holland tells Lindsey that the guard's family has been notified and a "suspect" is in custody, but Lindsey is off the project. Lindsey is stunned. He can find her, he says, but Holland says that's not necessary, that she's already been picked up. He's terminating the project, and she isn't Lindsey's problem anymore.

Angel, meanwhile, knowing that Darla is in trouble, is even more determined to go to her. Gunn offers to accompany him, but Angel turns down the offer. She asked for his help, he knows what she's going through better than anyone, and he can't turn her down, even though he knows the whole thing might be a trap.

At another time, Angelus did find her, in the midst of China's Boxer Rebellion. She holds a knife to his throat, ready to behead him. She can smell vermin on him, and it disgusts her that her "son" and lover has been surviving on animals instead of humans. But he insists he wants to be together again, he wants things to be like they were, and she can't bring herself to disbelieve him. . . .

In the Wolfram & Hart parking lot, Lindsey is dialing a cell phone and just reaching his BMW when a cord loops around his neck. Angel pulls it tight, lifting Lindsey off his feet. Angel wants to know where Darla is. Lindsey holds up the phone and lets Angel hear Cordelia answer it—he was just calling Angel to tell him. Lindsey isn't positive, but he believes she's been taken to an abandoned bank building. He gives Angel the address, and Angel warns that if Lindsey is lying, he'll be back.

Back in the chaos of the Boxer Rebellion, Angelus finds a family of missionaries—mother, father, older child, and an infant in a basket—cowering in an alley. He protects them from attack, and then hears Darla calling him. Leaving the alley, he lies to her, telling her that the alley contains only dead bodies. He suggests looking for something warm. Drusilla happens along, flushed with excitement—Spike has just killed a Slayer! Angelus is not pleased to hear this, but the newly important Spike misinterprets his reaction.

> "Don't be so glum, mate. Way you tell it, one Slayer snuffs it, another one rises. I figure there's a new Chosen One, getting all chosen as we speak. I'll tell you what: if and when this new bird does show up—I give you first crack at her."
>
> —*Spike*

Angelus wants to leave, claiming that the rebellion is boring him. They go, but Darla keeps a wary eye on Angelus.

Later, he comes into the house they're staying in, and Darla grills him. He says he's been out feeding, but she believes he's been at the docks, feeding only on rats. He counters that she's seen him kill men. She's noticed, though, that he only kills criminals and scoundrels. So she's brought him a test. She found the missionaries he protected from her and killed them all—except the baby. She offers that to him now, still in the white basket. . . .

Now, though, he's running to Darla—or driving to her. He roars into a tunnel under the abandoned bank building and leaps from his car just as two thugs are about to shoot her. As they fight, one of them slams her into a column, hard. Angel takes them out and turns to the unconscious Darla.

Lindsey walks toward his office at Wolfram & Hart and sees Holland talking to the security guard Darla "killed." Angry, Lindsey goes into his office, and Holland follows. He tells Lindsey that it had to seem real, that Lindsey had to believe it. Lindsey thinks Holland is fooling himself, that Angel is not going to have a moment of perfect happiness with Darla. He won't take advantage of her in her weakened state, and without that Angel won't come over to the dark side. Holland tells Lindsey that he doesn't expect physical intimacy. All he expects Angel to do is what he will try to do—save her soul.

RESOLUTION

Angel has taken Darla back to the hotel, where the rest of the gang finally gets a good look at her. When she wakes up, Angel sends the others away so he and Darla can talk. She's not sure how happy she is not to have been killed. But she asks Angel to make the pain stop, and she offers him her neck.

He refuses. Angry, she says that he promised to help her. He says he will, but not like that. She comes right out and says what she wants:

"Turn me back! My God! I can't bear this pounding in my chest for another instant!"   —*Darla*

Again, Angel refuses. She says she did it for him once. But he says that she didn't do him any favors by turning him into a vampire. He can't do it.

Darla disagrees. It's not that he can't, it's that he won't. But this is the Darla of 1900 talking, as Angelus looks down at the innocent baby in the basket. He snatches up the basket and crashes through a window, running away. . . .

And in the hotel, it's Darla who turns away from Angel, walking into the sunlight at the front door. Angel tries to stop her, but she goes anyway, warning Angel not to look for her again.

Case closed.

DOSSIERS

CLIENT Darla is the client. She is being held prisoner against her will by Wolfram & Hart, and she is in need of help on many levels.

SUSPECTS Lindsey McDonald is deeply involved in the plot to use Darla against Angel, but in fact he's also being manipulated by his boss, **Holland Manners**.

CONTINUITY

Angel demonstrates his drawing abilities again, shown in "Passion" and "Somnambulist." Angel's link to Darla and the Master was first revealed in the *Buffy* episode "Angel," in the early days of his relationship with Buffy. Cordelia urges Angel to solve the Darla problem without kidnapping her again, as he did in "Dear Boy." She also refers to Darla's stealth visits to the slumbering Angel, and Angel's ability to recognize Darla by her scent. Many of the historical scenes were parallel to those in "Fool for Love," the *Buffy* episode which immediately preceded "Darla" in the original airing. Spike was the narrator and provided the point of view for the "Fool for Love" scenes.

QUOTE OF THE WEEK

ANGEL: "Come on, guys. We're a detective agency. We investigate things. That's what we're good at."

CORDELIA: "No. That's what we suck at. Let's face it, unless there's a website called 'www dot oh by the way, we have got Darla stashed here dot com,' we're pretty much out of luck."

Angel tries to get the others to help him look for Darla.

THE DEVIL IS IN THE DETAILS

WEAPONRY

Necessity being the mother—a cord wrapped around a ceiling pipe

DEMONS, DEMONS, DEMONS

The Master, also known as Heinrich Joseph Nest, has been described as the most powerful of all vampires. Siring Darla, he puts in motion the entire chain of events that will bring Angel to Los Angeles centuries later.

THE VAMPIRE RULES

Vampires turn physically warmer—at least to a degree that can be sensed by other vampires—after feeding.

A vampire can sense through smell if another vampire has been feeding on humans or animals.

THE PEN IS MIGHTIER

FINAL CUT

When Wesley finds Angel drawing multiple sketches of Darla, in the original script he spotted a nude drawing and this exchange ensued—cut for length or good taste:

> **ANGEL:** "I've been . . . thinking. That's all."
> **WESLEY:** "Thinking?"
> **ANGEL:** "Yes. It helps me sometimes to think with my hands."
> **WESLEY:** "And occasionally . . . just the one hand?"

Makeup department head Dayne Johnson's team won the makeup artists guild award for "Best Period Makeup for a TV Series" for "Darla."

OUR HEROES

Tim Minear wrote and directed this episode, which was the second part of what The WB Network billed as a "Two hour *Buffy/Angel* event." He told us about the genesis of the story.

"The last time we saw [Darla], she looked a little conflicted. And [Angel] said, 'Your soul's gonna come back, and it's gonna start haunting you.' And what I pitched to Joss was, we should be exploring what it means for her to be human. She's been this other thing for four hundred years, suddenly she's brought back and she's no longer this thing, and she must be having some kind of identity crisis. And in order to do that I felt it was important to see what she was as a human four hundred years ago.

"Which meant flashbacks. My initial image was her having broken up her apartment, we're not sure why, she smashed all the mirrors, and Lindsey comes over and opens the curtains, and the sun hits her in the eye, and then we come down from the sun and it's whenever it was, 1602 or whatever. And we see her as a Puritan or whatever. So I pitched that to Joss, and he said, 'Well, I think that's very interesting.'

"However, that very night we were doing Spike's origin. Because what I was essentially pitching was Darla's origin story. Which is slightly problematic because of Angel not appearing in that for two hundred years. And so we hemmed and hawed and tried to figure out something else. And at some point I said, 'Why should we be afraid of this? Why don't we just do two episodes that are big history lessons? Because, in fact, these characters would have naturally intersected at different points throughout history, since she made Angel, Angel made Drusilla, Drusilla made Spike. So we know that there were some intersections in history.

"Then Joss came up with the thought that we could do it like *The Norman Conquest*, I think that's the name of the play. It's a play that's in three acts, but each act takes place at the same time. It's something like the first act takes place in the living room, and some characters enter the stage from the backyard, and have some interaction and then leave again. Then the second act takes place in the backyard, and at some point those characters leave to go into the living room, and we realize this is in the same time that that took place. And by the end of it you get the whole thing.

"So we knew that instead of doing something linear, that we would be able to tell things slightly out of order. Which actually worked out because of the way the timeline fell, that he would have had his soul back. Which then gave me the idea that this should be about him coming back to her.

"Joss had this image in his head of four vampires walking away from some burning city. That was the thing that was in his head. I came to him and I said, 'Here's a problem. At that time, Angel would have had his soul back and he would not have been with them.' And then that became the basis of the entire story, just so we could have that moment.

"I also said, 'Not only can we get that shot, Joss, that can be the one thing that repeats in both episodes.' Because otherwise each scene has a different point, at a slightly different time, but everything would be tied up in this one image of the Boxer Rebellion, and that one shot. So that the first time that we see it it seems like these four badass vampires, and Spike now an Alpha dog, and Angel just looking jealous, but the second time we see it, it's not jealousy, it's despair. And the first time we hear him say, 'Let's get out of here, this rebellion's starting to bore me,' it sounds like jealousy. The second time you hear him say it, you realize what he's really saying is, 'I gotta get some new friends.' So it was the same thing but it had a slightly different meaning.

"And the *Buffy* fans were furious for the first hour. They thought we had forgotten continuity and thrown it out the window.

"So I decided to pick something small and manageable for my directing debut: just six hundred years of history. But I also knew that it was all leading up to the moment where those two scenes started intercutting. 'Cause at the end, she says, 'Make me into a vampire again,' and he says, 'I can't.' And then it cuts back to her with the baby, and she says, 'What do you mean, you can't? You won't.' It was just that sort of intercutting which interested me."
—TIM MINEAR

Producer Kelly A. Manners talked about renting yaks for the Boxer Rebellion scene:

KELLY MANNERS: "I paid for the yaks because we really wanted to add the production value. So we really wanted the added production value of the yaks, and the animals. They were originally going to shoot China at Universal Studios, [but] at Universal, you're restricted to how much of Universal you can see. Our China got to be much bigger."

DAVID M. BURNS [ASSISTANT TO KELLY MANNERS]: "[The yaks] were three fifty a day."

KELLY MANNERS: "And then of course the wrangler for the yaks."

DAVID M. BURNS: "But you get a dozen chickens for seventy-five bucks."

KELLY MANNERS: "Chickens are cheap. But, see, chickens don't do me any good because David Boreanaz is scared of them."

Locations manager Kevin Funston explained some of the logistics involved in shooting two different but related shows at the same time:

"Because it was a crossover episode and both Angel and Buffy were going to be shooting in the same place, how did you coordinate that with the Buffy locations people? Did you just divvy up locations?"

KEVIN FUNSTON: "Yeah, basically we went through the producers on that and said, "We're going to shoot this for *Buffy*, and *Buffy*'s going to shoot this for us." The Gypsy camp was shot at the Disney Ranch, when we were out there. And the scene where she is in the house of the Master and she's dying, and he makes her a vampire, was shot in a building right there on the Disney Ranch that was just down the hill from where the Gypsy camp was. So they shot inside first, until it got [to be] night, and then they went outside and up the hill for the Gypsy camp. And we did shoot part of that for *Buffy*. And then when we were at the Boxer Rebellion, instead of having *Buffy* come out and re-dress the whole place, we shot the scenes they needed for the Boxer Rebellion for their episode. And then whatever we needed, they shot for us. They shot Universal for us, the European Street, and we shot the Boxer Rebellion out at Veluzat Ranch for them."

Julie Benz shared this insight into her "death" scene:

JULIE BENZ: "In the episode 'Darla,' where I'm dying, I asked Tim Minear if I could have a herpes sore on my mouth. Because, you know, she's dying of syphilis, and I wanted that on my face. I thought it would be fun. And then when David [DeLeon] put one on, he made it look so real, and I was like, oh my God, what was I thinking? I forget that they do a really good job—you ask for a herpes sore, you're going to get a really ugly one."

"A good argument for safe sex."

JULIE BENZ: "My nickname was 'syphilis whore.'"

SIX DEGREES OF . . .

Since "Darla" is a crossover episode, many of the actors have appeared on *Buffy* as well as *Angel*.

Mark Metcalf, who plays the Master in this episode, has appeared with Art LaFleur, the fake T'ish Magev in "Guise Will Be Guise," in two movies, 1997's *Hijacking Hollywood* and 1991's *Oscar*, both comedic crime stories.

TRACKS

Composer Robert Kral said that "Darla's Theme" is his favorite recurring theme on the show.

ROBERT KRAL: "In 'Darla' her theme recurs a lot, treated differently each time. By the end of that episode, her theme is in the low strings and it sounds more like a funeral: Angel is telling her he will not help her, that the two of them have no hope together and the episode reveals how vastly different they are.

"There is also Dru's theme. It's heard best in the 'Darla' episode. The essence of it was to convey a sense of playfulness, a touch of elegance, and several dashes of twistedness."

"How did the scoring work for the crossover?"

ROBERT KRAL: "For 'Darla' I raised the question of collaborating with [*Buffy* composer] Thomas Wanker as he would be writing music for scenes where there was a literal crossover within that scene. Tim Minear suggested we don't, as he wanted a completely different viewpoint. Wow, he's got great ideas! It was perfect because although these scenes literally met each other, we have a different perspective now. Angel and his gang bump into Spike. In the *Buffy* episode, Spike is in the middle of his own drama. In *Angel*, Drusilla has just become a vampire. A new theme for her reflects her playful twistedness. The scene is more about that than 'Hey, there's Spike!'

"A little later and we have a slow-motion climax during the Boxer Rebellion. In the *Buffy* episode this is very much in the moment of the rebellion; on *Angel*, it starts that way, the glory days of our vampire gang, then we realize Angel is in a world of his own: he's not so sure about all this. He can't kill humans anymore, Darla feels she's losing him, and the music is in their world in their minds, not in the rebellion at that point."

Kral submitted "Darla" as his Emmy-nominated episode for this season.

"I think 'Darla' is a fantastic episode: there's so much emotion, so much life-changing stuff in there, so much challenge between Angel and Darla as it juxtaposes when they were in the whirlwind glory days, to the beginnings of his inner wrestling between good and evil, to him making his stand and refusing to be an aid to evil at the end of the episode, with this incredible romance intertwined through it all: that thread that makes it hard to let go of her, but he does. I'm talking about the plot there, but that's the music too, that's how I think of it."

—ROBERT KRAL

"THE SHROUD OF RAHMON"

FROM THE FILES OF ANGEL INVESTIGATIONS
CASE № 2ADH08

ACTION TAKEN

Two detectives look through the one-way glass of an interrogation room at a murder suspect, a man slumped over a table as if exhausted. Their strategy planned, the officers go into the room and begin the questioning. Wesley raises his head from the table to tell them, in disjointed fashion, that he was only trying to warn someone, and then he grabbed her hard, and it all went "terribly wrong."

"He" should never have been there, Wesley continues. But he's the boss, and you don't tell the boss what to do. Besides, Wesley tries to explain, he helps people. Wesley is not himself right now, and he's not making himself understood, and the cops don't seem to be in any mood for word games.

WRITTEN BY Jim Kouf
DIRECTED BY David Grossman
GUEST STARS: Elisabeth Rohm (Kate Lockley), W. Earl Brown (Menlo), Dwayne L. Barnes (Lester), R. Emery Bright (Turlock), Tom Kiesche (Broomfield), and Tony Todd (Vyasa)
CO-STARS: Robert Dolan (Bob), Michael Nagy (Jay-Don)

Earlier that day . . . Wesley walks in to find Cordelia, whose hair is suddenly pitch-black instead of the dark brown he was used to, and cut differently. She claims that it's been this way for ten days, but she's not surprised that he didn't notice, being a man and all. Wesley's getting ready to go out to an opening with Virginia Bryce—a fact that has Cordy practically seething—but before he goes, he asks Cordelia about Angel.

Mostly what Angel has been doing is brooding about Darla, but he's not around right now, because he's off with Gunn, whose cousin "got involved in something pretty big—big meaning 'illegal.'" They've gone to help the cousin extricate himself from a jam. Wesley's just glad Angel's out. And it turns out he has an extra ticket for the opening, and Cordelia happens to be available, so they take off.

Elsewhere, Angel and Gunn hook up with Gunn's cousin Lester. Who hates vampires. A lot. He tells them that he accepted a driving job, but the crew he's supposed to be driving for is bringing in a "psycho vampire from Vegas," so he wants no part of the job now. They're robbing a museum, but he doesn't know where or when. Angel learns that the psycho vampire is named Jay-Don, and the name is familiar to him. Jay-Don is being picked up at the downtown bus at midnight. Gunn tells Lester to take his meeting, and Gunn will get him out before crime time.

When Lester leaves, Angel tells Gunn that he'll take over. He's very dismissive of Gunn, which Gunn does not appreciate, particularly since it's his cousin's life at stake. But Angel expects to be obeyed.

Angel goes home, and there's a blond woman in his apartment. But it's not Darla for a change—

it's Detective Kate Lockley. Kate wants Darla for the murder of the actor who played her husband Stephen when she was setting a trap for Angel in "Dear Boy." Angel tells Kate there are things going on that she doesn't understand, and warns her against getting in the middle of it. Kate, though, is in no mood to heed Angel's warnings.

Cordelia and Wesley return from their evening out—Cordy with a big cocktail sauce stain on her dress. Angel also notices the new black hair, then tells them about the meeting with Lester. He tells them he's going to take Jay-Don's place. Even Wesley has heard of Jay-Don, including the fact that he's colorful and extroverted—two words seldom used to describe Angel.

But at midnight, Angel is at the bus station. When Jay-Don comes out from underneath the bus, Angel greets him, pretending to be his driver, then stakes him. Sadly, Jay-Don's wardrobe turns to dust when he does, but Angel manages to save the sunglasses. Donning them and bright clothes of his own, he steps out to find Menlo, the demon who's really here to meet Jay-Don. Angel gets into character, doing his own version of a Rat Pack, Las Vegas hoodlum/vampire.

> **ANGEL**: "Yeah, you know, the trip was faboo. I love flyin' coach and what is that piece of junk?"
> **MENLO**: "You're funny, vampire."
> **ANGEL**: "We need to talk, bro'. Two things bringin' in the chicks: the do' . . ."
> (touches his hair)
> ". . . and the ride."

At the crew's hideout, Angel meets Vyasa, an enormous demon thug, and Bob, a uniformed (and human) security guard. They're still waiting for Lester, but then he arrives—only Lester, it seems, is now Gunn.

Angel's not at all happy to see him. They argue, *sotto voce* since neither one of them is who they are supposed to be and they're not supposed to know one another. Gunn asks what they're stealing, and Menlo tells them it's the Shroud of Rahmon, which is worth more than two million dollars on the black market. Working with a blueprint of the museum, they go over the plan. The shroud is inside a case that's stored in a vault. The vault has a thermal sensor, but a vampire, with no body heat, can go inside to turn the sensor off. "Jay-Don's" job is to disarm the sensor so the others can get to the case and carry it out.

As they go over the details, Angel sees a chance to get Gunn out and picks a fight. He wants to take the fight outside, but Menlo and Vyasa put a stop to that idea, drawing two guns (for Gunn) and a stake (for Angel). Angel doesn't want to spend the rest of the week with Gunn, but Menlo says that won't be a problem, as they're pulling the job tonight.

Back at the hotel, Cordelia and Wesley check museum collections online to see if there's anything that matches Lester's vague description of the crew's target. Eventually, at the Natural History Museum, they find a suspicious listing under "Recent Acquisitions"—something called the "Shroud of Rahmon," unearthed from a tomb.

The criminal crew is already on the move. They get to the museum, where the lock on a back door is held open with duct tape. Inside, they take an elevator to the basement, with security guard Bob using his key to bypass the security system. Another security guard, Earl, makes his rounds and comes across them, at which point Bob pretends to be a hostage. But there's not much reason to fool Earl, as Vyasa knocks him out cold with a single powerful blow. He's about to finish Earl when Angel stops him, warning him that if he kills the guard, the police will be that much more involved. Menlo settles it by duct-taping Earl.

They find the vault door. Menlo, who seems to have done this before, drills a small hole near the vault's lock mechanism.

At the police station, two plainclothes cops show pictures to Kate. One of the photos shows Bob aka "Robert Skale." Another depicts "M. James Menlo," a well-known safecracker. The third guy they don't know, but they've been told that Kate does. It is, of course, Angel.

Menlo takes a small vial of nitroglycerin from a padded case and prepares to insert it in the hole he's drilled. But Vyasa yells at him to hurry and Menlo, flinching, drops the bottle. Angel catches it on the toe of his boot, inches from the floor. He carefully puts the nitro in. They go around the corner and blow the vault door remotely.

In one of his books, Wesley has found some information on the Shroud of Rahmon. It's not cheery information.

> **WESLEY:** "Once, in 1803, the shroud was removed from its casing."
>
> **CORDELIA:** "And yuckiness ensued?"
>
> **WESLEY:** "Well, yes. The entire population of El Encanto went insane, mothers and children hacking one another to pieces, men roaming the streets like rabid dogs—"
>
> **CORDELIA:** "I get the picture. So in order to take his mind off the torment that is Darla, we sent Angel after a box that makes you crazy."

They decide to warn Angel about the shroud as soon as he comes back from his meeting. Which he's already late from. It occurs to them both that he's probably at the museum now, doing the crime, and they beat a quick exit.

With the vault door open, the body temperature-deprived Angel goes inside and looks at the sarcophagus-size box that contains the Shroud of Rahmon. And as he does, his eyes flash yellow, then he morphs to vamp-face and back. There's something very not-good about this whole shroud thing.

He disarms the thermal sensor so the others can come in. The box seems to have the effect of making the combative group argue even more. But in spite of their antagonism, they cooperate enough to pick it up.

Cordelia and Wesley have made it to the museum and found the duct tape on the lock. They go inside and start to feel woozy from the shroud's influence. They decide that they need to stick together, for safety's sake, and then immediately strike out in different directions.

Kate reaches the museum, sees the truck, and calls in for backup. But she goes in without waiting, gun drawn, ready for anything. Or so she thinks.

The crew continues hauling the really heavy case through the museum's corridors. At one point Gunn drops his corner and the box crashes to the floor, cracking a panel of glass on the top. Smoke issues from inside, along with strange whispering voices . . .

And now Kate is starting to feel lightheaded, too.

Angel and Gunn are at each other's throats again. Once again, Menlo separates them with his gun, wanting all hands to be carrying, not battling. But Bob, the security guard, points out that he needs to be tied up so he won't look like an accomplice. Menlo's happy to oblige. That's not enough, though. Bob wants to be hit, so it looks as if he were overpowered. And it has to look real.

This time, Vyasa obliges. Only instead of hitting Bob, he twists the human's head off.

Kate runs across Wesley, who is almost totally inarticulate by this point, jabbering about Kate's hair and the shroud and also, Kate's hair.

Meanwhile, Cordelia, equally under the influence, enjoys examining her reflection, admiring the size of her teeth, and she liberates a turquoise necklace from an Indian princess mannequin.

As the crew exits the elevator, Menlo panics, fearing they've left fingerprints behind. He dashes back into the elevator to wipe it clean. Angel, Vyasa, and Gunn continue on without him. But then Gunn can no longer carry his share of the load. While they argue, Wesley finds them. He maintains enough presence of mind to tell Angel that the shroud is dangerous and makes people bad.

Angel tries to tell him to get out, but before Wesley can go anywhere, Kate shows up, gun pointed at them. Vyasa starts toward her, but Angel stops him, claiming her for himself. Kate warns him to stay back. Angel's reply may or may not be in character.

"Whoa, okay. You got me. My life of crime is over, I'm goin' down. But first, a little impression: I'm a cop with a mission: to protect the innocent and rain on everybody's parade and obsess about my father's death *and bother people who are about to steal things*."   —*Angel*

He starts toward her again, Wesley trying to stop him. But Angel slams Wesley into a wall and morphs, charging Kate. She shoots, but he's too fast. He grabs her and sinks his fangs into her neck, drinking deep.

Kate's backup finally arrives. Entering a darkened hall, they find a barely conscious Wesley standing over a body. Then they see the body—Kate's, very pale, very still. They take Wesley into custody.

Back at the hideout, Gunn, Angel, Menlo, and Vyasa stagger in with the case. Menlo says they should open it—which Angel thinks would have been a good idea back at the museum, before they had to carry the box. Vyasa breaks the lid off and they take the shroud out. Imprinted on the shroud are the body and facial features of Rahmon, a demonic-looking being. Inside the box, Rahmon himself is a desiccated corpse. Greed finally overtakes everybody and they fight for the shroud.

Menlo starts shooting, and Vyasa slams the box into him, taking him out of the battle. Except that when Vyasa makes his play for it, Menlo, in his last moment of consciousness, shoots the big demon in the head. Now it's just Angel and Gunn. They struggle for a moment, before Angel says he knows what to do with it and yanks it from Gunn's hands.

He staggers outside with the shroud, barely able to hold himself upright. He dumps the contents of security guard Bob's liquid courage, a bottle of whiskey, on the shroud and flicks open a lighter. He drops it and the shroud is instantly engulfed in flames—the force of the explosion knocking the weakened Angel off his feet.

RESOLUTION

The detectives we met earlier are still interrogating Wesley, and they don't think much of his barely coherent story.

But as they're about to book him, Kate shows up—still pale, and wearing a coat that hides her neck—and instructs them to release Wesley.

A little later, she recalls what happened at the museum. Angel morphing and attacking her, sinking his fangs into her neck, Menlo ready to shoot her, Vyasa anxious to tear another head off. And Angel, face close to her ear, warning in a voice only she can hear to stay down, or they'll kill her.

Angel, whom she has come to hate, drank some of her blood in order to save her life.

Wesley and Cordelia contemplate the same conundrum. Having tasted human blood, even in a good cause, has Angel reawakened his bloodlust? As they consider this, Cordelia lies to Wesley, telling him that she returned everything stolen from the museum, even though she's still wearing the turquoise necklace.

And for his part, Angel sits in his apartment in the hotel, remembering the taste of Kate's blood. Case closed.

DOSSIERS

CLIENT Lester, Gunn's cousin, is the closest thing to a client Angel Investigations has. While obviously a small-time crook, Lester finds himself in over his head when he gets mixed up with Menlo and Vyasa's crew.

SUSPECTS Being basically a classic "caper" story, the episode is loaded with suspects. **M. James Menlo** seems to be running the show, with powerful demon **Vyasa** providing the muscle. Legendary psycho vampire **Jay-Don** is supposed to be in on the crime, but Angel takes him out of action early on to infiltrate the crew. **Bob**, a security guard at the museum who helps the crew circumvent the security system, becomes a victim as well when he tells Vyasa to "make it real." (All deceased.)

CONTINUITY

Kate mentions Darla's participation in the murders of innocents to lure Angel into her trap in "Dear Boy." Angel mocks Gunn for continuing to mourn the loss of Alonna in "War Zone," while Gunn expresses his continued anger toward those of a vampiric nature. The last time Angel is known to have consumed fresh human blood was in the *Buffy* episode "Graduation Day, Part Two," as Wesley reminds Cordelia. Drinking from Buffy was a desperate act to save his own life, as drinking from Kate was a desperate act to save hers. Angel uses fire to rid himself of a mystical problem. He'll employ this technique again in "Reprise."

QUOTE OF THE WEEK

"Okay, two words I don't like right off the bat, 'tomb' and 'unearthed.' People, you've gotta leave your tombs *earthed*."

Cordelia learns that university archaeologists have unearthed the Shroud of Rahmon from a tomb.

THE DEVIL IS IN THE DETAILS

EXPENSES

Cleaning bill for Cordelia's stained shirt
A bright shirt for Angel to wear when playing Jay-Don
The lighter Angel loses burning the Shroud

WEAPONRY

There are guns, stakes, a wall, and a lighter.

THE PLAN

A large portion of the episode has to do with planning a heist, but the only time the Angel Investigations gang actually talks about it is at the end, when Wesley and Cordelia perform a post-mortem on the previous day's disaster:

> **WESLEY**: "We had every good intention, of course."
>
> **CORDELIA**: "Right. Sending him into the path of a crazy-making, one-way ticket to evil-town death-cloth. Good plan."

DEMONS, DEMONS, DEMONS

THE VAMPIRE RULES

Vampire body temperatures are extremely low, making them ideal for circumventing all those body-temperature-reading security systems.

When humans are scared, it makes their blood taste salty.

THE PEN IS MIGHTIER

FINAL CUT

A reference to Wolfram & Hart's plot to use Darla against Angel was excised from the final aired version:

"Wolfram & Hart's plan, to scramble Angel's brain with eggs à la Darla till he can't even see straight, much less fight the Big Bad."   —*Cordelia*

Also cut was this exchange in which, after the premiere, Cordelia ducks behind the counter to change out of her stained clothes, and Angel claims to have done some research on museum acquisitions:

ANGEL: "Well, I did a little . . . I clicked the little . . . I turned on the computer."

CORDELIA AND WESLEY: "You did?"

ANGEL: "I know how to turn it on."

CORDELIA: "No, no—that's good. That's really—I can't talk to you with no pants on."

ANGEL: "You have no pants on?"

CORDELIA: "See, now that you know . . . it's weird, huh?"

POP CULTURE

❖ When Cordy and Wesley return from the premiere, after the cocktail sauce incident, this exchange occurs:

WESLEY: "I spilled it on her in front of Mr. Fat Chow Chou."

CORDELIA: "CHOW YUN FAT!"

ANGEL: (impressed) "You met Chow Yun-Fat?"

Chow Yun-Fat is the popular Hong Kong actor who starred in *Crouching Tiger, Hidden Dragon; The Replacement Killers; Anna and the King;* and many other films.

❖ Angel says of the flashy, psycho vampire Jay-Don, **"He ran with the whole Sinatra Rat Pack, never got over it."** Sinatra's Rat Pack included, among others, Dean Martin, Sammy Davis Jr., Peter Lawford, Joey Bishop, and more in the late-fifties/early-sixties Hollywood scene. They made a number of movies (and a lot of trouble) together, including *Robin and the 7 Hoods* and the original *Ocean's 11.*

❖ **"You know, I'm getting pretty sick of this vampire-killed-my-sister-so-now-I'm-all-entitled song. Don't you know any others? Like, say, 'MacArthur Park'?"** Arguing with Gunn in the museum, Angel gets personal and makes a pop culture reference at the same time. "MacArthur Park," written by Jimmy Webb, has been covered by a multitude of singers, but most prominently by singer Donna Summer, who had a huge hit with it in 1978.

❖ "The Shroud of Rahmon" is a classic caper story along the lines of those popularized by crime writer Donald E. Westlake. The viewer is led through the planning, the execution—and finally—the disastrous conclusion of a major crime. The only specific reference to a caper movie is a throwaway line referring to one of the all-time greats of the genre, when Bob, the security guard, says, **"I visited Topkapi once."** Topkapi is a well-known museum in Istanbul, but more germane here is the 1964 film of the same name about a heist set in that museum, for which Peter Ustinov won an Academy Award.

OUR HEROES

Charisma Carpenter talked about the rather dramatic hairstyle change that began in this episode and continued for the next part of the season.

"I felt that the long hair was somewhat juvenile, and she had gone through so much, and grown, and was ready for a change. And I felt that, also, I was having head sores because of the extensions that were in my hair. So I knew we had to go shorter, because my hair was no longer all one length and pretty cheerleader hair anymore. It was better to take it up in length. David Greenwalt was very concerned about how short. The length was fine, he said, 'No shorter than this.' And then I went to Chris McMillan, and Chris came up with the hairstyle. I had darkened my hair way before, but then when I cut it and it was dark, it was too rock and roll, too hard, for her. So we changed ultimately to the bob."

—CHARISMA CARPENTER

"When somebody that I love calls me on my behavior, I go to another level of intimacy with them. You may not in the moment, you may be defensive in the moment, but when you go back in your own silence and you think about it, you say, that's why I love them. Because they know me, and they're honest with me. And then, two seconds later he saves her life.

"So the doors get blown open again for her acceptance of Angel in her life. And even the nasty things he said in jest, or as a cover-up, were not a cover-up. They came from a place of integrity, which is why that shroud was so powerful. And his points were real. 'Oh, I'm such a tough cop. And I'm gonna shoot everybody up. And I'm gonna whine about my father.' And the fact is, that's what I've been doing, and it's a real smack in the face. I would never let him know it, but I think deep down inside, if there were other scenes, you know you'd see somebody going, all right, it's time to pull my act together here." —ELISABETH ROHM

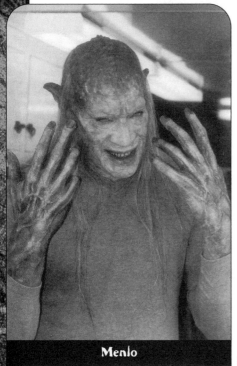

Menlo

This episode was a big one for Dayne Johnson, makeup department head, as he explains:

"'The Shroud of Rahmon' had Vyasa and Menlo in it. Which they worked a long period of time, you know, they worked like five days. When you get a demon or something that works like five or six days, that's a good stretch. We used that particular episode for our guild awards this year, our makeup artists and hair stylists guild awards. And we did get nominated for that show." —DAYNE JOHNSON

SIX DEGREES OF . . .

Tom Kiesche, who portrays plainclothes detective Broomfield, also appears as a vampire in the *Buffy* Season Five finale episode "The Gift."

Tony Todd, who plays Vyasa, is well known for his roles in science fiction and horror TV shows and movies, including appearances on *Star Trek: Deep Space Nine*. He also appeared in three movies based on Clive Barker's character Candyman, and in *Wishmaster*, written by Barker's friend (and *Hellraiser* screenwriter) Peter Atkins. Jerry Lambert, who owned Rick's Majick Shop in the Season One episode "I've Got You Under My Skin," was a music engineer on *Wishmaster*.

"THE TRIAL"

FROM THE FILES OF ANGEL INVESTIGATIONS
CASE № 2ADH09

ACTION TAKEN

Cordelia and Wesley are concerned for their boss. Angel has been down in the cellar of the Hyperion Hotel—a cellar with a history of badness—for an awfully long time. The strange clunking sound from downstairs does nothing to soothe their fear that he's still pining for a certain blond ex-vampire.

> CORDELIA: "Don't say 'Darla.' I am sick and tired of hearing about Darla. If I hear the name 'Darla' one more time . . . and he's not distraught, he's obsessed! And I thought you were going to be a man and talk to him about this."
> WESLEY: "I was a man—I said . . . things."
> CORDELIA: "Like what?"
> WESLEY: "Like did he prefer milk or sugar in his tea. It's how men talk about things in England!"

STORY BY David Greenwalt
TELEPLAY BY Douglas Petrie & Tim Minear
DIRECTED BY Bruce Seth Green
GUEST STARS: Christian Kane (Lindsey McDonald), Andy Hallett (Host), Sam Anderson (Holland Manners), Jim Piddock (Valet), Julie Benz (Darla), Juliet Landau (Drusilla)
CO-STAR: Evan Arnold (Shempire)

But as they discuss possible plans of action, the clunking noise stops and Angel emerges, a bundle of clean, dry laundry in his arms. He's oddly upbeat, even exuberant, which automatically makes Cordelia suspect that he's on drugs. He tries to set her mind at ease by explaining that he's given up looking for Darla. If she comes to him, fine. If she doesn't, that's okay too.

Cordelia and Wesley are trying to digest this new, non-broody version of their old friend when Gunn bursts in the hotel's front door, announcing that, at Angel's request, he has found Darla. Ignoring the murmurs of disapproval from Cordy and Wes, Angel strikes out with Gunn to get her.

Alone in her motel room, Darla looks at her own reflection in the mirror, as if still getting used to seeing herself. She tries lipstick on, wipes it off. Her sad self-examination is interrupted, though, by arrival of Lindsey, who has bribed the motel's manager to let him in.

Lindsey takes Darla back to the Wolfram & Hart offices, where Holland joins them. Holland is, as ever, cloyingly, falsely sincere when he tells her that she's not Wolfram & Hart's prisoner, but she is their moral responsibility. He hands her a manila folder, and she pages through the papers contained therein.

Whatever is on those papers doesn't exactly bring joy to her life.

By the time Angel and Gunn arrive at the motel, Darla is gone. Looking at her current digs, Angel remembers another time when she sought shelter against enemies and elements: France, in 1765.

Running from a lynch mob led by a man named Holtz, Angelus and Darla, sharing a horse, find a barn that promises some degree of safety. As it turns out, though, those who have been after them for their vampiric ways have followed them even here, and fire a flaming arrow through a window.

Back in Los Angeles, Darla, in her desperation, has lowered her standards in an attempt to be turned back into a vampire. Going to a bar where vampires hang out, she meets a loser who was made but apparently not schooled in vampiric ways. She persuades him—by promising to be his "immortal babe"—to make her. He takes her out into an alley behind the bar to do the deed, where Angel stakes him. Darla's furious at Angel's interference, but he doesn't understand why she isn't willing to try the human thing for a few months. Darla tells him that she doesn't *have* a few months—she's dying.

Thinking of France again, Angel remembers how Darla demonstrated her concern for his well-being. The barn under siege and their horse too tired to carry them both out, she slugs him with a flaming plank and rides off alone.

Managing to be more honorable than that, Angel brings Darla back to the Hyperion Hotel, much to the chagrin of Cordelia and Wesley. Here, he explains that Wolfram & Hart has told Darla that she's dying. Since it's Wolfram & Hart, though, no one but Darla believes it. However, she agrees to stay with Cordy and Wes while Angel investigates.

Angel's first stop is Lindsey's apartment. He kicks the door in, and Lindsey surprises him by inviting him inside. He tells Angel that the medical reports are real. When the human girl who became Darla was dying the first time, it was from syphilis. Now that she's human again, the syphilis is back, and advanced to such a degree that it's too late for antibiotics to help. Lindsey didn't want to believe it either, so he took her to more doctors, including his own personal physician.

Angel realizes then that, in his own, pathetic way, Lindsey loves Darla. The difference between them, Lindsey points out, is that he would do whatever he could to save her. Angel could save her, simply by making her a vampire again, but he won't. Angel is convinced that there's another way, and he's determined to find it.

Returning to the hotel, Angel tells Darla the news. In so doing, he has an inspiration.

And Darla sings for the Host, who is very impressed.

"Someone get my heart, that girl's ripped it right out. Okay. And I know I'm going to regret this. In fact, being prescient, I'm actually sure of it, but there is one way—it's a bit of a quest and it'll probably kill you."

—*Host*

He directs Angel to a particular Los Angeles swimming pool. Angel and Darla go there to find that all the water has been drained from it. But the Host told Angel he needs to "take the plunge," so Angel, in a serious demonstration of faith, dives headfirst into the empty pool. When he does, the floor of the pool opens up for him and takes him—and Darla—into a strange, stone-walled chamber, where they're met by an old-fashioned valet.

The valet explains the rules. If Angel wants to save Darla, he must complete three trials. When he does so, Darla will be "made whole." If he can't complete them, she dies instantly. Tough rules. To make them tougher, there's no backing out now that they've entered. To quit once they've come in is to forfeit her life.

For the first trial, unarmed combat, the valet takes away Angel's shirt and shoes. Barefoot and bare-chested, Angel is supposed to walk through a gate. However, between him and the gate is a massive, powerful demon named Tor, who, unlike Angel, is heavily armed. He has a broadsword and twin metal hooks set into lengths of thick, heavy chain. Tor has only one thing in mind—killing Angel.

In an antechamber, Darla is allowed by the valet to psychically observe the combat. What she sees is Angel getting the proverbial stuffing pounded out of him by his monstrous opponent.

But this is Angel, so he's able to overcome simple obstacles such as having one of Tor's hooks embedded in his leg. He yanks it out and uses the length of chain attached to knock the broadsword from Tor's grip. Beating Tor to the sword, he snatches it up and slices Tor cleanly in half at the waist. Having beaten the demon, Angel goes to the gate, which doesn't open. Then Angel turns to see that he

only thinks he's won—the demon is reattaching his lower half, almost as if putting on a pair of pants that just happen to have his legs already inside them.

He comes at Angel again, hooks whizzing through the air. Dodging the hooks, Angel manages to get his hands on one of them and skewers Tor with it. Cutting him in half once again, Angel uses the chain to bind Tor's top half to a torch pole high on a wall. Before the demon can reunite his parts, Angel hooks his leg and hangs his lower half from a different pole, some distance away. With Tor sectioned and separated, Angel really has won, and the gate opens for him.

The path leads Angel to his next challenge. He finds himself at one end of a long tunnel. At the far end is a door. Halfway there, a receptacle stands, but from where he stands he can't see what's in it.

The catch is, the tunnel—floors, walls, ceiling—is filled with hundreds of crosses.

Every step searing agony, Angel forces himself to run toward the far door. At one point, he falls, crosses burning his chest as well as his feet. He regains his footing, though, and continues all the way to the door.

Which is, of course, locked.

He looks back at the receptacle.

Running back to it, he sees that it's filled with water, and a key rests at the bottom. Of course, this is not just any H_2O; it's holy water. Angel thrusts his hand in, fishes around, and comes up with the key—and second-degree burns on his arm. Then it's once more across the floor of Christian iconography, feet burning, flesh steaming with every step. The key fits the lock, though, and Angel opens the door.

On the other side is another small stone chamber. Angel barely has time to look around before chains snake out toward him, clamping around his wrists and ankles and pulling taut. Angel is suspended, feet barely on the floor. Before him is a wall filled with small holes.

The valet joins him, congratulating him on his progress so far. As they talk, stakes emerge from the holes in the wall. Angel isn't happy. There's no way out of this one.

"Exactly. You . . . do understand? This third test has no 'catch,' as you put it. Death is the final challenge. We can't restore one life without taking another. You see? In order for Darla to live, you must die."

—*Valet*

Angel suggests they switch places, but the valet assures him that his own death wouldn't spare Darla's life. It has to be Angel. The stakes pull back, locking into a spring-loaded firing mechanism. The valet explains to Angel that he has to give his permission before they'll fire, that he has to accept his own death for Darla to live. The option is that he can refuse to die, walk away, and let Darla die. Angel won't do that, so the valet reminds Angel he has more to offer the world than Darla does.

Angel still won't budge. He's willing to give his own life to spare hers. The valet agrees, steps to the side, and the stakes are triggered. They fly at Angel.

In the antechamber where she was taken to wait, Darla screams, then opens her eyes to see a fully clothed Angel, the valet, and two statuelike demon guards standing before her. The valet congratulates Angel on having passed the third test. By accepting death, Angel has saved Darla's life.

The valet turns to Darla, takes her head in his hands—and hesitates. A worried look crosses his face. It seems that Darla has already been given new life, by supernatural means. She's already living her second chance, which is all the valet is empowered to give her. He's sorry, but there's nothing he can do for her. He dematerializes.

Angel snaps, going on a rampage of destruction. He overturns tables, smashes urns. Two statue-like demon guards try to restrain him but he takes them out and, in frustration, slams his fist again and again into a stone pillar, pulverizing it.

RESOLUTION

Back in Darla's motel, a forlorn Angel suggests another possibility. He says that maybe, because he has a soul, if he did bite her—

But Darla won't hear of it. She's decided to accept that this is her second chance, to die. The way she was supposed to die in the first place. Angel is surprised, and moved, by her courage. Still burned and battered, he holds her, not as a lover but as a dear friend he won't leave behind.

And then their moment of stillness is interrupted by three armed security guards kicking in the room's door. They attack Angel with a Taser, stunning him. Lindsey enters in their wake.

And he's brought a friend.

Confident and serene, Drusilla enters. She morphs, takes Darla in her arms, and sinks her fangs into her grandmother's neck. A moment later, lowering the weakened Darla to the bed, she cuts open her own breast and raises Darla's mouth to her wound. A restrained Angel watches in impotent horror.

Case to be continued.

DOSSIERS

CLIENT Darla is the client in this case—not a traditional client, by any means, but the one whose life is in danger, and whom Angel risks his own life—to no avail, as it turns out—in order to save.

CIVILIAN SUPPORT The Host sends Angel to the valet. It isn't clear if he knew exactly what Angel and Darla would be letting themselves in for.

SUSPECTS The valet, while also not a traditional villain, puts Angel in considerable peril, ultimately for no good reason. (Remains at large.) **Tor**, the demon, does his level best to kill Angel, only to be halved, twice, for his trouble. (Deceased.)

CONTINUITY

Holtz, the vampire hunter, is first mentioned in Angel's recounting of the events of 1765. Angel is leery of the Host's advice following the encounter with the false T'ish Magev in "Guise Will Be Guise." The Host reminds Angel of the treachery of his favorite bartender, Ramone, who had recommended the T'ish Magev in the first place. Angel and Darla's long and twisted road began with her siring him in an alley in *Buffy's* "Becoming, Part One," and led to his staking her in Sunnydale in "Angel."

Drusilla has not been seen in the States since Spike departed with her unconscious body in "Becoming, Part Two."

QUOTE OF THE WEEK

"I'm a channel surfer. Look, you're a big hunk of hero sandwich, you want to save the girl and I can see why." The Host seems reluctant to tell Angel what he sees when Darla sings.

THE DEVIL IS IN THE DETAILS

EXPENSES

Though Angel Investigations is unlikely to be billed, Angel trashes:
a table full of food
a big ceramic urn
an assortment of mystical paraphernalia, including skulls, candles, and a smaller urn
a stone pillar

WEAPONRY

Hooks and chains, and a broadsword.

DEMONS, DEMONS, DEMONS

THE VAMPIRE RULES

Darla has to explain to the uneducated Shempire how to turn, rather than kill, his victim:

> SHEMPIRE: "Well . . . I never actually did it to anyone before. And I was kinda out when it happened to me."
> DARLA: "I'll walk you through it. Drink. When you feel my heart start to slow, stop—"

272

THE PEN IS MIGHTIER

FINAL CUT

In the original script, the episode ends when Darla announces that she's ready to die, and Angel promises to stay with her until she does. The startling appearance of Lindsey and Drusilla was added later.

The Host apparently finds Darla just as attractive as Angel and Lindsey do, as evidenced by this line cut from the episode:

"Have her bathed and taken to my chambers . . . rrrrrrr."

POP CULTURE

❊ The script describes the Shempire:

Darla is seated in a booth at the back of this seedy bar. Across from her is a total SHEMP VAMPIRE (or "shempire"), he sports an eighties mullet hairdo. He bares his fangs and tries to talk all evil-sexy.

Shemp, of course, was one of The Three Stooges.

❊ When Darla wants to know why the Shempire has never taken a mate, he says it would be weird.

DARLA: "'Weird'?! It's mythic!"

SHEMPIRE: "No, you been readin' too much Anne Rice, lady. You got no idea how this thing works."

Anne Rice is the bestselling author of several vampire novels, including *Interview with the Vampire.*

❊ **"I mean, not only is she putting his life at stake, but ours. I'm sorry, but after four hundred years of death and destruction, seems to me you get voted off the island, am I right?"** Cordelia is not happy about having to share a roof with Darla. Being "voted off the island" is a reference to the hit CBS game show *Survivor.*

❊ **"It means: ohhh, Ground Control to Major Tom, we may not be able to save this bird."** Watching Darla sing, the Host offers his instant analysis. "Ground Control to Major Tom" is a line from David Bowie's 1969 song "Space Oddity."

OUR HEROES

Julie Benz was nervous about singing in the karaoke bar.

"That was, to me, a big challenge. I don't sing in public, at all. Barely sing in private. When they asked me to do it, I was like, what the hell, I'll try it; if it doesn't work out they'll loop it with somebody else. I'm always up to try things. I became an actor so I can constantly challenge myself and do things that you don't normally do in everyday life. And singing in a karaoke bar is not something that I do in everyday life. I was very nervous about that one. Terrified, actually, about it. It was very hard, because I'm very close to the crew and the rest of the cast. It was very hard to have to do it in front of people who matter to you in life. If it was a roomful of strangers I probably could have bluffed my way through a little better. My hands were sweating, the mike was almost slipping out of my hands because my hands were soaking wet. And it was very nerve-racking, but everyone was very supportive and loving and helped me through it."

—JULIE BENZ

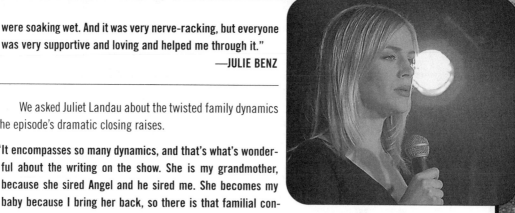

We asked Juliet Landau about the twisted family dynamics the episode's dramatic closing raises.

"It encompasses so many dynamics, and that's what's wonderful about the writing on the show. She is my grandmother, because she sired Angel and he sired me. She becomes my baby because I bring her back, so there is that familial connection as well. We are bound by this deep connection to Angel and our lengthy history. And there's the aspect of how one character's evil exacerbates the other. We bring out the worst, or what we consider the best, in each other."

—JULIET LANDAU

TRACKS

Darla sings "Ill Wind," written by Harold Arlen and Ted Koehler, from the Broadway show *Cotton Club Parade*. It was later heard in Francis Ford Coppola's film *The Cotton Club*.

Music coordinator John King told us about Darla's karaoke experience:

"On 'Ill Wind,' Julie Benz was to sing a karaoke version of that song, but unfortunately it wasn't available in karaoke. So what we had to do was to have Robert [Kral, *Angel*'s composer] do a new arrangement of it, and record it. Then we could bring Julie in and record her singing to his arrangement." —JOHN KING

"REUNION"

FROM THE FILES OF ANGEL INVESTIGATIONS
CASE Nº: 2ADH10

ACTION TAKEN

Calling for help, Charles Gunn helps a semiconscious Angel into the hotel. Cordelia and Wesley come running. Angel's barely coherent and badly hurt. Gunn explains that Angel managed to call him from Darla's motel room, and when Gunn got there the place was a wreck. He found Angel injured and Darla gone.

Angel clarifies—Darla, he says, is dead.

Rallying, he's able to tell the others that Drusilla is here, and that she made Darla drink. Wesley and Cordelia understand that this is bad news, though Gunn is in the dark as to just who Drusilla is.

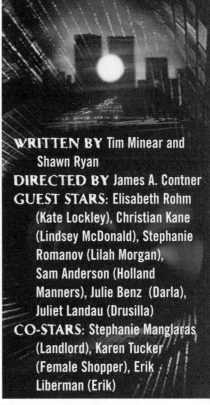

WRITTEN BY Tim Minear and Shawn Ryan
DIRECTED BY James A. Contner
GUEST STARS: Elisabeth Rohm (Kate Lockley), Christian Kane (Lindsey McDonald), Stephanie Romanov (Lilah Morgan), Sam Anderson (Holland Manners), Julie Benz (Darla), Juliet Landau (Drusilla)
CO-STARS: Stephanie Manglaras (Landlord), Karen Tucker (Female Shopper), Erik Liberman (Erik)

> GUNN: "Now these lawyers, they brought Darla back as human . . . but now this Drusilla vamp goes and bites Darla—"
> WESLEY: "So it would seem."
> GUNN: "Making her a vampire again."
> WESLEY: "That's the cosmological upshot, yes. Darla's human self has died. And sometime before dawn, unless Angel can stop it, she will rise again, a soulless demon."
> GUNN: "So that means . . ."
> WESLEY: "The clock is ticking."
> GUNN: "No, no. What I'm saying is . . . that means—the granddaughter remade the grandmother?"
> WESLEY: "Oh. Yes."
> GUNN: "Man, somehow that weirds me out more than the whole bloodsucking thing."

Angel manages to go into his office, rummaging through everything he owns in search of a stake. It's daytime now. Come nightfall, Darla will rise—and he intends to save her from that.

Angel downs a cup of blood to fortify himself. Cordelia's on the phone, trying to track down Lindsey via Wolfram & Hart, but she's just told that he's been in a meeting all day. Angel knows that's not true. Since it seems unlikely that Lindsey's at the office, though, Angel decides to go back to the lawyer's apartment. He's been invited in, after all—this time, when he kicks the door in, he can enter freely. The others offer to accompany him, but he turns them down. This is something he wants to do alone.

As it turns out, though, when Angel gets to the apartment, it's empty. Cleaned out. A landlord finds Angel inside and engages him in conversation. When Angel says he's trying to locate Lindsey because of a medical emergency, the landlord believes he's talking about Lindsey's English "cousin," who, she says, was very excited about getting the nursery ready for the baby, in spite of being way too thin to be healthily pregnant. Angel understands that the "cousin" was Drusilla. The landlord offered to show the odd English girl a two-bedroom, but she said she wanted her daughter to be born near the stars.

In a greenhouse, Drusilla prepares Darla for the moment of her rebirth, or re-rebirth, as the case may be. Lindsey watches as Drusilla prepares the body. Lilah and Holland show up, Holland offering, in all his smarmy false sincerity, to provide anything Drusilla might need. He tells Drusilla that they have a previous engagement they need to get ready for—and practically has to drag Lindsey away from the side of the dead but still lovely Darla.

Angel, Cordelia, Wesley, and Gunn debate the possible "nursery" choices that Drusilla might make. They consider a variety of options before Gunn makes the ultimate breakthrough, pointing out that there's another kind of nursery that combines the things she'll need: dirt, a starry view, and birth—a plant nursery. They decide to look for one that has some connection with the law firm, maybe a corporate supplier. And they come up with a greenhouse/penthouse on top of one of L.A.'s modern skyscrapers.

Angel goes in alone. He finds a mound of fresh dirt in a box, looking suspiciously like a grave. Clearing away some of the soil, he finds Darla underneath. He raises a stake to plunge into her breast. Angel doesn't want to do this, but he doesn't want to *not* do it more than he doesn't want to do it.

Before he can finish Darla once and for all, though, Drusilla slams him in the head with a garden spade. While they battle, destroying much of the greenhouse, Darla wakes, gasping and in pain. Angel and Dru manage to break the garden spade, leaving Angel with a pointy piece of wood in his hand. He dodges Dru and charges the grave—but it's empty now.

And Darla, emerging from the shadows, clamps a strong hand around his throat, causing him to drop the stake.

The fight continues until Darla leaps off the roof of the high-rise, disappearing into the darkness below. Angel turns back to the rooftop, but Drusilla's gone too.

Angel returns to the Hyperion to arm himself and his team. Drusilla and Darla, loosed upon the city—he knows it's a recipe for disaster. He wants to find at least one of them before they find each other again. Since it's a big city and there are only four of them, they'll start with the one solid lead they have—Wolfram & Hart.

At Wolfram & Hart, Holland talks to Lindsey about his party tonight. Lindsey doesn't have a date to bring—Darla, one supposes, being unavailable—and Holland tells him he needs to make time for healthy social attachments, emphasis on the healthy.

Drusilla emerges from the shadows of Lindsey's office, clutching a doll for comfort. She tells Holland, in her own unique way, about the fight, and warns that Angel is on his way to Wolfram & Hart. "He's very cross," she says. As they talk, Lindsey gets a call from security—a vampire is in the building. They start to take Dru to security, but when Lindsey opens the door, Darla stands on the other side. She comes in, practically spellbound, sniffing Lindsey and eyeing his neck as though it's a buffet. Then she throws him aside, clearing a path between herself and Drusilla. Darla grabs her granddaughter/mother, none too gently, and hauls her from the office.

Angel, meanwhile, drives like a madman through the Los Angeles streets. Wesley protests, but Angel's in a hurry. Then Wesley tells Angel to pull over altogether, because Cordelia's having a vision. "She should have done this before we left the hotel," Angel says, but he stops the car. Her vision will send them in the opposite direction, toward a young man she sees with a gun in his hand. Angel's not happy, but he knows that when The Powers That Be send Cordelia visions, they're important, so his argument is halfhearted and he turns the car around.

Elsewhere, one of L.A.'s shopping districts is the scene of a brawl between two young-looking women, Darla and Drusilla. Dru is genuinely puzzled as to why Darla seems so intent on tearing her head off. She thought she was doing Darla a favor by bringing her back.

Their fight blocks traffic, and finally a burly guy in a testosterone-fueled pickup suggests that the girls take their make-out session home. Darla's response is to vamp out and drain him, on the spot. When she turns back to Dru, losing the forehead and fangs, everything is fine between them. The old Darla—the vicious blood-sucking one—is back.

> **DRUSILLA:** "You're all new again."
>
> **DARLA:** "Let's go shopping."

Cordelia's vision takes the team to the garage of Erik, a young boy listening to death metal and preparing to sacrifice himself to the demon Morgog, gun in his lap and terror in his eyes. Cordelia tells Angel that the kid's ready to snap and has to be handled delicately, but Angel's version of "delicate" is to hurl the kid's boom box into his shrine, smashing both. Angel takes the gun from the kid, warns him against Morgog, and tells him not to kill himself. He empties the gun and throws it and the bullets into a barrel of motor oil. He's done.

Wesley doesn't agree. If The Powers That Be sent them here, the boy must need help. Angel's version of help seems a tad inadequate. Angel tells the others to stay and help all they want, but he has somewhere else to be.

In a clothing store, Darla and Drusilla are trying on clothing when they're interrupted by a cell phone that Drusilla has forgotten she carries. "Oo, I'm ringing, do you hear it?" she asks. "I'm ringing all over." Darla answers, knowing that it'll be Holland Manners. And it is. He's heard about their little spree—a saleswoman, bloodied and hurt, crawls past as they talk—and suggests that, while a spree might be fun, the ladies might be more entertained by a massacre.

When the conversation is over, Darla and Dru return to their shopping. But injured saleswoman ignores Darla's request for shoe advice for Drusilla's ensemble, so Darla snaps her neck, finishing her off.

At Wolfram & Hart, Lilah Morgan speculates that Darla and Drusilla will keep Angel busy for some time. Holland agrees—they won't need to worry about Angel for a while.

Cue Angel's entrance, crashing in through a plate-glass window. Holland offers his hand, as this is the first time he and Angel have come face-to-face. Angel rejects the hand, pointing out that Holland should be more careful about who he offers his hand to—an observation with which Lindsey has to concur. Holland tells Angel that he's Division Head of Special Projects. Angel asks if he means projects like Darla, to which Holland, in a surprisingly candid moment, replies that Darla is just a tool—Angel's the project.

Security guards enter, armed with vampire-specific weapons. Angel warns Holland that he could kill the lawyer before the guards could make a move. Holland knows that he could, but also that he won't—Angel has a reputation for not killing humans. Angel says that Holland barely qualifies. Innocent people die because of his games. But Holland says, "And yet, I just can't seem to care." Furthermore, he tells Angel that while Angel is wasting his time here, Darla and Dru are out painting the town red, as in blood. Angel doesn't think the guards are going to just let him walk out, but Holland says that they are. If they'd wanted Angel dead, he'd be dead. Instead, he asks security to escort Angel from the building. He'd do it himself, he says, except that he's running late for a wine tasting at home—to which Angel is, pointedly, *not* invited.

Lindsey accompanies Angel and the guards outside, where uniformed cops are waiting for him. They handcuff him and put him in a car.

Already sitting in the backseat, waiting for him, is Kate Lockley.

Kate tells him about the reports of carnage in a clothing store at Fifth and Hill, and the description of the two suspects, one of whom matches Darla. She knows she can't stop Darla, but she thinks maybe Angel can. It bothers Kate to believe in him, but she has no other choice. She uncuffs Angel and lets him go.

At Holland's mansion, Lindsey arrives, dateless, with flowers for Holland's wife. Catherine Manners tells Lindsey that the others are already in the wine cellar.

Holland, enjoying his expensive, ornate room and collection, is grandiloquent in his praise of his division's hard work. He tells the assortment of a dozen attorneys that the Senior Partners appreciate them, too, and he raises a glass of very costly 1928 Chateau Latour to Lilah and Lindsey for their efforts.

But he's interrupted by the arrival of Darla and Drusilla—blood at the corners of Dru's mouth. Apparently Catherine Manners made the mistake of inviting them in before Dru feasted on her. Holland, startled by this turn of events, is for once almost speechless as Darla explains to him that they've come to give Holland what he wants—a massacre.

Angel goes to the clothing store, looking at the scene of the spree. In a dressing room he finds a shopper, scared and hiding but unhurt. She says that she was lucky the vampires were in a hurry to get to a party—a tasting, more specifically, she recalls.

And at the tasting, Holland tries to use his patented sincerity gambit on the vamps. Darla's not buying it, still holding a bit of a grudge against Holland for raising her in the first place.

> **DARLA:** "You brought me back as human—a dying one at that—let me wallow with a
> soul, sent me crawling to Angel, begging him to restore me."
>
> **HOLLAND:** "Which he should have done right away. But I miscalculated, I thought he
> cared more than he did."
>
> **DARLA:** "Like you do."
>
> **DRUSILLA:** "Grandmum won't eat the double-speak."

Then Drusilla, sensing that the room was originally a bomb shelter, tunes out the conversation and listens instead to historic sirens.

Upstairs, Angel arrives. Catherine Manners, bleeding, wounded, sees him in the doorway and asks for help. That's all the invitation he needs to come inside. Downstairs, Holland sees Angel as his last hope and welcomes him.

Angel is here for Darla, though. He apologizes for not getting to her in time. He's sorry, but she's not. She really is the old Darla again.

The lawyers' desperation begins to show through. Lilah and Holland practically beg for help.

> **HOLLAND:** "Angel, please, people are going to die."
>
> **ANGEL:** "And yet, somehow, I just can't seem to care."

He closes and locks the heavy doors, trapping the lawyers in with the vampires they've brought to town. Holland shouts for Angel, but Darla picks him first, sinking her fangs into his neck. Listening to the sounds of carnage, Angel walks up the stairs and into darkness.

RESOLUTION

In his office, Angel tells the rest of the team what happened. They're stunned that he would just walk away and let the lawyers die. This is a different Angel than the one they're used to.

> **CORDELIA:** "You have to change the way you've been doing things. Don't you see
> where this is taking you?"
>
> **WESLEY:** "Listen to her. Right now the three of us are all that's standing between you
> and real darkness."
>
> **GUNN:** "You best believe that, man."
>
> **ANGEL:** "I do. You're all fired."

Case closed.

DOSSIERS

CLIENT Darla remains the client in this case, as she's the one in danger whom Angel tries to save. But he fails to do so.

VICTIMS The **burly guy** Darla feeds on is the first of many, including **various shoppers** and the **saleswoman** in the store whose neck Darla snaps and, by the end, what appears to be a large portion of the **attorneys** who comprise the Wolfram & Hart Special Projects Division.

SUSPECTS Drusilla, primarily, is behind the bloodshed this time out. Having remade **Darla**, the two of them go on a rampage.

CONTINUITY

Wesley, Angel, and Cordelia first learned about W&H's vampire detection systems in "Five by Five." They have thwarted them on several different occasions in different ways in "Blind Date," "Blood Money," and "Redefinition." Lindsey invited Angel into his apartment in "The Trial," for all the good it does Angel this time. Drusilla repeats the nursery rhyme she learned from her mother: "Run and catch, run and catch, the lamb is caught in the blackberry patch." She first chanted it in *Buffy*'s "Lie to Me," which also introduced Chantarelle, aka Lily, aka Anne Steele. Angel recalls Drusilla's fondness for the night sky in his mansion gardens in Sunnydale. His mansion is also mentioned in "Rm w/a Vu." Lindsey is unpleasantly reminded of Angel's forcible removal of his hand in "To Shanshu in L.A." when Angel declines Holland Manner's handshake. Drusilla calls Angel the "Angel-Beast," offering her own eerie glimpse into his jaunt to Pylea, perhaps?

QUOTE OF THE WEEK

"Am I right in guessing this Drusilla's got a set of teeth on her?"

Gunn tries hard to understand who's who in Angel's convoluted history.

THE DEVIL IS IN THE DETAILS

WEAPONRY

The standard weapons of vampiric battle are in the game: a stake, a sword, a crossbow, and an ax.

THE PLAN

Angel tells the team he's going to Lindsey's apartment to find Darla and Drusilla. The others offer to go along, since Angel won't be able to go inside, but Angel turns them down.

"So what's your plan? Stand outside his door and make remarks?" —*Cordelia*

Later, Angel announces that he's going to Wolfram & Hart. Once again, Cordelia has an objection.

"Hitting the pause button. Wolfram & Hart as in vampire detectors, a crack security system, and armed guards? Nice plan, General Custer." —*Cordelia*

Taking time away from Darla tracking to stop the kid from sacrificing himself to Morgog, Wesley and Gunn speculate on a deeper purpose for the interruption.

> **WESLEY:** "The Powers That Be must have had good reason to send us here."
> **ANGEL:** "I don't have time to figure that out."
> **GUNN:** "Maybe that's the plan. Maybe they're trying to keep you from going on this mission."

DEMONS, DEMONS, DEMONS

THE VAMPIRE RULES

Angel describes what happened when Drusilla made Darla:

"They made her drink . . . she didn't want to. You think you can resist. . . . But then it's too late. . . ." —*Angel*

When a vampire is made, she will rise after sunset on the following night. Before that, it is preferable, though not necessary, that he or she be buried in dirt, though the burial doesn't need to be deep or in an actual cemetery.

The vampire lineage as described in this case: Darla (the mother) made Angel (the son) who made Drusilla (the granddaughter) who made Spike (great grandson) and remade Darla (grandmother/great granddaughter).

THE PEN IS MIGHTIER

FINAL CUT

When Angel speaks with Lindsey's former landlord, she offers this assessment of her tenant, which was cut before airing:

"So sad to see him go. A lovely man. Always on time with the rent. Quiet and clean. Pity about the hand."
—*Landlord*

From the stage directions, when Angel locks the wine cellar doors on the lawyers and the vamps: Stunned looks all around. Even from Darla and Dru, but they're stunned with delight. They share a "that was so cool!" look.

POP CULTURE

❋ The script's stage directions describe the moment of Darla's rebirth:
  Bigger, uglier GASPS now. She's in big birth pain. She sits up in her grave, like Elsa Lanchester, her head darting all around the place.
  In spite of a film career that stretched from 1927 to 1980, Elsa Lanchester remains best known as the Bride of Frankenstein, and Darla's wide-eyed terror here is much like the Bride's stock expression.

❋ **"You had me at 'Everyone gear up.'"** Gunn is ready to roll out in pursuit of Darla as Angel passes out weapons. "You had me at 'hello,'" is a famous line from the Tom Cruise movie *Jerry Maguire*.

❋ **"Easy, boss. This kid's ready to snap, crackle, and pop. I felt it in my vision. . . ."** Cordelia warns Angel that the kid from her vision is on edge. "Snap, crackle, pop," is the slogan—and the names of the three mascots—of Kellogg's Rice Krispies cereal.

Chateau Latour, the wine that Holland serves at his tasting, comes from a well-respected vineyard in France, producing grapes for fine wines since 1718. A single bottle of Pauillac Chateau Latour 1928 can be had for a little over six thousand dollars.

OUR HEROES

Angel, who's been flirting with the darkness for a while, plunges in headfirst in this episode. Writer Tim Minear talked about how that came about.

"It was a breakfast meeting, it was David and Joss and me, and we were sitting there, and, 'How do we make this dark, broody guy dark and broody? How will anyone be able to tell?' And Joss said, 'We'll lock a bunch of lawyers in a room with Darla and Drusilla, and let them all die, and then fire everybody.' And our response was, 'Well, then, we should probably do that, because that sounds real interesting.' So we did that."

—TIM MINEAR

JAMES CONTNER: "Juliet [Landau] and I had a long talk about . . . how far to go with the character [of Drusilla]. There are certain instances where you see her kind of loopy in the episode, but we tried to see another side of her, to sort of flesh her out a little more, to see that she's not just off the charts all the time. Since we're dealing with a sense of history about their relationships, how much at one time they had meant to one another, and now they're brought together and sort of pitted against one another. To go around a lunatic all the time would kind of diminish the seriousness of the episode, which does have a very strong serious overlay. Again, with wacky moments. Also another marvelous actress, Juliet. She's a very studied actor, and she likes to work and experiment. She actually embraced the fact that she was able to do something different with her character. In fact, she called me after she saw the show, and said, 'You know, I've had more calls about my performance on that show,' and she thought it was the best show she'd ever done as that character. So I felt really good about that. I really felt I had a contribution in that. It was the one time where you do have an established character where you can actually make some changes, take it in a different direction. And she was very willing to do that. A lot of that also came out of an initial conversation with David Greenwalt, trying to do that with her character. I thought it worked very well. They were eerie together, especially in the scene where they end up in the wine cellar. Pretty creepy.

"And then, of course, there's that moment where Angel says, 'I just can't seem to care.' Which is huge.

"This is him going back over to the dark side, and really catching the audience, I think, off guard. Here he's sort of been moody and broody throughout this piece, but I don't think the audience had any inkling that he was just going to give up on these people."

"Did David have any qualms about that?"

JAMES CONTNER: "No, I don't think so. David is one of these actors we were talking about [with] natural ability. He also stays very true to the character and never likes to bring in a false beat, but there's no fun in playing the same thing all the time, for an actor on a weekly series. They relish those moments where they can be out of character, or take the character in a different direction for a few episodes. I think David had a lot of fun going to the dark side."

Elisabeth Rohm spoke about her brief appearance in this episode, turning Angel loose to go after Darla and Dru.

"Well, the thing is I don't know what really happened. I don't know that he got there and he decided that he was going to let them kill [the lawyers]. You know what I mean? I think, bad decision because I know my career is on shaky ground at this point. In the moment, I think, well, I tried my best. And maybe I have some self-doubt about Angel but in regards to my new quest as a cop and as a human being, I've made a decision to let Angel back into my life, and I intend to trust him. So even though he doesn't accomplish saving Wolfram & Hart, in the moment I heard about Wolfram & Hart I was disappointed that he didn't come through for me. I took it personally. You know, Wolfram & Hart is this evil place, so it's good they're all gone. So in a way it was a mixed bag of feelings. But later on, as my life becomes shaken again, I'll throw that into the mix and begin to blame him again." —ELISABETH ROHM

Julie Benz, now that Darla is a vampire again, has to appear in full vamp-face makeup, which is constructed differently on *Angel* than it was on *Buffy*.

"The prosthetic does a lot of the job. My prosthetic is sculpted to be pretty scary-looking . . . [so] it does ninety percent of the job for you. Unfortunately, you don't get much facial expression, though, you just get the one expression. I really try to move it, and that becomes hard, because then you have to overmove your face just to get a small response with the prosthetic on. I do find it very restricting. I have a really hard time with it. I can't see straight, I have to look up. That face speaks for itself, really. I could not do anything if I didn't want to, but I choose to try to bring it to life and make it more like it's not a prosthetic on my face but more of my face. I think I've found ways of manipulating it, but it is hard. Prosthetic days are not my favorite."
—JULIE BENZ

"I always really work with Wardrobe. All of the little details, including the Drusilla manicure, designed by Todd McIntosh, a specific manicure—when I was weak it was black with white tips, and since I've been strong again it's been red with white tips—all of those little details really do help shape and add to a character. In that episode we went on a shopping spree. Drusilla is experimenting, and the one look that looked a little bit rock and roll was kind of fun, because, again, it sort of brought back the Sid and Nancy analogy."
—JULIET LANDAU

Stunt coordinator Michael Vendrell shared some very strong opinions, including his belief that "stuntwomen are far superior to stuntmen."

MICHAEL VENDRELL: "Where a man is called upon, he's wearing boots and he can pad up pretty good. A lot of time, women are asked to do stair falls, car hits, in a dress. It's hard to hide pads when you're wearing a skimpy little dress. You can go on record saying Mike Vendrell thinks stuntwomen are tougher than stuntmen, by far."

"When you have Angel and Darla battling, are there different things you have to take into account?"

MICHAEL VENDRELL: "When they came to me about Darla, they didn't want Darla to look like Angel in their fighting styles. They said, 'What we want is for her to be very feral. Catlike. No martial art moves at all.' I watched some films on leopards, and how they pounce. So if you watch the way Darla moves when she fights, she more or less pounces on people. And if she hits, she has more of a swiping type of hit than a John Wayne punch. And when she fought with Angel in the greenhouse episode, if you watch, her and Drusilla both fight very similar. A little more feline on Drusilla, she's more like a cat. But I made Darla very, very strong, like twice as strong as Angel as far as physical strength. It's surprising to see this tiny little woman driving this man through the wall and up through the ceiling. So for shock value, that was kind of my idea to go that direction. And then Angel didn't know how to deal with this. Him and Darla had never fought before. So this was a situation where it's like, what am I doing now? How do I fight this person who I've known intimately? He has a soul, so he doesn't want to kill her. He had a lot of things he had to be thinking about. And thinking and fighting at the same time will get you killed."

TRACKS

"The biggest case of a last-minute change was at the end of 'Reunion.' Tim Minear was put in charge of the music approval for that week. However, when David Greenwalt heard the cue at the final mix, where Angel locks the doors on Wolfram & Hart, for their own massacre, David wanted a more epic-sounding moment there. We had a contorted, building orchestra thing. Tim was able to perform a change on the stage, but David ended up going back to the original version of the music. Sometimes that is the case when we provide several versions of a cue. A producer might ask for a different idea, sometimes it works better, other times we go back to the original version."   **—ROBERT KRAL, COMPOSER**

The music Erik listens to before Angel breaks his boom box is "Shock," by Fear Factory, from their 1998 CD *Obsolete*.

"REDEFINITION"

FROM THE FILES OF ANGEL INVESTIGATIONS
CASE Nº: 2ADH11

ACTION TAKEN

Angel has destroyed the team with two simple words: "You're fired." Cordelia, Wesley, and Gunn find themselves on the sidewalk in front of the hotel, trying to process what just occurred. They work though several stages of loss, including anger.

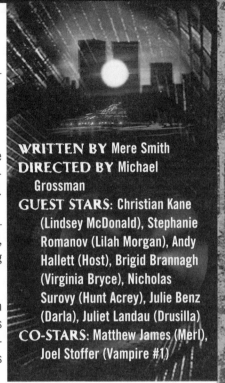

> "Darla. It's all about Darla. One thing you can say about Angel, at least he's consistent—it's always some little blond driving him over the edge." —*Cordelia*

The three go their separate ways, leaving Angel alone in the dark with his thoughts. Which seem of the grim, as he feeds his precious sketches of Darla into the flames of the hotel furnace. Having committed that act of catharsis, Angel pushes his workout routine to the limit in preparation for battle.

WRITTEN BY Mere Smith
DIRECTED BY Michael Grossman
GUEST STARS: Christian Kane (Lindsey McDonald), Stephanie Romanov (Lilah Morgan), Andy Hallett (Host), Brigid Brannagh (Virginia Bryce), Nicholas Surovy (Hunt Acrey), Julie Benz (Darla), Juliet Landau (Drusilla)
CO-STARS: Matthew James (Merl), Joel Stoffer (Vampire #1)

> "I'm not ready yet. Too many years sleeping in soft beds, living in a world where I don't belong. I can't fight them. Not yet. But soon." —*Angel*

Lindsey awakens on the floor of Holland's wine cellar to find that Darla spared him. His pleasure in being singled out to live is diminished when another survivor is discovered—Lilah, the constant thorn in his side.

Virginia Bryce gives a despondent Wesley a pep talk, first suggesting perhaps he can find something in his field of expertise—"renowned specialist in supernatural aid and rescue"—and then asking in what other areas he has skills. His answer is concise. "Not much."

Back at Wolfram & Hart, Lindsey and Lilah squabble about their very likely nonfutures, when they're interrupted by unexpected guests—Darla and Drusilla. Darla taunts Lindsey, claiming she kept him alive for romantic reasons, but then revealing her true purpose. They need a contact at W&H, and left both Lilah and Lindsey alive to see who fares better with the Senior Partners. Lindsey's inquiring about their plans for Angel causes Darla to react in rage, claiming her agenda might not even include Angel.

Meanwhile, Angel has expanded his training to include single-handedly taking out four sewer vamps with ease. He sounds more confident now. "I'm ready. I've got the moves. Now I need to know what theirs are."

That cutting-edge master of song, the Host, is on stage belting out "Lady Marmalade" when Wesley enters Caritas. Wes orders a bloodless Bloody Mary, having had enough of bloody drinks to last the rest of his life (see "Guise Will Be Guise"). He contemplates singing something from Cat Stevens to learn his path, when he bumps into Cordelia, visiting the karaoke bar for her own reasons. They have just confessed their embarrassment to each other when Gunn abashedly joins them.

Angel entertains himself by dipping a bound Merl, Wesley's stool pigeon pal, in and out of a sewer until Merl spews out his speculation about the possible whereabouts of Darla and Dru. Angel fails to compensate Merl for his valuable information, plus he leaves the parasite demon spinning, head down, by way of thanks.

Darla and Drusilla go out recruiting "muscular slaves" in a warehouse filled with demons and other monsters fighting for fun, à la *Fight Club*. Dru's warning of Angel's disguised presence interrupts Darla's spiel. Darla loses momentum for a moment, then recovers herself as Angel escapes into the night.

Back at Wolfram & Hart, Lindsey sees the softer side of Lilah briefly when she comes by his office and suggests they leave the firm immediately, on their own terms. She suggests they steal files for insurance, as Lindsey has done before. Lindsey steps in close, apparently in agreement—then scoops the concealed mike from her provocatively displayed cleavage. Blowing her a kiss, he suggests they stick out whatever happens.

Empties cover one of the illuminated tables in Caritas as Wesley, Cordelia, and Gunn spat over responsibility for Angel's behavior. There's only one possible outcome, and soon enough, they are up on stage, arms around each other, mangling Queen's "We Are the Champions." They either drive everyone else away or just close the bar down, because the Host approaches with no guidance, but with a nicely placed jacket to cushion Cordelia's head as she is slammed with a vision.

The three, instantly sobered, arrive at a dark alley, missing both the demon from Cordy's vision and its victim. A bit of astute detective work on Wes's part, involving sticking his hand into a vertical trail of blood, leads them to the top of the locked warehouse in which the demon has taken refuge.

At the hotel, Angel gathers up his gear and heads out into the night on a mission of his own, continuing to isolate himself by ignoring his ringing telephone.

And in another part of town, Drusilla wipes her fingers on her clothes, then puts them in her mouth, anxious to get any remnants of the eyeballs of the barkeeper she didn't care for off them. Darla is anxious to finish recruiting and move forward with her plans to destroy the city of Angel. Desperate to avoid any conversation about her ex, Darla impatiently hustles Dru along, not really listening to her insane rant.

"I see such pretty fire . . . And pain . . . so much suffering . . . The flames are lovely . . . they dance, and the fire licks like a cat . . . and the screams, oh, it's like star music . . ."
                                                                                                    —*Drusilla*

Angel arrives at Darla and Drusilla's destination, an auto repair shop, before they do, taking on the demons gathered there with dispassionate violence.

Wesley, Cordelia, and Gunn would just as soon rescue the bleeding woman they find without such violence. However, when the demon attacks, the trio rallies, making weapons out of the debris in the warehouse until they overcome the demon through sheer perseverance. Damaged and dazed, they survey their handiwork.

>**WESLEY**: "We should go before I pass out. Or possibly during."
>
>**GUNN**: "This thing nearly ripped us to shreds."
>
>**CORDELIA**: "Yeah, but out of everybody here, which one of us is the dead one?"

Darla and Drusilla arrive at the auto shop to find their potential henchmen a pile of demon parts and vamp dust. They quickly realize Angel is the cause, although they are puzzled by his demeanor.

Instead of leaping up to engage or join them, he rests on the hood of a car, the glow from a lit cigarette revealing the extent of damage he took in the fight. Darla greets him, and at first there is no response. Then he springs his trap, flicking his cigarette into the pool of gasoline at their feet. He departs without a second glance as Darla and Drusilla become undead torches.

Darla grabs a sledgehammer and the two screaming, burning vampires rush to a fire hydrant, which Darla smashes, releasing torrents of water. They huddle in the rain, a barely functional Darla trying to soothe the damaged Drusilla, who foretold the fire in her own cryptic fashion.

>**DARLA**: "That wasn't Angel."
>
>**DRUSILLA**: "He's gone! He's all gone! Oh, it hurts . . . it hurts . . ."
>
>**DARLA**: "Wasn't Angelus, either."

Lindsey and Lilah get a report of Angel's little acts of mayhem and arson the next morning just before they are called into the conference room. After pointing out their assets and weaknesses, Hunt Acrey, head of the firm's investigating committee, delivers a bombshell. They are to be the co-Vice Presidents of Special Projects, at least for the immediate future.

Wesley drops by the hotel to find Angel still in war mode. He tells his former boss that he, Cordelia, and Gunn will continue the mission, even without Angel. "Someone has to fight the good fight," Wesley says. Angel makes no response, and Wesley leaves with a disappointed look back. Angel resumes his knife practice.

"Let them fight the good fight. Someone has to fight the war."

—*Angel*

RESOLUTION

While Angel Investigations may have lost its nominal leader, Wesley, Cordelia, and Gunn demonstrate their dedication to the cause of "helping the helpless." Out of Angel's shadow, Wesley starts to show his leadership qualities.

Angel seems to have lost his purpose, following the many blows dealt to him since Darla's reappearance, lost chance for redemption, and enthusiastic return to her vampiric nature.

Case closed.

DOSSIERS

CLIENT The **girl** Wesley, Cordelia, and Gunn rescue is one of their most physically damaged clients. The wound to her stomach bleeds impressively all the way up a brick warehouse wall.

SUSPECTS The **anonymous demon** who assaulted the girl meets its end with a chair leg through its head. **Lindsey** and **Lilah** emerge from Holland's wine cellar with shiny new job titles. **Darla** and **Drusilla**, who seemed on the verge of triumph, have retreated to heal their wounds.

CONTINUITY

Wesley reminds Virginia that the less than ideal circumstances of their first meeting in "Guise Will Be Guise" included her role as a sacrificial pawn for her father. Hunt Acrey reminds Lindsey of his theft and assistance of Angel during "Blind Date"—acts which did not endear him to Wolfram & Hart. Lilah also gets her chops busted for losing potential recruit Bethany in "Untouched." Angel seems to draw inspiration on how to deal with Darla and Dru from his success with fire in "The Shroud of Rahmon."

QUOTE OF THE WEEK

"Earth to retards—you have an obsession, you pretty much squeeze it into your schedule no matter what."

Cordelia debates Gunn's theory that if she'd had more visions,
Angel would have been too busy to bother with Darla.

THE DEVIL IS IN THE DETAILS

EXPENSES
The owner of the auto repair shop better carry insurance
Cigarettes and gasoline for Angel
Way too many drinks for the gang at Caritas

WEAPONRY
There's a lot of it: throwing knives, a sword, the ratchet stakes, daggers, and crossbows, broken furniture.

THE PLAN
Angel's plan is to move from the defensive to the offensive.

"I'm not on their level. But I can get there. And when I do I'll be right up close. I'll bring the fight to them."

—*Angel*

Wesley starts assuming leadership for his team.
> **WESLEY:** "We start with the basics. First, we examine the area for any telltale signs of a particular kind of—yeuggh."
> **GUNN:** "There's different kinds of 'yeuggh'?"

DEMONS, DEMONS, DEMONS

Evidently demons can overdo the testosterone, just as humans can, if the fighting demons at the warehouse are any evidence. Most of the demons in this episode are of the generic big and burly type, whether getting their ears ripped off by Drusilla or having their plans spoiled by Cordy, Wes, and Gunn.

"Vampires . . . sloth demons . . . you know what's really, really evil? Tequila."

—*Cordelia*

THE PEN IS MIGHTIER

FINAL CUT

Cordelia expounds at length to Phantom Dennis about the personal distress she is suffering following Angel's decision. After a bit of her monologue, Dennis opens *TV Guide*, then turns on the television.

"Oh, I'm sorry, Dennis. Is my pain boring you? You dead guys are so insensitive."

—*Cordelia*

POP CULTURE

❖ **"I heard about your girls—Godzilla, Darcilla, whatever."**

Merl refers to the behemoth Godzilla, who first appeared in the 1954 movie *Godzilla, King of the Monsters!*

OUR HEROES

Alexis Denisof gave us his perspective on the change in Angel:

"As Angel slipped into the dark side, that alarmed Wes and the others. They tried and failed to help him, culminating in Angel firing everyone. That was a turning point. A trust was broken, and in so doing, Wes and the others were on the receiving end of Angel's flaws. He was certainly no longer a hero, or a partner, or even a friend. Though on a deeper level, I think it gave Wesley the chance to evolve and find qualities in himself instead of relying on Angel. Seeing Angel as imperfect was a catalyst for Wesley to take responsibility."

—ALEXIS DENISOF

Andy Hallett critiques Charisma, Alexis, and J. singing:

"That was hilarious. Extremely fun. They had a lot of fun doing it. Which, to me, is the best part. Making it look like it's fun and having it look fun on TV, well, that's great because you're accomplishing your goal. But when you're actually having fun doing it, that's even better. And they sure had a heck of a lot of fun doing that. They were messing around on stage and acting drunk. Charisma does it so well. They all do it well, but I love Charisma when she plays drunk. She's hilarious. I thought that scene was hysterical." —ANDY HALLETT

And Charisma Carpenter has her own take on that.

"I had fun playing drunk. Which always scares me, because I know there's probably alcoholics going, 'That is so not believable.' Or college students going, 'She needs to come hang with us for a little while, learn how to do it the right way.' There's always that fear that you're going to have to smoke, and you're going to look like you don't know how to smoke. And I don't smoke. The day's going to come when I'm going to have to smoke, and it's just going to be awful. I don't smoke, I don't like smoke, I don't like cigarettes. And people that smoke know that you're faking it. There's nothing worse than trying to look cool with a cigarette and just blowing it. Royally." —CHARISMA CARPENTER

"What's been your most dangerous stunt this season?"

MICHAEL VENDRELL, STUNT COORDINATOR: "I would say when we had to burn the two girls. Great burn. That was a tough burn, because . . . we lit them on fire twice. Once inside, where they totally got engulfed by flames, and then they had to come back outside and get relit again. So, 'Okay, we'll light you on fire and have flames eight feet above your head, we'll put you out, and then we're going to light you up again.' It's hard to find [stuntpeople] who'll do [burns] well. There's an art to being burned. Being lit on fire is hard enough, but then to be able to be relaxed enough to perform."

JULIE BENZ: "My stunt double Lisa Hoyle did all the actual fire setting. We were only involved in the aftermath, with the fire hydrant and the water. Lisa is an amazing stunt double. She looks exactly like me. And she loves doing that kind of stuff, so I let her do as much of it as she wants."

"What was your mind-set at the end of that, when Darla looks and says, 'That wasn't Angel . . . who was that?'"

JULIE BENZ: "To be honest, we were being drowned by ice cold water coming down on top of us. I think we were just trying to get to the end of the scene. She sensed that he wasn't Angelus. When she looks and he's smoking the cigarette, and he flicks it and lights them on fire, that's the moment when she realizes that she doesn't know what she's dealing with. Who is this? This isn't predictable Angel, and this isn't Angelus. This is like in-between guy. It's a little fear of not knowing who this person is. She can handle Angel, and she can definitely handle Angelus, but this person all of a sudden, it's like when you wake up and you realize you don't really know the person next to you. It's that realization of, wow, what happened?"

"Darla tends to sort of get impatient sometimes with Drusilla. Do you think she underestimates her?"

JULIET LANDAU: "I do. If she had listened to me about the fire we would have been in much better shape. You know, I'm pretty right on. I say things in sort of a poetic, unusual way, but she's been around me long enough to read between the lines. Somehow her own feelings for Angel and her own stuff, she started to get annoyed and not pay attention."

'I really enjoyed writing Merl. Because he's was just skeevy. He was so nasty. Angel doesn't talk throughout the entire episode, he only speaks in voice-over, [so in] the interrogation scene, Merl has to do all the talking, and Angel doesn't say a word. So it was really interesting to be writing Merl and having him be yammering on and not have to get anything from Angel. It was kind of like a puzzle. How do I do this? How do I have Angel interrogate him without saying anything? **—MERE SMITH**

TRACKS

From the stage directions:

. . . CRASHING into the upbeat music of "Lady Marmalade." (Or as the rest of us know it, "Voulez-Vous Couchez Avec Moi.")

Patti Labelle first released "Lady Marmalade" in 1973 as part of the glam rock group, Labelle. In mid-2001 the song was covered by pop sensations Christina Aguilera, Pink, Mya, and Lil' Kim for the *Moulin Rouge!* soundtrack.

"Most of the time I am supporting what is there, just adding a little color to the mood or feel of the scene. At other times my goal is to add what *isn't* there. In 'Redefinition,' for example, Darla is recruiting demons, and Angel is hiding amongst them in the crowd. Her dialog is all about the upcoming battle. But the music becomes sadly romantic. I'm bringing out the fact that the most important thing in that scene is that Darla's love is right beside her but she doesn't know it. It worked really well and shows how the music can add an element that isn't necessarily there." **—ROBERT KRAL**

"BLOOD MONEY"

FROM THE FILES OF ANGEL INVESTIGATIONS
CASE №: 2ADH12

ACTION TAKEN

Gunn and Wesley face off over the fate of the world—as determined by the roll of the dice in their fiercely waged game of Risk. Gunn wins the roll and is celebrating when a sleepy Cordelia strongly suggests they leave her and her apartment in peace. They demur, not wanting to be away if she is hit by a vision. Sure enough, as though on cue . . . wham! She tells them she has seen a demon in the sewers under a girls' school, and they depart, posthaste. And *nobody* is mentioning Angel.

Angel, meanwhile, walks the streets, lost in his own dark thoughts to such an extent that he runs smack into a young woman and the large box of clothing she's carrying. Angel apologizes and helps her gather the contents of her box and purse. He learns her name is Anne and the clothes are for the kids at the East Hills Teen Center, which she runs. They part ways, and the entire encounter seems innocent enough. Then Angel returns to the hotel, and adds her license and the contents of her wallet, which he has just lifted, to the surveillance photos of her he has on his wall—including one of her in animated discussion with Lindsey McDonald.

Wesley and Gunn, deep in a sewer tunnel, discover the two-headed giant demon Cordy sent them after is capable of shooting out flames through any gas-passing orifice. They charge anyway.

Angel bursts in on stoolie demon Merl in his untidy, bean bag-strewn lair. Angel is after information on Anne's connection to Wolfram & Hart, which Merl provides, explaining that they fund her center. Angel adds insult to injury as he departs, again not paying Merl *and* dissing his decor.

The decor may not be the best at the East Hills Teen Center, but at least it has a roof, four sound walls, and is clean, which is more than can be said for the streets and alleys of L.A. Anne attends to administrative duties, and looks up to see Angel with a bag of clothing to donate.

Anne takes Angel on a tour of her little shelter from the world, explaining they owe their continued existence to the recent intervention of the good souls at Wolfram & Hart. She also fills him in on their new fund-raising event—a Wild West Charity Ball at which the moneyed hand over their donations to TV stars dressed like bandits. Angel listens darkly—the same way he does just about everything these days.

WRITTEN BY Shawn Ryan and Mere Smith
DIRECTED BY R. D. Price
GUEST STARS: Christian Kane (Lindsey McDonald), Stephanie Romanov (Lilah Morgan), Sam Anderson (Holland Manners), Julia Lee (Anne Steele), Gerry Becker (Nathan Reed), Mark Rolston (Boone)
CO-STARS: Matthew James (Merl), Jeffrey Patrick Dean (Dwight), Jason Padgett (Holden), Jennifer Roa (Serena), Deborah Carson (Liza)

Merl's open door policy continues, as big bad blue demon Boone invites himself in, Angel style. Boone seeks information—he wants to know whom Angel's been asking Merl to keep tabs on. He departs, once he's intimidated Merl into revealing Angel's interest in Wolfram & Hart.

Lilah Morgan crosses the W&H parking garage at a rapid clip and gets into her car. She's a bit uneasy, and makes a point of double-checking the rearview mirror, which remains empty. But Angel is in her backseat. He smoothly congratulates her on her promotion, his manner more menacing than if he'd vamped and gone for an artery. Lilah tries to make a break for it, but his hand on her shoulder is enough to keep her in place as he assures her that all the old rules are abandoned. She has "screwed with" him, in his words, and now it's his turn to screw with her.

> **LILAH:** "Angel, please . . ."
> **ANGEL:** (cheerfully) "No, no, no."
> Angel leans in over the back of the seat, cheek-to-cheek.
> **ANGEL:** "The begging comes later."

Later, Lilah relays her little encounter to Lindsey, who is supremely unimpressed. After all, she's alive. Their bickering is interrupted by Lindsey's assistant announcing his unscheduled ten A.M. appointment—Boone. Boone enters, brushing past Lindsey and commanding, "Shut the door." Lilah and Lindsey remain unimpressed until Boone states his business with the Special Projects Division. He has unsettled business with Angel.

Turns out some eighty years ago, Boone and Angel engaged in extended fisticuffs in Mexico over the favors of a lady. Boone's ethics demanded he end the fight at sunrise when Angel was at an obvious disadvantage, but he also claims he was fighting at less than his best, and is anxious for a rematch. He knows from Merl that Angel is interested in Wolfram & Hart, and plans to intervene.

> **BOONE:** "When Angel comes for you, he's gonna find me instead."
> **LINDSEY:** "I like it. I like it and I'll tell you why. Because of the finding you instead part."

Remembering the long-range plans of the Senior Partners, Lilah cautions Lindsey against hiring Boone, but he shrugs off her admonishments. His philosophy? "If he's not going to play by the old rules . . . why should we?"

Drunk with victory and possibly beer as well, Wesley and Gunn bond in Cordelia's apartment. Cordy announces that she's been scouting out possible locations for a new office. There is much merriment and toasting, as they face the future in unison. All looks well for the Wyndam-Pryce Agency. Er, no, the Chase Agency. Well, perhaps the Gunn Agency?

Merl makes a polite enough entrance through his own door—when he is rudely tossed into the wall by some of Lilah's hired muscle, much to the detriment of his take-out dinner. Lilah tells Merl she's interested in the work he's done for Angel, and she and her bullies soon leave with the same info Boone heard—Anne Steele has been targeted.

Said target is working late in her office when a noise draws her into the main area of the teen center. The items in the darkness seem innocuous enough—Ping-Pong table, foosball table, vending machines, big dark brooding guy. Angel offers Anne a package, with all the surveillance information, and confesses to staging the previous night's "accident" to get her wallet. Anne is on her way to call the police but agrees to listen when Angel hits her vulnerable spot. He wants to talk about the shelter.

He's in the midst of speculation about W&H's plans when another door opens and Lindsey appears. Lindsey offers Anne reassurance, warning her that Angel is dangerous. Angel is amused by Lindsey; his expression changes to confusion when Lindsey is followed by Boone.

Boone pauses just long enough to give Angel "fair warning," then mystical metal coils wrap around his hands to form supernatural brass knuckles—a minor enhancement to his bulk and fighting prowess. Angel swiftly gets his can kicked and seizes his first opportunity to escape. Boone is ready to pursue, but Lindsey stops him, maintaining the illusion that they are there for Anne's protection. Boone is dissuaded only by the promise of a rematch soon.

Lindsey gamely continues in "sincere" mode, despite being surprised by Anne's ready acceptance of the supernatural, and her assertion that Angel is offering proof of Wolfram & Hart's plans to rip off the charity. He and Lilah meet outside the office to wonder a) if Angel has proof; b) how he managed to get it; and c) what he will do with it. They break off their conversation with the paranoid certainty they have given him more ammunition now by discussing it in a public place.

A battered Angel returns to the teen center, where Anne seems unsurprised to see him, even after Lindsey's claims.

> **ANGEL:** "What did Lindsey say about me?"
> **ANNE:** "That you were a bad man."
> **ANGEL:** "A bad man?"
> **ANNE:** "Well, a psychotic vampire who cut off his hand, harassed his firm, and was borderline schizophrenic. I was giving you the short version."

Anne very briefly touches on her vampire-groupie past, revealing that she used to think vampires were "the coolest" until she met one. But the existence of supernatural evil holds far less interest for her than obtaining funds for the teen center to assist help society's victims—whatever the cost. Angel asks for her assistance in crashing the charity ball and showing a videocassette he's taped that will aid in W&H's downfall, but she turns him down.

The ball is a gala event, with large crowds of the "haves" showing up to be "robbed" of a token portion of their wealth for the "have nots." A large screen in the background shows an avuncular (and late) Holland Manners, oozing charity, appearing in a video extolling the merits of the East Hills Teen Center. Lindsey checks that the hooded "vampire detector" is on the alert for Angel. A dazzling Lilah, flush with the implementation of her plan, introduces Anne to one of her bosses, an attorney named Nathan Reed, who slavers over her. She then moves to the podium and into the spotlight, kicking off the festivities as four young television stars in Western garb move into action, collecting funds at "gunpoint."

Up above the main action, Angel casts off his disguise—the cloak of the firm's vampire detector. He heads for a staircase but is intercepted by Boone.

Lilah has just moved into the thanks phase, looking happily at the tables groaning under the weight of the contributions, when a noise from the balcony draws the crowd's attention to Angel and Boone. Since this is a Hollywood crowd, the spectacular fight, including crashing over the railing and Boone's otherworldly appearance, is assumed to be part of the entertainment.

Lindsey and Lilah, who definitely know better, hurry to the combatants' sides. Boone looms over a winded Angel, then assists him to his feet and inquires after his well-being. Realizing they've been

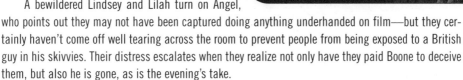

conned by Boone, who's really working with Angel, a frantic Lindsey and Lilah assume Angel has the incriminating videotape on him. Across the room, Anne inserts the tape into the player, as the two lawyers rush to stop her. They arrive too late to prevent the entire audience's viewing of the true nature of . . . what happens when video cameras fall into the wrong hands. Wesley and Cordelia are immortalized on film doing stupid human tricks.

A bewildered Lindsey and Lilah turn on Angel, who points out they may not have been captured doing anything underhanded on film—but they certainly haven't come off well tearing across the room to prevent people from being exposed to a British guy in his skivvies. Their distress escalates when they realize not only have they paid Boone to deceive them, but also he is gone, as is the evening's take.

RESOLUTION

Nathan Reed blasts the pair for their sequence of errors—losing the money, creating a scandal, and paying for Angel to be killed, against company policy. When Lindsey protests the last item, Nathan lays things out for him.

Angel is destined to play a key role in the Apocalypse, but they don't yet know for which side. Therefore the Senior Partners are invested in seeing he remains undead and as dark as possible, even if he kills staff in the process.

"As hard as it is to lose good attorneys . . . well, the truth is . . . you're both expendable. Angel isn't."
—*Nathan Reed*

Angel the unexpendable does some tasks in his office, then heads across the lobby to the stairs. He stops, and turns to face Boone in a final challenge, with the two million dollars from the ball at stake.

A beaten but triumphant Angel later delivers the loot to Anne at the shelter. There's some battle gore on it, but she is willing to look past that at the good it will do her kids.

Case closed.

DOSSIERS

CLIENT **Anne Steele**, the director of the East Hills Teen Center, receives assistance from Angel, theoretically for her benefit, but really for his own. The woman now known as Anne has been through many changes in the past few years, having been a vampire wannabe called Chantarelle (in the *Buffy* episode "Lie to Me"), a homeless waitress (in the *Buffy* episode "Anne"), and now as Anne, having assumed that name and a squalid apartment with Buffy's blessing. She has grown since then, becoming a pillar of strength for teenagers who find themselves in the plight with which she is all too familiar—living on the streets.

SUSPECTS **Lindsey** and **Lilah** get a little unexpected (and unauthorized) help from **Boone**, a large blue-skinned cowboyish demon. He says he crossed paths with Angel in Juarez in the "twenties," but since he plays up their feud to entrap Lilah and Lindsey, it's hard to tell how reliable this information is, especially if he means the 1920s, when Angel had a soul. A new "middle management" player from Wolfram & Hart, **Nathan Reed**, shows up to chastise Lindsey and Lilah.

CONTINUITY

Cordelia defends the "angel" on their business cards when Wesley disses it. She created the logo in "Lonely Hearts." Merl is understandably touchy around Angel after Angel's unorthodox—and non-paying—methods of extracting information in "Redefinition." Cordelia isn't the only reader of magazines where Virgina Bryce and Wesley's photos have appeared since "Guise Will Be Guise." Wesley on video is recognized by one of the Cowgirl actresses.

QUOTE OF THE WEEK

"Boo hoo. Let me wipe away the tears with my plastic hand."

Lindsey explains that he won't be brokenhearted if Boone actually kills Angel, in spite of instructions from the brass to let the vampire live.

THE DEVIL IS IN THE DETAILS

EXPENSES

Film and developing costs for Angel's surveillance of Anne

Most of the expenses are on Wolfram & Hart's side this time, including two-million-plus dollars inadvertently donated to Anne's center

WEAPONRY

Boone's metal coils seem to extend from beneath his skin, akin to X-man Wolverine's metal claws.

THE PLAN

Wesley and Gunn go for the straightforward attack on their sewer demon.

> **WESLEY:** "We'll take another look, and then we'll—"
> **GUNN:** "Die."
> **WESLEY:** "Wait, wait, wait, wait . . . till his back is turned . . . now!"

Angel requests Anne's help in exposing Wolfram & Hart.

"Help me. Get me into the party. I put this on, world sees a whole new side of Wolfram & Hart."

—Angel

Except, of course, Angel doesn't have the video at the party, and Boone helps him get in.

> **BOONE:** "You okay? I tried to cushion the fall."
> **ANGEL:** "I'll be fine."

LINDSEY: "What the hell are you talking about?"
ANGEL: (ignoring Lindsey, to Boone) "Thanks for getting me in."
(then, aside to Lindsey) "This place was like a fortress."

DEMONS, DEMONS, DEMONS

The **unseen and unnamed demon** Gunn and Wesley face is more than twenty feet tall, has two heads, and can breathe fire.

Boone is a very strong, blue-skinned demon who dresses and acts like a cowboy. He can extend metal coils around his hands like built-in brass knuckles. His current status is unknown.

AS SCENE IN L.A.

Anne's license shows she lives on Willoughby Avenue, which runs perpendicular to Santa Monica Boulevard and Melrose Avenue in West Hollywood.

"[The charity ball] was in Park Plaza, which is over on Park View Drive and Wilshire Boulevard. It's a very famous building in L.A. It's right over by MacArthur Park, and it's been used in a lot of different movies and television shows throughout Hollywood. It's also the building that we use for the exterior of our police precinct. So the establishing shot of the police precinct is the interior of where they did that auction."   —KEVIN FUNSTON, LOCATIONS MANAGER

THE PEN IS MIGHTIER

FINAL CUT

Cordelia's full "scene," shown on video at the charity ball:

"I gave you two children, Bill, and you leave me for a man?! No, don't speak, don't say anything—what is there to say? You said it all . . . WITH HIM!"

She looks at the coatrack with big teary eyes.

"I gave you two children, Bill . . . two children. I gave you two children."
(then, to herself)
"Then Bill the coatrack has his lines, blah blah blah, and then it's me again."
(acting)
"You DARE say that to me?! Oh!"

She slaps the coatrack, knocking a coat to the ground.

"Oops."

Cut to SNOW, then back on:

Cordy is cool and lovely now. She picks up a glass of MILK, looks at vid cam with the cool self assurance of a supermodel.

"Mmmm, milk."
(breezier)

"Mmmm, milk."
(sexier)
"Mmmm, milk."
(mysterious)
"Mmmm, milk."
(peppy)
"Mmmm, milk."
(surprised)
"Mmmm, milk."
(innocent child)
"Mmmm, milk."
A beat. Cordy puts the glass of milk down. "I don't get it. How am I not working?"

POP CULTURE

✳ Risk is a popular board game of world domination from Parker Bros. Gunn is on the verge of beating Wesley at the game in the opening scene of this episode.

✳ On the video, Cordelia appears to be rehearsing for a "Got milk?" commercial. Both David Boreanaz and Sarah Michelle Gellar have appeared in "Got milk?" ads.

✳ **"Price. Wesley Wyndam-Pryce."** Wesley imitates Sean Connery's James Bond delivery. Cordelia speculated that Wes would look "way 007 in a tux" in the Buffy episode aptly titled "The Prom."

OUR HEROES

Julia Lee (Anne) tells about the practical joke she played on David Boreanaz, the first day of shooting:

"We were getting ready to shoot the teaser where I am holding the box and I run into David on the sidewalk. One of the producers came up to me and said 'I have an idea, no, no, never mind.' And I said, 'Idea for what?' and he said, 'No, you're too peaches and cream.' 'Peaches and cream for what? What are you talking about?' 'Do you like jokes?' 'Yes, why?' 'Well, because I just have this idea, you know how you're going to do this scene and David is going to bump into

Toe Tags, Street Tags, Fake IDs:
TAKIN' NAMES

CORDY TAGS ANGEL: "Mr. I-Was-Alive-for-Two-Hundred-Years-and-Never-Developed-an-Investment Portfolio." ◆ "Pinocchio, this is a big deal." ◆ "The Dark Avenger" ◆ "The Dark Revenger" ◆ "Broody Boy" ◆ "Psycho-Wan-Kenobi" (as Angelus) ◆ "Mister I-Can't-Tail-the-Suspect-During-the-Day-Because-I'll-Burst-into-Flames-Private-Eye"

DOYLE TAGS ANGEL: "Mr. Obvious"

DOYLE TAGS CORDELIA: "Princess"

DOYLE'S STREET CREDS:
Cordelia: "Little Irish man" ◆ "Mister Too-Much-Cologne" ◆ "Mister Grouchy Pants"
The Lister Clan: "The Promised One"

WES'S TURN:
Cordelia: "Mister Don't-Talk-to-Me-Before-I've-Had-My-Flagon-of-Oat-Bran-in-the-Morning" ◆ "Ebenezer here"

DON'T LOOK TOO CLOSE AT THE PICTURE ID:
Angel: "I'm a veterinarian." ◆ "Herb Saunders, Baltimore" ◆ "Brian Jensen, Jensen International Holdings" ◆ Jay-Don of the Rat Pack
Cordy: "I work for a vaaaaa-entriloquist." "I'm Detective Andrews. This is Detective . . . Yeslew."

CORDY AND WESLEY AT THE OBSTETRICIAN'S: Mr. and Mrs. Pangborn

CORDY AND "DETECTIVE YESLEW" AT THE OCTAVIAN MATCHES: Mr. and Mrs. Winslow

CHECK OUT THAT SHIELD:
Kate Gets the Nicknames, too
"Cop lady" ◆ "Cagney and Lacy Kate"

ON STREET TAGS:
Gunn: "My name is Gunn. Angel sent me."
Cordy: "He's a great guy with a really fly street tag."

WESLEY AND CORDY:
Gunn Tags: "C-3PO and Stick Figure Barbie."

WHAT'S IN A ROSE?
"I like David. It's such a strong, masculine name. It just feels good in your mouth."
—CORDY ON DAVID NABBIT

"Name's Angelus."
—ANGEL, TO A BUNCH OF VAMPIRES

"I'm not an Angel. It's just a name."
—TO RYAN'S MOM

"You walked in here and called me by my first name. You never did that before. You wouldn't have had the nerve."
—HOLLAND TO LINDSEY

"You're Apt Pupil Boy!"
—CORDELIA TO PENN

"Angelus? I looked it up. It's all right there. 'The demon with the face of an angel.'"
—KATE TO ANGEL

"You don't have to be all Joe Stoic about his dying."—CORDY TO ANGEL, ABOUT DOYLE

Cordelia: "Paging Mr. Rationalization"
Gunn: "Paging Ms. About-to-Be-Thrown-out-of-a-Moving-Vehicle"

THE HOST WITH THE MOST:
"Mr. Tall, Dark, and Rockin'."◆ "Let's call him Angel, the vampire with *soul.*"

you, maybe after we rehearse and cameras are rolling and we're on our first take, maybe just don't say those lines.' 'Okay, what am I going to say?' 'Oh, I don't know, maybe you could make it up and just be you know be something completely different from your character. Something he just won't expect at all.'

"So they call action and nobody knows anything about this and I walk down the street and David bumps into me and I—it's completely out of character for Anne I think to swear, so she does, I got very upset with him and started screaming and yelling at him. And at first I think he thought he hurt me, that he injured me somehow and he backed up and sort of put his hands up in the air in a very defensive posture and his eyes were just big as saucers and he's staring at me. And then he starts getting the look in his eyes like 'Oh my God, she's completely insane!'

"And I just kept yelling and yelling and the extras are whispering and they're like, 'The actor and actress are yelling at each other and we don't know what's going on! Drama! Drama! Temperamental actors on the set!' And then finally I look at David and say, 'David, David, I'm kidding it's a joke, David are you okay?' And I gave him a hug and he did not know what was going on and I was really concerned that he was a) going to be upset with me forever or b) going to plot something out to get me back. Which I watched out for the whole rest of the day. Every day we were shooting, which he didn't. I'm still surprised that he didn't try to get me back. He just thought it was so funny."   —JULIA LEE

Do they or don't they? Writer Mere Smith on the Anne and Angel debate:

"That was actually a big debate. Does Anne recognize Angel? Does Angel recognize Anne? Because they had a brief exchange in 'Lie to Me,' second season. And so we had this, does he recognize her, does he not recognize her. And we were like, okay, it was three years ago, they said two sentences to each other, he's totally not gonna recognize her. So we went with that angle. I was sort of on the fence. I was like, you can't neglect the mythology. And Joss was like, 'Do you remember everybody you met three years ago, and shared three sentences with?' And I was like, 'Oh, fine, use logic.' I was kind of excited to get to take a *Buffy* character."   —MERE SMITH

Julia Lee offered her own interpretation of Anne's return.

JULIA LEE: "I think that although they didn't name the city that Buffy and I were in, my last episode on that show, I think everybody sort of knew that it was L.A. We have Sunnydale in California and L.A.'s a big city and it's close and it's the obvious choice, and now that Angel was in L.A. I know Joss was particularly interested in my character because he had told me that's really the theme of his show. That the underdog gets a chance to grow, to mature and to find a purpose in life, and he was really interested in pursuing that with my character. So when I met with him and David Greenwalt they discussed with me the idea of having Anne run her own shelter, and she decided to help out the kids that are now in the situation that she once was and give her a lot more purpose in her life. If you have a problem you go to Anne and she solves it, and that was exactly the opposite when I was Lily/Chantarelle. So we liked that idea a lot."

Trailers for Valentine, a thriller based on the Tom Savage novel, starring David Boreanaz, ran during the first airing of this episode.

"Did you have in your mind sort of a mental history of what she might have done or said or lived through between the time we last her, the time we saw her in Buffy and then when we see her on Angel? Did you imagine how she might have gotten to the point of running a shelter?"

JULIA LEE: "Well, yeah. I thought that after, I mean the last time we see Lily and she takes the name Anne, then Buffy gives her the apartment and the crappy doll, I think probably that is not the life that she wanted. It really didn't provide a whole lot of meaning for her and I think probably she struggled a bit more after that. I don't think things went straight up from there. I think probably she struggled and she probably hit the streets again and finally hit a point where she thought this is not livable. Nobody can live her life like this. So I imagine that she found some really nice souls at the shelter and had a really positive experience there and really felt a longing to be part of that. I think probably she took it up from there."

TRACKS

When Angel visits Anne at the shelter the first time, strains of "Legion" by Junkie XL from their *Big Sounds of the Drags* can be heard.

Someone at the charity benefit is hip to happening country music, and has selected "Let 'Er Rip" by the Dixie Chicks from *Wide Open Spaces* to contribute to the ambience.

"HAPPY ANNIVERSARY"

**FROM THE FILES OF ANGEL INVESTIGATIONS
CASE Nº: 2ADH13**

ACTION TAKEN

Alone in the hotel, the dark and brooding vampire broods darkly.

Cordelia and Wesley are busy removing trash from their new office, which only slightly improves its atmosphere. Banging her head on a dead hanging plant interrupts Cordelia's attempt at a pep talk; she insists there is no karmic significance to it. Gunn climbs over furniture to join them, and points out that the flyers he just distributed will do no good if a potential client tries to call. Their phone has no dial tone. Wesley attempts to resolve the problem.

> **WESLEY:** (O.S.) "Aha! Things are looking up! I think I found the right wire!"
>
> The lights go out. Total darkness.
>
> **GUNN:** "I'm so glad I met you guys. It's entertaining, really."

Angel, the vampire with insomnia, has fallen into a restless sleep that is broken by the sounds of the national anthem, beautifully performed by the Host. In the middle of the hotel lobby. He's come to wake Angel up—and because he just loves the lobby's acoustics. Angel is not pleased at being roused, especially by a "loud green demon" bearing news of the end of the world.

The Host recounts events from the previous evening at Caritas. It's a trying but uneventful evening for the laconic demon until a geeky grad student assumes the stage. Prepared for another mundane glimpse into someone's unremarkable future, the Host is stunned when he looks at Gene Rainy, the singer. Not only can he not see a future for Gene beyond 10 P.M. the following evening—he can't see a future for the world.

Angel, far from responding heroically to the news of the crisis, is skeptical. Which, in all fairness, may have to do with the less than spectacular results of following some of the Host's earlier directions, such as being sent to a phony T'ish Magev. Once persuaded, though, he sets out with the Host, hoping to find Gene at another karaoke spot.

Gene, the singing physics genius, is ensconced in his lab on a university campus. Lost in thought, he looks at his neatly assembled equipment and math equations with the expression of someone who has nearly grasped an important concept. Fellow students Mike and Val watch him through a window, Mike with envy and Val with compassion and a hint of something more. Val joins Gene. They're discussing his

STORY BY Joss Whedon & David Greenwalt
TELEPLAY BY David Greenwalt
DIRECTED BY Bill Norton
GUEST STARS: Andy Hallett (Host), Brigid Brannagh (Virginia Bryce), Matt Champagne (Gene Rainy), Darby Stanchfield (Denise), Mike Hagerty (Bartender)
CO-STARS: Victoria L. Kelleher (Val), Danny LaCava (Mike), Eric Lange (Lubber #1), Geremy Dingle (Student Clerk)

experiment, an attempt to freeze a moment of time out of the space-time continuum, when Gene's girlfriend Denise interrupts them. Denise and Gene greet each other warmly enough, but with no real intimacy, and confirm their one-year-anniversary dinner plans for the following evening. Denise and Val depart, leaving Gene alone with his project.

Angel and the Host arrive at their seventeenth karaoke bar of the evening. A guy on stage dourly sings "Greensleeves." Our heroes collapse onto bar stools and quiz the bartender about any regular clientele. With the aid of "For He's a Jolly Good Fellow," the Host determines that Gene is a regular—and the bartender steers them to the university campus.

In his campus lab, Gene makes a few adjustments to his equations, then enters instructions into his computer. His accelerators send out beams of energy to form a force field, into which a drop of mercury falls—and keeps falling. Discouraged, Gene shuts down the equipment and heads home, oblivious

to the Lubber demons who emerge from the shadows. The demons, better versed in theoretical physics than even Gene, move to the board and make a subtle change to the equation.

Discouragement and a funky smell fill the new office, despite Cordelia's attempt to revive their spirits by filling every available flat surface with candles. She, Gunn, and Wesley are sitting glumly behind their single desk when Virginia Bryce arrives in good spirits with a gift basket. Her treats are not enough to cheer the trio, but her news succeeds.

"My friend Patricia, her family's got this, like, big guy that's been harassing them, hanging around the house, getting scary and they'd be really grateful if someone got rid of him. . . ."   —*Virginia*

Gene returns to his lab and sees the new equations. Too excited by the potential for success to question the source of the changes, he resets the project. This time, the drop of mercury is suspended in the beam, where it is joined by three others. Frozen in time. Elated, he rushes out of the lab to share his good news.

Since it's daylight and Angel has to huddle under a blanket, the Host drives Angel to the university.

    ANGEL: "Where did you learn to drive?"

    HOST: "Just now, in your car. Not bad for a beginner, huh?"

    ANGEL: "You know what? You nearly got us killed four times."

At the university library, the Host hides in the stacks behind a Russian-English dictionary. They agree that, if spotted, he will claim to be a school mascot. Angel acquires several years' worth of yearbooks and such, looking for a photo that matches the Host's memory of Gene.

Val and Denise chat on a bench at the top of a staircase. Denise confides in Val that she plans to break off her relationship with Gene after dinner that night. She has enjoyed the relationship, but she doesn't find it fulfilling—"not the kind of love that lasts." Gene, unobserved, hears her reach this conclusion, and his heart is broken.

The Host finally finds a photo of Gene accepting a large grant for his work in physics. Armed with that knowledge, Angel asks the student clerk where he can find Gene's lab. The clerk is just pointing it out on a school map when something behind Angel startles the kid. A blasé Angel doesn't even turn around, assuming it's the Host. And that's when the Lubber demon clobbers him with his hunga munga.

In the lab, Gene is looking at a photo of him and Denise in happier times, when inspiration strikes.

The Lubber demon and Angel fight, violating all the laws of being quiet in the library. They scuffle, with a little interference from the Host, then the Lubber demon takes off. The Host fills Angel in on this brand of demon:

"Fanatical sect, awaiting a messiah who will usher in the end of all human life—a lot of your demons don't yak about it in mixed company but it's a pretty popular theology in the underworld." —*Host*

This adds further incentive to their urgent need to find and stop Gene. Their first stop is his lab, where they discover fellow student Mike, who is mystified that Gene's equipment is missing, and gives a brief description of its purpose: stopping time.

Mike doesn't seem to believe in the likelihood of the plan succeeding, but does speculate that if things were to go wrong, the whole universe would stop. Angel and the Host are sure Gene has his device with him, and get directions to his place. Gene, meanwhile, has been busily making preparations for his special anniversary evening—setting out candles, preparing dinner, and setting up the accelerators in the basement, with mirrors to reflect their force field around the bed.

Angel and the Host tear through the night streets of L.A. in the Angelmobile. Angel's relentless grumpiness continues, and the Host takes him to task for it. Goaded beyond his usual reserve, Angel finally lets loose verbally.

> ANGEL: "You wanna know what my problem is? I'm screwed. That's my problem. I can't win. I'm trying to atone for a hundred years of unthinkable evil and—newsflash—I never can. Never gonna be enough. Now I got Wolfram & Hart dogging me, it's too much. Two hundred highly intelligent law school graduates working full time driving me crazy why the hell is everyone so surprised that it's working? But no, it's 'Angel, why are you so cranky, Angel you should lighten up, you should smile, you should wear a nice plaid.'"

> HOST: "Oh, not this season, honey—"

Angel's rant of despair continues, and the Host points out that if they fail in their undertaking, Angel's in a pretty ugly emotional place to spend forever. And on cue, the opposition shows up, as a Lubber demon comes flying over the hood.

In the old money drawing room of Virginia's friends, the Bointons, Gunn pulls his battle-ax out of a dead Wainakay demon, trying to keep ichor off the expensive rug. Wesley is in his element, stalking about the room running down suspects in classic Agatha Christie tradition. Carrying a duck-headed cane, and tossing out uncomfortable bits of personal information about the family, he works his way through the facts to the conclusion that Helen Bointon summoned the demon. Cordelia helps restrain an escaping Helen, and the three are mighty pleased with their accomplishment.

Angel and the Host engage the attacking Lubber demons. Angel does his regular bit, employing his many varied fighting techniques. The Host uses an unexpected weapon against the two demons who charge him—singing a very long, very loud musical note.

Gene and Denise make small talk and don't consume much of his nice dinner. They move to the bedroom and soon are making love. Denise feels a sense of obligation to Gene, but Gene's purpose is more sinister—to reach a happy point in time that he can freeze forever.

Angel and the Host arrive at their destination, deducing the apparatus's location from the presence of the Lubber demons outside. Gene, reaching his critical moment of happiness, presses the button, and the force field surrounds the bed. Once it is engaged, a Lubber alters its settings, increasing the power. The force field starts to spread like a static big bang, threatening to stop time all over the world and not just for Gene and Denise. Angel heads for the basement, taking out Lubbers as he makes his way through the laundry and chairs to the device. As the field approaches, he disconnects something crucial, and the process reverses.

RESOLUTION

A stunned and resigned Gene hears those dreaded words from Denise. "Gene, we have to talk."

After she leaves, the Host and Angel visit Gene's apartment to explain the possible consequences of his actions. Gene is remorseful, and he and Angel bond over bad romantic experiences. Gene gets them some beer, and Angel speculates that Gunn, Wesley, and Cordelia are probably devastated by his behavior.

It'd be hard to tell though, as the new offices of Angel Investigations are filled with music and the sound of gainfully employed people partying with their friends and moving forward. A strange man stands in the doorway with a concerned look, and the three hurry to offer their services.

Case closed.

DOSSIERS

CLIENT For Angel: **the Host**, on behalf of the world. For the others: **Patricia Bointon**, Virginia Bryce's wealthy friend, whose family is being terrorized by a Wainakay demon. One brother has already been killed. The Bointons are the personification of "old money."

SUSPECTS For Angel: Inadvertent "criminal mastermind" **Gene Rainy**, who is being manipulated by the Lubber demons, who believe he is their Golden Child come to bring annihilation. For the others: **Patricia Bointon's family**, including her Curmudgeonly Father, Drunken Matriarch Mother, Dotty Aunt Helen, and Black Sheep Brother Kevin, one of whom secretly set the demon on his or her relatives.

CONTINUITY

Virginia, probably because of her father's mystical practices, knows a number of people (*wealthy* people) with problems of a demonic nature. Her contacts make a significant difference to the struggling agency. Part of the Host's difficult evening is training a new bartender, since Ramone—who was most skilled at crafting seabreezes—went MIA after betraying the Host and Angel in "Guise Will Be Guise." Angel's empathy for Gene's position—"the guy is a disaster at love and nearly destroyed the world: I can relate"—stems from his actions in Sunnydale in "Becoming."

QUOTE OF THE WEEK

HOST: "I don't know why you fired those three plucky kids. They were good company, not to mention: Cordelia, ooh, hot-o-rama. In the 'oh my sizzling loins' sense of the word if you know what I mean. And the British boy? He's going to be playing a huge—well . . ."

ANGEL: "Are you going to get to the end of the world or are you just going to chat until it does?"

The Host expresses his displeasure at Angel's firing of the team, and almost lets a spoiler slip about Wesley.

THE DEVIL IS IN THE DETAILS

EXPENSES

Cordelia, Wesley, and Gunn have a new office to pay rent on.

CORDELIA: "With all our money pooled together, we can stay here a long time."

WESLEY: "Twenty minutes?"

CORDELIA: "At least."

The Angelmobile may be due for a new transmission after the Host's first driving experience.

WEAPONRY

Lubber demons use hunga mungas.

"Angel is called upon a lot of times to use medieval weapons, when he's fighting with swords or axes or whatever else they can come up with. There was a weapon called a hunga munga that we had demons fighting with. A hunga munga is an actual weapon. It's not meant for hand-to-hand combat, it's actually a throwing weapon . . . from India. It was funny, because at the production meeting they said hunga munga, and everyone started laughing, and I said, 'No, no, no, it's a real weapon.' That's my job, I can fight with just about anything from a boomerang to a baseball bat."

—MICHAEL VENDRELL, STUNT COORDINATOR

THE PLAN

Angel and the Host base their plan on the only info they have on Gene.

> **ANGEL:** "Maybe he's just a guy who likes karaoke . . . maybe he doesn't know anything about you."
>
> **HOST:** "That'd make more sense. So what we should do is start with the other local karaoke bars, see if we can get a lead on him—if you're not too busy getting lawyers killed and setting girls on fire."

DEMONS, DEMONS, DEMONS

Lubber demons are a plain-dressing end-of-the-world sect with an astonishing grasp of physics.

A **Wainakay demon** goes after the Bointons, but only because a family member has hired it to.

AS SCENE IN L.A.

Locations manager Kevin Funston talks about the university setting:

"That was a very tough location. We ended up going down to Long Beach and using the Long Beach Public Library, which has a university setting. And we were fortunate enough to talk them into letting us shoot in their library during operation hours. So we started outside, on the grounds. It's a big plaza that surrounds all the city buildings there, and the city library, and they used that as the campus because it does look a lot like a college campus. And then they moved inside and shot in the library at night. Well, actually starting at around three o'clock. Long Beach tends to be a little easier to film in, because they're not overfilmed. Some of the locations in Los Angeles get so much filming that they get a little jaded, or they get kind of worn out. [Since] there is a thirty-mile radius that the unions and studios have set up to keep filming in, you try to always look for new locations, people that haven't had that kind of experience, that are really positive toward it, and it makes your job a lot easier."
—KEVIN FUNSTON

This episode, with its academic setting and complex physics, mentions several scientific stalwarts:

ALBERT NOBEL, the man responsible for inventing dynamite, established the Nobel Prize, which has recognized notable accomplishments in the fields of physics, chemistry, medicine, literature, peace, and economics through since 1901.

SIR ISAAC NEWTON, who made many important contributions to the field of math and physics in the 1600s, also practiced alchemy.

ALBERT EINSTEIN is probably the greatest scientific mind of the twentieth century. He's responsible for the special and general theories of relativity.

An event horizon is the boundary of a black hole. The Einstein-Podolsky-Tosen correlation is a paradox demonstrating quantum mechanics as an incomplete theory for describing our physical universe.

STEPHEN HAWKING is known for his work deciphering the laws of physics that govern the universe. His book *A Brief History of Time* was an international bestseller in 1992.

There. Don't you feel smarter now?

THE PEN IS MIGHTIER

FINAL CUT

Angel's original depressing love metaphor was more extended. "Well, you know, love . . . it's a fire. It burns you. Alive. Down to the bone. Then it turns the bone to ash and the cold wind just—"

POP CULTURE

❖ **"This garden hue and the horns *have* kept me out of some key public performances—just once I'd love to ring in a Lakers game with our national anthem."** The Lakers are Los Angeles's National Basketall Association team. The Host laments the limitations of being a demon.

OUR HEROES

Angel and the Host are this season's dynamic duo.

"Andy's a very honest person, so it makes it really enjoyable. His character represents a pretty interesting bond between the two of them. I enjoy it." —DAVID BOREANAZ

Alexis Denisof talks about the drawing room scene:

"I've always liked [the mystery] genre. It's so satisfying. You have this puzzle, and it's solved, and I think that was the key to that scene. It was one scene standing on its own. Very compressed. But that was the nature of it. So we create a mystery and a puzzle at the beginning of the scene, and then he solves it triumphantly by the end. And it was great fun. For me it was Poirot and Sherlock Holmes and Wimsey and a little bit of Peter Sellers too. I never like to leave Clouseau out of it." —ALEXIS DENISOF

Andy Hallett had an epiphany while filming "Happy Anniversary":

"And then, it wasn't until that episode, episode thirteen, that Angel and I were driving around in his car, it was toward the end of the night, and I'll never forget it, it was a Friday night, it was about one o'clock in the morning, and that's when this whole thing hit me. Because I had done twelve previous episodes, and I had seen myself on TV and everything, and it just didn't hit me until that night when we were in the car, driving around the big downtown L.A., and people were on the streets yelling at us, coming out of bars, and stuff, and the wind was blowing and the top was down and we were being towed around on a big truck. And that's when it hit me. I was like, wow, this is really cool. This is really cool. I'm really digging this. What a great experience. And it wasn't until that moment that I realized, you know, this is like what I've been waiting for." —ANDY HALLETT

"The Lubber demons came in the writing. They actually wrote that in the script, that they wanted them to look like—well, my interpretation was Mennonites [the script describes them as "sad-eyed fundamentalists"]. So what I did was I offered them three different looks from my Mennonite collection, which was band-collar shirts, in like an off-gray, all very plain, with waistcoats, cutaway black pants and boots. Very simple. And suspenders. And I also did like a plain off-white cotton shirt with a little

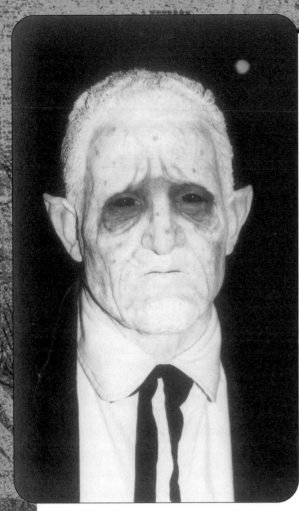

string bow tie, and that's the look they went with. And they wanted them to look like over-the-top fundamentalists. So we tried to do these ancient fundamentalists from the eighteen-hundreds who were coming into this world."

—CHIC GENNARELLI, COSTUME DESIGNER

SIX DEGREES OF . . .

Mike Hagerty, who played the bartender with literary ambitions and a great voice (according to the Host), has crossed paths with *Buffy* costars Seth Green in *Austin Powers 2: The Spy Who Shagged Me* and Michelle Trachtenberg in *Inspector Gadget*.

Conniving Aunt Helen was played by Norma Michaels, who also appeared in Season Three *Buffy* in "Doppelgangland."

TRACKS

Music coordinator John King had not yet defined what music would be used in the office party scene when it was shot. The cast danced to a selection from a crewmember's portable stereo, then he ended up matching their rhythm to "Hey Baby" from Mocean Worker's *Mixed Emotional Features*, rather than the reverse.

Don and Phil Everly made "Bye Bye Love" a hit in 1958. They were the *Real Everly Brothers*, as their album title declared.

"All by Myself" has been an anthem for the lonely for decades. The song was written by Eric Carmen and recorded on his self-titled album.

"Greensleeves," is a European ballad dating back to at least the mid-sixteenth century, making it even older than Angel.

The origins of "For He's a Jolly Good Fellow" are lost in history. The current version came from the United Kingdom in the early nineteenth century.

"THE THIN DEAD LINE"

FROM THE FILES OF ANGEL INVESTIGATIONS
CASE № 2ADH14

ACTION TAKEN

Angel walks through the dark, deserted hotel lobby, looking at the reception area where his team used to gather. In a fit of emotion, he shoves some random items off the top of the desk.

Things are quiet at the Agency With No Name as well. So quiet, Wesley is almost willing to invite trouble through the door. Sure enough, it arrives in the form of young Stephanie Sharp, escorted by her mother Francine. These are more friends of Virginia who are seeking experts in strange phenomena. Cordelia is full of blasé encouragement in the face of another potential big check, when an eye in the back of the girl's head blinks at her. Wesley and Gunn take a look as well, and they agree to handle the case.

WRITTEN BY Jim Kouf & Shawn Ryan
DIRECTED BY Scott McGinnis
GUEST STARS: Elisabeth Rohm (Kate Lockley), Julia Lee (Anne Steele), Mushond Lee (Jackson), Jarrod Crawford (Rondell)
CO-STARS: Cory C. Hardrict (Ray), Kyle Davis (Kenny), Camille Mana (Les), Darin Cooper (Police Officer), Brenda Price (Callie), Darris Love (George).

Outside on the streets, two young people flee an unseen enemy. They make their way to the East Hills Teen Center, where their desperation is enough to convince Anne to let them in, even though it's past curfew. As she shuts the door, there is movement in the shadows, and an expressionless police officer watches his prey take refuge.

Merl's lair is even more disheveled than usual as he moves around gathering up items and packing them. Angel's sudden appearance startles him, and Merl is impatient to divest himself of his last bit of information and get out of town. He tells Angel he's heard that Wolfram & Hart plans a significant meeting the following night at one of L.A.'s top restaurants. Merl points out that at least Wesley used to pay for his tips, and reminds Angel of all he has cut himself off from.

Anne tracks down Kenny and Les in the daylight to get a more complete explanation of their urgent arrival. At first Kenny tries to put her off, but then they tell her they were on the run from a cop who struck Kenny and injured Les's arm, though they were innocent of any wrongdoing. A concerned Anne decides to seek help.

Anne tracks Gunn down at the new office and brings him up to date. He agrees to investigate, and his vampire-hunting past comes up. He lets Anne know Cordy and Wes are aware of L.A.'s demons and such, and mentions the case they are working on. Cordelia suggests it's not that an unusual assignment for Angel Investigations, and Anne makes the connection.

> **ANNE:** "He tried to help me out a few weeks ago."

CORDELIA: (hopeful) "He did?"

WESLEY: "Really?"

ANNE: "But it turned out it was just a scam to screw this law firm."

CORDELIA: (mock cheerful) "Well. He hasn't changed a bit."

And it's back to the books, as Gunn and Anne leave.

Angel, perhaps goaded by the comments of the Host and Merl, is eavesdropping outside the office, and follows Gunn and Anne back to the teen center.

Gunn listens to the teens' tales of being mistreated by the police, then attempts to verify their stories. They are adamant that the attacks were unprovoked.

Outside, Angel has evidently heard enough and is moving away from the shelter when he is stopped by a man's authoritative voice. A police officer demands he present himself for search and arrest, speaking right over Angel's questions and objections. When Angel doesn't respond quickly enough, the officer hits him with his baton. Angel warns him off, then punches him, a blow that would land most men in the hospital. The officer is simply knocked down. The departing Angel is called back by the unanticipated sound of the officer rising to his feet, continuing his spiel as though nothing happened. The officer attacks with his club again, and Angel's defense includes a swift kick to the head.

Which detaches and flies away from the body, still speaking, as head and body decay into a rancid, moldering corpse.

Gunn has called for backup—not Wes and Cordy, but friends from the neighborhood, Rondell and George. Gunn is affronted when the two are already in the loop on the police problem, but they point out his preoccupation with being a "demon detective" has kept him from participating fully in the neighborhood watch. Even though things are tense, the three set out with a video camera to investigate, certain that their very appearance will draw out the cops.

Speaking of cops, Kate Lockley is hard at work at her desk, protecting and serving, when Angel approaches. They have a quick, tense exchange, in which Kate makes it clear she is not happy with Angel's recent actions with regard to Darla and Drusilla.

KATE: "Sounds like you enjoyed it. But then again, the whole murder and mayhem thing's always been right up your alley."

ANGEL: "If that's how you feel, then this probably isn't the best time to tell you I just killed a cop."

KATE: "I wouldn't make a joke about that in this building. No matter how immortal you think you are."

ANGEL: "Of course, this is the kind of cop that keeps talking even after he's been decapitated. I bet they don't teach you that in the academy."

He offers her the cop's badge, and she verifies that it's an official LAPD badge, belonging to a member of the Twenty-third Precinct who was fatally shot several months before.

In their offices, Cordelia and Wesley continue their research into the source of the extra eye on the Sharp daughter's head. Gunn calls in to share his plan, and they quickly conclude he would be better off with their help.

Kate takes Angel to the grave of slain officer Peter Harkes, where Angel points out that although the grave is six months old, someone has been moving the dirt far more recently. His theory, given the evidence: zombies. They check another officer's grave, and then a terrible fear strikes Kate. She tears across the boneyard to her father's grave, where Angel reassures her he rests undisturbed.

Anne and her helpers are settling in for the night when Cordelia and Wesley arrive at the shelter in search of Gunn. They quickly agree to divide forces, Wesley departing in search of Gunn, Rondell, and George, and Cordelia remaining behind to help with the shelter.

Anne is ready to shut the door for the evening when a thug named Jackson insinuates his way in over her protestations. Cordelia steps in to back Anne up, and is brushed aside for her trouble. Jackson, the epitome of bad news, heads into the rec room where he smoothly threatens a kid named Ray.

They say there's never a cop around when you need one. On the streets, Gunn, Rondell, and George are finding that to be true, having a surprisingly difficult time finding any police—in fact, the streets seem deserted. Their route has taken them to the edge of reputed gang territory, and they are just venturing in when the sound of a billy club tapping against something stops them. Rondell arranges his jacket so the video camera has a clear shot of events, as the cop asks Gunn to step to the wall. Gunn tries to determine what the cop's cause for stopping them is, but the cop is becoming more agitated as Gunn fails to comply with his instructions. Just as the cop raises his baton, Wesley rounds the corner, politely urging the officer to reconsider. The cop responds by drawing his sidearm and shooting Wes in the abdomen.

Gunn lunges for the cop, toppling him and knocking his gun to the ground. The cop regains his feet and starts to remove a second weapon from his ankle holster. He takes aim at Gunn, and more shots ring out—from his fumbled weapon, now in George's hands. Clearly George was acting in self-defense, but he is still shaken by the impact of his killing a cop. His shock quickly changes to terror as the dead cop starts to rise to his feet again, and the four quickly retreat from the field, a wounded Wesley relying on the others. As they disappear around a corner, the cop radios in for backup.

Gunn and the others duck into a nearby alley through a hole in the chain-link fence. While Gunn and Rondell minister to Wesley, George goes to call an ambulance.

Kate, Angel at her side, drops by the Twenty-third Precinct and uses her badge to try to get some answers about the current situation. The desk sergeant isn't forthcoming with answers, even to a fellow officer, but does remark on the recent significant decrease in crime, giving credit to the squad's captain.

Wesley does not look like a man with a high chance of survival, but Gunn reassures him as the ambulance arrives and they bundle him in. George and Rondell leave for the shelter on foot, but Gunn elects to ride to the hospital with Wesley and the paramedics. Police cars block their route, and when the driver gets out of the ambulance to negotiate a way around, the response is a hail of bullets. Gunn, in desperation, grabs control of the wheel, leaving the EMT to care for Wesley, and they evade the police long enough to reach the East Hills Teen Center. Over the protests of the paramedic, Gunn insists the shelter offers Wes's best chance at life. Unfortunately for Gunn, his plan actually has made the police officers' job easier, as all of their targets are now in one location.

Cordelia pushes past her shock at Wesley's injuries and immediately works to assist the paramedic in caring for him. Gunn suggests to Anne that she take protective measures, and she rallies the kids. Jackson doesn't assist in the preparations, preferring to rely on the gun in his waistband to solve confrontations, much to Gunn's distaste. Wesley's condition is rapidly worsening, and the paramedic is convinced he needs to be moved to a hospital, pronto. Cordelia agrees, and they assist Wes to the door—but when Cordy opens it, she sees a wall of blue uniforms and quickly backtracks.

Angel invites himself into the captain's office in the Twenty-third Precinct.

> **CAPTAIN:** "Who are you?"
>
> **ANGEL:** "Angel."
>
> **CAPTAIN:** "Well, Angel, if you need something, I'm sure someone downstairs can help you."
>
> **ANGEL:** "Actually, I need to talk to you."
>
> **CAPTAIN:** "About what?"
>
> **ANGEL:** "About some of your . . . more dead cops."

In response, the captain shoots Angel three times. Angel takes the slugs, vamps out, and throws the captain across the room. Finally, he pursues him into an inner sanctum, with a wall of photos of deceased cops who have returned to active duty, candles burning everywhere, and a kind of voodoo shrine to the dead cops. Angel roams the room in search of the linchpin of the reanimation.

Everyone but Wesley is engaged in defending the East Hills Teen Center from attack by the zombie cops, who come in from every angle like an all-cop revival of *Night of the Living Dead*. Jackson, looking out only for himself, tries to slip out an exit and is nearly brained before Gunn manages to save him. Cordy and Anne beat back one invasion, but things are looking grim as the sheer number (and indestructibility) of the cops allow them to gain the upper hand.

Angel checks out the various mystical trappings of the captain's setup, then raises an idol of a zombie god above his head before smashing it to bits. At the teen center, released from the magic, the zombie cops become corpses again. Everyone is frozen in a moment of relief before rushing to attend to Wesley. Angel reports back to Kate, who points out the irony that the zombie forces, as bad as they were, provided a safer neighborhood than the one Angel just restored. Angel is still at her desk when a gunshot report comes in from the hospital—with Wesley's name on it.

RESOLUTION

Wesley awakens postop to find Gunn sitting at his bedside, and they do a low-key version of their bonding hand slap. Angel watches their interaction through the hospital window, and turns away. Cordelia is standing there, but from the look on her face, she might as well be a million miles away. She coldly informs Angel he is neither needed nor wanted, and joins Gunn at Wesley's bedside without a backward glance, leaving Angel to exit the hospital, very much alone.

Case closed.

DOSSIERS

CLIENT The **kids on the street**, who are victimized by the zombie cops, are the clients in this case. Additionally, the **Sharp family** are clients of the unnamed agency, but that case is pending.

SUSPECTS The **captain of the Twenty-third Precinct** has determined his men will protect and serve to fit his ideals, even from beyond the grave.

CONTINUITY

Angel passed along Cordelia's designer shirt (which she wore in "Reunion") and other items when he met Anne in "Blood Money." Giving away her clothes was a major tactical error on his part. Kate has a difficult time bringing herself to trust Angel's judgment, given the bloody havoc Darla and Drusilla wreaked in "Reunion" after she trusted him to catch them. In Gunn's frequent absence, George and Rondell are emerging as the leaders of his old crew.

QUOTE OF THE WEEK

"Nothing says 'Aha, I'm on to you!' like being on the receiving end of a vicious police beating."

Cordelia has some doubts about Gunn's plan to catch a zombie cop.

THE DEVIL IS IN THE DETAILS

EXPENSES

Wesley's hospital bill
Broken video camera
Extensive damage to teen center

WEAPONRY

Chair leg, baseball bat, hammer, furniture, handguns

THE PLAN

GUNN: "All right, look, the plan's simple. I want you to roll the camcorder, wait for the cops to hassle us."

ANNE: "How do you know they will?"

GUNN: "'Cause we'll be the ones walking while black."

CORDELIA: "In order to find out if the police have been brutalizing and killing people in Anne's neighborhood, he's going to videotape the cops trying to brutalize and kill him."

WESLEY: "That can't be his plan . . . can it? I mean . . . that's really a . . . dumb plan."

CORDELIA: "Hey, Gunn graduated with a major in 'Dumb Planning' from Angel University. He sat at the feet of the master and learned well how to plan dumbly."

DEMONS, DEMONS, DEMONS

Something has attacked Miss Sharp and left her with a third eye in the back of her head, but Wesley and Cordelia's research into the problem is interrupted by trying to help Gunn.

Bullets don't seem to affect **zombies**, but decapitation is an effective method of re-corpsing them, as is destroying the source of their reanimation.

AS SCENE IN L.A.

Diaghilev, where Wolfram & Hart have a meeting planned, according to Merl, is one of Los Angeles's best restaurants. Located in a hotel in West Hollywood, it serves Franco-Russian fare, as evidenced by its name, which it shares with a Russian ballet celebrity.

THE PEN IS MIGHTIER

FINAL CUT

A later draft opened with Kenny and Les on the run from the cop, with none of the preceding scenes.

Angel originally took longer to discover the power source.

"How are you controlling them? Is it the entrails? I don't think so. Could you be controlling them with a sacred Manari candle? Nah. Red herring. I know, maybe it's the idol of Granath, the zombie god?"

—Angel

POP CULTURE

❖ The episode's title is taken from the phrase the thin blue line, referring to uniformed police officers protecting their city.

❖ **"Maybe we could buy one of those star maps, find out where Steven Seagal lives."** Before the Sharps enter the office, Wesley, bored, is eager for a fight of any kind. Steven Seagal was a martial arts coordinator on films before moving into starring roles in his own violent action flicks in the late 1980s.

❖ RONDELL: **"You've been moving on up, dog. Playing demon detective with your new family."** GEORGE: **"Deluxe apartment in the sky."** Rondell and George appear to be fans of TV's *The Jeffersons.* The show was a 1975 spin-off from *All in the Family,* and they do a riff on its theme song to goad Gunn.

❖ **"All right, look, all I'm saying is, you gotta let me get set up so they don't see me with this [the camcorder]. Cops see me with this and there's no way we're gonna Rodney King them."**

Rondell discusses the bad-cop entrapment scheme with Gunn and George in terms easily understood by members of L.A.'s African-American community. Rodney King was the center of a storm of national civil rights controversy in 1991. An amateur cameraman videotaped him being arrested and beaten by four police officers. Los Angeles erupted in riots when the officers were later exonerated.

OUR HEROES

Alexis Denisof discussed Wesley's being shot:

"It can be very challenging. I was really glad that they put Wesley in that situation. I think we found a sort of quiet, truthful way of playing that arc, of being shot. To me what was important—and this is something that's important all through the series—is Angel's the character who isn't human. He has supersensitive hearing, special eyesight, elevated senses, and special physical abilities. He's a quasi-superhero with super problems because of his past. But because of who he is I think it's important for the humans around him to be just that, to be very human. I took that episode as an important balancing for all the times that a vampire is staked and he gets up, or a demon is stabbed and doesn't notice, or a wound heals before your eyes. Again, it's clever of Joss and David to keep that in perspective, so that as a show, we're not always leaping tall buildings and flying off into the sunset. There are consequences for acts of violence. And for poor Wesley, we were in the middle of consequence. And it brought the characters very close. I think it bonded Wesley and Gunn."

—ALEXIS DENISOF

"We did [the shooting scene] a whole bunch of times. Alexis gives it to you as an actor on every take. . . . So you don't have to fake it. I never really thought of it as tedious, because he always gave it to me. And that's the same for everybody. All the actors I work with are like that.

"There was a scene where Wesley was put in the ambulance, and I stop the door and I say, 'I'm with him.' I wanted the camera to be really close to me at that point, because I felt like that was a turning point, where the bond was completely . . . but I think it still came across. But that's when I knew that I was really into this, and how he comes across. Because it was important to me at that moment. So now, to me, he considers Angel Investigations another part of his family. And this family is fighting on a higher level than his previous family was. We were all about self-protection. I'm still the general, so I can delegate orders, but I'm over here now trying to fight a bigger battle that I didn't realize I could be a part of."

—J. AUGUST RICHARDS

Julia Lee describes a favorite moment from the episode:

"They had the one scene where I got to wear knee pads and ankle pads because . . . I'm walking by the window and [a stuntman] reaches in and grabs my ankle. I drop to the ground and then Charisma comes over to help. We had to do it a few times and the director is just like, 'You know he's a stunt guy, don't be afraid to kick him.' And I kept thinking 'I don't want to kick his hand with my foot, I'm wearing tennis shoes,' and the director says 'Just don't even worry about it, just kick him as hard as you can.' And the guy says 'That's fine, that's what I get paid for, just do it.' I fell down and I just kicked with everything in me and of course it wasn't until afterward that he came up and went 'Wow, You weren't kidding on that, that was real.'"

—JULIA LEE

Property master Courtney Jackson sometimes invests lots of energy into what ends up being brief moments of glory.

"The episode with the zombie cops, remember the statue that [the police captain] got hit over the head with? We spent a lot of money and a lot of time, drawing this very cool idol, getting it approved, having it carved, having it molded, and having them poured so that we had a rubber one, and we had a real one, and then we had breakaway ones. And in the flash of an eye, it was gone. And you just sort of suck it up and go on. Because you're always thinking it could be the next time that you do get that big close-up, and your parents get to watch it and be all proud of you."

—COURTNEY JACKSON

SIX DEGREES OF . . .

Darris Love appeared in the dorm with freshman Buffy and her friends in "Fear, Itself" in Season Four of *Buffy*.

TRACKS

The youths at the East Hills Teen Center may not have much, but they do have their music. Background music includes "Ms. Jackson" by Outkast, "Who's Got My Back" by Seldom Seen, and "On a Mission" by Sucker Pump.

"REPRISE"

FROM THE FILES OF ANGEL INVESTIGATIONS
CASE №: 2ADH15

ACTION TAKEN

Angel makes his way through a dark tenement building, following faint sounds. He passes the detritus of discarded lives, through darker into darkest, where he pulls the cord of a hanging lightbulb to reveal a room full of . . . goats! He passes through the goats to the next room, where two worshippers are readying their sacrifice per the directions on the do-it-yourself sacrifice kit. They seem to have misplaced their ceremonial dagger, which is actually in the hands of the Dark Avenger. Angel goes into vamp mode and terrorizes them into revealing that they don't know what demon they are making the sacrifices to, but they do know the timetable—midnight is the deadline.

At Angel Investigations (sans Angel, of course), a proud trio presents the de-oculated back of young Stephanie Sharp's head to her mother. Mrs. Sharp departs, spawn in tow, declining to pay them and declaring they must be shams. Cordelia is affronted, but the wheelchair-bound Wesley is pragmatic.

WRITTEN BY Tim Minear
DIRECTED BY James Whitmore, Jr.
GUEST STARS: Elisabeth Rohm (Kate Lockley), Christian Kane (Lindsey McDonald), Andy Hallett (Host), Stephanie Romanov (Lilah Morgan), Sam Anderson (Holland Manners), Brigid Brannagh (Virginia Bryce), Gerry Becker (Nathan Reed), Thomas Kopache (Denver), Julie Benz (Darla)
CO-STARS: David Fury (First Worshipper), Chris Horan (Second Worshipper), Jolene Hjerleid (Singing Lawyer #1), Wayne Mitchell (Singing Lawyer #2), Marie Chambers (Mother)

> WESLEY: "Clearly it's easier for the Sharps to cast us as con artists, rather than accept the grim reality that Skilosh spawn nearly hatched full-grown out of their child's skull."
>
> GUNN: "Gee—wonder why."

Their business evidently concluded for the day, Gunn departs for his regular haunts, leaving a discouraged Cordelia and Wesley in his wake.

At Wolfram & Hart, lawyers are scurrying all over in preparation for the firm's big seventy-five-year review. Lilah is gung ho to make any possible improvements to her record, but Lindsey is tired of the game and willing to let his record stand. Lilah points out that said record includes the dangerous duo of Darla and Drusilla, whereabouts currently unknown. Lindsey counters with the observation that they are presumably still resting and healing from Angel's fiery attack, wherever they may be.

Angel, the vampiric blowtorch, is trying to persuade Detective Kate Lockley to initiate police action against the worshippers who are raising power for an unknown cause. Her reception isn't just icy, it's glacial, and when he presses the point, she tells him she is riding her desk until she meets with a review board. Even Kate herself is beginning to question some of her decisions. She's in trouble for letting Angel reach the captain of the Twenty-third Precinct, and feeling pangs of guilt over releasing him

317

after arresting him at Wolfram & Hart, only to find a wine cellar full of dead lawyers who'd been locked in with their executioners.

Darla—not missing after all—lounges on Lindsey's couch under a shawl, looking like she could use a roomful of lawyers for medicinal reasons. She has to settle for a bottle of human blood Lindsey removes from a bag. When Lindsey heads for the shower to remove the stench of his work, a surprisingly nimble Darla carries her drink over to his briefcase, and helps herself to the brief on the seventy-five-year review.

Caritas is having a busy night when Angel barges up to the Host, demanding information with his now usual charm. The Host points out that the stage is full for the evening, mostly with lawyers. His ethics won't allow him to directly share info from reading their auras with Angel, but he can tell him two bits he has overheard—the seventy-five-year review is on Friday, and it involves a Senior Partner.

Okay, that's news, but Angel still wants more, and he persists. He insists that getting to the Senior Partners is his destiny, to which the Host's reply is, "I haven't actually featured a destiny with you in it, lately. It's all a little murky." Finally acknowledging he has met with unstoppable determination, though, he shares two more tidbits—something called the Band of Blacknil is of import, and it has something to do with the "Home Office"—whatever that is.

Angel takes these new terms back to the office to research, but is unable to make any headway. Probably because he only has about four tomes left in the bookshelf, the rest having migrated to Angel Investigations' new home.

Angel bursts into the new office and makes a beeline for the bookshelf, where a furious Cordelia plants herself between him and his target. He removes one book, and she yanks it out of his hands, attempting to hand him a telephone directory instead. They have a test of wills for a moment, broken by Wesley's rising from his chair and telling Cordy to relent. Angel departs, book in hand. Cordelia rants.

> **CORDELIA:** "What a jerk."
> **WESLEY:** "Cordelia . . . ?"
> **CORDELIA:** "I mean, if it were anyone else, I'd just say—get laid, already!"
> **WESLEY:** "Cordelia—?"
> **CORDELIA:** "But no, not him. One decent boff and he switches back to evil psycho
>   vamp. Which, in a way, would be better for everyone—better for him, 'cause then
>   he'd get some, and better for us 'cause then we could stake him afterwards."
> **WESLEY:** "Cordelia! Ambulance."

And Wes, bleeding again from his abdominal wound, makes a return trip to the emergency room.

Kate Lockley's life is coming to an end, or at least it feels that way. Called before a review board to justify her behavior, she feels her badge slipping away. The board grills her about the loss of her father, her increasingly distant behavior, and her preoccupation with the unorthodox cases. Like someone caught in a slow-motion car wreck, she is unable to stop the sequence of events that ends with her gun and her badge on the desk.

Angel may be the same eternally youthful fellow he was in 1952, and Lucy Ricardo's antics may be just as funny frozen in a TV Land time warp, but the hand of age has taken its toll on Denver. The proprietor of the rare book shop immediately recognizes Angel even though he hasn't seen him since

'52, and explains that meeting a vampire who was interested in doing good for others turned his life around. Denver's enthusiasm dims a little when Angel tells him he walked out and let the Thesulac have everyone in the hotel, but he is still a font of information. He knows the Band of Blacknil is a ring used to move between dimensions. He theorizes the Senior Partner will manifest as a Kleynach demon, using the ring. If he is correct about the Kleynach choice, he also has the one item that can kill it: an ancient knight's armored glove. He is in the process of presenting Angel with the glove when he is killed with an antique sword. Angel steps forward to help, allowing Darla to use her vamp strength to add him to her macabre shish kebob. As Angel collapses to the floor, pinned by Denver's dead weight, Darla kicks him in the head and departs with the glove.

Virginia bustles around Wesley's apartment, providing tea and comfort as he rests on his couch in his bathrobe. His new bandages are prominent under the robe. They start out talking about his confrontation with Angel, but the topic soon becomes more general, and she reveals her deep discomfort with his job. Wesley, seeing where their conversation is leading, articulates it before Virginia can—she is breaking up with him.

No longer defined by her role as a cop, Kate comes home to find scant comfort in her awards and memorabilia from her time on the force. She pours herself a drink and lashes out at the shelves of items, stopping to gaze at a photo of her father, Trevor Lockley.

An ever-more-paranoid Lilah walks toward Wolfram & Hart the evening of the big review, flanked by a pair of bodyguards. Moments later, the guards are down for the count, and Angel has invited himself into the building, with Lilah his unwilling escort. As they step into the elevator, she notices him favoring his side, where he evidently is still suffering from Darla's skewering.

Cordy does some late-night office work when the phone rings.

> **CORDELIA:** "Good evening, 'Angphlmn' Investigations, we help the helpless. How can we help you?"
>
> **WESLEY:** "What in God's name is 'Angphlmn'?"
>
> **CORDELIA:** "Oh, there're just some names I'm not saying at the moment."

Wesley, his enthusiasm for "the good fight" considerably flagged by his wounds, both emotional and physical, is calling in to warn Cordelia he won't be in the following day. He comments on his surprise at finding her in the office in the evening, instead of out with her friends. She explains that "helping the helpless" has not left much time for a social life. They end the conversation on an artificially upbeat note, each trying to reassure the other of a more positive future.

Cordelia is about to douse the lights and call it a night when the phone rings again. She is prepared for Wesley calling back with more optimism, but her spirits are genuinely lifted when it turns out to be Mrs. Sharp, calling to say they have reconsidered the payment and can someone from "Angphlmn" come pick up a check? Cordy can't note the directions fast enough.

Sadly, it seems the Skilosh demons already know the way to the Sharps. Having done her bit in luring Cordy to the house, Mrs. Sharp is now dispensable to the demons, and she joins the rest of her family in a big pile o' death on the floor.

A Day-Glo pentagram dominates the center of the Wolfram & Hart conference room where an impatient Nathan Reed waits for Lindsey's co-vice president to show up. While they wait, a guard informs Nathan a vampire is in the building—on the same floor, in fact. Robed priests continue swinging their censers over the pentagram, which starts to shimmer. Lindsey spots Angel entering behind Lilah, and alerts the guards. Angel ducks security, dodging through the crowd toward a dark-haired woman in a red dress. When Angel pulls off her wig and douses her with holy water, a vamped, smoldering Darla is revealed.

Angel and Darla fight for possession of the glove, with Angel getting some assistance from the guards, who can only see evidence of Darla's vampiric nature.

None of the fighting has disrupted the arrival of the Senior Partner, and Nathan Reed goes to his knees, in obsequious mode. Angel strikes Darla with enough force to give the guards a chance to move in with their stakes. Lilah's call for Darla's staking is brought to an abrupt end by Lindsey's fist. Darla escapes staking but loses possession of the glove. Angel dons the glove and gets the just-formed Kleynach by the throat. The Senior Partner makes a splashy, abrupt departure from this dimension, leaving the laws of physics to hurl Angel, the glove, the demon's robe, and the Band of Blacknil out the window to a spectacular landing amid shattered glass below.

As most eyes watch Angel try to take flight, Lindsey frees Darla, who leaves after one unrepentant backward glance. Lilah, her perfect makeup smeared and her mouth bloody, glares at both of them.

Angel painfully rises from the ground and picks up the Band of Blacknil that the Senior Partner used to travel to this dimension. He slides it onto his finger with grim determination, and waits for some sort of transportation to the Home Office. Behind him, an elevator bell dings and doors slide open. Angel turns to the elevator, as the deceased Holland Manners slowly applauds his dramatic arrival.

Holland is immaculately dressed and bearing obvious Darla bite marks on his neck.

> **ANGEL**: "You're . . ."
> **HOLLAND**: "Holland Manners."
> **ANGEL**: ". . . not alive."
> **HOLLAND**: "Oh, no. I'm quite dead. Unfortunately my contract with Wolfram & Hart extends well beyond that."

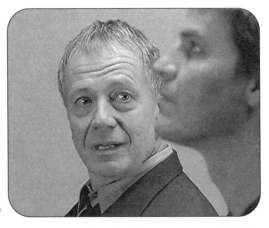

And they are on their way to the Home Office, with Holland playing elevator operator. Holland warns Angel that it's a one-way trip, then tries to engage the dour, committed vampire in a discussion of what he hopes to accomplish. Angel reveals that he hopes to bring the whole battle to an end by bearding the big bad Senior Partners in their den. Holland points out that while it certainly will mean an end to Angel's participation in battles, it won't mean an end to the ongoing struggle. And he reminds Angel he is supposed to play a significant part in a coming Apocalypse. Not that the W&H team really cares who wins in any given struggle—they are invested in the long-term spreading of evil through the mundane day-to-day existence of humanity. And with that, Holland announces they've arrived at the Home Office—and the doors open right where they closed at the beginning of the trip, onto the mall area filled with people engaged in their nightly routines.

RESOLUTION

Angel walks the streets of Hell, burdened by Holland's perspective. All around him he sees people generating their own little bits of darkness—a surly encounter with a coffee vendor, quarreling parents and children, or lovers fighting—darkness that comes from within themselves, not from any external force controlled by Wolfram & Hart. Around the city, the darkness touches Kate, as she goes to the medicine cabinet and removes a bottle of pills, and to Wesley, who lies alone in his apartment as the changing light from the TV screen silently flickers over him. Angel reaches the hotel to hear the telephone ringing, then Cordelia's familiar outgoing message on the answering machine, followed by Kate's despairing voice as she washes the pills down with alcohol. He gazes at the machine a long moment, then heads upstairs to his room.

An angry Darla is there ahead of him, eager to get the Band of Blacknil. Angel carelessly tosses it to the floor, then grabs Darla in a creepily passionate embrace when she dives for it. Still wary of this "new" Angel, she is hesitant to respond at first. Then she gives in, laughing at his apparent capitulation. He tosses her into the bedroom hard enough to shatter the French doors' glass, and she lands on the carpet in parallel to Angel's earlier landing. Then they are on the bed, and lost in the moment. Including *the* moment, Angel's nemesis.

Darla sleeps in the aftermath, but Angel shoots upright in bed, his face creased with anguish, as he stares out into the stormy night.

Case to be continued . . .

DOSSIERS

CLIENT **The Sharps**, who at first seemed like reasonable paying clients, stiffed Angel/Anghlphm Investigations for their work removing their daughter's third eye. **Kate's** desperate call to Angel goes unheeded in his present state of mind.

VICTIMS **Denver**, the beatnik bookseller who provided Angel with information and equipment on two occasions, half a century apart, meets his end at Darla's hands. **The Sharps** have been killed, having done their part to trap Cordelia.

SUSPECTS The **Skilosh demons**, thwarted in their efforts to produce spawn with the Sharp girl, arrange for their opposition to take her place.

Darla has been playing Lindsey as she waits for an opportunity to gain power, which presents itself in the form of the Band of Blacknil.

> "The ring's not about vengeance, Angelus. It's about power—we'll get to the vengeance part soon."
>
> —*Darla*

Given all the rumored nastiness associated with past reviews, the lawyers of Wolfram & Hart are surprisingly ungrateful that Angel has disrupted the visit from the Senior Partner.

CONTINUITY

Angel is probably going to hear about his torching of Darla and Dru for the rest of his unlife, as Lilah brings it up once again. Kate Lockley made judgment calls when her cases intersected Angel's, including in "The Thin Dead Line" and "Reunion." The consequences of those decisions are a significant factor in her being called before the review board. Denver assisted Angel in researching the Thesulac demon in "Are You Now or Have You Ever Been?" Holland and Angel discuss the prophecy from the Scroll of Aberjian, and Angel's role in preventing an apocalypse. Wolfram & Hart continue to work to steer Angel's loyalties to the dark side before that occurs.

QUOTE OF THE WEEK

"'Using a clean, diagonal motion, slit throat of sacrifice with the pre-blessed ceremonial dagger. Provided.' I didn't see that in the box—"

The second worshipper follows instructions carefully when sacrificing goats.

THE DEVIL IS IN THE DETAILS

EXPENSES

The ingredients of the restorative charm that removed the Skilosh eye from Stephanie Sharp's head include mandrake

Wolfram & Hart need to replace a window or two, as does Angel

Continuing medical expenses for Wesley

WEAPONRY

For the ritual, there's a ceremonial dagger. Denver has the glove, and Darla runs him through with an antique sword to get it.

> "Picked it up in seventy-five at a yard sale in Covina. Been using it as an oven mitt."   —*Denver*

Holy water is always useful.

THE PLAN

> **HOLLAND**: "So, what's the big plan, Angel? Destroy the Senior Partners? Smash Wolfram & Hart once and for all?"
> **ANGEL**: "Something like that."

DEMONS, DEMONS, DEMONS

Denver reaches the conclusion the Senior Partner will manifest as a **Kleynach demon** because of one of their handier attributes.

"Right. Kleynach. Lotta dark entities use the form of a Kleynach to manifest because a Kleynach doesn't have to rely on being conjured or brought forth. They can come and go as they please with that ring."
—Denver

Kleynach are also notoriously hard to destroy, being resistant to most attacks.

THE PEN IS MIGHTIER

FINAL CUT

The description of the first trip to the Sharps' was cut . . .

"Um, will you give me the address again? The British guy drove last time and there was a lot of 'Right side! Right side!' going on, so I don't . . ."
—Cordelia

Angel's elevator escort dished out the ultimate insult, also cut . . .

"For a man who's turned his back on his mission, you're awfully scrappy. I do so admire that. No messy moral philosophy, no guiding principles to muddle things. Just that pure, unpolluted human drive to win. You would have made an excellent attorney."
—Holland

POP CULTURE

❖ HOST: "I think the general angst is not so much about the review and more about the reviewer. And let's just say it ain't Rex Reed."
ANGEL: "What is it?"
HOST: "It's evil. It's dark. It's merciless. Actually, now that I say it out loud, sounds an awful lot like Rex, doesn't it?"
Critic Rex Reed's film and theater reviews notably appear in the *New York Post* and the *New York Observer.*

❖ "Most anything that can manifest in order to move in this dimension can be killed. Kinda the downside of being here. Well, that and the so-called 'musicals' of Andrew Lloyd Webber." The Host critiques Lord Andrew Lloyd Webber, the occasional toast of Broadway, who is the composer of musicals including *Cats, Evita, Jesus Christ Superstar, Joseph and the Amazing Technicolor Dreamcoat,* and *Phantom of the Opera.*

❖ "Jeez, Wes, zip-a-dee-doo-dah, all right?" Cordelia refers to Joel Chandler Harris's Brer Rabbit tales, which were worked into the 1946 Walt Disney musical *Song of the South*, and included the phrase "Zip-A-Dee-Doo-Dah" to express optimism. The song won an Academy Award.

OUR HEROES

Alexis Denisof spoke about the bittersweet relationship between Wesley and Virginia Bryce.

"They were sort of in that phase where they probably were falling in love with each other, or were about to, or already had. But it was decision time. Were they really going to let this go and become a relationship? Or were they going to pull back from it? Wesley's life pursuit got in the way and the bottom line was: that was more important. It was more important for him that he do that, and it was more important for her that she find someone who didn't have something in their life that was more important than her. Something had to give. I thought it was handled in a very human and real way."

—ALEXIS DENISOF

"We reprised a character from Tim's episode two, this season ("Are You Now or Have You Ever Been?"), Denver the beatnik hippie. And now he's an old man. But it was so cool to follow it, to keep him there, and in the same shop. And Angel looks exactly the same, but Denver has aged completely."

—MERE SMITH

"One of my favorite things that Angel does, and he doesn't do it enough, is, he'll be walking along the edge of a building, then he steps off. It's so cool when he does that, and Mike Massa has it down to an art. He'll fall three stories, straight as an arrow. It's terrifying. But Mike's got it down. He did the high fall the other night, when he hit the ground, he went off an eleven-foot ladder and landed on his face. Then in episode fifteen, he did a ninety-foot fall, just beautiful."

—MICHAEL VENDRELL, STUNT COORDINATOR

SIX DEGREES OF . . .

One of the would-be goat sacrificers is David Fury, a *Buffy* writer/producer who has also written *Angel* episodes, and acted professionally before becoming a writer.

TRACKS

When it comes to karaoke, lawyers are just as susceptible to choosing music from the seventies as real people. The members of W&H go with Peaches & Herb's 1979 hit "Reunited."

"EPIPHANY"

FROM THE FILES OF ANGEL INVESTIGATIONS CASE Nº: 2ADH16

ACTION TAKEN

A bit of déjà vu, as Darla sleeps in the aftermath of sex, but Angel shoots upright in bed, his face creased with anguish, as he stares out into the stormy night.

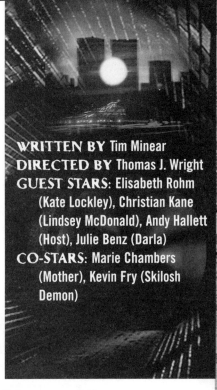

He pulls on a pair of pants and heads out into the storm that beats on the balcony, making a halfhearted attempt to pull on his shirt. Darla, roused from her slumber, drapes the sheet around herself and follows him out, encouraging him in his moment of transformation.

They stand in the doorway, sheltered from the external storm but not the storm of emotion. Darla reminds him she has just undergone a reawakening herself, and tries to talk him through his. He thanks her for saving him, and for a long moment she continues to believe she has restored the vampiric self the Gypsy curse undid. But that is not what he is thanking her for, and she is dismayed to realize he is still the vampire with a soul, despite their amorous activities.

WRITTEN BY Tim Minear
DIRECTED BY Thomas J. Wright
GUEST STARS: Elisabeth Rohm (Kate Lockley), Christian Kane (Lindsey McDonald), Andy Hallett (Host), Julie Benz (Darla)
CO-STARS: Marie Chambers (Mother), Kevin Fry (Skilosh Demon)

DARLA: "But we . . ."
ANGEL: "Yes . . ."
DARLA: ". . . and you . . ."
ANGEL: "I know . . ."
DARLA: "Then I . . ."
ANGEL: "Three times . . ."
DARLA: "You're not evil?"

Indeed, he is not. As he reached the zenith of their lovemaking, he also reached the nadir of his darkness, but still did not descend into losing his soul. Darla, insulted that she wasn't "perfect" enough, hopes to try again with different results, but Angel stays her hand, and quietly but firmly tells her to get out. Permanently. Because he will kill her the next time he sees her.

In the meantime, he is preoccupied with another blond. Angel rushes to Kate's apartment, bursting in when he gets no response, then drags her inert body into the shower with him. His tactics are successful in aborting her suicide attempt. A damp Kate thanks him, then tells him to get out, which he does.

Lindsey returns to his apartment, looking as though it's been a long night. He is somewhat surprised to find a pensive Darla there, and warns her that her attempt to gain power at the review has caused Wolfram & Hart to issue a "stake on sight" order for her. Lindsay devises a plan for her to lay low in response, part of which includes her moving from the couch into his bedroom—how handy! Darla is too intent on the Band of Blacknil she clutches to really respond to him.

She tells Lindsey that the ring, which has been disenchanted by W&H, is her payment from Angel, letting all that implies hang heavy in the air between them. Lindsey, who has reached the breaking point, demands she be more explicit.

The Host, clad in a stunning bathrobe, answers the dozen or so anxious rings of the doorbell after hours at Caritas. "I'm not deaf, you know!" he shouts. "Jeez. Keep yer pants on!" But when he sees his unexpected guest is Angel, he amends that. "Well, I see we're a little late with *that* advice . . ."

Angel spills the tale of the night's activities to the Host, who is only marginally sympathetic. He encourages Angel to move forward now that he has reached his epiphany, and reveals that Darla and Drusilla were destined to dine on uncorked lawyers with or without Angel's participation. When Angel asks why The Powers That Be didn't just direct him away from the whole thing, the Host reminds him of his whole recent attitude problem.

"Would you have listened? Besides, what makes you think they didn't? Over and over, and, as for example, over?"
                                                                                    —*Host*

Angel asks for further guidance, and the Host points out he already has someone for that job—Vision Girl, assisted by Wesley and Gunn. Angel isn't optimistic about his chances at getting back in the group's good graces—even less so when the Host shares that they may not survive the night.

Cordelia dismisses the cab driver who brought her to the Sharps', then looks at the dark house. She knocks, then enters through the unlocked front door. No one with her amount of exposure to things that go bump in the night would ever enter a place like this—unless they were extraordinarily fiscally responsible.

Cordelia moves through the darkened house to the kitchen, inquiring about the payment on the invoice she carries. She sees the dead family in the kitchen, and is about to wisely retreat when she is nearly knocked down by a powerful vision. The vision shows her in the kitchen doorway, attacked by a Skilosh demon. As she regains her normal vision—standing in that very kitchen doorway—the demon attacks. "Well, that was helpful!" Cordelia complains, addressing The Powers That Be.

She ends up against the wall in the living room, with a killer headache from the vision and the attack. The Skilosh hail her as one responsible for the destruction of their offspring, which she vehemently denies until she catches a glimpse of the third eye in the back of their skulls. They report they have also successfully located "the wheel-ed one."

"The wheel-ed one" is tidying his apartment when an unusual sound puts him on the alert. Wes maneuvers his wheelchair to the closet, where he manages to improvise with a broom to get down his shogun and shells without having to rise. He has the gun on his lap as he scans the premises for intruders, one of whom kicks the front door open. It's a frantic Angel.

ANGEL: "I've never been here before, Wesley! You have to invite me in!"

WESLEY: "Well, perhaps if you'd shown more interest . . ."

Angel points out the Skilosh invading his home. Wes quickly extends the necessary invitation, and the two of them dispatch the two attacking demons messily but effectively. There's a moment of shared relief, but only a moment before the walls are back between them.

Darla seems lost in her own world on the couch as Lindsey storms around the apartment, changing out of his rumpled suit as quickly as his artificial hand will allow. He tosses his keys on the coffee table, then goes into the closet, pushing past an assortment of Darla's clothes and his guitar to grab a pair of well-worn but neglected cowboy boots out of the back.

Angel and Wesley—still cleaning Skilosh goo out of his ear and hair—are in the Angelmobile in search of Cordy. Wes tries to reach her by telephone, but with no luck. Angel's oft-stressed lack of people skills and empathy are showing as he attempts to reconnect with Wesley.

ANGEL: "You know, it's kind of funny. I recently got a gut wound myself. Not a gunshot, like you got there, but, uh, it was kind of an antique . . . sword.

(beat)

Is what it was.

(beat)

Went deep.

(nothing.)

Yes it did. Hey, guess who stabbed me?"

WESLEY: "Dar-la?"

ANGEL: "Yeah."

Finally he gives up for the moment, and they just share the facts of the Skilosh demon case as they race toward the new office.

Cordelia is semi-eavesdropping on the Skilosh, hoping to figure out a way to escape, when they inform her that they have lost two more members of their tribe. She tries to conceal her elation, which is quickly replaced by fear anyway as they surround her, some of them restraining her while another positions itself to insert its proboscis into the back of her head. Once again, Cordelia is to be a breeding ground for demon spawn.

Angel and Wesley, who is keeping an eye on the street, unsuccessfully check the office for Cordelia. Angel carelessly suggests that perhaps she is enjoying an evening out with friends. Wesley observes that Angel's eagerness to entertain that notion simply demonstrates how little he knows the current Cordelia. They reach accord in their desire to find her, and move quickly to douse the lights and assume defensive positions when they hear movement outside.

They recognize Gunn before doing him any inadvertent harm. Gunn gives Angel the cold shoulder, while hailing Wesley with a complicated series of handgrips and much mutual acclaim.

GUNN: "So what's he doin' here?"

ANGEL: "I saw the Host at Caritas. He said my friends were in danger."

(A dry beat, then:)

GUNN: "So what's he doin' here?"

WESLEY: "He had an 'epiphany.'"

Gunn is curious about their nocturnal activities, and Wesley brings him up to speed on the Skilosh attack at his apartment. Wes and Gunn operate smoothly to determine Cordelia's likely whereabouts, while Angel makes several failed attempts to be helpful.

GUNN: "You check her pad?"

ANGEL: "I stopped by there earlier."

GUNN: "You enjoying your visit to 1973? I meant her *message* pad."

The carbon of the message pad shows the directions to the Sharps' home, and they all know that money is the perfect draw for Cordelia.

Cordelia, a recently unconscious mouse in the Skilosh's Sharp-cheese-baited trap, wakes up and gazes around the room. When she realizes she is getting a 360-degree view without turning her head, she rushes to the mirror to confirm her fear—and the sign of the Skilosh spawn is right there in the middle of her new haircut.

Angel, Gunn, and Wes are in the convertible on their way to her aid. Angel alternates between concerned glances in his rearview mirror and attempts to convince the guys of his renewed good intentions. The latter is not going well at all, as Gunn and Wesley both regard him with deep and deserved suspicion.

The uncomfortable silence in the car is broken by the crash of a Skilosh attack. Angel stops the car and gets out, commanding Gunn and Wes to continue to the Sharps' while he stands against the demons. The others hesitate for a moment, but Angel insists, "I'll be there. Just get to Cordelia." They acquiesce and drive off.

Angel stands in the street, ax in hand. He is ready to prove himself to his friends by standing against the assembled Skilosh, who converge on him with the surety of superior numbers before suddenly scattering. Angel has just a moment to wonder at their change of heart, before he is caught in the high beams of a speeding truck. Lindsey, face contorted into a grimace that would do a demon proud, knocks his vampiric rival down, then shifts into reverse and does it again.

At the Sharp home, Gunn assists Wesley as his wheelchair sticks in the grass, then peers inside to ascertain Cordelia's well-being. The good news is she's alive. The bad news is she has three eyes, and there are a lot of Skilosh around. Gunn and Wesley are concerned about the imminent emergence of Skilosh spawn from Cordy's noggin, and impatient for Angel to join them. When he doesn't materialize, they decide to enter and rescue Cordelia without him.

Angel is a little busy being repeatedly run over. Lindsey has burned a number of rubber donuts into the street as he circles his prey. For variety, Lindsey knocks Angel down with the truck, then gets out, sledgehammer in his good hand. He strikes Angel with the hammer again and again, demanding to know all the specifics about what happened between Angel and Darla. Angel rallies, and as Lindsey reaches into the truck bed for a stake, turns the tables. He attacks Lindsey verbally as well as with his fists. He stands over Lindsey, and with one decisive blow of the sledgehammer, makes Lindsey a one-handed man for the second time.

"Coulda been the other one. Just be glad I had an epiphany."   *—Angel*

And with that he helps himself to the truck and drives off into the night.

Cordelia, flanked by Skilosh in the Sharps' living room, sees Wesley and Gunn enter from opposite sides of the room, thanks to her new enhanced visual acuity. Her joy at seeing the cavalry soon turns to dis-may when she realizes her rescuers are captives as well. The Skilosh are targeting Wesley's and Gunn's heads when their ritual is interrupted by Angel driving Lindsey's truck through the front window.

While Angel, the truck, and the sledgehammer dis-patch Skilosh demons, Gunn and Wesley free themselves and perform the "deoculation" spell on Cordelia. Cordelia, a little confused, looks up to see all three men gazing at her in concern.

> **ANGEL:** "You okay?"
>
> **CORDELIA:** "No."
>
> **ANGEL:** "You're not?"
>
> **CORDELIA:** "No. You really hurt my feelings."

And with that, she leaves on the arms of the two she can count on.

RESOLUTION

Lindsey, footsore from walking home in the cowboy boots, finds his damaged truck outside the apart-ment building with a simple note on it: "Thanks." Inside the apartment, there is no Darla, and no sign of her possessions.

Kate visits Angel at the hotel, and they sit in the interior garden in a contemplative mood. Kate listens patiently to Angel's description of his recent revelations, and his rediscovered ideal of doing good daily for its own sake, not to score points off of law firms, or get credit toward his own redemp-tion. Angel may be the one who's had an epiphany, but Kate has had something very like one because of Angel's actions in saving her life.

> **KATE:** "I don't know what I believe but I . . . have faith. I think maybe we're not alone in this."
>
> **ANGEL:** "Why?"
>
> **KATE:** "Because I never invited you in."

Kate may be receptive to the new Angel, but Gunn, Wesley, and Cordelia are less than warm when he enters Angel Investigations. Angel apologizes. Wesley steps forward, leaning on a cane, to let Angel know they are resolved not to return to working for him. That's all right with Angel, who is there to request they allow him to work for them at their agency. His first task? Keeping Cordy from hitting the floor as she receives a vision.

> **CORDELIA:** "The usual Big Scary. Rising up in a housing project in Topanga.
>
> (eyes shifting as)
>
> And . . . why is it that I'm not on the floor this time?"
>
> **ANGEL:** "I've got you."

Case closed.

DOSSIERS

CLIENT Those mistrustful **Sharps**, including Mom and daughter Stephanie, are back. Virginia Bryce referred them to Angel Investigations, but evidently their connection with the Bryces is only based on their social standing and income, as they are in fatal denial about the things that go bump in people's heads. **Cordelia** could also be considered a client, since she is in danger and even is the subject of one of her own visions—albeit too late to do any good.

SUSPECTS **Skilosh demons** capture Cordelia and implant their young in her head. **Lindsey McDonald** lets loose on Angel.

CONTINUITY

Angel's painful, stormy, postcoital awakening is extraordinarily like his experience after he reaches "perfect happiness" with Buffy in "Surprise" and "Innocence." However skilled Darla may be, there is no such moment this time. Darla, with two turns at becoming an undead creature of the night ("Darla" and "Reunion"), consoles Angel when she believes he has re-lost his soul after their lovemaking. She loses him, but leaves with the Band of Blacknil, which was so significant in "Reprise." According to the Host, Darla and Drusilla's lawyer decanting in "Reunion" was preordained, regardless of Angel's choices. Cordelia is a demon-reproduction magnet, suffering impregnation in "Expecting," eyeball injection in "Epiphany," and prophecies of "Com-Shuking" in Pylea.

QUOTE OF THE WEEK

"I think I speak for everyone when I say—if all you're going to do is switch back to brood mode, we'd rather have you evil. Because then, at least—leather pants."

The Host has his own fashion-based response to Angel's epiphany.

THE DEVIL IS IN THE DETAILS

EXPENSES

Cab fare for Cordy
Someone is going to have to pay for repairs to:
Kate's front door
Wesley's apartment, including the ceiling/ floor of the apartment above

WEAPONRY

Wesley wields a shotgun against the invading Skilosh, while Angel uses one of Wesley's medieval axes. Lindsey tries to kill Angel with his multi-ton truck and sledgehammer, but Angel uses the hammer against Lindsey and drives the truck through the Sharp home, saving his friends.

THE PLAN

WESLEY: "We're going in there and we're saving our friend."
GUNN: "I say let's do it."
WESLEY: "One more thing—"

GUNN: "What's that?"

WESLEY: "I'm toppling over."

DEMONS, DEMONS, DEMONS

"**Skilosh**, a notoriously violent, asexual, self-replicating species of demon, has the distasteful habit of injecting its demon spawn into the cranium of a human host. One of the key diagnostic symptoms being the telltale third eye on the back of the host's head. If this condition is not arrested in time, a newborn Skilosh will erupt, fully grown, from the skull of its human host."

—Wesley

THE PEN IS MIGHTIER

FINAL CUT

Much of Angel and Wesley's extended discussion of the name of the agency was cut due to length.

ANGEL: "You kept the name. 'Angel Investigations.'"

WESLEY: "We're going to change it. But if you must know, we felt we had as much right to it as you."

ANGEL: "Oh. I mean, 'Investigations,' okay. But come on—"

(points to himself)

"Angel."

WESLEY: "Yes. But whatever good reputation that corporate name enjoys, is due to all of us. Not just—"

(mimics cadence)

"'Angel.'"

OUR HEROES

Julie Benz gets introspective about Darla and Angel's encounter:

"At the end of 'Reprise,' beginning of 'Epiphany,' they've come together as lovers, but he hasn't actually experienced that pure happiness.

"The difference in that one is that he wanted it more than she did that time. He wanted her. She didn't manipulate him. She makes a point of saying that, 'You wanted this, how could you not—you wanted it more than you've ever wanted it before. How could I have not made you happy?' And it devastates her. It just breaks her completely. It's the turning point for her. The whole season has led up to that moment. That moment of him wanting it, and then not experiencing that moment of happiness that she really thinks that she has given him. I think that ultimately, her soul mate really is Lindsey. In a very twisted way, they're both damaged. She can't get over Angel, [Lindsey] can't get over her. And they're both damaged goods, and ultimately, if she was smart, that's where she would turn to. But she just can't seem to get over Angel."

—JULIE BENZ

Renaissance man, music coordinator John King, demonstrated a different talent in this episode, creating the look for the Skilosh demons.

"David Greenwalt decided that he wanted to take a fresh approach to the makeup design on this monster, since it was going to be carried over from three episodes. I have a background in two and three-dimensional design, so David asked me if I would have a go at it. I thought it was a great opportunity and a challenge. He gave me the specs of what he was looking for—the key point being that it had to have an eye in the back of its head. So I sat down and just started knocking out some different ideas until I finally settled on something I thought was interesting and different. I thought, okay, these are the facial features, it's kind of humanistic, with a skeletal-like structure, but how can I make the eye in the back more interesting? I tried to figure out what the physiological aspects of having an eye in the back of one's head would be. And I took those internal mechanisms like the optic nerves, retinas, and muscles that that control eye movement and put them on the outside, just to be a little more disgusting."   —JOHN KING

Chic Gennarelli dresses them.

"The ideas for demon outfits come out of my head. That's another thing that just happens when I read the script. I read the script and I start formulating these ideas from their character, where they came from, what kind of look they have, makeup wise. My second thought is the makeup, so I have to get a sketch of what they're doing. And then I kind of build my ideas around that. And again, I like to use, sometimes, old, ancient looks with furs and leathers and stuff, and sometimes I like to use futuristic cords and nylon, and sometimes I like to mix them both together, which I did on the Skilosh guys. They were the ones with the eyes in the backs of their heads. They had like robes on, and fur vests, and fur boots, and their leader was very universal-looking, very gray and black and very tough. And they all wore corsets."   —CHIC GENNARELLI

Bad Boy Christian Kane identifies with Lindsey and his sledgehammer.

"I confronted Angel with a sledgehammer in [episode] sixteen. It was very very violent. I did all my own stunts on that, too. I loved it. David was at the premiere of *Valentine*, so I did it all with Mike Massa. It was awesome. Mike is David's stunt double, so we screw around. I grew up kind of a bad kid, so I know what's going on out there. I like it."   —CHRISTIAN KANE

Transportation director Robert Ellis found synchronicity in his choice for Lindsey's truck.

"When the script came out it mentioned a truck from Oklahoma, from his father's ranch. We didn't picture that. So that was really cool, another twist. My first choice was a brand-new truck, because the first thing I knew, it had to go through the window of a living room. So I was like, let's get something new so I can double it. And they liked it, but after a while they said, 'Let's get something with a little more character to it instead. We'd like to see something that came off the farm, that looked like it had been beat up, or it had been there awhile.' So the first truck I showed them was a bright red 'fifty-seven Ford [like David Greenwalt used to have]. [But they didn't like the red] so we took it to our boys at Studio Picture Vehicles and said, 'I need this truck a different color overnight, you guys. Please.' And they stood up and they sprayed it a primer red. Okay, now we need to find a double, because they actually want to crash it before they see it driving and running Angel down. But the funny part was, not only do they want to crash it first, but they want to see it crashed before it crashes. So now I've got to double the crash vehicle. I've got to have one pre-crashed and one to throw through the window. So we looked up a place, and we found places with fiberglass fenders. And we cut them, and made it look like the car was crashed before it even went through the window. We filmed it with a note on it that said, 'Thanks for the use of the car.' That was the first shot, which was the end. The second shot we shot was the truck going through the window. The third shot was the shot of it running Angel down before it went through the window. So we actually had to have three trucks. We pre-crashed it, and that pre-crashed one went through the window so the crashing would match exactly. When it landed, it had the same damage on it that it did when we shot the thank-you note in front of the apartment building. And I actually went out and found a toy 'fifty-six, and put it in a door and crashed it and put it on [David Greenwalt's] desk, crashed, with the windshield cracked."   —ROBERT ELLIS

Gunn's trust issues get some thought from J. August.

"In 'Epiphany,' how does Gunn feel when Angel comes to the office and apologizes, and says he wants to work for the group?"

J. AUGUST RICHARDS: "Well, see, Gunn doesn't take traitors well, so he sees Angel as a traitor, as a deserter. And so I don't trust him, I don't trust it, I don't trust an epiphany, you can't rely on an epiphany. Somebody who comes from the background that Gunn comes from needs concrete evidence to trust and believe in someone."

TRACKS

Robert Kral discusses one of the rewards of Angel's epiphany.

"Chris Beck wrote the Angel theme (which first appears in episode one) which is sometimes heard at heroic moments. It's a powerful theme and was used more often in the first season. Angel went very *very* dark for a lot of Season Two, and we held off using it. It's used only for very special heroic moments, so when it appears it's like an old friend you haven't seen in a while.

"We'd hardly heard that theme used at all in Season Two, then in 'Epiphany,' Angel returns at a very heroic moment. It was my intention that by rarely using it, when it is used it's that much more special."

—ROBERT KRAL, COMPOSER

"DISHARMONY"

FROM THE FILES OF ANGEL INVESTIGATIONS
CASE Nº: 2ADH17

ACTION TAKEN

Wesley, in his role as leader guy, is having a heart-to-heart discussion with Angel about the process of reassimilation. Angel looks as though he'd rather take a stroll on a sunny day. Wesley reaches a conclusion and releases Angel to mull things over at his new desk—a card table set up in the lobby. Oh, and before Angel mulls, the other three have coffee requests.

"Man, atonement's a bitch."   —*Angel*

WRITTEN BY David Fury
DIRECTED BY Fred Keller
GUEST STARS: Andy Hallett (Host), Mercedes McNab (Harmony Kendall), Pat Healy (Doug Sanders), Alyson Hannigan (Willow Rosenberg)
CO-STARS: Luis Contreras (Mexican Vamp #1), Luis Chavez (Mexican Vamp #2), Adam Weiner (Caged Guy), Rebecca Avery (Caged Girl)

A parked couple too involved with each other's tonsils to notice the robed figures creeping up on the car like something from an urban legend look up—too late.

Gunn, Wesley, and Cordelia engage in various re-nesting activities in the hotel when Angel descends from his daytime slumber. Angel, obeying a significant glance from Wes, approaches Cordelia and tries to initiate a conversation, but gets the complete deep-freeze. He tries to help her with a box, and for a moment it seems she may relent, then he realizes it's vision time.

Cordelia conveys the clearer bits of her vision to the guys—a large red avian and figures in blue robes in Lafayette Park. The guys take off in a hurry, Angel lingering just long enough to suggest Cordy take the rest of the night off.

Cordelia turns off the lights to head home when she hears something stir in the shadows. She screams in fright when a human figure appears, then screams in delight when she recognizes Harmony. After some brief catching up, when they both try to make their current situations sound as good as possible, Harmony confesses she has come to L.A. without a specific destination in mind. Cordelia immediately invites Harmony to stay in her apartment, to the blond vampire's delight.

Angel, Gunn, and Wesley arrive at the park and find the empty car. Wesley deploys the troops when a woman's screams provide a vital clue. They charge to the rescue, and dust the green-robed vampire responsible for her abduction. Gunn holds the robe and puzzles over Cordelia's apparent color error, although Angel is quick to defend her.

While Gunn scouts for remaining vamps or clues, Wes starts to call Cordelia and see if she can make progress identifying the arcane symbol on the robe. Angel confesses to sending Cordy home, and feels Wesley out on the idea of sending her flowers.

WESLEY: "Flowers?"

ANGEL: "Yeah. You know, to say 'thanks.' And 'sorry about the migraines.' Um, you know . . . 'I appreciate you.'"

WESLEY: "Yes, by all means. And while you're at it, pick me up one of those 'SORRY YOU WERE SHOT IN THE GUT' bouquets!"

ANGEL: "Right. Sorry."

Wes sagely tells Angel only time will help heal Cordelia's pain.

Maybe that's time and a little wine, as a very relaxed, bathrobe-clad Cordy sits on the couch with Harmony, and they crack up over their memories of their high school reign. Deep in her cups, Cordelia tries to express to Harm how she can be happier as a struggling actress helping the helpless than she was as the Queen of Mean, but gives up. She notices Harmony looking uncomfortable, in need of nourishment. Cordelia happily dials up her favorite pizza place, not noticing the hungry Harmony vamping momentarily as Cordy's bare neck nears her fangs.

Cordelia sleeps deeply, as one would expect of someone who experienced mind-numbing visions followed by alcohol. Harmony stealthily approaches her slumbering form—and Dennis the Alert slams the door behind her, bringing Cordy awake. An abashed Harmony apologizes for betraying Cordelia's trust, but explains she was irresistibly drawn to her friend. Cordelia, Ms. Enlightened, completely misunderstands, believing that Harmony was hitting on her, and shoos a relieved Harmony back to the couch, pledging her secrecy.

The next morning the enlightened one gets on the phone to Sunnydale, quizzing a befuddled Willow, who is trying to decipher Cordelia and brush her teeth at the same time.

WILLOW: "Okay, we are all clear on the fact that Harmony's a vampire, right?"

CORDELIA: "Ohhh! Harmony's a vampire! That's why she— Oh my God, I'm so embarrassed. All this time I thought she was a great big lesbo . . ."

After Willow brings Cordelia up to speed on her relationship with Tara, she warns a truly embarrassed Cordy to get some distance between her and Harmony. Cordelia agrees, but when she hangs up the phone, Harmony surprises her in the hallway.

Angel and Wesley work in the hotel lobby trying to make progress on the robe's origin. Angel answers the phone, and after talking to a rather frantic Willow . . . Angel and Wesley burst into Cordelia's apartment in prime Rogue Demon Hunter form. They arrive just in time to interrupt Harmony giving Cordelia a pedicure. Cordelia tells them that yes, she knows Harmony is a vampire, and no, they are *not* going to dust her friend. Wesley tries to persuade Cordelia to do the right thing, but Angel supports her, the strain almost visible as he tries to make amends.

The foursome return to the office, Harmony having passed up the chance to stay in Cordelia's haunted apartment, where they try to continue their research into the mysterious robed vampires. Well, Angel, Cordelia, and Wesley work, while Harmony spectates in an incredibly annoying fashion. Wesley is actually driven to grabbing a stake from a drawer after Harmony defaces one of his ancient texts, but Angel draws her away to safety. He offers her a big mug o' blood, which she reluctantly accepts, as it's porcine in origin.

Harmony, genuinely puzzled, tries to understand how Angel can resist his vampiric nature. Angel

SELECTIVE SLAUGHTER

Turning a Blood Bath into a Blood Bank

DOUG SANDERS

"Turn two...
the rest is food."

DOUG SANDERS
SELECTIVE SLAUGHTER

Turning a Blood Bath into a Blood Bank

seems hypnotized by her graphic description of the process, and relieved when the spell is broken by Gunn's entrance. Spotting the attractive blond, Gunn smiles and gives her a cute little wave. Cordelia's introduction leaves out the salient fact Harmony is a vampire, which Wesley rushes to include. Gunn's smile disappears. "Don't we kill them anymore?" he asks.

Angel, not wanting to reopen the "staking Harmony" debate, asks what information Gunn picked up. Gunn's sources reveal that there have been disappearances associated with robed vamps for weeks, but not a lot of buzz because there is no corresponding body count. Angel makes the intuitive leap—the missing aren't being killed, they are being turned. But by whom, and why?

The Whom—Doug Sanders, motivational vampire. The Why—to take part in his new scheme, built on a simple concept. "Turn two, the rest is food." Each one turns two people into vampires, they each turn two, and so on. Doug stands on a brightly lit stage with three screens behind him displaying his "snake in the triangle" logo and other important visual aids. His audience, composed of vampires in a rainbow spectrum of robes, seems highly receptive.

Gunn, Wesley, and Angel take the low-tech approach to narrowing their search field with a map and pushpin markers for disappearances. Cordelia is intent on the computer, and her diligence pays off as she discovers info on Doug via the Department of Justice Web site. They are about to take the next logical step, comparing Sanders's known meeting places to their map, when Harmony accidentally dumps her mug of sugar-laden pigs' blood over the keyboard. That's the temporary end of the computer, and nearly the end of Harmony. Cordelia draws her out of harm's way when she is struck by an insight—take Harmony to Caritas!

Harmony enthusiastically belts her way through her song with total disregard for the Host's tender musical sensibilities. "I think your friend should reconsider the name 'Harmony,'" he says. Cordelia and Harmony both expect enlightenment from the Host, but he simply tells Harmony she is already on her path, and Cordelia is her guiding star. The boys are hoping Cordy can be *their* guide; they have a finite area of the city they think is worth checking for any signs of the big red bird. Cordelia settles Harmony at the table, and then they head for the car, just the five of them. Five? Yep, Harmony has had an epiphany—she is supposed to be one of the white-hat team.

Team Angel rides down the street—Angel concentrating on the road, Wesley riding a surly shotgun, Cordelia trying to identify anything familiar, and Gunn trapped by a chattering Harmony. Cordelia sees a large exceptionally ugly bird statue, and they stop the car. Gunn points out the bird appears green, rather than red. They are about to give up and move on, when Angel makes his first right move of the evening, turning on a neighboring store's red neon sign, casting the bird in red light.

Wesley limps around the group issuing directions. He and Gunn will go around the building while Angel and Cordelia take the direct approach. Harmony? She can guard the car. When Harm's response is a little too enthusiastic, involving bloodletting, Angel takes a still-pissed Cordy aside to advise against trusting Harmony. Cordelia is not interested in his input, pointing out that having a soul didn't prevent him from being heartless to his friends. Angel gives up and they return to the group, where Wesley and Gunn report the only visible way into the building is through the front door.

Angel volunteers to go in as a Trojan vampire, but is reminded that between his soul and his rep, he would be identified. Cordelia has a solution: send Harmony in as their scout. She's a vampire, unknown in L.A., and seeking her purpose. Harmony vacillates, then agrees and heads inside.

Leader Doug is in his element, rewarding vamps for their successes with recognition from the crowd and choice selections from the cage of humans. Harmony joins the audience, trying to fit in.

In back, Team Angel starts to worry that something has gone wrong with the plan. Angel suggests helping Harmony if she has been caught in her espionage, but Gunn disagrees, opposed to the whole idea of saving vampires from other vampires.

Harmony makes a timely appearance and she invites them in, giving them the lowdown. She also thanks Cordy for her part in helping Harmony find her place in the universe as she leads them in the back of the theater. Wesley, impatient, cuts off her thanks to demand the whereabouts of the vamp cult. Double agent Harmony reveals they are all around them.

Doug steps out of the mass of robed vampires pressing in from all sides and praises Harmony for her accomplishment. Not only has she delivered the requisite "two to turn, one for food," but also Angel. Harmony is presented with a blue robe, and turns a deaf ear to Cordelia's enraged criticism. Doug confidently suggests Angel and Co. voluntarily disarm, and Wesley's response is a vigorous "KILL THEM ALL!"

Doug may be a natural motivational speaker, but he's no battle strategist. Despite their superior numbers, and perhaps hampered by the large number of relatively new undead, the vampires find themselves on the losing side of the pitched battle that ensues. Wesley and Gunn team up to dust the key-holding bloodsucker, and release the prisoners from the cage. Angel goes *mano a mano* with Doug, who keeps nattering even while they scuffle over possession of a fire ax. Angel ends Doug's pitch by decapitating him. Cordelia and Harmony roll on the floor, with the vamped Harmony ending up on top, the crossbow visible in Cordy's hand at her throat. Harmony contemptuously reminds Cordelia an arrow in the throat won't dust a vamp—Cordelia points out that's only half the story, and she has her second arrow aimed at Harmony's heart. Harmony pleads for clemency, and Cordelia relents one more time, warning the blond to get out of Los Angeles and stay out.

RESOLUTION

It's déjà vu in the Hyperion, as Wesley invites Angel into his office to discuss mending his fences with Cordelia. Angel is surprisingly receptive to Wesley's suggestions. The reason becomes clear when a shriek from the lobby is followed by Cordelia's exuberant entrance into the office, arms laden with new clothes from the bounty Angel has piled on her desk. She embraces Angel and dances off to a "new clothes" song of her own creation. A pleased Angel follows her out, leaving Wes to rethink his personnel skills.

Case closed.

DOSSIERS

CLIENT In the larger sense of the word, all of **L.A.'s innocents** who can get caught in Doug Sanders's scheme are the clients. In particular, **Harmony Kendall** comes seeking a new direction for her un-life.

SUSPECTS **Harmony Kendall**, former Sunnydale resident, was one of the "in-crowd" with Cordelia. The Cordettes were united in their appreciation of designer labels and harassment of lower beings. Harmony was attacked and turned into a vampire during the battle with Mayor Wilkins on graduation day. She remained in Sunnydale and had a brief romance with Spike before dumping the Buffy-pining Brit. Being a vampire makes her highly suspicious in the team's eyes, but Cordy's not about to turn her back on a friend.

The Department of Justice wants **Doug Sanders** for his part in a con game.

"This particular one was run by a motivational speaker and . . . lord help me, self-described 'life coach,' named Doug Sanders."
                                                                                    —*Cordelia*

CONTINUITY

Harmony was part of Sunnydale High's beautiful people, and a vacuous member of the Cordettes, who followed Cordelia. When Cordelia lost some of her social status by not only dating but being emotionally vulnerable to Xander Harris ("Lovers' Walk"), Harmony made a play for the position of leader of the pack. Harmony and Cordelia last saw each other battling the Mayor in "Graduation Day, Part Two," when Harmony was turned into a vampire. Harmony hooked up with Spike, and even inadvertently discovered the Ring of Amarra (which Spike followed to L.A. in "In the Dark.") Harmony left Spike and Sunnydale for L.A. following an ugly romantic confrontation with Spike, Buffy, and Drusilla in "I Was Made to Love You." Angel gave away Cordelia's clothes to Anne's street kids in "Blood Money," a fact Cordy discovered while assisting Anne against zombie cops in "The Thin Dead Line."

QUOTE OF THE WEEK

"You kidding? Free blood. And potato skins. Hey, I'm thinking about doing another number. What do you think: 'Candle in the Wind' or 'Princess Diana Candle in the Wind'?"

Harmony soaks up the pleasures of Caritas.

THE DEVIL IS IN THE DETAILS

EXPENSES

Cordelia's call to Willow

The page Harmony ripped from the ancient text will probably have to be restored rather than replaced

Cordelia's computer needs a new keyboard at the very least

Angel invests in lots of designer goods as balm for Cordelia's wounded spirit

---

"You know, you didn't just betray me, Angel. You didn't just hurt me . . . *You gave away my clothes!*"

—*Cordelia*

WEAPONRY

In battle against Doug's robed minions, the gang employs stakes, crossbows, battle-axes, and a fire ax—some of which is also used against them.

THE PLAN

CORDELIA: "So you thought you'd just bust into my house and kill my friend without giving her a chance to explain herself."

ANGEL/WESLEY: "Yeah. Pretty much. That was the plan."

DEMONS, DEMONS, DEMONS

Doug Sanders offers more proof that **vampires** maintain many of their least desirable human traits.

Harmony is still a sheep, following the strongest leader, just as she did back in ninth-grade remedial Spanish at Sunnydale High.

THE PEN IS MIGHTIER

FINAL CUT

The original opening, reminiscent of "Eternity" and "Reprise," played with a bit of misdirection.

We probably don't know where we are as we open close on Cordelia and Gunn, both scrutinizing something off camera.

GUNN: "Found 'em just like this. Blood all over."

CORDELIA: "*Dried* blood. This wasn't recent. No telling how long they've been here."

GUNN: (shaking his head) "Look, I don't care what darkside detour Angel goes off on . . ."

WIDEN to reveal Gunn holding up a couple of COFFEE MUGS with DRIED BLOOD caked inside and around the edges.

GUNN: "The man's gotta stop leaving his dirty cups all over the damn place."

The ending, as originally scripted, ends with Wesley a bit envious over Cordelia's new clothes. "I could use a DVD player," he announces.

POP CULTURE

✳ **CORDELIA:** "Whoa. Big bird."
GUNN: "Big Bird?"
CORDELIA: "Not the Muppet, dumbass . . ."
Gunn thinks Cordelia has seen Big Bird, Jim Henson's 8'2" yellow-feathered Muppet from *Sesame Street,* in her vision.

✳ **ANGEL:** "The red bird sculpture you saw in your vision—was it an eagle . . . a hawk . . . a falcon?"
CORDELIA: "What am I, the Bird Lady of Alcatraz? For all I know, it was a duck. A big, red duck."
Burt Lancaster portrayed the *Birdman of Alcatraz* in 1962. The movie of the same name was based on the true story of convict Robert Stroud (prisoner AZ #594). The multiple-murderer became fascinated with birds during one of his many terms in prison and even authored books on the subject.

The WB promoted "Disharmony" with the tagline, "Evil has never been so . . . blond."

OUR HEROES

Charisma Carpenter was happy to be back in scenes with David Boreanaz.

"I got to work a lot with David, which I haven't done, one-on-one, at all. And I loved it last episode because I got to tell him off. So 'Disharmony' was a great episode, because I got to be kind of colorful and yet put him in his place. And you got to see how much Angel means to Cordelia. You know, how much she was hurt by him, and that's always fun."
—**CHARISMA CARPENTER**

Mercedes McNab, reprising her role of Harmony from the *Buffy* series, draws parallels between the characters and the actors.

"Did you feel like there were any similarities between Harmony and Cordelia reuniting, and you and Charisma having a chance to work together again?"
MERCEDES MCNAB: "As the script was written, there weren't many similarities, because Charisma and I had always gotten along. And I'm definitely not trying to bite Charisma's neck. But I haven't seen her since we finished working together on *Buffy,* so that was similar in that way, in the amount of time in which I hadn't seen her. And our reunion, Charisma and I just fell right back into hanging out and being friends, so that was similar to the script as well."

"So the closest thing would probably be the scene where the two of you were sitting around doing your nails?"
MERCEDES MCNAB: "Yeah, sitting on the couch, reliving old stories and making each other laugh. Right before that scene actually, because she had to start the scene off hysterically laughing, to get her to laugh I would tell her jokes and tell her old stories that we used to laugh about when we

were younger. It was just really good to work with a new group of people that I hadn't seen or been with for a while. Because I'd worked with Alexis also, but not in a couple years. So it was nice to have some fresh blood, no pun intended."

Andy Hallett and Mercedes McNab on her "cacophony."

"Most of the time they make the people sound worse than they really are. Harmony does a crossover, and she comes and just tears a song to shreds. And she can actually sing quite nicely. I heard her, while we were fooling around on stage and so forth, and she was singing quite nicely, and they said, 'No no no no, it's got to be much worse.'"   —ANDY HALLETT

"Well, I used to sing, so it was interesting to try and sing really bad but not—I was watching the audience and I didn't want the audience to think I was trying to sound bad. Like I was trying to be a bad person singing sounding good. It was awkward, but it was really nerve-racking, because that was the first scene I shot on *Angel*. So I just got broken right in, I get up there and I'm just like, 'I really wish everyone had some earplugs. Get ready, folks.' I break right into song, and I was a little embarrassed and nervous, but I just went with it and used it for the character. And it was a lot of fun, and I think that scene turned out really well."   —MERCEDES McNAB

Think Harmony looked a little different vamped than she used to? She did.
Andy Sands, of Optic Nerve, explains.

"[When] we brought Harmony back, they specifically wanted us to modify her forehead, make it look more like an *Angel*-type forehead. We actually contacted the people at *Buffy* and said, 'Can we modify the forehead?' and they said 'Do whatever you want.' So we went in and we actually changed the mold."   —ANDY SANDS

TRACKS

The ill-fated couple necking in the car was listening to "The Evening Comes" by Study of the Lifeless while being attacked by the lifeless.

Harmony selects Barbra Streisand's "The Way We Were" for her karaoke performance, so the Host can do his "mind mojo." She is contemplating Elton John's tributes to blondes, "Candle in the Wind," or "Princess Diana Candle in the Wind" when she feels the call to join Team Angel.

While Harmony and Cordelia chat with the Host, strains of "Don't Say It" by Baba Googie and Rex are heard in the background. Baba Googie and Rex is music supervisor John King's band.

"DEAD END"

FROM THE FILES OF ANGEL INVESTIGATIONS
CASE №: 2ADH18

ACTION TAKEN

It's 6:45 A.M. in the City of Angels, and Lindsey turns off the traffic report on his alarm clock with the stump of his right hand. Another day to thank Angel for the fact he has to exercise extra care shaving, don a preknotted tie, and let his guitar sit neglected in the back of his closet.

The attitude is much more upbeat in the kitchen of the Kramer family, as Dad Joseph merrily plans his day and his wife and kids finish breakfast. The family heads for their cars, with Dad pausing just long enough to read a few stories in the paper, grab some school gear, and stab himself in the eye with a kitchen knife.

In the lobby of the Hyperion, Cordelia is hit with a vision of Joseph's action so acute it seems as if she is the one being deoculated. Angel rushes to her side and cradles her head on his knee as she sobs in reaction.

WRITTEN BY David Greenwalt
DIRECTED BY James A. Contner
GUEST STARS: Christian Kane (Lindsey McDonald), Stephanie Romanov (Lilah Morgan), Andy Hallett (Host), Gerry Becker (Nathan Reed), Michael Dempsey (Irv Kraigle), Mik Scriba (Sam)
CO-STARS: Dennis Gersten (Dr. Michaels), Kavita Patel (Nurse), Peter Gardner (Joseph Kramer), Stephanie Nash (Wife), Steven DeRelian (Bradley Scott)

Lindsey, Lilah, Nathan, and other fine upstanding members of Wolfram & Hart meet in the conference room to protect a poor public utility from angry bill payers. Lindsey proposes a solution that meets with favor from Nathan Reed and teeth-grinding envy from Lilah. Next item on the agenda? Angel. Lindsey is snappish on the subject, but Lilah fills Nathan in on Angel post-epiphany. They adjourn. Lilah rabidly accuses Lindsey of trying to kowtow favor at her expense. Seems there's a reevaluation in the offing—no more sharing of the Senior Vice Presidency of Special Projects, which at Wolfram & Hart generally means that one attorney will live and the other won't. A strangely dispassionate Lindsey is saved from Lilah by a summons to Nathan's office.

Nathan compliments Lindsey on his performance, and tells him a reward is in store—a mysterious, time-consuming reward.

Cordelia, bewildered and distressed by Kramer's self-mutilation, tries to help the men narrow down the field of investigation, but is having a hard time coming up with details. They divide up the more apparent avenues of investigation—hospitals, morgues, sewers—in hopes of rescuing their client and relieving Cordelia of her burden.

Lindsey sits on an exam table and tries to get information from the doctor who is obviously preparing him for an unknown procedure. Dr. Melman expresses surprise at Lindsey's ignorance, then explains. Lindsey is at the clinic to get a new hand.

Lindsey lies on the operating table while Dr. Melman and his crew work over him. Pretty standard operating chatter, until Melman asks for the Pockla, and a huge red-robed demon with skeletal hands emerges chittering through the door. It glides to the table and does some mojo on the seam between Lindsey's stump and his new right hand. Other than a faint line, there is no sign the twain were ever separate.

Gunn has worked his way unsuccessfully through a number of hospitals when Wesley and Angel return from their equally fruitless ventures. They all eye Cordelia with concern mixed with apprehension—they need more information, but how can they possibly ask that of her? Angel is designated.

> **WESLEY:** "Go ahead, probably best not to crowd her."
>
> **ANGEL:** "Me? You're the one in charge now."
>
> **WESLEY:** "You're right. That's why I'm assigning this one to you."

Cordelia and Angel reluctantly face the inevitable, and she strains to remember any helpful detail beyond the horror in her mind. The horror is amplified when she realizes Kramer had children. She sees the name of their school on a book bag, but having another clue does nothing to assuage her vision hangover. Angel solicitously asks if he can get her anything, and she snaps at him.

6:45 A.M. and the sun and radio awaken Lindsey in his apartment. He reaches out with his new right hand and turns off the alarm. He enjoys his restored freedom of two-handedness as he prepares for work. After his mundane morning tasks, he gives the new hand a real workout on his guitar.

Lilah's envy knows no bounds once she spots Lindsey's new, functional, *not*-plastic hand. She is wired into the company's finances enough to know how expensive the operation was, and to recognize what an investment Wolfram & Hart have made in Lindsey's future, which makes her own a little more precarious.

Lindsey and Lilah take a meeting with Nathan's old friend, chocolatier Irv Kraigle. Irv's righteous indignation at being sued by consumers of "cytoclistomene"-laden chocolate is soothed by Lindsey's clever proposal, one that leaves him legally blameless. Lindsey is in his element, spinning damage control, and writing "KILL KILL KILL" on his legal pad absentmindedly with his new hand. He abruptly leaves the meeting. Lilah seizes the moment when Lindsey falters, not bothering to see what threw him off the pace.

Back in his apartment, Lindsey experiments to see if the semi-automatic writing will reoccur, but to no avail. He even pokes a few bloody holes in the hand with a letter opener.

Angel collects an assortment of food from a deliveryman, and splurges on a one-dollar tip. He lays the food out on the reception desk, much to Cordelia's tired bemusement.

> **CORDELIA:** "What is going on here?"
>
> **ANGEL:** "I forgot what you liked."
>
> **CORDELIA:** "Why didn't you ask me?"
>
> **ANGEL:** "Well, you said why is everyone asking you if they can get you anything, and I didn't want to do that . . ."
>
> **CORDELIA:** "So you did this instead?"
>
> **ANGEL:** "Yup."
>
> **CORDELIA:** "I love you."

Angel's response is a big happy smile. Which causes a strange memory to stir in Cordelia—she remembers their client was happy about his eye right before he accessorized with a butcher knife. Gunn

343

and Wesley use concrete information from the Delancey School, which leads them to the Kramers' deserted house. The house is a dead end, professionally cleaned of all evidence. With nowhere else to turn, the gang heads for Caritas, to the dismay of everyone but Angel.

Lindsey and his guitar occupy the stage in the karaoke bar, and he has everyone in the room in his thrall. No, he hasn't done anything supernatural; he's just that good. The Host explains that Lindsey performed regularly before the loss of his guitar hand. Soon everyone but a petulant Angel is appreciatively listening.

Cordelia, Gunn, Wesley, and the Host shower Lindsey with praise as he leaves the stage, but he only wants to get an insight from the Host and get away from Angel as fast as possible. Lindsey accepts a drink, but doesn't stay to finish it, especially when told he and Angel are to work on discovering the answers to his questions together. The Host has a suggestion for Angel.

HOST: "'Cause right now he's got your case in the—forgive me—palm of his hand. Toodles."

GUNN: "If Lindsey's the lead, shouldn't we be following him?"

ANGEL: "You said the guy in your vision got a new eye, and Lindsey just got a new hand . . ."

WESLEY: "Right, then we should find out where the these transplants took place."

GUNN: "So we're following him, right?"

ANGEL: "Actually what we need to follow is his new hand."

Angel lifts a print from Lindsey's new hand off the attorney's discarded glass.

Lindsey follows his own trail, breaking in to Nathan Reed's office and opening files on Lilah and then himself. Bingo. He needs more information on the Fairfield Clinic, but now he has a starting point.

Angel works his own angles, getting a contact to determine that the hand's prior owner was one Bradley Scott, who served time for financial crimes. While Cordelia works on the computer's new keyboard to discover more about Scott, Wesley and Gunn quiz Angel about his sources. Angel confesses somewhat sheepishly that he no longer has Kate for inside information; he went to a private detective. Cordelia reports that Scott kept one appointment with his parole officer after his release, and hasn't been heard from again until part of him showed up on Lindsey's arm.

Lindsey and Bradley Scott's hand leave Nathan's office, and investigate some suspicious sounds from a room down the hall. He watches Lilah rummage through file cabinets and stuff some papers in her purse—which also holds some prescription bottles and a gun.

Lindsey's next stop is the apartment of Bradley Scott's parole officer, Sam. He doesn't know yet whose hand he has, but he's discovered that Sam will be able to help him find out. Lindsey talks his way inside using his connection to Wolfram & Hart, but is stumped when Sam demands a code word. When no code word is forthcoming, Sam clocks Lindsey upside the head with a pistol, then holds the gun to his head, pinning him against a table.

Paranoia from association with W&H has Sam on the verge of shooting Lindsey. Angel tosses a trash can through Sam's window, saving Lindsey's life and getting shot by Sam for his trouble. Keeping his grip on the lawyer, Sam peers out the window, puzzled by the disappearance of his second target. This allows Angel to get a rope around Sam's neck without violating the laws of vampires and invitations. Lindsey completely lacks gratitude, suggesting Angel has better things to do than save his life, like try to be the one responsible for ending it.

Angel has little patience for Lindsey's schoolyard antics, and he *does* have better things to do—like solve the case and relieve Cordelia's pain. He reminds Lindsey the case also involves him—revealing that Lindsey is wearing the hand of Bradley Scott—and starts questioning Sam, going vamp for added effect.

> **SAM**: "I'm not tellin' you zip. You can kill me but Wolfram & Hart'll do a lot worse."
> **ANGEL**: "Kill you? Why would I kill you . . . when I could live off you for a month?"
> **SAM**: "Dahhhhhh!"
> **ANGEL**: (pinches Sam's cheek) "Mmmm, can't you just taste that butter fat?"
> **LINDSEY**: "You're really gross, you know that?"

It works; a terrified Sam spills what little info he has: he only saw Bradley Scott once, then delivered him to a specified location.

Gunn and Wesley stealthily observe Cordelia, who obviously is still suffering the lingering effects of her vision. They quietly discuss the situation, and Wesley reminds Gunn of her hospital stay after Vocah attacked her. Without Doyle's half-demon constitution, Cordelia pays more of a mental and physical toll for the visions. Their concern rises when they hear her voice in conversation from the empty office, then ebbs when they realize she is on the phone with Angel, who reports progress.

Angel and Lindsey drive through Los Angeles in Angel's '67 GTX. Angel tells Lindsey about Kramer's eye, suggesting that he may have had the transplant done at the same place as Lindsey's work was done, then shifts to generally annoying Lindsey. They arrive at their destination, an innocuous-looking travel agency. Angel confirms with a bound and gagged Sam, riding in the trunk, that it is the right spot, and grabs a battle-ax. The lawyer and the vampire discuss the likelihood of high-level W&H security, then Angel tosses his battle-ax right though a Barbados poster, setting off an alarm. A quick battle goes in Lindsey and Angel's favor, and they move inside, then down a hidden staircase to a laboratory that would do Dr. Frankenstein proud.

Semitransparent chambers on both sides of the room each hold a human form—some intact, others missing limbs. Angel and Lindsey move through the room, drawn to the chamber containing most of Bradley Scott. Lindsey sees Scott and realizes they actually worked together at W&H in the early days, which increases his horror. He steps into Scott's line of vision, and the apparition struggles to speak.

> **BRADLEY**: "Kill . . . kill . . ."
> **LINDSEY**: "Kill who? Who do you want me to kill?"
> **BRADLEY**: "Kill . . . me."

Lindsey looks at Bradley and Angel, filled with indecision. Angel points out they have a finite amount of time before reinforcements appear, and Lindsey needs to act quickly, whatever that action may be. Angel walks to the side of the room with the people who haven't yet been vivisected, and starts freeing them. Lindsey apologizes to Bradley, then disconnects vital wires, shutting down the pod's life-sustaining functions. He continues down the row of dismembered souls, and then starts wreaking as much damage as he possibly can on the machinery.

Angel directs Lindsey to guide the whole people out of the building, then opens the valves of some handy oxygen tanks. A touch of a flame, and Angel hurries out of the travel agency just ahead of a huge explosion.

RESOLUTION

Angel, Gunn, and Wesley celebrate the closure of the case, a celebration tempered by the news Cordelia's still suffering some pain from the vision.

Lindsey, Lilah, and Nathan are back in the boardroom, this time with a gathering of Nathan's peers. Lindsey seems neutral; Lilah is wound tighter than a spring. Nathan gives a little speech filled with the formalities that look so nice later when the minutes are read, an effect spoiled when Lilah and Lindsey interrupt. Lindsey points out that obviously he has made the cut and she hasn't. The special determining factor? His evil hand.

Lindsey and his "evil hand" strut around the conference table, terrorizing the others. Nathan summons the security guard, but Lindsey and the "evil hand" disarm him, then shoot the guard in the foot with his own gun. Lindsey, gun in hand, holds everyone's attention as he tells them he believes they should've selected Lilah—oh, and by the way, he mentions the secret files Lilah holds on several of them. All in all, Lilah is far more devious, ambitious, and vicious; in other words, perfect Wolfram & Hart material.

"Me? I'm unreliable. I've got these evil-hand issues. And I'm bored with this crap. And besides, I'm leaving."

—*Lindsey*

And with one last completely inappropriate pinch on Lilah's behind, Lindsey departs.

Lindsey hauls his duffel bag and guitar case down to his pickup truck, dressed in his comfortable clothes, all signs of the smooth W&H drone left behind. He seems at peace with the world. Angel's come to watch him go—or to make sure he leaves—and they make small talk for a few minutes about the truck's still-damaged windshield. Lindsey prepares to drive off, and tells Angel he has no interest in returning to L.A.

"Good, I'm glad I didn't have to do something immature here. Don't drive too fast now, lot of cops out there."

—*Angel*

A dismissive Lindsey pulls out, the noisy truck bearing a large sign on the back: COPS SUCK. Case closed.

DOSSIERS

CLIENT **Lindsey McDonald**, the buttoned-down lawyer with the Okie singer soul, becomes Angel Investigations' reluctant client when their karmic paths cross thanks to The Powers That Be. Other peripheral clients include **Joseph Kramer** and **Bradley Scott**, the recipient and donor of random body parts.

SUSPECTS The long arm of Wolfram & Hart includes **the Fairfield Clinic**, where limbs are surgically and magically attached, and the unnamed laboratory, where parts are harvested.

CONTINUITY

Lindsey grabbed his cowboy boots but left his guitar in the closet when he headed out in search of Angel in "Epiphany."

QUOTE OF THE WEEK

CORDELIA: "Hi. You probably don't remember me. Cordelia. I know you're evil and everything but that was just so amazing."
GUNN: "That was kind of tight."
WESLEY: "Terrific, really."
ANGEL: "Is everyone drunk?"

Lindsey's singing provokes mostly positive responses from the gang.

THE DEVIL IS IN THE DETAILS

EXPENSES

Turkey, ham, roast beef, and vegetarian sandwiches, as well as soup and salad for Cordy
The private detective who came through with access to the NCIC and Bradley Scott's record
Sam the parole officer loses a window but acquires a trash can

WEAPONRY

Joseph Kramer uses a kitchen knife on his own eye. Angel uses oxygen tanks and fire to blow up the "travel agency" lab. Lindsey threatens his former colleagues with a handgun and shoots a guard in the foot.

THE PLAN

The Host's announcement that Lindsey and Angel should team up gets a less-than-enthusiastic response.

> **LINDSEY:** "I got a murderous hand on me and you're telling me to team up with the guy who cut mine off in the first place?"
> **HOST:** "I'm telling you what's what, sugar. What you do with it is up to you."
> **LINDSEY:** (to Angel) "I see you outside of this club, I'm gonna kill you."

DEMONS, DEMONS, DEMONS

Angel recognizes the **Pockla**'s insignias on the tapestries in the lab. He describes them as demon healers who know how to regenerate flesh. Oh, and *evil*!

THE PEN IS MIGHTIER

FINAL CUT

A scene with Cordelia, Wesley, and Gunn observing Angel after his night out with Lindsey for signs of reversion to the dark side was cut for length.

GUNN: "How you doin'?"

ANGEL: (so dark and grim) "How am I doin'? How am I doin'? How's it look like I'm doin'."

(The three exchange a look: uh-oh.)

WESLEY: "Angel . . . you need to get a grip on yourself."

ANGEL: "No, I need to get a grip on . . ."

(grabs Wes)

". . . you!"

(I'm not saying Wes hollers exactly like a girl as Angel bursts out laughing.)

ANGEL: "That was so great, the look on your faces."

CORDELIA: "That was not great. There was no greatness about that."

(She hits him with a book or something.)

ANGEL: "What, I can't have any fun?"

GUNN: "Didn't fool me."

(Gunn slips the stake he had in his hand back under the reception desk.)

According to the FBI Web site abstract: "The National Crime Information Center (NCIC) system provides a computerized database for ready access by authorized users to documented criminal justice information." They emphasize the "authorized." The private detective Angel hires uses a connection on the force to get information from NCIC, pointing Angel to Bradley Scott.

POP CULTURE

- **"That's an expensive operation. The shaman alone's a quarter mil—I guess they like you, they really really like you."** Lilah refers to Sally Field's flustered 1984 Oscar acceptance speech for *Places in the Heart,* which has become part of the national vernacular.
- **"Golly, Pilgrim, it sure is good to have you back in the saddle."** The Host channels John Wayne when congratulating Lindsey on his performance.
- **HOST: "Two enemies, one case, it's all coming together in a beautiful buddy movie kind of way."**
  GUNN: "They're supposed to work together on this?"
  LINDSEY: "Work with him? *Work with him?*"
  HOST: "Am I the only one who saw *Forty-Eight Hours*?"
  The Host suggests Angel and Lindsey think of themselves as Nick Nolte and Eddie Murphy from *48 Hrs.,* a 1982 buddy movie standard.

OUR HEROES

Building and Furnishing a Monstrous Lab 101 with Stuart Blatt:

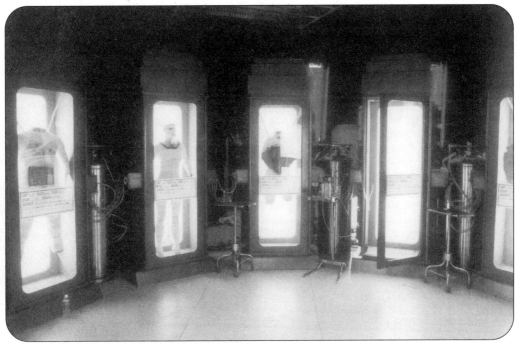

"We had the challenge of creating an underground cryogenics lab where the evil Wolfram & Hart are harvesting body parts. The [people] were to appear as naked. So we created our own versions of cryogenic chambers, and were faced with the challenge of how we put actors in there and obscure their particulars, without giving away the fact that we're just obscuring their particulars. So we were able to pump in a certain kind of smoke that sort of diffused as much as we could, and then we used discreet set dressing placed in particular areas to disguise unmentionables."

—STUART BLATT, PRODUCTION DESIGNER

Stunt coordinator Michael Vendrell helps fill the tanks.

"So tonight's the naked stuntpeople."

MICHAEL VENDRELL: "Which is a very funny story in itself. When they said we have to have five naked stuntpeople, I thought, oh my God, who am I gonna get to be naked. And they were quite sure, they couldn't be ugly naked people, we want attractive. So I went to Cheryl Lawson, who I just think is beautiful, she's radiant, she's beautiful. And I went to her and I kind of fumbled around, and I said, 'Cheryl, how would I go about asking a stuntwoman if they would mind doing a naked stunt?' She said, 'I'll do it.' So I go to Lisa [Hoyle] and I said, 'Lisa, would you . . .' and she said, 'Be naked? Sure, I'll be naked.' So it was a lot easier than I thought. Maybe because they're beautiful. For me, I don't think I'd take my clothes off."

James Contner reviews "Lindsey McDonald" and the "Hall of Horrors."

JAMES CONTNER: "Well, here's a character that started out kind of on shaky ground and sort of grew into this. Nobody knew where this character was going to go, or how many shows he was going to be in. This is a testament to Christian Kane, who plays the part. I think he really grew into the part and developed as an actor and really became a character that everybody liked. Or liked to hate. Whether you liked him or hated him, he was certainly an interesting character, who also had a chance to change in the course of things. He sees the light, in 'Dead End,' and realizes his role, as legal counsel to the dark world, is going nowhere. There's more to life, and he's tired of fighting these battles, and he wants to discover who he is. He's a guy who had a path in life, he became a lawyer, and got off on the wrong path, and now he wants to go off. I don't think we've seen the last of him. I can't say for a fact, but I know if the producers and writers have their way, they'd love to bring him back. I mean, I think the door's left open. I know David Greenwalt loves him."

"He and David Boreanaz played off each other so well. Those long pauses between them—they say a lot with a few words."

JAMES CONTNER: "That's been the thing I also like about this show. You're allowed to do those things. You're allowed to play moments. You don't have to be saying something all the time to convey what's going on between the characters. There's a subtlety to that kind of writing which you don't get in every series."

"We were on set almost to the exact moment you guys started shooting the naked stuntpeople. So how did that go?"

JAMES CONTNER: "Oh, that was scary. That whole scene just had such an eerie feeling about it. Coming in and finding all these tubes with these people being harvested for parts. It had a high creepy quotient factor to it. It's just great to see David and Christian, who have been arch-rivals and nemeses for one another for almost two seasons now, to find something to work together on, and sort of come to a meeting of the minds. Sort of one starting to understand where the other person's coming from. So you have this moment where they're actually working for a common goal, which is humanity. Which is kind of ironic, when one's a vampire and one's a lawyer. And it's all about humanity, it's all about saving these people. It's an ironic twist for the characters, and it's a wonderful moment. As simple as the parting scene is, it's one of those scenes where what's not said is as important as what's being said. You kind of just read between the lines."

SIX DEGREES OF . . .

Mik Scriba (Sam, the parole officer) plays a construction worker in 1998's *City of Angels*, which co-stars Colm Feore, who appears in *Pearl Harbor* (2001) with Eiji Inoue, the karaoke-singing "Japanese Businessman #2" in "Guise Will Be Guise."

TRACKS

Angel wants to sing Led Zeppelin's eight-minute "Stairway to Heaven," just to irk his team. Fortunately for them and the viewers, it's not necessary, as Angel's no Robert Plant.

Pretty girl on every corner

Sunshine turns the sky to gold

Warm, warm, it's always warm here

I can't take the cold

Streets littered with diamonds

Everyone is glistening

This whole world shines so brightly

I can't see a thing

She is pretty as a picture

She is like a golden ring

Circles me with love and laughter

I can't feel a thing

Bridge: Sky's gonna open

People gonna pray and crawl

Gonna rain down fire

Gonna burn us all

Sky's gonna open

People gonna pray and sing

I can't feel a thing

Executive producer David Greenwalt wrote the song that Christian Kane sings in this episode. It's called "L.A."

Christian Kane talks about getting to demonstrate his musical talent.

"I get to sing on this show, so it's kind of cool. That's the CD right there. David Greenwalt wrote it, but we recorded it, me and my guitarist. I'm a country singer. I have my own country band, Kane. Kanemusic.com, that Web site just came up, and man, there's been so many hits. We just opened it up and it went, bam, and it blew up, and we're like 'holy shit.'"

—CHRISTIAN KANE

Christian Kane also appeared as a struggling blues musician caught up in a star-crossed love affair in the 2000 made-for-TV movie *MTV's Love Song.*

FOR *ANGEL* SHOW, repeat third verse, bridge and go out saying, "I can't feel a thing, I can't feel a thing" and the third and final time just say, "I can't feel . . ." don't say "a thing" and go out on the E minor.
FOR LIVE PERFORMANCE, add one instrumental of a verse after first bridge.

"BELONGING"

FROM THE FILES OF ANGEL INVESTIGATIONS
CASE №: 2ADH19

ACTION TAKEN

The members of Angel Investigations dine out at a trendy restaurant, celebrating Cordelia's part in a national commercial shooting the next day. Cordelia is giddy with excitement, peering into the darkness for celebrities, and downing her food with enthusiasm. Angel struggles to be sociable and not air his gripes about the bill.

WRITTEN BY Shawn Ryan
DIRECTED BY Turi Meyer
GUEST STARS: Andy Hallett (Host), Amy Acker (Fred), Jarrod Crawford (Rondell), Darris Love (George), Brody Hutzler (Landokmar)
CO-STARS: Kevin Otto (Seth), Maureen Grier (Woman), Lynne Maclean (Claire)

"I'm not cheap, I'm just old: I remember when a few bob got you a good meal, a bottle, and a tavern wench."   —*Angel*

The table talk turns quickly away from Angel's days as a lout to strategies for disposing of the demon in Cordy's most-recent vision, a Haklar demon. Angel works hard to be included, but Gunn and Wesley steamroll right along. Scanning the diners, Angel notices something awry, and with that vampiric speed races across the restaurant to confront a woman about her choice of accessories. At a distance, at least, her shawl looks like a "Brahanian Battle Shroud woven from the skin of dead children." Up close, it merely looks expensive and like he is making a scene. Cordelia drags him back to the table, where they resume eating and try to avoid attention. Moments later, the diners are treated to the spectacle of Cordelia throwing up her expensive appetizer—too many long hours and vision hangovers to put raw fish on top of.

At the hotel later, Wesley calls his father to wish him a happy birthday, an onerous task that strikes a heavy blow to his self-esteem. When Gunn inquires into the well-being of "English, Sr." Wesley rallies to cover his filial disappointment.

Angel enters Soundstage 6 in search of Cordelia, but is distracted from his purpose by a pretty blond in a bikini . . . standing in front of an artificial beach. Angel, who hasn't seen direct sunlight since his encounter with the Mohra demon, basks in the studio-created sunlight. Cordelia is not pleased to discover him there, nor to hear he has questions about her vision.

Before Angel can get to the point, the director arrives and inspects Cordelia. He is not pleasant or kind about what he sees, in a petty tyrant way, criticizing a very pretty Cordelia in a very revealing string bikini made of seashells. Angel objects to the director's high-handed treatment,

resulting in a panicked Cordelia intervening for the second time in as many days. She resignedly tells Angel the info he seeks, then heads for makeup.

Back at the Hyperion, Wesley gives Gunn the lowdown on the "Haklar with two As." Amateur cameramen George and Rondell drop in unexpectedly, in search of Gunn's truck, with or without Gunn in it. Gunn gets ready to accompany them on their vampire-dusting trip to MacKenzie Park. Angel arrives with the Haklar's location, and Gunn makes the hard choice to accompany Wes and Angel rather than George and Rondell.

Angel gathers arms to slice and dice the Haklar, taking his bad mood out on the weapons. He shares his experience on the set with Wes and Gunn, describing how the director treated Cordelia like chattel.

> ANGEL: "And you know what the worst part of it is? She took it. When was the last time Cordy took crap from any of us?"
>
> GUNN: "Never and the day after never."
>
> ANGEL: "Exactly. He's also got her wearing this flimsy swimsuit that covers . . . like nothing."

And all three get that "straight guy picturing scantily clad woman" look on their faces. They break out of the moment guiltily, grabbing weapons to dispose of the Haklar.

Inside Caritas, the Host holds center stage, regaling the assembled humans and demons with a beautiful rendition of "Superstition." When the stage behind him starts to ripple, the audience figures it's part of the entertainment. A huge, ugly, tusked, drooling demon emerges through the resulting portal, prematurely ending the song and throwing the peaceful bar into chaos.

The Host stares at the demon with fear and a glimmer of something more. The beast charges through the terrified clientele and disappears into the night, leaving the Host to reassure customers in an insincere fashion.

Cordelia, in full beach-babe mode, smoothes sunscreen onto another actor's back, assisted by the bikini-clad woman who failed to make an impact on Angel. Unfortunately Cordelia is not making an impact on the director, who obviously hired her for some T&A, not her ability to act as though the sunscreen is the best product on the market *ever*. Cordy's acting talents serve her well as she swallows the tears that threaten to fall at his abuse.

She is sitting quietly on the ottoman in the Hyperion lobby when Angel and Wesley return from their Haklar slaying. Angel apologizes for interfering in her acting job, and she forgives him, still unhappy about the day's events.

"I just wanted to act, that's all. For them to like me because I was good. I never wanted to feel like this."
                                                                                                    —*Cordelia*

She asks about their undertaking, and Gunn. They explain that Gunn left separately to look in on George, Rondell, and the others, after they successfully killed the Haklar, no thanks to the power walkers it was about to devour. One power walker, taking political correctness to a new nadir, struck Wesley in the Haklar's defense. They all glumly consider the difficulties of life in L.A.

The Host fails to break the gray atmosphere with his request that they immediately track down and kill a Drokken that appeared via portal in his club. Wesley, Mr. Demon Encyclopedia, has never heard of a "Drokken," but the Host glosses over the details and emphasizes his request—kill it.

The club-goers emerging onto the nighttime streets and fatally encountering the Drokken would probably echo that sentiment, if they were alive to do so. The Drokken kills and consumes two men before turning its attention to a terrified woman a short distance away.

Wesley and Angel continue to try to get Drokken details from the less-than-forthcoming Host, and decide to try to search the area around Caritas for lack of a better plan. Cordelia looks ill, and they realize she isn't having a sashimi flashback, she's having a vision.

In this vision, Cordelia sees a young woman with long dark hair and an apple necklace working in the public library. She examines a large volume from one of the shelves, puzzling out the words. As she does so, a portal opens up behind her. The young woman screams in terror, and the portal sucks her in.

She relays this to the others, who immediately seize on the common link to their Drokken problem—a portal! They head out to the library, the Host tagging along resignedly.

Gunn has reached his home turf and found it unusually quiet. The sentry he quizzes is unresponsive, and he makes his way past the graffiti-covered empty hallways to a room filled with his crew. Gunn makes his way to the front of the room, the others parting before him so he is walking a gauntlet of silent stares. Rondell crouches next to a couch that supports George's corpse, and quietly reveals the bite marks on George's neck.

Angel and the Host scour the public library with Wesley and Cordelia in search of the woman from Cordy's vision, or other clues. They encounter Claire, a librarian, who rationalizes the Host's appearance as makeup for the children's program, and identifies the woman they seek. The Host wanders off to check out the venue as the rest follow Claire to the checkout desk.

Winifred "Fred" Burkle disappeared from the library's foreign language section five years before. Cordelia positively identifies a picture of her, and they learn she was studying to be a physicist. They investigate the foreign language section, and the Host catches up with them as Cordy finds the book she saw Fred reading in the vision. Without thinking, Cordelia rushes to read from the book, and the portal opens again behind her, much to the Host's terror and dismay.

Another traveler arrives in L.A. via portal. This one is tall, green, horned, red-eyed, and armed. He battles briefly with Angel, two warriors getting each other's measure, until the Host identifies him as his cousin, Landok.

> **ANGEL**: "You know him?"
>
> **HOST**: "Yeah. But just because I know his name doesn't mean you can't knock him unconscious. Please, continue."

But it's too late. The cat's out of the bag, and the demon's out of the portal. Landok, who prefers the more formal "Landokmar of the Deathwok Clan," is cousin to the singing green demon, originally known as "Krevlornswath of the Deathwok Clan."

Despite "Lorne's" attempts to disengage from the

conversation, a few telling truths emerge: Lorne is held in contempt by the family, most of whom assume he is dead anyway. Wesley in particular is enjoying the airing of someone else's dirty family linens. Lorne rallies and boasts to Landok that he is participating in the hunt for the Drokken. Landok is more than willing to assist, and volunteers his services tracking their dangerous prey, which he reveals can best be killed with a weapon dipped in thromite. Lorne points out the problem—there is no thromite in this world.

Meanwhile, Gunn struggles with extended-family issues of his own. Rondell blames him for George's death and doesn't hide his feelings as they build an impromptu funeral pyre for their fallen comrade.

Elsewhere, Landok uses his trained hunting skills to attune himself to the Drokken. Angel seems impressed by this demonstration, but Lorne scoffs at the "golden spawn." Lorne gives Angel a quick rundown on his problems with his home dimension—most of which make it sound rather like a paradise to Angel.

> **HOST**: "Talk about screwed-up values. A world of only good and evil . . . black and white, no gray? No music, no art, just champions roaming the countryside looking for justice? Bor-ing. Got a problem? Solve it with a sword. No one admits to ever having actual feelings and emotions, let alone talking about them. Can you imagine living in a place like that?"
>
> **ANGEL**: (longing for one) "Not really."

Cordelia and Wesley speculate on Gunn's continued absence, but are not tempted to investigate after the drastic consequences of the past. Cordelia is a little distracted anyway as she tries to get more of a big-picture handle on the case than just finding and dispatching the Drokken. Landok's endeavors are successful and he prepares to lead them to the Drokken's location and the future meals, aka people, it has stored. Landok also gets in a few more hits about Lorne's lifestyle choices.

The Drokken selected a dark pallet yard for its pantry. The gang pulls up in the convertible, top down, and Wesley is puzzling out the best strategy when Landok leaps out and disappears into the darkness in pursuit of the beast. Angel grabs a sword from the car and follows suit.

The Drokken appreciates their lack of a plan, as it leaps on Landok and buries its teeth in his shoulder. Angel charges in, but his not-dipped-in-thromite sword is not doing much damage. The woman the Drokken brought with it escapes deeper into the wooden maze. Wesley and the Host arrive with flares from the car. Landok demands his cousin help him regain his sword, despite the fact that his venom-infected wound is sure to be fatal.

The Drokken tires of playing with Angel and knocks him aside to pursue the woman. Angel follows it, and after a moment Wesley does as well. They use Wesley's flare for illumination among the pallets, not realizing the Drokken is above them. They divide to find the woman and demon, and Wesley succeeds at both.

The Drokken charges Wesley, knocking him to the ground, and the woman uses its distraction to escape into the dark again. Wesley force-feeds the Drokken his flare with no noticeable result. The Drokken moves in for the kill, and Angel knocks it away from Wesley at the last moment. They engage in another round of battle, which Angel ends by piercing the Drokken's neck with his thrown sword. Angel stands victorious over the body, exhausted, filthy, and triumphant. "That was fun," he says.

RESOLUTION

Landok and Lorne bicker over whether Lorne will perform their people's last rites if Landok dies. Cordelia intervenes with an inspiration—if they send Landok home, he will survive, and she thinks she knows how.

The cousins, Angel, Wesley, and Cordelia seek out the portal spot at Caritas, and set Landok and the book up in front of it. Farewells are said, and Landok reads from the book. The portal opens again, and the green warrior disappears. The Host proposes collective voluntary amnesia, and Angel and Wesley agree. Cordelia doesn't respond—probably because she is no longer in Caritas, but in a strange, creepy world unlike our own.

Case pending . . .

DOSSIERS

CLIENT

The Host is the client again, hoping to obtain their help in disposing of the Drokken without mentioning any messy details like the fact that he hails from the same dimension.

"You're still a knight for hire, yeah? Well, I'm hiring. I need you to kill something. I suppose you'll want the particulars, so here they are. It's called a Drokken."　　　　　　　　　　**—Host**

VICTIM

Vision Girl does an excellent job of describing the missing **Fred**. "She's tall . . . brown hair down to about here . . . glasses . . . pretty. She wears a locket . . . it's shaped like a ball . . . or an apple, I think."

Fred wears the apple in subtle tribute to Sir Isaac Newton and the apocryphal story about his discovery of gravity.

CONTINUITY

Wesley was fired by the Watchers Council between "Graduation Day, Part Two" and "Parting Gifts." The whole Angel Investigations staff was fired by Angel in "Reunion." Wesley became the de facto leader while the team was split, and Angel has deferred to him since reuniting with the team in "Epiphany." The Host and Angel teamed up to prevent the end of the world in "Happy Anniversary," and tracked their client through a university library. Gunn's involvement with Angel Investigations continues to impinge on his time with his old gang, who last appeared in "The Thin Dead Line," helping to save Wesley after he was shot by the zombie police officer. Cordelia is dressed in a revealing outfit, treated like a slave, and called "princess" by the commercial director. Sounds like Pylea.

Have You Seen Me?

Winifred "Fred" Burkle

Hair: Brown
Eyes: Brown
5' 7"
Medium Build

MISSING!

Since May 7, 1996

Last seen at the Stewart Branch Public Library

If you have any information

Please Call　(213) 555-0455

QUOTE OF THE WEEK

LANDOK: "The same Krevlornswath of the Deathwok Clan who refused the ancient tradition of hunting and gathering?"

HOST: "I'll let you in on a little secret, Landok. While the rest of you boys were off hunting, I was down at the waterhole chatting up the senoritas, gathering a little love."

LANDOK: "Your cowardice even extended to the sacred joust."

HOST: "For the last time . . . not a coward. I just saw both sides of the joust. How are you supposed to joust someone when you partially agree with their point of view?"

THE DEVIL IS IN THE DETAILS

EXPENSES

Angel spent $19 on Cordelia's sashimi couscous appetizer, plus the other trendy treats and a nice bottle or two of wine at the dinner celebration. Wesley places a long distance call to the UK on the office line.

WEAPONRY

Battling the Drokken, the team uses battle-axes, a scimitar, and a sword.

DEMONS, DEMONS, DEMONS

Haklar demons sound exceptionally nasty. Gunn describes it as a "big bloated thing," and Wesley is quite well informed on them.

> **WESLEY:** "The Haklar, descended from the Klenzen Order of demons, can weigh as much as three tons as an adult male. It awakes from its hibernation during alternating full moons only to feed and mate, often simultaneously. Incapable of traditional speech, the Haklar race has learned to communicate with each other via a complex pattern of carefully timed facial tics, not dissimilar to our own Morse code. The Haklar prefers a warm moist clime where it can—"
>
> **GUNN:** "Wesley?"
>
> **WESLEY:** "Yes?"
>
> **GUNN:** "I meant, how we go about killin' it?"
>
> **WESLEY:** "Oh. Your standard slice and dice."

"Funny story, according to my informant, liver-eating Haklars have different feeding grounds than the people-eaters, and I need to know which kind it was so I can track it down and kill it."

—Angel tries to get more information out of a tired and sick Cordy.

The **Drokken demon** is enormous, with blue-green skin and a cannonball-shaped head. Drokkens eat humans—ravenously. The best way to kill it is with a weapon dipped in thromite—failing that, one has to hit it very, very hard. Its bite contains poison fatal to Pyleans.

THE PEN IS MIGHTIER

FINAL CUT

Although lines were added in the final aired version, Angel's response to Cordelia remained unchanged in the closed captioning when the episode aired.

> **CORDELIA:** "Celebrities. They won't put 'em out here in the 'B' section, they'll put 'em back in the dark."
>
> **ANGEL:** (added) "Not like here where it's brightly lit and open and everyone can stare at you and . . ."
>
> **ANGEL:** (original) "It's a little exposed . . ."

POP CULTURE

❋ **"I didn't hire you to play Ophelia. Show the cleavage. Say the line. Got it? Or do you want to waste more of our time?"** The commercial director—or, as Angel calls him, "Mr. 'Hey, I'm L.A. Director Shooting A Commercial, So I Must Be The Center Of The Universe' Guy" disses Cordy's performance by comparing her to Hamlet's *Ophelia*.

❋ **"This reading room—to die for. Raked stage, rocking chair, fabulous colors. I'm tempted to just show up tomorrow morning with Harry Potter."** The Host is impressed by the library from which Fred disappeared. J. K. Rowling's novels about a young wizard attending a seven-year school have a huge audience worldwide and have caused some to proclaim a renaissance in children's reading. The first book in the series, *Harry Potter and the Sorcerer's Stone,* was released in the U.S. in 1999.

❋ **ANGEL: "I don't do big and crowded."**
HOST: "Mr. Elton John hits the first few keys of 'Yellow Brick Road,' I defy you not to feel like the only other person in the room."
The Host suggests Angel attend an Elton John concert with him. The singer/songwriter performed his Oz-alluding song on 1973's *Goodbye Yellow Brick Road.*

❋ **"Krv Drpglr pwlz chewrt strplmt dwghzn prqlrzn lffrmtplzt. Yeah, Pat, I think I'd like to buy a vowel."** Cordelia reads from the portal-opening book. If she doesn't succeed in commercials, perhaps she can be a game show host's assistant, like Vanna White for *Wheel of Fortune.*

❋ **ANGEL: "Lorne?"**
HOST: "Yes, Lorne. If you must. Though I generally don't go by that, because, well—"
(gestures to face)
"Green."
CORDELIA: "Hunh?"
ANGEL: (laughs) "Right. Lorne Greene."
(off Cordy's look)
"*Bonanza*? Fifteen years on the air not meaning anything to anyone here? Okay, now I feel old."
Although Angel seems to prefer his many books to television, he watched enough episodes of the Western ranch saga, *Bonanza*, to immediately understand the Host's dilemma. Lorne Greene starred as Ben Cartwright, and Michael Landon played his son "Little Joe" during the show's 1959-1973 run.

The Pylea Quartet is rife with references to the land of Oz. L. Frank Baum, who billed himself as "the royal historian of Oz," introduced the fantastic land and its inhabitants in 1900 when he published The Wonderful Wizard of Oz.

OUR HEROES

Alexis Denisof grows thoughtful about Wesley and his father.

"The show opens with Wesley realizing it's his father's birthday, and he has to call him and wish him a happy birthday, and on the one hand he's very excited to tell him about how he's running this fantastic operation, and lives are being saved, and good is being done. On the other hand, he's terrified to even speak to his father. And . . . it goes badly. His father leaves him feeling bad about [his life], and . . . this causes a prolonged confidence crisis in the character, which will be redeemed in the new world. We'll go into that arc with a lot of insecurity, and going back into an area that's an old nemesis of Wesley's, which has to do with his self-confidence and his ability to make clear, good decisions and be confident about them, and believe in himself and the others around him." —ALEXIS DENISOF

Amy Acker is shown for the first time, in a very brief vision scene. She talked to us about joining the regular cast in the third season.

"It was actually a pretty cool thing. Almost as soon as they cast me, they told me they were thinking about making Fred a regular for the next season. But it was pilot season and I was going to be doing a few things, so they had to make up their minds fairly quickly. So the process was much faster than usual. The producers can take a long time to decide if they want to hire you for the next season. But since I was about to commit to some other projects, they made the deal very fast. So that was a lucky thing." —AMY ACKER

J. takes a look into the heart of Gunn:

"In 'Belonging,' how did you find your grief for Gunn to express when George dies? He's already seen so many people he cares about die."

J. AUGUST RICHARDS: "It's cool because any time something like that happens, I think the character goes back in his mind to his sister. [He's] seeing the same situation occur, because Gunn can't let anybody go. So when George dies, I feel directly responsible, because I said that I would be there and I wasn't there. That's the heart of the character, in a sense. He kind of moves out of a place of guilt and responsibility. Which is so different from me. That's who he is."

Another dimension to the Host, as revealed by Andy Hallett.

"And it's not until this episode . . . where you do see a different side of the Host. The Host has always been large and in charge, and fully in control of every situation, especially in the bar. And now you're going to find that he is not, because he's very very very secretive about his past. Doesn't want anyone to know about his past, because everyone in his hometown apparently was mean to him, so that's why he got out of there. So when this beast shows up, [and] later his long-lost cousin shows up, he doesn't want anyone knowing about his past. You do see this real nervousness throughout the script. He's frightened, and it's just a completely different side to the Host." —ANDY HALLETT

"OVER THE RAINBOW"

FROM THE FILES OF ANGEL INVESTIGATIONS
CASE Nº: 2ADH20

ACTION TAKEN

Inside Caritas, the portal is closed. Landok is gone. And so is Cordelia. Angel panics, searching around for a hiding Cordelia, then grilling the Host, who is panicking pretty well himself.

Cordelia gets her bearings as well as she can in the new dimension, looking at the strange twisted trees, the two red suns above her head, and the complete lack of Angel, Wesley, or anything else familiar. She yells for help, then thinks better of it. Maybe closing her eyes and clicking her heels will help? Nope. She starts to relax and orient herself when she spots a giant hairy hellbeast eyeing her from a rock. Screaming seems like a good idea again, and she runs into the unknown, with the beast in hot pursuit.

WRITTEN BY Mere Smith
DIRECTED BY Fred Keller
GUEST STARS: Andy Hallett (Host), Amy Acker (Fred), Susan Blommaert (Vakma), Persia White (Agnes), Daniel Dae Kim (Gavin Park), Michael Phenicie (Silas)
CO-STARS: Brian Tahash (Constable), William Newman (Old Demon Man), Drew Wicks (Blix)

Angel grabs the book and readies himself to leap through the portal in hot pursuit of Cordelia. Wesley advises research and preparation before they do anything rash.

> **ANGEL:** "I don't wanna research, all right? I wanna jump through the big swirly hole thingy and save Cordelia."
> **WESLEY:** "We might never be able to get back!"
> **ANGEL:** (meaningfully) "It's Cordy."

Wes yields to the inescapable logic, Angel reads from the book, and the Host ducks behind the bar. They are all prepared for just about anything—except the actual result, which is nothing. Angel tries again without success, then tosses the book to the floor in frustration. Wesley suggests returning to the research idea again. The Host cautions them that perhaps they shouldn't be so eager to travel to his dimension, where it's not good to be human.

Cordelia rapidly discovers just that, as the hellbeast knocks her to the ground, then pins her there and waits for its master like a good hunting dog. Trensiduf of the Gathwok Clan, an old demon man, appears and praises Seekul for finding a "cow." Cordy barely has time to protest before she is bound, gagged, and hauled off to market.

360

At the Hyperion, Angel works to get more information from the Host while Wesley seeks answers in his many reference books. The Host doesn't have many answers about how to get from dimension A to dimension B; *his* trip was strictly serendipitous.

ANGEL: "But then . . . who opened the portal?"

(The Host holds up his hand like he's going to "make it talk.")

THE HOST: "Gift horse."

(he opens his hand's "mouth")

"Mouth."

(He deliberately turns his head away.)

Lorne purchased the building he arrived in, and erected Caritas. Angel presses for more details on Pylea, which the Host describes as a close second to Hell. Angel, who has a personal basis for comparison, is doubtful, but the Host provides an impassioned description of his home world's major failings—no music!

Research Boy is struck by an insight. The portal at Caritas did not open a second time because its natural psychic energy was depleted by the two recent uses. The one in the library may be "cold" as well, so they need to find a different gateway to the Host's world. And they need to take measures to ensure when they arrive in Pylea, they arrive together.

The fourth potential traveler chooses that moment to check in, much to Angel and Wesley's relief. Gunn's face is solemn. He knows Cordelia's missing and they're working on a rescue attempt, but he bows out. The loss of George weighs heavy on him, and he can't commit to an undertaking which may prevent him from ever returning to his original crew. He sits quietly in the War Wagon for a while before driving off decisively.

Angel thinks the Host is being empathetic when he agrees with Gunn's choice to stay. Actually, Lorne is being *emphatic*, stressing his complete and unequivocal dedication to remaining in this dimension. He leaves in search of an informant who can lead the others to a hot spot.

In Pylea, Cordelia is unceremoniously hauled into a village square and bartered to Vakma, an unpleasant old demon woman. The old demon man places a collar on Cordelia's neck, then cuts her bonds. Her protestations of independence are abruptly cut off when Vakma shocks her with the collar. They head out of the square, and a pretty brown-haired human woman watches the departure from her concealed location.

A different pretty brown-haired young woman is doing the psychic phone line thing when Lorne enters her cubicle. She disconnects her caller, and greets the Hollywood-incognito Host with a hug. Aggie is a walking contradiction, someone with real psychic powers working in an industry full of frauds. She knows the reason for the Host's visit, but urges him to explain in his own words. He fills her in on the need for a "hot" portal location, for the others to use.

AGGIE: "And you're not going with them."

HOST: "Aggie, I'd rather have a hydrochloric acid facial. I'd rather invite a hive of wasps to nest in my throat. I would rather sit through a junior high school production of *CATS*—do you see where I'm going with this?"

AGGIE: "Not to Pylea."

HOST: "Exactamundo."

Aggie is sympathetic to his position, but tells him that without his presence in Pylea, the trip to rescue Cordelia is doomed. Besides, he really should make one last trip to clear up those inner-demon issues that are clouding up his aura. Like many psychiatrists, the Host himself has a counselor, of sorts.

Wesley has found out more about portal travel, including the idea that iron or metal will serve to keep travelers together. Angel suggests handcuffs, which Wes seems to have readily available, but would rather not say too much about. Two piranhas in business suits interrupt their studies. Attorney Gavin Park and his associate deliver the latest salvo from Wolfram & Hart—the firm plans to buy the Hyperion when Angel's current lease expires in six months. Angel, focused on Operation: Rescue Cordy, barely takes the time to turn vampface and kick the lawyers out.

Cordelia, meanwhile, dressed in rags, is more than ready to be rescued as she works at the unpleasant task of mucking out the flehegna stables.

"I wanna be in my bed. I wanna order some Thai food. I wanna read the latest issue of *Marie Claire*. I wanna be doing anything but *SHOVELING DEMON HORSE POO!*"

(*ZAP!*)

"AHHH!"

(whispers)

"Woman has ears like a bat."

—Cordelia

Cordy's had enough, and starts to tug at the collar, hoping to remove it. From her hiding place, Fred urgently stops her, telling her if she succeeds in removing the collar, her head will go with it. Cordelia intermittently pretends to continue shoveling while conversing intently with Fred, who seems a bit incoherent, but better informed than the new arrival. Cordelia tells Fred about her trip by portal, but before Fred can follow up on this interesting information, the constable and his men forcibly remove Fred from the stable. They leave Cordy facedown in the muck and drag Fred off to face punishment for disabling her own collar and running away.

On Earth, Angel is completing a call with "if we don't come back" details when the Host makes it back to the Hyperion with the hot spot info. Wesley has an actual "Eureka!" moment, and they are ready to head to Pylea.

While in Pylea, Cordelia and Vakma shop, but Cordelia takes no pleasure in her favorite activity for once. Maybe because she is laden with all of Vakma's goods and the old demon woman snaps at her every time she opens her mouth. Things aren't improved when she is hit with a vision of a villager under attack from a Drokken. Instead of Cordy's warning being met with gratitude, she finds herself surrounded by superstitious villagers shouting about cursed cows.

Angel, Wesley, and the not-fully-committed Host drive close to the gates of a movie studio, enjoying the L.A. night air with the top down. Angel asks Wesley for reassurance that the metal of the car is enough to ensure their safe travel. Wesley is "almost" positive the car will work.

Gunn arrives, having had a change of heart after hearing Angel's telephone message, and after a last, futile attempt by the Host to stay behind, the four males buckle up. Wesley reads from the book, and they drive into the portal. The portal closes and nothing remains—except the book they open portals with.

The Angelmobile emerges into a beautiful meadow under Pylea's two suns. Angel's reflexive attempts to dodge the sunlight dissolve into amazed curiosity when he shows no signs of bursting into flames. Wesley pinches Angel's cheek to study this fascinating phenomenon. Gunn loses some of his enthusiasm over the portal ride when Wesley lets slip that they ran a risk of emerging a "freakish, four-man Siamese twin." The Host instructs them to hide the car, and they comply, Angel giddy with the gift of sunlight. "Can everybody just notice how much fire I'm not on?" he says. Gunn and Wesley do their elaborate handshake thing, and wonder about Cordelia's well-being.

A valid concern, as Cordelia finds herself the object of unwanted attention from the villagers, Constable Narwek, and priests. The constable verifies that Cordelia's vision proved true, and she protests quickly that she only reports the visions, she doesn't cause the events. Silas, a red-robed priest with a booming voice, announces they will conduct tests to ascertain that Cordelia bears the curse—tests involving a table full of torture devices.

The Angelmobile concealed under branches, the guys gather their belongings and prepare to travel into the nearest village on foot. Lorne leads the way, followed by Gunn and Wes, who calls back to Angel to bring the book with him. Everything comes to a dead stop as they realize no one has seen the book since they left L.A.

> **GUNN**: "Who had the book?"
> **WESLEY**: "Angel!"
> **ANGEL**: "Wesley!"
> **WESLEY**: "No I didn't."
> **ANGEL**: "No I didn't."
> **WESLEY**: "Yes you did."
> **ANGEL**: "Yes you did."

Wesley deduces that the book is probably tied to the dimension it opens portals in, therefore it could not travel to Pylea with them. Lorne is not consoled by the insight, but Angel rallies the troops by reminding them their priority is to find Cordelia before returning home anyway.

Cordelia has never appeared in more dire need of rescuing as she lies on the floor post-testing in a ball of pain, barely reacting as Silas proclaims the positive results. Two priests gather up her unresisting form and bear her away.

The Host leads them into the village and leaves the humans watching from an alley as he drops in on an old friend. It takes about thirty seconds for him to come running from the "friend's" house, with the owner in hot pursuit, shouting for his fellow villagers to join him in pursuit of the traitor/deserter/betrayer. The Host nimbly leads his gang through the alleys into the village square, where they are immediately surrounded on all sides.

The members of Angel Investigations have faced tough odds before. They charge into battle with little hesitation, Wesley prematurely confident of their victory. They end up bound and battered, kneeling in the middle of the square facing the constable.

The constable remembers Krevlornswath of the Deathwok Clan, evidently with distaste, and queries Lorne about his companion "cows." Krevlornswath's defense of his friends is definitely outside party lines, and he is hauled away for interrogation. When Angel and Gunn protest their mistreatment, the constable beats them, obviously hoping for more justification to continue. Wesley advocates diplomatic restraint.

Now in a dungeon, Gunn struggles with his bonds, while Wesley thoroughly inspects the walls in search of an escape route. Both ventures meet with defeat. Angel listens at the thick door for any useful tidbits and gets enough to determine that Cordelia arrived and received unwelcome attention. Despondent over their friend, they allow themselves to be led, in wrist manacles and ankle hobbles, from their cell and to the castle for sentencing.

RESOLUTION

They are surprised to discover a more-or-less intact Lorne in the castle antechamber. They confer briefly about their options, which are severely limited. The constable interferes with their conversations, expressing his delight with the Host's misfortune and imminent execution.

The doors open, they enter the royal chamber, and swing into action on Angel's count of three. They are still severely outnumbered and outclassed in the weapons department, but they are desperate to save Cordelia from the terrors of . . . being queen?

Case pending . . .

DOSSIERS

CLIENT Angel Investigations' own **Cordelia Chase** is their motivation for stepping through the looking glass and over the rainbow. The missing librarian **Fred** is in Pylea as well.

SUSPECTS The victims in this case seem to have brought about their own problems through the untrained use of portal-generating books.

CONTINUITY

Angel steps out into the sunshine for the first time since "I Will Remember You." He was briefly in sunlight in "In the Dark."

QUOTE OF THE WEEK

FRED: "I forget, it's not important. But if you take the collar off, bad things'll happen to your head, like it'll implode, so don't take the collar off, okay? 'Cause I can't talk to you if you don't have a head, okay?"

CORDELIA: "Okay. Are you a human?"

THE DEVIL IS IN THE DETAILS

EXPENSES

Someone is going to have to pay a hefty library fine for the loss of the book.

WEAPONRY

For lassoing those cows, there are self-binding throwing cords.

From the script:

A small table is wheeled forward, on it lots of rusty-looking pointy ouchy things.

The villagers also have axes, pitchforks, large bludgeoning tools, and swords.

DEMONS, DEMONS, DEMONS

Pylea is inhabited by a number of different-looking demons:

Seekul, the hellbeast that catches Cordelia, bears a strong resemblance to the hellbeasts summoned to disrupt Sunnydale's prom, with mottled skin and a reddish-brown mane. Unlike the hellbeasts in Sunnydale, though, Seekul is more of a hunting dog, trained to fetch but not to destroy.

Pylea's inhabitants come in a rainbow of colors—green, red, purple, etc. The social classes of the soldiers, villagers, and priests are based on their appearances.

AS SCENE IN L.A.

There's no place like . . . Paramount Studios?

"That was another big location that we did. They came to me and said, 'We need a Hollywood landmark where we can go through this portal,' and originally they wanted to do the Mann's Chinese Theatre. But to close down Hollywood Boulevard on a Friday night just wasn't going to happen. So we decided on the Paramount gate, and we decided we were going to try to close down Melrose. And it was touch and go for a while, because when you try to do something like that, the EIDC which pulls your permits and allows you to do those things, and the Department of Transportation has to okay all of that, and closing down Melrose is a major artery.

"So we had to get signatures because we were going to go late, and we had to get the okay of the DOT and the EIDC, and then also, fortunately, since [we already shoot] on the Paramount lot, they were accommodating in letting us do that. And we found out the day before that we were going to be allowed to do it. We were going to be allowed to close down Melrose and shoot that scene where Angel and the boys go running right toward the gate.

"Paramount did say they didn't want us to use their logo, so one of the things they did, tricks of the trade, they blotted out the Paramount logo with a little tree branch above the camera. When they pull up you can see the gate, but you can't see the Paramount logo which is right on the gate. They don't have to use any CGI, it was just a very simple thing that the producers decided to do to take care of that problem of not showing the Paramount logo." —KEVIN FUNSTON, LOCATIONS MANAGER

THE PEN IS MIGHTIER

FINAL CUT

The Host's opportunity to spread the Yiddish vernacular for "complaining" was cut due to length.

> **CONSTABLE**: "Krevlornswath of the Deathwok Clan, you and the cow trash are not to speak."
>
> **HOST**: "Aw, debunch your panties, Narwek. We weren't 'speaking,' we were just kvetching."
>
> **CONSTABLE**: (suspicious) "Ka-vatching? What is this?"
>
> (The Host opens his mouth, then thinks better of it.)
>
> **HOST**: "Forget it."

POP CULTURE

❉ The episode's title comes from Judy Garland's wistful song longing for another land and another life that lies somewhere "Over the Rainbow" in Oz in the 1939 movie.

❉ When Cordelia first arrives in Pylea, she tries a trick she learned from *The Wizard of Oz*. The Wicked Witch of the West's ruby slippers transport Dorothy Gale back to Kansas in the movie when she clicks her heels together three times.

❉ **"I wanna read the latest issue of *Marie Claire*."** The women's fashion magazine was published internationally for several years before debuting in the U.S. in 1994.

❉ **"Yes, it's a beautiful day in the neighborhood all right."** The Host, impressed by how much Angel seems to enjoy Pylea, evidently caught episodes of *Mister Rogers' Neighborhood* as well as *Bonanza* since coming to this dimension. Fred Rogers started treating preschoolers to gentle stories in 1966.

❉ **HOST: "Just remember, keep your head down. Xenophobia's kind of a watchword where I'm from."**
GUNN: "I don't get it. Why are they afraid of Xena? I mean, I think she's kinda fly."
Gunn gets confused by an apparent reference to the Warrior Princess who ruled syndicated TV for seven years before sacrificing herself to save 40,000 souls.

❉ **"Back up, Copernicus. That's suns. Plural."** The Host, pointing out the multiple suns of Pylea, refers to Polish astronomer Nicholas Copernicus, who laid the foundation for the modern understanding of our universe. He probably would have noticed something different about Pylea immediately.

❉ **"Of course I didn't know it was music—all I knew was that it was something beautiful and painful and right. And I was the only one who could hear it. Then when I wound up here and heard Aretha for the first time . . ."** The Host refers to Aretha Franklin, "the Queen of Soul," and one of Andy Hallett's musical heroes.

OUR HEROES

There are some advantages to Pylea, according to David Boreanaz.

"It was great. It was good to be outside, be in the sun. It was fun. Our call times were early. Six A.M. instead of having a three o'clock [in the afternoon], and going till four in the morning. But that doesn't happen all the time."
—DAVID BOREANAZ

More on Gunn's extended family from J. August:

"Episode twenty, after George dies, that's a really cool episode for me because that's when Gunn initially says that he's not going to go with them to rescue Cordelia, because he feels so torn between what's happened with his crew, and leaving them behind and saving Cordelia. So at that point, he decides that . . . Cordelia is a part of the family. I can't just let her die. I can't let her down. So he makes a very huge decision . . . to go to this other world and risk never coming back. It's not that he favors one family over the other, but I think they're all a part of his family, and it's one family. That's how I see it."

—J. AUGUST RICHARDS

Amy Acker was able to clear up one of the Big Questions:

"Is Fred going to be Angel's love interest?"

AMY ACKER: "I really don't think so. I doubt it. She was a scientist, studying physics, and I think she's there to help discover things, like Wesley and Cordelia do. But she'll also be readjusting to reality. 'TACOS!' She's a little nuts when she gets back, and I figure she's going to have a very hard time getting used to life in Los Angeles again. She'll see things in a very different way from everybody else. Plus I think she'll get to fight a lot. I've studied combat and I think that's part of why they wanted me."

"How did you show her as crazy without going over the top?"

AMY ACKER: "It's difficult because of the way we have to make our marks and things like that. For example, when I'm talking to Cordelia through the hole in the stable wall, I could peer directly through the hole, which is what I normally would do. Then I had to keep that sense of being off-balance. I hesitated a lot, and I let her giggle at inappropriate places. They let me keep my Texas twang, to give her another point of departure. All those years trying to lose it! But it was a lot of fun."

Costume designer Chic Gennarelli found vast inspiration in designing the costumes for the inhabitants and visitors of Pylea.

"David [Greenwalt] calls me one day and says, 'We need to talk about the end of the season.' I thought, oh, boy, this sounds exciting. He told me that they were inventing this other dimension. They weren't positive where they were going, it was unfolding as it happened. And he gave me some parameters of what he thought they were feeling, which was a medieval kind of setting with industrial overtones. [It] was exciting for me, because . . . I love period work. It's . . . what I'm trained in. And for me to mix real period with fantasy was the ultimate challenge. Because period is easy to do. It's already been done, all you have to do is copy it. But to mix it with a fantasy, futuristic, other-dimensional world, and demons intertwined in it, it was really exciting.

"So the first thoughts were of color, fabric, what we wanted this dimension to look like. What color the people were going to be. Every time they created a new character for the show, they were a different look. And since demons run this other world, they were all in masks. So I was able to decide the look, which was total soft color, dirty, worn, ripped, aged, medieval look. Not much prettiness going on at all with the village.

"I had to buy a lot of silk linen, to make burlap sacks out of, for Charisma, because I didn't want her to wear wool or burlap. So it's all made out of silk. So when you see her slave outfit, and you see her all dirty and messy, just know that that's silk. And she was just fine. A little cold, but she was fine.

"They wanted a warrior set. Each little farmland area has their own little group of warriors. So we did a warrior set, a mix of Roman and Greek and early European, all mixed together. It was really a lot of fun.

"Then they wanted palace guards. I wanted the village and the village people and the slaves to be all in their beige tones, and dirty browns, and maroons, and charcoals, and chocolates. And then I wanted the castle people to be in black and silver. And I really wanted the distinction of the tough palace guards, with the strong colors, so I put them in knee-high, black leather, modern lace-up boots. With modern black leather pants. And then over that, we did medieval chain mail, and Roman leather vests, actually.

"There is where the mix starts, because of the modern boots. Everything was in heavy leather, thick soles, and laces, which are not period correct but fantasy correct. And that gave me my industrial look. The villagers, of course, were all in medieval garb, even to the shoes. It was all period correct.

"But then when you got to, the Deathwok farm warriors, they had thick, modern, buckled, brown boots to go with their period costumes. Again, mixing the two sensations. Then we had priests in the castle running this whole place. So we've got the browns and tans and greens and grays of the village, and then we have the black and silver on the guards, and then we have the priests in—it's a very horrible way to describe it, but it is stomach-blood red. It's got a lot of brown in it, but it is a red.

"Then they decided that Cordy has a vision. So they make her into the Princess Queen, and here I wanted to really go a huge departure from everything else that we've seen so far in this other dimension. The realness of the monk-cloth fabrics, the colors, the tones, the softness of the fabrics, the steel of the vests and the silver, and I wanted her to be totally out of place.

"The first outfit, when we reveal her as the princess, I wanted to be colorful. I also wanted to really sock them with this industrial futuristic feeling. Her first costume [is] made out of silver and foil holograms that are pyramids. So when she moves, each one of these little holograms changes color and changes into a pyramid. Which, for my aesthetic view of the show, this is the fantasy part that doesn't have anything to do with anything in this place, but somehow these people, these priests are capable of coming up with this kind of outfit.

"So that's what I was going for, and I think we achieved it." —CHIC GENNARELLI

Pylea meant a lot of extra work for Dayne and the makeup crew.

"As far as the last few episodes go, once we went out into the other world, it dealt mostly with our Host character, Andy Hallett. It basically switched gears into the fact that we could shoot during the daytime, and Angel could be out during the daylight and didn't burn. So it meant we had to get up a lot earlier.

"I had days where I had manpower of up to like sixteen extra makeup artists just to handle some of the crowd scenes and some of the green characters that we used in the background, that looked like Andy. With the red horns and green faces, green hands, green legs, whatever skin showed through their wardrobe, we had to do that. So there were a couple days per episode where I had at least twelve to sixteen makeup artists come in and help me out."

—DAYNE JOHNSON, MAKEUP DEPARTMENT HEAD

Amy Acker tells us about the fun to be had at Paramount, where *Angel* is shot.

"I share a trailer with J. He asked me right away what kind of music I like, so I would like what he played in his part of the trailer. He made a CD for everyone called the Unofficial *Angel* CD. Every track was named for a character. Mine was "Let's Get Crazy." David's was "I'm a Soul Man." Cordy was "Visions" and J. was "Living for the City." Wesley was "Englishman in New York," Andy was "Music" by Madonna, and Darla was "Back to Life" by Soul II Soul. He gave one to everybody on the crew." —AMY ACKER

SIX DEGREES OF . . .

Persia White appeared as Aura, aka Girl #3, in "Welcome to the Hellmouth," *Buffy*'s premier episode. Aura is the unfortunate girl who discovers a vampire corpse in her locker. While we don't learn if Aggie shares the Host's musical talents, Persia is a musician, working on an album of "alternative rock, rap, and art fusion."

Amy Acker appeared in the 1999 miniseries *To Serve and Protect*; Michael Attanasio was the Unit Production Manager, and also worked on *Miami Vice*. So did Vern Gillum, who directed "I Fall to Pieces" for *Angel*. He also directed episodes of *Baywatch*, as did *Buffy/Angel* directors and writers Reza Badiyi and Bruce Seth Green.

"THROUGH THE LOOKING GLASS"

FROM THE FILES OF ANGEL INVESTIGATIONS
CASE N⁰: 2ADH21

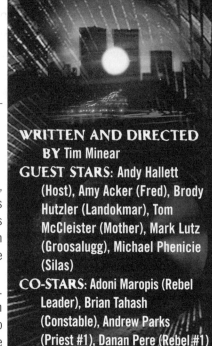

ACTION TAKEN

Having been brought into the throne room against their wills, Angel, Wesley, Gunn, and the Host try to fight with the guards who have taken them prisoner. But a familiar voice freezes them in their tracks. Cordelia. Alive and well. Wearing a crown and a gauzy outfit, and sitting on a throne. Not looking like someone who needs rescuing.

Cordelia confirms that, yes, she is now the ruler of Pylea. Wesley's suggestion she command the guards to release them is countered by the constable asking the princess's approval to gut them. Cordelia is not interested in gutting, but maybe some groveling? No? All right, then, off with their heads! The

WRITTEN AND DIRECTED
BY Tim Minear
GUEST STARS: Andy Hallett
(Host), Amy Acker (Fred), Brody
Hutzler (Landokmar), Tom
McCleister (Mother), Mark Lutz
(Groosalugg), Michael Phenicie
(Silas)
CO-STARS: Adoni Maropis (Rebel
Leader), Brian Tahash
(Constable), Andrew Parks
(Priest #1), Danan Pere (Rebel #1)

guards raise their swords to comply . . . and Cordelia countermands her order with a breezy "kidding."

Cordelia, power trip over for the moment, commands the constable and his guards to free the prisoners and leave them in her presence. He reluctantly complies. Wesley, Gunn, and the Host charge across the room, ecstatic to see food, and gobble ravenously. Angel seeks enlightenment from Cordelia, who explains that the priests tortured her, then named her ruler. Wesley puzzles over that for a moment, but the Host understands—Cordelia and her visions fulfill the terms of a prophecy.

"A prophecy. Great. Because those always go well . . ."

—*Angel*

It seems good old Silas and his group, the Covenant of the Trombli, have been in charge of the dimension for thousands of years. Their prophecy speaks of a messianic being with visions from The Powers That Be, and Cordy fits the bill.

Cordelia isn't that dismayed to hear about the lost book and unknown portal locations. After all, L.A. is home, but she's not a princess there. She is surprised, though, by the sight of Angel admiring himself in a full-length mirror. Angel seems bemused by the condition of his hair—which the others assure him is how it always looks.

Wes takes charge, delegating Lorne and Angel to visit the Deathwok Clan and ferret out information about other portals while he uses Cordelia's royal pull to visit the priests' library. Unbeknownst to the new princess, some of the priests dispute her royal status, but Silas has a plan—once Cordelia participates in a "Com-Shuk," she is disposable.

As Angel and the Host approach the Deathwok farm, they see some clan members wrestling. A particularly large, bearded specimen hurls another to the ground, then turns at the sound of Lorne's voice. Once she verifies Krevlornswath's identity, she spits in his face, loudly proclaiming her shame at his behavior.

"Your father was right. We ate the wrong son."   —*Mother*

Angel is stunned by her appearance and embarrassed for Lorne. The Host takes the abusive reception from his maternal unit pretty much in stride. He tries to get right to the point—can any family members remember seeing a portal around the time of his disappearance? His mother remembers the

family's happiness that he had vanished. She shouts for his brother, Numfar, to demonstrate the Dance of Joy. It's about what one would expect from a demon raised in a dimension with no music.

With that, she is ready to dismiss her prodigal son and his "cow" companion. However, Landok, returned from Los Angeles and recovered from the Drokken poison, hails Angel as a great warrior—probably the son Mother always wanted. He even rates a Dance of Honor from Numfar. Angel loses his leather duster, which is replaced by Pylean warrior garb, and is hauled off to the village square to recount his heroic exploits.

In the castle library, Wesley is in his element deciphering the trick to the seemingly incomplete volumes set before him. They are written in "trionic," with one thought being spread over three volumes. He sees no immediate references to portal locations, but he does decipher some passages about the Cursed One "Com-Shucking" with a "Groosalugg." Wesley arranges some of the volumes on the table into a disturbingly familiar order, and they rethink the idea of seeking assistance from priests whose sacred books bear the symbols Wolf, Ram, and Hart.

Angel has already told the enrapt villagers the story of evil Dr. Meltzer and his disembodied hands, and follows it with the tale of chopping off Lindsey's hand, to great applause. The Host suggests they hit the road, but Angel, perhaps a bit tired of all the brooding and atonement, is game for more time with the admiring throng. When Landok invites Angel to join the Bach-nal and swing the crebbil, Angel follows without a moment's hesitation.

Even with the unknown prospect of Com-Shuking before her, Cordelia is indifferent to Wesley's pleas to leave the castle and the priests' area of influence. Silas joins them in the throne room with updates for the princess: the Groosalugg is on its way from the Scum Pits of Ur for the Com-Shuk.

> **SILAS**: "The Com-Shuk is the Mating Ritual."
>
> **GUNN**: "I told you it was dirty."
>
> **CORDELIA**: "Yes, exactly. The Mating Ritual. Which is . . . great. It's been a really long time since I've had a good . . . Com-Shuk. So I'm just gonna run out for a minute because . . . 'cause I wanted to . . . get it a gift. And ya know, Groosaluggs, hard to buy for. So I should hurry."
>
> **SILAS**: "I must insist you not leave the palace, Majesty. The rebels are about. There are rumblings."
>
> **CORDELIA**: "Rebel rumblings?"
>
> **SILAS**: "We've doubled the palace guard."

Silas departs, and Cordelia needs no further urging to leave.

In the village square, villagers carry Angel on their shoulders, standing him on a platform and handing him an ax. Shouts of "Swing the crebbil!" fill the air, and the fugitive Fred is thrust across the chopping block before him.

Landok and the other members of the Deathwok Clan wait for the mighty war hero to decapitate the "cow," a great honor. Angel stalls, and when he sees they are committed to Fred's death, swings into action. He grabs the young woman and backs up on the platform, the odds of him and the crebbil prevailing against the villagers in the tiny category. Lorne provides an extremely unlikely rescue by breaking into song, causing his family and former neighbors to fall to the ground, covering their ears and writhing in pain. The palace guard is made of sterner stuff however, and one knocks the Host out despite his singing. Angel and Fred escape on a handy horse.

Cordelia, laden with booty, follows Wesley and Gunn to a trapdoor that leads to the sewers—the only real escape route, now that the castle guard has been doubled. The men go first into the stinky pit, and Cordelia adjusts her treasures before following. Silas catches her, and she quickly makes excuses. He listens impassively and gets to the point—she needs to prepare to meet the Groosalugg. She abandons her escape and heads to meet her fate.

In the meantime, Angel and Fred have put enough distance between them and the village that Angel suggests switching from their stolen horse to maneuvering on foot. He and Fred dismount, and he sends the horse trotting off. Fred gazes at Angel for a long moment, and says, "Handsome man. Saved me from the monsters. Bye." She tears off into the woods.

Angel follows, trailing her to a cave. It's obvious Fred has been here a while, and not only adapted the natural crevices and pools to suit her needs, but also used the walls as a sort of natural chalkboard. They are filled with indecipherable equations.

Fred frantically adds to the wallpaper, not reacting to his presence. When his reassurances that she is safe with him draw no response, he asks her why she doesn't want to talk to him.

"Because. You're not real. Or I'm not real . . . somebody here isn't real and I suspect it's you. So, if you're not real then that means my head came off back there and so I'm dead now. Dead. And with me being dead and you not being real I can hardly be expected to have some big conversation at the moment because it's just a little too much pressure, all right?!"

—Fred

Angel explores the cave as she works, idly handling different objects, including a California driver's license for Winifred Burkle. He makes the connection to Cordelia's vision, and tells Fred he knows who she was back in L.A. and that he has the means to take her back to that life. She embraces the dream for a moment, then turns somber and loses hope. Because this is Pylea, and "Bad things always happen here. . . ."

Back at the palace Cordelia sits on her throne, surrounded by her attendants, who make sure every detail of their princess is Com-Shuk ready. Her exterior may be ready, but her interior is far from it as Silas announces the arrival of the Groosalugg. The disgusting figure of a bentback demon enters the

doorway. Before Cordelia can devise a way out of the throne room and far away, the actual Groosalugg enters, casually telling the bentback to set his things anywhere. Ah, the Groosalugg, the undefeated champion of Pylea. Cordelia takes in the sight of the muscular, long-haired, strong-jawed, incredibly handsome male figure approaching to kiss her hand.

Intent on bringing Fred back to L.A. with them, Angel convinces her to meet his friends. Fred and Angel make their way from her cave toward the castle. They are in a rocky area when more of the palace guards ride down upon them. Angel shoves Fred to safety, and tells her not to be afraid of what she might see. Then for the first time in this new world he morphs—and is transformed screaming into an AngelBeast, as the vampire demon inside him emerges in its purest form.

The good news for Fred: the AngelBeast savagely dispatches the guards, chewing bloody bits of one as the last one mounted desperately rides away. The bad news for Fred: the AngelBeast shows no sign of recognition or humanity as it turns its gaze on her. The AngelBeast backs Fred up against a rock, no defense possible. It leans into her, bits of guard hanging from its teeth, and menace in its snarl. Suddenly, responding to an unknown sensation, it bounds away from a shaken Fred, leaving her alone.

In her throne room, Cordelia listens raptly to the Groosalugg's tale of his impure, half-cow lineage. She is smitten. They compare his story of being driven from his village with her story of her father's poor choices involving the IRS. The Groosalugg confesses he contemplated suicide, and Cordy's response is, "Get out!" This being another world and her being princess and everything, she is taken quite literally. She amends her inadvertent command to ask the Groosalugg to stay, to their immense mutual satisfaction.

Constable Narwek demands the princess process his prisoner, the unhappy and gagged Lorne. Her distracted command for him to take matters in his own hands has him shouting for the executioner, which gets Cordelia's attention back on task. She hurriedly pardons the Host, then shoos him out of her tête-à-tête.

Gunn and Wesley, lost and tired, are wandering the woods. They stop to get their bearings, and Wesley hears something stalking them. The dynamic duo stand back-to-back, ready for action, and the AngelBeast obliges them. It knocks them apart and Wes to the ground, stayed from its killing blow by Gunn hurling rocks at it. The AngelBeast turns its attention to Gunn, giving Wesley a glimpse of Angel's tattoo through its tattered shirt. Wesley shouts the bad news, and it's unclear how long Gunn can defend himself without having to try for a fatal blow.

Fred changes the dynamics of the situation by drawing the AngelBeast's attention with a bloody fist. She carries a leather pouch, donated by a former palace guard, filled with blood. She backs into the woods toward her cave, and the AngelBeast follows.

Wesley and Gunn assess the situation while Wesley applies a mud poultice to Gunn's wounds. Gunn rises and the two prepare to resume their journey—which is the cue for the rebel cows who have watched them from hiding to emerge and capture them.

Fred leads the AngelBeast back into her cave and past the reflective pool. The AngelBeast attacks his reflection, at first fiercely and instinctively, then more deliberately, reaching to touch the reflection of his hideous appearance with a clawed hand. Then he morphs, and a semi-catatonic Angel in his human form trembles on the cave floor as Fred reaches out a soothing hand.

In the palace, the Groosalugg's adoration starts to chafe at Cordelia, who admits to feeling like a bit of a fraud as a princess. The champion reassures her that actions matter more than titles, and points to her pardoning of Lorne as evidence she deserves her job. Cordelia, inspired, sends for parchment to start using her powers to change the world to reflect her ideals. Silas and the other priests react poorly to this inspiration, and conceive a way to rein her in.

RESOLUTION

In the rebel camp, the ragtag members debate their options. Wesley, who is bound but not gagged, gets their attention. Over Gunn's protests, he offers his and Gunn's services as messengers to the palace, since they know the princess. The rebels consider this idea, and decide a more persuasive way to deliver a message to Cordelia is by writing up a list of demands, shoving the list into the mouths of Wesley and Gunn, and putting their severed heads on sticks outside the princess's window. Wesley deflates, and Gunn asks, "Have I mentioned just how glad I am I decided to leave my people behind in L.A. so I could come here to die?"

The tables have turned in Fred's cave, with Fred attempting to console Angel, and him reluctant to respond. Finally he does, sharing his deep distress that the hideous beast inside him not only emerged, but also was seen by his friends. Fred reassures him that although she's seen the beast, he is welcome to stay with her.

Cordelia and the Groosalugg are using parchment, a feather quill, and the throne room floor to change their world. Silas enters, and dismisses the Groosalugg without ceremony. He has a covered silver platter brought in. Cordelia protests his high-handed actions, and attempts to reassert the power of her position.

> **CORDELIA:** "But I'm the princess—"
>
> **SILAS:** "The princess, like the Groosalugg, is a tool of the Covenant. Nothing more. You will do what we tell you to. If we tell you to mate, then you shall mate."
>
> **CORDELIA:** "You can't force us to . . ."
>
> **SILAS:** "If we tell you 'silence,' then you shut your cow mouth."

She persists in disagreeing with Silas until he presents her with the ultimate argument for her cooperation: the Host's head on the silver platter.

Case to be continued . . .

CONTINUITY

Landokmar tells the tale of Angel and the Drokken's battle in "Belonging." Angel tells the village children about chopping off Lindsey's hand in "To Shanshu in L.A." Landokmar requests that Angel repeat the story of evil Dr. Meltzer from "I Fall to Pieces." The Groosalugg learns a lot about Cordy's past. She refers to her previous experiences as the bearer of demon spawn in "Expecting" and "Epiphany." She tells him about her family finances being seized by the IRS prior to "The Prom." And she mentions her work in the suntan lotion commercial in "Belonging." Gunn reminds Wesley of his choice to accompany him and Angel and Lorne to Pylea, rather than remain in L.A. with his crew ("Over the Rainbow").

QUOTE OF THE WEEK

MOTHER: "Each morning before I feed, I go out into the hills where the ground is thorny and parched, beat my breast and curse the loins that gave birth to such a cretinous boy-child!"

HOST: "My Mother." Lorne takes Angel to the old homestead.

THE DEVIL IS IN THE DETAILS

WEAPONRY

Angel is offered a crebbil, an executioner's ax used during the Bach-nal celebration. The palace guards are armed with the usual assortment of period weapons.

DEMONS, DEMONS, DEMONS

Cordelia gets the story of the **Groosalugg**'s life in Pylea as a half-demon in bits and pieces.

> **GROOSALUGG:** "For my people, to be part cow is to be less than whole. There was nothing I could do to prove my worth. I was incapable even of performing husbandly duties with any of the females of my tribe."
>
> **CORDELIA:** "Oh, you mean, you're . . ."
>
> **GROOSALUGG:** "Anatomically equipped to mate only with a human."
>
> **CORDELIA:** "Good to know."
>
> **GROOSALUGG:** "I was cast out of my village. Cut off from my life-givers, forced to make my way on my own."

He threw himself into early battles in hopes of perishing, and acquired the Covenant's title of "Groosalugg—the brave and undefeated" by default.

The Groosalugg's valet is a hideously ugly **bentback demon**. A bentback named Mordar sang at Caritas once, much to Lorne's dismay.

As the **AngelBeast**, Angel's skin turns green and studded with bony, outthrust horns—a truly fearsome sight.

AS SCENE IN L.A.

Not all exteriors in Pylea were on soundstages.

"They came to us and said, 'We need another world.' They wanted some woods that looked kind of witchy, or kind of spooky. And there's a great set of woods out at Hidden Valley, which is Lake Sherwood, at a ranch called Rancho de la Fresno. And when Cordelia arrives in the other world, that's where she appears, in what we were calling the Witchy Wood. And where the demon beast comes and licks her and everything. It's a really interesting and kind of spooky, magical look, and that's what they wanted, and there's not a lot of that in L.A. Some of the other woods, when Angel and the boys arrive, was over at Ventura Farms, which is a big ranch complex that has a lot of different looks. And that's also where the rebel camp was. And then the episode where he's riding on a horse and he comes around a rock, that's over at Ventura Farms. The Pylea village is Veluzat; that also was the Boxer Rebellion. They re-dressed it and I have to say Stuart Blatt, who's the production designer, has done a great job when it comes to that little area there. And then they did the CGI castle up on the hill there. In Tim Minear's episode, which I believe is episode twenty-one, they went back to the Witchy Wood over at Rancho de la Fresno, where they kind of show the entrance to the cave where Fred's hiding. From there, they went back to Ventura Farms and shot, and the village of Pylea. Those were basically the three different locations that we used for the last three episodes."

—KEVIN FUNSTON, LOCATIONS MANAGER

THE PEN IS MIGHTIER

FINAL CUT

The Groosalugg's gift for his princess did not make it on screen.

"Just put those anywhere."

(His valet, the bentback, deposits the wet, squishy tentacles.)

"Majesty . . ."

(re: tentacles)

"I bring you tribute from the kill. The Mogfan Beast is defeated. The Scum Pits of Ur are safe once again for travelers."   —*Groosalugg*

POP CULTURE

❖ **"Off with their heads!"** In *Alice in Wonderland,* the Queen of Hearts was fond of commanding, "Off with their heads," to punish transgressions such as planting the wrong color roses. Princess

Cordelia echoes the sentiment when her friends are brought before her, but quickly reveals that she was kidding.

❖ **WESLEY:** "Fascinating . . . a hart."
CORDELIA: "That's not a heart. It's a Bambi. And we expect him to read this teeny tiny print?"
WESLEY: "No, no. Not H-E-A-R-T. H-A-R-T. The male red deer, or 'staggard,' is often associated with rural mysticism."

Felix Salten's 1923 novel *Bambi, A Life in the Woods* told the story of a young deer prince. Cordelia, one suspects, probably is more familiar with Walt Disney's 1942 movie.

❖ **"Well! You're just a regular Hans Christian Tarantino, aren't ya?"** The Host refers to Hans Christian Andersen, who wrote some of the saddest well-known fairy tales. He created more than 150 stories, including "The Little Mermaid" and "The Snow Queen," between 1835 and his death in 1875. Writer, director, producer, and actor Quentin Tarantino is known for the consistent over-the-top violence in his projects. Lorne sees Angel's graphic tales of life in L.A. for the village children as a bizarre mix of the two.

❖ **WESLEY:** "Shhh—"
GUNN: "You havin' a Blair Witch moment?"

The Blair Witch Project was a 1999 pseudodocumentary film about three students lost in the woods without the skills to follow the river out and about the spooky things which happen to them. Pylea has plenty of Witchy Woods.

SIX DEGREES OF . . .

Numfar of the Deathwok Clan, who does the Dance of Joy and the Dance of Honor, is played by Joss Whedon.

OUR HEROES

"What did you think when you saw the script and learned you were going to be the AngelBeast?"

DAVID BOREANAZ: "Jeez, I didn't want to be in the makeup, I'll tell you that. It was pretty horrifying. It was a pretty ugly thing. Which was really pretty much the theme for this whole season, though. The way he was the whole season. So he came to grips with his problem."

"How long did your makeup take?"

DAVID BOREANAZ: "[About three and a half hours.] I was only in that thing once. I couldn't deal with it. The stuntperson was in that more than I was."

The Groosalugg's name evokes Sergio Aragones's "Groothe Wanderer," a mighty–but mighty goofy–warrior who succeeds in battle despite himself. He was created by the popular <u>Mad</u> magazine cartoonist as a humorous homage to <u>Conan the Barbarian</u> and has starred in dozens of comic books.

The Venerable Monarch of Pylea, General of the Ravenous Legions, Eater of our Enemy's Flesh, Prelate of the Sacrificial Blood Rites, Sovereign Proconsul of Death, talks about life in a metal bikini and tiara.

"Is there anything special you'd like to say about being a fairy princess?"

CHARISMA CARPENTER: "It's bitchin'. It's great to be queen. It's a lot of fun. But it's also very binding, and cold [since these episodes were shot in winter]. When it's snowing and there's ice on the camera cases, that was interesting."

"Is it more like playacting, these last few episodes?"

CHARISMA CARPENTER: "Yeah, it feels surreal. Like, these last few episodes have felt so epic and grandiose. I feel like Elizabeth Taylor may have felt as Cleopatra. I'm told that I wear it well, so maybe all those years of practice came off. One of the grips, actually Matt Mania, who's key grip, he always calls me 'Princess' anyway, and so now that I have a crown on I haven't heard the end of it. And I think he means it as a compliment."

Amy Acker talks about her first days on the set.

"Everyone gets along well. The first day of my second episode, my first scene was sitting on the horse behind David. We were supposed to kind of trot into the frame. But David decided to play a little joke on me. He made the horse just really run, and I started to fall off the back. I had my arms around his waist so I pulled him down, too, and we just sort of fell in slow-motion to the ground. I went first, and then David fell on top of me. All very slowly; it was so weird.

"He really apologized. The next day we were both really sore. And someone told me to go see this man standing off to one side. I thought he was going to give me a massage, so I sat down in this chair and waited for a nice massage. But he grabbed my head and gave me a twist! He was a chiropractor! So those were two days on the set of *Angel*."

—AMY ACKER

Dressing Princess Cordelia continues to be a pleasure.

"What I wanted to do was make her, of course, as sexy as possible, and as revealing as the producers wanted it, so I designed this kind of princess slave girl outfit. And I called a company up in Berkeley, California, and they actually made [it] for me, out of gold coins—actually, they're not gold, they're probably brass coins, but they are real coins, and they're all antiques. [The producers] said it was okay to leave her in the same outfit and just rip the skirts off, and I said, 'I don't think so. She needs a little sex outfit.' So then we did the gold coin outfit. The whole thing, from the crown, which has little hearts in it, to her top which is all the gold coins, and the skirt overlay is all gold coins, and the gold chiffon, and the shoes with the straps, like Lucite platform five-inch heels with gold straps up to her knee. I just can't tell you how happy I was. It came out better than I thought. And she's so spectacular-looking anyhow, that I think it's really going to do the show perfect to have that bit of beauty there. So that was Cordy, and that was really the crowning jewel to this whole event."

—CHIC GENNARELLI, COSTUME DESIGNER

And Dayne Johnson worked on her knight in shining armor, the Groosalugg.

Original script description:

A quite literal BRONZE GOD—half human, half something else. But all the best halves. Bronze metallic skin glowing, pure blue eyes flashing. Dressed in Lancelot gear.

DAYNE JOHNSON: "He's not colored anymore. He has normal skin—they nixed all the colors—and he has blue contacts and he has long hair."

"That's very different from what we saw."

DAYNE JOHNSON: "Yeah, they changed it. I [think both] I myself and the producers felt that painting him a color kind of lost some of the sex appeal. Which I think was a good move. That made him sexier, and you could see his features and see his eyes and see things better without him being colored. We went through gold, and we went through silver, and after silver we stopped."

"With Angel *basing everything on 'strict reality' except for the last three episodes, does that make it easier or harder?"*

KELLY MANNERS: "Well, reality makes it easier, because everything's here. To go out and find another world, a medieval world at that, is tricky. For example, we need an exterior of a castle on this, and I actually considered the idea—there are some castles around, but they're outside the zone. So instead we're doing it all through the magic of CGI and a miniature. We're building a miniature castle. And then we have our castle wall, which is on stage. So reality is much easier, because to go find a building or a subway tunnel or an alley is very easy. Go find a medieval village, not so easy. A castle wall, with dirt and greens, is going to cost you about twenty thousand dollars."

DAVID M. BURNS, ASSISTANT TO MR. MANNERS: "But it's a well built wall."

STUART BLATT: "The guy who made our model is Greg Jein. He worked on *Close Encounters* and *Star Wars* and *Star Trek* and *The Mists of Avalon*, and lots of big, really cool projects. He's been on Academy Award-nominated crews."

"How much time will it be on screen?"

STUART BLATT: "Maybe ten seconds, maybe four seconds."

"How much will be actually built?"

STUART BLATT: "Two sides. We just want to give one perspective from one angle. We shoot low up on the hillside."

"What's your favorite part of your job?"

STUART BLATT: "Figuring out how to present and achieve the bizarre things they come up with

379

in the scripts. The most fun thing is really to be able to deliver something that seems totally impossible. A Chinese rebellion. A medieval village. A miniature of a castle. Most TV shows don't reach our magnitude. They don't attempt as much as we do."

"If you did it on the cheap, would it be a matte? Would it be CGI?"

STUART BLATT: "No, this was proven to be much cheaper than a matte. We still have to do CGI work. Loni Peristere still has to take this image, once they shoot it, and composite it onto a plate shot of the village, so we can have the village in the foreground and the castle up in the hills in the background. So there's still work to do. But he's not having to create this. He's not having to do a 3-D rendering or pay for a matte painting. It's going to cost a minimum of ten thousand dollars for a matte painting. So we'd rather do this and get more vantage points out of it. With a matte painting you can't really get any other vantage point than what you paint, whereas here, with a literally three-dimensional model, you can move the camera around it, and sort of creep along one of the walls, or up one of the walls, or up one of the turrets to one of the windows."

TRACKS

"Tim and I spent a lot of time working on a sound for the Bach-nal event in the village square. He wanted tribal elements, and a hint of *Planet of the Apes* with horn-type battle calls etc. You might hear a little of 'Stop! In the Name of Love' during an action scene in 'Through the Looking Glass.' It was Tim's idea, and I thought it wouldn't work. That's why he's the ideas man: it worked great! Lots of fun working on the music for that episode!"   —ROBERT KRAL

"Stop! In the Name of Love" is an effective weapon against the Deathwok Clan, as well as a huge hit for Diana Ross and The Supremes.

"THERE'S NO PLACE LIKE PLRTZ GLRB"

FROM THE FILES OF ANGEL INVESTIGATIONS
CASE № 2ADH22

ACTION TAKEN

Cordelia sobs over Lorne's severed head. The last thing she expects, as she wishes she were home, is for him to open his eyes and agree with her.

"My people, the fun-loving Deathwok Clan, you cut off our heads, we just keep on a-tickin' until you mutilate our bodies—obviously they haven't gotten to my body yet, probably a backlog in the mutilation chamber, so if we move quickly and quietly—"
—*Host*

**WRITTEN AND DIRECTED
BY** David Greenwalt
GUEST STARS: Andy Hallett (Host), Amy Acker (Fred), Brody Hutzler (Landokmar), Mark Lutz (Groosalugg), Michael Phenicie (Silas), Tom McCleister (Mother), Lee Reherman (Captain)
CO-STARS: Jamie McShane (Rebel Two), Adoni Maropis (Rebel Leader), Danan Pere (Rebel One), Alex Nesic (Slave One), Andrew Parks (Priest One), Whitney Dylan (Slave Wench)

Cordelia needs directions from someone, but Markello, the first slave, seems like a bad choice. He hurries from her royal presence to report her distress to Silas, who is coordinating hunting parties with the captain of the palace guards. Their objectives: Gunn, Wesley, and Angel. They are particularly anxious to dispose of Angel, not just because of his rescue of Fred, but also because they connect his act with the rebel uprising.

PRIEST ONE: "He is a Van-tal, a drinker of blood—he can only be killed by fire, decapitation, or a wooden spear through the heart."

SILAS: "Perhaps all three, just to be thorough. Take a tracker beast to the woods where he killed your men, hunt him down."

CAPTAIN: "It shall be done, my lord. I will personally bury my spear in his rump."

Silas points out that Angel's heart is "where a cow's is," in the chest. After the captain leaves, suspecting a little rebel espionage in the palace, Silas rewards Markello for passing along key information by causing his head to explode. Silas gloats over the master device connected to all of the slave collars, by which he can do the same to any of the slaves.

Heads are about to part company with their bodies in the rebel camp as well. Wesley and Gunn, locked in stocks, kneel awaiting the fatal blow. Their lives are saved by the arrival of the palace guards, whose attack prevents the rebels from beheading the very men the guards intend to kill. The two rise, contemplate escape, then throw in their lot as best they can to join the rebel defense.

Fred prepares a Pylea-style breakfast as Angel still agonizes about the appearance of his internal demon. She may be crazed, but she has a strong practical streak, as she points out that internal demons are pretty much universal, and he shouldn't let his prevent him from interacting with others.

Meanwhile, The Light That Shines in Darkness Upon [The] Land summons a serving wench for some mutilation chamber assistance.

CORDELIA: "You have served me long and loyally these last two and a half . . . days, I'm very fond of you, Lamara."

SERVING WENCH: "Marelda."

CORDELIA: "I knew that."

SERVING WENCH: "Of course you did, Exalted One, you know all. You must cut my tongue out of my worthless skull."

CORDELIA: "No! No cuttin'. What is it with you people and mutilation?"

SERVING WENCH: "We don't have a lot of entertainment, M'um."

Cordelia asks Marelda to guide her to the mutilation chambers, but evidently that is against royal protocol. Time for Plan B: Cordelia gets her wench to disrobe, and catches the Host peeking.

Angel enjoys the sunlight that makes its way into Fred's cave. They discuss the pros and cons of life in Pylea. Pro: daytime activities, reflection. Con: the AngelBeast. Angel changes the subject to Fred's messy equations, and she tells him she's made innumerable attempts to correctly proclaim the "constant representations of a mathematical transfiguration formula" and open a portal home, but none have worked. He theorizes she has succeeded, but the portals have opened elsewhere—like near the Deathwok farm.

They are so deep in conversation the attack from the captain and some select palace guards takes them by surprise. Angel fights using all the skills his two-plus centuries have given him, but even so his human body fails him. He resists the impulse to change to the AngelBeast, and the captain takes advantage of this to shove him to the cave wall, a spear through his chest. Fortunately for Angel, the captain lacks practice at dusting vamps, and misses on his first few efforts. Things look grim, until intrepid Fred uses a handy rock to knock the captain unconscious. Not knowing Angel's nasty habit of getting repeatedly pierced and recovering, she rushes to his side, pleading with him not to die.

The soldiers, despite their superior weapons, have underestimated the rebels and lost. There have been casualties on the rebels' side as well, including their erstwhile leader. The remaining rebels set Wes and Gunn free, convinced by the "enemy of my enemy is my friend" philosophy. Wesley proposes a search for Angel, but Gunn counters with the suggestion they ally forces with the rebels, increasing their options for storming the castle. Besides, thinking of his recent loss back in L.A., he doesn't want to leave without helping if they can.

Fred prepares herbs for Angel's wounds, but with his vampire healing factor they are hardly needed. He confesses he doesn't want to change into the AngelBeast again for fear that he won't be able to change back. Fred insists he's not a beast, and the captive captain laughs at her naïveté. Fred is ready to feed him to the local Drokken, but Angel wants information. The news is discouraging—Cordelia is destined to die post-Com-Shuk, and Lorne has been beheaded. Angel is finally motivated to leave the cave, over Fred's protests.

> **FRED**: "They'll kill you and you'll turn into the beast—maybe not exactly in that order."
> **ANGEL**: "My friends are in trouble."
> **FRED**: "But the beast, I know you don't want them to see you that way . . . I'm not afraid of it like everyone else—"

The captain proves his loyalty to the priests by slipping his bonds and lunging with his knife. He cuts Fred's arm before Angel kills him with his own knife. Now it's Angel's turn to care for an injured Fred.

Cordelia makes her way through the bowels of the castle to the mutilation chamber. From the sound of things, it's just part of the entertainment, with the torture chambers nearby. The Head is with her in a bucket. Whoever is in charge of mutilations is not too tidy, as there are various icky substances on the floor and demon body parts are haphazardly piled in the corner. Including some parts wearing a fashion statement unique to Earth, to the Host's dismay. Clearly his body has already been destroyed. He's about to start his own eulogy when a sound causes them to duck deeper in the shadows. Cordelia is vastly relieved to see the Groosalugg instead of an enemy.

The contradiction of the Host's still-active head and dismembered suit are resolved by the Groosalugg, who acted on his own impulses rather than priests' orders for the first time, and gave Lorne's body to Landok to bear safely to the Deathwok farm. Cordelia, nearly as happy as the Host, warmly embraces the Groosalugg, proclaiming him a true hero.

The rebels are fervent but disorganized and quarrelsome about the best approach to the castle. Wesley intervenes with a few choice observations, and swiftly finds himself promoted from kibitzer to uneasy leader of the rebel forces.

> **WESLEY**: "Why do people keep putting me in charge of things?"
> **GUNN**: "I have no idea."

Angel, having disposed of the captain's corpse and dressed Fred's wound, is ready to leave. He and Fred exchange farewells and he exits the cave—only to return momentarily asking for directions. In spite of her reluctance to leave the security of her cave, Fred volunteers to show him the way.

The Groosalugg and Cordelia's romance is set aside for a theological discussion, as he frets about his rebellious act. She points out that defying evil is a good action for a hero, and they should plan more ways for him to act against the priests. The Groosalugg, smitten, protests his unworthiness to take her visions upon himself when they mate. Surprisingly Cordelia, far from being pleased at being relieved of her gift from The Powers That Be, nixes the idea.

> **CORDELIA**: "Groo . . . I can't give up my visions. I like them. Okay, I don't like the searing pain and agony that is getting steadily worse."
> **GROOSALUGG**: "You are pure human, you are not meant to carry such a burden."

CORDELIA: "Maybe not, but I'm not ready to give 'em up, either. They're a part of who I am now. They're an honor. And you know, the visions, they only last for— GWAAAGGGGGG!"

And Cordelia gives an abrupt demonstration of what it means to receive a vision, ending up in tears in Groo's arms. Her vision, although she lacks details, is of him in a battle to the death with the AngelBeast, who she does not recognize, in his green-skinned, horned glory, as her former boss.

Wesley has plans for the Groosalugg as well, as he applies himself to the task of rescuing Cordelia. As Champion of the Land, the Groosalugg must battle all challengers. Wes carefully studies the sketch of his enemy's other "big gun," the Slave Killer Console. The rebels agree Silas must not get a chance to use it, but despair at entering the well-guarded castle.

Angel, Fred right beside him, is suddenly in their midst, unchallenged. He introduces Wesley and Gunn to Fred. The rebels investigate their shabby border guards, leaving the friends with a quiet moment together. Everyone is eager to return to L.A., and Angel mentions Fred's portal skills. Unfortunately Fred's response is rather manic, leaving Wes and Gunn concerned for their fate.

More reunions take place as the sentries bring in Landok. He explains his burden to Wes and Gunn, who haven't heard of Lorne's decapitation, and the four take a solemn look at the head. Angel, Wesley, and Gunn mutter a few inadequate words, and the Host promptly rebukes them. The three go flying back in surprise, with only Fred taking a talking disembodied green demon head in stride.

Landok leaves for his clan's home in search of his kinsman's body. Wesley and his ragtag rebels plan to storm the castle, both to free the slaves of their control collars and to rescue Cordelia. A quiet, determined group gathers around the campfire that night, knowing not everyone will survive their undertaking.

Now a sober leader, Wesley gives Angel his assignment—lure the Groosalugg out from the castle by issuing a challenge, then kill him. Angel protests, as only the AngelBeast will be able to prevail against the Groosalugg. Wesley has taken that into account, but clasps his friend's shoulder and expresses confidence in his ability to suppress the beast after. Angel and Fred slip off into the night.

Gunn asks if Wesley is really that sure about Angel, and Wesley tells him he isn't, but he needs Angel to believe in himself. Gunn is left wondering if this new, coldly efficient Wesley is really an improvement over the old one.

Groo has helped his princess, still stricken from her vision, onto a couch instead of the floor—a move an impatient Silas interprets as progress toward the Com-Shuk. The priest, who has reinforcements, is ready to forcefully encourage Groo and Cordelia to mate. A potentially ugly scene is prevented when Silas and the Groosalugg are called to investigate a disturbance in the village.

Angel, with Fred coaching from the wings, issues a formal challenge to the Groosalugg, then follows it up with some old-fashioned name-calling. The incensed Groosalugg's battle fever is fanned by Silas whispering inflammatory lies about Angel's evil intentions toward Cordelia in his ear. Not even the heartrending pleas of his concerned princess can prevent him from heading to answer the challenge.

Once the Groosalugg is out of the castle, Wesley and the rebels implement the next stage of the plan. Blatant frontal attacks are staged in several areas at once by kamikaze rebels, as Gunn, Wesley, and a few others take advantage of the guards' distraction to scale the castle walls.

The Groosalugg enters the village square and marches to Angel's flaming torch, holding his hand in its flame with no evident pain—to Angel's distress. Fred, hiding behind some handy curtains on a vendor's wagon, wishes Angel well against his formidable opponent. Groo attacks Angel with a weapon in each hand, then kicks him halfway across the square. Angel hits the ground hard, and the Groosalugg charges him again.

The Groosalugg batters Angel around the square like a kitten with a particularly determined mouse. Fred urges Angel to change, but he resists.

Wesley and Gunn fight their way through the castle. They catch a glimpse of Silas, but he evades them. Silas rushes to the relic room, where he has stashed Princess Cordelia for safekeeping, and blames everything that is going wrong in his little world on her and her fellow humans. He backhands her into the bookcase and makes his way toward the Slave Killer Console.

Groosalugg, frantic over the threat he believes Angel presents to his beloved princess, uses a "cow binding" device to fasten Angel's right arm to a handy post. Angel is vulnerable to his repeated assault, until the AngelBeast emerges and he breaks free.

Wesley and Gunn burst in on Silas and Cordelia. They have no range weapons, and there is no way for them to reach Silas before he triggers the Slave Killer Console. But a revived Cordelia becomes a Warrior Princess, grabbing a sword and chopping off Silas's head.

> **CORDELIA:** "These guys stay dead without a head?"
>
> **REBEL #1:** "Oh yeah."

Next item on her agenda—rescuing Groo from the beast she saw in her vision. They rush to the village.

In the square, the AngelBeast has pinned the Undefeated Champion's head to the ground with a clawed hand, and is ready to deliver a killing bite. He hesitates, and returns to Angel's handsome human form, determined not to let the beast overpower the man. Cordelia and her retinue arrive, shouting for the fight to end.

Angel is thanked for his nobility by being knocked back by Groo, who would probably continue his assault if his arms weren't full of a purple-cloaked princess declaring to the world her love for him. She hardly spares a glance for Angel or anyone else, except to declare an end to slavery and request a medic for Groo.

RESOLUTION

Angel makes one more trip through Pylea's daylight to the Deathwok farm. Lorne, back in one piece, smoothes his rough clothing with distinct distaste. It's a touching moment, as the Mother of the Vile Excrement bids adieu to her offspring. Angel and the Host bid a hasty retreat before being forced to witness Numfar doing the Dance of Shame.

Angel and the Host share a contemplative moment. The Host realizes he now understands why the psychic Aggie said he had to leave L.A. for Pylea one more time—so he would appreciate L.A. And with that he breaks into song, flattening random cousins as he and Angel stroll back to the palace.

Cordelia commits a few final royal acts: destroying the Slave Killer Console, reminding the priests their days of enjoying slavery are over, handing off the country—but not her visions—to the  Groosalugg, with a long kiss full of unfulfilled potential. When Fred announces that they are ready to make the portal leap, Cordelia makes a grand exit, her subjects prostrating themselves before her as she passes by.

WESLEY: "Should people bow in a free society?"

CORDELIA: "These things take time."

There's a bendy-flashy-whoosh-bang, and the portal opens in Caritas. The Angelmobile doesn't exactly fit in the bar, and there are a few table and chair casualties, but they are home. Angel, Cordelia, Wes, Gunn, and Fred make their way to the Hyperion, Cordelia filling Fred in on the forgotten luxuries of life in L.A., like tacos and soap.

They come through the French doors from the garden, and Angel is beaming as though he is standing in a ray of sunlight. The light drains from his face and the whole group stills as they see a small, sad, redheaded figure on the ottoman. Angel takes one look at Willow's sorrowful expression and instantly knows. "It's Buffy."

Case closed.

CONTINUITY

Cordelia apologizes to Lorne for his decapitation as a result of her challenging the priests in "Through the Looking Glass." Wesley apologizes to Gunn for his imminent decapitation as a result of his boasting about knowing Princess Cordelia in "Through the Looking Glass." Lorne mentions his psychic friend, Aggie, largely influencing his decision to return to Pylea in "Over the Rainbow." Willow's appearance follows Buffy's selfless sacrifice in the *Buffy* episode "The Gift."

QUOTE OF THE WEEK

"I realize this is a bit of a shock but I can explain . . . take it easy . . . okay, get it out of your system . . . good, that's good . . . you'll have to breathe sometime—GOOD LORD, SHUT UP, WOMAN!! It's not like I have hands to cover my ears here, ya know."

The Host's head tires rapidly of Cordelia's extended scream.

THE DEVIL IS IN THE DETAILS

EXPENSES

Full repairs to Caritas

WEAPONRY

The beheading stocks are a popular meeting place in Pylea. The locals have short swords, axes, long swords, and bows and arrows.

The Groosalugg, a professional champion, has a large mobile weapons rack he brings to meet Angel's challenge. His first attacks on Angel are with mace and bludgeon.

THE PLAN

Gunn is cool even under the executioner's ax.

> **GUNN:** "I've got a plan."
> **WESLEY:** "Oh thank God! What is it?"
> **REBEL #1:** "One . . ."
> **GUNN:** "We die horribly and painfully, you go to Hell, and I spend eternity in the arms of Baby Jesus."
> **WESLEY:** "Oh."

When Wesley becomes the rebel leader, his responsibility weighs heavily upon him.

> **GUNN:** "I'm only gonna say this once. The guys you send to create these diversions are going to die."
> **WESLEY:** "Yes, they are."
> Gunn's a little taken back by that.
> **WESLEY:** "You try not to get anybody killed, you wind up getting everybody killed."

DEMONS, DEMONS, DEMONS

Even in the demon-ridden world of Pylea, vampires of a sort exist. Unlike the dominant species of the world, **Van-tals**, as they're called, are like "cows" in that their hearts are in their chests rather than their rumps.

THE PEN IS MIGHTIER

FINAL CUT

Cordelia made an accidental connection with the slaves in the original script.

> **CORDELIA:** "Oh, the shrieking . . . it's a Royal Meditation I do to help me focus on the great affairs of state that I must manage."
> She takes a deep, thoughtful breath and SHRIEKS!
> **CORDELIA:** ". . . clears out all the pent-up, uh . . . where I come from we call it meck-flookenbahhhggg, you wouldn't understand."
> **SLAVE ONE:** "Ahhh, sexual sorrow."
> **CORDELIA:** "What are the odds."

POP CULTURE

✴ "**. . . we just keep on a-tickin' until you mutilate our bodies . . .**" The Host adapts the Timex tag line to his own benefit. They described their watch's durability by "takes a licking and keeps on ticking."

❊ **"Can you keep a secret, Geraldo?"** Her Infallible Majesty mangles Marelda's name into that of the infamous moustached television journalist.

❊ **"Hi. And thank you from the bottom of my neck on down. So where's the rest of me?"** The trauma of being decapitated with a missing body caused the Host to quote Ronald Reagan's most famous line from *King's Row* and the title of his autobiography, *Where's the Rest of Me?* In the movie, the former actor-turned-president wakes up to find that both of his legs have been amputated.

❊ **GROOSALUGG: "What is this 'reconstruction'?"**
CORDELIA: "Gunn, you want to field this?"
GUNN: "It means sayin' people are free don't make them free. You got races that hate each other, you got some folks gettin' work they don't want, others losin' the little they had. You're lookin' at social confusion, economic depression, and probably some riots. Good luck."
Reconstruction is the term for the period following the American Civil War in which United States citizens adjusted to the new status quo.

❊ **ANGEL: "Can I say it? I'm going to say it."**
WESLEY: "Say what?"
ANGEL: "There's no place like . . . Willow?"
Angel is interrupted before he can complete the line that sends Dorothy home from Oz in *The Wizard of Oz,* a 1939 movie starring a young Judy Garland, and based on the popular novel by L. Frank Baum.

OUR HEROES

Since Fred accompanies the gang back to Los Angeles at the end of Season Two, we asked David Boreanaz about her future.

"She's a great character. I don't think that [her future role is] one I can discuss fully. I do know that she was a scientist before she went to the other world. Relationships as far as romantic relationships are concerned, I don't think that would be really one for Angel's plate, only because it's more like a brother-sister relationship between the two of them. She'll get back into being a scientist again."

—DAVID BOREANAZ

J. August comments on Gunn's lessons in leadership.

"I think [Gunn] becomes more comfortable and solid in terms of his relationship with the Angel Investigations crew. It's not that he's left his crew behind, but there's another journey developing, and he's got to be okay with that. And also, by the end of this season, I think that Gunn learned that people die, that it happens, and it's not necessarily [his] fault. Because Wesley says to me, in the last episode, essentially, 'You know, if you try to save everyone you end up killing everyone.' And I think that Gunn really hears those words, and takes them to heart, and kind of forgives himself in some ways."

—J. AUGUST RICHARDS

Fred's cave gave the production designer an opportunity to play in Wonderland.

"I had a lot of fun doing our cave. You weren't hampered by conventional restraints of [set] building, [where] I need something to be [specifically] eight feet long, [or] two feet long, etcetera. This was very freeform, and I stood in there for a day or two with our construction coordinator, Ted Wilson, and we talked about where we wanted the arches to go, and where we wanted the pool of water to go, and how we wanted it to be a sort of Alice in Wonderland kind of hole that came out above ground. And then his carpenters went to work on that, and we brought in a special foaming guy who had done all the foam work on Planet of the Apes and The Grinch, and he spent two days fully foaming the set and creating all the large roots, the stalactites and stalagmites, and the pool of water."

—STUART BLATT, PRODUCTION DESIGNER

And the fantasy extended to the rest of Pylea.

STUART BLATT: "This was great, this was a great way to end the season for us. Within the medieval world, we were sort of bracketed by references from real medieval times, and other movies that have obviously gone before us and created medieval times. But what they wanted out of these scripts was a somewhat fantastical, storybook kind of land that these really bizarre things were happening in. So it gave myself as a designer and my whole crew a chance to create just really, really phenomenal sets. We built everything from a great throne room in the castle, where Cordelia is the princess, to a dungeon, to catacombs, to a cave, to passageways throughout the castle, to a large exterior wall of the castle that rebels are going to be scaling over on ropes. So it's been a really great capper for the season, to create something that is just so far out of the ordinary for us."

"Sometimes when you watch a fantasy movie, it seems very odd. How do you make it seem fantasylike without making it seem silly?"

SB: "That has a lot to do with Kevin Funston, who's our locations manager. I rely heavily on him to find places that are not only going to be easy to get the company in and out of, because that's one very key aspect of his job, but you want to find something that's going to further the story, and not just say, 'Okay, this was easy to shoot, but it didn't help the story in any way.' And we said, 'We're looking for someplace with really creepy woods. We're looking for someplace that would be really vast openness. We're looking for someplace that would really create a sense of isolation.' And he was able to find some great locations for us to take a look at. We found these great woods, that we called the Witchy Woods, which was just a corner of a farm out in the Westlake Village area. But back in the corner of it, the guy had a couple acres that were just totally magical, as far as old giant rocks that are as big as a house, crazy gnarly trees that look like something right out of either *Babes in Toyland* or *The Wizard of Oz*."

"Rain is always a factor. Unfortunately, when we were shooting at our little village for this show, where we had another big fight between Angel and the Groosalugg. This time, we really would have preferred not having rain, and it just rained like hell. But unfortunately, because we're in the medium we're in, very rarely do we ever cancel a shoot. We've never cancelled or stopped on *Angel*."

—KELLY A. MANNERS, PRODUCER

Propmaster Courtney arranges for bloodless mayhem.

COURTNEY JACKSON: "It's amazing, the amount of historical replicas of all kinds of weapons. You're able to buy them on the Internet. There are also a tremendous amount of craftsmen, people involved in Renaissance fairs and that kind of thing, who love doing swordwork and axework. There's an incredible guy, Tony, at The Sword in the Stone, here in Burbank, who can make pretty much anything that I can show him a drawing of, if he's got the time. And he does weapons for all the big movies. He's done blades for *Zorro* and all that kind of stuff.

"So you come up with different resources for weapons, and then you'll find something, and make sure that it's going to work with the stuntpeople and the director, and that our actors like it. And then sometimes you'll have to change the blade, make it an aluminum blade so it's very easy to wield, because a steel blade's much too heavy, and it makes you look very manly when you can take a big sword and wield it all over. And then make a rubber copy so that it's nice and safe."

"In set dressing, the philosophy is sort of, it doesn't matter if it's right, as long as it looks right on camera. But that's mostly distance. Is that not true in props, because you don't know if they're going to get the close-up?"

COURTNEY JACKSON: "It needs to pretty much be right. I mean, there's definitely times when you know something's going to be background, like when we had the rebel camp, and everybody's fighting. They've all got rubber weapons. If you were close in on some of this stuff, where they're actually hitting each other, you're going to see that they're rubber. But we've got extras in the background, and there's ninety of them or something, and you want to make sure they're safe, and it looks fine. Because you're really concentrating on the actors. But an actor holding something, you want to make sure it's just right."

"How difficult is it to be doing all this, and be doing it mobile?"

SANDY STRUTH, SET DECORATOR: "It's very hard. It's a lot of work. It doesn't really matter whether it's away, or on stage, because you have to take it to your location anyway. You have to go someplace, load a truck, and whether you take it here or take it there, it's more that you have to then, you're doing so much in so many different directions. Those episodes are busy, so it's nice to just come here and dress all the stages all the time. But it's nice to go to a location because a location has special things about itself, that can be a nuisance but can also make it something different. So that you get to work around that, even if it's poison oak, which we had to deal with when we were out in the woods in the last few episodes. And I'm allergic to poison oak, so I sort of sat in my car and pointed. I don't know how they did it shooting, I can't imagine what it was like shooting in poison oak. But the locations were good, they had lots of rocks and good trees. I think it's kind of fun, because we get away enough, you don't get so soundstage crazy."

Producer Kelly A. Manners believes in realizing ambitions.

"Well, for me it's weird how the whole season worked out. Because these shows are impossible. Every time we finish one with success, Joss and David raise the bar, and they make the next one just that much more impossible . . . These last three shows, where we went to this other world, I mean, we've had sixty extra makeup men over the course of a show. That's unheard of in episodic television. It's been a great joy and a great pain in the ass all at the same time. Now that it's over, you look back and you just go, 'Wow, how in the heck did we manage to pull it off?'" —KELLY A. MANNERS

TRACKS

"How does one compose for a world without music?"

ROBERT KRAL: "I raised the question in spotting about how there is no music in Pylea. The producers really wanted another world type sound that might remind us of The Princess Bride, Willow, and fantasy movies featuring castles, etc. The character of Fred has her own very special theme, played on recorder. It's kind of lonely and haunting, evocative. It becomes very important musically and dramatically when she stops Angel from tearing Gunn apart!"

SIX DEGREES OF . . .

Former American Gladiator Lee Reherman (the captain) played "Krause" in *Last Action Hero*. Persia White (Aggie Bellfleur) appeared in the movie in an uncredited role. Arnold Schwarzenegger played the title character, and also appeared in 1994's *True Lies* with Eliza Dushku (Faith).

Whitney Dylan, who plays the serving wench Marelda, played Lysette Torchio in "The Zeppo." Lysette was fond of Xander's uncle's car, but not that taken with *him*.

DAVID BOREANAZ: "Angel"

David Boreanaz was born in Buffalo, New York, and raised in Philadelphia, Pennsylvania. He was inspired to act by Yul Brenner's performance in *The King and I*, which he first saw when he was seven years old. After he graduated from Ithaca College, he moved across the country to California to pursue an acting career. David often mentions his mother and father as being very influential and supportive of him. His father's long-term job as a weatherman on Philadelphia station WPVI also inspired David to give the industry a try.

Before becoming Angel, David's acting resume was rather short. *Macabre Pair of Shorts* in 1996 lists him simply as "Vampire's victim." His small roles in *Aspen Extreme* and *Best of the Best II*, both released in 1993, went uncredited. He appeared as Frank, Kelly's cheating biker boyfriend, in a 1993 episode of *Married . . . with Children* titled "Movie Show."

After the success of *Buffy* and *Angel*, David's first starring role in a major movie was *Valentine*, released in 2001. It was loosely based on the book by Tom Savage. David has also appeared on *MadTV*, both times credited as playing himself. He lent his voice to two episodes of *Baby Blues* in 2000. His role was billed simply as "Bizzy's boyfriend." His next film is *I'm with Lucy*, currently scheduled for theatrical release in 2002.

"What's with all the teasing about your hair?"

DAVID BOREANAZ: "The joke was the fact that I couldn't see my reflection, so my hair is all over the place. That'll probably be an ongoing theme. There's got to be something."

"When Angel is going through dark times, as in 'Darla,' where he went close to the edge, is that hard on you as an actor? When you're in these brooding, dark places all day, is that hard to let go of?"

DB: "Well, I'll tell you, it was pretty enjoyable when I was doing it. I think sometimes you enjoy playing broodiness, sometimes you don't. For me to go back to being broody may be difficult sometimes. It's not an easy thing to do, it can be painful at times, but you just go through it. Be as truthful with it as you possibly can. Showing up is the hardest thing. You have to be able to show up. When you show up, you never know what's going to happen. But that's the most difficult part about work in general, is showing up. That goes for any kind of occupation."

"When you're in a different kind of an attitude with one of the characters, does that affect your off-set interactions?"

DB: "No. Once it's done, it's done. I don't cross the line. I'm doing a scene, I do the work, and once it's a wrap, I'm done."

"What about the people with whom you're working during the day? Like, say, you're sitting in your chair. Do you maintain the mood?"

DB: "No, no. I pretty much stay as loose as I possibly can. I'm not into that whole getting-ready thing. I have a good time and I turn it off."

"What is something that you haven't done on the show yet, that you wish would come up?"

DB: "I'd just like to see him grow. Honestly, everything he's done so far I've enjoyed, so there's not really one thing. Maybe, like, golfing or something. I'd like to involve something with an antique shop."

"Alexis thinks it should be scuba diving in Bermuda."

DB: "Yeah, I'm sure he'd love that."

CHARISMA CARPENTER: "Cordelia Chase"

Charisma Carpenter did not initially intend to pursue a career in acting, but fate intervened. To earn money for college, she was waitressing at a restaurant; her plan was to become an English teacher. But a commercial agent discovered her while she was waiting tables, and she has since appeared in more than twenty commercials.

Her first break in television came with a guest appearance on the popular series *Baywatch*. Shortly thereafter, she landed an audition for Aaron Spelling, who cast her in the role of Ashley in the series *Malibu Shores*. Her early work also included a role in Full Moon Entertainment's *Timemaster*.

Born and raised in Las Vegas, Charisma's family moved to Mexico when she was fifteen. She had studied classical ballet since the age of five and pursued dancing as part of her high school curriculum by commuting between Mexico and San Diego to take classes at the School of Creative and Performing Arts.

Carpenter currently resides in Los Angeles with her two golden retrievers. A fitness enthusiast, her outdoor interests include in-line skating, rock climbing, hiking, and skydiving.

> "[as Cordelia] I think I'm more inclined to stick up for Angel, and more inclined to stick up for my crew, you know, my family. So I think the reason why that is, is because I have the visions, and the last episode of first season, I got a taste of what kind of pain there is out there in the real world, and that deepened me. Well, my character. Because I don't have visions in real life. But I do believe there's pain out there."
>
> —CHARISMA CARPENTER

GLENN QUINN: "Allen Francis Doyle"

Glenn Quinn moved to the States from his hometown of Dublin, Ireland, at age nineteen, and soon landed a role on *Roseanne* as Mark Healy. Swallowing his Irish accent, he was so convincingly American that his "guest star" role lasted years—until the series ended in 1997.

During *Roseanne*, he was also tapped to star in *Covington Cross*, a short-lived but critically acclaimed series that died young and stayed pretty. That series' early demise was mourned, but for Glenn it was probably just as well, since doing two series at once—on different continents—was pretty much guaranteed to make him die young and get wrinkly.

Quinn also showed his range as an actor with his role as the corrupt music executive, Ben, in the VH-1 movie *At Any Cost*, which aired in August 2000.

His feature credits include *Shout*, a coming-of-age movie, as well as *Dr. Giggles* and *Live Nude Girls and Men* (aka *Some Girls*). He also recently completed a feature titled *Sticks & Stones*.

Glenn lives in Los Angeles, where he co-owns a nightclub.

ALEXIS DENISOF: "Wesley Wyndam-Pryce"

Alexis Denisof has a varied background filled with travel and acting. His mother's side of the family hails from Philadelphia (the family seat of David Boreanaz as well). His father's family were Russian immigrants. His childhood mostly took place in Seattle (including a stint with A Contemporary Theatre, otherwise known as ACT). Then it was off to boarding school in New Hampshire and subsequently off to Europe for a grand tour.

David Boreanaz Charisma Carpenter Glenn Quinn Alexis Denisof J. August Richards
And Benz Christian Kane Stephanie Romanov Elisabeth Rohm
Sara erson
Julie Nab
Davi enter
Glen hards
And Kane
Step Rohm
Sara lavin
Eliza rsters
Julia Le Nab
Charism hards
Julie B Acker
Stepha ellar
Carey erson
Juliet L Burr
Matthe anaz

There London piqued his interest, and both the London Academy of Music and Dramatic Arts and the Royal Shakespearean Company can claim him as an alumnus. He soon found himself in shows such as *Hamlet*, cast opposite Ian McKellan. He stayed in the UK for a decade and a half.

Once back in the US, like many actors, Alexis had small roles here and there. He filmed the pilot for *Ghost Cop*, which was not picked up. He was in George Harrison's music video for "Got My Mind Set on You." He snagged a one-shot gig on *Highlander*. Other film and television credits include *Murder Story*, *Dakota Road*, *First Knight*, *True Blue*, *Halcyon Days*, *The Misadventures of Margaret* (which appeared at the Sundance Film Festival), the HBO TV movie *Hostile Waters*, and a trio of Sharpe television movies: *Sharpe's Revenge*, *Sharpe's Justice*, and *Sharpe's Waterloo*.

Then came Wesley. *Buffy the Vampire Slayer* was in the middle of its third season when a new Watcher named Wesley arrived. Alexis's British accent was convincing. The character was initially supposed to be killed off after only two episodes, but Joss Whedon kept him alive through the end of the year.

Once the season ended, though, it was apparent Wesley was no longer a part of the main arc, with Buffy having quit the Watchers Council. He worked in an independent film, *Beyond City Limits*, with Alyson Hannigan, and two more films, *Rogue Trader* and the TV movie *Noah's Ark*, in which he played Noah's son Ham.

The next fall, Alexis got a call asking if he'd be willing to reprise his role as Wesley—on *Angel*. Alexis happily made the leap from *Rogue Trader* to Rogue Demon Hunter.

J. AUGUST RICHARDS: "Charles Gunn"

Raised in Bladensburg, Maryland, (a suburb of Washington DC), J.'s career got an early boost: In a summer camp in the Catskills, he was spotted by a casting director who gave him a guest-star role on *The Cosby Show*. Soon after, he moved to Los Angeles to attend U.S.C.

He finally got another break on his birthday, the last weekend of his last semester at school: He would be performing in a touring educational show called "Chemi Palooza."

J. has made guest appearances on series like *The Practice*, *Chicago Hope*, *Any Day Now*, and *Nash Bridges*, and he starred in NBC's critically acclaimed miniseries *The Temptations*. His film credits include *Why Do Fools Fall in Love*, and *Good Burger*. He also appeared in the Mark Taper production of *Space*.

Looking with gratitude at his blossoming professional life, the actor attributes much of that success to an acting workshop where he studied under Eriq La Salle (*ER*) and Michael Beach (*Third Watch*).

"They really made me confront my demons. I told them what roles I had difficulty playing and they made me play them," he explains. "It was such a great way to gain confidence and lose self-imposed limitations."

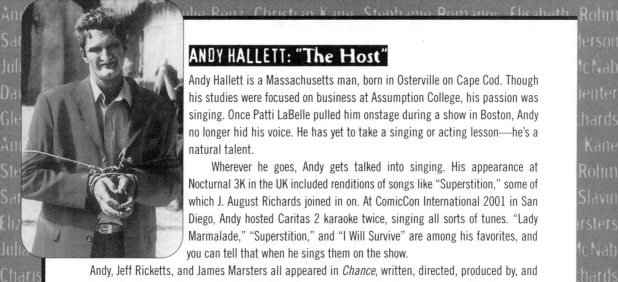

ANDY HALLETT: "The Host"

Andy Hallett is a Massachusetts man, born in Osterville on Cape Cod. Though his studies were focused on business at Assumption College, his passion was singing. Once Patti LaBelle pulled him onstage during a show in Boston, Andy no longer hid his voice. He has yet to take a singing or acting lesson—he's a natural talent.

Wherever he goes, Andy gets talked into singing. His appearance at Nocturnal 3K in the UK included renditions of songs like "Superstition," some of which J. August Richards joined in on. At ComicCon International 2001 in San Diego, Andy hosted Caritas 2 karaoke twice, singing all sorts of tunes. "Lady Marmalade," "Superstition," and "I Will Survive" are among his favorites, and you can tell that when he sings them on the show.

Andy, Jeff Ricketts, and James Marsters all appeared in *Chance*, written, directed, produced by, and starring Amber Benson (Tara, on *Buffy*). Musician Grant Langston, who played guitar in "To Shanshu in L.A.," played multiple tracks in the film (some of which were written by Amber and her sister, Andy).

AMY ACKER: Winifred "Fred" Burkle

Like Christian Kane, Amy Acker was born in Dallas, Texas. She attended Southern Methodist University. Throughout her time there, she acted in a number of SMU-produced plays. She was nominated for best leading actress by the Leon Rabin Awards for *Therese Raquin*.

Post-graduate roles included three appearances on *Wishbone*, a PBS series for children, and *To Serve and Protect*, a TV miniseries. In addition to joining *Angel* as the newest member of the cast, she has finished filming *Groom Lake*, directed by William Shatner, and stars in *The Accident*.

JULIE BENZ: "Darla"

Julie Benz has a distinguished career in film and TV. Some of her TV credits include *Fame L.A.*, *Married . . . with Children*, *Sliders*, *Roswell*, and others. She will appear on a new series, *Taken*, debuting in 2002. Her film work includes *As Good as It Gets*, with Jack Nicholson, *Jawbreakers,* and *Satan's School for Girls*.

Six degreeing: Julie Benz and Danny Strong (Jonathon, on *Buffy*) were both in *Scream If You Know What I Did Last Friday the 13th*. The film also featured Majandra Delfino from *Roswell*. Julie played a recurring character on Season One of *Roswell* as Agent Topolsky.

"At one point you said, 'Even fake blood makes me want to faint.' And Darla's scenes have actually gotten a lot bloodier. How do you cope?"

David Boreanaz   Charisma Carpenter   Glenn Quinn   Alexis Denisof   J. August Richards
Andy Hallett   Amy Acker   Julie Benz   Christian Kane   Stephanie Romanov   Elisabeth Rohm
Sarah   erson
Juliet L   cNab
David E   enter
Glenn   hards
Andy H   Kane
Stepha   Rohm
Sarah   Slavin
Eliza D   rsters
Julia Le   cNab
Charis   hards
Julie E   Acker

JULIE BENZ: "I keep trying to remind myself it's fake blood. I had to drink out of a bottle of blood in an episode, and even though it was red syrup, it was pretty gross. I mean, the whole concept of drinking blood makes my stomach turn."

"And yet, you have to look like you're really enjoying it."

JB: "Acting. I get over it real fast. But I can't stand the sight of blood. I can't even stand somebody talking about an injury that they've had. If someone tells me a story about breaking their leg, automatically my leg starts to hurt, and I start having sympathy pains."

"How, then, did you deal with the burn scene and the scars from Season Two? Was it hard to have that makeup on?"

JB: "Yeah, but I made lots of jokes. I looked like a surfer girl who didn't wear sunblock. Those burns were pretty intense. But it's not the makeup so much that bothers me. Looking in the mirror looked like it hurt really bad, and I did have the sympathy pains, but I get through it with humor, really. I walk around making jokes. We always have a lot of fun."

CHRISTIAN KANE: "Lindsey McDonald"

Christian Kane was born in Dallas. During his childhood, his family lived in various parts of the southern U.S., including Oklahoma. His dad was a rodeo rider and a musical influence on his son. At an early age, Christian learned how to sing and play guitar.

After high school, Christian headed to the University of Oklahoma. His interest in the performing arts grew, and he moved to the land of stars and heartbreak— Southern California. After some odd jobs, he won the leading role of Ryan Legget in the television series *Fame L.A.* (1997). The show only lasted one season. Two years later he landed another leading role, that of Wick Lobo on *Rescue 77*. This WB show was cancelled, but not without Christian getting some more footage on his presentation reel and turning the heads of more casting directors.

EdTV, a 1999 box office hit, featured him as a production assistant. Later that year, he tried out for *Buffy the Vampire Slayer*, for the role of Riley Finn. The job went to Marc Blucas.

When *Angel* was spun off, there he was as wicked lawyer Lindsey McDonald. The fans loved to hate Lindsey, and the character recurred throughout the first season. On hiatus, Christian filmed *Summer Catch* with Marc Blucas and Freddie Prinze Jr. Then it was time for *Angel* once more, and Christian's gig as Lindsey continued. He even was able to show off his vocal and instrumental talents in the 2000 MTV television movie *Love Song*, and paid homage to his cowboy roots in the 2001 TNT television movie *Crossfire Trail*. He also appeared in an episode of *Dawson's Creek*.

His film career continues to grow, with a role in the forthcoming *Life or Something Like It*. He performs locally in L.A. with his band, Kane, to ever-increasing critical and popular acclaim. He's asked often if Lindsey will be returning to *Angel*. He reports, sincerely, that he has no idea . . . but then again, he's used to lying on the job!

STEPHANIE ROMANOV: "Lilah Morgan"

Like Charisma Carpenter, Stephanie Romanov was born in Las Vegas. Also like Charisma, she had an Aaron Spelling gig, in *Models, Inc.* It was, in fact, her first TV appearance. She was discovered by Elite Modeling agent John Casablancas at the age of fifteen, and she modeled extensively in Europe and New York for magazines such as *Elle*, *Bazaar*, *Vanity Fair*, and *Vogue*. Her varied career includes many guest-star and recurring character appearances on TV series including *Just Shoot Me*, *Homicide*, *Nash Bridges*, *Early Edition*, and others. Her film appearances include *Spy Hard*, *Menno's Mind* (for Showtime), and *13 Days*.

ELISABETH ROHM: "Kate Lockley"

Elisabeth Rohm was born in Germany and raised in New York City. She still holds her dual citizenship. She studied writing and European history at Sarah Lawrence College. She landed a role in the drama department's production of David Henry Huang's *Bondage*. After that, she was hooked on acting.

One of her early credits was a role in Dick Wolf's Fox pilot, *The Invisible Man*. Following that, she worked in a miniseries titled *The 60s*, as well as a BBC miniseries, *Eureka Street*.

She starred in the Wall Street drama series *Bull* and she currently is on *Law and Order*.

Elisabeth loves to travel and ride her horse.

> "I really believe that you've got to have other interests in life. I believe that in order to have a well-rounded life, and in order to be fulfilled and not take things too seriously, you have to give yourself the balance of having lots of different things in your life. I think it's something that I've always worked hard on, to . . . have other things going on in my life. I'm trying to produce films, I've written a book, and I'm really active in other ways."
> —ELISABETH ROHM

SARAH MICHELLE GELLAR: "Buffy Summers"

Sarah's a New York girl, an only child with close ties to her mother, and a motherly figure to her friends. Her first movie appearance was in 1983 and she continued to get work throughout her childhood and into her teenage years with TV movies, television shows, and commercials galore.

She received a Daytime Emmy for her role as Kendall Hart on the soap opera *All My Children*. Only a few years later, scripts for the TV series *Buffy the Vampire Slayer* were making the rounds, and Sarah showed up . . . to try out for the role of Cordelia!

After *Buffy*'s first season wrapped, Sarah was off in North Carolina filming *I Know What You Did Last Summer*. Films continue to pepper her resume, including

399

Scream 2, Cruel Intentions, Simply Irresistible, Scooby-Doo, and *Harvard Man.* She's hosted *Saturday Night Live* twice and appeared in surprise guest spots other times. Maybelline uses her as a spokesmodel; and Kula Shaker and Stone Temple Pilots have both featured her in their videos.

Just as Angel has dropped by Sunnydale, Buffy has visited Angel's world via crossovers, including "I Will Remember You" and "Sanctuary."

CAREY CANNON: "Sister Oracle"

New Yorker Carey Cannon attended Carnegie-Mellon for a degree in theater, and she worked onstage in New York for about eight years after graduation. *Angel* was her first TV gig. She met Amy Britt, the casting director for *Buffy,* at a casting workshop, and eventually read parts for both shows. The Sister Oracle role was the first good fit.

Carey has also appeared in an independent film titled *Cops on the Edge: Episode 89.*

"In the episode where we died, there was an actor . . . who played the demon [Vocah]. [He] had a lot of makeup and red eyes, and he was a big guy anyway in a dark cape; and my 'brother' and I were painted gold, and in our togas, and there's a lot of sitting around and waiting. In . . . scenes where there are demons, or David is in vampire makeup . . . you're in a world that you can so easily buy as having these creatures in it. And being one of them yourself.

"But then [you look] around and see grips and PAs [having] donuts, and people grabbing coffee. Having been on TV sets and movie sets and stuff before, the disparity between the real world of making a TV show, and the characters, was really pronounced. And so I do have this image of everybody kind of standing around craft service tables in their prosthetics and makeup and trying to figure out how to eat with fangs, sipping soda through a straw. It's one of the stories I told my friends. You're with vampires and demons and stuff, and yet, you're just doing your job. It's just strange."

—CAREY CANNON

RANDALL SLAVIN: "Brother Oracle"

Randall Slavin has had a long and distinguished film and TV career, appearing in such series as *Roseanne, The Practice,* and *CSI;* feature films including *Legends of the Fall* and *The Sleepy Time Gal;* and the TV movie *Glory, Glory.*

ELIZA DUSHKU: "Faith"

Eliza Dushku has been working as an actress since she was in middle school. One of her first jobs was in a feature film entitled *That Night.* She often talks about her supportive parents and brothers, one of whom, Nate, is also an actor. She loves her hometown of Boston, where she learned American Sign Language and participated in theater work.

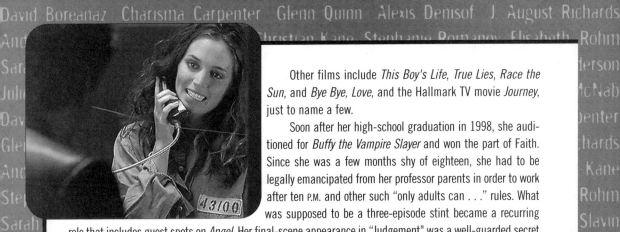

Other films include *This Boy's Life*, *True Lies*, *Race the Sun*, and *Bye Bye, Love*, and the Hallmark TV movie *Journey*, just to name a few.

Soon after her high-school graduation in 1998, she auditioned for *Buffy the Vampire Slayer* and won the part of Faith. Since she was a few months shy of eighteen, she had to be legally emancipated from her professor parents in order to work after ten P.M. and other such "only adults can . . ." rules. What was supposed to be a three-episode stint became a recurring role that includes guest spots on *Angel*. Her final-scene appearance in "Judgement" was a well-guarded secret throughout the summer leading up to the season premiere, and pleasantly surprised the audience when it aired.

Her movie *Bring It On* opened at number one at the box office in August 2000. Her most recent films are *Soul Survivors* and *Jay and Silent Bob Strike Back,* a Kevin Smith flick. (Kevin Smith affectionately calls her "Duck Shoot.") On the horizon are *City by the Sea* and *The New Guy.*

SAM ANDERSON: "Holland Manners"

Veteran actor Sam Anderson has appeared in many films, including *The Stand* and *Forrest Gump*, and TV series including *The Golden Girls*, *Hill Street Blues*, *Remington Steele*, *Star Trek*, *L.A. Law*, *ER*, *Picket Fences*, *The West Wing*, *Chicago Hope*, and *The X-Files*—just to name a very few.

JULIET LANDAU: "Drusilla"

Native Angelena Juliet Landau studied theater in London and completed her degree at North Carolina School of Arts. She was a professional ballerina for five years and is a member of the Actors' Studio.

After costarring in Tim Burton's *Ed Wood* with her father, Martin Landau, Juliet starred opposite Whoopi Goldberg and Armin Mueller-Stahl in New Line Cinema's *Theodore Rex*. She was next seen starring on *Buffy* as Drusilla, a vampire sired by Angel. Joss Whedon describes Dru and her lover, Spike (whom she sired), as "the Sid and Nancy of the vampire set." Brought back by popular demand, she appears on both *Buffy* and *Angel*.

Juliet just completed a starring role in the feature film *Carlo's Wake* and a costarring role in the underground film, *Citizens of Perpetual Indulgence*, with Joe D'Allesandro and Holly Woodlawn of Andy Warhol fame. She can also be seen in *Life Among the Cannibals*, *Ravagers*, *The Grifters*, *Direct Hit*, and *Flipping*. She's also appeared on the TV shows *Millennium* and *La Femme Nikita*.

Her theater credits include roles in *Uncommon Women and Others*, *The Pushcart Peddlers*, *Billy Irish*, *We're Talking Today Here*, the West Coast premiere of *Irish Coffee*, and the world premiere of the musical *The Songs of War*.

401

"When they did the big crossover episodes, what was it like to be back working with David and James again after being away?"

JULIET LANDAU: "It was so much fun. Working on that crossover was like working on a huge period movie. The wardrobe that Cynthia Bergstrom did for me was just amazing. One of my costumes, the costume I wear when I make Spike a vampire, was actually from the movie *Titanic*, and Gloria did my hair in all those period dos. Getting to step back in time and fill in some of the back story that we knew had existed, to actually film it, was really amazing. And then of course it was just loads of fun to be back with those guys."

JAMES MARSTERS: "Spike"

James Marsters, who has appeared on *Buffy the Vampire Slayer* as Spike, the punk rock vampire, became a cast regular for the fourth season of *Buffy* in addition to making guest appearances on *Angel*.

Born in the logging town of Greenville, California, and raised in Modesto, California, Marsters always knew he wanted to be an actor. From his debut as Eeyore in a fourth-grade production of *Winnie the Pooh*, he went on to study acting at New York's prestigious Juilliard School. He began his professional career in the theater, performing in stage productions including *The Tempest* and *Red Noses* at Chicago's renowned Goodman Theater. He appeared in an original play titled *The Why*, which was produced by Noah Wyle of *ER* fame. He was also seen in *The House of Haunted Hill*, a horror film.

James made his onscreen debut guest-starring on the television series *Northern Exposure*. Soon after moving to the Pacific Northwest, he landed the prominent role of an ill-at-ease priest on the series, which was cast locally in Seattle. He was inspired by the success to move to Los Angeles and within months was sinking his proverbial teeth into the role of Spike in *Buffy the Vampire Slayer*.

James enjoys playing the guitar, watching football, and spending time with friends at the beach. He currently lives in Los Angeles.

JULIA LEE: "Anne Steele"

Julia was fourteen when she started to study acting, eventually completing college at UC Irvine with a degree in theater.

Her professional career took off in 1997. That year and thereafter, she found work in television (*Buffy*, *Angel*, *Charmed*), and in musicals and plays *Into the Woods*, *The Tempest*, and *The Crucible*. She appeared in feature films as well, including *Ophelia Learns to Swim* and *Diablo*.

Julia enjoys her stunts and action scenes. Between takes on *Angel*, she and J. August Richards would sing "Say My Line" to the tune of "Say My Name" by Destiny's Child. She also loves how strong her character is now, how Joss has enabled her to mature, change, and grow.

THOMAS BURR: "Lee Mercer"

Thomas Burr is a relative newcomer to acting. In addition to *Angel*, he has appeared on the TV series *Good v. Evil*, *Fame L.A.*, and *Time of Your Life*. His feature work includes *The Hunted* and *BraceFace Brandi*.

"How did you come to get the role of Wolfram & Hart attorney Lee Mercer?"

THOMAS BURR: "I had auditioned once or twice for *Buffy*, for parts that I went back for but never got, but the casting directors—who had hired me for a show called *Fame L.A.* and a couple independent films—they knew me. So they actually requested me and called me in. I went in and auditioned for David Greenwalt and one of the producers, and then they had me back one more time and offered me the role. I think the reason they had to create that part [of Lee Mercer] was because their original lawyer, Lindsey, who was in one of the earlier episodes, was not available. So because of that situation they had to create a character that I think they were just gonna use that once, until [Lindsey] was free again. And then luckily they asked me back for little things here and there."

"What sort of qualities do you think they were looking for that made them think of you? Do you do weasely and slimy really good?"

TB: "Apparently I do it okay. I think they wanted someone who was emotionless. As a matter of fact, that was the one thing that they told me, was that they were looking for someone who just had absolutely no emotional attachment to what he was doing."

"The only feeling you get from him is ambition."

TB: "Right, exactly. And certainly cold, snippy, all of those things."

MATTHEW JAMES: "Merl"

Matthew James comes to *Angel* practically straight out of the gate. His previous experience consisted of two feature films, *Tattoo Boy* and *Decline of Western Civilization II: The Metal Years*.

"What appealed to you about this role?"

MJ: "Well, it's kind of a sleazy type of guy. It was a Huggy-bear role, you know, like on *Starsky and Hutch*."

"What trait do you find dominant in Merl, his demonic nature or his bent toward being sleazy? Do you think Merl's the kind of guy who would have been that way no matter what?"

MJ: "Well, you know, it comes from the upbringing. I guess he's not like an evil, evil person. As you can see, he gets his ass kicked all the time, so he's not really like a tough guy."

MERCEDES MCNAB: "Harmony Kendall"

Mercedes has been with *Buffy the Vampire Slayer* since the beginning. The character of Harmony recurred through Seasons One, Two, and Three as a Cordette.

She visited Los Angeles in the *Angel* episode "Disharmony," in which the Angel gang finally learn that she has been turned. A hilarious end scene was cut, which had Harmony in Mexico, trying to explain the "Turn two, the rest is food" policy to others.

Picture a young Mercedes with two braids and you might remember her from the two *Addams Family* movies of the 1990s. Mercedes was the Girl Scout in *The Addams Family* and then Amanda in *Addams Family Values*. She's guested on such TV shows as *Harry and the Hendersons; The Adventures of Brisco County, Jr.; Too Something; Diagnosis Murder; Smart Guy; USA High; Touched by an Angel;* and *Walker, Texas Ranger.* Other film work includes *Savage Land*, *The Fantastic Four* (as Sue), and *White Wolves III: Cry of the White Wolf.* Two of her standout roles were in the TV movie *Escape from Atlantis*, in which she had some scenes akin to Cordelia's Princess of Pylea stint, and in the 2001 TV movie *Beer Money*.

"I think that [Angel's] world
is so evolving and ever-changing . . .
so tempestuous that it lends itself to being
different in every episode. The overall
theme is trying to find some sense
of making him a mortal in an
immortality kind of world."

—David Boreanaz